LIKE A FIERY METEOR

LIKE A FIERY METEOR

THE LIFE OF
JOSEPH F. SMITH

STEPHEN C. TAYSOM

THE UNIVERSITY of UTAH PRESS
Salt Lake City

Copyright © 2023 by The University of Utah Press. All rights reserved.

 The Defiance House Man colophon is a registered trademark of the University of Utah Press. It is based on a four-foot-tall Ancient Puebloan pictograph (late PIII) near Glen Canyon, Utah.

Names: Taysom, Stephen C., author
Title: Like a Fiery Meteor: The Life of Joseph F. Smith / Stephen C. Taysom
Description: Salt Lake City : University of Utah Press, [2023] | Includes bibliographical references and index.
Identifiers: LCCN 2023003138 | ISBN 9781647691271 (hardcover : alk. paper) | ISBN 9781647691288 (paperback : alk. paper) | ISBN 9781647691295 (ebk)
LC record available at https://lccn.loc.gov/2023003138

Errata and further information on this and other titles available online at UofUpress.com

Printed and bound in the United States of America.

*For Lindsey, the bringer of all good things. And for our children,
Rex, Reagan, Summer, Steele, and Grey, the stars in our sky.*

*For my father, Colonel Michael S. Taysom, USAF (RET.).
1941–2021, the fieriest of meteors. I miss you, Dad. For my
mother, Cheryl Smith Taysom, who has never doubted.*

*For Stephen J. Stein, 1940–2022, teacher, mentor, and friend.
Thank you for showing me how to balance
my love for scholarship and family.*

Contents

A Note on Sources | ix
Preface | xi
Acknowledgments | xv

Introduction | 1
1. Bloodlines | 4
2. From Missouri to Nauvoo | 19
3. The Murders of Joseph and Hyrum Smith | 33
4. Pioneer Days | 47
5. Upon the Isles of the Sea | 67
6. Returning to Utah and Finding a Wife | 93
7. Mission to the British Isles | 102
8. Marital Discord, Domestic Violence, and Divorce | 128
9. JFS the Apostle, JFS the Polygamist | 144
10. Mission President in England, Losing the Lion | 162
11. Exile | 198
12. "We were unsettled as a Quorum" | 217
13. An Emerging Gospel Scholar, Iosepa, and the Manifesto | 228
14. The Ever-Tightening Knot of Utah Politics | 244
15. Politics, Economics, and Polygamy Collide | 260
16. Presiding High Priest, 1901–1918 | 286
17. The Complexities of Religion in a New Century | 316
18. From Salt Lake to Sharon | 321
19. Dusk | 352

Afterword | 359
Notes | 361
Bibliography | 425
Index | 433

Illustrations follow page 216

A Note on Sources

The vast majority of the primary source material for this book is derived from the Joseph F. Smith Papers housed at the archives of the Church of Jesus Christ of Latter-day Saints in Salt Lake City, Utah. This collection is numbered as MS 1325. For the sake of brevity, in the notes I typically refer to this as the "JFS Papers, LDS Church History Library." I provide box and folder numbers when available. Other collections from the LDS Church History Library are labeled in their complete form followed by the abbreviated "LDS Church History Library."

Preface

Who is Joseph F. Smith? He is generally known among Mormons as the young, fiery son of Hyrum Smith who drove a team of oxen across the plains with his widowed mother, Mary Fielding Smith, and who, after her death, engaged in a period of juvenile delinquency that climaxed in an assault on his teacher carried out in defense of his younger sister. Following this, so the story goes, Brigham Young sent the fifteen-year-old on a mission to Hawaii to try to set him straight. While in the islands, he developed a lifelong love of all things Hawaiian, had a famous dream about being "late but clean," and generally came to his religious senses. On his way back to Utah he found himself confronted by a mob who, as the lore has it, ominously demanded to know if he was a Mormon, to which he supposedly replied that he was, "died in the wool, deep blue, through and though." Mormons might also be able to tell you about his exile in Hawaii in the 1880s and his testimony before the Smoot hearings in 1904.

The basic folklore of JFS's life ends with his "vision of the redemption of the dead," which he received a month before he died in 1918. Many Mormons would know these things, and, frankly, that is a great deal more than they probably know about Lorenzo Snow or Heber J. Grant, the LDS Church presidents between whose administrations JFS's fell.

I have spent several years studying JFS, and the things I've learned have been surprising. In this book I have sought to bring an immediacy to JFS's story that has been lacking. His journals and letters, and those of his family members and friends, reveal a surprisingly complex figure, and this complexity troubles the entrenched folklore about his life. For example, he never had much genuine affection for Hawaii or Hawaiians, and what little he did have showed up only late in life. He was far more deeply attached to England and the English people, among whom he served as a missionary and twice as a mission president.

JFS did, indeed, have an anger problem, one that he struggled with all his life. But he also struggled with despair and sorrow. A romantic plagued with crippling sentimentality and separation anxiety, he mourned for his children in florid and unabashed lamentations that men like Brigham Young and Wilford Woodruff

xii   *Preface*

would have found puzzling. He could also be stunningly insensitive one moment, and literally overcome and crippled with empathy the next. His first marriage ended in divorce amidst accusations of domestic violence and mental illness. He held deeply ambivalent feelings about Brigham Young, the man who brought him into the upper echelons of church leadership. JFS respected Young's position as leader of the church, but deeply disdained his doctrinal authoritarianism.

This list could extend for pages, but the point is that JFS, like all human beings, defies easy description and simply refuses facile categorization.

In this book, I follow the model used by Joseph Ellis in his award-winning biography of Thomas Jefferson: "My approach is selective, but maintains a traditional commitment to chronology. My goal is catch Jefferson at propitious moments in his life, to zoom in on his thoughts and actions during those extended moments, to focus on the values and convictions that reveal themselves in these specific historical contexts, all the while providing the reader with sufficient background on what has transpired between sightings to follow the outline of Jefferson's life from birth to death."[1] I determined which periods of JFS's life to examine in deep detail and which ones to approach from a much broader angle according to two basic criteria. In order to merit detailed attention, a period has to be (1) well documented by JFS himself and (2) not thoroughly discussed in biographical material already published on him. I have done my best not to duplicate that work to a burdensome degree.

There is, obviously, a silent third requirement that leads to the inclusion of material that I, for whatever reason, find interesting. As Ellis did with Jefferson, I selected for close scrutiny the periods of JFS's life that are both important and sufficiently documented. In the years I have spent excavating the remaining traces of JFS's life, I have been drawn to an examination of his responses to his environment, rather than a quest to place him within the broader world. I certainly do make a point to contextualize JFS's experiences, but I privilege his own point of view.

The nature of biography requires the creative deployment of scholarly tools, including shifts in methods and narrative scope within the work itself. Biography is fundamentally delimited by lifespan, but obviously not everything within that period is equally well documented, equally significant either to the subject or the biographer, or novel enough to warrant inclusion in a new work. Some periods in JFS's life are totally occluded, others are available only through memories, and still others are known only through a combination of solid, but spotty, documentary material and informed conjecture. It is at these dark junctures where I have chosen to take excursions into theoretical or historiographical terrain.

For example, almost nothing exists to tell us about JFS's early childhood, but there is literature that can tell that help us understand what his childhood was like and what it meant during that period, and in those places, for people *like* JFS. Similarly, when dealing with his early adolescence, we are dealing with reminiscences, so it is appropriate to explore what scholarship has to tell us about the role that the intervening years between an event and its recollection have in shaping memories. Sometimes, particularly for his later years, we have access primarily to JFS's public life through sermons or his own published writings. His journals and much of his correspondence from his presidential years, for example, remain closed to researchers. For other periods, however, JFS left us with an almost constant stream of journal entries and letters that let us into his public and private lives on a daily basis for years at a time. When the documentary record produced by JFS is thick, my interpretation of his words drives the narrative. When they are thin, problematic, or nonexistent, other factors shape the discussion.

Some biographers choose to present their work thematically rather than chronologically. While this approach provides the reader with a convenient pathway to topics of interest, it sacrifices the sense of change that readers can better appreciate with a chronological narrative. This book moves chronologically, with themes such as family life, religious beliefs, doctrinal contributions, and so forth woven throughout the narrative.

An explanation is perhaps necessary to justify my approach to covering JFS's presidential years. I mention this here because I am certain that some readers will go straight to that period of JFS's life with few stops in between. Those years have garnered more scholarly attention than all the other periods of his life combined. This is natural, of course, since his primary claim on history is as the president of the LDS Church. There are other reasons though, including the length of his presidency.

In the history of the LDS Church up to the time of this writing, only three presidents served longer terms than JFS. Brigham Young's tenure was substantially longer, but most of JFS's predecessors served less than half as long as he did. In fact, JFS served as president six times as long as his immediate predecessor, Lorenzo Snow.

Scholars are also drawn to the period of JFS's presidency because of its eventful nature. The political, economic, and religious worlds of Mormonism all weathered tectonic shifts in the first two decades of the twentieth century. Government involvement in the church's sugar interests, the Reed Smoot hearings, World War I, debates about Prohibition and social reform, and similarly significant events framed JFS's presidential years. On the doctrinal front, JFS produced what is now the final section of the Doctrine and Covenants, the last major canonized revelation in Mormonism. Finally, as with every LDS Church president, JFS's term ended with his death, which is always a major focal point in any biography.

All of these factors, taken together, account for the relatively high interest in this part of JFS's life. Students of economics, politics, scripture, ritual, polygamy, and ecclesiology are all drawn to JFS as president. The fecundity of scholarship on this period presents some challenges to a biographer. The most basic problem is that one must find a way to write about these years without either reinventing the wheel or presenting readers with a warmed-over mélange of previous scholarship.

xiv *Preface*

Naturally, the insights of other scholars must be taken into consideration, and they are, but mostly in a quiet way, and usually in the notes.

For all of the scholarship on JFS as president, most of it is really about something else. The developments in church education, the standardization of priesthood organization, changes in the interpretation of the Word of Wisdom, and a major increase in church building projects (including the church administration building and the Hotel Utah) have all been well-documented. The final chapters of this book are primarily concerned with bringing to the reader a sense of immediacy, a front-row seat to JFS's struggle to find his way through these challenging years.

Readers will find only brief background on things such as the Smoot hearings, Utah politics, religion in the Progressive era, the intermountain sugar industry, church economic development, and similar subjects. The avalanche of events during JFS's presidency threaten to bury him and keep his personality out of our view. The remedy is to keep as closely focused on JFS as a person as we possibly can.

Readers are directed to the notes for references to the scholarship on other topics related to JFS. Thomas Alexander, Leonard Arrington, Kathleen Flake, Jonathan Stapley, Paul Reeve, and others are expert guides and I will, in turn, guide you to them. In the final chapters of this book, however, I hew unusually close to the sources produced by JFS himself, primarily letters since his journals are largely unavailable, and the journals and letters of close associates and relatives. Contextualization is provided, of course, but it is limited. There is just enough historical context provided to understand JFS's personal reactions without drawing our attention away from our study of JFS the man. I have tried not only in the last chapters but in the entire book to bring JFS's thoughts, feelings, and daily activities to the fore.

Acknowledgments

I have been working on this book for ten years, and in such a vast span of time, I have accrued many debts. Too many, in fact, to fully acknowledge here. Nevertheless, there are a few people who merit special mention.

Ben Park first encouraged me to pitch the idea of this biography to the University of Utah Press. It was there that I met John Alley, who enthusiastically issued me a preliminary contract and patiently shepherded the book for several years before his retirement. His replacement, Tom Krause, was also very helpful during his time at the press. Alexis Mills undertook the herculean task of copyediting the book, and she improved it tremendously. I wish also to thank the anonymous reviewers who read the manuscript and offered both praise and useful criticism. Kristine Haglund, Arle Lommel, and Brian Whitney each read the entire work and offered valuable suggestions for improvement. The same is true of my cohort in the Young Scholar of American Religion program and our mentors, Laurie Maffly-Kipp and Doug Winiarski. I am grateful for the support of my colleagues in the Department of Philosophy and Comparative Religion at Cleveland State University, particularly Matt Jackson-McCabe, Sucharita Adluri, and Stephen Cory. I could not ask for a warmer professional home.

A very special thanks is due to Ardis Parshall. She has helped me in so many ways over the entire course of this project that she should probably be listed as a co-author. She is a gifted researcher and scholar whose generosity and friendship has known no bounds.

On a more personal note, I want to thank my friend, mentor, and dissertation director, Stephen J. Stein and his wife, Devonia. Although I finished my graduate work many years ago, Steve and Devonia kept close track of my family in the interim. Steve passed away just as this book was nearing completion. The scholarly world lost a true giant, and I lost a dear friend. Nevertheless, his influence is found in this book, and in everything that I do.

I wish also to thank my parents, Mike and Cheryl Taysom. They supported me, encouraged me, and pulled me through some very dark days and I love them.

Acknowledgments

My father died before he could read this book, but I hope that it would have made him proud.

Finally, I want to thank my wife, Lindsey, and our children, Rex, Reagan, Summer, Steele, and Grey. I can be a trying domestic presence, often leaving my wake awash in books, papers, and Diet Coke cans. I always clean up after myself, eventually. But they are patient enough to wait. Lindsey has been my partner, friend, critic, and an enthusiastic fan of this book. The kids have brought me greater pride and joy than they can even imagine. I love all of you.

Introduction

"I was born," Joseph F. Smith wrote, "13 days after the betrayal of my father, Hyrum Smith, into the hands of the mob. I have inherited much of my mother's <u>love</u> for the enemies of my people."[1] If I had to limit my biography of JFS to a single representative two-sentence sound bite, this would be the one. In it, JFS reveals the three great pillars around which the woven cord of his life was wrapped: his father's death, his mother's life, and his ever-present sensitivity to what he viewed as the ceaseless vicissitudes heaped upon God's chosen people. Like all of us, JFS was a complex individual. This book is an attempt to understand how he interacted with the worlds he inhabited.

This is not the first book written about JFS. He has been the subject of two previous biographies. The first, published in 1938, was written by his son, Joseph Fielding Smith Jr.[2] Although JFS Jr. had access to all of his father's papers and journals, his book lacks adequate citations. It is still helpful to modern biographers, however, that JFS Jr. quoted liberally from his father's journals that are currently unavailable. However, the book is a hagiography written by a loving son. It is as much a manual for how to be a good Latter-day Saint as it is the story of JFS's life.

The second biography, published in 1984, was written by Francis Gibbons.[3] Gibbons served for decades as the secretary to the LDS Church's First Presidency, and he has written biographies of all of the presidents of the church through Howard W. Hunter. Gibbons's book is also devotional in nature, and it is a fairly shallow treatment. He uses few if any nonpublished primary sources, relying largely on sources quoted in the earlier biography. Both books were written for a casual LDS audience seeking faith-promoting portraits of LDS leaders. They have filled that capacity admirably.

At the other end of the spectrum, there is a biographical essay about JFS written by Scott Kenney based on extensive research he did in the 1970s.[4] Titled "Before the Beard: Trials of the Young Joseph Smith," the article fits within the genre recently described by biographer Oleg V. Khlevniuk as "archival exposés."[5] When previously forbidden documents are suddenly made available, as they were in the 1970s in the

2   *Introduction*

LDS Church archives, there is a temptation to use the documents to portray the (usually beloved, revered, or powerful) subject in such a way that only the sensationally negative aspects of the figure are revealed. It is not that the material is false, but the presentation is crafted in such a way that culturally negative behaviors are given far more narrative weight than anything else. Both hagiographies and archival exposés suffer from the same malady: they tend to be one-dimensional and deeply invested in the "morality" rather than the "humanity" of their subjects.

In 2012, JFS was the subject of a Brigham Young University church history symposium from which a proceedings volume was published.[6] Although the symposium was hosted by BYU and generally assumed a devotional posture toward JFS, the essays in this collection are generally of good quality and cover a wide range of themes. I have made extensive use of them as important secondary sources, a fact made clear in the notes.

This biography is quite different than the previous works in that it is a scholarly work, written without a faith-based agenda and intended primarily for scholars of American religion and Mormon studies. However, the nature of JFS's life pressed me to explore a much broader range of subjects than religion in general, and Mormonism in particular. The reader will find lengthy discussions of the cultural constructions in nineteenth-century America, including those surrounding death, childhood, masculinity, and gender roles. The book also addresses issues of domestic violence, American missions, religion, and politics; JFS's role in defining and elevating the LDS doctrines of family, temples, and the afterlife; his dualistic worldview and its implications; masculinity and JFS's personal propensity toward violence; his role as a doctrinal systematizer; colonialism; and the ironic relationship between his sexual activity and sexual conservatism.

I hope readers will come away from this book with a greater appreciation for the complexity of JFS's character, a better-developed sense of how he interacted with his historical contexts, a clearer idea of the roots of his character traits, and a more robust sense of his humanity. JFS's story is astonishingly complex, and almost any decade of his life could itself be the subject of a single long volume. But this book is a celebration of that complexity and an exhilarating voyage, which, as the best biographers know, can generate more questions than it answers.

A note on names: Anyone who has written about, or read, early Mormon history knows that names get confusing very quickly. The number of variations on the name "Joseph Smith" is mind-boggling. This book is about Joseph F. Smith, the son of Hyrum Smith, the nephew of Joseph Smith Jr. (the founder of Mormonism), the grandson of Joseph Smith Sr., and the father of Joseph F. Smith Jr. (known to most Mormons as Joseph Fielding Smith) and Hyrum M. Smith. He is also the half brother of John Smith; the cousin of the apostles George A. Smith, George Albert Smith, and John Henry Smith; and the grandfather of Joseph F. Smith II. On his mother's side, he is the nephew of Joseph Fielding.

In an attempt to simplify this situation, I refer in this book to Joseph F. Smith by his initials, JFS. I admit that this is an unconventional approach to one's biographical subject, but this is something of an unusual situation. When I refer to Joseph Smith or simply Joseph, I am referring to the founder of Mormonism, Joseph F. Smith Jr. When I write about Joseph Smith's father, I refer to him as Joseph Smith Sr. I refer to Joseph F. Smith Jr. as JFS Jr. or Joseph Fielding Smith, which is the name by which he was known when he, too, became church president. I refer to JFS's father as Hyrum Smith or Hyrum.

I refer to JFS's mother, Mary Fielding Smith, as Mary Fielding when discussing her life before her marriage to Hyrum Smith, and usually as Mary after her marriage. I refer to JFS's son Hyrum as Hyrum M. Smith or Hyrum M. When referring to JFS's uncle Joseph Fielding, I use his entire name. JFS's grandmother, Lucy Mack Smith, is referred to as Lucy Smith or Lucy. JFS's sister, Martha Ann Smith Harris, is referred to as Martha Ann. All other Smiths are referred to by their first name, middle name or initial (depending on popular Mormon usage; for example, George Albert Smith and George A. Smith), and last name. All other persons are referred to by their full names, with case-appropriate middle initial/name, on first usage, and their last names in subsequent usages.

1 | Bloodlines

Joseph F. Smith came from English stock on both sides. The Smiths and the Fieldings were both religious families that valued charismatic experience over institutional religious expression. Both families came to North America for largely religious reasons, although they did so more than two centuries apart. JFS's most famous family members, of course, were those of the immediately preceding generation of Smiths. Too often, the Fieldings are overlooked or ignored. JFS's personality, however, was at least as much a product of his Fielding side as of his Smith side. Any thoughtful exploration of his life and thought must take into account the various familial histories and influences that shaped him. But JFS, traumatized as a child and orphaned as a teen, was left largely to his own devices to try to make sense of his experiences and create his identity. We must begin with the ancestry, with the raw materials that created JFS's first and most basic identity.

Although JFS would spend much of his life as an outsider in American culture, his family roots reached deep into the American past. Exactly 200 years before JFS was born, his first Smith ancestor to arrive in North America crossed the Atlantic from England. Puritans were leaving England in great numbers during the 1630s in an effort to escape the brutal anti-Puritan policies being enacted by William Laud, the archbishop of Canterbury, from 1633 until 1640 (he was executed in 1645). Young Robert Smith, only twelve years old, made the journey and settled in Massachusetts.[1] JFS's grandmother, Lucy Mack Smith, was a native of New Hampshire, with even deeper Puritan roots than the Smiths had. She was descended from several Mayflower passengers and many members of separatist John Lathrop's congregation. Lathrop and his coreligionists left England in 1634 and founded the town of Barnstable, Massachusetts.[2]

It is of no little consequence that the Smith/Mack story begins with a dramatic flight from the perils of religious intolerance. JFS's life would, in some ways, mirror that of his ancestor Robert. For generations, the Smiths lived and worked in Massachusetts. JFS's paternal grandfather, Joseph Smith Sr., was born in Topsfield, Massachusetts, in 1771. He and his wife, Lucy, settled in Vermont, where he tried his hand at farming and importing ginseng from China. Smith showed no aptitude for either agrarian or other commercial pursuits, and ended up losing a great deal of money on poor investments.

The family was peripatetic, moving seven times in fourteen years. Finally, in one more attempt at a new start, the Smiths, like so many New Englanders at the time, trekked west into the wilds of New York. In the Palmyra-Manchester area, they settled on a 100-acre farm. By this time, the family had grown to include eight children, with a ninth arriving after the move.

The Smith family arrived in New York with nothing. They worked a variety of jobs in the Palmyra area in addition to their attempts to farm. By 1825, the family had moved into a home in the nearby town of Manchester, one of the first houses in the area to be plastered. They were moving up the economic ladder and even refused a very substantial offer of $1,500 for their house. Contemporary accounts coupled with archaeological findings from the Smith home indicate that the family lived at a middle-class economic and social level.[3]

Religion played a major role in the family life of the Smiths. New York was part of the "Burned Over District," an area of western New York that was repeatedly convulsed with the Protestant religious revivals that accompanied the Second Great Awakening. Beginning around 1800, a major shift in the American religious landscape began to take shape. The emergence of a religious marketplace that followed the disestablishment of religion by the U.S. Constitution led to the demise of the dominance of Calvinist Congregationalists and Anglicans, and gave prominence to Baptists, Presbyterians, and Methodists who preached an Arminian theology.[4]

During the Second Great Awakening, emotion came to be viewed as a legitimate religious idiom, and the charisma of ministers came to matter much more than their formal training in divinity. The revivals were interdenominational, with Baptists, Methodists, and Presbyterians jointly hosting these events, which had as their chief goal the salvation of souls through acceptance of Christ as their personal savior. Once the revivals ended, however, tensions emerged among the evangelical congregations that were a permanent part of the town. The revivals converted people to a sort of generic evangelical Christianity, leaving the local Methodists, Baptists, and Presbyterians to fight over the newly saved souls, with each group striving mightily to bring the new converts into their own denominations.

The Smith family had long maintained a strong interest in the supernatural, although not in organized religion. This was particularly true of the family patriarch, Joseph Smith Sr. Historian Richard Bushman, describing the religious tensions within the family, noted that "Lucy's only explicit reservation about her husband was his diffidence to religion."[5] Lucy had gravitated toward the Methodists, while other members of the family favored the Presbyterians. Still others, like Joseph Smith Sr., found little use at all for organized religion. Like that of the nation in which they lived, the Smith family's "religious culture was too eclectic" for them to fit neatly into any religious taxonomical scheme.[6]

6   Chapter 1

The Smith Brothers and the Founding of Mormonism

It was this tension over religion, both within his community and inside his own family, that led Joseph Smith Jr. to seek out God to find out for himself which of the various churches was the "true" one. In 1820, he retired to a wooded patch on the Smith property and posed the question to God through prayer. The result of this attempt became the origin point of Mormonism. Smith claimed that heavenly beings appeared to him, one of whom identified himself as the resurrected Jesus Christ and instructed him that he should not join any of the Christian churches because they had all fallen away from original Christianity and lacked the proper authority to bring souls into the kingdom of God.[7]

Three years later, Smith claimed that he was visited by another resurrected being, this time a man named Moroni who had been part of a pre-Columbian Christian culture that had lived, and been destroyed, in the Americas. Centuries earlier, according to Smith, Moroni had deposited gold plates with a record of these people and their religion in a hill not far from Smith's home. In 1827, Smith claimed that he was given permission by Moroni to take possession of the plates for the purpose of translating them into English and publishing them as the Book of Mormon. The first copies appeared in 1830.

That same year, Smith organized his own church, which he claimed he did under command from God. He presented himself as a prophet and a seer, a man chosen by God to speak for the divine and to restore the original true religion that was taught to Adam and Eve. The entire Smith family joined the new church, including Joseph's older brother Hyrum. Hyrum and Joseph developed an intensely close relationship that grew stronger as the new church faced vicious persecution. In 1844, the brothers died together in a jail in Illinois, the victims of an armed mob.

JFS, Hyrum Smith's son, almost always recalled his father and his uncle together, only rarely speaking of one without mentioning the other. His habitual reminiscence of them in tandem is probably justified by the historical record: it was as a team that Joseph and Hyrum Smith built up the Mormons' first gathering place at Kirtland, Ohio, near the shores of Lake Erie, established and tried to defend settlements in Missouri during the mid-1830s, and founded the city of Nauvoo, Illinois, in 1839 before being jailed and murdered together in 1844.

Although Joseph and Hyrum Smith are so closely associated in Mormon memory, and were nearly inseparable during their lives, they were distinct individuals with quite striking differences in personality. Hyrum Smith was born on 9 February 1800 in Vermont. He was slightly better educated than Joseph, having had the opportunity to attend Dartmouth Academy for a short time. Hyrum was a compassionate and sensitive man who rarely showed anger. His mother noted that as a boy he was "rather remarkable for his tenderness and sympathy," traits that would follow him into adulthood. Unlike Joseph, Hyrum had a disposition toward introversion and was almost always deferential to Joseph, who was almost six years Hyrum's junior. Hyrum married his first wife, Jerusha Barden, in 1826. Jerusha was well-liked by the Smith family. She bore six children, two of whom died in childhood, before she passed away in 1837.[8]

The Fieldings, Mormonism, and a Marriage

Hyrum's second wife, JFS's mother, was Mary Fielding. Mary was born in Bedfordshire, England, a small rural county in south-central England with a history of religious turbulence dating back to 1650, when John Gifford founded a Particular Baptist congregation there. From 1653 until 1660, the Baptists actually occupied the local Anglican chapel. A century later, the Methodists found in the Bedfordshire soil a fertile missionary field. The Fieldings were active participants in Bedfordshire's "second rise of Methodism," a period that lasted from 1791 until 1831.[9]

Mary Fielding was born in 1801 in the tiny hamlet of Honeydon. From a young age, she was interested in religion; when her older brother left England for Canada, Mary's letters to him display keen interest, particularly in religion with an apocalyptic flavor. In 1833, she wrote with obvious excitement that local preachers were dwelling "upon the subject of our Lord's second advent" which brought "man to the saving knowledge of truth as it is in Jesus." In the same letter, Mary reported the presence of an "enlightened Jew" in the area who had made an extensive study of "their records," including, of course, the "Hebrew Bible." This mysterious stranger informed the people of Bedfordshire that there was "every reason to believe that the Mesiagha will appear within 7 years." Mary assured her brother that she was aware of the gravity of the subject and that it should be broached only with the utmost caution. She noted that the preaching of the "enlightened Jew" and his messianic message had become "a very prominent" subject among the people of Bedfordshire and that "the good effect of preaching this doctrine has been very considerable here."[10]

In 1834, Mary followed in her brother's footsteps and emigrated to Toronto, Canada, where her sister Mercy also came to live. It was in Toronto that the Fieldings met another English expatriate, a Methodist preacher named John Taylor. Taylor was born and raised in the Cumberland Lake region of far northern England, and although trained as a wood-turner, he was an autodidact with a keen mind and insatiable curiosity. Taylor was also obsessed with religion but found the Church of England stifling.[11] Like the Fieldings, Taylor was most strongly attracted to Methodism, and he became an exhorter for that faith at the age of seventeen. In Canada, Taylor's religious seeking had continued, and he started his own Bible study group. The group attracted a large number of like-minded seekers and was seen by the local Methodist establishment as a bastion of unauthorized and potentially dangerous zeal. Soon, Taylor's license to preach was revoked.

Taylor's experience was not an uncommon one; during the antebellum period in the United States and Canada, the newly powerful evangelical mainstream

8   Chapter 1

proved remarkably prone to fissures. Founded on the central idea that emotion was more important to religious experience than intellect, Baptist and Methodist congregations sometimes struggled to control the forces that they themselves had unleashed. The Holiness movement, for example, was established by Methodists who had found that their particularly strong and charismatic emotionalism was too much even for the average Methodist to endure. Taylor, too, had found that Methodism, a persecuted dissident group when he first encountered them in England, was acquiring the trappings of institutionalization. Groups like Taylor's threatened the stability that was becoming increasingly important as Methodism rose to prominence.

Taylor's group was particularly focused on the church organization described in the New Testament. He and the Fieldings were thus actively searching for an institution that looked like the church in the New Testament and which claimed authority directly from God. It was into this environment that Mormonism was introduced by Parley P. Pratt, who had been sent on a proselytizing mission to Canada by Joseph Smith in 1835. The message that Pratt bore of a new dispensation, a new prophet, revelation, and restored authority resonated deeply with Taylor and members of his congregation. Taylor spent a considerable amount of time shadowing Pratt, watching him speak and observing at least one apparently miraculous healing. Taylor brought Pratt to meet Joseph, Mary, and Mercy. After he agreed to preach only "old Bible" religion at a meeting, the Fieldings agreed to attend. Whatever Pratt said at the meeting must have dispelled any doubts the Fielding siblings had previously entertained regarding Mormonism. In May 1836, Taylor and his wife, Leonora, were baptized along with the Fieldings.[12]

Soon after their baptisms, the Fieldings moved to Kirtland, Ohio. Mercy married Robert Thompson in May 1837. Joseph Smith requested that the couple return to Canada as missionaries, where they would remain until 1838.[13] Mary remained in Kirtland without her siblings. She displayed a deep loyalty to Mormonism and an almost reverent attitude toward the Smith family. She believed that the Mormons were the true, chosen people of God and that satanic forces were constantly attempting to destroy the work. In the summer of 1837, Mary wrote that she did

> not expect in the least that Satan will give up the contest. No, he'd work
> in the children of this world, and also in the hearts of the children of the
> kingdom wherever he can find access to them, until he is bound. O may
> the Lord preserve us from his subtle power and keep us to that day.[14]

Mary was also convinced that those who became Satan's puppets in the persecution of the "saints" would meet with grisly ends. In the fall of 1837, she wrote to her sister that a family whose matriarch had recently spoken against the church was killed in a carriage accident near the temple. Mary observed that the woman "is gone to prove whether it is the church of Christ or not."[15]

Predictably, the origins of JFS's personal traits and worldview are most often searched for in the life of his father. It is clear, however, that many of his most basic assumptions about the world had their grounding in his maternal inheritance. Mary Fielding's letters, written before her marriage to Hyrum Smith, display certain habits of mind that would later find full expression in the life of her only son. JFS clearly inherited Mary's embattled posture and her way of viewing the world as the site of cosmic combat, both physical and spiritual, between the forces of evil and the forces of good in which she and her family were major combatants.

Like his mother, JFS had no problem seeing the devil's work being done by human hands, and neither of them hesitated to damn the evildoers in the most profound terms. It is significant that Mary demonstrated these habits of mind before she had personally experienced any significant persecution. It seems clear that, for both Mary and JFS, the experience of persecution worked together with a preexisting attitude about the nature of good, evil, and suffering to produce a particularly acute sensitivity to any insult, real or imagined.

In 1837, Mary took time to describe the Smith family: "Joseph and Hirum [*sic*] I know best and love much."[16] Very soon, her relationship with Hyrum would take a dramatic turn. His first wife, Jerusha Barden Smith, had borne him five children and was heavily pregnant with the sixth when Hyrum left Kirtland to attend to some church business in Missouri. While he was away, tragedy struck. One October day, Hyrum opened a letter from his brother Samuel. "Dear brother . . . Jerusha died this evening about half past seven o'clock. She was delivered of a daughter on the First or Second of this month."[17]

Jerusha's obituary noted that her loss was "severely felt by all" but hastened to add that she had died a good, dignified death, surrounded by loved ones and maintaining "her senses to the last." The obituary also contained what it claimed were Jerusha's last words, which consisted of a message to the absent Hyrum. "Tell your father," she spoke from her deathbed, "that the Lord has taken your mother home, and has left you for him to take care of."[18]

Hyrum must have found the prospect of caring alone for such a large family, including a new infant, astonishingly challenging. Even with a large extended family around him, the burdens on a single man of his importance and with so many demands upon his time would prove difficult to bear. Although low with grief, Hyrum returned to Kirtland as soon as he could. No historical evidence has been found to help us reconstruct just how he came to court Mary Fielding, but they were married just weeks after his return. A persistent family tradition holds that Joseph Smith sought a revelation from God about the matter and was told that Hyrum should take Mary Fielding as his wife. Although this story is frequently cited in published histories, there is no contemporary evidence to support it. It is, however, not an unreasonable idea. Smith was frequently asked by members of the church to inquire of God about some matter or other. Given the anxieties that Hyrum felt, it would have been in character for him to ask his brother, the prophet, for some divine guidance.

However it came about, on Christmas Eve 1837, Hyrum married Mary Fielding. She had no relatives to share the day with. Her sister Mercy was in Canada and her brother Joseph had returned to England. On that cold day near the shores of Lake Erie, she became a Smith. She also became a stepmother to six children, and the burden must have been heavy. Her own mother, who also was a second wife and a stepmother, had warned Mary against "entering into the important and responsible situation of Step Mother."[19] In the coming years, Mary would complain to Hyrum about the difficulties she endured as a mother to his children with Jerusha. In 1842, she signed a letter to him as "your faithful companion and friend but unhappy stepmother M. Smith."[20]

Whatever the burdens of stepmothering were, Mary would also give birth to her own children with Hyrum. Very shortly after the wedding, she became pregnant, and she gave birth to her first child and only son, Joseph Fielding Smith, on 13 November 1838. She was thirty-seven years old. In the blink of an eye, Mary had gone from being an interested observer of the Smith family's turbulent and often tragic life to being a full-fledged participant.

The Tumultuous Mid-Nineteenth Century

JFS was born at a time of not only tremendous upheaval within the relatively small world of Mormonism, but also at a time of great change in the United States and the world. He was born less than two years after Andrew Jackson left office, and he grew up in a nation that continued to labor under Jackson's shadow for decades. Jackson was the first president who did not emerge from an elite background; he never knew his father, was orphaned at fourteen, lacked many educational opportunities, and carried the scars of war. He represented the new American ideal of social egalitarianism. Jackson, that "most contradictory of men," embodied the heaving seas of antebellum American culture.[21] According to one of his most insightful biographers, Jackson viewed his presidency as part of a larger "struggle against privilege." In fact, he "knew only struggle ... His struggles defined him."[22]

Struggle also defined the new nation, just as it would come to define Mormonism and JFS. The first half of the nineteenth century saw major changes in politics, and also in economics, transportation, and religion. The nation expanded westward at an astounding rate. Between 1810 and 1820, the American population west of the Appalachian Mountains doubled, and five new states entered the Union.[23] The American political foundations crumbled and were then rebuilt. An American economy emerged that brought new meaning to the notion of boom and bust. During these years, much of what transpired was in fact a struggle between privilege and poverty. Scholars have dubbed this the Market Revolution, and it brought with it unforeseen complexities, not only in terms of economics, but also touching on social and political life. As historian Christopher Clark renders it, "new public as well as private spheres, new collectivities and communities as well as individualism grew out of the profound economic and social transformation of the early nineteenth century."[24]

Transportation and publication revolutions during this period changed how much people knew, and how soon they knew it. JFS was born into an environment that was turbid on almost every level, from the familial to the global. By the time he died in 1918, the world had become a markedly different place than the one into which he was born. As a world traveler, missionary, cultural observer, and eventually an ecclesiastical leader for a church scattered all over the globe, JFS spent his life in constant contact with the forces of change that convulsed the long nineteenth century.

Considering again the local environment into which JFS was born and raised, particularly in his earliest years, the most important of the many changes was the radical transformation of religion in the United States. Historian Jon Butler has referred to these years as an "antebellum religious hothouse" because of the tremendously diverse religious world that seemed to emerge almost overnight.[25] But revolutions are expensive because entrenched cultural interests dislike change. The rise of new religious movements such as Mormonism and the arrival of wave upon wave of Jewish and Catholic immigrants to American shores generated a response in the form of nativism.

Nativists—mostly from the lower class of white, native-born, European-American Protestants—employed a wide variety of tactics, including violence, in their quest to preserve what they viewed as "American" virtues. Anything that was not white, Anglo-Saxon, and Protestant became the enemy. Nativists were particularly venomous toward the Irish Catholics who began arriving in the United States in the first half of the nineteenth century. In 1834, at the same time that the Mormons were dealing with violence in Missouri, a Protestant mob attacked and burned to the ground an Ursuline convent in Charlestown, Massachusetts. Historian Katie Oxx has argued that nativism represented "a volatile mix in which bigotry was conspicuous and disputes were resolved through bloodshed."[26]

Violence of this type was commonplace in nineteenth-century America, and it certainly was not limited to Mormons, or even to religion. Cities faced an increasing threat from riots, and mob violence was so common that a term emerged to describe it: "mobocracy." In 1835, the *Southern Times* of South Carolina noted that "the whole country seems ready to take fire on the most trivial occasion," and the *Richmond Whig* in Virginia observed with alarm "the present supremacy of the Mobocracy," while Philadelphia's *National Gazette* opined that "the horrible fact is staring us in the face that whenever the fury or the cupidity of the mob is excited, they can gratify their lawless appetites almost with impunity."[27]

Many histories of Mormonism focus on the Mormon experience of violence without tying it to the larger antebellum culture of mob violence that was so prevalent in America. Viewing Mormonism this way inevitably and unnecessarily distorts the picture by ignoring the dialectical relationship between American culture and Mormonism. The fact is that Mormonism, particularly the attitude of nineteenth-century Mormons toward "the world," cannot be understood by focusing on only half of the conversation. It is simple enough to argue that persecution became an important rhetorical theme within Mormonism because Mormons were persecuted. But since the widespread, violent persecution of other religious and ethnic groups did not result in those groups defining themselves largely by their persecution experiences, one must ask what was different in the Mormon experience.

Perhaps this crucible of violence had a more profound impact on Mormons than upon other groups because Mormonism was forged and framed within it. Mormonism had no identity prior to persecution; it developed its identity in conjunction with persecution and violence. Decades after the threat of physical violence had largely passed, Mormons clung to a communal identity grounded in a narrative of persecution and martyrdom, largely because their core sense of communal self was organized around those ideas. This is important not only to the history of Mormonism, but especially to the self-formation of JFS, who would all the days of his life view the world as a dangerous place, a trap set by Satan and baited with particular malevolence toward the Mormons.

For JFS, the boundaries between his own identity and the communal identity of Mormonism were blurred. He was born at a moment when Mormonism seemed to be in an existential struggle for survival. In the early 1830s, Mormons built communities in Kirtland, Ohio, and Missouri. Kirtland thrived as the Mormon population increased. Mormons built a large new temple reflecting the increasing size and complexity of the church's ecclesiastical and ritual structure. Although there were several instances of anti-Mormon violence, including a brutal attack on Joseph Smith in which he was tarred and feathered, for the most part the Mormons lived in relative peace from 1831 to 1837.

That peace began to unravel in the months leading up to JFS's birth. The Panic of 1837 exposed weaknesses in Smith's financial banking system, an organization called the Kirtland Safety Society. Under President Jackson, the second National Bank of the United States had lost its charter. The Bank of the United States provided stability to the country through its twenty-nine branches; however, it was also the largest corporate entity in the United States and so became a favorite symbolic target of Jacksonians. Without a national system of currency, localities filled the vacuum, and instability inevitably followed.

Senator Thomas Hart Benton lamented the sudden emergence of a "wilderness of local banks," each of which issued its own currency. The inherent instability and riskiness of this arrangement was made clear by Jackson's refusal, beginning in 1836, to take anything but silver or gold for federal land purchases.[28] Like many similar institutions around the country at the time, the Kirtland Safety Society was not licensed by the state and was therefore more vulnerable to the frequent changes in the economy than chartered banks were.[29] The church suffered a major financial scandal as a result of the society's collapse, and church membership became polarized. Not for the last time, previously stalwart followers took Smith's financial failure as a sign that he was a fallen prophet. One-third of the church's general authorities left the church. Kirtland was in shambles.[30]

The Mormons Move to Missouri

The Mormons' experience in Missouri was far more brutal than in Ohio, and the trouble began almost immediately upon their arrival. Smith declared on 20 July 1831 that God intended for the Mormons to establish the holy city of Zion in Jackson County. This would be the New Jerusalem, the place to which the righteous would gather to escape the imminent calamities of the end times. The city of Zion, according to Smith, would be the location of a massive temple complex where Christ would reside after his return to earth.

Smith's 1831 revelation was both grandiose and provocative. Speaking in the voice of the Lord, he said,

> the land of Missourie . . . is the land which I have appointed and consecrated for the gathering of the Saints. Behold, the place which is now called Independence is the centre place, and the spot for the Temple. Wherefore, it is wisdom that the land should be purchased by the saints and also every tract lying westward . . . and also every tract bordering by the prairies [and also] the church [must] buy lands in all the regions round about.[31]

The revelation further commanded the Mormons to establish a mercantile concern and a printing office.

In 1831, Independence, Missouri, and its environs were every bit a frontier. Earlier settlers saw in the Mormon migration to Missouri a potential occupying force, powerful enough to band together and control the local economic and political spheres. Although they found Mormon religious ideas bizarre, their chief concern was how much power the Mormons would gain, and how quickly they would use that power to displace Missourians. The revelation made it clear that Smith and the Mormons had ambitious plans for the region that involved buying up as much land as they possibly could. The wording of the revelation itself carried a threatening tone. Consider, for example, the way the main city is described: "the place which is now called Independence." That "now" suggested that a new order was rolling in, and that this order intended to change the political, economic, religious, and even toponymic features of the area.

The mixture of frontier edginess and Mormon aggressiveness formed a volatile concoction. It is no surprise that mutual antagonism characterized the relationship

14   Chapter 1

between Mormon settlers and the Missourians in Jackson County from the very beginning. Soon, rhetorical disputes gave way to violence. In 1833, the Mormons were driven by force from Jackson County. They established successive communities in Clay, Ray, Daviess, and Caldwell Counties, but were driven out of each of them. Finally, in the fall of 1838, Missouri governor Lilburn Boggs issued an order mandating that the Mormons be driven from the state or face "extermination."[32]

Almost simultaneously, the Mormon settlement at Kirtland was collapsing, bringing Joseph and Hyrum Smith to Missouri. The Smith brothers arrived in Far West, Missouri, at the worst possible time. The Mormon experience in Missouri was so dark that Joseph would eventually write to a reporter that

> it would take more time than I can devote to your services, at present, to describe the injustice, the wrongs, the murders, the bloodsheds, the thefts, misery and wo [sic] that have been committed upon our people by the barbarous, inhuman, and lawless proceedings of the State of Missouri.[33]

When Joseph and Hyrum arrived in the late summer of 1838, organized and semi-organized conflicts began to erupt between Mormons and Missouri militias. The Mormon War, as it was somewhat grandly named, involved several armed skirmishes between Mormons and Missouri militia units. It began on 6 August 1838 when a large group of Missourians attempted to block Mormons from voting in Gallatin. A violent melee ensued in which no one was killed, but dozens were seriously injured. From that moment, relations between the Mormons and Missourians, already tense, began to deteriorate rapidly. Violent rhetoric and violent actions flowed freely from both sides. Mormon homes were burned, livestock stolen, and men shot.

In mid-October, a series of raids was launched on Missourians in Daviess County during which Mormons looted stores and burned approximately fifty buildings to the ground.[34] Richard Bushman, the preeminent biographer of Joseph Smith, somewhat charitably observed that some "militants took the Prophet's call for self-defense to extremes," a fact that did not help ease the situation.[35] It was becoming increasingly clear, however, that the situation was spiraling out of control, and the Mormons could not adequately defend their settlements. On 30 October 1838, the small Mormon settlement at Hawn's Mill was attacked by a well-armed force of Missourians who killed men, women, and children with equal viciousness. In the end, seventeen Mormons died, and thirteen were wounded. The war ended at Far West, Missouri, when Joseph Smith surrendered and was taken into custody.[36]

With the end of the Mormon War, the Mormon sojourn in Missouri was effectively over, but it would live on in the collective memory of Mormons forever, and it would haunt JFS, who only lived in Missouri for a few months, for the rest of his life. Joseph and Hyrum Smith, along with several other prominent leaders, were arrested and charged with several crimes, including treason. There is little doubt that Mary, perhaps for the first time, felt the full weight of her role as stepmother, a role she had been warned by her mother not to take.

The Incarceration of Joseph and Hyrum Smith

In November 1838, a hearing was held in Richmond, Missouri, to determine who among the accused Mormons should be held over for trial. Joseph and Hyrum were incarcerated in the Liberty jail in Clay County. It consisted of an upper floor, where the jailer lived, and a basement, or "dungeon," where prisoners were held. The lower room was less than six feet from floor to ceiling and approximately fourteen square feet. It was extremely cramped and very cold. The prisoners slept on logs and ate food that frequently made them ill. The food, which Hyrum believed to have been poisoned, had such an effect "upon our systems that it vomited us almost to death, and we would lie sometimes two or three days in a torpid, stupid, state not even caring or wishing for life."[37]

For his part, Joseph raged. He wrote vituperative letters castigating the Missouri authorities and even asked aloud why God would allow such injustice to befall his prophet. If Hyrum was correct in his recollection, the Smith brothers were being held as insurance to guarantee the departure of the Mormons from the state. A great deal more was at stake than just the ramifications of Mormon behavior during the Mormon War. Whatever the intention, the effect was that Mormons fled to yet another state, Illinois this time, in search of safe harbor.

From December 1838 until April 1839, the Smith brothers endured hellish conditions in the prison, conditions made all the harder to bear by the knowledge that the Mormons were now completely friendless and without a home. Mary and all of the Smith children were living with her sister Mercy and her daughter in a rough-hewn log home. Mercy's husband, Robert Thompson, had fled into the wilderness in November 1838 to hide from some Missourians.[38] He did not emerge for three months, leaving Mary and Mercy without a man in the house.

Hyrum doubtless had his new child and the rest of his suffering family on his mind. According to one source, he learned of JFS's birth from his father, who had asked what the child should be named. Hyrum replied that he should be given a blessing by Joseph Smith Sr. when he was eight days old, and that he should be named Joseph Fielding Smith. In the nineteenth century, it was a common Mormon practice to bless babies on the eighth day of their life, so this is not an implausible scenario. However, the source is an autobiographical reminiscence written some seventy years after the fact, so it must be treated with caution.[39]

Hyrum first laid eyes on his son on 29 January 1839, when Mary and Mercy visited the jail and brought the baby with them. According to one account of the visit, Hyrum held the baby, and JFS "received a blessing under his hands."[40] This blessing is commonly interpreted to have been the "naming and blessing" ceremony practiced by Mormons. Although it remains unclear if this traditional account and its interpretation are accurate, at least one historian, after careful research, concluded that "it is likely or highly probable that Joseph F. Smith was blessed by his father Hyrum on January 29 or 30, 1839."[41]

Mary's Motherhood and JFS's Childhood

The earliest known document to contain JFS's name is a letter written by his mother to his father in April 1839. "All the children seem very fond of him," she wrote of JFS. "He grows fast and is very strong and had two teeth when a little more than two months old." While pleased with his physical development, Mary expressed some concern over JFS's appearance. "You may not think him handsome," she wrote, "but it seems to me intelligence seems to beam forth from his eye and countenance. He begins to show signs of a good mind."[42]

While JFS was growing teeth and beaming intelligence, his older half brothers John and Hyrum Jr. were keeping themselves busy with other things. Mary reported to Hyrum that the older boys "often talk of doing great things to the mob for keeping Father away for so long."[43] Although Mary probably found such talk mildly amusing, it takes on a decidedly more tragic cast when backshadowed by Hyrum's murder. The boys' use of the term "mob" to describe those who they believed to be keeping their father captive is instructive. In the broader Mormon culture, the term was being used increasingly to describe any and all persons or entities who opposed the LDS Church. To the Smith boys, as to so many others, the "mob" must have seemed to come in never-ending waves to harm them and do violence to their families. JFS's earliest environment, then, was one in which mobs were real, dangerous, and ripe targets for vengeance.

As difficult as the Joseph and Hyrum Smith's time in the Liberty jail must have been, the Mormons' situation would get much worse. JFS was thus a child born in a time of war and social dislocation, to a family that was itself under great strain. His mother was newly married to an important historical figure and suddenly the stepmother to six children; his father was freezing and vomiting in a filthy dungeon in Missouri; and his religious community was once again, but not for the last time, marching homeless at the point of a gun. Tellingly, Mary was firmly of the opinion that "no one felt the painful effects of their confinement [in the Liberty jail] more than myself."[44] The birth of her first child coupled with the long-standing illness that crept in soon afterward did make her life particularly miserable.

During the months after Mary wed Hyrum, she must have felt nearly invisible, swallowed up by the massive, misfortune-prone extended Smith family, surrounded by children born to another woman. The identity she carved out for herself in that world was tinged with a sense of martyrdom. As was her natural inclination, she felt the world was unjustly singling her out for suffering, and she impressed that mindset on JFS. During the early months of his life, Mary was unable to care for and feed him, so Mercy stepped in and took over the nursing duties, a feat made possible by the fact that she had given birth to a daughter the previous summer. Mary remained bedridden for months with a chronic pneumonia-like illness. She eventually left Far West and went to the Illinois town of Quincy, where the Mormons were living in what was, in effect, a large refugee camp.[45]

Mary's tendency to call attention to her suffering was a trait that she would never be rid of. In fact, the Fielding family was characterized by, more than anything else, two overarching traits: an almost preternaturally deep and fiery religiosity and a hotly defensive temperament. These traits were never more prominently displayed than when conflict erupted within the family over Mormonism. Not all of the Fieldings of Bedfordshire found the message of Mormonism as appealing as Mary, Mercy, and Joseph did. Their brother James, in particular, found reason to object.

When Joseph Fielding returned to England as a missionary in the summer of 1837, he was keen to introduce James to the "restored gospel." He had some reason to hope for a warm reception because James had been reading letters from Joseph to his congregation, and the congregation was showing considerable interest. Sadly for him, things did not go as he had hoped. According to Joseph, he and the other missionaries were allowed to preach at James's pulpit until they started to become appealing to the flock. "The people," Joseph wrote to Mary, "began to believe more and more [and] this made Brother James begin to fear." James demanded that the missionaries leave his church and take their book of "fables" with them.[46]

A surviving letter from James to Joseph opens a window on the Fielding family dynamics. James began his letter by calling Joseph an "aggressor" and then accused him of trying to poach from his flock; being dishonorable, credulous, and cowardly; and having lost his "immortal soul."[47] He concluded by inviting Joseph to discuss matters face to face, but he cautioned that the meeting "better not be here" because it would certainly "endanger the quiet" of James's friends.

The tone of the letter is peculiar, with its sense of martyrdom, the comparison of the author to the persecuted Christians of old, acknowledgment of anger as a legitimate emotion in the cause of truth, the view that there is a one and only truth and anything deviating from it is idolatry, and a thinly veiled, but clearly threatening, invitation to "discuss" matters. Joseph concluded that the entire ugly event was for the best because it demonstrated that the "more it is oppressed, the more Truth is manifested."[48] James would no doubt have agreed. Each brother believed he was being persecuted by the other for and by religion. The relationship between oppression and truth was clearly part of the worldview of the Fielding family well before JFS arrived.

As peculiarly intense as this exchange is, it is uncannily similar to letters that JFS would eventually write. His letters to his cousin Joseph Smith III are

18   Chapter 1

particularly reminiscent of the exchange between the Fielding brothers. The Smith family, too, had their squabbles, but they were generally limited to interactions with William. On the whole, the Smith family culture tended toward cooperation, mutual support, and forgiveness. The Fieldings seem to have had a family culture that embraced insults as an opportunity to affirm identity and proclaim ultimate correctness. There are clear antecedents to JFS's attitudes toward religion and life in the story of his mother and her siblings.

Mary Fielding Smith collected and nursed grudges, as did her brother James, and for the few remaining years of her life after she married Hyrum, she would never want for opportunities to gather them. Nor would Mary's grudges and the anger and indignation that they generated die with her: they would burn forever in the breast of her only son. Added to his own increasingly traumatic experiences, JFS's indignation on behalf of his much-wounded mother formed a personality that could be as brutal as it could be loving, as violent as it could be comforting, and as earthy as it could be spiritual.

Consider a brief autobiographical account that JFS wrote in his journal around 1890. Recounting the now-famous story of the mob who ransacked his home, he wrote that "A company of men led by a Methodist preacher named Boyard, entered [the] house, searched it, broke open a trunk and carried away papers and valuables belonging to my father." JFS noted that he, a tiny infant, was asleep on a mattress and "entirely overlooked by the family" as they scattered. The intruders, also not noticing JFS, picked up another mattress and stacked it on top of the bed on which he was asleep, "completely smothering me up." He was finally remembered and thought to be dead, but he miraculously survived the ordeal. Before finishing his account of the incident, JFS made a point to mention that another man, Harlow Redfield, was also present. He noted with obvious satisfaction that Redfield, who later ended up with the Mormons in Utah, came to Mary's home to explain himself and try to excuse his actions. "My mother," he wrote, "could not swallow it, as she plainly told him."[49]

This particular story is occasionally published in Mormon periodicals in order to demonstrate the power that God exerted on behalf of this special infant. JFS's telling of the story serves a much different purpose. Quite simply, he is naming names and lionizing his mother's frank dismissal of any attempt at reconciliation. Moreover, his autobiography skips over the Nauvoo period almost entirely and ends with his arrival in the Salt Lake Valley in 1848. Nearly half of the pages in the document are dedicated to the various wrongs done to Mary. It is telling, indeed, that when he sat down to pen a reminiscence, fifty years after the events transpired, and with such a full and varied life from which to choose experiences, JFS chose to tell the story of the wrongs perpetrated against his mother. When it came to his mother's enemies, he never forgot and never forgave.

2 | From Missouri to Nauvoo

Although Joseph F. Smith was only an infant when his family left Missouri, the shadow of the events that transpired there followed him into adulthood. In order understand why Missouri and, later, Nauvoo, Illinois, came to figure so prominently in JFS's life, especially as he grew older, we may look to a theory of religion developed by Thomas Tweed. Tweed argues that "whatever else religions do, they move across time and space. They are not static. And they have effects. They leave traces. They leave trails. Sometimes those trails are worth celebrating.... Sometimes trails are sites of mourning." Tweed calls the trails left behind by the movement—both figurative and literal—of a religious tradition "sacroscapes."[1]

Sacroscapes help religions make sense of the changes that they make, especially those that are involuntary. Western religions, in particular, hold tightly to the concept of an unchanging God and an accessible "Truth." Changes, whether of ritual, doctrine, or status, pose potential problems. Successful religions, meaning those that are historically persistent, find ways to make necessary changes to remain viable within a given cultural and historical context while simultaneously explaining away the changes as nonexistent, unimportant, or as epiphenomena that are changes in appearance only, and which are actually in service of a larger, unchanging phenomenon.

This dyadic system of constant change and adjustment in response to historical contingency on one hand, and an internal rhetoric of constant stasis on the other, is particularly apparent in nineteenth-century Mormonism. Few religions in history have "moved," using Tweed's multivalent sense of that term, so much in so short a time.[2] The nineteenth-century Mormon sacroscape includes various moves from one type of family system to another and back again, from one type of conception of God to a much more radical one, from a centrally based Zionic ideal to a more diffuse one, and so on. Mormons moved not only from New York to Ohio to Missouri to Illinois, but also from Europe and the Pacific to the United States. All of this, and more, makes up the sacroscape. JFS's stories about his life became the lens through which later generations of Mormons would wander the trails of

20   Chapter 2

joy and, more often, of trauma and tragedy. It was in that capacity that JFS left his accounts of Missouri and Nauvoo, and those accounts can only be understood and analyzed with the notion of the sacroscape in mind.

JFS opened one brief autobiographical essay about his early years in blunt fashion: "November 13th, 1838. This is the date of my birth. I was born in Far West, Caldwell County, Missouri, 13 days after my father was taken prisoner by the mob."[3] His story starts in the crucible of persecution at the hands of the mobs in Missouri. Missouri found a lasting and active place not only in Mormon memory, but also in the Mormon view of the future.

Despite the humiliating string of defeats and evictions that occurred throughout most of the 1830s, and despite the ignominious imprisonment of their leader and prophet, Mormons never let Missouri go. There are two basic, related reasons for this. The first is that the early revelations established that God wanted Independence as his city, where Christ would one day return and rule personally on earth. The language in those revelations was so specific and so forceful that they simply could not be ignored no matter how grim the actual situation was. Second, a revelation received by Joseph Smith in 1834, after the Mormons had been driven off of their lands in Jackson County, was given increasing weight in subsequent years.

Smith's 1834 revelation spoke of the "redemption of Zion"—that is, the reclamation of Mormon lands—"by power."[4] According to the revelation, "the blessing which I have promised after your tribulations, and the tribulations of your brethren [is] their restoration to the land of Zion, to be established no more to be thrown down." This promise of a redemption of Zion and a return to Missouri remained vivid throughout the nineteenth century. Many individuals were promised as part of their patriarchal blessings that they would live to return to Missouri in preparation for the Second Coming of Christ. As late as 1916, such a blessing was given to Alma Owens, a resident of the small Mormon hamlet of Iona, Idaho, which stated that Owens would "build up the center stake of Zion on this continent."[5]

JFS's brief sojourn in Missouri had an outsized impact on him and on Mormonism in general. He incorporated memories of the period—including things he had heard from others but could not have actually experienced—into his own reminiscences. His recounting of his family's experience in Missouri offers crucial insight into the dynamic and malleable nature of memory. By looking at the tone, characters, incidents, and narrative structure of JFS's reminiscences, it's possible to get a sense of not only what may have happened in the past, but also the factors that shaped his memories and the collective memory of the Mormon people.

Mary and Hyrum Smith were not reunited until 22 April 1839.[6] After leaving Missouri, however, their time together would prove relatively short-lived. Hyrum and other church leaders immediately began searching the state of Illinois for a place in which the Mormons could resettle. On 1 May 1839, church leaders agreed to purchase land in and around a small town on the Mississippi River called Commerce.[7] It was a ramshackle collection of log cabins and a few stone houses located on a swampy flat at the bottom of a prominent bluff. Joseph and Hyrum moved to Commerce in the middle of May. By 18 May, the area was being surveyed for plot division. Wilford Woodruff arrived in late May and recalled, "Commerce is beautiful for situation though there is but two or three dwellings in the town as yet."[8]

Although it is clear that Joseph occupied one of the log homes, the location of Hyrum's dwelling is less well-established. He probably moved into one of the stone houses, where he lived with his family until April 1840, when they established a farm east of town. Although the horrors of Missouri had only recently been left behind, Woodruff gauged an optimism among the Mormons. "Notwithstanding the Saints are driven from city to city & from place to place yet they are not discouraged but are determined to build a city wherever their lot is cast showing themselves to be industrious & determined to maintain the kingdom of God."[9]

Soon after settling in Commerce, Joseph renamed the town Nauvoo, which he said is a Hebrew word connoting peace and beauty.[10] The refugees from the Mormon War in Missouri began to settle in Nauvoo in large numbers by 1840. By early 1841, converts from the church's missionary efforts in Great Britain also began arriving. Church leaders launched a campaign to bring as many Mormons as possible from wherever they were living to resettle in Nauvoo.

After the painful and costly years in Missouri, the Mormon leaders were determined to do everything within their power to ensure the safety and security of Nauvoo. One of the most important steps in this direction was the establishment of the Nauvoo Charter. W. W. Phelps, writing on behalf of Joseph Smith to a news reporter, accurately described the charter as endowing the leaders of Nauvoo with "as liberal powers as any city in the United States."[11] This document allowed Nauvoo to raise its own militia and to start its own university, and Mormons governed the city as they saw fit. Ultimately, however, these measures, which were intended to create a safe haven for the Mormons, would contribute to the circumstances that led to the murders of Joseph and Hyrum Smith and the collapse of Nauvoo.[12]

The town grew rapidly and within three years was second only to Chicago among Illinois cities in population. A massive temple was being built on the bluff, and the once-dilapidated flats now housed a variety of businesses and many homes. Immigrants continued to flow into the city, especially from Great Britain, until the mid-1840s. Joseph Smith was also introducing new doctrines, particularly those relating to the temple. He began teaching that living persons had a responsibility to be baptized on behalf of their dead ancestors. This concept of proxy work for the dead would later be applied to other things besides baptism.

Smith also began introducing certain members of his inner circle to the practice of plural marriage. He probably began practicing plural marriage himself in Kirtland, Ohio, in the 1830s, but it was not until the 1840s, in the relative safety of Nauvoo, that Smith began encouraging other men to do the same.

The nineteenth century saw the rise of many Christian primitivist groups that sought to recreate the church as it was described in the New Testament book of

22   Chapter 2

Acts. Scholars sometimes lump Smith in with this group; however, he was seeking to restore what he thought of as the original religion, an entity that stretched far back beyond historical Christianity. This original religion, Smith believed, had been taught to Adam and Eve by angels. Over time, the truths of the pure religion were lost and had to be restored again through divine revelation given to prophets.[13]

The periods during which "the true religion" was upon the earth were called dispensations. Smith believed that with the death of the New Testament apostles, the authority to act in the name of God had been removed from the earth, and without prophetic guidance, the human race descended into a period of religious confusion and darkness. He also believed that he had been called as the first prophet of the final dispensation, and that he would help restore the truths lost as a result of the deaths of the original apostles.

According to Smith's teachings, this particular dispensation differed from all others in two principal respects. First, Jesus Christ would return to earth at the end of this dispensation to destroy the wicked and establish his personal reign of righteousness. Second, during the final dispensation, every teaching, practice, doctrine, or belief that had ever been part of any previous dispensation would be restored to the earth through the instrumentality of living prophets. It was only in the final dispensation that everything would be restored and new things revealed, things that had been "hid from before the foundation of the world."[14]

The roots of Mormon polygamy, the practice that would play such a profound role in JFS's life, grew from this concept. Joseph Smith knew that Abraham had multiple wives, and he became curious about that. According to Smith, he asked God to tell him if a restoration of plural marriage was in order.[15] This may have happened as early as 1831, although no contemporary documentary evidence exists to establish a reliable timeline. In July 1843, Smith dictated a revelation that outlined God's views on plural marriage.[16] JFS was not yet five years old when his uncle spoke the words of this revelation that would irrevocably set the course of his life.

The revelation on plural marriage was originally written down in a failed attempt to convince Joseph's first wife, Emma, of the principle's divine nature.[17] Hyrum, ever the optimist, believed that if Emma saw a revelation from the Lord, she would be more accepting of the fact that Joseph had married other women, which Emma knew about.[18] In fact, she may have been present at some of the sealing ceremonies.[19] But her patience with her husband's experimentation had worn thin, and by the summer of 1843, she was refusing to embrace the principle.[20] Emma had discovered that her husband had taken six wives already that year, five of whom were living in the house with Joseph and Emma at the time.[21] Her reaction to the news of her husband's marriages was understandably negative. Joseph spent three hours on July 12, 1843, dictating the revelation, which Hyrum then took to Emma. Hyrum was shocked when he found himself on the receiving end of "the most severe talking to [of] his life."[22]

From Missouri to Nauvoo 23

Although the mission to convert Emma to the principle of plural marriage failed, the fact that the revelation had been committed to paper marked an important shift. There was now a tangible artifact to which Mormons could point, not only to justify plural marriage as an approved act of God, but also as a practice instituted by Joseph Smith. In the years after the creation of the Reorganized Church of Jesus Christ of Latter Day Saints in 1860, under the leadership of Joseph Smith's son Joseph Smith III, Emma and her sons claimed that Brigham Young was the one responsible for polygamy, and that her husband had neither taught nor practiced it.[23] JFS kept up a decades-long and contentious correspondence with his cousin on the matter.

In reality, Joseph Smith had gathered around him a close group of confidants to whom he introduced a constellation of new theological and liturgical items centered on the rituals that would take place on a larger scale once the Nauvoo Temple was completed. This small group, originally consisting only of men, met in Smith's office, his store, and private homes. The group referred to itself as the Quorum of the Anointed or "the Quorum."[24] It was in this context that Smith introduced the concepts of eternal family relationships, ritual work on behalf of the dead, the political kingdom of God, and plural marriage. It was also during this period that he introduced what he called "the endowment."

The origins of the endowment ritual are mysterious. The phrase "endowment of power" had been part of the Mormon lexicon since the 1830s, when a revelation promised that an endowment of power would be poured out on the Mormons in the Kirtland Temple. But in Nauvoo, the term took on a very specific meaning. On 4 May 1842, Smith summoned nine men to his store. On the upper floor, he introduced them to a new ritual that enacted the entirety of the human experience, from before the creation of the earth through the expulsion of Adam and Eve from the Garden of Eden, with a focus on the laws that all men (and, later, women) must covenant to obey in order to return to the presence of God.

The endowment consisted of two basic parts, an "initiatory" ritual that involved washing the body and anointing it with consecrated olive oil, and the lecture/covenantal portion in which individuals were taught the way back to God's presence.[25] Smith intended that the rituals would eventually be performed in the Nauvoo Temple, but for the next three and a half years they were performed in other places, including Joseph's store and various private homes. As part of the endowment, initiates were not only given access to hidden knowledge, but also instructed to wear a specially marked undergarment.[26]

Historian Jonathan Stapley argues persuasively that "Joseph Smith's revelation of the expanded temple liturgy in 1842 and 1843 was associated with an expanded cosmology in which kinship, priesthood, government, and salvation became synonymous." This "cosmological priesthood," as Stapley calls it, revolutionized Mormonism.[27] During the 1830s, there was little that separated Mormons from other

24   Chapter 2

low-church American Protestant denominations in practice. After Nauvoo, that was no longer true. The Mormonism that JFS would know, love, and preach all over the world was largely the Mormonism of the cosmological priesthood, born in the crucible of 1840s Nauvoo.

Hyrum did not learn of his brother's "reinstatement" of the practice of polygamy until sometime in the spring of 1843. In mid-July, he begged Joseph to commit the revelation to writing.[28] In August 1843, after Mary gave her consent, Hyrum took his first plural wife, Mary's sister Mercy Fielding Thompson. Mercy found the idea distasteful at first. "This subject when first introduced to me tried me to the very core all my former traditions and every natural feeling of my heart rose in opposition to this Principle." However, when Joseph told her that she had been "called by direct revelation from Heaven through Brother Joseph the Prophet to enter into a state of Plural Marriage with Hyrum Smith the Patriarch," her belief in his prophetic gifts overrode her revulsion.[29]

With her acceptance of plural marriage, Mary gained admittance to the elite Quorum of the Anointed. She was initiated on 1 October 1843.[30] From that time forward, Mary was often present at meetings of the quorum and assisted in the ritual of washing and anointing other women who were invited to join. She participated actively in the meetings but, unfortunately, left no record of her participation, so we lack her reflections on what these rituals meant to her. Hyrum and Mary's participation in meetings of the quorum was a significant, but largely secret, component of their religious lives in Nauvoo. Many decades later, JFS would serve for years in the Endowment House in Salt Lake, then as president of the Salt Lake Temple, and he regarded temple ordinances as among the most important work performed by the entire church. He was devoted to the form of the rituals he had first experienced, believing them to represent unchangeable revelations from God, and he was adamantly opposed to any proposed changes.[31]

After Hyrum married the widowed Mercy, he took her and her daughter, Mary, and made them part of his household. Richard Bushman suggests that Hyrum's abrupt course reversal on the issue of polygamy may have been helped along by the promise that Hyrum could be sealed, by proxy, to his deceased wife, Jerusha Barden.[32] Whatever the reason, and however it was that he actually learned of the practice, Hyrum embraced it wholeheartedly, just as he had every other teaching that had fallen from his brother's lips.

It is no surprise that Hyrum accepted the doctrine of plural marriage with little coaxing. While some men, notably Brigham Young, claimed to have deep revulsion toward the practice, he submitted to Joseph's new doctrine with little resistance. Even though Hyrum was seven years Joseph's senior, Joseph had always been the more dominant one in the relationship. Part of this was a matter of temperament, but part of it was simply the fact that Joseph was the one who had the visions.

Although Hyrum maintained complete solidarity with Joseph, he began to show signs of the internal and external stresses that pressed upon him and his brother beginning in 1843. Even his youngest child, Martha, noticed. She described her father in the final years of his life as "always anxious and sober" and "seldom cheerful."[33]

Childhood on the Mississippi

JFS's childhood in Nauvoo, Illinois, is accessible only through a re-creation of the general historical context because very few mentions of him exist from this period. We do know that his membership in one of the most important families in Nauvoo would have granted JFS an elevated status relative to other children his age; that he loved to walk the streets of the city, sometimes with his father; and that he and his siblings also spent time with their grandmother, Lucy Mack Smith, at her home in Nauvoo.[34] They were most amused by Lucy's practice of sending her dog to the store. Carrying on his back a basket and a grocery list, the dog would in due course return with a basket full of the things Lucy needed.[35] Most of the time, however, JFS could be found at his family's farm.

More ominously, there was also on the property a "little brick outhouse" in which JFS would frequently hide "to keep from going to prison."[36] Already by the age of three or four, he was hiding from his enemies, even if they were more imagined than real. This suggests some important things about the development of JFS's personality. First, his earliest years were spent in two worlds, one represented by the fields and streets of town, the other by the brick outhouse. The first world was the happy and prosperous world of Nauvoo, with its green fields and bustling dock—the world in which his uncle was king and his father was prince. This world surged with optimism as the church continued to grow, and the gleaming temple on the bluff continued, slowly but surely, to rise.

JFS's other world was one in which his uncle and father were hunted villains who not infrequently had to go into hiding to evade the Missouri officials who would sometimes come to Nauvoo seeking to extradite them.[37] Having never stood trial on the charges for which they had been held in the Liberty jail, Joseph and Hyrum remained liable to arrest. This was also a world in which violence could be inflicted on Mormons with impunity. The Missouri conflict had left indelible scars on the collective Mormon psyche, and the most prominent symptom was a chronic insecurity and, ironically, a tendency toward intolerance of dissent that occasionally turned violent. JFS picked up on that insecurity and transferred the threat of arrest aimed at his father and uncle onto himself.

JFS never recorded what went through his mind as he secreted himself in that fetid little brick box, but we know that he never forgot being there. We can safely conclude that the twin emotions of fear and anger, as powerful as they are primitive, surfaced early in his life. Unlike most children, who learn eventually that there is no monster under the bed, JFS learned early and often that the brutality he

26   Chapter 2

feared was very real, and that it could reach out and snatch happiness away from him with shocking caprice. Throughout his life, he was constantly being forced to deal with the tension between the world of the fields and the world of the box, and he was ultimately responsible for making theological sense of this tension.

Life in Nauvoo

JFS's family life was dominated by his mother, whose domestic burden was considerable. By 1842, Mary was responsible for six children ranging in age from one to fifteen, only two of whom were her biological children. Even in the most ideal circumstances, such a domestic arrangement would present distinct challenges. In the pressure-cooker environment of Nauvoo, tensions were bound to lead to conflict of one type or another.

In the fall of 1842, Hyrum apparently found occasion to criticize Mary's approach to his older children to other people in Nauvoo. When word inevitably got back to her, she was both deeply wounded and embarrassed. Mary wrote Hyrum, who was out of town, a letter describing a variety of more or less banal domestic happenings. But after she had apparently finished it, she began writing a lengthy postscript:

> I feel as though I could not close my letter without telling you how hard I feel it to bear to have my character scandalized and published round the neighborhood as an Oppressive Stepmother to your children, and this taken from your own mouth. I had supposed that you were tolerably well satisfied with me as a mother to your children. But after taking upon myself such a task purely out of sympathy and for so long doing everything in my power, and that conscientiously, for their comfort both in your absence and in your presence it gives me the very worst kind of feelings to hear you say that the children have no Mother. The consideration that you had confidence in me has generally been an encouragement to me to the best I could, and I believe it out of power to do better than I have done, especially after what I have heard, which I must say has tended to lessen my Parental feelings for your family.... I am not conscious of committing one act of oppression upon one of your children since I knew them, and I know that those who have lived with me since the commencement will lay no such thing to my charge tho I am English.[38]

Her sister Mercy was also apparently targeted for criticism, and Mary defends her in the letter against the charge of "interference" with the Smith children. Although I have added punctuation to the letter for ease of reading, that postscript contained virtually no periods. Mary even apologized at the end of the letter for the degree to which her normally fine grammar had deteriorated under the heat of her indignation.

It is unclear just how upset Hyrum was with Mary's parenting. He may have made an offhand reference on a frustrating day, or he may have held sustained ill feelings about it. What is interesting is that Hyrum complained to others in Nauvoo, most likely his extended family, rather than bringing his complaint to Mary herself. But he had more than met his match in Mary Fielding. The letter is, in many ways, a microcosm of her personality. It showcases her eloquence, devotion, her refusal to be cowed or intimidated, her facility with razor-tongued rebuke, her dedication to her church, and her loyalty to her husband. It also flashes a hint at the outsiderhood that her Englishness set upon her. It is all too often overlooked that JFS was half English—that he was raised by a woman with a "foreign" accent. Just how much Mary's national origin affected her standing within the Smith family is only to be guessed at; however, her letter leaves readers with no doubt that it was an issue that weighed on her mind.

Despite his occasional misgivings about Mary's heavy-handed parenting style, Hyrum maintained an unusually busy schedule. He played major roles on the committees handling immigration and temple construction. Thousands of British converts were arriving in Nauvoo every year, and it was up to Hyrum to help them find work and housing. His time-consuming responsibilities on the temple committee included managing work schedules, securing tithed labor from local Mormons, and directing the fund-raising efforts for the temple.[39] Hyrum also traveled frequently on church assignments. He spent a great deal of time in Mormon settlements across the river in Iowa, where he gave lectures on religious subjects and tended to church members' spiritual development.

In the fall of 1840, Hyrum and Joseph's father died.[40] At the time of his death, Joseph Sr. had been serving as patriarch to the church, whose main responsibility was to lay hands on the heads of church members and pronounce patriarchal blessings. These blessings, which are still given today, generally consist of telling individuals which tribe of Israel they are descended from and then providing an oracular narrative of what the future of the individual may hold. The day before his death, Joseph Sr. laid his hands on his son's head and said, "I seal upon you the patriarchal power and you shall bless the people."[41] All members of the church desiring such a blessing would now have to receive it under the hands of Hyrum. Further adding to his workload, Hyrum was called in January 1841 to be assistant president of the church. In the revelation calling him to this position, he was pronounced a "prophet, seer, and revelator," and Joseph Smith's chief deputy.[42]

Dodging external threats, managing immigration and temple construction, handling internal legal and ecclesiastical conflicts, and performing his duties as patriarch to the church and assistant church president left Hyrum little time for family life. Mary would have spent her time caring for the children, which involved not only preparing meals but also sewing and mending all of their clothes. The

28   Chapter 2

family was rambunctious and generally happy.[43] In May 1841, Mary and Hyrum's last child was born, a girl they named Martha Ann.

Religious life in Nauvoo has proven surprisingly difficult for historians to reconstruct. The eminent historian of Mormonism Marvin Hill once wrote that "when I was asked to consider religion in Nauvoo and began looking over my research notes which filled many large boxes, I found that very few of them deal directly with religious subjects." He concluded that in Nauvoo, to a far greater degree than in Missouri or Kirtland, Ohio, the boundaries between "religious" and "secular" collapsed. "Seen in this context," Hill wrote, "everything that occurred at Nauvoo of a social or political nature was essentially religious."[44]

Mormon religious practices would not become fully routinized and standardized until several decades later, after the move to Utah. Even then, it took decades for the religious and the secular to begin to clearly separate. In Nauvoo, explicitly religious activities such as scripture study, prayer, doctrinal discussions, and so forth were largely private or semiprivate affairs. It was not until 1844, for example, that an attempt was made to implement Sunday school. Mormons met weekly for sacrament meetings, often held in private homes with just a few families present. Gatherings of all the Mormons in Nauvoo and the surrounding areas, which were called conferences, were held twice a year. These conferences were opportunities for the sustaining of church officers, an activity that allowed Mormons to feel part of the larger organization of the church. It was mostly at the conferences that Mormons felt "part of a church larger than their own family or small congregation."[45]

Church leaders, including Joseph and Hyrum Smith, began speaking more frequently in open-air groves near the temple site. Mormons flocked by the hundreds to these gatherings, anxious to hear the prophet of the restoration, the man for whom many had cut family ties and crossed oceans. George Laub, a convert to Mormonism from Pennsylvania, left a record of what these Sunday sermons sounded like to an average rank-and-file Mormon at Nauvoo.

> We was taught by the mouth of the Prophet from Sabeth to Sabeth, who spoke with great power and much ashurance. He expounded the Scripture so that it could not be misunderstood for plainness. He also told us the will of the Lord concerning our present situation and State. He told us how to walk before the Lord and leade a happy life.[46]

In addition, Laub remembered that Joseph Smith taught that Mormonism was the unique vessel of truth in all the world, and that "the various denominations know nothing about God or Jesus Christ or of the Father or of faith or of truth or of knowledge as it consists in God & etc." But Joseph Smith promised that he would "sow the true principles of the docrin [sic] of Jesus Christ in its purity."[47]

Laub did not rub elbows with Nauvoo's elite, and he likely knew nothing of the Quorum of the Anointed or plural marriage at the time he was listening to Joseph

Smith deliver his sermons. What Laub's journal demonstrates is that, despite the revolutionary teachings and practices emerging in the highest echelons of Nauvoo society, Smith's 1840s sermons were very much like those of the 1830s: they highlighted his gift as a revelator uniquely positioned to teach the scriptures and to instruct his followers in the finer points of the moral life, all within a distinctly sectarian context. Although JFS remembered attending meetings, he left few records about his religious experiences during these years.

When the Nauvoo Temple was completed in 1845, religious life briefly shifted to a much more intense, ritually oriented enterprise centered on the new ordinances of the endowment and sealing. Throughout the entire Nauvoo period, perhaps the most important vehicles for dispensing religious information, communicating societal norms, and generally forging a unified culture among the constant stream of new immigrants were two newspapers published by the church: the *Times and Seasons*, which was primarily concerned with religious matters, and the *Wasp*, later named the *Nauvoo Neighbor*, which served as a general-information newspaper.[48] The papers carried reports of conference sermons, letters and editorials from church leaders, scriptural materials (including the texts that would eventually be published and canonized as the Book of Abraham), and information about housing and other practical and logistical matters of interest to new immigrants. The majority of new converts who were moving to Nauvoo from Britain and elsewhere during the 1840s probably had very little knowledge or understanding of the church's origins, doctrine, and scriptures. The *Times and Seasons*, especially, helped to remedy that knowledge gap.

Although religious practice was both diffuse and pervasive in Nauvoo, church organization was increasingly structured. There was a stake in Nauvoo, with a stake presidency and a high council. There was the First Presidency, and also the Quorum of the Twelve Apostles. Each of these entities was responsible for similar functions but in different geographical areas. In the 1840s, for example, the Quorum of the Twelve had authority only in areas in which no organized stake existed. Although the quorum slowly gained power in Nauvoo, members of that group were frequently assigned as missionaries to the eastern United States or abroad. Below the levels of general and stake leadership were local units. The church in Nauvoo was divided into wards that corresponded to geographical areas. Within each ward, various quorums of priesthood-holding men were organized. These quorums met whenever the need arose. Some of them were responsible for holding ecclesiastical courts for erring members of the ward.

There are few records to tell us about JFS's childhood beyond the fact that he attended school in a little brick store on the south side of Water Street.[49] During his childhood in Nauvoo, there would have been a multiplicity of parenting styles and attitudes toward children. In JFS's family of origin, matters of discipline were most likely left to his mother, but we have no reliable evidence that would allow us to reconstruct those family dynamics. Central to the story of JFS's upbringing, however, is the issue of masculinity.

30   Chapter 2

In the early nineteenth-century world in which JFS was raised, ideals of masculinity and femininity were clearly demarcated. Boys, especially in rural communities, were often assigned tasks that were both physically demanding and allowed them to remove themselves from the watchful eyes of their mothers in and around the house. Boys were encouraged to fight, race, play pranks, compete, and even, according to one scholar, "torture small animals."[50] JFS was no exception. In fact, his particularly traumatic childhood, coupled with the early nineteenth-century model of masculinity that he imbibed and embodied, would lead him to carry some of those aggressive traits into adulthood. In the context of marriage, family, and community life, JFS's often childish displays of aggression were out of place and problematic.

JFS's own memories of Nauvoo are historically suspect because they are inevitably reconstructed through the lens of the trauma of his father's murder. In the essay about his childhood that was published in the *Utah Genealogical and Historical Magazine* in 1916, JFS described Nauvoo as both "beautiful" and "dismal." He recounted the majesty of the temple, but pointed out that no one could afford to buy corn.[51] These impressions formed a braided rope of feelings that represented the conflict JFS felt about Nauvoo. On one hand, it was the birthplace of the Mormonism that he defended his entire life. On the other hand, it was the scene of his greatest personal trauma. One senses that JFS's published memories of those years seem far too clear, too crisp and sharp, to be the genuine memories imprinted on a three- or four-year-old mind. The recorded memories themselves are worth considering in detail, however, because they tell us something about what Nauvoo came to mean to JFS as he matured.

Unsurprisingly, all of the memories that JFS recounts from the Nauvoo period include his father. In one story that he told multiple times, he describes a visit from his father and uncle:

> While I was a little boy, one day I think it was just about the noon hour, we were anticipating, or my mother was anticipating, the return of my father from somewhere for he and Joseph and been in concealment away from the mob, and I was looking for them. I went out to the bank of the river, close to the old printing office. I sat on the banks of the river, and presently, I saw a skiff starting out from the other side of the river. The river there is a mile wide. They rowed on across the stream until they landed close to where I stood. Out of that little skiff the Prophet and my father alighted and walked up the hill. I joined the hand of father and we went to my mother's home, the home of my father. They both went into the house and sat down. They chatted and talked with each other, and while my father was changing his clothes—I suppose his collar and cuffs and things of that kind—Joseph the Prophet sat there. He took me on his knee and trotted me a little and then he looked at me a little more carefully and finally he said "Hyrum, what is

the matter with little Joseph here?" "Well," he says, "I don't know. What do you think is the matter?" "Why, it looks like he had not a drop of blood in him." "Oh," Father says, "that is because he has been living on milk only" for up to that time, I had hardly eaten anything harder than milk. I was living on it. I do not know whether that had the effect of making me white or pale, but that was the condition I was in and that was the remark the Prophet made. I never forgot it.[52]

The detail of this story is impressive. JFS sets the stage with the touch of a master storyteller. His audience would have heard stories of Nauvoo, and the imagery he conjures up takes them with him back to the banks of that river, "a mile wide." The image of the child's hand in his father's is poignant; the audience would have known the tragedy of that gesture, that JFS's hand would reach forever after to the hand of his father, a hand that he would never find again. The fine-grained description of Hyrum's pedestrian actions—changing cuffs and collars—is mesmeric in its humanizing effect.

Joseph Smith's role in this story is intriguing. He is a shadow at first, outside of the intimacy of Hyrum's home. He does bounce the young JFS on his knee, but he only speaks in the service of the pathos that JFS is crafting for his audience. The pale little boy with nothing but milk to nourish him is foreshadowing the storm that the audience knows is rushing inexorably toward him.

The second memory is almost certainly more fiction than fact.

> One day during cold weather, my father took me by the hand and led me down the road to a little brick building. It was not much larger than ... a little beehive, but it was the best they had at that time, and in it was a little sheet-iron stove. I remember the looks of it just as well as if I had seen it yesterday. There I remember the Prophet Joseph, my father, Brigham Young, Sidney Rigdon, and Willard Richards, and there were a number of others. They met in that hovel to consider what they should do with the obligations that rested in their hands, from those that had been despoiled of all they had in the world.

Many Mormons owed money to the church and to church leaders, but they were now incapable of repaying the debts because of the devastated conditions that obtained after the exodus from Missouri. JFS recalled that as they sat in that room, with the actual debtors' contracts, Joseph Smith "opened the door of the stove and stuck them in, and I saw them burn."[53]

If such a meeting took place, it most certainly would have occurred before April 1842, at which time Joseph Smith declared bankruptcy. That would mean that JFS could have been no older than three and a half. I have no doubt that JFS believed sincerely that he remembered this event. The fact is, however, that this would have been nearly impossible. We have in this case a memory that he created from some fragmented recollection that reflects his sense of what Nauvoo was all about. The memory, however, contains elements of the grand narrative that JFS believed undergirded his entire life. It paints the Mormons as victims who refused to claim victimhood. By destroying the notes and forgiving the debts, Joseph Smith was, in a sense, refusing to further the aims of the "mobs" through self-sacrifice. By the time JFS told this story, the Smith brothers had long since been enshrined as the martyrs of Mormonism, from whose blood the seed of the church sprang. It is not surprising, then, that JFS fashioned a memory that echoed the themes of martyrdom and self-sacrifice.

3 | The Murders of Joseph and Hyrum Smith

Once Hyrum Smith accepted plural marriage and the revelation began to circulate in written form, the internal situation in Nauvoo, Illinois, began to deteriorate rapidly. Like so many other events in LDS history, the story of the last year of Joseph's and Hyrum's lives have been documented over and over again. In 1843, the well-founded rumors of polygamy and polyandry were growing in strength. The church was, once again, plagued by high-level internal dissent, and one can draw a straight line from the expanding practice of plural marriage to the murders of the Smith brothers on 27 June 1844.

Although polygamy presented the greatest obstacle for some church leaders, two other developments also raised objections. One of these was Joseph Smith's increasingly elaborate belief in a political kingdom of God. He had established a secret Council of Fifty, yet another elite group of Mormons, and a few non-Mormons, who would govern the country after Smith was elected U.S. president. His serious attempt to run for the presidency in 1844 fueled fears among some Mormons that he intended to completely dissolve the boundaries between secular and sacred. Finally, Smith's now-famous King Follett discourse offered a radical new theological schema that diverged sharply even from Mormon conceptions of God that had emerged in the 1830s.[1]

The unlikely-named King Follett, who had been a friend of Smith's and a civic leader in Nauvoo, was killed when a bucket of rocks fell on him. Smith spoke of his friend in a sermon on 7 April 1844, but he spoke of much more than that. This sermon presented Smith's idea that God was a being who had once lived on earth as a mortal being and who had, by adhering to certain laws and principles, ascended to godhood. Smith suggested that it was the privilege of all human beings to become gods and goddesses if they followed the same pattern. The discourse has been interpreted in various ways by scholars in the century and half since it was presented. What is important for our purposes is that while most Mormons either paid no attention to it or embraced it as yet another astonishing revelation from their dynamic prophet, others reacted less enthusiastically.

34   Chapter 3

Even before the King Follett discourse, Smith believed that there was a plot to take his life.[2] In May 1844, several of his opponents set up a newspaper printing operation in Nauvoo. The paper, called the *Nauvoo Expositor*, was published only once, but it contained accusations about the practice of plural marriage, something that Joseph Smith was still publicly denying. The *Expositor* caused a fair amount of panic among the Smiths and their associates, precisely because the allegations about polygamy were true. But Joseph Smith had lost control of the narrative: the *Expositor* spun the story of plural marriage as one of secret lust and sexual license. However, the 1843 revelation, which was not a public document, makes clear that Smith preferred to nest his practice and teaching of polygamy within the context of ancient religious practice and an ever-expanding web of eternal family relationships.

Smith had grown accustomed to dealing with hostile newspapers over the years; he had been mocked in print since before the church was even organized. Newspapers in nearby Carthage and Warsaw, Illinois, had been growing increasingly vituperative in their calls for the expulsion of the Mormons. The *Expositor*, however, represented a special case. This was a newspaper operating within Smith's own city, and it was being run by former trusted associates. To exacerbate matters, the editors of the *Expositor* framed the publication not as an exposé, but as a call to repentance directed at Smith. The editors argued that they were left with no choice but to publicly "explode the vicious principles of Joseph Smith."[3]

Smith's supporters saw in the *Expositor* the same evil hand that had so badly abused them in the past. During a fateful city council discussion about what to do about the paper and its allegations, Phineas Richards drew a connection from the worst of the previous persecutions right to the publication of the *Expositor*; he "said that he had not forgotten the transaction at Haun's Mill, and that ... his son then lay [in a well] without winding-sheet, shroud or coffin."[4] Richards avowed that he refused to sit still while he saw the same spirit "raging in this place." To him, the publication of the *Expositor* seemed "much murderous at heart as was David before the death of Uriah." John Taylor asked, "Will you suffer that servile, murderous-intended paper to go on and vilify and slander the innocent inhabitants of this city, and raise another mob to drive and plunder us again as they did in Missouri?"[5]

Clearly, the persecution narrative provided Smith with the emotional and political support to move. He himself argued that the *Expositor* was simply another attempt to destroy the church. Many Mormons believed this argument. Joseph Hovey, for example, wrote that Smith's enemies "concocted a plan to destroy the Prophet by publishing a paper that was as foul as hell itself."[6] Hovey's recollection represents the common view held by most Mormons in Nauvoo.

Although the established narrative of persecution that had taken shape most vividly after the Missouri period seemed to fit the *Expositor* situation as well, the situation was not so simple. The narrative was complicated by two factors. First, the accusations in the *Expositor* were true; the material was presented in terms and at a time that were unfavorable to Smith, but these were not lies. Second, Smith's

The Murders of Joseph and Hyrum Smith 35

decision, enacted through the agency of the Nauvoo City Council, to destroy the press and all available copies of the *Expositor* was an act of desperation so grandiose that it raised questions about the scope of Mormon power and the propriety of allowing it to exist within the borders of the state of Illinois.

Although the murders that would soon follow represent the most despicable impulses of antebellum American vigilantism, Smith had made himself vulnerable to this treatment through his own mishandling of the dispensation of knowledge regarding plural marriage and his foolhardy decision to destroy the *Nauvoo Expositor*'s printing press. As Dallin Oaks and Marvin Hill remarked, in a virtuoso act of understatement, "the question of ultimate authority was at issue in western Illinois in the 1840s."[7]

In the court at Carthage, Chauncey Higbee, one of the *Expositor*'s publishers, and others swore out complaints against Smith and his accomplices for the destruction of the press.[8] Smith used his control over the Nauvoo courts to secure a writ of habeas corpus. In the meantime, responding to rumors that local militias in Warsaw and Carthage were preparing to march on Nauvoo, he deployed the Nauvoo Legion and declared martial law. As the pressure, and danger, mounted, the Smith brothers initially fled Nauvoo and crossed the Mississippi River into Iowa. They planned to use Porter Rockwell as their "guide" to the "Rocky Mountains."[9] They understood that if they surrendered themselves to the legal authorities in Illinois, they would be placing themselves at the mercy of a wide variety of legal and extralegal forces, and would be in grave danger.

When Rockwell returned to Nauvoo to secure horses for the journey, he encountered a distraught Emma Smith, who pleaded with him to try to get Joseph to change his mind.[10] Hyrum, too, was having second thoughts, but when Rockwell returned and told Joseph about Emma's request that he return, Hyrum also expressed his opinion that they should demonstrate greater faith in God and trust that he would see them through any difficulties that might arise in Illinois. All of this was enough to convince Joseph Smith to write to Illinois governor Thomas Ford, promising to surrender himself and the fourteen others charged in the destruction of the press if his safety could be guaranteed. The men then recrossed the river.[11]

This chain of events ended in the jail at Carthage, Illinois. The Smith brothers had secured a promise of protection from Governor Ford, so when they arrived in Carthage on 25 June 1844 along with John Taylor, Willard Richards, and others, they were locked in a room on the second floor of the building that served as the Hancock County Jail. But two days later, the promised protection disintegrated. An armed mob of between 100 and 200 men with blackened faces mounted an attack on the jail. Members of the mob may have been drawn from the militia at Warsaw, Illinois, a town that was feverish with anti-Mormon sentiment.[12]

Charging up the narrow stairway leading to the room that held their victims, the vigilantes smashed against the heavy wooden door. Gunfire soon erupted. Hyrum was the first to fall. He was attempting to brace the door shut with both arms when a slug penetrated the door and lodged in his face. The force of the shot knocked him onto his back, but left enough life for him to mutter, "I am a dead man." He was shot several more times, although it is unclear which wounds proved fatal.[13]

Joseph attempted to fight back, but he was badly outgunned; his tiny pepperbox pistol was simply no match for the guns and rifles of the mob. After taking fire from assailants within the jail as well as from those outside, he stumbled, mortally wounded, to a window, where he shouted a Masonic distress cry, "Is there no help?," and fell to the ground below. John Taylor also took two slugs but managed to survive. Richards somehow emerged from the melee unscathed.[14]

Aftermath of the Murders

Early on the morning of 28 June 1844, Joseph F. Smith heard Dimick Huntington shout to his mother, Mary Fielding Smith, through the window of her bedroom, "Hyrum is dead!" "I remember," he recalled, "the exclamation that my mother made," and that "it was a misty, foggy morning; everything looked dark, and gloomy, and dismal."[15]

The actual attack on JFS's father and uncle probably lasted no more than a couple of minutes, but the wound that it would leave on JFS's mind and soul would stay with him for the rest of his days. In some ways, his mind was never far from that room in the Carthage jail. Despite several trips that brought him close, he did not visit the room in which his father was murdered until 1906. JFS found the experience so harrowing, even after many decades, that he nearly became physically ill.[16]

The murders of Joseph and Hyrum Smith left the Mormons in Nauvoo in a state of shock. After all of the close calls, all of the imprisonments, all of the pursuits, and all of the persecution, the two brothers had suddenly ran out of luck; they were dead and gone. More than 10,000 Mormons in Nauvoo and the various satellite Mormon villages in the area were now left without a prophet, without their founder and leader, without the living symbol of their faith.

Most of the members of the Quorum of the Twelve were not even in Illinois at the time of the murders. Wilford Woodruff, Brigham Young, Heber Kimball, and many others were scattered throughout the eastern United States trying to drum up support for Joseph Smith's U.S. presidential bid. News reached Young, who was in Boston, and the other members of the quorum slowly, and most were hesitant to believe the initial reports.[17] Rumors mixed with fact, adding to the confusion. On 11 July 1844, Woodruff wrote in his journal that he was still unsure just exactly who had been killed. He knew that Joseph and Hyrum were dead, but he also noted reports that Willard Richards and W. W. Phelps had been shot.[18]

The story was national news. On 9 July 1844, the *New York Daily Tribune* carried a report of the murders, which noted that although "the deepest grief and affliction pervade the city [of Nauvoo] ... there appeared to be no danger of the burning of Carthage."[19] The *Indiana State Sentinel* held up the murders as an example of the runaway violence in the United States: "The actors in this disgraceful transaction are probably confined to a few desperate characters who are determined to ride over the law to effect their object."[20]

The bodies of Joseph and Hyrum Smith were returned to Nauvoo, where they were washed, dressed, and prepared for viewing. Joseph's body looked relatively good. Hyrum, however, with the bullet wound to his face, was a much more macabre sight. JFS was lifted up so that he could gaze into the coffin and see what was left of his father. The memory of his father's brutalized, violated, decimated face never left him. Nearly as disturbing must have been Mary's emotional breakdown at the sight of the body. A writer who had visited the home earlier in the day described her as being "stupefied with horror" as she "unsteadily approached the coffin. With the children clinging to her, she fell on the body, asking Hyrum if he were really dead, holding his head in her hands, kissing his mangled lips and shrieking."[21]

The feeling of helplessness that overcame JFS at that moment was something he never wanted to experience again, and the anger generated by this encounter with his father's corpse animated him for the rest of his days. Some 10,000 people shuffled somberly through the front parlor of the Mansion House to view the bodies. After the public viewing, the bodies were removed from the coffins, which were filled with sand and buried at a funeral the next day. The reason for the subterfuge lay in the price that remained on Joseph's head. There was a bounty on him, and it would be paid if he were brought back to Missouri, dead or alive.

The larger Mormon community in Nauvoo reacted to the murders with a mixture of grief and rage. Like most religious groups, Mormons had to integrate a catastrophic disappointment of their prophetic expectations into their self-understanding. One of the mechanisms of reintegration was the lore that sprang up emphasizing Joseph Smith's foreknowledge of the event. This narrative, which persists into contemporary Mormonism, has Joseph proclaiming as he rode out of town toward Carthage, "I am going as a lamb to the slaughter but I am as calm as a summer's morning. I have a conscience devoid of offense to God and all men. I shall die innocent, and it shall yet be said of me, 'He was murdered in cold blood.'" It is not possible to know if Smith ever said this because no accounts of it predate his murder. The earliest known account was published in the 5 July 1844 edition of the *Times and Seasons*.

JFS's activities during the period between his father's murder and his family's departure from Nauvoo in 1846 are not documented. His son Joseph Fielding Smith wrote that "Between the time of the martyrdom and the time of the exodus from Nauvoo ... life was spent in the depths of wearisome toil."[22] The documentary record allows us to say little more than that, and JFS was still very young and had no reliable memories upon which to draw. His mother, Mary, left no journal. John Smith, JFS's older half brother and later patriarch of the church, wrote an

38   Chapter 3

autobiography that moves immediately from the murders in 1844 to the departure of the family from Nauvoo in early 1846. It is likely that much of life carried on for JFS as it had before.

The family continued to live on the farm, and while Hyrum's absence was doubtless keenly felt by everyone, he had not been an active presence in the home during the last years of his life. Mary's brother Joseph moved into a building on the farm, and in early 1846, Mary was married to Heber C. Kimball in the Nauvoo Temple. Kimball and Young had started marrying the various widows of the Smith brothers in an effort to ensure that they were not left without some protection. Mary left no record of what this second marriage meant to her, but Lucy Walker, one of Joseph Smith's plural wives, was also married to Kimball, and she recorded that

> the contract when I married Mr. Kimball was that I should be his wife for time, and time only, and the contract on the part of Mr. Kimball was that he would take care of me during my lifetime, and in the resurrection would surrender me, with my children, to Joseph Smith."[23]

In all likelihood, Kimball's arrangement with Mary was similar. This was not a marriage in any romantic sense of the term; there would have been no sexual relations, and the two never lived together. Kimball was simply claiming responsibility for the general care of these widows.

Mary, for her part, had little to do with Kimball and managed affairs mostly on her own. JFS's memory of the period between his father's murder and the evacuation of Nauvoo left no doubt about that. "By the massacre at Carthage," he recalled, "she was left the sole guardian of a large family of children and dependents, for whom by her indefatigable exertions she provided the means of support."[24] JFS remained fiercely protective of the memory of his mother as a completely independent widow for the rest of his life. When Kimball's son Solomon showed JFS a draft of a biography of his father, JFS expressed outrage at the implication that Mary might have received some material assistance from Kimball. "No man supported my mother from her widowhood to her death," JFS fumed, "and anything to the contrary is not true."[25]

JFS was probably unaware of the drama unfolding all around him, even though he would have certainly detected his mother's intense sadness. There is evidence that Mary and Mercy participated in initiatory and endowment rituals in the newly completed temple. Once the temple was completed, members of the Quorum of the Anointed were generally endowed again and sealed to their spouses and children for eternity, and they then worked to endow and seal others. In an act of great generosity of spirit, Mary stood proxy for Hyrum's first wife, Jerusha, as Hyrum and Jerusha were sealed for time and eternity. Mary was sealed, again, to Hyrum and to her children on 26 January 1846.[26] JFS was present, along with his sister and all of his half siblings, as they knelt around an altar in the temple and were sealed to

Hyrum. JFS and Martha were then sealed to Hyrum and Mary, with Brigham Young standing in as proxy for Hyrum. It is interesting, and strange, that JFS never mentions this experience. He would have been seven years old and possibly retained some memory of it. Perhaps it was something that he felt was too sacred to speak about publicly. In any case, it marked the first moment in a lifetime of temple service, first in the Endowment House in Salt Lake City and later as president of the Salt Lake Temple.

Outside of the family circle, however, major changes were happening, and fast. With the death of the Smith brothers, the church faced a disorienting leadership vacuum. Joseph Smith had, over the course of his life, designated several possible successors. The ambiguity of his intent led to what has come to be called the "succession crisis," which played out in the late summer of 1844.[27] The apostles had all finally made their way back to Nauvoo, with Brigham Young as their leader. Young believed that Joseph had intended the Quorum of the Twelve to govern the church. This meant, of course, that although Young would not be president of the church, he would be the leader of the church's governing body.

Contesting Young's leadership was Sidney Rigdon, who was baptized in 1830 and had been an associate of Joseph Smith's since December 1830. Smith had appointed Rigdon to be one of his counselors in the First Presidency in Kirtland. In Nauvoo, however, their relationship became strained. When Smith was drawing a group of associates close to him and instructing them about, among other things, plural marriage, Rigdon was not there. Although admitted to the Quorum of the Anointed, his participation was, at best, half-hearted. This stemmed, no doubt, from what he saw as the folly of Smith's evolving theological ideas and the practice of polygamy, something that Rigdon refused to accept.

In 1843, Joseph had tried to release Rigdon as a counselor to the presidency, but Hyrum had prevailed on his brother to show mercy and allow him to remain in place. Church members generally sided with Hyrum. Joseph was frustrated and angered, but he honored the prevailing opinion. In June 1844, however, he asked Rigdon to go to Pittsburgh to take charge of a small branch of the church there. One cannot help but interpret such a move as a way to be rid of him without violating the wishes of the larger church membership.

By the time he returned to Nauvoo on 3 August 1844, Rigdon had already become something of an outsider. For six days, the apostles and Rigdon moved about Nauvoo, trying to settle on a solution.[28] Rigdon and Young finally squared off in a series of public outdoor meetings held in Nauvoo on 8 August. Rigdon spoke to the assembled Mormons first, claiming that he, as the last remaining member of the First Presidency, should be the "guardian" of the church. Although in retrospect it appears that Rigdon was no match for Young, the situation on the ground in Nauvoo at the time probably looked a little different. As historian Ron Walker has pointed out, "Rigdon's claims were not easily put aside. He still held many Church titles and was easily among the most accomplished of the Saints."[29]

Rigdon gave a persuasive speech, but he was upstaged by Young, who had entered the meeting unseen and taken a seat on a stage opposite Rigdon. When Young finally spoke up, everyone turned to see the man who had been absent from Nauvoo for four months. His natural charisma and force of personality, coupled with his argument about the keys of the kingdom resting with the apostles, won the day. When put to a vote, the vast majority of Mormons chose Young and the apostles.

Although most members of the church followed Young, several significant splinter groups also formed.[30] Rigdon wanted to establish a rival church and entered into talks immediately with some Nauvoo residents who disliked Young. On 8 September 1844, a court was held in which Rigdon was tried for his membership in the church. Most of the assembled leaders felt that Rigdon was unstable and had lost the trust of Joseph Smith in the years before his murder. Young reminded the group that Rigdon would have been gone already if Hyrum Smith had allowed all of the evidence against Rigdon to be presented during the 1843 deliberations. Rigdon was then excommunicated. There were others who gathered followers around them, including James Strang and the ever-problematic Smith brother William. Although not insignificant, these groups failed to seriously fracture the main body of Mormons who had lined up behind the leadership of Brigham Young.

Once the succession question was more or less settled, Young turned his attention to the tasks that had always been the most pressing in Nauvoo: building the temple and managing immigration. Immigrants were continuing to arrive, mainly from England, and Young continued to pour church resources into construction of the temple. Beginning in the fall of 1844, Nauvoo entered a relatively peaceful period. In January 1845, Young decided that, even though the state legislature had repealed the Nauvoo Charter, the Mormons should remain in Nauvoo and finish the temple.[31]

In August 1845, Young wrote in a letter to Amos Fielding that "three or four days more will complete the shingling of the temple, and the dome is nearly all up and the inside work is in rapid progress." In fact, he noted that "more has been done on the temple . . . this season than in any one season before." Enough grain had been produced to support not only "the city, but also all that will come in this fall." Even major residential projects continued, with "several large and good houses" coming to completion that summer.[32]

Even as Young wrote that letter, however, yet another Mormon settlement was about to collapse. In the same month that Young said God was telling him to remain in Nauvoo, the Illinois legislature crossed partisan lines to repeal the Nauvoo Charter. Nauvoo was growing increasingly vulnerable to the anti-Mormon groups in Hancock and Adams Counties. At one point, Governor Ford personally warned Young that it would be best for the Mormons to move on, arguing that he simply did not have the manpower to avert bloodshed in Nauvoo if the anti-Mormon militias decided to attack.[33]

In September, Young and other church leaders sent a letter to the "Quincy Committee" and Governor Ford declaring that in order to avoid the horrors that accompanied the flight from Missouri in the winter of 1838–1839, the Mormons intended to leave Illinois in the spring. Young, however, put some conditions on the removal. He requested that all help be given to the Mormons in the disposition of their property and that no violent action be taken to force their departure earlier than the spring of 1846. On 1 October, representatives from nine Illinois counties met in Carthage to consider Young's letter. Unsurprisingly, the committee accepted Young's document of surrender. Young immediately began planning what would become one of the largest mass movements in American history.

At the same time, certain residents of Hancock County were not willing to abide with "patience" the removal of the Mormons. Mormon settlements outside of Nauvoo were coming under attack. In September, one attack left forty-four buildings burned to the ground, and Young sent more than 130 wagons to the Green Plains area to begin shuttling refugees into Nauvoo. He and his associates began to understand that time was not on their side.

After Young announced that Nauvoo was to be evacuated, the residents sprang into action. Bathsheba W. Smith recorded that in the fall of 1845, "nearly every family was engaged in making wagons." Part of her home was used as a workshop in which the wagons could be painted.[34] Young and others studied maps of the American West. Young's genius as an organizer and leader matched perfectly the needs of the moment.

Even while planning their exit from Nauvoo, the Mormons continued to work on the temple. It was finally completed in late 1845. The rituals of endowment and sealing that were originally available only to the relatively few members of the Quorum of the Anointed were now accessible to all Mormons willing to live by the requirements of worthiness. Between December 1845 and February 1846, 5,000 individuals participated in the endowment rites.[35]

These rituals, performed inside the massive temple, served several vital functions for the Mormon community. First, the rituals suggested that they would help recipients resist evil and find protection from danger. Second, they provided initiates with the specific ritual knowledge that they would need to get to heaven when they died, and a way for them to be united with all of their loved ones in the spirit world. Both of these were no doubt welcome ideas for people preparing to head out into a hostile and brutal environment with no destination in sight. Third, the temple rituals allowed Brigham Young to create a covenant community, something that he knew he would need to rely on if he was to successfully organize and motivate thousands of people from diverse backgrounds. Finally, the increasing pace of temple rituals served as a mechanism for Mormons to help explain why they were being attacked.

These temple rites were far more elaborate than previous rituals performed within Mormonism. In the temple, special robes were worn, unusual ritual clothing

42   Chapter 3

that contributed to the otherworldly atmosphere. Special handclasps and sacred (and secret) key words were learned. The initiates received new names never to be spoken. Through all of this, the Nauvoo Temple rites were creating a community. Everyone made the same covenants, obtained the same sacred promises, and agreed to invest everything in the cause of God. Those communal ties would have to provide the foundation for the grueling and spare years ahead. Like so many others, JFS would often dream of this sacred clothing and these holy rites, dreams that would sustain him through almost impossibly trying difficulties.

The Abandonment of Nauvoo

On 8 February 1846, the temple that the Mormons had sacrificed so much to build was abandoned. The sacred veils came down. The plants, furniture, and other decorations were removed. Church leaders had worked themselves to exhaustion in the sacred confines of the temple, many days working around the clock to assist their fellow worshipers in entering the full covenantal fellowship of the saints. Now they turned their backs on the temple and walked away. Wilford Woodruff delivered an emotional speech before leaving Nauvoo and wept as he crossed the Mississippi and saw the temple abandoned on the bluff. Brigham Young had no time for sentiment. He never even looked back.

With the closing of the temple, Mormonism entered a period of diaspora unlike any it had experienced before. The founding prophet and many of the earliest church leaders were either dead or estranged from the largest body of the saints, and Brigham Young's Mormonism began to take on the cast of a frontier society. Things would never be the same. For most of the next decade, Young would work to recast Mormonism as he built a kingdom-like territory in the Great Basin. It was in this diasporic, liminal environment that JFS would shed his childhood and develop into a lean and wiry young man. The only thing he brought with him from his childhood was the memory of his father's mangled face and the massive web of events that led to his murder. As a man, JFS would find the need and the opportunity to express both the rage that never seemed to cool and the equally intense religious devotion to a faith for which his father died. He was never able to fully disentangle the two.

Young's dealings with the Smith family were proving less successful than his other endeavors. Emma Smith held a deep-seated disdain for Young, and the feeling was mutual. Emma resented Young for his enthusiastic endorsement of plural marriage. Young, for his part, disdained Emma for what he saw as her subversion of Joseph's revelations, and because her sons would not leave Nauvoo.[36] Mary Fielding Smith, on the other hand, accepted Young as the church's de facto leader, so when Nauvoo collapsed, she prepared to follow him.

Before the Mormons were ready to leave, armed groups of anti-Mormons decided they could not wait any longer, and attacks against Nauvoo began.[37] The first group of Mormons began evacuating Nauvoo in early February 1846. This vanguard company included Young and members of the Quorum of the Twelve and their families. In what seems, in hindsight, to be an astonishingly optimistic plan, Young had decided to leave Nauvoo early in order to allow the pioneers to reach the "rocky mountains" in time to plant crops. What he did not imagine was how very difficult the immediate journey across Iowa would be.

Joseph Fielding returned to Nauvoo, where he and his sisters Mary and Mercy would remain through the summer of 1846 "for want of means to get away."[38] In May, Mary had auctioned off "the interest" of Joseph, Sarah, John, Martha, and Jerusha in Hyrum's considerable property holdings in and around Nauvoo.[39] To complicate matters, Hyrum's oldest daughter, Lovina, now a married woman, demanded a share of the estate. After lengthy negotiations, Mary finally sold off the property for the ridiculously low sum of $900. She gave $200 to Lovina and used the remaining $700 to prepare to leave Nauvoo with her family.

Property prices were so low not only because buyers knew that the Mormons were desperate to be on their way, but also because Nauvoo had become a hotbed of crime and ruffianism. The summer and fall of 1846 were violent times in Nauvoo. The violence reached a peak just as Mary and her family were leaving the city. JFS remembered lying on the banks of the Mississippi River as cannon balls whizzed overhead and crashed around Nauvoo. In September, Joseph, Mary, Mercy, and the children crossed the river with a total of nine wagons, six of which belonged to Mary, two to Mercy, and one to Joseph. Martha Ann maintained a vivid memory of the departure: "We left our home, just as it was, with all the furniture, in fact everything we owned. The fruit trees were loaded with rosy peaches and apples. We bade goodbye to the loved home that reminded us of our beloved father everywhere we turned." After bidding a tearful goodbye to Lucy Smith, the group "crossed the River on a skiff in the dusk of the evening."[40]

Martha Ann's vivid memory of the fruit on the trees is a moving symbol of beautiful things that might have been, but could never be. Life with a father and a mother in a comfortable home had, by the time she penned that memory, been replaced by life in a hardscrabble and unforgiving desert wilderness. Leaving their childhood comforts and dreams behind them, the children of Hyrum Smith faced a terrifying future. The group that crossed the Mississippi River that September consisted of twenty-seven persons, twenty-one head of cattle, and forty-three sheep. These Bedfordshire farmers and their offspring were now American pioneers. By this time, JFS's half brother John Smith had reached Winter Quarters on the Missouri River near Omaha. Learning that his family had just begun the arduous trek across Iowa, John quickly returned to help them. He was fourteen years old.

JFS and his entire community were once again forced exiles. Records for this part of JFS's life are scant, but it is clear that this diaspora forged his identity as a forced immigrant alienated from two imagined communities, Zion and an idealized and righteous America. This profoundly shaped his nascent worldview. "Diaspora"

44   Chapter 3

is a slippery term, and there is some scholarly debate about just what it means and how it should be applied as an analytical category. We might profitably think of diaspora as a forced exile of a community from a real or imagined homeland to which they plan to return.

The study of communities in diaspora reveals a great deal about community formation, but it also involves understanding how memory works as a cultural device for community construction and maintenance. In the Mormon case, we can imagine a diaspora that begins with the declaration that Independence, Missouri, was the city of Zion, to which all the righteous were commanded to gather in preparation for the Second Coming of Christ. As we have seen, the attempts to build an actual brick and mortar city in Missouri failed over and over again for most of the 1830s. However, the idea of constructing the city of Zion in Missouri remained part of Mormon thought into the twentieth century. The possibility of a return to Jackson County was a living idea for Mormons throughout the nineteenth century. The experience of building and then losing a city in Illinois was a continuation of the diasporic chain that had its genesis in Missouri in 1833, when the Mormons were expelled from Jackson County.

The Mormons under Brigham Young meet the two basic criteria of a diasporic community—forced exile from a real or imagined homeland and an articulated desire to return to that homeland—so we must think about what kind of diasporic community they created. Historian Jurgen Osterhammel has pointed out that "diaspora formation as a result of mass migration was ubiquitous in the nineteenth century." Diaspora, he argues, is an "important type of discontinuous social space ... a community that lives outside of its real or imagined land of origin, yet still feels loyalty and attachment to it."[41] Africans, Jews, Irish, Chinese, Indians, Parsi, and countless other nineteenth-century groups underwent also forced mass migration. In order to provide a more fine-grained taxonomy, Osterhammel identifies four general diasporic types: victim diaspora, labor diaspora, trade diaspora, and cultural diaspora.

Nineteenth-century Mormonism is best understood as a victim diaspora of the sort experienced on a much larger scale among European Jews and Armenians in the nineteenth century. In Europe, as nation-states emerged and greatly reduced the number of discrete, independent political entities, many minority populations found themselves forced out of areas where they previously enjoyed all of the privileges of community membership. In the case of Mormonism, there are at least two specific moments when not only cultural hostility but also governmental hostility forced them into exile. The first is the infamous "extermination order" issued by Lilburn Boggs in Missouri in 1838. The second is the communication from Illinois governor Thomas Ford explaining that he could, and would, do nothing to stop the Mormons from being attacked and forced to leave Nauvoo.[42] In both cases, in fact, military power was brought to bear on the Mormon communities.

The Murders of Joseph and Hyrum Smith   45

That the Mormons were forced into exilic migration is beyond dispute. What complicates matters is that they did not identify with only one community. In addition to being Mormons, for example, they were also Americans or British citizens. In a sense, the expulsion of the Mormons, first from Missouri and then from Illinois, presented moments of community formation. Each individual had, at those moments, to make a choice between the Mormon community being exiled and the larger non-Mormon community doing the exiling. To choose Mormonism under such circumstances certainly must be read as a statement of preference with regard to communal identity. There is no question, for example, that the American Mormons who fled west across the freezing Mississippi in 1846 saw themselves as more Mormon than American.

The homeland concept that is so important to diasporic communities manifested in two general forms among nineteenth-century Mormons. The first, as we have already discussed, was the dream of returning to Missouri in order to "redeem" it and build the city of Zion. The second homeland to which the exiled Mormons dreamed of returning was an idealized version of the United States. Mormon rhetoric from the Utah period did not reject the United States per se. In fact, almost immediately after arriving, church leaders began a campaign for Utah to be admitted to the Union. What Mormons rejected, at least rhetorically, was the wayward America that had strayed from the vision of its founding documents when it allowed the Mormons to be persecuted and exiled. Osterhammel suggests that in diasporic communities "an idealized myth of this (purported) homeland is cultivated down the generations, sometimes including plans to revive or rebuild it."[43]

In the Mormon case, the mythos of a return to Missouri works in tandem with a deeply ingrained idealization of America that persists among American Mormons even today. Mormons believed, before they were a diasporic community, that America was chosen by God as a sacred place whose God would be the one revealed by Joseph Smith. It was a nation that would be protected as long as it remained righteous. Once Mormons became a diasporic community at the bloody hands of non-Mormon Americans, they could not disavow America. Rather, they imagined that they would, eventually, be the instruments for reviving its true, righteous soul as God intended for it to exist.[44]

This rhetoric of a fallen America being redeemed by Mormonism emerged only after the experiences in Missouri. In the decades after the expulsion from Nauvoo, this lore became increasingly familiar. A wide range of sources, some of extremely dubious provenance, claim that Joseph Smith believed the United States was somehow "fallen" and in need of redemption. One of the more reliable accounts along this line came from Parley Pratt, who claimed that Joseph Smith said,

The government is fallen and needs redeeming. It is guilty of Blood and cannot stand as it now is but will come so near desolation as to hang as it were by a single hair!!!!! Then the servants goes to the nations of the earth, and gathers the strength of the Lord's house! A mighty army!!!!!! And this is the redemption of Zion when the saints shall have redeemed that government and reinstated it in all its purity and glory!!!!!!!!!!!!!!![45]

Smith was similarly quoted as saying,

Even this nation will be on the verge of crumbling to pieces and tumbling to the ground and when the Constitution is on the brink of ruin this people will be the staff upon which the nation shall lean and they shall bear the Constitution away from the very verge of destruction.[46]

Soon after the murders of the Smith brothers, several of the apostles wrote a letter that appeared in the 15 July 1844 edition of the *Times and Seasons*. The letter pleaded with the people to remain calm, trust in God, forgo any planned acts of vengeance, and believe that the Smiths were now working in the spirit world to move the work forward. More importantly, however, the apostles wrote, "as to our country and nation, we have more reason to weep for them, than for those they have murdered; for they are destroying themselves and their institutions."[47] This sentence contains a microcosm of at least one part of the Mormon diaspora/ homeland dynamic. At first, the apostles refer to "our" nation, but the orientation then shifts, and they reposition themselves as exiles when they refer to America and Americans as "them" and "they."

Mormons had once believed that American institutions were good, but the murders of Joseph and Hyrum Smith represented the "destruction" of those institutions; the pollution of the pure fountain dictated that "we" must now view the homeland as an external entity, a "them" rather than an "us," something from which a reluctant uncoupling must be achieved. The task of making the Mormons and the Americans an "us" again would fall, in large measure, to the elderly JFS, a man who was only five years old when the apostles' letter was penned.

JFS, then, grew up in a diasporic community that shared, and nurtured, an identity grounded firmly in the soil of persecution and trauma, and which simultaneously dreamed of a return to two imagined homelands—homelands that would require a violent redemption to both restore the community to its God-intended place and destroy the enemies that had driven them out. Apostle Orson Pratt neatly set forth the Mormon diasporan mindset as he left Illinois in 1846: the Mormons, he said, were now on their own, heading "far from the abodes of what is falsely called *civilization* and *Christianity*."[48]

4 | Pioneer Days

Leaving Nauvoo with his family in the spring of 1846, Joseph F. Smith would have had no idea that he was part of a massive, unprecedented, worldwide mobilization of peoples. Jurgen Osterhammel points out that the nineteenth century was like "no other epoch in history" in terms of "long-distance migration on such a massive scale"; the rate of voluntary international migration for the period 1815–1914 was nearly three times greater than for the years 1945–1980.[1] The entire world, it seemed, was moving, and most of that movement was westward.

JFS was not moving voluntarily, and he was surrounded by a veritable sea of displaced persons. In North America, the Mormon Trail was one of several overland routes west that were becoming crowded by the late 1840s. Approximately 40,000 children were among the various overland companies heading to California, Oregon, Utah, Colorado, and elsewhere.[2] Historians have found that the life of a child on the American frontier was a double-edged sword, and JFS, like countless numbers of his peers, would feel both sides. On one hand, frontier children lived a life of "self-reliance, inner-directedness and early independence," but they also felt "withering poverty, dispiriting routine, and personal entrapment."[3] Before any of that could happen, JFS had to make it across Iowa.

Perhaps the most difficult stretch of the journey from Nauvoo to the Rocky Mountains was the slog across Iowa. Brigham Young and his party, having left Nauvoo in February 1846, did not arrive at the Missouri River until June. Bad weather hampered travel. Most of the people on the trek had no experience with wagon travel, and delays inevitably resulted. The circumstances were so dire that some of the leaders began to adapt the Nauvoo Temple prayer rituals for use in the "wilderness." In Nauvoo, as part of the meetings of the Quorum of the Anointed, and later in the temple itself, the participants engaged in something they called "the true order of prayer." Dressed in full temple robes, the members of the circle would make certain sacred ritual gestures and then assume a special ritual posture as they prayed vocally. On 4 April 1846, after a prolonged period of terrible weather, Heber C. Kimball performed a variation of this ritual by himself. He told Emmeline B. Wells

48   Chapter 4

that he had "on Saturday evening went into the woods by himself, offered up the signs of the Holy Priesthood, and prayed to the Lord that the storm might abate and the sun shine forth in his majesty and for the health, prosperity, and salvation of the camp of Israel."[4] Kimball was unsurprised when the prayer was answered and the sun came out.

The use of elements of the temple prayer liturgy became common on the journey west and provided a crucial link between the temple rites introduced in Nauvoo and the ones that would be performed in Utah. This is an example of the tremendous capacity for adaptability that has always been a hallmark of Mormonism. The abandonment of Nauvoo and the pressing tasks that accompanied life on the trail could easily have resulted in a communal forgetting of rituals that were deemed irrelevant. However, Mormons like Kimball continued to make the temple symbols and rites relevant in new and challenging contexts, thereby preserving the central role of these practices in Mormon thought.

Young, for his part, was furious at the delays and not in a pleasant mood when they finally made it across Iowa. The Mormons immediately began to create a temporary settlement on the western side of the Missouri River. They called the place, optimistically, Winter Quarters. Mary Smith's company, including seven-year-old JFS, arrived there in late November 1846.[5] JFS would remain there until the spring of 1848. That period, between his arrival at Winter Quarters and his arrival in the Salt Lake Valley, is the only period of his life that JFS would think about with an almost unrestrained romanticism. He learned to work with and love horses, and also how to do pastoral work. The physically demanding labor that JFS mastered during his pioneer period remained a part of his life until very old age.

The quality of life in Winter Quarters depended to a great degree on one's social station. Houses began to go up in the late fall of 1846. Those occupied by church leaders tended to be wood-framed rather than simple log homes. People lived in everything from these larger homes to caves carved out of the nearby hills. Many lived in tents. By the end of December, Winter Quarters consisted of "538 log cabins, 83 sod houses, and a population of 3,483."[6] Joseph Fielding and John Smith built a house for Mary Fielding and Mercy Thompson. The Smith house was a fairly decent abode by Winter Quarters standards; it was sixteen feet square, one story, with clapboard siding and a sod roof. The structure had a dirt floor, however, and only the sod and clay chinking kept the icy winds at bay.[7]

Winter Quarters was divided into twenty-one wards, and the bishop of each was responsible for collecting tithing and other offerings that could be used to help sustain the growing number of poor arrivals. Mary was a member of the thirteenth ward. A mill was built, as was a basket factory, both of which provided employment opportunities. Skilled craftsmen were always in demand as well. For those who could not find work in Winter Quarters, they had the option of going south to Missouri to find temporary labor. Mormons also made trips to St. Joseph, Missouri, to purchase supplies and foodstuff.

One such trip loomed large in JFS's memory. Along with his mother and uncle Joseph Fielding, JFS headed from Winter Quarters to St. Joseph, and he had the privilege of acting as a teamster, probably for the first time. The trip was unremarkable until the journey back to Winter Quarters. The party camped along the Missouri one evening, turning the oxen out to graze in their yoke. In the morning, they were nowhere to be found. JFS and his uncle searched for hours in vain. According to JFS's recollection of the event, Mary calmly told the men to eat the breakfast that she had prepared and she would find the oxen herself. Although skeptical of her ability to do what they had failed to, the men watched her wander off. JFS noted that, across the river, a group of cattlemen were driving a herd in the opposite direction. As Mary walked in search of the oxen, one of the men called out to her that he had seen the animals and that she was going in the wrong direction. Mary ignored the man, who repeated himself. As JFS phrased it, Mary "walked on as though she were on the 'straight and narrow path.'" Soon she discovered the oxen tied up. JFS concluded that the cattlemen had stolen the oxen during the night in the hopes of selling them at market and had intentionally tried to misdirect Mary so that their plot would not be discovered.[8]

The stories that JFS remembered and chose to retell all share certain characteristics. Perhaps the clearest commonality is their emphasis on good versus evil. The stories always have a hero and a villain. JFS saw the world in strongly dualistic terms, and the ubiquity of enemies in his memories suggests that he was plagued by a vivid sense of being under siege. Another shared characteristic of memories from his early years is the role played by his mother. She was, in JFS's recollection, a woman who could do what men could not, who could discern truth from lies, and who would not be intimidated off of the "straight and narrow path," even by a frontier-hardened cowboy.

Brigham Young's Pioneer Personality

The entire focus of life in Winter Quarters was preparation for the journey farther west, one that would require as much preparation and as many saved resources as possible. People remained there until they could afford to leave. Pioneer companies began leaving Winter Quarters on 5 April 1847 and would continue to do so until it was abandoned in 1852. Winter Quarters is probably best remembered among Mormons today as a place of great physical suffering, particularly due to disease. Richard Bennett has estimated that the death rate in Winter Quarters in 1846–1847 was around 10 percent. He concludes that "disease and death were omnipresent, exacting a vicious toll on almost every family."[9]

It is no surprise that people wanted to leave Winter Quarters as soon as they possibly could, and too many made the mistake of pestering Brigham Young with requests to accompany the first company out. Enraged by the clamoring, Young addressed the inhabitants of Winter Quarters in unforgettable language, verbally abusing them in a petulant rage.

> You poor stinking curses, for you are cursed and the hand of the Lord shall be upon you and you shall go down to hell for murmuring and bickering. This people means to tie my hands continually. They are already coming to me saying can't you take me along? Don't leave me here, if you do I am afraid I shall die, this is such a sickly place. Well I say to them, die, who cares. If you have not faith to live here you will die over the mountains.[10]

This type of discourse came to be Young's signature rhetorical posture. In 1847, though, this kind of speech from a leader would have been new to the Mormons.

Joseph Smith, while known to occasionally throw darts at his audiences, had never approached the level of hostility and disdain that Young showed for his followers. JFS was growing up along with a new, harder Mormonism—one that was designed to wring every ounce of energy, grit, courage, will, and vision from its adherents. Anger, aggressiveness, violence, adventurousness, courage, toughness: these became the cardinal virtues of diasporic Mormonism. Young invented and embodied the prototype of such Mormonism, but JFS was perfectly suited by temperament and experience to thrive in this environment. However, even in a world that prized such obviously "masculine" Mormonism, JFS stood out as almost too Mormon.

Mary's sister Mercy was among the fortunate few who were able to leave Winter Quarters in the first immigration season. On 18 June 1847, she left for the Great Basin as part of the Daniel Spencer/Perrigrine Sessions pioneer company, which included 186 persons and seventy-five wagons.[11] The company arrived in the Salt Lake Valley in late September. Mary could not have been thrilled at the prospect of living on roots after traveling more than a thousand more miles, but her commitment to the cause never wavered.

Back at Winter Quarters, JFS found opportunities for work and adventure beyond anything he could have imagined. He was particularly fond of his work as a "herd boy." His job consisted of moving cattle from the herd ground to other areas to feed, and then driving them back again. On one such occasion, in the fall of 1847, he and a friend encountered "a gang of Indians stripped to the breech-clout, painted and daubed, on horse-back . . . charging at full speed toward us." In the confusion that ensued, JFS's young companion fled, shouting "Indians! Indians!" while JFS rode to the front of the herd in an effort to keep them from scattering. He was motivated by his knowledge that these cattle represented his only opportunity to escape "the horror of being compelled to remain at Winter Quarters." In a scene worthy of the most ostentatious western film, JFS tried to drive the herd toward home while staying ahead of the Indians. Eventually, his horse "ran out of wind," and two Indians came up on either side of him, took him by the arms, lifted him off his horse, and "chucked" him to the ground. Several other horses jumped over the dazed boy. At that moment, a group of Mormons armed with pitchforks intervened and drove off the Indians. JFS was nine years old.[12]

This event is significant, but so is the manner in which JFS told it. At the beginning of the incident, JFS was accompanied by an older boy, whom JFS describes as "almost a young man grown," a "very sober and steady boy," as well as two other youngsters around his own age. The older boy, Alden Burdick, had left them to go and gather some hazel nuts. As JFS tells the story, he is not only the hero who has to take the place of an absent (semi)adult, but also the one who is forced to face the threat alone when the cowardice of his companions overwhelms them, and they deliver him into the hands of the enemy. This was a scenario that JFS was familiar with, and it formed a sort of template for other experiences as he recollected his life.[13]

JFS's turn to leave Winter Quarters finally arrived on 7 June 1848. Together with his siblings, his mother, his uncle Joseph Fielding, and more than 600 others, JFS left the outfitting post under the leadership of Mary's husband, Heber C. Kimball. Mary's group was among the last to arrive at the staging area. She and her brother Joseph had difficulty with their oxen because the animals were young and not accustomed to being yoked to a wagon. Kimball visited and urged Mary and Joseph to start as soon as possible. The family had suffered through a brutal winter, and many of their animals had died. The group lacked enough animals and teamsters for all of the wagons and so ended up having to attach one of the wagons to the back of another one.

Seven wagons, including a carriage, had all been brought from Nauvoo and were now ready to be put to the most severe test imaginable. One seasoned pioneer who had already been to the Salt Lake Valley and had returned to pick up his family unhelpfully informed the group that "it was great Folly to attempt to go as we were fixt."[14] But not wanting to spend another winter at the dismal camp on the Missouri, and being "anxious to go with the church to the Valley," Mary pressed on anyway.[15] By the time she arrived at the main body of the camp, things had already taken a rather sinister turn. The group left the next day.

At the very start of the journey, a character came into contact with the Smith family who would loom large in many of JFS's reminiscences.[16] Cornelius Lott arrived at the staging ground at the same time Mary and JFS did. Daniel Davis, who was standing watch that evening, recorded the event innocuously enough: "Bro Cornelius [Peter] Lott & Sister Mary [Fielding] Smith the Wife of the Patriarch Hyrum Smith Each With their Family, came to camp."[17]

What happened next would kindle anger in JFS's heart toward Lott for the rest of his life. However, there are two Cornelius Lotts that need to be acknowledged. One of them joined the LDS Church during the Kirtland period, was part of the Danite band in Missouri, served as a bodyguard to Joseph Smith, managed Smith's farm in Nauvoo, and became his father-in-law through plural marriage. This Lott

52   Chapter 4

was also a frequent participant in Brigham Young's prayer circle after the death of Joseph Smith. In Utah, he managed a church farm for two years before his death in 1850.

Then there is the Lott that existed primarily in JFS's memory and imagination. That version was a raving madman. The events that occurred at the staging ground, or at least JFS's perception of them, formed the basis of one of his most enduring memories and marks the emergence of his will to violence. Late in his life, he recalled the incident as one "I shall never forget and have not yet forgiven." According to JFS, Heber Kimball came to visit Mary and brought the leader of the group of fifty to which she and her family had been assigned. Lott, as captain of the company, pointed out the obvious disadvantages that Mary and her party faced given the poor state of their equipment and their shortage of animals. As JFS remembered it, Lott told Mary that she should wait another season so she could outfit properly. Otherwise, "you will be a burden on the company the whole way and I will have to carry you along or leave you on the way."[18]

One might be forgiven for seeing Lott's point. Mary's group was ill-prepared for the journey and short on able-bodied men but long on women and children. Lott clearly did not want to take responsibility for a group so full of potential liabilities. The tone, however, of this "disconsolate harangue" could make JFS's blood boil even half a century later. For her part, Mary replied with cool self-assurance. "Father Lott," she said, "I will beat you to the valley and will ask no help from you either." Lott was nonplussed and, no doubt angry at being publicly humiliated by a woman, assured Mary that she could not, in fact, make it to the valley without help and that the "burden" for that help would inevitably devolve on Lott himself. JFS felt "greaved" at the "harsh and disencouraging" tone of Lott's "cold bluff."[19]

It was against the backdrop of Lott's encounter with Mary and her promise to get to Utah without the help of any man that JFS told what would become one of the most famous stories in LDS pioneer history: the healing of the oxen. According to JFS, at a point somewhere between the Platte and Sweetwater Rivers, "one of our best oxen laid down in the yoke as if poisoned and all supposed he would die." Lott duly appeared, began to gloat over the unfortunate scene, "blustered about as if the world was about at an end," and said to Mary, "I told you you would have to be helped!" According to the story, Mary calmly knelt by the ailing animal, prayed for its recovery, and poured holy consecrated olive oil on it. The ox regained his strength, stood up, and continued the journey. This scene was repeated three times, "to the astonishment of all who saw and to the chagrin of Father Lott."[20]

But this was just the beginning of the Lott saga. In the same autobiographical fragment recorded in his journal, JFS told another story about Lott. One day, as the camp was resting the livestock, an obviously agitated Lott began asking the assembled group, "Is all right in the camp?" When Mary responded that all was right, Lott pounced, shouting, "All is right is it? And a poor woman lost?!" Lott was convinced that a woman from the camp had gone missing, but Mary assured him that the woman was not missing, nor was she in danger; she had merely traveled ahead a few miles to visit with her mother in another camp. JFS pointed out in his account of the event that the woman was sickly, a "charity case" who was traveling with Mary's family. Indicating the rising importance of the Word of Wisdom at the time he was writing about the incident, JFS also emphasized that the woman had a great love for "<u>snuff</u>" and, having run out, had sought out her mother in another part of the wagon train to see if she could replenish her supply. JFS claimed that this angered Lott beyond all reason, and he shouted, "I rebuke you Widow Smith in the name of the Lord! She is missing and she must be sent for!" Mary, always calm in her son's stories, simply replied, "Alright, she shall be sent for." Somehow JFS's half brother John was selected for the task. After navigating "droves of ravenous wolves" with shining eyes, John found the woman safely in the company of her mother. Lott, again, is shown to be the fool, and Mary the wise and faithful voice of reason.[21]

John Smith later included a slightly different version of the incident in his brief autobiography.

> At about sundown, when were camped on the Platte river, it was reported that a woman was missing. Without ceremony, I took my coat on my arm and a piece of cornbread in my hand and started up the road. I had not gone far when I came up with a dead [animal] carcass, which was covered with wolves, fighting and howling. I walked past as fast and as quietly as possible.

John recounted that he passed about twenty such scenes before he stopped for the night with some friends he came across. The next day he "found the lost woman safe with her mother."[22]

The basic elements of these stories match, but the discrepancies are instructive. John's version is much less dramatic, includes no account of any doubt about the woman being missing, and does not so much as hint that Mary Smith knew where the woman was. In fact, he does not mention her at all. According to John's version, it was his decision, made immediately, to head out after the lost woman. Clearly, the hero of John's story is John himself. It is a simple adventure story about a boy dodging wolves on the Overland Trail.

The hero of JFS's story is Mary. But the key difference is that John's story has no villain. JFS's story is much more grandiose in scope; it is a morality play. In JFS's version, Lott singles Mary out, in front of everyone else, in an attempt to humiliate her and depict her as either ignorant or heartless. It was a setup. Lott was asking if all was right just so he could insult her. But Mary proved that she was neither ignorant nor heartless by demonstrating her superior knowledge (knowing the whereabouts of the woman) and her superior heart (allowing her stepson to brave the wolf-infested prairie in search of the not-lost woman). That, at least, is how JFS remembered the event.

54   Chapter 4

But Lott was not done tormenting Mary just yet. It is worth reproducing here a lengthy section of JFS's written memories of another event in order to convey the tone and tenor of the piece.

> On reaching the last crossing of the Sweetwater, to the best of my recollection, three of Capt. Lott's ablest oxen and his best mule laid down near the camp-ground and died. This was a sore trial to the old man, and a very great loss as he was obliged to get help in order to proceed. I heard him say, "It looks suspicious that 4 of my best oxen should lie down in this manner all at once, and die, and everybody's cattle but mine escape!" and insinuated that somebody had poisoned them through spite. All of which was said in my presence and for my especial <u>benefit,</u> which I perfectly understood, altho' he did not address himself directly to me. It was well for Father Lott, I was only a stripling of 9 years of age, and not a man, even four years later such an occurance would have cost the old man dearly, regardless of his age, and perhaps been a cause of regret to myself. My temper was beyond boiling, it was "white hot" for I knew his insinuation was directed or aimed at my mother, as well as I knew that such a thing was beyond her power even had she been as well as I, and all the camp. At this moment I resolved on revenge for this and the many other insults and abuses this old fiend had heaped upon my mother, and should most certainly have carried out my resolution had not death come timely to my releaf and rid the earth of so vile and despicable an incumbrence.[23]

Here we have a most significant document. JFS, an apostle in the LDS Church, admits that he would have sought violent revenge and possibly would have killed a man for insulting his mother. This is not the only time that he remembers being prepared to murder someone on the basis of a perceived insult. And, as we will see, there were others less fortunate than Lott who crossed paths with JFS as an adult and suffered violence at his hands. Note that the insult from Lott is, at worst, an insinuation. Note also that JFS believed he was being singled out, as if the words were being communicated to him almost secretly from Lott. Even after so much time had elapsed, his interest in the story had not waned.

There is some reason to believe that JFS may have misinterpreted some of these events, or misremembered them, or both. This is particularly true of the incident involving Lott's dead livestock. There seems to be no reason whatsoever for JFS to conclude that Lott's lament at his relatively bad fortune was aimed at anyone unless he had already created a narrative that fit that conclusion. The incident is not mentioned by any of the other members of the pioneer company in either their trail journals or their autobiographies.

These stories about Lott, as narrated by JFS in the early 1890s, shed some light on his own personal myth. There is, in this entire set of stories about Lott, a peculiar sense of obsession. JFS is convinced that Lott was obsessed with harassing him and his mother, but it is absolutely clear that JFS is, himself, obsessed with Lott—not as a person, but as a symbol. Cornelius Lott is portrayed in these stories as an archfiend consumed with an evil and cruel need to inflict pain and suffering on Mary Smith. Lott plays the role of the stock villain, and Mary is the innocent victim. Lott persecutes Mary, and his faithlessness leads him to doubt and devalue her, while his superior social standing allows him to humiliate her. Lott represents a powerful, faithless, and relentless tormenter. Despite his position and the apparent weakness of his victim, he is ultimately humiliated and disgraced by the power of God as manifested through Mary Fielding Smith. The stories show Lott to be unworthy, both intellectually and spiritually, of his position of power.

In some ways, JFS's stories of Lott versus Mary are of a piece with how he viewed his own experiences throughout life. He always felt that he was in danger of humiliation and persecution by those more powerful, but less worthy, than he was. It is possible that one reason JFS resisted "forgiving" Lott was that it would have eroded one of the major touchstone narratives upon which his life was based. The Lott saga gradually became less about memory and more about morality.

The earliest known instance of JFS referring to Lott is in a letter that he sent to his half brother John in 1861. JFS was serving a mission in England, and he and John had had a falling out over the sale of land. JFS wrote to John about forgiveness and reached back to the incident: "The hardest thing for me to forgive is wrapped in the memory of C. P. Lot! yet even <u>that</u> I forgive, tho' I never will forget it." "My memory," he added, "is keen upon these things."[24]

By the time JFS wrote his formal reminiscences of the Lott incidents, he had been a church leader for decades. He had, in fact, been responsible during part of the 1860s and 1870s for managing the massive emigration/immigration machinery that brought Mormon converts from Liverpool to the United States. In that capacity, JFS had been responsible for giving counsel that was very much like what he heard Lott say to his mother. As we will have the opportunity to witness, JFS spared no feelings when denying unprepared European emigrants access to the Mormon emigration companies. It is curious, and revealing, that even those experiences did not allow him to put the Lott event into some kind of perspective.

Clearly, JFS would have rejected a comparison between himself and Lott out of hand. There are several reasons for this. First, when it came to his mother, no criticism was to be brooked. He revered her to a fault. Any cross word or sideways glance in her direction was, in JFS's mind, an act so transgressive that it bordered on blasphemy. Even if the criticism was warranted, JFS viewed it as very nearly a sin. Second, and more importantly, JFS believed to the end of his life that showing weakness to an enemy, even in the form of compassion, was a sin. To forgive Lott would elevate weakness to a virtue, and that was something he could scarcely afford to do.

In December 1894, not long after he penned the memoir that included the stories about Lott, JFS attended what he hoped would be a regular event marking the anniversary of Joseph Smith's birth. He encouraged those who had known Smith to share their memories of him, and he acknowledged that the number of people in that category was rapidly shrinking. JFS started things off by sharing a memory of his own. He told of playing marbles with his cousin Alexander Smith in front of Joseph Smith's Nauvoo House residence. Suddenly, the door flew open, and a man came flying toward the boys "right off the end of Joseph Smith's foot." After telling this story, JFS defended the event against an imaginary critic who might wonder how someone who had experienced such sublime heavenly manifestations as Joseph Smith had could treat another person with such violence. JFS's response to his own question tells us a great deal. Joseph Smith, he said,

> was tried beyond endurance many a time by false brethren, by false accusers, by wicked men, by mobs and murderers and evil creatures that sought his life. There was never a moment of his life that he was free of such things as these, being hounded, and abused, and insulted by wicked men; and he had been *less of a man* if he had not kicked Josiah Butterfield out of his house that day.[25]

JFS chose to tell a story about Joseph Smith that would allow him to explain his own view of masculinity, and it reveals much about how he saw life. Josiah Butterfield was, like Cornelius Lott, a symbol of the constant persecution that JFS endured, and in justifying Smith's actions by invoking the issue of what it meant to be a "man," he was quite plainly explaining *himself*. To allow Lott to pass into history unchastened would have, in JFS's mind, made him "less of a man."

The issue of masculinity will surface repeatedly through this study of JFS's life. Part of the reason for this is that conceptions of masculinity became extremely important markers in the American West. Historian Richard Slotkin has identified several features of masculinity as they appeared in nineteenth-century literature and histories, collectively known as "the myth of the frontier." A standard character in this myth is the man "converted from farmer to fanatical man of violence by the iron of personal wrong in the form of persecution, oppression and murder."[26] JFS was not fanatical in his violence, but he was violent, and he was violent for exactly the reasons discussed by Slotkin. He also came to embody what Slotkin calls the "two dominant strains of American mythology":

> the sacred, Biblical mythology of Christianity, with its fables of sin and atonement, salvation and missionary labor and apocalypse, and the secular myth/ideology of the Frontier, with its canonical fables of savage war and rescue, paradise lost and Eden rediscovered, [and] regeneration through violence.[27]

Because of a unique set of circumstances, JFS was, by the end of his life, a man who carried several levels of symbolic meaning. Due to his relationship to the "martyrs of Mormonism," and because he was raised as a religious refugee on the American frontier, he represents a most unusual specimen among LDS presidents. Unlike any other Mormon leader before or since, JFS presented a personality that combined deep religiosity, a sensitivity to and self-perception of persecution and living martyrdom, and violent masculinity in one vexing, fascinating, and ultimately inscrutable persona.

JFS's personality was forged in a migration unlike any other in American history. Wagon trains had been traveling across the North American continent since 1830. By the early 1840s, a deep national interest in wagon travel and family migration to the American West had developed. Fueled by largely false newspaper reports claiming the ease with which the Rocky Mountains could be crossed, thousands of Americans headed west.[28] Mormons were thus an important part of a much larger movement of peoples to a variety of locations in the West. But Mormon pioneering differed from other types in several ways. Mormon pioneer companies enjoyed far greater organization than did other pioneer groups. Pioneers traveling to mining fields or homesteads worked their way west in ad hoc groups of individuals and families who came and went, but with whom they did not share any particular bond. The Mormon pioneer experience, by contrast, was a communal effort, and groups of Mormons traveled under company leaders and, theoretically at least, worked together for a common goal. More importantly, this was a religious movement.

There were other pioneers who also saw their travels as part of a religious mission. Various benevolent societies, for example, headed to the Pacific Northwest and elsewhere to bring a Christian presence to the frontier. One of the most prominent of these was the Methodists' Oregon mission, which had as its goal the conversion of Native Americans and wayward fur traders. But the Mormon pioneer connection to religion was deeper, more primal. Mormon pioneers viewed their trek not as just another move brought on by the prospect of economic gain, nor even as an opportunity to spread their faith, but as an "exodus." They viewed themselves as God's chosen people, seeking refuge from the wickedness of the world by following a modern-day Moses into a desert wilderness.

Mormons viewed their migrations west as an important part of a sacred story that was unfolding under God's direction in the nineteenth century just as it did in the Sinai Desert thousands of years earlier. The rules for the trek were spelled out in a document that would become Brigham Young's only canonized revelation. Known as "The Word and Will of the Lord," the text was produced in January 1847 in Winter Quarters. Mormons believed that this document represented the literal words of Jesus Christ, given to them via their prophet Brigham Young. The revelation stated that the Mormons were to "be organized into companies, with a covenant and promise to keep all the commandments and statutes of the Lord our God." The document specified that there would be groups of 100, 50, and 10, each with a captain. The revelation also reaffirmed that the Mormons were leaving because "thy brethren have rejected you and your testimony, even the nation that has driven you out; And now cometh the day of their calamity, even the days of sorrow." In order for the Mormons to make it safely across the plains under the protection of God, they were told to avoid "evil speaking" of one another, stealing, taking the name of God in vain, and fear. They were instructed to sing, dance, rejoice, pray, care for the widows and orphans, and use good judgment in deciding who should start out and at what time of year.

Much to Young's chagrin, people sometimes fell short of the instructions in the revelation, and he found himself calling the pioneers to repentance on a regular basis. Stealing seemed to be a particularly vexing problem, significant enough for Young to declare, "I swore by the eternal Gods that if the men in our midst would not stop this cursed work of stealing and counterfeiting, their throats should be cut."[29] Whatever the shortcomings in adherence to the rules, the fact that rules existed at all set the Mormon pioneer endeavor on a different footing than all others. Pioneering was an incredibly challenging task. For Mormons, it not only included the normal hardships of life on the trail, but also required the blending of individuals from widely diverse ethnic, religious, social, and economic backgrounds into a well-functioning unit. Not the least of the challenges facing the Mormons was the large number of children on the trail, including JFS.

A Migrating Childhood

What was it like for JFS to experience childhood and adolescence in such an environment? Beyond his own much later recollections, there is little in the way of good historical evidence to answer such a question, although there are sources that allow more general speculation. Only in the last two decades have scholars become interested in what childhood was like in the American West. Elliott West's pioneering work on this subject invites us to reconsider how the frontier shaped children and created or encouraged certain personality traits. "For all their variety," West wrote of emigrants headed west, they all had one thing in common: "they had imagined something compelling out there and had been willing to seek it out. Emigration was a sifting. It made for a society heavily weighted with persons of a particular bent."[30]

But children experienced the journey and settlement very differently than their parents did. Children typically lacked a well-developed sense of what was normal and thus accepted the harsh conditions of the American frontier much more smoothly than older individuals. The children who pioneered the American West were still in the process of developing a strong sense of self, "a sense of who they were and what was to be expected of life." They were, wrote West, "still being shaped [when they arrived in the West] and part of that shaping came from how they responded to what was around them." The result, according to West, was that the children who made their way west grew up as "a distinctive generation."[31]

A child growing up in the American West was shaped by three overarching influences: the geography, the motives that underpinned the migration and settlement, and the striking mix of cultures that was represented in nearly every town in the region. For JFS, it is clear that the West's categories of influence had a direct bearing on his development. The land in which he eventually settled was near the Great Salt Lake in the arid Great Basin, along the western front of the Wasatch Mountains. JFS came to view the treeless desert and cool canyons as normal, and this view emerged when he traveled outside of Utah. He learned horsemanship and farming and husbandry in ways that would have been completely alien to his parents and their peers. He understood irrigation. He was raised in and inhabited a physical landscape that could hardly have been more different from the one that nurtured his parents. It became, as West noted, "the original measure for the rest of their lives, and that measure was one their parents would not have known."[32]

West goes to great lengths to demonstrate the wide range of motives that impelled migrants westward in America. He argues that, like geography, the reason behind the move west would shape a child on the frontier in particular ways. A child who moved for economic reasons, for example, would be different from a child who moved in order for a parent to recuperate from an illness in a "cleaner" environment. We need not belabor the obvious point that JFS's migration was both forced and religious at its root. For those reasons, he came to view his particular environment as a blessed and sacred space, prepared by God himself for the Mormons. For JFS, as for the children that West studied, place and purpose were inextricably linked. This also points up a striking difference between Mormon and non-Mormon settlements in the West; most settlers moved out of their original settlement within ten years—most Mormons did not.

Finally, West argues that the stunning cultural diversity of the American West helped shape this new generation of Americans raised on the frontier. During the nineteenth century, "the West was the most cosmopolitan part of the nation, with between a fourth and a third of its people born outside of the United States."[33] This trend was magnified in Utah. English, Welsh, Scottish, Danish, Swedish, Polynesian, and Norwegian emigrants rubbed elbows with American-born Mormons in most of the Mormon settlements in the West. Ethnic boundaries, while important, were superseded by religious devotion and a shared vision. JFS grew to adulthood in a world where he likely heard foreign languages on a regular, if not daily, basis. One wonders how old Hyrum Smith was when he first heard a foreign language, and how many languages met his ears during his forty-three years of life. Whatever the answer to those questions, it is absolutely certain that JFS bested him in both categories by a wide margin.

Part of JFS's significance in Mormon history stems from the hydra-headed fact that he was the last church president to have personally known Joseph Smith, and the first church president raised in the Great Basin. As West's work has so helpfully illustrated, the second part of that fact is more significant than we are

60   Chapter 4

likely to realize. JFS was not just a Mormon who happened to live in the American West. He was a frontiersman, a child of the American West who was surrounded by religious devotion, cultural diversity, and environmental hostility. Consider the contrast that such a childhood and youth presents when JFS is set next to Brigham Young, a Vermonter; John Taylor, from the north of England; Wilford Woodruff, a Connecticut Yankee; and Lorenzo Snow, a native of northeast Ohio. None of these men were born Mormons, none of these men carried the "blood of the prophets," none of these men were westerners. JFS was the first, and last, of his kind. It was a journey unlike any other.

The Valley of the Great Salt Lake

The next phase of JFS's journey began on 23 September 1848, when Mary Fielding Smith and her party arrived in the Salt Lake Valley. The region had been home to Mormon pioneers for just over a year. For centuries, various Native American peoples had inhabited the area, and they were eventually joined by Spanish explorers. Mountain man Jim Bridger was the first known European American to visit the Great Salt Lake. He arrived in the Salt Lake Valley in the fall of 1824. Other explorers passed through the area in the 1830s and 1840s, including Jedediah Smith, Joseph Walker, and John C. Frémont. Although no significant number of pioneers had settled in the Salt Lake Valley before the Mormons arrived in 1847, the path west was well-enough trod by groups going to Oregon and California that the Mormons had only to break approximately one mile of new trail on the entire journey from Winter Quarters.

Once they reached the valley, they immediately began attempting to plant crops and build a fort. Approximately 2,000 Mormons spent the winter of 1847–1848 in the Salt Lake Valley.[34] The immigrants never stopped coming. Every summer and fall brought new families. By 1853, nearly 16,000 more people had reached the valley.

JFS's family spent their first Utah winter in the fort constructed by the first group to enter the valley the year before. According to JFS, most of the new arrivals lived in their wagons until spring.[35] When the weather broke in 1849, church leaders began to lay out settlements and assign building and farming lots. Although Mary, Mercy, and their brother were all granted lots in the main settlement, the "city," Mary felt the need to have a farm. She built a cabin in the city but chose a spot in the East Millcreek area, about five miles southeast of the fort, for a farm. In the spring of 1849, JFS planted a couple of grain fields a short distance west of their new home, in the vicinity of what is now 2700 South and 700 East.[36] In 1849, this area was a wilderness, and one cannot help but notice Mary's desire to spend most of her time apart from the main body of the community. Her reasons for this are not known, but clearly she did not enjoy a particularly exalted status as the widow of Hyrum Smith. Utah Mormonism was Brigham Young's Mormonism, and he was not willing, yet, to allow a Smith to muddy things up by rising to social or religious prominence.

Mary remained relatively close to Heber C. Kimball, who baptized Martha Ann in 1849.[37] It was in Kimball's house, in the fall of 1852, that Mary died. She had not enjoyed particularly good health since at least the late 1830s, and in the fall of 1852, she fell ill with what she thought was a cold. As weeks went by and her condition worsened, she moved in with the Kimball family. Mary succumbed to illness on 21 September 1852. It always gave JFS a cold sort of comfort to know that his mother outlived Cornelius Lott by two years.

The funeral service was a small affair held at Kimball's home, with Brigham Young presiding. Young's sermon was both personal and theological. He told the assembled family members that they would do well to try to match Mary's dedication to God's cause and to rejoice in the knowledge that she was now reunited with her husband in an unimaginably glorious paradise. To the shattered children, Young said that they should not worry. He related a story in which Joseph Smith had told him, "I have no fears concerning my children. God will take care of them and if it needs be he will hide them up in the rocks of mountains. They will do well enough." He said Hyrum's children, too, could expect the same care under divine watch. Young demonstrated considerable thoughtfulness to JFS's half siblings when he reminded Jerusha Smith's children that she, too, was a righteous woman whose life was cut short. Moving into a theological mode, Young taught the group that the spirits of human beings, both good and evil, remained upon the earth. Mary's spirit was close, and so was Hyrum's. Young concluded his remarks by directing a blessing to the children: "God bless you. I feel to bless you with all the power and influence I have."[38]

Kimball finished the meeting with a very moving tribute to Mary, in which he said that she had fulfilled the roles of mother, father, and even bishop in her tireless work on behalf of those in her care. He said that during the final two months of her life, Mary expressed a desperate wish to live for the sole purpose of continuing to care for her family. She knew she was going to leave them orphans, cast upon the mercy of the community for their very lives. "I know she has gone to peace, she has gone home," Kimball said. Then he made a somewhat strange comment. "I never heard her to murmur against Brother Brigham in life." If that was true, it certainly put Mary in a vanishingly small group. If nothing else, Kimball's remark is indicative of how much the world of Mormonism had tilted toward Young since the death of the Smith brothers.

JFS would always harbor a low-key resentment toward church leaders regarding the treatment of his mother, and he maintained throughout his life a general sense of having been on the wrong side of a class divide in early Utah. At a social gathering at the home of Heber J. Grant in 1900, JFS told the group that "for years after he reached Utah, he never had enough to eat," a fact made more galling when he attended a "sociable" at John Taylor's home in 1851 where a "feast" was laid out. He had, he told his listeners in 1900, "never forgotten that circumstance."[39] With the exception of Heber Kimball, JFS wrote, Mary "received no support from either the church or any human being ... while on the other hand she contributed largely to the support of others besides supporting her own family."[40]

He echoed the same sentiments sixty years after his mother's death, when he wrote to his grieving sister-in-law, Asenath Richards Grover, that he could empathize with her because he, too, had suffered, being "left fatherless, by violent, lawless crime, and only a little later left also motherless. And that in times of poverty, and practically friendless and homeless."[41] That JFS and his siblings were orphaned and impoverished is well-known. That the children of Hyrum the martyr would find themselves "friendless" in the new world that Mormons were creating in the Rocky Mountains may shock some, but it helps explain JFS's later insistence on absolute loyalty to family and his belief that everyone he met was assumed to be an enemy, pending evidence to the contrary.

JFS's recollection of his mother's treatment during her years in Utah carries the strong sense of injustice that is so common in his reminiscences, and it echoes the resentments expressed at Mary's shoddy treatment by Young and others in Nauvoo after the death of the Smith brothers. There is some evidence that John Smith was also suspicious of Young's attitude toward the Smiths. In an 1856 letter he wrote to JFS, he said their sister Jerusha was being courted by a young man named William Pierce. John expressed indignation that Pierce would attempt to marry Jerusha without John's permission. He was especially angry because Pierce had been "adopted" into Young's family.[42]

Until 1894, Mormons performed rituals of adoption by which one could join the family of a prominent church leader. The general idea was that the larger the family one had, the grander life would be in the hereafter. "The Pierce family," John reminded JFS, "belongs in Brother Brigham's family, and he [Young] would like it first rate to get one of father's daughters into his family and leave father without any kingdom."[43] It seems unlikely that Young was trying to steal Hyrum's "kingdom" in this way, but it is clear that in the 1850s Hyrum Smith's sons felt that their family was in grave danger of being airbrushed out of the Mormon hierarchy.

We do not know if JFS felt the sting of injustice at the funeral, or if he, like John, honed that sense as the years passed. What we do know is that JFS ran from the house sobbing. For a child who had already endured such significant trauma, he must have felt very nearly alone in the world. The only close family member he had left was Martha, but extended family members reached out to the children to give them encouragement if nothing else. In early 1853, JFS received a letter from Agnes Pickett, the widow of Don Carlos Smith. Pickett had left Utah and was living in California. "I feel to mourn with you the loss of your dear mother," Agnes wrote, adding that "you must try and comfort each other and be good children and do what you know would please her if she was with you and then you will do alright."[44] Among other things, JFS knew this meant that he was responsible for protecting Martha. He knew the world was full of enemies and dangers, and he would ensure that his younger sister would be protected by his hand.

Just a few months before his mother died, JFS received a patriarchal blessing. These blessings remain an important fixture in LDS culture. They represent a sort of mild divination coupled with a declaration of group membership. The patriarch declares which tribe of Israel the person belongs to, and then proceeds to speak a blessing that predicts some of the things that may happen to the person in life. Often, these blessings carry promises of missions, marriages, children, and church service, as well as warnings to avoid sin and evil. On 25 June 1852, JFS sat down, and his uncle John Smith placed his hands on JFS's head and pronounced his blessing. Toward the end, Patriarch Smith told JFS that he would "live to take vengence on those that have slain your Father."[45] Nathaniel Ricks, the first scholar to attempt an analysis of this document, suggests that this line of the blessing might productively be read symbolically; that is, not as referring to literal revenge, but as a form of revenge that might play out in another way. Ricks argues, for example, that the LDS Church's purchase of the Carthage jail and its repurposing of it as a center for missionary work might represent the fulfilment of the promised vengeance.[46]

Ricks may be correct, but it is difficult to imagine that JFS would have assigned such a capacious meaning to the prophecy. One can reasonably believe that JFS saw this not only as a promise, but also as the imposition of a responsibility. Five years after the blessing, while on a mission in Hawaii, JFS wrote a letter to his cousins Agnes and Josephine in which he gave clear voice to his views about revenge: "The blood of our fathers that lies spilt is fresh in my sight. Their murmurs from the tomb are in my ears. And urge me to the sprit of revenge!" The letter gathered speed as JFS grew increasingly agitated. "Men have wronged me! And I feel it. It makes me desperate. It blackens my countenance with hatred and malevolence. You may perhaps think I ought to suppress such feelings. I say no, encourage it! Nourish it and let it grow."[47]

These do not sound like the words of a young man content with symbolic vengeance. Even accounting for the hyperbole inherent in all teenage angst, JFS clearly felt deep, dark, and violent feelings toward the world that murdered his father and, indirectly, killed his mother. But the letter also reveals that JFS viewed himself as a protector of the honor of the larger Smith family. With the death of his mother, JFS was now responsible not only for settling the scores of the past, but also for carrying the burden of shielding his young sister from the endless dangers that lurked in this new frontier world. And it was a violent act performed in her defense that would send him on his next grand adventure.

The Orphan Missionary

We know very little about JFS's life between the time of his mother's death and his assignment to the Sandwich Islands as a missionary in 1854. In a reminiscence

64   Chapter 4

published in 1887, JFS links the two events: "My mother died, September 21, 1852 aged 51 years and 2 months and in April, 1854, I was called to take a mission to the Sandwich Islands."[48] During the interim, he lived first with Hannah Grinnells, the woman who had been assisting Mary's family since before JFS was born. Grinnells died the next year, and JFS spent 1853 living with some of his older siblings and his younger sister.

According to his own recollections, JFS spent most of his time engaged in duties and chores typical of life in pioneer Utah. He cut and hauled wood from the nearby canyons, and helped with planting, harvesting, and irrigation. Just as he had in Winter Quarters, JFS spent most of his time protecting the family's livestock, which were not only at the mercy of the elements but also constantly being harassed by the large population of wolves. JFS was proud of his work during these lean and lonely years, writing many years later that in his years as a herd boy he never lost a single "hoof" "by neglect or carelessness on my part." He would recall that those early years in Utah, before his mother's death, were times of "boyhood joys and sorrows" that were stamped in "fadeless colors in my mind."[49]

JFS came to view these years through a patina of sentimentality, and he remembered his time at the "old log schoolhouse" where he endured the "shambling tuition" of his teachers and also attended "testimony meetings."[50] The building, he wrote on another occasion, "holds a place in the warm cranny of my heart reserved for early memories."[51] At other times, JFS seemed to resent the limits that his impoverished upbringing placed on his education. "When I was a little boy," he wrote in 1875, "and should have been going to school ... I had to travel on the plains and camp in the deserts with no home but a wagon or a tent and no teacher to teach me." Even when he found a home in Utah, he "was obliged to herd cattle, plow and irrigate and harvest and go to the canyons to get wood [and when] I went to school it was [only] for 3 months and three weeks." For the rest of his life, he believed, he was "learning at a disadvantage."[52]

JFS was growing to maturity in an unforgiving place, and with very little in the way of family support. He admitted, in 1888, that he was totally out of control during these years. "After my mother's death there followed 18 months—from Sept 21st, 1852 to April, 1854 of perilous times for me. I was almost like a comet or fiery meteor, without attraction or gravitation to keep me balanced or guide me within reasonable bounds."[53] Although he does not mention any specifics about his transgressions of "reasonable bounds" in that letter, it was during this period that one of the most famous events in JFS's early life transpired, and one to which he was almost certainly referring in his letter to Samuel Adams.

The story of JFS and the schoolmaster has moved from history into legend. It is worth taking a brief look at the story and its sources to try to make a judgment about its historical accuracy. The basic story holds that one day, as Martha Ann was about to be punished by the schoolmaster, JFS intervened and beat up the teacher. Then, the story goes, Brigham Young sent JFS, only fourteen years old, on a mission to Hawaii in an effort to channel his aggression.

It is difficult to discern the balance between fact and fiction in this story. Mention of the event does not surface in the historical record until the late 1880s. Sources include the letter to Adams and a recollection from JFS's friend Charles Nibley in which Nibley says that George A. Smith told him in 1867 that JFS was sent on a mission because he "licked the teacher."[54] The Nibley reminiscence is the only source that contains JFS's account of the incident. I can find no mention of the beating in any of JFS's sermons or writings.

The closest thing to any direct acknowledgment of the event that can be definitively traced to JFS is found in an article published in the church periodical the *Contributor*. Written with the cooperation of JFS, the article mentions that he attended school at the beginning of the 1853–1854 school year, but that "two or three weeks after the opening the teacher, whose name was D.M. Merrick, fell into disgrace and the school was closed." The author of the article then adds that Merrick was, in JFS's opinion, a fine teacher "in spite of his faults."[55] It makes little sense to think of a teacher surviving an assault by a student as a "disgrace." It is equally strange that the school would have closed because of such an incident. If the disgraceful incident was, in fact, the beating, it is clear that JFS was not interested in having the details aired publicly. It is also clear that he felt that whatever happened to end Merrick's tenure as a teacher was his own fault.

In any case, the 1895 *Contributor* article is far too vague to tell us anything, in and of itself, about what happened. One might expect to hear something of this event from the other major player in the story, Martha Ann. For some reason, she did not include any reference to the event in her autobiography, and it is likewise omitted from a biographical sketch published by her son in 1924. All of the detail comes from Charles Nibley's account of what JFS told him—an account that was not published until 1919, one year after JFS's death.[56]

Remarkably, Nibley reconstructed a lengthy "quote" from JFS, and it is this statement that has been uncritically attributed to JFS for nearly 100 years. To be clear, it is Nibley's *reconstruction* of what he claimed to be JFS's explanation of the beating that was published by Joseph Fielding Smith Jr. in 1919 in his edited compilation *Gospel Doctrine: Selections from the Sermons and Writings of Joseph F. Smith*, and published again (and attributed as a direct quotation) in his 1938 biography of his father. All subsequent citations of the event, as recently as 2012, go back to one of those two sources, and none of them mentions the fact that the quote is actually from Nibley, although some of them do mention that it was mentioned in Nibley's reminiscences. Those two facts indicate that writers place an inordinate amount of trust in Nibley's memory.

Given the large span of time over which the details of this story trickled out, and the distance between the event, which was probably in fall 1853, and the possible

Chapter 4

oblique allusion to it in 1888 and Nibley's recollection of JFS's story in 1919, it is difficult to make a judgment about the relationship between the altercation with the teacher and the mission call. JFS was certainly capable of accosting his teacher. He admitted many times, in word and deed, to possessing a temper that could turn violent. Late in his life, JFS described this temper as a "species of madness," a weakness that led to "hasty, premature, and unsound acts."[57] JFS learned to despise that dimension of his personality, praying at the age of thirty-nine that "God, [would] hasten that glorious day when the feeling to ... punish, to retaliate, either for real or fancied wrongs, shall have perished from our natures!"[58] That particular "species of madness" would afflict JFS for most of his life, and the incident with the teacher is the first recorded occasion in which his temper led him to commit an act of violence. It is certain that he was called on a mission at an unusually young age.

There is no definitive link between the two events, but the circumstantial evidence is strong. We know, for example, that Brigham Young did send young men on missions if he felt that their behavior was out of hand. In 1865, Oscar Lyons wrote to his uncle George A. Smith, from his mission in the eastern United States, that he suspected Young had issued his mission call out "out of spite, on account of that affair at the Social Hall. Be it so or not, I thank him for it as it has changed me from a 'wild mountain boy' to a thinking man."[59] Here we have evidence that not only connects Young with the use of missions to tame "wild" boys, but also connects George A. Smith to this practice. JFS's close relationship with George and the fact that Nibley recalled that it was George who told him that JFS had been sent on the mission because of his attack on the teacher all come together to provide a strong historical argument for the assertion that JFS was sent to Hawaii because of the incident.

JFS's own impression, however, was that Heber Kimball was the motivating force. In 1888, he wrote, "I shall always thank God and Heber C. Kimball for that mission."[60] Although the call would naturally have been approved by Young, it is most likely that JFS is correct. Kimball, who by dint of his marriage to Mary had responsibility for JFS, probably brought the matter to Young's attention and suggested the call.

5 | Upon the Isles of the Sea

There are several reasons why a biography of Joseph F. Smith must linger on his first missionary experience in Hawaii. First, his service as a proselytizing missionary in the Hawaiian Islands was the capstone event of JFS's childhood and adolescence. His first two decades of life are unusually dense with watershed experiences, as we have seen already. The murder of his father, the geographical dislocation from his home in Illinois, the events attendant to crossing the plains, a new life in the exotic biome of the Great Basin, and the death of his mother all occurred within an eight-year span. As difficult as life had been for JFS before his mission, in Hawaii he faced trials and difficulties that tested him in ways that even the traumatic events that had hammered him since boyhood had not.

Second, JFS's time in Hawaii would become a touchstone for him throughout the rest of his life. It became so important to him, in fact, that he actually imported into his memory of his Hawaiian mission events that occurred at other times in his life. The most famous of these is a dream that he had, which remains a famous and oft-told tale in LDS general conference addresses. In the dream, which I will examine in greater detail later in the book, JFS found himself rushing to a meeting with his dead uncle and his father. He stopped to cleanse himself, and upon reaching the house where his relatives were, he was mildly reproved by Joseph Smith for being late. JFS responded that he may be late but "I am clean." JFS first told this story in 1918, and it was published in *Gospel Doctrine*, a collection of his thoughts, and again in Joseph Fielding Smith's 1938 biography of his father. From 1918 until the present, the dream has always been placed in the context of his dreadful hardships in Hawaii. A close reading of JFS's journals, however, indicates that the dream actually occurred years later, while he was serving a mission in Great Britain. It did not happen in Hawaii but, it seems, it *should* have. The mission possessed a kind of gravitational pull on JFS's memory.

Third, the mission and the role of JFS's memory of it in his later life signal a major shift in how Latter-day Saints would come to view the role of a mission in a young man's life. In the nineteenth century, there was no typical, or expected, missionary experience. Many men served multiple missions of widely varying duration,

68   Chapter 5

from a few months to three years. Most of these missionaries were adult men with wives and children, and the vast majority of them did not volunteer for service. The call to serve a mission most often came, unbidden, from church leaders. Some men never served formal proselytizing missions.

During the nineteenth century, and the first half of the twentieth, missionary service was not viewed as a particularly important part of the move from youth to adulthood. Unlike the current atmosphere—in which formal missionary service carries pressing cultural implications for things such as finding a marriage partner, and in which many men, and some women, view their time as young missionaries as the defining period of their religious development—nineteenth-century Mormons simply did not view mission experiences that way. Women, for example, were not encouraged to marry only "returned missionaries" as they are today. Missions tended to be ongoing events, even disruptions, in the lives of some Mormon men, but they were not typically viewed as conclusive or formative, nor did they function as a sort of credentialing rite of passage as they do today.

JFS's mission experience foreshadowed its centrality to his own self-image as a Mormon and, as a man, the role that missions would play in a later era. As in so many other ways, JFS's experience in Hawaii was anomalous and out of step with the broader religious world in which he functioned. Modern Mormons almost certainly better understand the significance that JFS attached to his missionary service than did his contemporaries.

Fourth, it is during his Hawaiian mission that we get our first deep, extended look at JFS's life through his own eyes, rather than solely through the eyes of memory. JFS emerges through his journals and letters in his own words. In the process, he reveals to us, for the first time, what he was thinking and doing *when* he was thinking and doing them. Although only a teenager, JFS reveals through his words a young man of astonishing complexity. Tenacity, humility, insecurity, searing intelligence, stunning ignorance, cultural arrogance, keen observational skills, love of nature, viciousness, physical courage, strength, gifted writing, intense curiosity, a natural sense of drama, an innate ability to effectively project personal power, profound religiosity, anger, sentimentality, bravado, a bent toward the romantic, vindictiveness, cruelty, and love—all of these mingled stormily within this slight young man. Although any human being is little more than a churning sea of contradictions masquerading as a coherent whole, JFS was unusually complex.

Finally, exploring JFS's missionary years in Hawaii provides an opportunity to survey the larger context of Hawaiian history in the 1850s, providing a more robust sense of the larger world in which JFS's life played out.

An Unexpected Call

On the morning of 6 April 1854, JFS's name was read, along with many others, at the church's general conference. These men were being called on missions to a wide variety of locations around the world. "Joseph Smith (son of Hyrum)" was called to labor in the Sandwich Islands. JFS began his long journey to Hawaii the next month.

During the first leg of the journey, from Salt Lake to the Mormon settlements in southern Utah, JFS and his fellow missionaries were accompanied by Brigham Young and other church leaders. Young was on a tour of the various settlements, and JFS had the opportunity to view Young in action up close. It took the group a week to reach the settlement of Fillmore, located 148 miles south of Salt Lake City. Young addressed the settlers and "took the liberty to give a man by the name of A. J. Steward a tremendous tongue-lashing for some misdemeanor of his in surveying the city of Fillmore."[1] Although Young had a well-earned reputation for his surliness, he also had a knack for knowing exactly what tone to use in any given situation in order to get the best results. The business of settling the far western frontier was a serious one, and Young understood that vinegar often produced better results than honey.

The group left Fillmore and continued south to Cedar City, where they encountered the apostles Parley Pratt and Ezra Benson. Pratt, who was headed to California, continued on with the group as they turned west. They reached Las Vegas on 29 May 1854, and by 10 June they had made it to San Bernardino, California. Soon they were in San Francisco. There, "under the presidency and direction of [Pratt]," JFS began his official missionary service.[2]

San Francisco underwhelmed JFS, who described it as "little more than a village on the sand hills."[3] However, the missionaries found a variety of jobs to earn money before they set sail for Hawaii. JFS also enjoyed the opportunity to spend time with his aunt Agnes, the widow of Don Carlos Smith, and his beloved cousin Ina, who had made a home in the San Francisco Bay area.[4]

Although JFS enjoyed the company of his aunt and cousins, his aunt's husband, William Pickett, rubbed him the wrong way. JFS was particularly irritated by Pickett's incessant and vulgar screeds against Brigham Young and other church leaders. One day, after single-handedly lifting Pickett's stuck wagon back onto the road, JFS took him aside and said, "I am a better man than you are, and now, sir, if you once more open your mouth to me against Brigham Young or others, I will knock the daylight out of your head."[5]

JFS—tall, lean, broad-shouldered and well-muscled from his life as a frontier orphan—had already by the age of fifteen developed the capacity to project a physically menacing presence when it suited him. He would find plenty of suitable occasions in the years to come. In 1854, however, his temper and relatively thin skin impeded what little missionary work he had time to do in San Francisco. According to one of his companions, after his first day of proselytizing, JFS asked to be excused from that duty because he "could not offer a Book of Mormon without having to listen to a burst of blasphemy and a tirade of falsehood and abuse to my Uncle Joseph and I cannot be peaceable and hear it."[6] Remaining "peaceable" in the presence of real and imagined insults would prove a struggle that JFS carried to the grave.

Hawaii and Colonization

Hawaiian history had been turbulent since Polynesian groups had first settled the islands sporadically between 400 and 1,000 CE. Before the first known European contact with Hawaiians in 1778, the islands were ruled by chiefdoms that found frequent cause for tribal warfare. Captain James Cook's arrival had an astonishing impact on Hawaiian demographics and, thus, everything else from politics and economics to religion and family structure. Scholars have not yet reached a consensus regarding the population of Hawaii before Cook arrived. Estimates range from 500,000 to more than a million. Whatever the original number, the census carried out by Christian missionaries in 1832 revealed that only 130,000 Native Hawaiians remained. They also discovered that deaths exceeded births by two to one.[7]

This "great dying," as it was called, was due largely to European diseases being introduced to the islands by a wide variety of visitors. As Sally Engle Merry describes it, Hawaii in the early nineteenth century "lay at the crossroads of a dizzying array of peoples engaged in the expansion of capitalism and European imperial power"; in addition to "merchants from Britain, France, the Netherlands, and the United States," there were also "goods [being] traded in Spanish dollars brought from Chile and Peru; and Chinese merchants and sugar masters settled in Honolulu to trade or moved into the wet valleys to grow rice or sugar."[8]

Another epidemic in 1848 led to an even greater loss of population; perhaps as much as 30 percent of the remaining population perished. The demographic collapse naturally led Hawaiians to begin questioning their own cultural systems. The catastrophic decline in population led to the widespread belief, held most importantly by Kamehameha III, that the Hawaiian "race was headed toward extinction."[9] Motivated by this fear, the king introduced sweeping changes to age-old traditions of land ownership.

In 1850, the Kuleana Act was passed. For the first time, ordinary Hawaiians could buy, own, and sell land. Although the intention was to provide an incentive for Hawaiians to remain on the islands and attempt to revive their culture, the unintended consequence was that large amounts of land quickly ended up in the hands of Christian missionaries. A great many rural-dwelling Hawaiians found themselves both landless and homeless. It was to this class of dispossessed persons in particular that Mormon missionaries directed their message.

The dizzying pace of new crises made it clear to the Hawaiians that, whatever else might be going on, their notion of "pono" was failing. "Pono" refers to, among other things, the cosmic equilibrium that permits life to flourish. It was this breach of cultural expectation that helped early Christian missionaries gain a foothold in the islands, not just religiously but also politically. After the death of King Kamehameha I, who had united the island tribes in 1810, the new rulers sought out European help. King Kamehameha II and his stepmother, Kaʻahumanu, sought to fend off challenges to Hawaiian sovereignty by adopting Euro-American laws and governmental systems. Among other things, the Hawaiian leaders "hired more foreigners to design a constitution, bill of rights, and a set of law codes based on models drawn from New England and other parts of the world."[10]

Around the same time, Kamehameha II violated the important concept of taboo by engaging in "profane eating"—meaning he ate at the same table as his female counterparts. According to Hawaiian historian Jonathan Kay Kamakaw-iwoʻole Osorio, the violation of taboo and the introduction of Euro-American style "prohibitionary laws" not only "altered traditional morality and custom, but also resulted in the Natives' abnegation of their own culture and values as well as their reliance on foreigners to tell them what was pono."[11] Historian James Haley goes further, arguing that the shattering of the taboo represented the death of the Hawaiian religious system, and although "the common people continued to revere their household gods, the old religion was ended."[12] Haley argues that this is "the only known time in the history of the world when a people threw over a long-established religious system with nothing to replace it."[13]

While Haley may be overreaching on this point, there is no question that Hawaiian society was suddenly without a comprehensive religious culture just when such a system was desperately needed to help make sense of the seismic shifts that were rocking all dimensions of Hawaiian culture. Into this religious vacuum stepped the Christian missionaries. The success of Protestant Christian missions in Hawaii in the early nineteenth century can be explained, in large measure, by what Osorio describes as the Christians' ability to "promise life when death was every-where ... [and when] their own religion could not prevent them from dying."[14]

Hawaii had been the site of Christian proselytizing for decades by the time JFS arrived in 1854. Protestant missionaries arrived in the South Pacific in 1797 and began missionary work in Hawaii in 1819. In 1822, Christian missionaries acquired a printing press for the publication of tracts and periodicals. The next year, Keōpūolani, the queen mother, converted to Christianity and publicly renounced Native Hawaiian religious practices.[15] Just the year before JFS's arrival in Hawaii, the American Board of Commissioners of Foreign Missions had declared the islands "Christianized."[16] Fully one-fourth of Hawaiians identified as Christian by 1853.[17] The Mormons believed that fact made the need for missions there even more urgent. Whereas Christian missionaries believed they needed to save the Hawaiians from "savagery," Mormons believed that they had to save Hawaiians from savages and "apostate" Christianity.

Recent scholarship on Christian missionary work in Hawaii has shown that there were significant differences among the various Christian approaches to missionary work in the islands. Of particular importance are the differences between Protestant missions and Mormon missions, in both purpose and function. As Laurie F. Maffly-Kipp has demonstrated, the Mormon view that all other forms of Christianity were apostate and essentially wicked gave a unique flavor to Mormon missions in Hawaii. The missionaries were there to save the Native Hawaiians not only from their natural ignorance, but also from the added layer of false belief that had been foisted upon them by Protestants.

Mormon missionaries did things differently than their Protestant counterparts. Most importantly, they lived in much closer contact with the Native Hawaiians than the Protestant missionaries did. Maffly-Kipp suggests that this "intimacy" was largely the result of poverty: the Mormons could not afford to live on their own. Regardless of the cause, the result was that Mormons found themselves "compelled to conform to local practices and power dynamics, rather than immediately trying to change them."[18] Mormon missionaries were thus less obviously erosive of Native Hawaiian culture than the Protestant missionaries were. This dynamic, coupled with the estrangement of the Mormons from the American government, made Hawaiians less likely to link Mormon proselytizing with American imperial and colonial goals.[19]

Like the more politically entrenched Protestant groups, the Mormon missionaries became remarkably successful in Hawaii. Of course, they did not enjoy the influence that their religious rivals had among the Hawaiian elite, a fact that made their missionaries even more appealing to that segment of the Hawaiian population that was not only suffering terrible demographic losses, but also feeling marginalized by the new Hawaiian/Christian political and legal systems. Mormons found this success relatively early in their history, with missionaries landing in the islands only three years after Brigham Young's arrival in the Salt Lake Valley.

Mormon missionary work in Hawaii began formally in the fall of 1850. That year, several Mormon men who had been working in the California gold fields were issued assignments to travel together to Hawaii as full-time proselytizing missionaries. The youngest of the group, at twenty-three, was George Q. Cannon, a nephew of LDS apostle John Taylor who would one day become an apostle and member of the First Presidency himself. But in 1850, he was just a young man with very little experience and no idea about where he was. When he later explained the situation, Cannon identified the major challenges of Mormon missionary work in Hawaii as Mormon ignorance, Protestant influence, and Protestant cultural knowledge. "We landed upon these shores complete strangers," he recalled, "totally ignorant of the language, customs, and prejudices of the people among whom we landed, with a strong influence to contend against, and that, wielded by these well acquainted with what we were ignorant of."[20]

Cannon and his nine companions began splitting up and working in different areas almost immediately after their arrival in November 1850. While most of the men began by trying to teach local whites, Cannon, laboring in Lahaina on Maui, had quickly decided that he and his two companions would try to learn the Hawaiian language and take their gospel to the Natives.[21] In December 1850, Cannon wrote in his journal that he "felt a great anxiety to be able to talk with [the Native Hawaiians] and impart unto them the glorious truths of which we are the bearers, they seem to be bound down by the [Protestant] missionaries in Temporal as well as Spiritual Affairs."[22]

Cannon made astounding progress in his language training and began translating the Book of Mormon into Hawaiian, a task that would bear fruit when the first Hawaiian translation was published in 1855–1856. The difficulty of the language may have helped land JFS in Hawaii. By 1853, Cannon's successor as mission president was requesting younger missionaries because the language "is difficult for an adult foreigner to learn," and the English-speaking missionaries' facility with the language varied "in proportion to their ages."[23]

The first wave of Mormon missionaries in Hawaii set the stage for JFS's mission work in several ways. First, as noted above, the missionaries began to concentrate almost completely on Hawaiian-language proselytizing. Second, they gave Native Hawaiians responsibility for leadership as congregations began to form. Third, like the Protestant and Catholic missionaries, they launched various "civilizing" efforts that usually focused on education and the imposition of Euro-American standards of dress and etiquette. Finally, the Mormon missionaries in Hawaii transplanted their concept of a Zionic "gathering place," first articulated in the 1830s. The idea was that the righteous should gather in a place where they could all live together and better avoid the evils of the world.

The Hawaiian gathering place was officially approved by Brigham Young in the fall of 1853, and the roughly 3,000 Mormons in Hawaii were encouraged to move to the new colony on the small island of Lanai. It was hoped that this place would serve as a place of refuge for Hawaiian Mormons as they awaited the ultimate goal of migration to Utah.[24]

JFS in Hawaii

JFS's time in Hawaii, which lasted from the fall of 1854 until the spring of 1858, is among the most frequently cited periods of his life. For modern Latter-day Saints, JFS's mission is a touchstone that has grown in importance as the practice of sending young men and women on missions has become an expected part of LDS life. JFS's mission is often held up as a quintessential mission experience, complete with poverty, sickness, miracles, faith, language mastery, perseverance, and the solidification of the missionary's testimony.

JFS himself, in an 1888 letter to Samuel Adams, expressed his belief that "My four years mission to the Sandwich Islands restored my equilibrium, and fixed the laws and metes and bounds which have governed my subsequent life."[25] His letters from Hawaii reveal that he was somewhat more conflicted about what the mission meant. He gloried in following the difficult path of discipleship, but he also felt that he had been "cast into the world" and denied the opportunity for education.[26]

There can be no question that JFS developed and demonstrated in Hawaii a wide range of traits, habits, contradictions, and ideals that would form the pattern of his remaining decades. Very late in his life, he wrote that he would "never cease to be grateful for the experience, hard as it was at times."[27]

Various aspects of JFS's mission experience have been dealt with by other biographers in a wide range contexts. I intend to place his mission within the broader context of Hawaiian history while focusing on a limited number of texts produced by JFS during this period in an effort to understand not only his experiences, but also his mindset as he moved from childhood to adulthood both biologically and spiritually.

On 8 September 1854, JFS set sail on the schooner *Vaquero*, headed for Hawaii. The trip took eighteen days, during which a fair amount of seasickness plagued the group. This must have been a tremendously exciting experience for JFS. The group disembarked on 27 September at Honolulu on the island of Oahu. "As a boy of 15," JFS recalled, "I first set foot on the soil of Hawaii, where then stood the little village of Honolulu, principally a native town built of grass houses with crooked little roads with now and then a comfortable dwelling inhabited by the whites."[28] JFS and the other missionaries enjoyed their first real bath in weeks at King's Falls (now known as Kapena Falls).

The next day the group wandered around the city, attempting to get their bearings and adjust to the new culture. They found a sprawling city with a much greater European and American presence than they had expected. Silas Smith, a distant cousin of JFS, was also with the group and recorded his impressions in his journal. In addition to the friendly "natives," he noted the presence of "merchants who have emigrated to the Island for the purpose of obtaining gold and silver which is probably the only god they worship." Even worse was "the class of people who style themselves as missionaries to the heathen." Silas pointed out that these missionaries appeared to live a life of "luxury," a fact that he took as clear evidence that they were "successful in fleecing their flock."[29]

On the group's first day in Hawaii they encountered the three basic strands of society: the Native Hawaiians, the merchants, and the politically and economically powerful Christian missionaries. It is likely that the young men had been prompted by Cannon and other earlier missionaries about what to expect, particularly in regard to the Christian missionaries. As one missionary wrote in an 1854 letter to a friend in Utah, the LDS missionaries had experienced a "fair sample of the bad effects arising from the influence some of the [Protestant] missionaries have over some of the officers of government."[30]

The missionaries, most of whom, like JFS, had grown up in the arid American West, were astonished at the number and variety of trees and other types of vegetation on the islands. Silas Smith recorded in his journal the presence of exotic fruits such as lemons, oranges, figs, and coconuts.[31] After a day of sightseeing, the missionaries spent the following day in meetings with their mission president, Philip Lewis. At one of these meetings, Lewis assigned each missionary to labor in a specific area.[32]

The earliest extant letter written by JFS is one he wrote to his sister, Martha, on 17 October 1854. Although he says almost nothing about his journey or about the islands, the brief letter tells us a great deal about JFS as a green missionary. He expressed an almost urgent need for prayers on his behalf. "You must remember me in your prars day and night whare ever you are or what ever sircumstances you may be placed in," JFS implored. Despite his youth, he demonstrated his natural inclination to teach and lead and provide advice. He reminded Martha that her first priority should be education, "so that I may find a well lirned girl when I git home." Despite the obvious rawness of his education and the vastness of his inexperience, he did not hesitate to promise Martha that if she would "take notice of my coun-cil ... you will be blest."[33] Two weeks later he wrote again, this time to Martha and Jerusha, entreating Martha to "keep your temper to yourself" and reminding them that he thought of them "day and nite."[34]

JFS's first missionary area was the island of Maui, and almost immediately upon arriving, he fell seriously ill.[35] Around the same time, he wrote a letter to George A. Smith that left little doubt about his sense of purpose: "I know that the work in which I am engaged is the work of the true and living God and I am ready to bear my testimony of the same at any time or at any place or in whatsoever circumstances I may be placed."[36]

Although it is not clear how much JFS knew about Mormon doctrine at the start of his mission, he almost certainly had not read the Book of Mormon all the way through, and some of the things that make up the core of Mormon theolog-ical and soteriological teachings today were still very much in flux during the 1850s. Missionaries had no set lessons from which to teach. The material to be taught was left entirely to the discretion of the missionaries, who probably focused primarily on the role of Joseph Smith as the prophet of a new dispensation, the Book of Mormon as evidence of the divinity of Smith's calling, the divinity of Jesus Christ and Christ's disavowal of all religions beside Mormonism, and the doctrine of the "gathering of Zion." In all of JFS's years as a missionary and mission president, these were the main elements of his teaching.

Despite his youth and the often difficult circumstances in which he found him-self over the next four years, JFS's resolution to share his faith with the Hawaiian people never flagged. He became extremely ill during this period and found himself under the care of Sister Mary Hammond. JFS's letters to his half brother John contained enough references to his illness that John became concerned "pertaining to [JFS's] bodily health"; he worried that the "the climate and food wood not agree with you and wood be likely to keep you sick for I knowed it was not what you had been used to."[37] After JFS recovered, he began studying the Hawaiian language, firm in the conviction that God wanted him to bring the message of Mormon Christianity to the Native Hawaiians. JFS later estimated that, through a combi-nation of the "gift of tongues" and dedicated study, he had mastered the Hawaiian language "a hundred days after landing upon those Islands."[38]

In 1908, JFS wrote to one of his sons, then serving his own mission in Hawaii, that "it is true that I readily learned the language," and even though the other

76   Chapter 5

missionaries were older, "not one of them got ahead of me" in language capability.[39] His memory on this point was accurate; a report from a mission leader to Brigham Young in 1855 indicated that "Brother Joseph can speak [Hawaiian] as well as some elders after being here 2 years. He bids fair to make a stir on these lands, awaking up old Israel and calling upon them to gather together."[40] JFS reported to George A. Smith that, in March 1855, he could "chat quite freely with the natives" and had given sermons in Hawaiian.[41]

It is clear from the facility with which JFS continued to use Hawaiian for the rest of his life that he learned the language well. In fact, in April of 1855, a fellow missionary wrote that "Some of the brethren who came here first (I mean of our company) have advanced considerably in the language and are speaking publicly. Among these, the most forward in the language is Joseph [F.] Smith, son of Hyrum."[42] Only months after beginning his study of the language, JFS could confidently speak Hawaiian publicly. In the days before LDS missionaries underwent formal, systematic, and semiprofessional language training, this was quite an accomplishment—and another sign of the high level of JFS's raw intelligence.

Since the first wave of LDS missionaries arrived in Hawaii, new missionaries had been studying a Hawaiian grammar, and in 1853, Jonatana Napela, a Hawaiian convert of some means, opened a small language school for the missionaries in his home.[43] However, the grammar and the school still provided only the thinnest of educations. Although proud of his language skills, JFS learned that he was often partnered with less-skilled missionaries, leaving him to do the bulk of the work.[44]

Facility with the Hawaiian language became the most prominent measure of a missionary's success during the 1850s. In 1855, B. F. Johnson and "Brother Karren" left Hawaii after serving there for two years. One of their colleagues pointedly noted that "Brothers Karren and B. F. Johnson were not successful in getting a knowledge of the native language. Consequently, their means of doing much good on their mission was quite limited." Although Karren baptized an astonishingly high number of Hawaiians, more than 200 in two years, Silas Smith concluded that because "he was not able to converse with them, he could not give them much instruction pertaining to the laws and regulations of the Church. Consequently, they were no better after their baptism than they were before."[45] JFS's devotion to gaining fluency in Hawaiian thus had more than practical implications among his fellow missionaries and leaders, who viewed it as evidence of the young man's spiritual power.

Learning the language was one thing, but as in Cannon's time, there was some division among the missionaries serving with JFS about the usefulness of preaching to the Native Hawaiians at all. Some missionaries took the view that the Hawaiians lacked the moral and intellectual capacity to understand and implement the Mormon message. Although this attitude was founded on a bedrock of racism, there is no doubt these missionaries were also influenced by the natural human tendency to follow the path of least resistance. Taking the message to Native Hawaiians meant learning the language and living with, and like, the poorer people on the islands. JFS, characteristically, followed the path of greatest resistance.

JFS's single-minded devotion to missionary work not only increased his fluency in the Hawaiian language and the numbers of baptized Hawaiian converts, it formed an important element of JFS's personality. Given his inherent passion and drive, it is conceivable that JFS could have found himself on any number of other paths that would have resulted in a very different life for him. Although he was clearly committed to Mormonism from early on, it was his time in Hawaii that solidified his faith and created a new dimension of his personality, that of a religious preacher and leader, which otherwise may not have emerged.

JFS learned in the spring of 1857 that he had been assigned to move from the island of Hawaii to Molokai, which, although it "could be worse," had a reputation among the missionaries as "a hard field to labor in." He anticipated the task unflinchingly. "One thing is certain," he wrote in a letter, "I never shall shrink from my duty as long as I can keep the spirit of Mormonism about me, for I know better."[46]

Despite his lack of any substantial formal education, JFS demonstrated a knack for written and spoken English, including a large vocabulary and a syntactical instinct that would set him apart from many of his contemporaries in later church leadership. His physical and intellectual talents were all put to good use during his four years in Hawaii. Apparently JFS also demonstrated significant leadership potential. Naturally, his family connections did not go unnoticed. Brigham Young's nephew, John, served with JFS in Hawaii and wrote to his uncle that "Brother Joseph Smith is filled with the Spirit of his Father, and his voice is raised boldly and loudly in defense of Zion's cause."[47]

In March and April 1855, JFS traveled extensively, raising that bold and loud voice in the branches around east Maui. He gave frequent sermons in Hawaiian during this excursion. The tour was cold and rainy, he had to cross swollen, dangerous streams, and he frequently spent days at a time in wet clothing.[48] His tirelessness, grit, and ability to inspire flagging missionaries and recalcitrant converts alike attracted the attention of the mission leadership.

By the summer of 1855, JFS had regained his health and described himself as "fat and stout" and perfectly able and willing to "throw all the boys down that there are in the valleys [Utah]."[49] It was at this point that the sixteen-year-old was appointed president of the Maui conference. At that time, LDS missions were divided into conferences, which consisted of smaller units known as districts. Conference presidents were responsible not only for the missionaries, but also for church members. This represented a significant responsibility, far outstripping modern LDS missionary assignments such as zone leader. Conference presidents operated as quasi-independent ecclesiastical leaders, more akin to modern stake presidents. They oversaw everything from the construction and maintenance of church meeting facilities to disciplinary proceedings. Contact with the president of the mission was sporadic, so conference presidents were expected to make their own decisions about weighty issues.

78   Chapter 5

JFS's confidence in the discharge of his responsibilities was remarkable, and it stood in stark contrast to the personality and abilities of his older half brother, John. Six years JFS's senior and then serving as church patriarch, John did not take kindly to JFS's admonition that one should speak "in publick when called upon." That was fine for JFS, who was good at it, John wrote, but "I have experienced that little thing which is cald diffidence."[50] John's reluctance to speak was so strong that he had even refused repeated requests from Brigham Young to offer the closing prayer at the church's most recent general conference. John wrote to JFS that while he had managed to say the sacramental prayers a few times in public and given a prayer or two, "as to preach[ing] I have not done that yet and I fear I never shall make much of a preacher."[51] John believed that his "thick num scull ... cannot free my mind neither writing or in speaking [even] if it was to save my neck from the gallows."[52] By contrast, even as a teenager JFS demonstrated significant gravitas in his public speaking and the performance of his ecclesiastical responsibilities. Three "foreigners" who attended a Sunday sacrament service in the summer of 1856 learned this first-hand when they watched the seventeen-year-old "storme for some time," administer the sacrament, and then excommunicate nine members of the congregation.[53]

Excommunication was a much more common practice in nineteenth-century Mormonism than it is today. During JFS's time in Hawaii, members could be excommunicated from the church by a vote of the congregation, and excommunications became a regular part of his religious duties. He noted, for example, that in the course of just a few months in the summer of 1856, more persons were excommunicated from his conference than were baptized.[54] In a practice that mirrored the Reformation meetings being held in Utah, JFS presided over meetings in which entire congregations were called upon to publicly confess their sins and seek forgiveness. One such meeting occurred in July 1856. JFS's description of it is, by his standards, unusually detailed and worth quoting at length.

> attended morning meeting, called on those—guilty—to confess their sins at which several arose and repented and prayed for forgiveness. and those who would not should be cut off, or god would never bless me nor them, if I neglected to tend to the business commited to my charge. thus boath old and young got up and confessed, some that they had "sined unto death," (whoredoms) others that they had quareled and fought, &c &c, after all had been done, and I gave them some pertinent remarkes pertaining to their future duty, and wellfair, the sacrement was adminstered, and the meeting closed, all appearantly feeling well, and satisfied, with how had been done. This was the first clenzing the branch had undergon for some time, and you may depend, some foul stuf had collected.[55]

JFS clearly took his responsibility for the welfare of these souls seriously, and he firmly believed that if he knowingly allowed any sin to go unpunished, then his own

Upon the Isles of the Sea 79

salvation would be in jeopardy. Even in these very early years of what would become a lifelong ministry, JFS demonstrated a tendency to explicitly tie soteriology, ritual, priesthood authority, and scripture together into something like a systematic whole. He abhorred fragmentation, insisting that each of these elements relates logically to all of the others. That need to make all of the pieces fit into a coherent whole required some measure of "religion-making."

Not all Mormon leaders in the nineteenth century approached religion this way. Most were comfortable with a messier and more ad hoc posture. JFS's insistence on this practice would be transmitted to his son, JFS Jr., who as an apostle and church president himself would construct a uniform, systematic theological and practical matrix that would become *the* normative form of Mormonism in the twentieth century. The roots of that were on display in miniature on that sultry Sunday in July 1856.

When JFS assumed his first leadership position in the summer of 1855, he had to face a number of seemingly intractable challenges. He took a clear-eyed view of the mission's current state, concluding that it was "rather weaker than it has been for some time before, or since the rise of the Church on the Islands," something that he intended to "change for the better."[56] According to a report issued by the church in 1856, crop failure the previous year had led to debt, "which hampered efforts to gather the Hawaiian saints to the gathering place where they could be free from hireling missionary organizations and other contaminating influence of licentious civilization."[57] These early efforts to gather the Hawaiian saints first to a settlement in Hawaii and, eventually, to Utah in the face of tremendous logistical, sectarian, and economic challenges unquestionably helped prepare JFS for the work he would perform on a much larger scale in the 1870s as president of the European mission.

At times JFS found himself in the middle of horrifying personal crises in the lives of the Hawaiian converts. One night he and his companion were awakened by a woman and her son who told the harrowing story of having barely escaped a rapist, a man from the neighborhood who had forced himself into her home. JFS handled the situation by assembling the LDS congregation, telling them the story, and then enjoining them to "horse whip him out—run him off."[58] The would-be rapist should have counted himself fortunate not to have been caught and dealt with by JFS himself.

After eight months, JFS was reassigned to the island of Hawaii, where he held leadership positions in the Hilo conference. In the spring of 1857, he was assigned to Molokai. Unfortunately, very little source material dealing with JFS's first two years in Hawaii exists. The journals for this period were destroyed when a young missionary from Australia named Clem Hurst accidentally set fire to the mission home.[59] Although the fire wiped out a great deal of historical material, it did yield a bit of information. After hearing of the fire, JFS wrote a list of the things he had lost. Because the trunk that burned up contained nearly all of his possessions, the list helps us understand his material poverty. The trunk itself was a treasured possession, a gift from his cousin Ina, and it had contained

80   Chapter 5

> 1 pair of 5 dollar pants, never worn, 1 $4.00 cotton vest never worn, 1 coat (linnin), 7 shirts some new, 4 pair of garments new also, one bran new native Kapa, one suit of Temple clothes bran new, also one suit belonging to George Spiers, several pair of stockings, 1 neck handkerchief, 2 bookes of Mormon one 2 dollers and a half and the other priceless, no charmes could have bought it, two Bibles one Testiment, 1 docterin and Covenents, 1 voice of warning, "history of the Perciscutions of the Church of Jesus christ of latter day saints," "Spencers letters""A glance at Scripture and reason""Pearl of great Price" and numirous other small books and pamphlets on the faith of the Latterday saints, some 20 or 30 No. of the Deseret News, 40 or 50 letters from my Brother, sister, and friends in general, two midle sised journals, "pasportes, Blessings" &c&c, a deguarian likeness of my father, uncle Joseph and Brigham Young, a presant and priceless to me, shaveing utensils, compleat, and bran new, two native vocabulary, and other native books, if this was all it would be better than it is. I had gathered a great many curiosities of the Sandwich Islands which would be interresting to me and my folks at home. Well these dear earned fiew things is gon and not one saved, and now I am destitute.[60]

In some ways, it is surprising that JFS owned as much as he did. Almost all of these items were gifts, and no doubt the most painful loss was the book that he says was "priceless." This happened to be an early European edition of the Book of Mormon that had belonged to his father. Even after so many years, so far away from Carthage, it seems that JFS could never stop losing pieces of his father.

The loss of his personal possessions made a difficult situation much worse. In the 1850s, conditions for missionaries were much more difficult in Hawaii than in Scandinavia or Britain. JFS spent a great deal of time traveling by boat or, more commonly, on foot or horseback over "uneven and difficult" terrain that boasted "scarcely no roads."[61] American missionaries often, probably to their surprise, found themselves fighting off shivers. One of JFS's contemporaries lamented that the "native houses are made of grass and they will not admit any fire inside. Consequently, they are not very pleasant in the rainy season."[62]

JFS also noted with some regularity the scarcity of food. In 1855, his half brother John learned the hard way that his complaints about only having "corn dodger" to eat after a rough harvest drew no sympathy from JFS. The two brothers maintained a complex, and often fraught, relationship throughout their lives, with JFS feeling both superior to and protective of his elder brother. In this early example, so typical of their interactions, we are left to wonder exactly what JFS wrote in response, but the general sense of what must have been a fierce reply is evident in John's next letter. In that, a very obviously chastened John wrote, "I feel sorry that you cannot get any doger, and flour, bread, buckwheat, pancakes, any milk or butter [that] we are blessed with at the present."[63] John learned from this exchange that hardship is relative and that missionary life had done nothing to blunt JFS's

JFS's View of Hawaiian Culture

By 1856, the church was slowly gaining a foothold in the islands. Following the model of Protestant missionaries, the Mormons established an "English school" at Palawai and were calling Hawaiian converts to serve as missionaries.[65] JFS did not shy away from noting with some frequency the various Native Hawaiian customs, rites, and traditions that he found offensive and uncivilized. In January 1856, he recorded two incidents that struck him as particularly unsavory. The first involved a baby who had been abandoned by its parents, presumably because of poverty. JFS reflected in his journal that before the whites arrived, "they would at the birth of a child choak it to death" unless the mother had particular affection for the child, in which case it would be buried alive.[66]

Stories of Hawaiian infanticide loomed large in the European imagination, not least of all because the practice did not exist before European contact. Jeffrey Tobin has persuasively argued that "infanticide was a myth that Cook and his crew carried to Hawai'i," and within "several decades ... Hawaiians accepted the myth of their own practice of infanticide." Stories of infanticide spread rapidly, especially among white Christian missionaries, a fact that prompted Tobin to caution that "missionary rumours of Hawaiian infanticide should be read sceptically."[67] JFS, of course, did not actually see any such act of infanticide, but the presence of an abandoned child triggered an immediate association with the alleged practice.

The second event was similar to the first in that JFS rendered Hawaiian practice "savage" by analogy. "The natives," he wrote, who were apparently short of meat, castrated some goats and served up the testicles. JFS could scarcely contain his disgust and contempt: "this is what I call eating live flesh, or the next thing to cannibalism."[68] Despite the popularity of testicle consumption among groups worldwide, JFS interpreted it as an act of desperation so depraved that had there been no testicles to consume, there was little if anything to keep the "natives" from consuming each other.

JFS's view of Hawaiian Mormons was not much sunnier. This is an area of potential controversy because, later in his life, he spoke with some affection for Hawaii and its people. In fact, Nathaniel Ricks argues that JFS's love for the Hawaiian Mormons was a major fact of his first mission there. He notes that JFS was the beneficiary of some generosity from the Hawaiians, and that he wept when he left the saints on Maui in 1856.[69]

These observations notwithstanding, JFS's attitude toward Hawaii and Native Hawaiians as recorded in his journals and letters from the 1850s was overwhelmingly negative. The temptation to read his later, more positive views back into the

82   Chapter 5

1850s is understandable, but the documentary record on this point is clear. "The native saints," JFS wrote in an 1857 letter, "seem very torpid and sluggish in regard to the work."[70] He also found the presence of animals in the Hawaiian dwellings disgusting. During a Sunday service in 1856, he told the assembled congregation that "it is bad enough to live as you do without living with na popoki! na Sliʻo!! me na paaa!!! (Cats! doges!! and hoges!!!)."[71]

JFS was offended by the "filthy" way they lived, and by the skin diseases he frequently mentioned in his journal. Many of the Native Hawaiians, he wrote, "were rotten!—and stunk with diseas!" and he claimed to have slept in places so filthy that "should my hog sleep [there] my stumache would forbid me eating of it."[72] Much of this JFS laid at the feet of the converts' ethnicity, as when he wrote to his cousin in 1857 that "they are still Hawaiians and according to present prospects I can draw no other conclusion that they will ever remain so."[73]

In JFS's opinion, all of this squalor was nothing more than a physical manifestation of an infected spiritual wound. "This nation," he confided in his journal, "is rot[t]en, and stink[s], because of, and with their own wickedness."[74] In his mind, there appears to have existed a difference, if not a total mutual exclusivity, between being Mormon and being Hawaiian. Among the Hawaiian converts, JFS noted that only "a _few_ are alive," meaning reborn. He saw himself as not just bringing Mormonism to the Hawaiian people, but also giving them a chance for rebirth, an opportunity to leave behind not only the "man of sin" but also the Hawaiian traits that JFS found so distasteful. He believed that they could, if they wanted it badly enough, become newly "alive" as Mormons. Yet JFS frequently reported visiting areas where branches of the church had once been established only to find that most, and sometimes all, of the congregation had ceased to participate.

In 1857 JFS set out on a day-long journey to visit a branch at Waialua. When he asked to see the branch president, he was "informed he had left the Church."

> [W]e sucseded in geting a mormon to lead us to the meeting house, this we found transmogrified into a Carpenters Shop & was full of rub[b]ish, boards, Tools &c, &c, &c, &c, we soon prevailed in geting it cleaned out. I sent for the prest. of the Branch, asked him his reasons for leaving the Church, he said because the rest were leaving, and his mind changed &c. I gave him a good preaching to warning him, of his perrilous situation, his forfeiture of all blessings &c, but it seemed wors[e] than throwing words away to talk with him.[75]

That same year, JFS visited the village of Kawaluna and found "the Saints, if I can call them that, all redy to leave the church but one or two." He accommodated their wishes by excommunicating twelve of them.[76]

Although the Hawaiians' lack of church participation could be explained by the relatively remote locations of the branches and the corresponding infrequency of visits from missionaries, JFS interpreted apostasy as another sign of the Hawaiian temperament and further evidence that he was working in a "degraded land."[77] Throughout his time in the islands, he never stopped thinking and writing about the Hawaiian mindset. In fact, in May 1857, toward the end of his mission, he mentioned in his journal that he had spent "four or five hours" conversing "upon the subject of this people's degeneracy."[78]

This was not just the hasty judgment of youth. More than a decade later, after listening to a returning missionary describe the situation in Hawaii, JFS concluded that "the curse of the Almighty seems resting upon the Islands for the indolence and wickedness of those who reside on them."[79] As he had during his years there, he placed the blame on both the Native Hawaiians and the purveyors of "so-called Christianity," upon whom he cast "some very severe but deserved strictures" because they introduced the "damning and corrupt practices" of the Europeans.[80]

This is not simply a matter of JFS demonstrating rank bigotry or ignorance. One must keep in mind the extent to which he and other missionaries needed desperately to make sense out of their experiences in this strange land. They did this, in part, by finding ways to connect it with their own mythos. For the Protestant missionaries, this manifested in a sense of urgency to usher the Native Hawaiian converts into leadership positions. This, it was believed, "would lead to an upward direction [i.e., a more Protestant Christian worldview] ... to the native mind."[81] The Mormon missionaries had a different intellectual template to assist them.

When King Kamehameha III died in January 1854, Silas Smith noted that the lamentations of the Hawaiian people were the most mournful heard since "the days of Moroni at or near the Hill Cumorah where the Nephites were destroyed by the Lamanites."[82] It is likely that the Book of Mormon's typology of lazy, sensual, warlike Lamanites was projected by JFS and others onto the Hawaiians they encountered. At the very least, the Book of Mormon provided a template that linked nakedness, dark skin, the wanton consumption of beasts, shiftlessness, and sensuality with wickedness.

According to the Book of Mormon, both the Lamanites and the Nephites descended from civilized life to complete depredation because they rejected the truths taught by their prophets. JFS believed that Hawaiians had similarly devolved. In a letter to a cousin, he warned that Hawaiians had, "before they were known to the world," reached the "apogee of their civilization," but "now only a portion of their rapid strides to the summit remains to be retraced, when they reach the goal from whence they started." JFS assured his cousin that "when you hear of the purity, splender and magnificense, the advancement, civilization, educational proficiencies &c, of this people, you may deside, that it is an ironicl discription, of the same, it is all a hoaks, there is no trouth in it."[83]

Such attitudes had been expressed by LDS missionaries in Hawaii since they first arrived. One of these early missionaries, Henry Bigler, wrote that "the Hawaiian race was once a favored people of the Lord and must have had the law of

84   Chapter 5

Moses and observed its teachings but through transgression they fell into darkness, error, and superstition, as regards the true God."[84] JFS's cousin and mentor wrote, "We feel to empathize with you and your fellow missionaries," who were called by God "to climb through all the filth, degradation, exposure and disease, vermin and dirt of that degraded race of the descendants of Israel."[85]

George Cannon made very similar remarks in a letter he wrote to Brigham Young in March 1854. He wrote that it was almost more than the missionaries could do "to arouse this people from the stupor and lethargy into which they have fallen, in consequence of the long night of darkness though which they have passed." Teaching the Hawaiians, wrote Cannon, required all of the persistence and patience that one had to use when dealing with children, except the Hawaiians "are not only like children, but they have traditions and superstitions that children do not."[86]

JFS, and all of his contemporary missionaries, believed that these "savage" traits could be reversed only through conversion to, and punctilious application of, the principles taught by the Mormon missionaries. Well before JFS arrived in Hawaii, mission leaders were arguing that the Hawaiian saints had no chance of living "righteously" in their native context. In February 1854, Cannon approved a plan to send Nathan Tanner back to the United States to gather funds for the purchase of a vessel that, they hoped, would allow them to launch a systematic migration of Hawaiian converts to San Bernardino, California. When Tanner left Hawaii for San Francisco the next month, he carried a letter explaining that "the Island saints are exceedingly poor, and the influence of example, education, and habits, renders it extremely necessary that some change should be effected in their location and circumstances, to render the great amount of labor expended upon this mission of lasting benefit."[87]

Although the gathering of Hawaiian converts in California was abandoned in favor of the creation of a Hawaiian Mormon colony at Lanai in the late summer of 1854, the rhetoric about the corrosive effects of Hawaiian culture on Mormon converts persisted.[88] When JFS wrote a report of his mission upon his return to Utah in early 1858, he stated that the missionary work in Hawaii "seemed to be progressing as effectually as we could wish ... [until] the work of gathering commenced about this time many became dissatisfied." The resistance to gathering, JFS argued, was so severe that "the decrease [in membership] was marked and rapid" and "beyond our power to recover it."[89] Although he provided no further elaboration, it is significant that JFS marked as the moment of most precipitous decline the very moment when Native Hawaiians were being asked to shift a part of their identity away from Hawaiian and toward Mormon by gathering in a Mormon colony.

In the same report, JFS provided an overview of how he imagined the religious life cycle of the Hawaiians that he encountered. They began, of course, as nature worshippers, then "tryed Calvinism, Catholicism, and Mormonism and [when] all had failed to meet their anticipations ... they would return to [worshipping] the Sun, Moon, Stars, Thunder, Lightening, Rain, Fishes, Beasts, Birds, Stones, Treas, Wooden images, or the volcanoes." JFS's attempt to portray the chaotic nature of

Upon the Isles of the Sea   85

Hawaiian religion by listing off nearly every natural feature he could imagine was augmented by his observation that "almost every individual had a god of his own." JFS did offer one positive insight, however: the multiplicity of Hawaiian forms of worship had led to a widespread attitude of "liberty" and "respect" among the Natives toward unfamiliar religious practices.[90]

In 1855–1856, Kīlauea, a volcano on the Big Island of Hawaii, produced a lava flow that threatened to overrun the town of Hilo. As the lava slowly moved toward the town, residents grew frantic. JFS later enjoyed telling a story that, while almost certainly false, reveals his opinions of both Hawaiian religion and Protestant Christianity. "I witnessed one of the grandest eruptions of Kilauea ever seen," he wrote to his nephew many years later. "It was in 1856, and molten lava flowed down to within about eight miles of the town of Hilo, frightening the inhabitants away from their homes." He then said that Titus Coan, a Calvinist minister and also an amateur volcanologist, "was greatly exercised over the threatening aspect of the approaching lava, he called fasts, and prayer meetings and sought by his (so called Christian) faith to avert the impending doom." When these measures proved fruitless, Coan "lost all hope and flew to a Native Kahuna, whom he implored to invoke the clemency of the 'God of Pele' by the offering of sacrifices. This he did, and soon afterwards the flow of molten lava ceased and so the town escaped." JFS regarded Coan's alleged defection to heathenism as little more than a cosmetic change. "The providences of God are not much moved or changed either by heathen sacrifice, or the invocations of a minister of an apostate religion."[91]

JFS's various duties and adventures during his years on the islands did not preclude him from keeping in close contact with family members and friends. His first letters represent the earliest extant primary sources produced by JFS. Even as a teenager, he demonstrated his lifelong tendency to offer advice that must have brought forth at least some eye-rolling by the readers. In later years, he would frequently lecture, via letter, his wives and children about mistakes in grammar and spelling, and give them unsolicited advice on everything from scripture to toilet habits. "I could give you much council," the teenaged missionary wrote to his younger sister, Martha, "that would be beneficial to you as long as you live upon this earth."[92] JFS expressed to Martha his belief that "if you have any trials to put up with, remember that it is to try you and to see if you are of <u>Smith grit or not</u>." In such circumstances, JFS wrote, "sho your Smith and that good, too when it comes to the pinch."[93]

This letter opens a unique window into JFS's mindset. By the summer of 1855, he had conjured up an explanation of and purpose for his life's problems: he had created an ideal identity as a Smith, and he clearly believed that something in the universe intended to challenge his claim to that identity. This worldview would harden as he aged, and never altered. He spent the rest of his life "showing his Smith."

JFS believed in cosmic dualism: everything was either good or evil, and this, too, is revealed in his letters from Hawaii. In a single letter he illustrated both dimensions of this dualism. In 1857, while traveling from one island to another, JFS

86   Chapter 5

found himself in rough seas with only "one-fourth inch of pine boards between us and the tremendous, dreadful, yawning grave of thousands of poor, ill-fated beings." He explained that the only thing that saved him from death was his trust in God, a power that will "deliver all who will lean upon it." Following closely on the heels of this providential act, however, was a diabolical one. Arriving at his destination, JFS discovered that more than thirty dollars had been pilfered from the church, an act which he attributed to the "devil" who "exerts his utmost power to thwart everything that we attempt to do."[94]

In Hawaii, JFS grew so accustomed to receiving correspondence that he made note in his journal of those occasions when none arrived.[95] The letters often left him in a nostalgic mood. Despite the traumas of his childhood, JFS's struggles in Hawaii led him to look back "at the seenes of my childhood and call to mind the happy by-gon days I have spent with my friends and brethren, it seems but yesterday."[96] In 1856, he noted the passing of the July 24 holiday commemorating the arrival of the first Mormon pioneers in the Salt Lake Valley in 1847 by remembering "the many good and plesant 24ths I have spent among my friends and relatives at home."[97] He contrasted those apparently good times with "the change that has taken place since that time," a change that left him on an island thousands of miles from home, often lonely, frequently ill, and always stressed out.

That same year he sat down and recorded his misery on Christmas Day, on which he "said nothing to nobody—and received the same in return."[98] Much later in life, after serving twice as president of the European mission, JFS would write that "no man can fill a mission unless his heart and mind are in it, for failure and vexation are the inevitable results of a mind divided against itself."[99] But in the fog of a lonely Christmas, far from home, the teenager allowed his mind to divide. JFS engaged in an almost Dickensian fantasy of what Christmas must be like among his friends in Utah, "all enjoying themselves at the festive dance, playing [making themselves sick feasting on] the abundance of nature's productions while I am here feasting on poi."[100]

JFS's foul and clearly envious mood resolved itself into a sort of gloomy hope. "All I have to say," he concluded, is that "my turn will come sometime if it ever does, and then I will make [up] the lost time."[101] He looked to the New Testament for comfort, noting that "I must content myself and obey the voice of the good sheepherd that said 'he that loveth his Father, his Mother his friends his lands &c, more than he loveth me he is not worthy of me.'"[102] With his father and mother both long dead, and no real home left behind, one wonders exactly what JFS was nostalgic for. Certainly he missed his sister, Martha, more than anyone else, but his longing for home seems rooted most fully in the sense of community that existed among the Mormons in Utah.

For JFS, his time in Hawaii carried exilic overtones, and he felt deeply that Utah and Mormonism and his own identity were all inextricably melded together. In July 1856, he described a dream he had using the terms "home" and "house" in ways that suggest the degree to which he identified those concepts with the LDS

Church as an institution and with Utah as a place.[103] When recounting the dream, JFS described the bowery and the old tabernacle as "houses," and Utah as "home," but the only person named in the entire dream was Brigham Young. This deep emotional attachment to Utah as his home and LDS leaders as his surrogate family, displayed so clearly in the dream, never left him.

The depth of JFS's emotions may have contributed to the development during his time in Hawaii of a loquacious, almost purple-prose style that is at once melodramatic and charming. Even in his personal journal, he takes pains to use as many adjectives as possible when describing almost anything.

> The wind was high and the sea calm, we sailed off quite brisk allmost under "bear pools." we ware not, however, long to enjoy the sweet entiripations [anticipations] of so speedy a journey as presant prospects indicated, for we ware soon left in a compleat callm, the sails flittering and flop[p]ing at each rock of our appearantly or seemingly deserted and forsaken craft. we ware alone and in silence. the howling of the wind had seased, and and [sic] the swol[l]en wave had sank to its level, and all was still, but now the luminary of midnight had arisen to a considerable highth. its silvery rays shone softly upon the unrippled sea, which threw around us the most loving, and majestic of all sceneries. on our left & right ware the riseing hills of Maui & Lanai towering far above the milky clouds that hung thickly beneath their sum[m]its, and yet a little farther on ware the towering peakes of Maunakea and Maunaloa of Hawaii, with their snowy mantles spread by the hand of nature never to be removed, standing, to defy the tempests of ages gone by and to come. and from it[s] bowels ware belching forth the liquid flames of everlasting torment as is made known by our good and self righteous priests of this progressive and enlightened age.[104]

JFS's mission journals also reveal a young man with a puckish sense of humor and love of wordplay, even in the face of significant difficulties. When his shoes gave out, he noted that he had to spend an entire day acting as a cobbler. "Poverty is the mother of inventions," JFS wrote, "and I think before long it will lead me into the commencement of all trades,' and of course 'the master of none.'" Continuing the joke, he observed that "the oldest daughter of Fortune is Miss Fortune, and she is acquainted with many."[105] On another occasion, he tried to do a little farmwork, but "in conciquence of my laying out so much strength, the hoe handle refused doing its duty by 'parting' its ligneous particals under the preponderations of my muscular arm!"[106] There is an undeniable playfulness and charm in these entries that might have been even more pronounced in his personal interactions, or perhaps it was in writing that he felt most comfortable indulging in silliness, something that would fade in his later years.

As time went by, JFS spent more of his downtime reading. He displayed an unusually high degree of intellectual curiosity about a wide range of subjects and

88   Chapter 5

also regularly read the LDS newspapers the *Western Standard* and the *Deseret News*. In those he would have read the history of Joseph Smith as well as sermons by church leaders. He kept a close eye on political and cultural developments in Utah, noting in one journal entry, for example, that George A. Smith had been appointed to lobby in Washington, DC, on behalf of Utah statehood, and in another that 149 missionaries had been called and that "Indian depredations" were troubling some Utah settlements.[107]

However, JFS's interests ranged beyond ecclesiastical and local Utah matters to include such diverse topics as natural philosophy, psychology, medicine, the Crimean War, popular novels such as *Fernley Manor* and *The Unknown Heiress*, a biography of George Washington, and "The Hystory [*sic*] of Bread."[108] When he found anything he judged to be "of importance, or pleasing," he cut it out and saved it.[109] JFS's curiosity wandered beyond the purely intellectual from time to time. On one occasion he "tryed my hand thatching in the native stile, and I flattered myself it was done well."[110]

Long-Distance Romances

Many of JFS's friends and relatives wrote to him regarding potential romantic avenues to be pursued upon his return to Utah. Some of these correspondents warned him that the pool of eligible bachelorettes was ever-dwindling, and they offered to put a good word in with one or two favored prospects. It is difficult to know exactly how JFS felt about these matters. He typically responded politely, but noncommittally, to the invitations, and he generally kept silent on the matter in his journal. The fact that he did not marry any of the women mentioned in the letters might provide some insight into how seriously he took the entire subject. There was, however, one person that JFS exchanged flirtatious letters with during the latter part of his mission: his beautiful and sophisticated cousin Josephine Smith, the daughter of Don Carlos Smith, who occupied a special place in his heart.

Josephine and her mother had decided to remain in California, and she had a somewhat cool relationship with Mormonism. Later known as Ina Coolbrith, she would go on to fame as the first poet laureate of California. She was born Josephine Donna Smith, but went by her childhood nickname, Ina. She began using the last name Coolbrith, her mother's maiden name, as an adult.

JFS was clearly captivated by her, although such feelings may have been troubling to him. In one "private" letter to her that he wrote while on his mission, he asked her to "remember me not as a lover." Ina replied coyly that "a little alteration makes a very good reply."[111] In response, he wrote that "I sometimes long to see you again, and to see the time fly thinking that each fleeting moment brings us nearer to the time we shall greet each other's presence again not to separated." Although he felt well enough, he wrote, he "might feel better if my sojourns in isolated parts were ended, and I were with you. You might think I had rather not be hear, you are right." He closed the intimate letter with an equally intimate coda: "I go to bed and dream of Josephine, and the good time coming."[112]

JFS's relationship with Ina was deeply conflicted, and it remained so for the decades that they corresponded. He was apparently attracted to her, however vaguely, in a romantic way. He also maintained an almost avuncular sense of responsibility for her spiritual welfare, so he often took her attitude toward Mormonism as a personal insult. In 1855, he confided in his sister, Martha, that Ina and her family were not to be emulated because of the "kind of Mormons ... they are." The situation with Ina's religious beliefs was troubling, but JFS vowed to "better it someday." To that end, he "wrote a letter to [her] and gave her a rite good Mormon sirmon."[113]

But to JFS, Ina was more than a lost soul to be reclaimed. In a subsequent letter, he confided that he felt sympathy for young men in Utah who were being called on missions after they had become engaged but before they were married. He imagined that it must be difficult to "forgo the plesures of perhaps strongly anticipated conjugal or connubial joys and participations ... so assiduously sought for and so much desired." It comes as no surprise that JFS, as a typical eighteen-year-old, could empathize so strongly. He expressed hope that, although reports of marriages seemed ubiquitous, "there will be some few left for those who like myself are debared from the priviledge that others—perhaps more fortunate—are now enjoying." JFS added, somewhat unnecessarily, that "I have thought some upon this subject myself of late."[114]

But no matter how attracted JFS may have been to Ina, her attitude toward Mormonism appalled him. Their 1857 correspondence, which contains tender and even romantic undertones, eventually turned nasty. Ina directly challenged JFS on the subject of plural marriage. She had come to believe that plural marriage was sinful, and even accepted the idea that Joseph Smith, their uncle, had been killed in 1844 as a punishment from God for introducing the wicked practice. Ina even quoted a section from the Book of Mormon in which God, through the Nephite prophet Jacob, forbade the practice of polygamy.[115]

JFS felt insulted and betrayed. Ina seemed to see him as "some lackey," her "country cousin." She had insinuated that he was too ignorant to be familiar with the Book of Mormon and was "unconscious of my real existence and did not know but that which every boday said was thus and so." He threatened her with hellfire and damnation if she failed to repent of her slanderous remarks about Joseph Smith, and he used his collection of newspaper articles on LDS history to bolster his defense of plural marriage. His anger turned personal as well. Ina had complained to JFS that she had written many letters to his siblings in Utah but had heard nothing in reply. JFS took the opportunity to observe that given "the spirit of injustice and cold-heartedness with which you write to me, I do not blame them for keeping silent."[116]

JFS accused Ina of being "totally ignorant of what would bless you" and wrote that reading her opinions about Utah and Mormonism caused his blood to "congeal" and led him to feel "sickened and ghastly when I read such infernal fiendish, nefarious, despicable falsehoods and hellish lies of the blackest and most diabolical hue." Ina, in his "disinterested" opinion, had been "duped ... by fiends condemned to the bottomless pit, whose treachery and perfidy are utterly unfathomable." Further irritating JFS was Ina's casual mention of the murder of Parley Pratt, which she also linked by implication to the sin of polygamy.[117]

By sheer coincidence, Ina's letter arrived on the same day that JFS learned of Pratt's murder. JFS had known him, although not well, and had traveled with him on the early stages of his journey to Hawaii in 1854. In his journal, JFS wrote that "to endever to speak my feelings upon this subject would be fearful ... he died a martyr for the cause of Truth. He has conquered the world, Death, and the Devil and his name is ratified in the Arch Ives of Heaven."[118]

JFS responded to Ina's rather insensitive mention of Pratt's death with predictable vigor, expressing shock that she had spoken of the matter "As if a mear ruffian had deceased!" Pratt, railed JFS, was "a prince [who] died a martyr," and his "assassins will mildew, moulder, and rot and sink forever into the vortex of naught!" And then, as quickly as the storm arose, it vanished; with no hesitation in his pen, JFS continued: "since I last wrote you, I have received the announcement of [JFS's sister] Martha's wedding. Love to all, J. Smith."[119]

This letter, written by JFS just as he reached adulthood, and just as he began to emerge more fully in the documentary record, sheds some light on his complex relationship with Ina. It shows us something of the intimate sexual longings of JFS's adolescent and lonely heart. It also gives us a glimpse into his advanced knowledge of LDS history and scripture, especially with regard to the practice of plural marriage. Finally, it further cements our impression of JFS as a man of both tenderness and temper, and it demonstrates the bathetic shift from operatic indignation to pedestrian blandness that became a hallmark of his rhetorical style.[120]

JFS's contempt for other Christian missionaries on the islands grew sharper over time, and he had no dearth of occasions to engage with them. The two main areas of contention were doctrine and competition for converts. On one occasion, JFS recorded in his journal that four Mormons had "left the Church and gone back to the whore of the Sandwich Islands," as he called the collective Protestant presence in Hawaii.[121] Frequently he reported the presence of "Calvinists" at LDS meetings. JFS usually took such opportunities to preach against one of the hallmark Calvinist doctrines, predestination. One such occasion occurred in the summer of 1856:

> four foreigners ... attended meeting. I heard that one of them believed in foreordination and that "whatsoever a person done in the body was all right, as he was fore-ordained to do so, conciquently he could not be punished for murder, theft, lying, &c, beyond the boundries of this world" &c, therefore I spoke somewhat upon that subject.[122]

A few months later, JFS reported that he "had a 'confab' with a calvinist member—proved to him his folly and ignorance and returned home."[123] JFS relished the opportunity to engage in sectarian fisticuffs, and he clearly took pride in his ability to, at least in his view, best his older, better-educated opponents.

Other interactions made JFS's "confabs" with the Calvinists seem tame by comparison. At times, JFS lashed out in his journal at the hypocrisy of ministers who, while condemning Mormon plural marriage practices, surrounded themselves with "mid-night whores" while they "blush and crimson at the plain and honest Mormon saint, and the practices of the ancient prophets and all that's good—at the same time practicing—sub race—the most heartless, unchaste and abominable dieas [sic] of the damniable regimen." One can almost feel JFS begin to thrum as his pen picked up speed. "You poor, soulless, withered, Blighted miscreants and stuble and refuses of debauchery! How dare you articulate a sound of goodness, lest it smite you! How long will ye listen and not hear, see and not understand, know and yet be moste unfathomably ignorant! You poore Devils."[124]

As with so many other aspects of his life, JFS's fiery indignation at the Christian world's dim view of plural marriage first found form and expression during his years as a missionary in Hawaii. What made him bristle so indignantly at assaults on plural marriage in 1857, when the practice was, for him, still an abstract concept, would make his blood boil in later decades when the attacks became something to take personally.

In 1857, during the final summer of his mission, JFS did comparatively little proselytizing. He spent those months at the LDS settlement at Lanai, a situation that greatly improved his mood. He ate somewhat more heartily and spent his days doing farm chores. He mended fences, tended corn, and fed livestock. He continued to preach on a variety of issues, including "the subject of persecution [and] the blessings derived therefrom."[125] The familiar rhythms of life in a farmlike environment seemed to comfort him. He even took the opportunity to hunt wild goats with his companion Simpson Molen and some Hawaiian guides. JFS was astounded at how hard it was to kill the goats, with one of them surviving not only multiple gunshots, but also a fall from a high cliff.[126] In a strange irony, while JFS was spending 11 September 1857 on a treacherous hunting trip, some of his fellow Mormons back in Utah were engaging in what would be known as the Mountain Meadows Massacre.

In addition to hunting and farmwork, JFS spent the last days of his Hawaii mission reading novels and newspapers, reading and writing letters, and mentally preparing himself to return to life on the mainland. On 29 September 1857, JFS prepared to leave Lanai for the port of Lahaina, where he would book passage to Honolulu and from there back to California. While saying his goodbyes, JFS was moved by the outpouring of emotion that the assembled native saints demonstrated. Of all the weeping Hawaiians, the one that captured JFS's attention was a "little boy—Kamohaalii." The boy had been living with JFS and Molen for "several months," and JFS thought that he "seemed to feel as tho' he trod alone some banquet Hall that all but he had deserted, and that he had parted for ever with his only friend." JFS "could hardly bear to leave the little fellow, and never would if I had means to take him."[127]

This scene is as revealing as it is moving. One can imagine few others as well-suited to empathize with the little orphan boy than JFS. All of his life, his heart broke for orphans and for the friendless and the lonely. It does not require any exotic psychological speculation to see how JFS saw himself in people like Kamo-haalii, and over the course of the coming decades, he would see many of them. JFS would never stop trying to rescue the little boy that he once was, wherever in the world he saw him.

JFS borrowed thirty dollars from Silas Smith to pay for his trip back across the Pacific, which commenced at 12:30 p.m. on 6 October 1857. JFS noted with no obvious sentimentality that "the shores of Oahu fast receded in the distance."[128] The voyage back held little in the way of excitement, although JFS made sure to note that he alone was spared the ravages of seasickness. The worst thing he experienced was "a very disagreeable sensation, produced by pestiferous smells of boiled meat and onions from the Gally."[129]

During the voyage JFS read Harriet Beecher Stowe's 1852 novel *Uncle Tom's Cabin*. It may have been a conversation starter, because he ended up in an involved discussion with an English traveler on the issues of "slavery, the origen of the Negro . . . and the design of God in creating man."[130] Unfortunately, JFS recorded nothing in his journal about the views he expressed during the course of this conversation, although, indefatigable missionary that he was, he left the Englishman with a pamphlet about Joseph Smith and Mormonism.

JFS's eagerness to get back to Utah stemmed not only from a desire to reacquaint himself with family and friends. He was also eager to join in preparations to defend Utah from the federal army, which was threatening to invade. Three days before JFS left Hawaii, a letter arrived from Brigham Young requesting that all missionaries "that could be spared" be released and that they "hasten to our midst" to assist in the "warm times" that were expected to ensue shortly. Young wrote that he "would never sit still and see the people driven and abused as here-fore," to which JFS answered, in his journal and his heart, "Amen to this."[131]

JFS sailed into San Francisco on 14 October 1857. There he and the other returning missionaries met with George Q. Cannon, who encouraged them to get back to Salt Lake City as soon as possible. JFS sailed down the coast to Santa Cruz, where he linked up with a group of Mormons headed to San Bernardino. Once there, he briefly reunited with Agnes Pickett and Ina Coolbrith, but was unable to convince them to continue with him to Utah. To cover the costs of his travel, JFS worked as a teamster for the overland company. He arrived back in the Salt Lake Valley on 24 February 1858.[132]

6 | Returning to Utah and Finding a Wife

The political, religious, and cultural environments changed a great deal during Joseph F. Smith's time away from the Salt Lake Valley. Four events in particular helped to shape the atmosphere into which JFS reemerged: the concerted push toward Mormon economic self-sufficiency, the handcart disaster of 1856, the Mountain Meadows Massacre of 1857, and the Mormon Reformation of 1855–1857.

The Mormons in Salt Lake City walked a fine line between resistance and cooperation with "gentile" economic interests. Non-Mormon businesses had been present in Salt Lake since 1849, a development that rankled some church leaders. Mormon residents in Utah needed manufactured goods of all kinds, but these were only available at vastly inflated prices due to a variety of circumstances, including the high price of overland shipping and the high markup placed on the goods by retailers.

In an effort to combat the presence of gentile businesses, Young approached the problem in two ways. First, he instituted and heavily promoted the importance of "home industry." His goal was to educate Mormons, the vast majority of whom made their living as farmers, in various crafts and trades. Young believed strongly that self-sufficiency in manufacturing, even on a small scale, would help Mormons remain free from entanglements with non-Mormon elements. To this end, the territorial legislature in 1856 incorporated the Deseret Agriculture and Manufacturing Society to train Mormons to produce clothing, household goods, and other necessities.

Second, Young attempted to fight the high price of goods shipped overland by creating the Brigham Young Express and Carrying Company. Although the company folded in 1858, it is proof of Young's unflagging desire to exert influence over all aspects of Utah's economic life.[1] Salt Lake City, in particular, had been the site of acute economic and political conflict for years, but by the time JFS returned home, it was more intense than it had ever been.

The handcart disaster is one of the most famous stories in all Mormon lore, one that continues to be used by church leaders to inspire Mormons today. JFS learned of the tragedy from his half brother John. In November 1856, John wrote to JFS that "there are two companies of handcarts back the other side of Fort Bridger in the snow and there has been a good many perished."[2] Poor planning and excessive

94 Chapter 6

eagerness on the part of newly arrived immigrants had led to a late start for several handcart companies from Nebraska. Caught on the plains late in the season, they encountered a series of early snowstorms. Despite Brigham Young's organization of a major rescue mission that lasted more than a month, more than 200 pioneers perished.[3]

If the handcart disaster came to represent dedication in the teeth of starvation and hypothermia, the Mountain Meadows Massacre represented something far darker, and something that the church spent more than a century trying to forget. On 11 September 1857, a group of travelers from Arkansas cut through Utah on their way to California. At a spot in southern Utah known as Mountain Meadows, approximately 100 unarmed men, women, and children in this traveling party were murdered on the orders and at the hands of a group of local Mormon leaders and militiamen. Initially, many believed that local Native Americans were responsible for the murders, but the truth of Mormon involvement soon became clear.

What remains unclear is the exact motive for the massacre, but the travelers arrived in Utah just as news of Parley Pratt's murder was rolling through the settlements. The fact that they were from Arkansas, the very state where Pratt was murdered, probably played a role in the attention that they garnered. The Mormon Reformation and the impending Utah War, both discussed below, no doubt contributed to a tense atmosphere. All of these factors probably coalesced into the bloody crime at Mountain Meadows. Historians disagree about Brigham Young's foreknowledge of the event, but sources seem to indicate that he did not order the massacre. However, he may have impeded its investigation.[4]

JFS had also missed the period of retrenchment known as the Mormon Reformation. Although Mormons had undergone periods of reformation before, nothing as ritually and rhetorically complex and persistent had ever before been seen in Mormon communities. The Mormon Reformation lasted from the fall of 1855 until about 1857. During this period, church leaders introduced a range of measures designed to shake the rank-and-file Mormons out of what Brigham Young and other leaders believed to be a spiritual stupor. Church meetings often involved a call for public confession, something that JFS had been doing in Hawaii before the reformation in Utah got underway. Mormon men were assigned as home missionaries to visit their neighbors and ask them a series of questions known collectively as the Mormon catechism. The catechism asked about things as varied as adultery, family religious practices, and bathing frequency.

Rebaptism, already a staple of Mormon ritual life, took on a new urgency during the reformation. In an unprecedented move, the church suspended the administration of the sacrament of the Lord's Supper for six months beginning in November 1856 due to the Mormons' alleged unworthiness. Young abrogated this basic ritual of the church "to afford [Mormons] space and time for repentance, restitution, and, when ready, for a renewal of their covenants."[5] Church leaders traveled throughout the Mormon settlements delivering blistering sermons aimed at convincing listeners of their deep unworthiness before God and the corresponding need to repent. Jedediah Grant said, "The wrath of God burns against us owing to the filth and abomination that exists here."[6] Occasionally, Young and other leaders would bring up the possibility of the need for "blood atonement," which, for some Mormons, meant that certain sins are so serious that forgiveness is possible only via self-sacrifice.

JFS knew about the reformation because his half brother John wrote a panicky letter to him in November 1856 detailing his experience at a reformation meeting.

> There was some hard questions asked about committing sins of every description and any man that was guilty of adultery, theft, lying, murder, and many others too numerous to mention had to confess there and agree to do so no more and a curse was put on any one that lied there to cover his sins. Now Joseph one word to you be careful what you do and do nothing but wright and do not go to sleep on your mission for fear of the displeasure of our Beloved President Brigham Young and your god.[7]

There was little chance that JFS would "go to sleep" on his mission. In fact, the calls for public confession, the large-scale excommunications, and the relentless calls to repentance that were characteristic of the Mormon Reformation were staples of JFS's ministry in Hawaii.

It is clear that these four events, among other, lesser, ones, created an environment fraught with tragedy and tensions of a hundred kinds. Whatever his sentimental, homesick fantasies of Utah had been while he was in Hawaii, the reality JFS faced upon his return was one of deep uncertainty, fear, hostility, and potential (and sometimes very real) violence. For better or worse, JFS seemed to thrive under such conditions. Throughout his life, he met adversity without surprise. The world, as JFS saw it, worked from a script, and in that script he was always the underdog, the oppressed, the righteous voice in the wilderness of wickedness. There could not have been a better place nor time for JFS to return to than Utah in 1858.

By the time he arrived home, the energy that Mormon leaders had been pouring into the reformation had been redirected toward a much more immediate threat than spiritual torpor: the U.S. Army was coming to Utah with orders to quell a "rebellion."[8] Mormonism in general, and polygamy in particular, had garnered a good deal of press attention while JFS was away. In 1856, polygamy had famously been conjoined with slavery as one of the "twin relics of barbarism" in the Republican Party platform.[9] In early 1857, James Buchanan assumed office as president of the United States and immediately found that the Utah Territory would be a headache. He received waves of letters from federal officials who had left their posts in Utah. The territorial officials who had been assigned there complained that any non-Mormon governmental presence was a sham, and that Young ruled as a brutal tyrant with flagrant disregard for federal law.

96   Chapter 6

The press in the eastern cities seized on this discontent and fanned the rhetorical flames with gusto. In July 1857, Young learned that 2,500 U.S. soldiers were escorting a new territorial governor as well as other newly appointed officials to Salt Lake City. JFS learned of this development when he received a shocking letter from John, who claimed that "there is 2500 soldiers coming out here to hang Brigham Young and all of his associates and also all those that will not put away polygamy."[10] In the fall, Lot Smith led bands of Mormon riders on harassment raids against the federal troops. Although they burned many wagons, no one was killed.

In early 1858, Young decided on his course of action. He would continue to harass and delay the army in the canyons east of the city while the entire Mormon population would move south to Utah Valley. Young ordered that the foundations of the Salt Lake Temple, then in the early phases of construction, be covered up and the construction site filled in. While Young did not literally scorch the earth, he certainly gave the federal party the impression that they were arriving to govern a ghost town.[11]

JFS, of course, eagerly anticipated the opportunity to defend his people. We know precious little about his service in the militia, known as the Nauvoo Legion, during the Mormon War. In fact, the only source that sheds any light on it is a short piece of a larger essay that JFS wrote for the *Deseret Evening News* in 1901.[12]

> When I reached home, all Utah was aflame with the war spirit. Johnston's army was in winter quarters east of the Wasatch Mountains, and the local militia, called out by President Brigham Young, who had placed the Territory under martial law, were preparing to resist the impending invasion of Salt Lake City; the success of which meant to the inhabitants of this peaceful region ... a repetition of the bloody scenes through which our people had passed in Missouri and Illinois.

JFS met personally with Young, who assigned him to "Col. Callister's cavalry command in Echo Canyon." That night JFS unpacked some pig iron that he had purchased in Las Vegas and spent the evening casting his own bullets. However, despite ranging over a wide swath of territory over the next few months, he never had to use them. His time in the Nauvoo Legion was spent escorting various federal officials into the Salt Lake Valley as both sides tried to hammer out a settlement that would avoid undue drama and bloodshed.

JFS was also assigned to guard the empty city of Salt Lake after the move south. This duty required relatively little beyond showing up for roll call at 6 a.m. every other morning, but he expressed in a letter to his sister the strange feelings that came over him as he looked at the empty city. "The city, houses, and country look deserted and lonely," he wrote, adding that "everything wears a lonesome, dreary aspect."[13] JFS's most exciting assignment during the Mormon War was

Returning to Utah and Finding a Wife 97

undoubtedly the opportunity he had to ride as part of Porter Rockwell's unit as they spied on army movements at Camp Scott in what is now southwest Wyoming.

Once it became clear that there would be no actual war, JFS left military service and headed for Provo, where his siblings, and almost everyone else, had migrated in April 1858. JFS spent most of his time helping various family members prepare for the move back to Salt Lake City. While he was in Provo, he became reacquainted with one of his Smith cousins, sixteen-year-old Levira. The daughter of Samuel Smith, Levira and JFS bonded over more than their shared last name. Just as JFS was born to Hyrum's second wife, Levira was born to her widowed father's second wife. In July 1844, just one month after the murder of his more famous brothers Joseph and Hyrum, her father died of a "bilious fever."[14] Levira was an infant so never knew her father.

In early 1859, JFS wrote a rather melodramatic letter to Levira declaring that he was filled with "embarisment and diffidence" as he attempted to "delineate ... the throbbings of my heart." He wrote about how he had developed romantic feelings for her beyond those of "cousin and friend," and that he wanted her to let him know, with total honesty, how she felt about him. JFS also drew on his lifelong sense of persecution in his bid for Levira's affections. He noted the many "disadvantages" he had faced since birth, his familiarity with nothing but "scanty means," and his constant battle against numerous powers "arraid against me." JFS suggested that a rejection by Levira would be yet another injustice, adding the impediment of "the course of true affection" to fate's lengthy list of kicks to JFS's existential head. He certainly made his best case, leaving the strong impression that he was madly in love with young Levira.[15]

Historian Scott Kenney has suggested that JFS's romantic move toward Levira was somewhat disingenuous. Kenney's main piece of evidence is a scathing letter from the irate father of Jane Fisher, the sister of John Smith's wife, Hellen. Jane was one year younger than JFS, and the two knew one another quite well. John's marriage to Hellen in 1853 drew them closer together. JFS and Jane corresponded during his time in Hawaii and occasionally engaged in flirtatious exchanges. Jane's father claimed in his letter to JFS that the two had been engaged to be married, and he suggested that JFS broke off the engagement at the behest of Heber C. Kimball. Kenney writes that JFS "began pursuing his cousin ... three days after that rebuke."[16]

It is true that JFS wrote his feelings to Levira three days after receiving Fisher's seething missive, but there is no evidence to suggest that he was so craven of character as to invent feelings where none existed. In fact, Fisher did not possess any evidence of any engagement, probably because none existed. It is entirely plausible that JFS and Jane discussed marriage, and she certainly mentioned it in the letters she sent to him in Hawaii, but there is no compelling reason to believe that they were engaged. Jane's father was also the father-in-law of JFS's brother, so he may have heard talk about the alleged engagement from family sources who knew less than they thought they did. Had they actually been engaged while JFS was in

Hawaii, as Fisher seemed to believe, it is strange indeed that they would not have married before early 1858, when Fisher's letter arrived.

There must have been rumors of an engagement, however, because in the summer of 1857, JFS wrote to his sister Martha assuring her that he was not "bound to anyone" because he had not yet encountered a potential wife "in whom there is a spark of heavenly fire that burns and blazes in the dark hour of adversity and that is willing to share [my] humble lot."[17] At the same time that Jane was apparently claiming to be engaged to JFS, he was writing to Martha of his abject terror of wedded life. "It does seem curious in the extreme to me why folks go so headlong into [marriage]," he wrote, considering that by doing so they bring "willingly down upon themselves ponderous grievances and a world of trouble from which they may never extract themselves." In an eerie foreshadowing of his own first marriage, he wrote that the thought of the potential "miseries and heart-wrending scenes of discontent, discord, and bitter unhappiness" that a bad marriage can inflict caused him to "quake ... to the center."[18]

The evidence thus suggests that JFS was not engaged to Jane, although she may have been telling a different story. Fisher's letter is, for the most part, the understandably irate ventings of a father with an emotionally wounded daughter. He naturally took her side in the matter and painted JFS in almost demonic colors. No doubt the relationship between JFS and Jane was more complex than her father's letter implies. However, Fisher does say something interesting in his letter that would prove sadly prophetic—not for Jane, but for Levira. "I believe," Fisher fumed, that "she would have married you and dragged out a few miserable years in broken hearted wretchedness [due to JFS's] tyrannical jealousy and self-importance." Whatever the nature of his relationship with Jane, JFS followed the happenings in the Fisher family closely enough that he could, in 1907, provide his friend Samuel Adams a detailed summary of which Fisher siblings had died, where the living siblings resided, and the size of their families.[19]

JFS married Levira in April 1859, but their union would be a largely unhappy one, and one of the darkest domestic periods in JFS's life. Levira suffered from some form of mental illness, almost certainly major depression, and, as we will see, JFS was overseas for most of their marriage. When he was around, he found her difficult to deal with, and what Fisher accurately described as his "tyrannical jealousy" led him to act out violently toward her. But things were still moving along well one year into the marriage when JFS received an unexpected call to resume his missionary service, this time in Great Britain.

Between his return to Salt Lake City and his departure for England, JFS not only married but also occupied new ecclesiastical positions. In March 1858, he was ordained to the priesthood office of the Seventy, the group charged primarily with missionary work, and in the fall of 1859, he was ordained to the office of high priest and called to serve on the high council of the Salt Lake stake. High councils consisted of twelve high priests who served under the stake presidency. In this position,

Returning to Utah and Finding a Wife 99

JFS would have been a part of ecclesiastical courts that tried Mormons for their membership in the church on charges ranging from adultery to congregational infighting. None of this would have been new to JFS given his extensive experience as a district president in Hawaii.

Service on the Salt Lake stake high council certainly provided another opportunity for JFS to interact with high-level church leaders, and there is no doubt that his burgeoning administrative and oratorical skills did not go unnoticed. His appointment to the high council was part of a larger reshuffling in which the entire group was dissolved and reconstituted with "active young men, who could efficiently discharge the duties of High Councilors ... more in accordance with the principles of the truth than some very old men can, under existing circumstances."[20]

The men installed in 1859 shared something besides relative youth. Most of them were closely related to prominent Mormons, including Orson Pratt Jr., eldest son of Apostle Orson Pratt; Edward Partridge Jr., son of the first bishop in the LDS Church; Samuel W. Richards, nephew of Willard Richards; Joseph W. Young, nephew of Brigham Young; Claudius Spencer, son of the former Nauvoo mayor and then-current president of the Salt Lake stake, Daniel Spencer; and Franklin Woolley, the son of Samuel Woolley, a prominent Salt Lake bishop and business leader. But JFS's service on the high council lasted only six months. In April 1860, at the general conference, he was called to travel to Great Britain to serve another proselytizing mission.

JFS's financial situation remained tenuous. Since December 1858, he had been employed as the sergeant at arms for the Utah legislature, a job which paid so little that he relied exclusively on external support for his mission. He left the Salt Lake Valley for Britain on 27 April 1860. JFS's characteristic sentimentality no doubt made it difficult for him to part with his new wife and the comforts of home that he so often longed for during his years in Hawaii. The parting was made easier because his good friend, cousin, and now brother-in-law, Samuel B. Smith, had also been called to serve a mission in Europe. Even as he crossed the plains though, JFS had difficulty keeping his mind off of things at home. From a camp on the Sweetwater River, he wrote to Levira asking her to "find out if possible if the cows have been found and if the mare is safe."[21]

Levira also found cause for worry in the warning of an astrologer whom she and JFS had consulted before he left. According to the astrologer, because Samuel's birth month was August, he was in particular danger. Although the warning was vague, it was enough to stir Levira to mention it. "You will please caution Samuel," Levira wrote, "and be cautious yourself."[22] Nothing else is known about the couple's interaction with the astrologer, but it is certainly surprising given JFS's later view that astrology and similar phenomena originated with the devil and should be scrupulously avoided.[23]

Samuel and JFS paid their way across the plains working as teamsters for a group that included a dozen missionaries plus two members of the Quorum of the

Twelve: Amasa Lyman and Charles Rich. In his journal, JFS noted his pleasure at having made good time, reaching Florence, Nebraska, in forty-one days. But before he could reach his mission field, he had to revisit the past in ways that proved deeply emotional. In Nebraska, JFS met his half brother John, who had been in the Midwest since the previous fall preparing to help his sister Lovina Walker finally make the move to Utah. One of Hyrum's children with Jerusha Barden, Lovina was eleven years JFS's senior, and he had not seen her since he was eight years old. Obviously, he lacked deep emotional bonds with her, but meeting Lovina put him in mind of his father and prepared him for the next phase of his journey: his return to Nauvoo.

Apart from reconnecting, however tensely, with his Smith relatives, JFS used his brief time in Nauvoo to meditate on the strangely mixed emotions that the place forced on him. He visited the site of the temple and Hyrum's farm, complete with the still-standing barn where he used to play. "It is impossible to describe," he confided in his journal, "the overwhelming and very peculiar sensation produced upon my mind in once more beholding the old playgrounds of my infant days." Seeing Nauvoo, walking on the very "streets my father walked," struck JFS as both "dear and dreadful." Dear because Nauvoo served as the repository for "sacred memories," but dreadful because of the "dread scenes that are ... to my memory clear as day [that] brought gloom and Horror upon the honest world and filled 10 thousand hearts with grief and woe!"[24] The power of the experience must have been almost overwhelming, but JFS left Nauvoo fortified by memory and communion with his "father's dust," ready to continue his journey to England.

JFS traveled through Chicago, Detroit, and Albany before finally arriving at "the great metropolis" of New York City on the Fourth of July. Despite the recent Utah War, he did not take the opportunity to disparage the United States as one might have expected him to do given the atmosphere back home. Rather, he joined wholeheartedly in the celebration of American independence by attending a "grand and imposing" fireworks display, which he judged "the grandest sights I ever saw."[25] JFS spent ten days in New York, where he made a point of proselytizing in order to get "a little practice in the line of my duty."[26]

JFS was once again feeling the pangs of homesickness. The unreliability of mail service meant that often letters written weeks, or months, apart would arrive in one big bundle. The writer had no idea what was happening and was left to wonder if someone's failure to reply was a personal snub or a postal snag. In New York, JFS was waiting to hear from Levira, finally pleading with her to "write upon receipt of all my letters" because "I long to hear from you." In the same letter he revisited the subject: "be sure to write. Tell me all of the particulars of your prosperity."[27]

JFS's anxiety on this score reflects an important new reality in his life: for the first time since his mother died, he had something to lose. He clung desperately to his relationship with Levira, which at that stage consisted mostly of the fantasy of the newly wed; relatively unfamiliar with one another, each is able to project qualities onto the other that they desire a mate to have. Growing familiarity erodes this habit. Had JFS remained in Utah, it is probable that the eventual demise of his marriage would have been hastened. As it happened, however, Levira and JFS remained pen pals for years before spending any considerable time together living as husband and wife. It is evident in their letters throughout his time in England that, while they shared family connections and acquaintances, they lacked close familiarity.

7 | Mission to the British Isles

On 14 July 1860, Joseph F. Smith and his traveling companions boarded the steamship *Edinburgh*, and for twenty-five dollars he crossed the Atlantic. The journey took just under two weeks. Unlike his earlier, stormy sailing in the Pacific, JFS found the trip to England remarkably smooth, noting that not one person succumbed to seasickness.[1] JFS set foot on the Liverpool docks on 27 July. After passing through the "very tedious custom house ordeals" and finding the mission office at 42 Islington Street, the first thing he did was take a bath, followed shortly by a trip to purchase some new clothes, including "a hat vulgarly called a stove pipe." These items were followed in short order by tailored coats.[2]

Victorians in Britain were obsessed with respectability. For them, "respectability was a much broader process than merely compelling the working classes to accept middle-class standards of decorum. It meant working people themselves wishing to create security, cleanliness, and safety for their families, asserting a social status, and 'keeping up appearances.'"[3] In Victorian Britain, hats were an essential part of a man's wardrobe, and the top hat represented the pinnacle of prestige.[4] Clothing signaled class and occupation, and Mormon missionaries in Victorian Britain went for as lofty a look as they could manage. Many could not afford tailored clothing and so relied on the new second-hand clothing trade.

When JFS and his associates arrived in England, people at the mission office said they looked like "wild beasts and monkeys" and directed them to the nearest ready-to-wear clothing stall. JFS took on the trappings of the Victorian middle class with some trepidation and self-consciousness. In a letter written to Levira shortly after his arrival, he mused,

> You had ought to see me now as I am bent over the desk writing to you. I think you would hardly know whether it was Joseph or not. Let me describe him as he sits. Here he is, hair shinggaled, tall stove-pipe hat, stiff collar and, in full English style, all set and in full trim to go forth a regular English Mormon preacher!

JFS marveled at how, with a little "starch and costume," a "hail, hearty, rugged mountain boy [from] way off Deseret" could be made to appear "classed up." He promised to send a picture of his hat as soon as possible.[5] JFS's turn to third person is most unusual for him and likely represents an effort to cope with the rapidity with which he was transforming himself into another person in another world. He had not yet caught up with himself.

Predictably, JFS's attitude toward his work in Britain contrasted sharply with his approach in Hawaii. This is not to say that he did not find "wickedness" in abundance in Liverpool. On his second day in the city, he took a walk through "the main thorofairs of the Town" and saw things that "defy description," although he did go on to describe them as "horrible."[6] But this was not endemic degeneracy of the kind he believed he saw in Hawaii. This was, apparently, simply evidence that human beings are prone to sin. Britain represented a more important field of labor because it was the center of church business in Europe, and it was supplying most of the Mormons to the Mormon culture region.

In the nineteenth century, the United States and Europe constituted an "overarching Atlantic model of civilization" in which the United States "did not rank equally in global cultural and politics" with Britain.[7] In Hawaii, JFS saw a degraded culture, one he, in his early years, looked down upon. English culture, by contrast, represented to JFS a lofty symbol of civilization. Along with most of the world in the nineteenth century, he looked up to the English with their massive railroads and factories, and their sprawling empire.

JFS also had personal ties to Britain because his beloved mother was a native, and many of her relatives still lived there. In fact, his uncle Joseph Fielding had been one of the first LDS missionaries in Britain and served as the president of the British mission from 1838 to 1840. JFS was inclined to view the British with a far greater measure of charity than he did the Hawaiians for many reasons, not least of which was that the British, in his view, may have been singing the wrong religious lyrics, but unlike their Hawaiian counterparts, they were familiar with the basic tunes. Britain, JFS wrote in his journal, "was not a heathen land, but a civilized, an enlightened, a religious, a Christian country."[8] Although he saw a good deal of suffering among the poor classes in industrial Britain, he never made the kinds of sweeping generalizations about their overall moral standing or personal habits the way he did about Hawaiians.

Missionary work in Britain had begun in 1837, when Joseph Smith called Heber C. Kimball, Orson Hyde, and Joseph Fielding to travel to England and preach. The aim of that first mission was not only to make converts, but also to "gather" them into the Mormon communities in the United States. In the summer of 1837, Kimball and Hyde baptized the first British converts in the town of Preston in Lancashire. Preston had the distinction of being the birthplace of the water frame, a cotton-spinning device invented by Richard Arkwright in 1769. Arkwright's invention led to the establishment of cotton-processing centers, such as Manchester, in the north of England.

The missionaries met with astonishing success in Preston and the surrounding area. By the spring of 1838, 1,500 English converts had accepted the message of the Mormon missionaries. They had also stirred up controversy among local clergy and the regional press. Joseph Fielding prevailed upon his brother, Rev. James Fielding, to allow the missionaries to speak to his congregation of dissenting Primitive Episcopalians. The reverend came to regret inviting the Mormons to speak because his flock apparently found their message appealing. In addition to the "Fieldingites," two other small dissenting sects in the Preston area lost a fair number of members to the LDS missionaries. It soon became difficult for Mormon missionaries to find pulpits from which to preach their message.[9] This left them to preach in private homes. Hyde and Kimball left Britain in April 1838, leaving Fielding behind as president of the British mission.

While much of JFS's experience in Britain in the early 1860s contrasted with his Hawaiian experience, similarities also surfaced. As with his mission to Hawaii, his arrival in England followed closely on the heels of social, economic, political, and religious changes that had remade the culture. Both Hawaii in 1854 and Britain in 1860 were new worlds in which older ways of thinking about and being in the world had changed virtually overnight. The Industrial Revolution left England littered with factories of various kinds, and its imperial interests contributed to a booming import/export trade both economically and culturally. England was also convulsed with social activism on issues ranging from temperance to child labor. In the 1850s, the Church of England "was roused from its Georgian torpor" and spent the decade building churches at a rate not seen in England since the fifteenth century.[10]

In 1851, the national census revealed that England had become the world's first urban country, with more than 54 percent of the population living in cities. In France the number was only 19 percent. One-fourth of the population lived in cities of over 100,000 people, many of those in the newly burgeoning northern cities of Leeds and Sheffield, and the all-important port city of Liverpool. The Britain that JFS found in 1860 was a Britain reborn in the grime of the Industrial Revolution. Historian Simon Gunn noted, "The city was the fulcrum for the major changes overtaking British society in the nineteenth century; it was on the very cutting edge of capitalism and modernity."[11] And nowhere was this truer than in the northern industrial cities where JFS spent almost the entirety of his first mission to Britain.

The fruits of industrialization in Britain were staggering. Between 1850 and 1870, "total production nearly doubled. The length of the railway line doubled, as did the number of passengers, while freight tripled. The tonnage of steamships increased nearly 600 percent."[12] And it was in Liverpool that most of the action took place. Liverpool was a cotton city at the heart of a cotton empire, and the demand for cotton had completely restructured the city's socioeconomic landscape. Liverpool's docks on the Mersey received thousands of cotton-bearing ships every year and sent out goods produced from that cotton in Lancashire mills further inland. JFS had landed in "the epicenter of a globe-spanning empire."[13]

Liverpool's population grew from 82,430 in 1801 to 429,881 in 1860. Urbanization on this scale and at this pace created both challenges and opportunities for the Mormon missionaries. In this new world of railroads and factories and all the changes that such developments implied, JFS's missionary work had three main foci: strengthening and stabilizing existing branches of the church, encouraging and helping to prepare church members to emigrate to Utah, and proselytizing.

Britain's new social landscape brought striking religious changes as well. In Liverpool, the 1851 religious census revealed that while the Church of England remained the city's single largest denomination with about 76,000 people in attendance, 96,034 individuals attended other churches. But the Church of England's dominance in the more rural areas and in the urban south of England did not carry over to the northern cities. In places like Preston, Liverpool, and Manchester, people found the religious messages of the Calvinist Methodists, the Wesleyan Methodists, the Baptists, and dozens of other churches appealing. According to historian Robert Tombs, the Methodism of the Fieldings, in particular, "positively thrived on socio-economic change—including population growth, industrialization, migration, and social mobility." Further weakening the Church of England in the northern cities was the presence of large numbers of Irish emigrants who had crossed the Irish Sea to seek employment in the booming industrial cities. By 1851, more than 50,000 Irish Catholics were regularly attending church services in Liverpool. As Tombs observed, "English religion no longer consisted of a national church with a few licensed dissenters, but of some ninety churches and sects."[14]

The stage was set in Victorian England for Mormonism to make its appeal. In order to attract converts in such a boisterous and fragmented landscape, missionaries needed to present something different, something bold, something that spoke to the revolutionary conditions that the English people were facing. They also needed publicity, and that was something that the British press provided in spades. Almost from the beginning, the press in England lampooned Mormons, first for their audacious proclamations about new prophets and gold plates. Later the press portrayed the missionaries as lusty creepers invading English villages and scouring homes in search of brides for their polygamous harems in the far-off deserts of America.

Although much of the anti-Mormon literature and rhetoric turned people away from the faith, it also amplified Mormonism over the din of competing religious factions. JFS took a keen interest in anti-Mormon publications, even sending copies of one serial, "Jesse the Mormon's Daughter," home to a puzzled and disgusted Levira. He claimed that he sent it "for the benefit of those who wishes to see what fools the world is made up with," but it was also strong evidence for the fame of Mormonism.[15] "Mormonism" quickly became a household word in parts of England and Wales, and that publicity, however negative, was worth a great deal. Attacks against Mormonism in Britain, just as in the United States, provided the church with an important rhetorical opening. Persecution was read as evidence

106   Chapter 7

of the divinity of the church. Why else, they asked, would we be so hated by a wicked world?

When Brigham Young and Wilford Woodruff arrived to take charge of the mission in 1840, they sought to capitalize on both the boom in religious periodicals and the growing interest in Mormonism by establishing what would become the longest continually published periodical in LDS Church history. *The Latter-day Saints' Millennial Star* was far more than a religious newspaper. It was the main instrument through which information flowed from Utah to the missionaries and church members in Britain. Like many newspapers of the time, the *Millennial Star* included various stories gleaned from other sources, but the bulk of the material consisted of publications of sermons from church leaders, notices on immigration, information on arriving and departing missionaries, and editorials produced by mission headquarters that frequently addressed the interaction of Mormonism with British culture.

In 1858, the *Millennial Star* published an editorial that made this very case. "It is the universal practice of Editors to refuse a 'Mormon's' statement admission in their columns," the piece read, a fact that proves "conclusively the determination that exists to put them down by keeping the truth hid as long as possible."[16] In the same issue was a lengthy letter from British mission president Samuel W. Richards that he had submitted for publication to the *Daily Telegraph*. This, the paper seemed to suggest, is what the editors do not want you to know.

Mormonism's pugnacity served the church well in the rough and tumble of English religious life—and to be important in English religious life was to be important in many other areas as well. Religion in England during this period provided a crucial beam around which the ships of politics, economics, and social life were built. More than any other factor, it was religion that dictated how British men voted and with whom they associated. Religion had begun to take on new meaning for many Britons. No longer content to passively attend Anglican services and then retire to the cricket pitch, Britons by the thousands were finding an outlet for their religious zeal in a wide variety of social causes. Temperance, animal protection, the abolition of slavery, Sabbatarianism, prison reform, and the criminalization of sexual deviance were a few of the causes that religiously motivated people undertook.

In 1860, Britain still occupied a special place in Mormon consciousness. As JFS's travel companion Amasa Lyman wrote, "The brethren from home, as they touch these shores, seem to be filled with the fire of the work."[17] JFS and his associates were the first new missionaries to arrive in England since "the recall of the Elders from Zion at the time of the Utah Expedition." The *Millennial Star* called their arrival "a new dispensation in the British Mission," and JFS and his cousin Samuel earned special notice. At a banquet held to honor the new arrivals, at least one person was deeply impressed by the "presence of the sons of Hyrum and Samuel Smith and the nephews of Joseph, our prophet" and found it impossible to "be forgetful of the great dead" in the presence of "these their natural relics."[18]

Even two years later, the novelty of seeing the son of Hyrum Smith had not worn off. One observer noted in the *Millennial Star* that he was "much pleased with brother Joseph [F. Smith]; he reminded me much in appearance of his father, whose example he seeks to follow."[19] After a tour of Denmark in 1862, JFS's old friend William Cluff wrote to tell him that the Danish "Saints" not only "often speak of" his visit "in the highest terms of satisfaction and pleasure,"[20] but a large number of them prevailed upon Cluff to hang a photograph of JFS on the wall of the mission office in Copenhagen "where they can see you occasionally."[21]

At this point in his life, in his early twenties, JFS was not yet a general authority, but he was famous for being Hyrum's son. There is no evidence to suggest that he courted these comparisons to his father and the attention that they brought, but he certainly had to live with them. If anything, JFS entertained a sense that he was underestimated by nearly everyone. "I have a tolerable high opinion of myself," he wrote to Levira, adding that he was "necessitated to hold myself in high estimation as no one else would."[22]

This fame by association was clearly a mixed blessing. On one hand, JFS felt blessed to have the "sacred blood" of the "prophets" in his veins. But on the other hand, he must have had a keen sense of pressure to perform coupled with a potentially muddled sense of identity, especially before his call to the First Presidency. Up to that point, and to a lesser degree after, most members of the church would describe JFS only in relation to another person, Hyrum Smith. The psychological toll of this linked identity must have been substantial. But it also opened doors, first in mission leadership in England and, later, when Brigham Young found himself in desperate need of a "natural relic," to leadership at the highest level.

On 28 July 1860, JFS received his first assignment, which was to serve in the Sheffield conference.[23] Located on the River Sheaf about 100 miles east of Liverpool as the crow flies, Sheffield was a steel town. Like Liverpool's, its population had exploded during the Industrial Revolution. JFS first served in the city of Hull, which was within the boundaries of the Sheffield District.[24] He set about visiting the branches of the church in the area, preaching at meetings to which "strangers" were invited, visiting Mormons who had fallen away, and encouraging those Mormons with the means or skills to emigrate to Utah to do so as soon as possible. Because Mormonism had been present for so long in Britain, there was a wide variety of Mormons. Some younger adults had been born into the faith. Many active members had split their families up so some could emigrate while the others remained behind to earn more money. Many longtime Mormons had ceased to participate in church activities but remained convinced of Mormonism's truth, while other former members had become openly antagonistic. JFS had to use different skills to deal with each type of church member under his care, and he did so with great skill.

Learning experiences abounded, as did somewhat less edifying activities. Victorian Britain crawled with entertainment and entertainers of all kinds. Some events were religious, others clearly secular, and many were industrial in nature, but all of

108   Chapter 7

them belonged to the family of spectacle, and JFS could not get enough. The theater had changed considerably in the early decades of the nineteenth century. Although attending the theater had been an educated, upper-class British leisure-time pursuit for centuries, by the time JFS arrived in Britain, interest in the theater had surged among working-class people. This not only led to an expansion of the number of venues in which plays could be performed, but also changed the content and tone of the productions themselves. "What this new audience wanted," wrote historian Patricia Pulham, "was spectacle, excitement, music and dancing."[25]

Prior to urbanization, rural English village life bristled with various, and usually rowdy, forms of entertainment that differed greatly from the refined arts found in the cities. After industrialization brought thousands upon thousands of rural Britons into the cities, working-class theater productions reflected a hybrid of the rural taste for excitement with the upper-class form of theater. In the course of just one month, JFS attended nearly a dozen such events. The first of these was a debate between a Reverend Brindly and the "Celebrated Infidel, or 'Secularist,' Joseph Barker."[26] Barker was an eccentric religious seeker who earned a transatlantic reputation for his preaching against conservative religion and his abolitionist activism. By 1861, however, he had switched his views on religion and began to publish in favor of traditional Christian morality. JFS could not have known it at the time, but he had the opportunity to see one of Barker's final performances as an "infidel." He also attended "Mademoiselle Veroni's Vocal, Musical, and Magical Entertainments," which "were well performed except one trick which thro accident proved a failure."[27] He also visited a local steel mill and gathered with other spectators to observe the launching of "the great Steam Ship 'Munster,'" where "one man's legs were broken by a rope that caught him as the ship slid out."[28]

JFS's next stop was the Queen's Theater in Hull. He developed an abiding affection for plays during his years in Britain, and he remained a regular theatergoer throughout his life. During his first mission to Britain, JFS attended the theater at least twenty-six times and saw a wide variety of plays ranging from farces and pantomimes to Shakespeare. He saw *Hamlet* on three occasions.[29] His first trip to the Queen's Theater, however, was not to see a play. The attraction was William Wallet, a clown who, because he once performed for Queen Victoria, in 1844, referred to himself ever after as "The Queen's Jester."[30] Although he had nothing to say in his journal about Wallet's performance, the ceremonial opening of the "People's Park" in Hull made a tremendous impression on JFS. He excitedly noted that "15,000!!" people gathered to watch the mayor's tree-planting ritual, followed by a tightrope walker and "blazing rockets and fireworks." "Everything," JFS recorded, "was on a grand scale, except for the accommodations for the Public, which were poor."[31]

Despite his love of entertainment, JFS never lost sight of why he was in Britain: to share the "restored gospel" with those who would accept it, and then encourage those people to emigrate to Utah. However, JFS found preaching in English hard work. Accustomed to missionary work in Hawaii, which allowed him to hide, as it were, behind a foreign language, he found himself feeling somewhat more vulnerable in England. In a letter to William Cluff, his old missionary friend from his Hawaii days, JFS confided that although he had preached many good sermons in Hawaii, in England, "I have not got to be much of a preacher yet." After preaching his first sermon in England on 12 August 1860, he was not entirely pleased with his performance. He felt that his sermons would be stronger if he could preach in "native" Hawaiian instead.[32]

That first sermon also provided JFS a lesson in the importance of diplomacy. Preaching to a large crowd, he proclaimed that the authority of the ancient apostles now rested with the leaders of the LDS Church. Someone in the audience shouted "Blasphemy!," and, JFS later recalled, this was "too much for my boyish temper to bear." He immediately began aggressively debating the audience, whipping them into a frenzy that resulted in a wave of angry Englishmen rushing the stage, but JFS and his companion managed to escape. In a letter written decades later, JFS said the angry crowd made him recognize the need to avoid "showing any temper when reviled" and to "moderate my fervor and be more diplomatic in the presence of a mixed crowd."[33]

Just a few months into his mission, JFS was called to preside over the Sheffield District. "I am no little surprised at my appointment," he wrote in his journal, adding that it caused him "to feel my weakness more and more."[34] Perhaps to ease his discomfort, he immediately called his best friend and brother-in-law, Samuel B. Smith, to preside over the Bradford conference.[35] As in Hawaii, the mission in Britain was much more than the proselytizing arm of the church. In areas without organized stakes, missions represented the official ecclesiastical form of organization. Each mission was divided into districts, which were, in turn, composed of conferences. Within the conferences were the basic ecclesiastical units, the branches.

As president of the Sheffield District, JFS assumed responsibility for the spiritual welfare of missionaries and church members in the Sheffield, Bradford, Hull, and Lincolnshire conferences. His letter of appointment specified his duties in detail. First, he was to watch over the people in the district in both spiritual and temporal affairs; second, it was his responsibility to see that directions from the mission presidency, often published in the *Millennial Star*, be implemented in the branches of the district; third, he was to call and set apart local church leaders as well as local men to serve as part-time missionaries; fourth, he would have to police the teaching in the various branches to ensure that nothing was taught except material from the scriptures that comported with doctrines and policies from the First Presidency and the mission presidency; fifth, he was given the heavy responsibility of excommunicating members of the church who violated moral standards or otherwise disturbed the church and its peaceful operation; and sixth, he was required to make sure that no preaching in the branches tended to "oppress the poor" by requiring that they pay tithes or other offerings. Finally, JFS was to see to it that "as far as they can," the members begin making "deposits" toward the cost of emigration.[36] In effect, JFS served in a capacity that was the equivalent of the twenty-first-century Area Seventy.[37]

JFS wrote to Levira to tell her about his new calling. "My headquarters," he noted, "is to be wherever I am most needed."[38] His time as district president was indeed filled with travel. By 1851, Britain boasted one of the most extensive railway systems in the world, covering more than 10,000 miles.[39] The railroads, together with a vast canal network, were "remarkably effective in connecting most communities in Britain."[40] JFS's most time-consuming activity was, in fact, travel because he was assigned "an extensive field." "Mostly I travel by rail and water the long distances," he wrote Levira, and he marveled that "this whole country is almost a complete network of rail-roads. There is scarcely a village or town but there is a railroad running through it or near it."[41]

While railway lines connected the major cities and larger towns and villages, the multitude of smaller cities and villages scattered across the English countryside had to be accessed by road or footpath. Since JFS did not so much as set foot inside a buggy until 1863, he walked a great deal.[42] Although he characterized his walks as consisting only of "short distances," he typically walked several miles each week to lay hands on an ailing church member or to speak at a meeting. On occasion, his ambles took him considerably farther. In 1862, for example, he twice walked more than seventeen miles to attend meetings.[43]

JFS found that he was needed for a great many things. Of course, he preached a great deal, but even when it went well (something he denoted by recording in his journal how "free" he felt during a given meeting), it was his least favorite part of missionary work. "There is nothing I have to do," he wrote Levira, "that is more tiring and exhausts me more than preaching."[44] Before the advent of electronically amplified sound systems, speakers had to rely solely on their biological vocal equipment to reach their audiences. JFS found that while his natural tendency to "talk loud when I speak publicly" was a benefit, his lungs were weak and he could "do with a stronger pair."[45]

No matter how draining or onerous he found the task, JFS preached night and day during his British mission. He was careful to note in his journal each time he spoke, but he recorded the topics of those sermons only rarely. This makes it somewhat difficult to develop a clear and comprehensive picture of what he preached about. Those sermons for which we have a subject include general topics like "the necessity of knowing and practicing true principles," "the duties of the saints," "tithing," and "the sacrament," as well as emigration-specific sermons such as one on "the hardships to be encountered by the saints gathering to and living in the Valleys."[46]

Since missionary work had begun in Britain, the goal had always been to get the new Mormons to emigrate to where the rest of the Mormons lived. JFS and his fellow missionaries did everything they could to stir up enthusiasm for emigration, which sometimes was not an easy sell. And if they ever let up, mission leaders were quick to put them back on track. George Q. Cannon specifically instructed JFS in

Mission to the British Isles   111

early 1861 to increase his preaching on the subject in the city of Leeds.[47] Cannon wanted to capitalize on chain migration, in which some family members emigrate first, thus providing increased incentives for the remaining family members to follow. On one occasion, Sunday services were held at the home of a church member where JFS read to those assembled "a letter to the group from the host's sister, who is in the valley."

In addition to the frequent encouragement and sermons he gave on emigration, JFS was charged with assisting Mormons in raising funds for the trip and reporting to the mission president how many individuals from his district would be leaving. During emigration season, which usually began in April, JFS would personally accompany people from his district onto the ships in Liverpool, ensuring that they were settled and prepared for the arduous voyage to come. Upon "securing the berths," he would often call the group together for church services. Because ships often did not leave on time, JFS would remain in Liverpool until the ship sailed, returning to the vessel as often as he could to visit and calm the emigrants' "anxiety to get underway toward the Home of the Saints."[48]

Aside from preaching on emigration and tithing, JFS occasionally broached more complex doctrinal subjects like "the different glories, and how we could obtain the greater."[49] Although he does not mention it in his journal, he very likely touched on the topic of polygamy in his sermon on the "glories." No doubt the basis for this sermon was a revelation that Joseph Smith recorded in which he was shown that the afterlife consisted of "degrees of glory" that corresponded to the spiritual state of each individual. The more righteous someone was, the greater their degree of glory would be. This revelation was part of the LDS Doctrine and Covenants. By 1860, most Mormons believed, and were taught, that in order for a person to reach the highest of all degrees, what JFS refers to as "the greater," that person had to enter into an authorized plural marriage.

If JFS did talk about plural marriage, it would probably have been to a small group, and such occasions would have been rare. One of the most prevalent anti-Mormon ideas circulating in England concerned the alleged intention of Mormon missionaries to seduce English women and girls, bring them to Utah, and add them to their collection of wives. In truth, missionaries were repeatedly counseled that they were sent to Britain "to preach and not to get wives."[50] This did not stop JFS from teasing Levira about it, however. In 1861, he apologized for being too busy to write and expressed his confidence that Levira would forgive him, "unless I tell you how I have fallen in love with the girls, how they have drawn my attention from you and how lost I am to the Syren beauties of Old England!"[51]

Although JFS was not preaching much "deep" doctrine, that does not mean it was not on his mind. In 1861, he received a Bible as a gift from a local member of the church. The first thing he did, on the very day that he received it, was to "commit the last chapter of Malachi to memory."[52] Later that year, he memorized the first five verses of the fifth chapter of the Book of James.[53] While most Christians, and,

112   Chapter 7

indeed, Jews, would find these odd choices, JFS found both familial and doctrinal appeal in these texts. The material in James, of course, is the text that Joseph Smith said led him to seek wisdom from God, and from which came "the First Vision." The last chapter of Malachi, which consists of only six verses, was part of what Joseph Smith said that the angel Moroni quoted to him in 1823. "Behold," the text reads, "I will send you Elijah the prophet before the coming of the great and dreadful day of the Lord, and he shall turn the heart of the fathers to the children, and the heart of the children to their fathers, lest I come and smite the earth with a curse." Joseph Smith claimed that this prophecy had literally been fulfilled in 1836, when Elijah the prophet appeared in the temple at Kirtland, Ohio, and conferred upon him the authority to do ritual work on behalf of the dead. And in Nauvoo, it was this same scriptural text that Joseph Smith would point to as the foundation for Mormon ritual work on behalf of one's kindred dead. Fifty-seven years later, in 1918, just one month before his death, JFS would cite this same scriptural passage in his "Vision of the Redemption of the Dead," which would be his only contribution to the Mormon canon.

JFS had to deal with a variety of problems as president of the district, ranging from the banal to the demonic. The first thing he discovered was that the situation among the Latter-day Saints in Sheffield was less than ideal. Missionaries were having trouble paying rent, and church members were finding various ways to violate Mormon standards of conduct. In addition to the usual problems related to sexual sin, including child sexual abuse,[54] JFS faced a larger, more systemic problem of general malaise, and he had to personally attend to the "priesthood" in Bradford who were "playing Hob," British slang for causing mischief.

JFS took time to try to smooth over various local disagreements, such as when he visited "Bro. Hadyson, who felt hurt by some counsel given him by the brethren."[55] Releasing branch presidents and calling their replacements also often fell to JFS. As in Hawaii, some congregations simply stopped showing up. For example, "the brethren and the Hull branch were falling away."[56] A large percentage of baptized members no longer engaged with the church on any level, and those who did "have been feeling low for some time past."[57]

JFS also laid hands on the sick on a weekly basis, and even more frequently during a smallpox outbreak during the fall and winter. He claimed to have contracted a "slight" case of it himself, having "lived among it for days, laying hands on those who were like masses of corruption." He found that associating with and blessing people took a physical and an emotional toll on him. He recalled that one day he blessed an old man and a young child, and after blessing the man, Avram Varley, JFS "felt as though half of my strength was gone."[58]

JFS's tenderness is one of the many contradictions in his character. He fought—with his pen, his sermons, and his fists—nearly his entire life. He could also be cold, condescending, and even cruel. Another part of him, however, registered sadness and responded with depression and compassion. In 1860, he recorded his deep sadness at witnessing a child "taken with fits." "The poor little thing," JFS confided in his journal, "did seem to suffer intensely."[59] He often took care to note in his journal the illnesses and deaths of children. In later years, he would lose many of his own "lambs," his heart shattering with each death. But even before he was a father, the suffering and death of children resonated in him with unusual strength.

As in Hawaii, JFS found that the devil was alive and well in Britain, and possessing the bodies of British Mormons on a semi-regular basis. He never doubted that he lived in a world in which unseen forces swirled around him. Angels and demons formed as substantial a part of his lived experience as bricks and dirt. In October 1860, a morning meeting had barely commenced when a woman "was possessed of an evil spirit." The woman's face contorted, and she emitted "strange murmurings" as JFS and others attempted to cast the spirt out through the laying on of hands. Although she apparently recovered, during the evening meeting she "was again afflicted with the evil one." JFS does not mention performing the exorcism ritual again; he simply notes that "a good many strangers were in attendance and were very attentive and all stayed till meeting was out."[60]

He displayed a similarly untroubled attitude when, almost exactly a year later, "the meeting in the evening was disturbed a little by a woman possessed of a devil."[61] Another year passed and he again had occasion to perform an exorcism when in the middle of a "good meeting ... the Devil thought we should not have it all our own way, so he attempted to disturb us by afflicting one of the Sisters with his evil power, but we laid hands on her Twice, and rebuked him after which he left her."[62]

For JFS and many of his contemporaries, casting out the devil was no more remarkable than laying hands on an ill person and watching them recover. In JFS's worldview, the devil was real and had power to inflict physical harm. In January 1863, he slipped while descending a flight of stairs, and the first thought to "flash thro'" his mind was "the Devil wants to hurt me, but I'll watch myself."[63] JFS would have viewed these events as natural and expected. Similarly, he casually mentions two occasions when members of a congregation spoke in tongues.[64] Such things provided more evidence for JFS of the reality of God, Satan, the efficacy of Mormon priesthood authority, and, ultimately, the truthfulness of the LDS Church as evidenced by the presence of the specific gift of casting out evil spirits.

Not all of the enemies JFS faced on his mission came from the ranks of Satan's army. In a letter to Levira, he confessed that he had engaged in a frightening act of bloodshed so horrible that it "perfectly disconnected him." JFS wrote two pages about his work as a "midnight assassin" before revealing that the wholesale slaughter in which he engaged was not of men, but of bedbugs.[65] One can only imagine Levira's response to the lengthy jape. JFS's humor, so prominent in his letters home from Hawaii, still emerged in Britain, if somewhat less frequently. He particularly enjoyed wordplay and puns. When, after a delay of six months, JFS received a letter from Levira, he responded that the letter arrived "just in time to save me from committing Susan Cide."[66]

114   Chapter 7

At times, especially when writing to his friend Samuel Adams, JFS's humor could lean ever so slightly toward the bawdy. They often communicated via poetry, and JFS sent this poem to Adams in the summer of 1861.

> You seem to think your Wife the means
> Of keeping you in "time" & "trim"
> Of brightening up the slumberous beams
> Reflecting from your rhyming dreams!
>
> 'Twas Love & fancy, in _me_ wrought
> The wonderous working of the thought
> That stir'ed the Soul with hot desire,
> To "wake the muse," to rhyme aspire.
>
> And when the object of the flame
> Was wone, the Summit gained,
> The joy excelled so much the fancy
> That rhyme was nought compared with "Nancy."[67]

JFS's brief foray into mildly bawdy poetry paled in comparison to the time he spent doing religious work of all kinds. In Britain's tumultuous religious environment, he frequently took the opportunity to speak with, and listen to, ministers from a variety of Christian faiths. Church of England ministers and representatives of various dissenter groups were his most frequent contacts. These experiences elicited a range of responses from JFS. Most often he reacted with fiery indignation at the "sectarian prejudice, ignorance, and conceit, and passionate hatered [sic] to the Truth."[68] At other times he employed humor to express his feelings of religious superiority, as when he stopped to listen to an itinerant preacher and "got tracted, warned, and slightly bored" before continuing on to his dinner appointment.[69] His visit to a Methodist revival meeting elicited a similarly supercilious response: "_more_ folly and confusion and foolery I _never_ saw. It is wonderful, to see to what extent human folly will go, unguided and unchecked!"[70] Occasionally, however, if he found a minister who would listen without rancor, JFS would respond in kind. He wrote, "I had a long conversation with a church of England minister and Scripture-reader whom I found very reasonable in his conversation, and liberal in his views."[71]

Toward the end of his time in England, George Q. Cannon alerted JFS to the arrival in Britain of missionaries from the newly formed RLDS Church who asked if the LDS Church would "open [their] meeting houses for [them] to set [their] views before the people," a request that Cannon flatly refused. This was an unusual move since it was a common practice for churches, even Mormon ones, to allow ministers from other denominations to occupy their pulpits. When an RLDS missionary pointed this out, Cannon replied that he "did not view him, and those with whom he associated, in the same light as I would an honest, sincere, sectarian minister of any denomination."[72]

Although JFS never seems to have come into contact with representatives of the RLDS faith, Cannon's letter to him exposes the unique challenge that they posed to the LDS Church. The RLDS missionaries wanted to publish a tract by "The Prophet Joseph Smith," meaning Joseph Smith III, capitalizing on the fact that they had Joseph Smith's son and namesake at the head of their movement, while the LDS Church had few Smiths in high office, and none of Joseph Smith Jr.'s descendants. JFS labeled the new movement "a fraud—a base counterfeit having only a form and color of the true coin, but not the metal"; he considered it not only spurious but a bastardized form of religion, "an attempt by apostates to compromise with the world," ultimately aiming to "root out and destroy the Kingdom of God."[73] The LDS Church would spend the rest of the nineteenth century trying to respond to the RLDS challenge, something that would carry profound implications for JFS and his future life's work. In 1863, however, Cannon's admonition to JFS was to refuse to "play their game" and to "<u>let them severely alone</u>."[74]

The Mormons in the Sheffield District did not meet solely for religious purposes; they maintained an active social calendar as well. Usually twice a month, but sometimes more often, the Mormons would hold a "tea party," usually at a rented space or at the home of a church member. JFS loved these events during which the assembled group would play games, tell stories, eat, and sing late into the night. (In April 1861, JFS attended five of these tea parties.) One party was held in a "branch [that] numbers a little more than a hundred, and there were more than two hundred took tea, old and young. After tea, as is a custom here, the evening was spent in a very aggregable manner by singing songs, hymns, and glees; recitations and preaching. Sister Cook favoured us with music on a harmonium engaged for the occasion."[75]

Mormons even adapted the growing British theater movement to tell their own story. One production, entitled "Priestcraft in Danger," dramatized "the introduction of the gospel in England in the year 1837."[76] Despite JFS's later reputation as a somewhat surly and supercilious individual, he proved during his years in Britain that he could also completely lose himself in the joys of socializing. In 1862, probably during one such event, he was among the first to hear a hymn written by a local knife grinder. "We Thank Thee, O God, for a Prophet" had humble beginnings in the Sheffield District.[77]

Despite his extensive experience as a world-traveling missionary and burgeoning autodidact, JFS occasionally expressed significant self-doubt. Certainly, no one would know to look at him that he was anything but supremely confident, something of which he was acutely aware. He hinted as much when he wrote that he was "naturally proud," but not as proud as people thought. "Folks judge me rather harshly on this point," he complained, because of "certain peculiarities I have which are modified on becoming ... acquainted with me."[78] In private, among friends,

116   Chapter 7

JFS could sometimes express vulnerability, especially about what he felt was his "rough, untutored" nature.[79] Often this took the form of self-deprecating humor of a type that hinted at certain insecurities. He wrote, for instance, that he only rarely suffered from headaches because "there is but little in it to ache," and any pain experienced there was likely due to a vain effort to "aspire to mimic heads of weight."[80] He assured Levira that he would never go bald because "that is generally a consequence of study and hard thought, two evils from which I am remarkably clear!"[81] Sometimes, however, JFS dropped the joking tone and gave vent to sincere, and overt, feelings of inadequacy. In 1875, he wrote that when he left on his first mission in 1854, he "had never written a letter in my life, and did not know how to write a dozen words." After more than twenty years of practice, he wrote, "I can just write to be understood."[82]

Although sensitive about the crudity of his education, JFS seemed more deeply concerned with his masculinity. More than once, he referred to himself as "one who hoped to be a man" but remained a child.[83] These fears seemed to surface in letters written around the time of his birthday. Just after he turned twenty-four, he wrote,

> I cannot tell why it is, but I do not like to think I am getting older. But the fact is too apparent to admit of a doubt. I would not so much mind if I knew I grew in other things as well, and in proportion with my years, but I do not flatter myself with any such folly as to think this is the case.[84]

Earlier, he wrote a letter to Levira in which he seemed to be bordering on panic. JFS noted that he was "still poor Joseph and I see no likelihood of becoming anything else."[85] He mused that Levira, no doubt, would "love to see me grow to be a <u>MAN!</u>" At the time JFS wrote this letter he was twenty-two and had been an orphan for nearly ten years, yet he still felt that he had not reached manhood. He longed to be able to grow into manhood under the "tuition of such men as we have here." In the letter, JFS indicated that Cannon, an apostle and then-president of the European mission, made a fine model of manhood and was an example of "true nobility [and] real, unfeigned greatness."[86]

Throughout his life, JFS would link religiosity with masculinity. Although he does not reveal what occasioned the April 1861 letter, it is clear from its unusual tone and contents that something was eating at him. After praising Cannon in the most florid terms for his manliness, which JFS equates with spiritual purity, he wrote page after page about his own moral weakness. "No night could be so dark, no pit so deep as to hide my shame!" he wailed. Then he asked himself, "Why [do I] grovel in the filth of degradation?" At some point in the letter he ceases to address Levira and writes directly to God. "O! My Father, give me strength to rise above the weaknesses of the flesh, to govern myself ... to shake off from my soul the influence and power of sin, to become holy and pure in thought and deed."[87]

Clearly, something had happened about which JFS felt deeply disturbed, but he never mentioned what it was. However, it is reasonably safe to assume that JFS, a young married man living an ocean away from his wife, would occasionally entertain sexual thoughts and feelings, which may have left him conflicted and possibly guilt-ridden. Whatever the cause, the letter is remarkably passionate and allows us to glimpse a dimension of JFS that is so often occluded. He always presented himself to the public as an almost invulnerable being, not necessarily self-righteous, but certainly more righteous than most. In his April 1861 letter to Levira we see his fear, his vulnerability, and, apparently, his guilt over some sinful "thought or deed." JFS believed that true manliness was found only in total moral restraint, and that indulgence in things of the "flesh" was a sign of nagging childishness.[88] He concluded the letter with a comment on the conflict that he believed raged in the heart of every person: "let us develop the good which is within us, and crush the evil that contends against it."[89]

While JFS spent his time in Britain adjusting to missionary life and contending against the evil within himself—all while living in what was then one of the most exciting places in the world—Levira was undergoing her own struggles, including adjusting to life without a husband. She had not been married long enough to have come to rely solely on JFS's support, but the interruption of the life they had begun together naturally proved unpleasant for her. She worried about him and was particularly concerned with his tendency toward overexertion in the pursuit of frivolity. One time in New York, JFS came across a device that allowed an individual to test his ability to lift weight over his head. Always a very physical man who remained proud of his strength and fitness all his life, JFS could not pass this up. He wrote to Levira, excitedly reporting that the test proved him to be as strong as he ever was.[90]

Levira, however, was unimpressed. In response to his triumph in the test of strength, Levira offered "a few words of caution": "I hope you will not go lifting anything heavy and hurt your back," she chided. Anticipating his response, she continued, "I do not like to hear you say that you can lift so much and not hurt you[rself] either for if you do not feel it at the time, you will feel it sometime." She encouraged him to "preserve your strength for I do not doubt but you will need all you have got sometime and perhaps to lay out to a better advantage than just lifting for amusement."[91] JFS detested physical weakness and cowardice, but we learn through Levira's words that even at the age of twenty-one, he "suffered with [his] back" in a chronic fashion that she feared would return.

Levira's seemingly endless rounds of banal chores were occasionally interrupted by notable events, and her letters to JFS never failed to include them. Levira was a keen reader of the "signs of the times," including a windstorm that caused massive damage to the settlements of Ogden and Farmington, north of Salt Lake City. After noting the heavy losses incurred by those in the path of the storm, she waxed

Chapter 7

apocalyptic, noting that "this is nothing compared to what will take place if judgments commence," judgments which "we need not think to escape."[92]

In addition to being JFS's wife, Levira was also his first cousin, so as a Smith, she shared his deep resentment toward those who, she felt, were responsible for the deaths of Joseph and Hyrum Smith. She reflected on this after learning of the death of George A. Smith Jr., who "died a martyr to the cause of truth … with many others of our family."[93] "Oh, how long ere the wicked will have to pay the penalty of their crimes? How long ere the 'United States' will have to come forth and atone for the abominable deeds which they have committed?" she asked. In answer to her own question, she offered a simple answer: "not long."[94]

George's death also touched a nerve in JFS, who claimed "never did I feel grief so keen." He was particularly troubled by the potential life that his cousin could have lived. "He might have lived, lived for years!" JFS lamented. As if trying to convince himself, he wrote that "we cannot recall the past," and even though that is an "awful sentence," the living must get on with life and "let rest" what has been.[95] Although doubtless sincere in his sentiment, JFS would never come close to letting his own past rest.

Prone to melancholy that would eventually descend into incapacitating depression, Levira struggled to find peace. Her letters also hint that she may have been somewhat afraid of JFS. He would confess many times to having struggled with his anger, and Levira had by that point seen it in action.[96] She had a "likeness" made of herself and enclosed it in a note in which she expressed her hope that JFS would "not give me a downright scolding for daring to be so presumptuous as to do such a thing without being requested … though I almost fear that you will." He also severely chastised her for wasting paper. How, he asked, did she come up with an idea so ridiculous and wasteful as to "write half a dozen lines 8,000 miles!" "Let me teach you a lesson," he wrote, "I want LETTERS, not POST-SCRIPTS."[97]

Levira recognized that she could be thin-skinned and wrote of her desire to toughen up "with time, so that I can take a scolding and not hurt my feelings in the least." However, she reminded JFS that "cross words from you have fell like ice upon my heart, and yet I have feigned to care nothing about them." She never admonished JFS for being harsh with her, and tended to cast the blame back upon herself. "I hope from this time forth and forever I may never do or say anything that will cause you to disregard my feelings."[98] She often wrote about her unworthiness to have such a righteous husband, and of her good fortune to have JFS "to point out to me the right path and guide me therein."[99] She seemed to crave direction, guidance, and validation, but her admonition regarding JFS's back suggests that this subordination was not absolute. Although Levira tended toward feelings of inferiority, JFS's personality leaned the other way. In the coming years, this confluence of personality traits would prove disastrous.

In the early 1860s JFS did occasionally "scold" Levira, much as he would do with his later wives, and he could be sharply critical of others, especially when it came to the written word. Upon receiving a letter from Joseph Rich, for example, he snidely recorded in his journal that the letter was "fraught with writing characteristic of the person."[100] He also, somewhat ironically, chided Levira for being hot-tempered. When she wrote to JFS about an altercation she had with a neighbor, he responded that he was

> sorry to hear that brother Amy has turned so much against you, but I hope you have given him no cause…, it is our duty to give all the credit to individuals that they deserve for their kindness and good actions, and regard their faults with all the charity we can exercise. Mr. Amy is not all bad. He is getting old, and perhaps age contributes largely to the cause of his ill-temper and peculiarities. We must overlook such things in all, and always increase our stock of charity.[101]

Such advice may have been somewhat hard for Levira to swallow, coming as it did from a man who also wrote,

> We must 'pray for them that hate us and despitefully use us' and for our 'enemies.' I pray that my enemies, and those who do evil be cursed with the sting of their own iniquity and receive the reward due for their demerits. This is as good as I can feel towards them. And it is merciful."[102]

He added that while George A. Smith said that Levira "ought" to be paid for the damage that another man's cattle had done to her property, JFS found such an approach cowardly and useless. "I am sorry to say," he wrote, that the man in question "ought to do several things which has been the case for a long time to my certain knowledge but he 'ought to yet' and will 'ought to' as long as the old man lives, which I could pray to be not very long."[103]

Aside from occasional flashes of temper, JFS's letters to Levira consisted largely of well-meant but somewhat generic-sounding expressions of affection, as when he wrote that she was "the best little wife and friend I ever had," coupled with slightly condescending admonitions and occasional theological musings. In the same letter he wrote that he hoped that their "lot may be a blessed and happy one," and that she would "not neglect any opportunity to enjoy [herself] so far as is wisdom, but don't be foolish." After writing a few sentences dealing with "time and eternity," JFS wrote, "I don't design preaching you a sermon, but sometimes we preach for want of something else to say."[104] It may seem odd that he felt pressed to fill conversational silence in writing, but he occasionally expressed his view that having purchased an entire page, and having to pay to mail it, he was obliged to fill it up.

That JFS's go-to silence filler was "preaching" is both revealing and thoroughly unsurprising. In his mind, at least from the time of his mission in Hawaii, everything was linked to, and anchored in, his understanding of Mormonism. For him

120   Chapter 7

it represented ultimate reality, and the worth of everything else was determined by the degree to which it complemented his faith. He fell back on theological discourse naturally. JFS's letters were generally shorter and less detailed than Levira's, a fact not lost on either of them. JFS excused himself by claiming that he had "no time" and could not produce lengthier letters even if he "had the disposition to [write] more."[105] When one compares JFS's letters with his journal entries, something else becomes apparent. He rarely told Levira about his leisure activities, making little mention of the truly extravagant events he attended, including at the Surrey Music Hall, which included "singing, dancing, tight rope dancing, dialogues, gymnastics" and an "elephant performance." Nor did he share with her his excitement at witnessing a "display of pugilism" and getting a close look at "Jim Mace, the renowned pugilist, and his belt." Probably mindful of Levira's dissatisfaction with being left to toil in the desert while JFS went roaming, he chose the safer course and kept his outings to himself. This, however, would have left him with a good deal less to say given the relative frequency of his outings to the theater, parties, museums, agricultural fairs, circuses, and even freak shows.[106]

Levira Falls Ill

Levira went through several periods of mysterious ailments. In retrospect it seems likely that she probably suffered from mental ailments that today might be diagnosed as major depressive disorder, bipolar disorder, generalized anxiety disorder, and more. But during her lifetime, the science of the mind and the emotions was embryonic, at best, and this led to misunderstandings that could only have crippled her further. Although she showed few physical signs of illness, she would become incapacitated for weeks at a time. JFS described her as always appearing "grave and sedate ... with now and then a gleam of sunlight suffusing [her] countenance."[107]

Levira expressed reluctance to share her suffering with JFS. Although she certainly needed the support, she knew that he struggled with how to respond. She pleaded that she would give anything "if you only knew how difficult it is for me to write to you especially when I am compelled to say so little respecting myself for fear of distressing your feelings." After months of keeping "silent as possible in regards to myself not wishing to tell you any of my troubles or anything that would be calculated to disturb your mind or cause you to worry about me," she was ready to open the floodgates. Her pent-up feelings spilled onto the page as she told him that her "health is miserable and has been for a long time," that she had been the target of attacks by Satan, who "has exerted his powers to destroy me," and, finally, that she "could not endure for one year to come what I have endured during the past time of your absence from home, no I cannot! One look at my poor, pale face, and wasted form would convince you of that."[108] It was the last letter she would write to JFS for six months.

Mission to the British Isles

JFS never knew quite how to respond to news of Levira's suffering, a harbinger of dark conflicts to come. Compounding matters, Levira could be frustratingly fickle about the tone of JFS's letters, such as when she informed him that she was too depressed "to take a joke, so you must not joke me a great deal."[109] In response to her brutally honest letter, JFS admitted that he was "a poor hand to speak comforting words" but wanted Levira to know that he felt "sorrowful sometimes when I think of you as you have had to suffer, and endure sickness and perhaps sometimes privations while I am separated so far from you, but I cannot help it"; he wished things could be different, of course, but was always "willing to bow in obedience to [God's] will."[110]

In late 1861, Levira's health began to seriously falter. Fortunately, she came under the care of Zina D. Young, who had been a plural wife of Joseph Smith and then a plural wife of Brigham Young. Aunt Zina, as JFS called her, informed him that Levira had spent weeks at a time unable to get out of bed or function. Many nights they would stay up and read scriptures together. During this period, Brigham Young himself laid his hands on Levira's head and gave her a blessing of health. After directing Zina to purchase "Warm underclothing," shoes, and other items for her, Young confided to Levira that he intended to make a "giant" out of JFS.[111]

Zina wrote to JFS and admitted that although they were practically strangers, she felt she had come to know him as she read his letters aloud to Levira and other members of the Young household. Unsurprisingly, she related to JFS primarily through his relationship to his father, Hyrum, and his uncle Joseph Smith. "I have watched you and your Kin with much interest," she wrote, and she said his letters confirmed for her what she "fondly anticipated, begin[n]ing to develop itself in your lineage."[112] Zina assured JFS that Levira would soon be able to attend church meetings and, in due time, return to live with her mother. Zina's letter moved JFS deeply, and he described it as a communication from "an angel of peace" that "went far to allay my fears and to inspire within me hope and faith and opened a fountain of gratitude in my heart that never can be dried! God Bless her and our Beloved President!"[113]

Zina's letter was not just filled with praise, however. She also offered the gentle but crystal-clear suggestion that JFS should take a moment to write a letter to Young expressing his gratitude. Three days after receiving the letter, a trepidatious JFS put pen to paper, offering thanks for Young's "kind and fatherly care" of Levira. "Accept my warmest, <u>heart-felt</u> thanks for your very great kindness to me and Levira," JFS continued. "I trust I may some day be worthy of such kindness. I feel deeply endebted to you but you can imagine better than I can say, my humble, but sincere and fervent gratitude." With that out of the way, JFS reported that his mission was going well, and the work was moving along at a satisfactory pace. He complained of a cold, but noted that "Brethren from the Valley are, in this country" prone to them, and he "had hardly known what it was to be free from a slight

122   Chapter 7

cold since I have been here." [114] He told Young that while there was no shortage of willingness to emigrate, the English "saints" lacked means. He predicted that the group preparing to leave in 1862, which numbered about 150 from the Sheffield District, had only enough to make it as far as Florence, Nebraska.

Although during his time in Britain JFS expressed less melancholy homesickness than he did when he was in Hawaii, he made it a point to tell Levira that he "was not homesick."[115] It seems his increasing maturity helped, as well as his knowledge that he had a home to which he could reasonably hope to return, with a wife and a future. However, on 24 July 1862, he made one of the few nostalgic entries in his journal. "This is the 15th anniversary of the entrance of the Pioneers into the Valley of the Great Salt Lake," he wrote, adding, "I have thought many times of my folks at home today."[116]

Trying Times in England

JFS did, occasionally, find opportunities in his busy schedule to brood more seriously. Birthdays seemed to be particularly hard times. When he turned twenty-three, he noted how many of his birthdays had been spent away from home: "this is my second birthday in England. my 16th and 17th and 18th birthdays were Spent on the Sandwich Islands, my 19 in California on my return home, my 20th & 21st at Home & my 22nd and 23rd in England."[117] His twenty-second birthday, 13 November 1860, had been far worse. It dawned "rainy and disagreeable," a condition that seemed to match his emotional state. While reading the *Millennial Star*, he happened upon his mother's obituary. JFS had never before read this document, and doing so left him to reflect bitterly on his past.

> She died on the 21st Of September 1852, aged 51 year[s], & 2 months [and] left a family of 5 Children, 2 Boys, & 3 girls, and an old man, blinde, and decriped [decrepit]. also, an old lady, whome we called "Aunty"—Han[n]ah Grinnels—who had lived in the family for nearly 20 years. in 4 years after mother's death, the old man—George Mills—and 'Aunty' were resting in the 'Silent Toomb.' the three oldest, and the youngest of the children, were married, and I 5,000 miles from what only a short time before was a peaceful lovely <u>home</u>, now broken up and its inmates Scattered."[118]

JFS always viewed his early years, from the death of his father until his own marriage in 1859, as a period of disintegration. In his response to his mother's obituary, he crystalized these feelings in terse but freighted prose. Things fell apart, and the vicissitudes of life laid waste to the world JFS believed could have been. His father's family lay in fragments, disjointed by death and, interestingly enough, marriage. He did not bother to note that his father's family had begun to fracture with the death of Jerusha Barden, the biological mother of all but one of JFS's siblings, and that this rupture brought Mary Fielding and, obviously, himself into the Smith family. For JFS, Barden always remained something of a shadow, a woman who never quite fit into his own concept of his father's story. Even when the opportunity presented itself, he often refused to identify her by name. In 1911, JFS introduced himself to an inquiring correspondent by first identifying his mother, then his father, and then, in the process of describing his mother's "struggle for subsistence," he mentioned that she was the mother of two children and the stepmother of "five others born to [her husband] of a former wife."[119]

To bring Barden clearly into focus would mean that Mary Fielding would be second and, somehow, lesser. JFS could not have allowed such a concept to find purchase in his memory or imagination. In fact, throughout his life, he resented what he viewed as ingratitude on the part of his half siblings. "Where would my father's children [by which he meant Hyrum's children with Barden] have been today, but for her? They do not appreciate their position now—which they owe to her."[120] No matter the reason behind his view that his father's family really started with his marriage to his mother, Mary, examining JFS's mental picture of an entropic family of origin may shed light on the strong emphasis he would later put on creating and maintaining a strong family identity among his own descendants. We will revisit these themes as we examine JFS beginning his own family and growing in power and influence. For now, it is sufficient to note that in his early twenties, he saw that he would have to begin again, to finish what his father and mother started.

Tension between JFS and his half brother John proved something of a distraction during his first year in England. Mary Fielding Smith had owned three properties in the Salt Lake Valley: a lot northwest of the temple block in the city and two parcels of farmland to the south. David Taylor, a friend of JFS's living in the Salt Lake Valley, offered to farm some of his land in his absence to keep the lots in working order and to provide for Levira. One day in the fall of 1860, Taylor happened upon John Smith working the land, and Taylor suggested that JFS wanted him to work the land instead. Taylor obviously touched a nerve because he unexpectedly found himself on the business end of a tirade. John informed Taylor that as long as JFS was not around, he would decide what happened to the land, and if that meant that he wanted it farmed, he would decide who farmed it, and if he wanted to sell it, it would be sold. A chastened, and probably confused, Taylor reported the incident to Levira, who, in turn, wrote to her husband in November 1860 to tell him that John was telling people that the land was under his complete control until JFS returned. Furthermore, Levira suspected that he intended to sell the city lot without consulting JFS. "I think something aught to be done, and that too right away," Levira wrote, "or else you will have nothing at all to come home to."[121]

JFS had worried that something like this might happen. In August he had written to George Smith asking him to make sure that Levira was not left at his

124   Chapter 7

half brother's mercy. "I would like at least the East lot to be kept . . . for Levira's use while I gone from home," JFS requested, adding that he was trying to avoid dealing directly with John because "I want no more feelings and I fear there will be if means to provide for Levira is left in John's hand."[122]

George's response was probably less helpful than JFS had hoped. He counseled JFS to focus on his mission rather than on matters at home.

> I think that it is not best for you to have any uneasiness on the subject for while on our missions we have to let things out of our reach take care of themselves. Any misunderstanding between you and John in relation to business affairs can be adjusted on your return.[123]

Furious and indignant, JFS ignored this counsel, put aside his concerns about "feelings," and went after John directly: "I understand by letter that you are trying to sell the City Lot," he wrote, despite the fact that he owned

> one half of it and I do not wish to "sell out." in regard to the Jorden Land, I think that my feelings should be consulted as to its disposal. I told you what I thought was right about that in my last letter. I do not see why you disregard me and my wants, for I have not only a claim on you to respect them, but I have a right to claim it. I want that you should let me have control of a portion of the land. I am not particular to an acher [acre], but I cannot (I am discouraged to try again) trust my intrest to your car[e].[124]

The complex mix of anger and love that he felt toward his half brother comes through clearly in the letters. "Why have you not written to me in answer to my letter?" JFS demanded, adding that he imagined it had something to do with the fact that "you respect so little my feelings."[125] He also expressed his resentment about their past relationship, in which "in consequence of your age, and my respect for you as my older brother every liberty and advantage, and all I had claim upon has been at your mercy and control."[126]

JFS also used rhetorical questions to impugn John's previous behavior. "Have you shown me impartial justice? Answer it yourself." He had run out of patience regarding John's failure to consult him about the disposal of the land, and JFS warned John that "Forbearance is a virtue, but there is a point beyond which it ceases to be a virtue," adding, ominously, that "I am not over virtuous in this." JFS made his request crystal clear so as not to be misunderstood: "I wish David Taylor—if he chooses—to take care of the East Jordan, and the City lot, for me, or if you choose, the East and half of the west Lot—over Jorden, and you may take the City lot in your own care. One of these two things I claim to be my right, till I get home."[127]

Mission to the British Isles   125

John apparently ignored those instructions because a few weeks later JFS wrote again. This time he was less aggressive and spent some time trying to explain the tone of his previous letter.

> You must excuse me for writing ... as I have done. The Truth is John if we say what we think, there is nothing hidden, and then if difficulties arise we have the satisfaction of knowing that we did our <u>best</u> to prevent it. The surest way to prevent 'feelings' is to have a good understanding about everything. You understand what I mean, and my motto is, have the spirit to resent a wrong, and a <u>heart</u> to forgive it.[128]

This motto revealed JFS's apparently lifelong belief that resentment and forgiveness could coexist. In the end, John refused to let Taylor farm the land, and he left it to "lay waste" when he himself left on a mission to Scandinavia.[129] JFS would not hear from John again until February 1862.

The spat over the land, as David Taylor found out the hard way, was part of a much larger and more profound and complex dynamic that existed between JFS and John. Throughout his life, JFS outshone his older half brother. He had a keener mind, a quicker wit, and a bolder, more confident presence. There is reason to suspect that he felt superior to John. JFS, who repeatedly wrote that many of his best qualities came from his mother, saw in John's lack of these qualities evidence that he suffered from not being both a Fielding *and* a Smith. At the very least, he tolerated a condescending attitude toward John among his friends. In 1862, after John received a mission call to labor in Europe. William Cluff, JFS's mission companion from Hawaii, noted in a letter that John's mission would be a "good school for him" because he needed to "learn how good it is to be away from home and friends." "How do you think John would stand what we have went thru on the Islands?" Cluff sneered, concluding, "I bet it would tame him a little. What say you?" When JFS suggested that John might be sent to Italy, Cluff found the idea laughable. "If he goes to Italy, as you suppose he will not get off without 'running the gauntlet' a few times."[130] We do not have JFS's response to this letter, but it is reasonable to conclude that Cluff would not speak about John in such terms if JFS had not displayed a tolerance for such banter.

John did not go to Italy but was called instead to Scandinavia at the direct instruction of Brigham Young. Sending the patriarch to the church on a mission out of the country was an unusual move, but Young felt that because John "was given to rowdyism," he was best sent away.[131] Among other things, Young had recently heard complaints against John by one of his wives, who accused him of "neglect," and Young responded by offering to grant the woman a divorce.[132] In early 1862, Young suggested, in the first of several attempts to remove John from office, that George A. Smith replace him as patriarch. George, however, "did not see any necessity for him

126   Chapter 7

becoming Patriarch." John duly left Utah for Scandinavia but resumed his position as patriarch to the church upon his return.

A Tense Meeting with the English Fieldings

From the moment JFS landed in England, he had looked forward to meeting his mother's family. He longed to forge connections with those who shared his mother's blood. He found encouragement from George A. Smith, who wrote, "I think it will be a good thing for you to visit your Fielding relatives and feel after them."[133]

In the spring of 1862, JFS spent a considerable amount of time doing just that. The Fieldings who remained in England had rejected Mormonism, but they seemed more or less willing to welcome their American nephew into their lives. JFS's aunt Martha was by far the warmest and most welcoming, and she wept when she laid eyes on him. However, Mary Fielding Smith's brother Rev. James Fielding was suspicious of JFS and often confronted him on religious matters.

Over the course of their visits, JFS expressed a desire to develop at least some form of familial tie with him, but James rejected the idea on the grounds that no friendship could exist "when people entertained religious views in opposition to each other." When JFS first met James, his uncle asked him if he was in England on "a religious errand." When he replied in the affirmative, James pounced: "You do not preach all of your doctrines in England." JFS responded that he did preach all of them, but did not practice all of them. Tired of dancing around the subject, James finally declared, "Polygamy is against the law!," to which JFS simply replied, "It is in England."[134]

JFS was taken aback by such aggressiveness, stridency, and tactlessness, but he was truly puzzled at the Fieldings' reaction when he requested that they provide him with their "likeness." His aunt Martha refused to do so because she believed it was a sin. James likewise refused and told JFS that "he had concluded not to have the likeness of the children taken" for the same reason. He then intimated that JFS's interest in obtaining photographs of the family members was somehow connected to baptism for the dead. The exact nature of James's suspicion is unclear, but he mentioned that both Mary Fielding Smith and Joseph Fielding had previously requested "the pedigree of the family, as they had in view baptism for the dead." James proudly told JFS that he refused "to send the information."[135]

JFS developed a disdain for James and the "Religious views" in which he "was most wonderfully bound and cramped up," in part because James baited and hectored him constantly. On one occasion, when JFS stopped by for dinner, James, apropos of nothing, suddenly "began to read me some comments he had made on the writings of P. P. Pratt." James took particular aim at Pratt's book *A Voice of Warning*, which happened to be one of JFS's favorites. When that approach failed to draw sufficient anger from JFS, James proclaimed that if "Ten Thousand Angels should come down and testify before [my] face that Joseph Smith was a prophet of God, [I] would not believe them." Somehow, probably for his late mother's sake, JFS managed to shrug off the abuse, which had turned from theological to personal. James then left with an associate to attend a prayer meeting. As a parting shot, he said he wished for JFS "all the prosperity and blessing, the Lord in his Mercy saw was good for me."[136] JFS noted in his journal that the "sarcasm" was not lost on him.

Although JFS generally refused to argue with the Fieldings, he often recorded his unspoken thoughts in his journal. After being told by James that he was prepared to "go to [Jesus] in a moment," JFS wrote, "I thought, it was a pity he should stop here with that chance before him."[137] The things that JFS disliked most about James were his aggressiveness, his condescension, his intransigence, his self-righteousness, his insistence on the superiority of his own particular interpretation of scripture, and his refusal to take counsel from those he considered inferior; ironically, JFS's enemies would later accuse him of the same things. In his worst moments, JFS had more in common with James Fielding than either of them would have cared to admit.

JFS had been expressing his eagerness to get back to Utah for some time. "You can expect me next summer," he wrote Levira in May 1862. "I shall be glad to go home the next emigration." In March 1863, George Q. Cannon informed JFS that he would be released in the spring, after all the emigration business had been tied up.[138] He expected, in fact, to leave no later than May, but Cannon, who had come to rely heavily on JFS's advice regarding mission business, requested that he wait until he could escort the apostle's wife back across the Atlantic. "I tell you Vira," JFS wrote ten days before he left, "I want to go home. And once I make a start, which must be a good one after so much preparation, not so much besides a blue streak will be seen of me until I fetch up somewhere in the neighborhood of East Temple Street."[139]

JFS would be bringing more than just memories home from Britain. He would also bring a four-year-old boy named Edward. JFS had adopted him after the boy's mother died and the father vanished. Edward would live as JFS's son until his death in 1911, but as researcher Kevin Folkman has pointed out, "little has been known in the church at large about Edward Arthur Smith, and he is barely acknowledged in the current biographies of Joseph F. Smith."[140] This is due, in part, to the paucity of source material dealing with Edward. He surfaces occasionally in letters and journal entries, but the circumstances surrounding his adoption and his early years with JFS remain something of a mystery. What is clear, and totally unsurprising, is that JFS would empathize deeply with the plight of a young son of an absent father and a recently deceased English mother. Given his own background and his innate tenderness toward children, JFS must have been deeply stirred by both the boy's circumstances and his own strong desire to be a father.

8 Marital Discord, Domestic Violence, and Divorce

Joseph F. Smith arrived back in New York City on 6 July 1863 and found himself in the middle of what would become known as the New York Draft Riots. The riots began as a protest by lower-class whites, mostly Irish, against the policy that anyone who could pay the government $300 was exempted from conscription, thus ensuring that the poor would end up dying in disproportionate numbers in the ongoing Civil War. Soon the rioting spread and became an opportunity for whites to attack African Americans throughout Manhattan. JFS witnessed much of this firsthand. "The negrows were assaulted wherever found, and beaten and mauled to death. The police dared not interfere only where they were in sufficient numbers to ensure safety from the mob. Several policemen were killed, some beaten to a complete jelley."[1]

JFS ventured out into the streets where he saw "a Negrow Boarding house had been attacked by the mob and torne down and all that would burn thrown out into the Street and set fire to." He was awakened in his hotel room by the sound of breaking class, gunfire, and the screams of women and children. Although he dressed and went to the lobby, prepared for any contingency, the riots ended as abruptly as they had begun, and JFS was able to continue preparing to travel west.[2]

JFS left New York City by train on 24 July 1863. He found rail travel in the United States quite poor compared to what he had grown used to in Britain. In Illinois, JFS noted in disgust that the train "hurried along at a most fearful speed over the worst road I ever saw. The English government would not allow an Engine to run upon such a line at all."[3] The rough ride notwithstanding, JFS made it to Florence, Nebraska, the place where rail and river travel stopped and walking began. JFS arrived back in Salt Lake City the first week of October.

JFS's return to Utah marked what he hoped (falsely, it turned out) would be the beginning of a stable life with Levira. When he returned, as when he left, he was destitute. Brigham Young, to the consternation of many, publicly called for donations for JFS. Young sought to raise at least $1,000 to help him establish himself after being away for so long. Young's boosterism was not common, and it demonstrates his ongoing interest in JFS. In the end, the fundraising campaign yielded very little except for the antipathy of many residents of the Salt Lake Valley. In all, JFS collected $77.50 in U.S. currency, $5.25 in gold and silver specie, and a "wild California pony" valued at $50.[4]

Worse than the financial situation, however, was the state in which JFS found Levira. He expressed shock at the sight of the "emaciated, enfeebled" woman who was "a mere shadow of her former self." Levira was suffering from hallucinations and "had grown so low that by many she had been given up." Apparently, JFS faced the task of trying to care for her alone. Through the fall and winter, he stayed by Levira's bed, from which she would not move for weeks at a time. This not only exhausted JFS and blunted his opportunities to "again mingle with old friends," but it also kept him from holding down a job. He admitted to George Q. Cannon that after two months of little sleep and constant monitoring of Levira, he had "become weary of life myself." In the same letter, JFS reported that, slowly, Levira was cycling out of her deep, crippling depression and beginning to recover her "health and her reason," allowing JFS to begin trying to figure out how he was going to make a living.[5]

No sooner than JFS had turned his attention to that task, however, he received a visit from Young. He could not have been thrilled to learn the purpose of the visit, although his loyalty to Young would never permit him to express such an opinion. Young asked JFS, who had been back from his three-year mission in Europe less than six months and had a very ill wife and no clear means of support, to return to Hawaii.[6] This was no ordinary assignment, however. Since the recall of missionaries from Hawaii in 1857, things in the islands had taken a strange turn. In 1859, a New Yorker named Walter Murray Gibson arrived in Salt Lake City. Gibson, who had "dreams of [a] Pacific empire," had been attempting to convince federal officials, and then Mormon officials, that the tension between the two could be eased if Mormons could emigrate to New Guinea.[7]

Young never seriously considered such a plan, but he found Gibson's flattery and eastern credentials appealing. Wilford Woodruff attended a lecture in which Gibson said

> the salubrity of that Country was so great that you pull any kind of herbage you can find and bind it on any tree so that it would stay and it would take root & grow. Said He I have seen fifty kinds of herbage grow upon one tree of Different kinds like the misseltoe. He spoke of several diferent kinds of fruit which he had No knowledge of before which were vary [sic] healthy.[8]

Gibson had joined the LDS Church in early 1860, and he told those assembled for the occasion that he had been a prisoner—innocent, of course—in a Dutch prison in Java. While in prison, "He had a Dream which showed him his Escape, his return to the United States, his visit to Utah & Dreamed that some saints returned with him to the Malays Islands, And He is now Here & has Embraced the Gospel."[9] Young took this very seriously.

A few days later, in the presence of Woodruff and other church leaders, Young took out a map and pointed out the places where Gibson claimed to have traveled. He told the group that Christ's ancient apostles undoubtedly preached to the "Malays," and that some remnant of "the Israelitish traditions were [still] among them."[10] Gibson had free access to Young, and in March, having been a member of the church less than two months, he received his endowment.[11] After serving a short mission in the eastern United States, Gibson returned to Salt Lake City, where he made the unusual move of calling himself on a mission. Woodruff noted in his journal that at a meeting in November 1859, Gibson announced to an audience including Young that "he was about to take another mission. Was going to Japan, Siam, & the Malay Islands. He has had an invitation by the Historian of Japan to visit that Land. Is intimately acquainted with the King of Siam & has been Strongly invited by the princes & Chiefs of the Malay Islands to visit them."[12]

The fact that these claims were nonsensical blustering is clear in retrospect, and in 1868 the *Deseret News* publicly denied that Gibson had been encouraged by church leaders.[13] But the truth is that Young found Gibson credible and potentially useful, and so, according to Woodruff, "Blessed him & said He would go with a Commission to all Nations upon the Earth & he should go with his good will & blessing."[14]

Signs of Gibson's charlatanism might have been detected earlier if anyone had been paying attention. In addition to the outlandish claims that he continually made about his personal connections with political leaders the world over, someone showed up in Salt Lake City looking for Gibson while he was in the East. The visitor told Young that Gibson owed him money and had been hiding from him for some time. Young defended Gibson's honor, and once it became clear that impugning him would mean impugning Young's judgment, no one, including Young himself, was willing to raise any objections. So it was that Gibson went on his way. Young, fatefully, asked Gibson to stop off in Hawaii to check on the status of the church there before continuing on to the Far East.

When Gibson stopped off in Hawaii, it was the last time he would ever follow instructions from Brigham Young, and it was at this point that things went awry. Gibson discovered that without missionary support from Utah, the church in Hawaii had fallen into chaos. Perhaps 3,000 members lived there, but only about 1,000 still identified as Mormon. Gibson reported to Young that, as far as he could tell, there were only three non-native Mormons in the whole of Hawaii. He then took it upon himself to take over the church there, and he soon began refusing to answer Young's letters. Gibson, it turned out, had run amok. He not only set himself up as the "high priest" to whom the Hawaiians related as they would to a king, but he also began selling priesthood offices, using church money to purchase lands for himself, and introducing new ritual and theological innovations.

Around the time JFS was spending sleepless nights at Levira's side, reports reached Young of Gibson's mutiny. Alarmed and angry, Young decided to send a party to investigate the situation, depose and excommunicate Gibson, restore order, and purge the church of any new rituals and beliefs. He chose the highest-ranking people he could spare to head the mission, the apostles Ezra T. Benson and Lorenzo Snow. Naturally, he would have preferred to send George Q. Cannon, who spoke Hawaiian and had helped open missionary work there, but because Cannon remained a world away in Liverpool, Young needed to look elsewhere for linguistic and cultural advisors for the expedition.[15] Chief among those Young wanted for this job was JFS.

In addition to his linguistic skills and familiarity with Hawaiian culture, JFS knew Gibson. By his own admission, he had become "very intimate with Gibson and his two sisters" during his sojourn in New York City in 1860.[16] That was enough to qualify him for the job. And, Young informed JFS, he would remain in Hawaii as mission president after the fiasco with Gibson was sorted out. The First Presidency set apart JFS for this latest mission on 29 February 1864.[17] Young summoned JFS to his office and gave him a blessing before he set out, promising him sufficient wisdom to discern truth from deception, setting him apart to "take charge of the mission when the Apostles" leave, and informing him that "your name shall be had among the nations of the earth for good and evil."[18] This last portion clearly echoes the words of Moroni to Joseph Smith Jr., proving once again that JFS marched forever beneath the shadow of the Mormon martyrs.

On his way to Hawaii, JFS stopped over in California and reunited with Ina Coolbrith, although the encounter seems to have been somewhat strained. Coolbrith found him secretive and gloomy, a far cry from the boy she had seen come and go from Hawaii in the 1850s. She was so troubled by this change in demeanor that she wrote him a letter in which she held nothing back. "Drop the mask!" she demanded. "Open your mouth and talk," and stop "going 'round with that long face of yours, as if there was nothing but sorrow in God's universe."[19] Few people would ever feel so free to critique JFS in such an aggressive manner, but Coolbrith's frankness shows us just how much the recent years had told upon JFS.

Another Mission in Hawaii

JFS soon found himself once again fighting seasickness as he crossed an ocean alone. Young had authorized Levira to travel to Hawaii, but she decided to go to San Francisco to await JFS's return. She arrived in California months after he left on his mission, getting to the coast in the fall.

JFS's letters from this period reveal that he missed Levira more than he had at their first parting; in one of the first letters he wrote, he made the frank admission "I did not think so much about you all the time I was in England, as I have done

132 Chapter 8

since I left you, three weeks ago."[20] One wonders how Levira, ever sensitive to implied criticism, and still quite unwell, took this remark. Nonetheless, JFS's letters to her during his second Hawaiian mission are far more heartfelt and romantic in tone and content than those he wrote from England. They are longer, more creative, and far warmer.

Probably contributing to this change in tone was the fear that Levira's life seemed endangered by her continuing illness, and part of it no doubt stemmed from JFS's distance after he had the brief opportunity to renew their relationship. Whatever the reasons, Levira and JFS reverse roles in these letters compared those they wrote during the British mission. Here, Levira comes across as far more open about her dark state of mind and ill health, and less concerned with how JFS will react. For his part, JFS seems almost desperate to prove that his feelings for her are deep, abiding, and genuine.

It is difficult, if not impossible, to read these letters outside of the shadow cast over the historical record by the agonizing divorce that we know looms in their near future. It is, perhaps, too easy to see in the letters of 1864 the foreshadowing of the catastrophe of 1867. That risk notwithstanding, it appears that JFS knows the relationship is strained, and he seems to be going out of his way to try to soothe it. Levira, however, appears to be far less concerned with JFS's opinion of her than she was before. He clearly wished he could be with her, but he was torn between his loyalty to Brigham Young and the church, and his growing uneasiness about the state of their marriage. In his letters, he did his best to argue that his almost constant absence from her on church business would, in the long run, benefit both of them. Levira disagreed.

JFS's worry over Levira's condition and disposition temporarily abated when, on 27 March 1864, the party arrived in Honolulu, where JFS enjoyed a "good meal of poi." It is worth remembering that during his first mission, poi had come to represent the hardship of his life on the islands, and he complained frequently about having to eat it. But in 1864, poi tasted like sweet nostalgia. "Six years ago I crossed this water, then gladly bid farewell to these lands," he wrote to Levira, and though he "thought never to return . . . here I am."[21]

JFS had grown a great deal even since he had left Britain, and a new and completely self-confident JFS emerges on this second sojourn in Hawaii. In a May 1864 letter to Levira, he described himself in the third person as a "gentleman who might have seen much for [his] years," who exhibited a "lofty, genteel, and easy manner," and "self-confidence" rooted in "experience and good sense." He was "good looking" with "manly features," and a "joyous countenance."[22] This letter is remarkable because it provides a rare glimpse of significant development and change in JFS's personality. When he arrived in Britain in 1860, he felt somewhat embarrassed by his lack of education, his dusty provincialism, and his lack of "manliness." By 1864, those deep self-doubts began to give way to a new perception of himself as a man of the world, a man of style, a man of experience, a man of wisdom, and, finally, and most importantly, a man. Although JFS rarely backed away from a challenge, even in his early years, this stronger sense of self would, in the coming decades, contribute to more intense conflicts than he had ever before experienced. Not until his old age, when he came under the sometimes vicious scrutiny and lampooning of the national press, would he again be plagued by feelings of inadequacy and weakness.

JFS's newfound confidence proved necessary for dealing with the situation that confronted him in Hawaii. Gibson had proclaimed himself prophet and "had ordained twelve apostles, high priests, seventies, elders, bishops." He had even invented a new office: "priestess of the temple." Gibson had also commanded the Hawaiian Mormons to turn over their worldly goods and whatever money they had to him, after which he would provide for them according to their needs. With these funds, Gibson purchased about 6,000 acres of land in the Palawai District. Benson and Snow demanded that Gibson sign the land over to the church, but he refused, arguing that "he had not been sent here by the Church" and had "acted on his own responsibility for what he had done."[23]

Both of those statements are technically true: it was Gibson, not Young, who initiated his mission to Asia, and he certainly had been acting under his "own responsibility" the entire time. There was no doubt that Gibson had acted in bad faith—both in his claims to Young and other leaders about his conversion to Mormonism, and his loyalty to the church and to the Hawaiian Mormons to whom he lied.

It took very little time for JFS and the others to deal with Gibson, at least as far as his influence in the church was concerned. It became clear that Gibson had convinced many Mormons that he possessed special, supernatural powers, and that he used this as an important means of control. One thing Gibson did to orchestrate this perception was to create a sacred shrine composed of various shrubbery forming an enclosure around some mysterious stones. Taking a cue from the stories of Moses in the Hebrew Bible, he told everyone that this shrine was too sacred to be touched or entered, and that anyone doing so would be struck dead. The settlement buzzed with stories of children who had accidentally contacted the shrine and "had dropped dead." When JFS learned about the site, he commandeered a horse and headed straight for it. To the horror of the surrounding witnesses, JFS angrily attacked the shrine, sending the shrubbery skyward and climbing all over it. When he did not immediately perish, JFS made the then-unnecessary observation that the shrine was nothing more than "a teepee of brush and poles," dealing a serious blow to Gibson's credibility among the Hawaiian Mormons. Soon, Gibson's little settlement was deserted, and his followers left to try to rebuild their lives.[24]

Getting rid of Gibson would prove to be the easiest of the missionaries' several tasks. They also had the responsibility of "travelling through the mission, re-organizing the branches and ... establishing the church anew, instructing and encouraging the Saints, baptizing new members, and correcting the many erroneous

134   Chapter 8

ideas and principles introduced by Gibson."[25] Snow, Benson, JFS, and the others did not have many options when it came to dealing with Gibson. They confronted him in a public meeting in which both sides took turns making their respective cases in front of the gathered Hawaiian Mormons. At first, Gibson seemed to have the advantage and the support of the majority of the Hawaiians. Elder Snow, sensing the dynamics of the meeting, arose and informed everyone that if they wished to remain members of the church, they had to renounce Gibson, leave the settlement, and confess their sins to JFS, who would be left in charge of the church in Hawaii.

Next they excommunicated Gibson and made sure that everyone knew that he had gone rogue. This meant that JFS had to speak to congregation after congregation, informing them of Gibson's fate and correcting the unorthodox beliefs and practices that he had introduced. He also had to deal with the difficult task of finding new places for some of the congregations to meet because Gibson had sold many of the church's meeting houses. More importantly, they had moved the de facto headquarters of the church from Palawai to Laie and were encouraging church members to gather there. (The Laie plantation would be JFS's hiding place during the polygamy raids of the 1880s, and it was eventually the location of a temple.)

Benson and Snow left two weeks after excommunicating Gibson, and JFS spent the next few months as the leader of the church. He visited branches wherever they were located and tried to ensure that they were running in as orderly a manner as possible. He left Hawaii in October 1864.

Just before leaving the islands, JFS wrote to Samuel H. B. Smith that he was preparing to "take up the line of march once more for home, tho' it almost seems that my home is the wide world."[26] It is no wonder he felt that way. By the time he became president of the LDS Church in 1901, JFS had spent more time on missions overseas than any previous church president, a record that still stands and will probably never be equaled. Though he was raised in the chaos of frontier life and death, he developed and never lost the sense of himself as a citizen of the world.

A Return Home, but No Reunion

When JFS arrived in California, on a foggy day in early November, he no doubt was anxious to be reunited with Levira. She had been staying with relatives, including Ina Coolbrith's family, since September. He was disappointed to learn that she was not in the city, having left to spend some time "in the country," so JFS visited Ina Coolbrith instead. What he could not have known is that the joyful reunion he hoped for would never happen.

Because Levira feared that she was not well enough to make the journey back to Utah in the cold weather, she did not want to return to Utah with JFS. Her aunt Derinda Kimball, whom JFS despised, tried to convince him to leave Levira behind until the spring; JFS would have none of it, remarking that "if she could stand it to come out, she could stand it to go back." Levira acquiesced, but they only got as far as Dutch Flats in northern Nevada. There, her health grew worse, and JFS consulted with some local women about the best course of action. After talking to Levira, they insisted that she was too ill to continue and should return to San Francisco. JFS accordingly put Levira on the next wagon train back.[27]

Almost as soon as Levira arrived back at her aunt's house, she began to bleed heavily. This greatly disturbed both of them because Levira believed she was in the early stages of pregnancy. The bleeding continued for a week, and a doctor informed her that she had probably miscarried the child.[28] Whether that is what happened or not is impossible to know. What we do know is that she continued to bleed heavily off and on for more than six months, a condition that kept her in bed much of the time and which contributed to a worsening of her depression.[29]

JFS, upset and lonely, continued on to Salt Lake. On 18 December 1864, he reported his mission to church leaders and other interested parties in the tabernacle on Temple Square, but he continued to worry about his own lack of employment.[30] Brigham Young remedied that immediately. On the evening of 22 January 1865, he ordered that Thomas Bullock, a longtime Church Historian's Office employee, be fired and replaced by JFS.[31] Mormons believe they have a sacred duty to keep a history of their church, and the Church Historian's Office in Salt Lake City was the hub of this operation. The office collected records, wrote a history of the church, and engaged in similar tasks. Young's reason for firing Bullock was the implausible claim that "I Believe Dr [Willard] Richards used to take any papers he could lay his hands upon for waste Papers whether they are valuable or not & I believe Thomas Bullock will do the same, & I dont want him in the office any longer."[32]

Richards, who had not only served as church historian but was also was a member of the First Presidency, had died in 1854. Now, more than a decade later, Young was accusing him of misconduct and implying that Bullock would engage in similar behavior. Even Wilford Woodruff found this hard to swallow, recording in his journal that he had "never known either Richards or Bullock [to] destroy any valuable papers But always looked upon them as faithful honest men."[33] Young could certainly be capricious, but the firing of Bullock was an unusually callous act. Clearly, he was willing to go to great lengths to ensure that JFS had a steady job doing work that would bring him into close contact with members of the church hierarchy.

JFS's work for the Church Historian's Office was largely clerical; he took dictation from Woodruff and George A. Smith, organized documents, and ran errands, but he also shoveled snow. Occasionally, he would participate in the writing of church history, using documents such as Young's letter books and Woodruff's journals as primary source material. JFS's position also provided him with the opportunity to speak in the tabernacle on subjects such as "the great ascendency of the

136 · Chapter 8

Latter-day Work."[34] He also worked in the Endowment House as a recorder and an ordinance worker, in which capacity he oversaw the performance of the various rituals. The Endowment House was where Mormons went to participate in the sacred rituals of endowment and sealing, as well as baptisms for the dead.[35]

Although his work kept him busy, and JFS enjoyed occasional outings to the theater in Salt Lake City, he was becoming increasingly concerned about Levira. Almost from the beginning of this most recent separation, he had been displaying a monumentally paranoid and jealous attitude. A letter from Levira in January 1865 reveals that JFS suggested that she had returned to California to facilitate some sort of romantic dalliance.[36] Apparently this was not the first time he had alleged such a thing during their married life, as would eventually become clear during their 1867 divorce.

Levira responded to the allegation with pronounced indignation and a warning:

> it is unkind of you to imagine so base, and cruel a thing of me and to upbraid me for circumstances and afflictions which I am powerless to avoid. . . . But it is not the first time my heart has been pierced by similar insinuations. If you are still inclined to doubt my virtue, <u>sir</u>, you are perfectly welcome to enjoy your very exalted opinions of your wife. But beware you do not drive me to win the <u>game</u> of which it would seem I have won the <u>name</u>.[37]

When JFS was not angrily accusing Levira of infidelity, he was sulking about his loneliness. He agonized over his separation from her. She had initially been staying with Agnes Smith and Ina Coolbrith, but JFS learned, to his dismay, that she had left in early 1865 and taken up residence with her maternal aunt Derinda and Derinda's husband, Hazen Kimball, who had left the LDS Church and moved to California in the late 1840s. Derinda found JFS repellant; she was disgusted that a pair of cousins had married, and she "hoped that [Levira] would never have a baby by him."[38]

Levira had moved in with the Kimballs because she could no longer take the verbal abuse dished out by Ina's stepfather, Mr. Pickett. Levira apparently moved back in with Ina at some point, but the Kimballs insisted on visiting her, and Ina worried that this could seriously damage her reputation among San Francisco society. In the early months of 1865, however, Ina continued to reassure JFS that Levira was not being unduly influenced by the Kimballs or anyone else. In fact, Ina was growing frustrated at Levira's refusal to do anything at all, good or bad. She eventually concluded that Levira was a "hypochondriac" and said she was "worse than a child"; she had no energy, no interest in anything, and brooded constantly, yet no one could find anything physically wrong with her. Of course today we recognize these symptoms as anhedonia and psychomotor retardation, two classic symptoms of major depressive disorder. But to Ina, and those around her, it seemed that Levira just needed to shake herself off and get on with her life. Still, despite all Levira's ailments, Ina concluded that she remained "pure-minded, honest and true."[39]

In May 1865, Dr. C. White, who had been treating Levira, wrote to JFS about her condition. He believed that she was suffering from "chronic inflammation of the womb," which he judged to be "of long standing." However, he noted that Levira's "much shattered nervous system" was improving. On a point that would become important during the couple's divorce proceedings, the physician noted that Levira's recovery was being hampered by her "neglect" and "disobedience" of his recommendations, but even this had proved only a minor impediment. He cleared her for a return to Utah in June.[40]

JFS responded to this news with a mixture of excitement and thinly veiled anger. He wrote to Dr. White of his relief that Levira had shown signs of improvement and exclaimed that "it would be the greatest happiness of my life to once more see my wife in the possession and enjoyment of sound mental and physical health. She has suffered immensely."[41] But JFS had more to say that was less convivial. After thanking the doctor for providing Levira with months of free medical treatment, he tartly concluded, "I flatter myself with the belief that under my protection and personal care she would be better off—healthier—than she is today. I may be mistaken, but I think not." JFS's contempt was directed largely at the Kimballs and what he viewed as their evil influence over Levira, but he disliked physicians anyway, so he could not have been pleased with the idea that he was in a position to have to rely on charity from a "gentile" doctor.[42] As he later put it, he preferred his doctor to be "a man of faith & little medicine."[43]

JFS's mood grew increasingly foul as the weeks passed. In fact, his resentment over the "unwelcome, unwished for and hateful separation" careened rapidly toward bitterness.[44] He complained that he was living "the life of a hermit" who "cares for nobody and goes nowhere."[45] In response to one letter that no longer exists, Levira wrote that she feared JFS "could do something desperate" because his letters indicated that he was "dreadfully out of temper."[46] When she asked him why he felt so angry, he wrote,

> You have treated lightly my counsel, to say the least and you have not seconded my wishes, but you have opposed me in your feelings and by your words. This is what weighs me down, but all evil shall have an end. If you had placed confidence in me, acted upon my counsel, stuck to me as almost any other true woman and wife would have done to her husband instead of being lead [sic] by the advice of others, who are not your true friends or given way to the silly whims of silly minds, you would today have been richer, healthier, happier, better and more beloved by true friends. When I met you in San Francisco, if you had felt right, or enjoyed the good spirit, you would have said "now Joseph, you know I am weak, and I would like to spend a little time here, but whatever you say do, that is right, and that

138   Chapter 8

we'll do!" Was it so? No Vira, you knew better than I did what was write [*sic*]—you did not ask my counsel, I took the liberty to counsel as I thought it was my right—you were offended. My advice was not welcome. You did not offer to be one and united with me regarding coming home as untimely and at last consented in anger after it had been put off to the latest moment. I never consented for a moment in my feelings for you to stay, but I saw you did not want to come and I was determined you should have your own way at the sacrifice of my own feelings. These are a few things that have troubled me, that have made me sorrowful. I know you were delicate and not strong, but I would have taken care of you as not many could, and you would and could have stood it as well as going back if your mind had been set on staying by me and going home.[47]

Levira did not always sympathize with JFS's sulkiness about her absence. In fact, she took the opportunity to remind him that the shoe was usually on the other foot.

You are just tasting of my feelings while you were in England, only not so long nor in the same circumstances. Yet it gives you some little idea of what a married life is like without a husband or a home. If I can stand all that I have had to endure, I think you can stand it until I can come home.[48]

The bickering continued via letters throughout June 1865, with Levira insulting the moral fiber of the population of Utah, accusing JFS of habitually "getting a person down and keeping them down," and finally concluding, "You do not know me."[49] JFS countered by saying that she was just making excuses for remaining in California. Levira grew increasingly bold as well. She gave JFS a "warning" that "if you make yourself morose and cross I will not love you."[50]

It was clear by the summer that Levira did not want to return to Utah. The tortured state of her marriage—as well as her conviction, shared with her aunt Derinda, that JFS was contemplating taking a plural wife—added to her reluctance to move back. In a letter written 27 July 1865, Levira hinted that she knew someone was trying to get between her and JFS, someone she probably suspected of courting her husband, and she warned him, "Do not try to make a fool of me." She wrote, "You think perhaps I don't know that there is an influence against me, a strong one, too!" And she made it clear that she was not interested in any such plans. "Let anyone, no matter who, undertake to step between you and me, when I am there to defend myself, and you'll find that as Levira has been meek and gentle, she can also be rash and wild."[51]

The entire dramatic first half of 1865 is worth pausing over. Most treatments of JFS's life skip this period, but a close examination of his and others' letters provides us with a wealth of insight into his mindset. He was clearly uncomfortable when he felt unable to control his life circumstances, and doubly so when he felt he could not control his wife. It is also clear that JFS desperately wanted the relationship to work out, but only on his terms. Levira's increasing independence and willingness to contradict her husband were probably not only infuriating but also embarrassing for him. In a letter to Levira's brother Samuel, JFS sculpted his narration of the circumstances that led to Levira's remaining in California in such a way that made it seem as if he were the one making the decision: "I left Levira in California because the weather was so cold she was afraid to come with me."[52] A minor deception, perhaps, but a telling one.

The final humiliation came in late July, when Levira telegraphed Brigham Young himself and arranged for him to pay her fare back to Utah.[53] JFS was furious and, again, felt insulted. Now twenty-seven, his life had consisted of one chaotic storm after another, and wave upon wave of loss and displacement. And just when he thought he could finally introduce some stability into his life, he seemed to feel that yet another person he loved had let him down. Levira did not die, as his parents had, but JFS knew he was losing her, or his imaginary version of her, in an equally profound way.

In some ways, Levira was a symbol of the possibility of a reconstituted existence in a new world where life and settled abundance would replace death and rootlessness. It appears that JFS felt he could not bear to lose that dream again, so when he realized that he had to give it up, it exposed the darkest shades of his character. In later years, JFS treated his wives differently from the way he treated Levira, perhaps in part because they did not bear the weight of expectation that he had placed on Levira and were not so symbolically important to him.

JFS Takes a Plural Wife

Perhaps unsurprisingly, JFS's reunion with Levira in Utah was not a particularly happy one. Levira spent considerable time living at her mother's home while JFS continued working at the Church Historian's Office and Endowment House. He was also trying to build a house.

In the spring of 1866, JFS took a plural wife. Very little can be said with certainty regarding the circumstances surrounding this development because no contemporary records remain. Tradition holds that JFS was instructed by Brigham Young to make the move, and this is probably true. In a response to an inquiry from Samuel H. B. Smith regarding a rumor that he had married again, JFS replied that it was true, and that he "had no other object in view other than to obey counsel." He reported, possibly disingenuously, that Levira "has so far performed her whole duty most nobly and good," and that she seemed fully in favor of entering into the "principle."[54] JFS also claimed that Levira was present at the marriage, or sealing, ceremony and "freely gave her consent thereto."[55]

Julina Lambson, the sixteen-year-old who became JFS's first plural wife, was the niece of his mentor and supervisor at the Church Historian's Office, George A. Smith. At the time, the office was located in George's home, and it was there that JFS and Julina first met. She noticed that he was quietly paying close attention to her, and she "thought he was the most handsome and finest man [she] had ever seen."[56] JFS proposed to her in a hallway, but she accepted only after obtaining permission from her uncle. In the Church Historian's Office journal for 5 May 1866, JFS himself noted that the "sealing" to Julina took place in the Endowment House "7 years to the day since he married his cousin, Levira A. Smith."[57] (In fact, JFS and Levira had married on 5 April.)

Very soon after the wedding, Levira moved in with her mother. She returned briefly, but apparently moved out permanently in August 1866. We can be certain that she was gone for good by December 1866 at the very latest because a doctor contacted JFS asking for payment for treatment he had administered to Levira at her mother's house between December 1866 and March 1867. When presented with the bill, JFS responded that he "knew nothing about it" because "previous to that time, she left my home and was acting entirely upon her own responsibility in defiance of me and my express wish, intending from the first to procure a divorce."[58] These facts stand in contrast to representations that JFS later made, as well as published family "memories" about the timing of Levira's departure from the family.

Years later, JFS claimed that "it was not until long after the second marriage [to Julina Lambson] that my first wife was drawn from us." In a genealogical publication from 1976, a descendant stated what must have been the long-standing family belief that Julina and Levira "got along well together until Julina's first baby was announced," at which point "Levira's mother ... filled Levira with thoughts that Joseph wouldn't love her as much now."[59] Neither of these statements comports with contemporary historical evidence. It is clear that JFS was correct in claiming that Levira did not leave because of polygamy; after all, the problems in that relationship long predated his marriage to Julina. However, there is no reasonable way to construe the phrase "long after" to fit the fact that she left, at most, a few months after the marriage. As to the charge that Levira left only after the announcement of Julina's pregnancy, it simply is not possible. Julina's first child, a girl named Mercy Josephine but nicknamed Jode, was born 14 August 1867, which meant she could have been "announced" no earlier than December 1867, at which time Levira was already living with her mother.

Although all of these developments no doubt exacerbated the situation, it is unfair to lay the blame at the door of Levira and her mother. JFS did his best, however, to locate the cause of the divorce outside of his own control. His first marriage failed, he said, "not on account of domestic troubles, but for other causes." Joseph Fielding Smith lists those causes as his father's frequent absences due to missionary work and "interference on the part of relatives."[60]

Marital Discord, Domestic Violence, and Divorce   141

While JFS's frequent extended absences and the involvement of family members no doubt played a part in the breakup, evidence produced at the time of the divorce by both Levira and JFS demonstrate beyond all doubt that rather serious domestic troubles played a major part. The sad details of the marriage's disintegration were recorded and preserved because the fighting between JFS and Levira attracted the attention of Brigham Young. Throughout the summer of 1867, JFS and Levira exchanged nasty letters full of petty bickering about the ownership of sheets, blankets, photographs, and letters. JFS wrote to acknowledge receipt of "two handkerchiefs, a roll of brown tape, a small pasteboard box with sundry trivial articles rather the worse for wear, which you have so graciously forwarded to me." In the same letter, he responded to a request from Levira for sheets and a quilt, saying, "[T]hey belong to me, were made and paid for with wool from my sheep, without one stroke of yours," and he refused to return them.

What angered JFS the most, however, was Levira's "brazen impudence manifested in two lines of [her] note, that in relation to '[his] cow Cherry'!! contemplating the deliberate effrontery intended."[61] JFS had a special sentimental connection to Cherry that lasted into the 1870s (when he finally ate her), an attachment that Levira seems to have been mocking. Levira claimed that she had nothing else belonging to him and requested that he "be kind enough to destroy" the letters she had written.[62] Obviously, he did not.

Divorce

Finally, in August 1867, Young intervened to settle the dispute. He requested that Levira provide him with a statement outlining the problems in the marriage as part of her attempt to secure a "just and righteous settlement" and her "lawful share" of JFS's property. In her statement, Levira painted a profoundly unflattering portrait of JFS, claiming that from the earliest days of their marriage he had refused to provide her with the necessities of life, and that he had behaved cruelly toward her, embarrassing her in front of friends and family. She noted that he had a habit of "commanding" rather than "asking," and mocked her mental struggles by saying that she "ought to have a hole bored in the top of [her] head and some manure put into it for brains." She said JFS was impatient and physically threatening, and that his jealousy brought out the worst in him. She claimed that he once insinuated that her inability to have children made it possible for her to "whore it up" without anyone "being the wiser."[63]

Levira also recounted another incident that occurred when JFS found her alone in her room with a "gentile" named Harris, whom she claimed was simply reading to her. She said that when JFS discovered them, "he called me a d__m whore a little damned illegitimate whore and a liar and if he ever caught a man in my room again

142   Chapter 8

there would be bloodshed if he had to swing for it, he threw my chair back against the stove." But as disturbing as these threats of bloodshed are, even more disturbing are Levira's accusations of actual violence. She claimed that on one occasion after she and JFS reunited in Utah in 1865, he had ordered her to remain in bed according to her doctor's instructions. When she got up to investigate the sound of a band playing outside, "He immediately came in with a rope which he doubled four or five times and struck me five or six times across my back notwithstanding I begged of him not to strike me."[64]

Young immediately provided JFS with a copy of Levira's statement and invited him to respond. This is made clear by JFS's handwritten responses on the letter itself. Thirteen days later, he submitted his own statement to Young. JFS denied some things, especially the charge that he refused to provide for her, but, in the main, his statement was calculated to contextualize rather than deny. He admitted telling Levira that drilling a hole in her head and filling it with manure would "be an improvement," but he insisted that she knew it was spoken "in jest." He similarly admitted that he had, in fact, threatened to murder any man he caught with his wife, and admitted, "I do believe that if I had been armed I would have done violence."[65]

JFS knew that shooting any man "caught with his wife" would have drawn little attention from Young or anyone else in the 1860s. Even a decade later, the *Deseret News* published an article titled "Adulterer Shot" that reported on a case in Pennsylvania in which a husband murdered his wife's lover by shooting him in the head. "The sympathy of the people," the piece concluded, "seems to be altogether with [the shooter]."[66] Given this context, JFS's unflinching ownership of his threat to kill a suspected adulterer is not surprising.

On the most serious point—Levira's accusation that JFS beat her with a rope—he hedged a bit. He admitted that he hit her, but not "5 or 6 times," and not with a rope. Rather, he said, it was twice with a branch from a peach tree no bigger around than "the butt of an office pencil." JFS claimed that he had no choice because Levira was out of control, raving like a lunatic, "insane or possessed," running outside in her nightclothes and refusing to rest in bed as the doctor had ordered.[67]

JFS's framing of the incident is important because in the nineteenth century, the abuse of women was tolerated, but only within certain parameters. Widely accepted Anglo-American legal ideas dating back to the eighteenth century granted a man the right to "chastise" his wife through violence "as long as he did not inflict permanent injury upon her." This "doctrine of chastisement," as it was known in legal circles, held that a husband, "as master of the household, could command his wife's obedience, and subject her to corporal punishment or 'chastisement' if she defied his authority."[68] Wives and children held basically the same legal status with regard to corporal punishment: a husband and father was responsible, legally and morally, for the behavior of his dependents and therefore had the responsibility to discipline them in any way that did not result in serious injury. JFS's description fits his actions into this rule of discipline, claiming that his actions were not likely to cause injury in violation of the doctrine of chastisement. Furthermore, he was careful to point out that the beating was a correction given because she had defied his authority, refused to follow doctor's orders, and was, in his own words, "like a willful and disobedient child."[69]

From our modern perspective, these distinctions are meaningless, but from the perspective of nineteenth-century American cultural norms, the differences in Levira's and JFS's accounts are anything but minor. Men were sometimes subjected to beatings and/or jail terms when they violated the doctrine of chastisement by beating a wife in public, doing serious injury to her, or beating her without any obvious attempt to reform behavior. JFS framed his version of the events to demonstrate that his actions did no significant physical harm, occurred in private, and were an attempt at reform rather than an expression of spite, acts of revenge, or simple anger. He was thus assumed to have acted within his prerogatives as a husband, and no action, ecclesiastical or otherwise, was taken against him. However repugnant such acts were, it is the unfortunate fact that they found a great degree of legal, cultural, and even ecclesiastical acceptance in 1867.

On 4 January 1867, JFS and his wife Julina received their second anointings, the holiest ritual of the LDS Church, under the hands of Heber C. Kimball.[70] Levira moved to California, where she filed for divorce from JFS on the grounds of adultery with Julina Lambson.[71] He did not see her again until 1871, when she "arrived from California in a state of insanity."[72] That may have been the last time he ever encountered her, but not the last time he mentioned her. In a letter written nearly a decade after the divorce, JFS comforted a man with a seriously ill wife by telling him that he understood because he had been in a similar situation. "The Lord raised her up" from her sickbed, he wrote, "but alas!" her physical healing did not result in lasting happiness. In fact, JFS suggested that she might have been better off had she died: "I could have withstood her burial more complacently than much that I have been compelled to witness. To me, death is preferable to apostasy."[73]

JFS rarely mentioned Levira, and for the rest of his life he referred to Julina as his first wife, but on the very rare occasion that his marriage to Levira came up, it was clear that he remained sensitive about the issue. As late as 1909, he was asked if it was true that he "divorced or put away" his "first wife." JFS denied it, presumably on the grounds that Levira divorced *him*, adding that "this is a matter that in no legitimate way concerns the curious nor the meddler into private family affairs."[74]

9 | JFS the Apostle, JFS the Polygamist

Joseph F. Smith's entry into plural marriage was an important event for a variety of reasons, one of which is that it opened the door for his advancement in the hierarchy. Although not all Mormon men had multiple wives, almost all of those who held the position of bishop or higher had at least two. All of the church's apostles practiced plural marriage during this period.

It is possible that Brigham Young encouraged JFS to enter the practice because he planned on moving him higher up in the hierarchy. JFS was actively participating in the prayer circles of the general authorities who met regularly upstairs in the Historian's Office—a sign of his increasing prominence.[1] On 1 July 1866, Young, John Taylor, Wilford Woodruff, and George A. Smith, each of whom was an apostle and/or a member of the First Presidency, held their prayer circle in the Historian's Office. Rounding out this group was JFS, who up until that time had held no higher church office than member of the Salt Lake stake high council.

After Young finished the prayer, he arose from his knees and removed his ritual apron, part of the holy robes worn during the prayer circle ceremony. Suddenly he stopped in his tracks and announced that the "sprit constrains me" to ordain "Joseph F. Smith to the apostleship. And to be one of my counsellors."[2] Young polled the others to see if any of them disagreed and, finding unanimity, he performed the ordination and "the setting apart" on the spot.[3] In the blink of an eye, JFS had become the first member of the Joseph Smith Sr. family since his father to assume a place in the First Presidency. From this moment, the trajectory of his life would change dramatically, and he would be able to carve a legacy of his own out of the mountain of his father's memory.

It is not clear why Young decided to take this action when he did. There were no vacancies in the First Presidency, but it was not unusual for extra counselors to be added from time to time. Perhaps, as he stated, Young felt that some supernatural force had demanded the action be taken, and he simply complied. However, there may have been another force at work. Young knew that two of Joseph Smith's sons, Alexander and David, were planning to come to Utah in August on a proselytizing mission for the newly formed Reorganized Church of Jesus Christ of Latter Day Saints.

RLDS missionaries had been in Utah since 1863, but the Smiths' visit represented something very different for the members of the RLDS Church and for Brigham Young. Joseph Smith III had been unimpressed with the efforts of the first RLDS missionaries in Utah since their arrival in 1863, and at the church's 1866 general conference, he proposed that Alexander Smith be appointed head of the mission in Utah. Roger Launius, Joseph Smith III's biographer, has argued that the RLDS president "believed that the stature of the martyr's son functioning for the RLDS in Utah would intensify the missionary effort and build a solid base of [RLDS membership] in the intermountain West." Until Young directly instructed his people to stay away, they had "flocked" to Alexander's meetings.[4]

While impossible to prove, it is not unreasonable to surmise that Young worried that the presence of Joseph Smith's sons, personally bearing witness that Joseph Smith III now had a church and was the rightful heir to his father, might have a certain appeal to Latter-day Saints living in Utah. Young would surely have recognized that he could never match Joseph Smith's mythological status in the minds of the Mormon people, but he had managed to carve out a special place for himself as the rescuer of Joseph Smith's church. But what if that church no longer needed rescuing? What if a Latter-day Saints Church with a man named Joseph Smith at its head were able to successfully reestablish itself?

I doubt that Young feared a mass exodus from Utah, but I also suspect that bringing JFS into the First Presidency one month before Joseph Smith's sons arrived in Utah for the first time was not mere coincidence. Whatever Young intended, the move reminded Utah Mormons that not only did they, unlike their RLDS cousins, practice all of the principles introduced by Joseph Smith—most importantly, polygamy—but they, too, could lay claim to the Smith bloodline. Little surprise, then, that in JFS's first public sermon after being installed as a member of the First Presidency, he singled out Alexander Smith as a representative of evil:

> I have seen and conversed with men, have known the feelings of their hearts and seen that they were just as full of the darkness of hell as they could be. So full and firmly rooted were they in darkness and ignorance and in a determination not to receive the truth that, though angels and ministering spirits had taught them, they would still have preferred to remain in ignorance and unbelief. I was forcibly reminded of this a short time ago, when in conversation with Alexander H. Smith. Do you suppose an angel would convince him? He said that no human testimony could convince him. They will not receive the testimony of men, yet they will quote and reiterate the testimonies of men whom we know to be as wicked and corrupt as the devil; but when Prophets and Apostles ordained under the hands of the Prophet Joseph, and who are carrying out the very plans and purposes made manifest

146   Chapter 9

through him, bear testimony of these things, their testimony is rejected, for they will not receive the testimony of men. It is simply this—we will not have the truth, we cannot bear it, and you cannot force it upon us—we do not want it.[5]

While the presence of Alexander Smith in Utah in 1866 did not end up having a significant impact on either the LDS or the RLDS Churches, Young continued to wage a war of words with Joseph Smith III and his representatives for decades over the question of Joseph Smith Jr.'s involvement with polygamy. Young would yet find ways that JFS could become an important agent in that conflict.

After his divorce from Levira, JFS's life went on largely as before. He continued to work in the Historian's Office and the Endowment House, and, in apparent contrast to his relationship with Levira, he delighted in Julina and their daughter, Josephine. But with Levira gone, Young urged the newly monogamous JFS to find another plural wife. How he settled on Sarah Richards is unclear. Family lore holds that JFS and Julina together drew up a list of eligible women and they agreed on Sarah.[6] Sarah and JFS married on 1 March 1868. Like Julina and JFS, Sarah was well-connected to the elite first generation of Mormons. Her father was Willard Richards, an early convert to Mormonism and a counselor to Brigham Young in the First Presidency until his death in 1854.

The marriage to Sarah came at the same time as JFS's first major assignment as a general authority of the church. He, Wilford Woodruff, and a few others were instructed by Brigham Young to move to Provo, a town in Utah Valley some forty-five miles from Salt Lake City. Young was unhappy with the way Provo was being governed. The most commonly cited reason for his displeasure is that an outlaw environment was developing in Provo, with violent crime and vigilante activity on the rise. But Young was also concerned with the reluctance of some of Provo's leaders to commit to trading only with Mormon-owned companies.[7]

As the completion of the transcontinental railroad drew closer, Young was "anxious to promote economic growth and cultural sophistication" on the one hand, while "maintaining a covenant kingdom" on the other. He made several moves intended to make these goals viable, including reintroducing the Relief Society for women and Schools of the Prophets for men.[8] While JFS strongly supported the latter, he expressed ambivalence over the former. He told the Salt Lake 16th Ward Relief Society that he "did not understand . . . the entire object of the organization of these societies," hinting that mothers, "often . . . having sole charge of their families" in the absence of their missionary husbands, did not need anything to draw them away from their domestic duties.[9]

On the economic front, Young announced a boycott of "gentile" businesses and introduced the idea of a widespread merchandising cooperative under the name Zion's Cooperative Mercantile Institution (ZCMI). Local towns with their own CMIs would feed into the central ZCMI.[10] Young's desire to ensure that "gentile" businesses found no customers in Utah found some resistance in Provo. His response was to send a cohort of trusted men to Provo and have them elected to the city council and other ecclesiastical and government positions. Young announced his intentions at a meeting of the Salt Lake School of the Prophets on 31 January 1868. Wilford Woodruff recorded in his journal that "President Young Nominated Abram O. Smoot to go to Provo as President, Mayor & Bishop of that Place & John Taylor as Judge and a Number of Others as City Councillors."[11] On 10 February, less than two weeks after Young announced his plan, an election was held in Provo. To no one's surprise, all of Young's candidates were elected to the exact offices he had chosen for them.[12] Consequently, JFS set up temporary housekeeping with Sarah in Provo, leaving Julina behind at their permanent home in Salt Lake.

JFS spent most of his time traveling with Smoot throughout the settlements in Utah Valley, holding meetings at which they explained how the cooperative movement worked and its importance to the prosperity of the church, and encouraged Mormons to "subscribe for shares."[13] The pitch must have been persuasive because the residents of Provo and the surrounding settlements "subscribed for shares in a spirited manner."[14] In Provo, JFS and Sarah moved in to a ten-by-ten-foot adobe house, and he found work at a cabinet shop for thirty cents an hour. He worked at the shop whenever church or city business lulled, and he also took the opportunity to make furniture for the small adobe home.[15] Not long after JFS finished making the furniture, Young ended the experiment and called JFS and the others back to Salt Lake.[16]

Even while living in Provo, JFS had made occasional trips to Salt Lake, usually on business, but occasionally for recreation. In October 1868, he was delighted to attend a reunion of the living members of Zion's Camp, a grueling march from Ohio to Missouri during which many died or became very ill, which was a seminal moment in LDS history. JFS met with twenty-nine veterans of the march, including the oldest, eighty-nine-year-old John Duncan. For JFS, moments like this mingled the mythic past of the church with his own family history, and he found them mesmerizing.[17]

That same month all of the members of the First Presidency and the Quorum of the Twelve Apostles assembled in the same place for the first time in more than thirty-two years.[18] Since the Kirtland period, members of these groups had been on missions or otherwise unavailable for general conferences. Wilford Woodruff recalled that the last time they had all convened was in a tense meeting at Heber C. Kimball's home in Kirtland. Disgusted by the squabbling, Brigham Young had "prayed to God that that Quorum might never again meet until they Could meet in peace."[19] This story has to be read with caution, however, since Woodruff himself was not present and not yet a member of the Quorum when the meeting took place. But Woodruff saw the 1868 reunion as evidence that unity had returned.

In fact, only three of the men present at the meeting in Kirtland were still living: Orson Pratt, Orson Hyde, and Young himself. Brigham Young Jr. was called to fill a vacancy in the Quorum of the Twelve, relieving JFS of being the least senior

148   Chapter 9

member of the group.[20] To mark the occasion, the First Presidency and the Twelve assembled on 11 October 1868 to have a photograph taken by Charles Savage. The image is striking, with Brigham Young, John Taylor, Lorenzo Snow, Orson Hyde, Orson Pratt, George Q. Cannon, and the others all in the same photo. The men are seated in wooden chairs, with the three members of the First Presidency at the front and Young in the center. The apostles are seated behind them in a rough semicircle.

At the far right of the group sits JFS, slightly reclined and turned away from the others, his position providing a relatively rare view of his entire frame. We see a broad-shouldered man with large feet, eyes that appear almost black, a receding shock of dark hair, mutton-chop sideburns, and a moustache. His position on the very edge of the group probably mirrored his feelings. Most of the men in that image had been members of Mormonism's founding generation, personally acquainted, as adults, with Joseph and Hyrum Smith. These men had built the temples in Kirtland and Nauvoo, and had led the exodus to the West. JFS felt close to very few of them, but he held all of them in a regard that bordered on reverence. There is no doubt that, in 1868, he still saw himself as an outsider, but if he felt intimidated, he did not show it.

On 9 February 1869, less than a year after their marriage, Sarah gave birth to their first child, a girl named Sarah Ella. Six days later, the baby died. JFS would lose thirteen children during his lifetime, and each loss torched his soul.[21] Sarah Ella's death opened a door to a level of suffering that JFS had never before known. The loss of his parents had been heartbreaking; the loss of his children would prove soul-crushing. He lost his first child when he was thirty and would continue to lose them until 1918, the year of his own death. He lost five children between 1877 and 1886 alone.

In the case of Sarah Ella, JFS grew desperate to determine the cause of her death. He wrote to Sarah's half brother, Heber J. Richards, a young doctor, explaining the circumstances surrounding the baby's death and asking for answers. JFS believed the child had been born prematurely, but Richards disagreed, writing that "you are mistaken in its birth being premature. A child is considered viable after the seventh month." Rather, Richards believed the child probably died from "atelectasis pulmonum which is the medical term for imperfect expansion of the lungs. Every child should be made to cry as hard as it can that it may completely expand its lungs."[22]

Just over a year later, JFS's first child, Josephine, whom he called Jode, became ill. JFS continued his work at the Endowment House but was distracted by the child's declining condition. When at home, JFS would hold her on his lap and feed her strawberries and cold water. When she did not improve, JFS grew increasingly distraught: "I have no appetite, my sympathy and solicitude for my darling little Josephine, has greatly bowed my spirit." Despite such oppressive feelings, he wrote, somewhat uncertainly, that "I think I have received a testimony that she will not die."[23]

The next day, 6 June 1870, as JFS reluctantly prepared for work at the Endowment House, he spoke to his little daughter, telling her that she had not slept much the night before. After giving him a hug and a kiss, she said, "I'll sleep today Papa." But JFS would never see his daughter alive again. When he returned from the Endowment House that evening, she lay dead, and he nearly broke down. He poured his grief into his journal in the form of a prayer to Jode, complete with the traditional language of prayer:

> Oh, my Jode, my heart is nearly broken for the loss of you. You came to me when my heart was wrung in a time of deep trouble, sorrow, and affliction, like a golden sun-beam of joy. Thou wert a green oasis in my hitherto desert life.... Thou didst make me a better man. For thy sake I loved humanity, earth, and Heaven, more. Thou didst draw me nearer unto God, and purify my heart."

He implored his daughter to "in thy spirit visit me ... do my bidding and ... watch over us."[24]

In less prayerful language, JFS recorded his almost unspeakable pain at seeing his "little earthly angel gone, my heaven on earth removed, the brightest stars of my hope obscured, darkening all of my mortal existence." His heart had been "rent to the core, the tenderest fibers shredded by the cold and cruel hand of death." Each time JFS entered the house, the pain exploded again, causing him to conclude that "home has lost its brightest charm for me, no pattering little footsteps, no beaming little black eyes ... no soft little arms and hands to clasp me round the neck [nothing but] a vacant little chair, her little toys concealed, her clothes put by." In a haunting image, JFS described how he would "wander through the rooms," "look in vain," hear "no sound." "All is vacant," he wrote "lonely, deserted, desolate"; he found nothing but "the one desolate thought forcing its leaden, crushing weight upon my heart, 'She is not there! She is gone!'"[25]

Of all the losses JFS endured, the death of his firstborn child had one of the most profoundly deep and long-lasting impacts, and he resented attempts by well-meaning friends who encouraged him to temper his grief. Eliza R. Snow, in particular, rankled JFS when she suggested that "manhood" called for a more "stoical" response. This advice, he said, far from helping to ameliorate his grief, "fell like a grindstone on my heart."[26]

In violation of the gender norms of his day, JFS refused to hide his tears, although he had decidedly mixed feelings about them. He lacked the capacity to compartmentalize strong emotions, particularly anger and grief, and as a result, expressions of rage and tears became part of JFS's public persona, something that became more obvious as he aged. With the tears, however, always came doubts about his masculinity. After one public display of tears, he wondered aloud to the congregation, "I don't know if I will ever get over being a baby or not."[27] But more

150   Chapter 9

tears came on 8 June 1870, when JFS and Julina buried their daughter in Salt Lake in a fourteen-dollar glass-lidded coffin.[28]

More than a decade after JFS's death, Julina wrote that he

> never got over losing his first born.... She came to us when he needed comfort, and she filled the bill.... When she died we had another baby girl Mamie which he used to take in his arms, walk the floor, and cry. I have had eleven children, he has loved them all with as great a love as a human could have, but he never got where he could talk of [Jode] without tears in his eyes.[29]

The journals of JFS and Julina provide important clues about JFS's emotional state at the time of Jode's birth. The despair and desolation they describe also undoubtedly relates to his divorce from Levira. JFS hoped that his daughter would help ease the pain of yet another loss, only to have her become another lost part of himself. He noted also that the child made him more empathetic to those around him. Jode's life and death may have done a great deal to cool and bank JFS's temper, at least as far as his family was concerned. After she died, he apparently never laid a hand on any of his wives again, and only sparingly used corporal punishment on his children.

Confronting death, either in his own family or among his friends, always led JFS to make clear expressions of his religious views. Because religion suffused all aspects of his daily life, he did not often pause to make note of it; his religion was as much a part of him as his own appearance, and just as unlikely to generate self-reflection. After Jode's death, JFS, to an extent not evident before, saw illness in his children as an evil rather than something natural—an idea that was in tension with his belief that God had chosen to call his loved ones back to heaven.

When his daughter Mary became "very sick" in the fall of 1870, JFS did not seem at all conflicted about the cause. After watching the child vomit and suffer all night, he "laid hands on her, anointing with oil, rebuked the disease, and the Destroyer, commanding the blessing of life upon her." After this, "she seemed better," JFS recorded, "and I felt greatly relieved myself."[30] His tendency to frame illness and death in explicitly religious ways highlights not only the depth of his faith, but also the particular aspects of Mormon theology that seemed to attract him the most: the ongoing conflict between good and evil, and the eternal nature of the family.

JFS, perhaps like all parents in similar circumstances, romanticized his children any time death took them from him. In the winter of 1907–1908, many years after his first such loss, JFS lost two loved ones within the span of three months. In December 1907, his thirty-six-year-old daughter Leonora died, and in March 1908, his daughter-in-law Louie Shurtliff passed away. In a spate of letters written just after Louie's death, JFS took the opportunity to praise these two women as "two of the choicest souls" who ever lived. Louie was "young, accomplished, and beloved by all." She and Leonora were "the most perfect women it has ever been my privilege or good fortune to know." No one, he wrote, could be as "pure and true and good" as these two women.[31] In one of the letters, this one to a distant relative not of the LDS faith, JFS also extolled the virtues of his children still living. "Not one of them," he wrote, "has ever darkened the door of a saloon, a pool room, a gambling house, or place of ill repute; not one has ever used intoxicating drink or narcotic drug."[32]

JFS's tendency to review the righteousness of his posterity when death was on his mind goes far beyond the typical lionization of the dead by the living, perhaps because so many of his family members died during his lifetime, beginning with his father and ending with the death of his son Hyrum just months before his own death. JFS believed completely in the doctrine of eternal families, which had been introduced by Joseph Smith in the 1840s, but was ill-defined for decades. Until Wilford Woodruff ended the practice of dynastic sealing in 1894, most leaders had viewed the object of that practice as the creation of spiritual dynasties that would continue in the afterlife. It was common for prominent LDS leaders to "adopt" non-related persons into their patriarchal sealing chains because church policy disallowed the sealing of children to parents who had died without being baptized into the church.

JFS, while not disavowing the doctrine of adoption, was among the earliest LDS leaders to imagine the sealing doctrine in a strictly familial, rather than dynastic, sense. His emphasis on the eternity of the family unit, including children born to a couple on earth, was not a true innovation, but it can rightly be regarded as an elaboration on the principles outlined in Doctrine and Covenants 132. That revelation does not depict the sort of specific, eternal family-based heaven that JFS's adaptations of the sealing practice codified.

In 1890, the First Presidency and the Quorum of the Twelve decided that people could be sealed to parents who had been baptized but who died out of full fellowship of the church. JFS thought this did not go far enough, arguing that "children should be sealed to their parents even when the latter died without a knowledge of the gospel, and thus the connection with our ancestry should be extended as far back as it was possible for each."[33] There existed a problem in JFS's view, however. If parents had not embraced the gospel or had died outside of the faith, how could their worthiness be established?

Perhaps JFS's most enduring contribution to Mormonism was his 1918 revelation about the redemption of the dead, which solves the problem of how believers could be sealed to those who had not embraced the gospel. For JFS, the key to making this dream of eternal families a reality was the faithfulness of each family member to the sealing covenants of the temple. His review of the "worthiness" of his children after the deaths in 1907 and 1908 was rooted in his most pressing desire, which was that after death the most egregious wrongs inflicted upon him in life—namely, the untimely deaths of those he most deeply loved—would be permanently reversed unless unrepented sin blocked the path.

Confronting the Sons of Joseph Smith

The summer of 1869 saw the return of some of Joseph Smith's sons to Utah. Unlike the 1866 visit, this trip erupted into a brief but intense confrontation that played out publicly as well as privately. Alexander Smith returned, this time with his younger brother, David, who was born after his father died. On 17 July 1869, the Smith brothers faced Brigham Young and more than a dozen other LDS leaders, including JFS. Almost immediately, the meeting took a predictable turn toward hostility. By the time it was finished, Young had called Emma Smith the "damndest liar" on earth, and the "Smith boys" had returned the favor by insisting that Young had built his empire on the lie of Joseph Smith's polygamy. After concluding that the Smith brothers' "mission is to destroy the Church ... the foundation of which their father has laid," the group unanimously refused Alexander and David an opportunity to speak at the Salt Lake Tabernacle.[34] Undaunted, they found another venue in Corinne, a town in Box Elder County settled by non-Mormon railroad employees.[35]

It fell to JFS to counter the Smith brothers' claim that Joseph Smith never practiced nor taught plural marriage. He expected to find mountains of evidence directly linking his uncle with plural marriage, but to his shock discovered instead that people had been most circumspect in writing about the subject during the Nauvoo period. "I was astonished," he later wrote to Orson Pratt, "at the scarcity of evidence, I might say almost total absence of strict evidence upon the subject as connected with the Prophet Joseph himself." He could "not find a word, except for the revelation itself, showing that the Prophet was the author, under God" of the principle of plural marriage. Failing to find anything in the written records, JFS decided to collect "affidavits of as many as I know of ... who received personal instruction or commandment from the Prophet respecting the subject of celestial marriage."[36] These sworn statements, although far less effective than documentary evidence from the 1840s, would have to do.

The public exchanges between the cousins were brutal. JFS not only presented the historical evidence in the form of the affidavits, but he became so angry that he wandered off-script and accused Emma Smith of bearing a large part of the responsibility for the murder of Joseph and Hyrum, and that this stain would remain on her soul "until burned out by the fires of hell!" "This is hard," JFS acknowledged, "but I want these men to know that if they come here to raise their party, we will give them facts, and some of those facts will cut, and if they don't want them told, let them go away and keep their mouths shut." JFS expressed utter disgust and frustration at the brothers' "insolence and misrepresentations."[37]

With the weight of historical truth on their side regarding Joseph Smith's involvement with polygamy, Young and JFS would have been better served to leave Emma Smith's reputation out of the debate. Making wild and unfounded accusations, and generally disparaging the character of their opponents' mother, appeared unseemly and a bit desperate. It also gave her sons an issue to focus on other than Joseph Smith's polygamy. But JFS had found it difficult to curb his dim view of Emma throughout his life. For example, he once recorded in his journal, approvingly, a story about her that he heard from a man named Wellington Coolidge. Coolidge told JFS that he had been sealed by Joseph Smith to several women, and that he had recently visited Emma and broached the subject with her. According to Coolidge, Emma insisted that Joseph Smith had "abandoned plurality of wives before his death." When Coolidge offered his testimony to the contrary, Emma retorted that if she were wrong, her husband "was worthy of the death he died."[38] There is no way to verify Coolidge's claims, but they clearly rang true to JFS, and he accepted the story as more evidence of Emma's villainy.

Despite the drama, little of consequence resulted from the Smith brothers' sojourn in Utah, although it did provide JFS an opportunity to clarify just what he disliked most about the RLDS movement. The Smiths left Utah for California in November 1869, having managed to woo away only a few Brighamites, but they had shown they could hold their own in hostile territory.

JFS's personal dislike of his cousins had continued to solidify during the summer and fall of 1869. In August, JFS published an extract from Joseph Smith's journal in the *Deseret News*. While not addressing the Reorganized LDS Church directly, the extract helped to establish two facts: first, that Joseph Smith had intended before his death to establish Mormon settlements in "the mountains," and, second, that "to get salvation, we must not only do *some* things, but *everything* which God has commanded." JFS added the italics to his uncle's words, clearly intending to suggest that the RLDS Church's refusal to gather in the Rocky Mountains, along with their willingness to follow only "some" of God's commandments, would have met with disapproval from Joseph Smith, and they would "be damned at last."[39]

JFS continued to engage with the Smith brothers on the issue of plural marriage until 1914, when Joseph Smith III died. In JFS's view, the RLDS Church represented a far more malignant threat than even the sectarian world of false Christian churches. He often claimed that its goal was to destroy the true church established by Joseph Smith. While that is clearly an uncharitable and false interpretation of its mission, a close look at why JFS believed this provides a clue about what he saw as the absolute anchor of Mormonism. It was not plural marriage per se. Rather, "they strike at the very foundation of the work of God which Joseph Smith lived and died to establish, namely the sealing power," of which polygamy was only one type of "eternal union of husband wife." Without the power to seal families together, JFS asked, "what more are we than the sectarian world?"[40] "The miserable, apostate Josephites are a bad lot," he wrote, and he claimed that his "cousin, Joseph Smith, told me he preferred [to believe that Joseph Smith did not practice polygamy] and to maintain it as long as he could by any means fair or foul," regardless of the facts. JFS could not understand his cousin's mindset, asserting that he himself was "for the truth tho it awake the dead!"[41]

154   Chapter 9

As part of his ongoing surveillance of his cousins and their activities, JFS kept a close eye on the publications of the RLDS Church and any visits the cousins made to Utah. In 1872, he wrote to George A. Smith to get a formal rebuttal to claims made by David Smith at a meeting in Salt Lake that emissaries of Brigham Young, including George A., had made repeated visits to Joseph Smith III requesting that he come to Utah and take Young's place. JFS noted that this charge surfaced repeatedly in "one or more of their pamphlets." He wrote, "Having heard this, I feel that to be silent would make me to some extent particeps criminis if it is false." In order to avoid becoming an accomplice, JFS sought to "solicit from you or from President Young a statement of the facts of the case."[42]

Possibly because of his years working in the Historian's Office, as well as his frustration in 1869 at being unable to find much documentary evidence linking Joseph Smith to plural marriage, JFS insisted that any rebuttal provided by Smith or Young on the subject be provided "in writing." He wanted the historical record to be clear about Young's attitude toward the sons of Joseph Smith, recognizing that such a contentious issue might well outlive Young and cause potential problems for the church when it came time to name Young's successor. George A. Smith duly produced a denial of the charge, labeling it "a false fabrication without the last shadow of truth," and JFS filed the response away at the Historian's Office.[43]

A decade later, JFS would find that written response and the affidavits he had collected useful. In April 1879, Emma Smith died. Six months later, the RLDS newspaper, *The Saints Herald*, published an interview that Joseph Smith III had conducted earlier that year. In it, Emma was asked directly if Joseph Smith "had anything like [the revelation on plural marriage]? What of spiritual wifery?" Emma flatly denied the existence of any "revelation on either polygamy or spiritual wifery," and claimed that Joseph "had no other wife but me, nor did he to my knowledge ever have."[44]

After reading the interview, JFS decided that he could not remain silent. He responded by publishing in the *Deseret News* many of the affidavits that he collected in 1869, which he argued "should offer convincing proof to everyone who reads it, that the martyred Seer not only taught but entered into the practice of plural marriage."[45] It would also, JFS hoped, prove Emma Smith a brazen liar.

JFS and Territorial Government

In the 1860s and 1870s, JFS took an active role in territorial politics. In the fall of 1865, he won a seat representing Salt Lake City in the Utah House of Representatives. He took his oath of office on 11 December 1865 in rooms that "were neatly and comfortably furnished."[46] JFS was reelected six times, and he solidified his reputation as a principled man with a fiery temper. The secretary of the legislature, J. C. Reed, described him as "decisive in his remarks, contending for the right

JFS the Apostle, JFS the Polygamist   155

without fear or favor from any party." Reed warned that JFS was "especially active at wrestling [and] unless you want a fight, do not be prevailed upon to call him a liar."[47]

From 1872 to 1874, JFS served on the Salt Lake City Council, where he first drew the attention of the always hostile *Salt Lake Tribune*. In August 1872, the paper described him as having "a bad temper and worse taste," and being "a bitter and narrow minded fanatic" whose "affectation of superiority and sometimes positive insolence" rendered him "most unworthy" of a place on the city council.[48] JFS, the paper proclaimed, was a "natural ruffian and outlaw whose fanaticism leads him to distort all the images in the world's kaleidoscope, and to imagine that [all] others are robbers and rogues."[49]

In 1873, JFS introduced a resolution, adopted by the city council, that barred the *Tribune* from sending a reporter to council meetings "until that paper shall cease lying about and misrepresenting us and our proceeding." The *Tribune* responded by publishing a woodcut likeness of JFS with the caption "Elder Joseph F. Smith, how he appears in his sublunary state, the champion of the Church and the opponent of free speech, the man whose zeal outruns his discretion."[50] This would be the first, and by far the mildest, of many lampoonings that JFS would get in both the local and national press. Over the decades, there is a certain symmetry in both laudatory and derisive descriptions of him. While the opposing sides clearly disagreed about JFS's moral worth, they described his personal traits identically.

JFS did not record much about the nature of his business in the territorial legislature, but he did record his feelings about what he viewed as perpetual federal interference. Naturally, he held the federal appointees in disdain, and in the early 1870s he took a particular dislike to J. Wilson Shaffer, an Illinois politician appointed territorial governor of Utah by President Grant in 1870. Shaffer went to great lengths to antagonize the Mormon population by inserting himself into their affairs in a way that no previous official had done. After reading correspondence between Shaffer and Daniel H. Wells, JFS noted in his journal on 29 October 1870 that Shaffer was "showing himself more and more an ass."[51] Two days later, Shaffer suddenly died, an event that met with JFS's hearty approval. "Gov. Shaffer is dead, thank God," he wrote, eulogizing the governor as "a low, debauched, vulgar, senseless, ignorant curr, and the Lord be praised that his vile, despicable existence has terminated."[52]

With the coming of the railroad, the introduction of the cooperatives, and the reintroduction of the Relief Society and the Schools of the Prophets, Utah underwent significant changes. In the April 1870 general conference, JFS outlined a list of fundamental truths that, in his opinion, constituted the core of Mormon orthodoxy: the divinity of Christ, his resurrection from the dead, eternal and celestial marriage, and "eternal increase" of posterity. Stripped to its barest bones, Mormonism consisted of the belief in "Christ and Him crucified and Joseph and him martyred," and any church member denying these had "apostatized and denied the faith."[53]

JFS repeatedly emphasized that the standard of Mormon belief could be met only by those who could say, "I believe in my eternal Father, I believe in the Prophet Joseph Smith, I believe in the doctrine of Christ which we have received."[54] An apostate, in JFS's opinion, was "two-fold more the child of hell" than one who never believed.[55] "I love a man or woman who does right," JFS told the October 1896 general conference, "but when he turns away, Amen. He must go his own way." He agreed with George A. Smith that "the railroad has had the effect of causing some to apostatize and others will follow, but there never was a time when the prospects of Zion was better."[56]

Despite his optimism about Zion's prospects, however, JFS always found it nearly impossible to love those who left Mormonism; indeed, he could almost never view them as anything but enemies. In the summers of 1868 and 1871, JFS accompanied Brigham Young, George A. Smith, and others on tours of Mormon settlements in Cache Valley in northern Utah. The church leaders viewed politics, economics, and religion as parts of one comprehensive issue, and the sermons they gave to Mormons in Cache Valley reflected that. In addition to preaching temperance and testifying about Joseph Smith's prophetic mission, they also made it a point to encourage naturalization among the Mormons to argue for the need to secure legal title to the lands upon which they lived and farmed.[57]

At every stop in Cache Valley, it fell to George A. Smith to push naturalization, and it was sage advice. In the nineteenth century, becoming a naturalized U.S. citizen was a relatively simple affair, and becoming citizens and holding title to land would strengthen the Mormons, both individually and collectively, against efforts by the U.S. government to dispossess them of their property. For the same reason, Brigham Young encouraged people, especially polygamists, to make proper wills. Polygamists who died intestate left behind a hornet's nest of contention and difficulty that frequently disrupted families and forced church authorities to sort things out. Sensing the general reluctance to even contemplate such a possibility, Young reminded audiences that "no one was obliged to die because he had made a will."[58]

In 1871, JFS and the other LDS leaders met with the local School of the Prophets in Paris, Idaho, and the main topic of discussion arose from a question asked by a member of the group. The man wanted to know whether "a man will get as great a salvation with one wife as with many."[59] The relationship between plural marriage and one's standing in the afterlife had been of interest to Mormons since the 1840s, but even in the 1870s there were still many unanswered questions. Young fielded the question but provided a less than crystalline answer. "A man can obtain as complete a salvation with one wife as with ten," he said, but it would not be as "great or numerous." George A. Smith added that anyone who rejected the "principle of celestial marriage," by which he meant polygamy, "would be damned, go to hell, and remain there eternally."[60]

While the local brethren tried to sort through these answers, Young moved on to the less abstract topic of the proper way to cut and harvest hay. JFS spent a fair amount of time encouraging men to build roomy homes, procure sewing machines, and use water-powered spinning wheels whenever possible, all of which would provide women with "time to study and improve their own minds and the minds of their children." He admonished mothers to educate themselves, especially on the topic of "surgery," because "many children's lives are lost through the ignorance of parents."[61]

After the stop in Paris, Idaho, Young told JFS to visit the settlements in the south end of Cache Valley. One of the main themes in the discourses of other leaders during this trip, however, was tithing. It seems that a fair number of Mormons believed that Young's interest in tithing had more to do with enriching himself than with furthering the work of God. Young responded to these rumors strongly enough that JFS made note of it. "How long will it take to prove to the people that I can support myself?" Young asked one group, pointing out that not only did he not live on tithing, but that he paid two dollars to the Tithing Office for every dollar that he took out, and furthermore, he had supported himself in Kirtland, Missouri, and Illinois and had "preached every summer."[62] JFS likely also sermonized on the importance of tithing, but no one could ever accuse him of dipping into the tithing coffers to support a luxurious lifestyle.

While in northern Utah, JFS took time to indulge in his love of fishing and pulled quite a bounty from local streams. He also paid close attention to the quality and details of any buildings he happened to pass by or enter. In Logan, at the end of the trip, JFS recorded what for him must have been the highlight of the entire visit, a reunion with missionaries with whom he had served during his first mission to Hawaii, including his beloved friend W. W. Cluff. He returned to Salt Lake Valley on his own, on horseback, while the rest of the group took the train from Ogden.[63]

During the early 1870s, JFS's family continued to grow. In 1871, on New Year's Day, Daniel H. Wells sealed Edna Lambson to JFS in the Endowment House.[64] Edna was the nineteen-year-old sister of his wife Julina, and she had lived with the family on and off since her mid-teens. Many years later, in a letter to Susa Y. Gates, JFS described his ideal wife as possessing

> good stature, good features, good temper, kindness of heart, charity, intelligence, patience, consideration and thoughtfulness, honesty, sincere religious convictions, modesty with firm resolve, and <u>Spirit</u>, with love and reason, and such attainments as will contribute most to the happiness, comfort, and peace of society.[65]

And, as usual, he compared and contrasted all women with his mother, Mary Fielding Smith, who remained "the standard in my mind of the purest womanly metal." She was, he continued, "the refined, pure gold of womanhood; wise, intelligent, faithful and indomitable. I have never met her equal."[66]

JFS may have known what he wanted in a wife, but his ideals duly submitted to reality. No woman could have ever met his "gold standard," probably not even his

158 Chapter 9

mother if JFS could ever have seen her realistically. As with most of his marriages, JFS seemed to expend little energy in his search for another wife, preferring instead to marry young women with whom he already had regular contact. On the last day of January 1871, Sarah gave birth to a daughter named Leonora. The baby was born at 4:45 a.m., and by 7 a.m., JFS was back at work at the Endowment House.[67]

The next year, Edna gave birth to her first child, Hyrum M. Smith, and Julina gave birth to a daughter, Donnette. In early 1873, Sarah gave birth to a son named Joseph Richards Smith. In an attempt to keep up with this expansion, JFS spent much of his spare time building and furnishing a house suitable for such a substantial brood, including shutters, dressers, stovepipes, hundreds of pounds of nails, chairs, and basins. Whatever JFS couldn't make, he traded for or, as a last resort, purchased. His skill as a carpenter and an all-around builder of things was remarkable given his lack of formal training, and the growing family benefited from his innate skills and tireless work ethic.[68]

During the early 1870s, JFS's life was more stable than it had been since the years before his father's death. Although he kept a punishing schedule of ecclesiastical, political, and personal work, he had managed to establish a home, nest within it a growing family, and remain basically anchored. During this period, he continued to develop interests and methods in the field of theology and doctrine that would come to characterize his entire life. Unlike many of his contemporary church leaders, JFS was reluctant to speculate overtly on doctrinal matters that ranged outside of the scriptures or the revelations of Joseph Smith. Because Mormonism had yet to be thoroughly doctrinally homogenized on an official level, many leaders felt free to speculate on a wide variety of theological topics, but JFS resisted this.

Ironically, one of the most powerful influences on JFS during these crucial years was Orson Pratt. Although Pratt is known for his theological combat with Brigham Young, and he certainly never shied away from speculation, JFS was obviously deeply impressed by what he saw in him. Most influential was Pratt's emphasis on the importance of systematic theological ideas. For Pratt, unlike Young, one test of doctrine was how well it fit within the larger system of accepted theology, which consisted of scripture and Joseph Smith's teachings.

It is this emphasis on religion as a system—a coherent whole, a machine with complementary moving parts—that sets JFS apart from so many other LDS Church leaders. In his first published sermon, which appeared in the *Deseret News* in early 1867, he said that one need only to examine all the "systems" of every "sect and religious denomination in the world" to find that "such a system" exists only in Mormonism.[69] This was a far more sophisticated method of doctrinal elaboration than those employed by Brigham Young.

JFS's journals in the early 1870s are replete with references to Pratt's ideas and their scriptural foundations. Even if we limit ourselves to examining his journal entries for three months in the spring and summer of 1870, we find the record thick with references to Pratt's style and content. These are representative of dozens of such entries between 1870 and 1873. JFS was almost singularly impressed with Pratt, praising him dozens of times as a man with "great power, and spirit,"[70] able to give "strong and spirited testimony,"[71] and someone who gave "most powerful and rich discourses"[72] that were "thorough and able"[73] in organization and effect.

JFS especially liked it when Pratt looked to the scriptures, as when he spoke "on the 29 ch. of Isiah [sic] verses 18 to 21, comparing the evidences in favor of the Bible & of the Book of Mormon";[74] when he admonished his listeners "to memorize passages of the Scripture on various subjects, for thus the Lord had commanded, that we may be like Timothy of old";[75] and when he delved, using a combination of biblical material and Joseph Smith's teachings, into that uniquely Mormon subject of "Baptism for the dead, the turning of the hearts of the fathers to the children & the hearts of the children to the fathers."[76] JFS's deep admiration for Pratt is evident not only in the laudatory statements, although those are important. He also wrote in his journal that Pratt should be "blessed for his labors and Testimony, he is a strengh [sic] to many,"[77] and he finished one entry with "God bless that man, and his testimony forever."[78]

JFS in later life and, a generation later, his son JFS Jr. would be the ones to whom church leaders and lay persons alike would turn for answers to vexing doctrinal questions. But before that, on the rare occasion when JFS looked for answers, he turned to Orson Pratt. Once, when some RLDS missionaries quoted one of Joseph Smith's early revelations about "one mighty and strong" who God would send to set in order "His house," and another who would attempt to "steady the ark" and be struck down for it, JFS found himself a bit "befogged." The RLDS missionaries argued that "the one mighty and strong" was Joseph Smith III, and the ark-steadier was Brigham Young. JFS found this problem so unsettling that he wrote to Pratt and asked, "Who is meant?"[79] In all of JFS's personal writings, I have found nothing to match the frank intellectual and spiritual humility displayed in this request. There could hardly be a clearer sign of JFS's respect and admiration for Pratt than the fact that he turned to him, out of all the potential church leaders, for answers to a scriptural mystery.

Evidence of JFS's interest in the doctrine of salvation for the dead includes the special notations he made in his journal whenever a sermon on the subject was delivered, something he rarely did with other topics. His work in the Endowment House doubtless fueled his continued interest in the subject and his ongoing efforts to understand the doctrine behind it. JFS summarized his understanding of the doctrinal underpinnings of work for the dead this way: "All that died without a knowledge of the gospel that would have received it if they had the chance are entitled to a fullness of glory through the ordinance, etc. But those who have a chance and do not obey it in the flesh can only receive the terrestrial glory."[80] Although he indicated that these ideas came from the writings of Joseph Smith, he had taken up the mantle and would continue to work them out until the moment of his own death.

160   Chapter 9

In many ways, JFS was maturing. His sister, Martha, wrote in 1873 to express her gratitude for him, for he had "filled as near as could be the place of a Father" to her.[81] His role as a father figure not only for his children but also his sister and, to a certain extent, his much younger wives led JFS to develop more conspicuously the traits he imagined a good father should have. He took this role particularly seriously in large part because of his own experience as a fatherless child. For all of his emotional fire, JFS's paternal instincts tended toward patience, solicitousness, calm—if frequently pointed—advice, and physical affection. Nonetheless, JFS's rage, the demon that helped destroy his first marriage, had not been conquered.

The McKnight Affair

On New Year's Day 1873, JFS nearly beat a man to death. The day started out fine enough, with him officiating in the sacred rituals of baptism for the dead and eternal sealings at the Endowment House. Upon returning home, however, he decided to visit his neighbor, James McKnight, a relation by marriage. JFS loathed McKnight, and he was furious that his neighbor's livestock continually "trespassed" on his land and ate his feed. According to his journal entry, JFS walked up to McKnight's door and demanded "a settlement."[82] McKnight was having none of it. He refused to give JFS any "satisfaction," and then issued an insult. At this, JFS wrote, he "administered a salutary chastisement" by beating McKnight senseless with a walking stick and leaving him bleeding in the street.[83]

When McKnight's wife went over to her cousin's house later that day to find out what had happened, JFS informed her that her husband ought to consider himself lucky. After all, if McKnight hadn't suddenly found the strength to crawl away, JFS had "intended to turn the butt-end of his cudgel" and apply it to his head.[84] JFS did, however, apologize, and McKnight agreed to drop the charges. But the beating was a severe one. McKnight bled internally and remained unable to leave the house for weeks. Even a year later, he was still in pain, and several doctors told him that the beating had probably taken years off of his life.[85]

A year later, McKnight and JFS had another dispute, which led McKnight to write a lengthy and somewhat rambling letter to JFS that detailed—among many other wrongs, such as shooting chickens, stealing land from the elderly, and animal abuse—the brutal beating of January 1873. McKnight observed, accurately, that JFS was a man who "if not for his religion, would be a desperado!" Apparently, JFS had originally sought forgiveness by claiming that his temper got the better of him. McKnight wrote that the "life-long plea of inherent and uncontrollable frenzy" that JFS had used to explain his behavior "for a quarter century past" was no longer a valid excuse. A man of JFS's age and station in life, he wrote, could no longer use his volatile temper to "screen moral law and mental imbecility."[86]

JFS dismissed the letter as full of lying, abusive, and slanderous language.[87] In fact, several letters that McKnight wrote to the *Salt Lake Tribune* were so vicious that the paper refused to publish them.[88] But the attack on McKnight was probably the most violent of JFS's adult life and could have had serious repercussions for him had McKnight not backed off. JFS simply could not find a way to escape his anger. "The worst enemy I have is my temper," he wrote to Edna in 1875, "and I fear no man but Joseph F. Smith."[89]

McKnight, never the most stable person, took the feud with JFS public, writing articles in the *Tribune* and making more noise than probably was prudent under the circumstances. He also wrote directly to Julina, accusing the Smiths of intentionally building their "stable, cowpen, chicken yard, and hog range" within feet of his front door, flooding his home with a "noisome and unbearable ... fetid smell."[90] In November 1875, JFS attended a meeting at which McKnight was excommunicated from the church "for lying, stealing, and other infamous practices."[91]

After McKnight was excommunicated, his wives left him. Bereft and friendless, he moved to the state of Washington and remarried, but he spent the rest of his days bitterly brooding over his treatment by JFS and the LDS Church. In 1904, two years before his death, he wrote a letter to his son describing the "diabolical treachery" that left him "robbed, stripped, plundered, betrayed, the victim of the foulest conspiracy." He claimed that at the heart of the conspiracy stood JFS, "the very man who had attempted, absolutely without cause or provocation to murder me!" McKnight believed that JFS and unnamed others had planned to "assassinate" him, and only "the interposition of Jehovah" had saved his life.[92]

It is clear that in the case of James McKnight, JFS had behaved abhorrently, knowing that he was far more powerful, both physically and politically, than McKnight could ever dream of being. It is inexcusable that he used those advantages to exploit McKnight in ways that reverberated through decades of the man's life and the lives of his family members. When McKnight died in 1906, JFS was president of the LDS Church, whereas McKnight's memory had been all but erased from the minds of his former associates.

It is beyond debate that the episode with McKnight and JFS's treatment of his ex-wife Levira represent the nadir of JFS's behavior over the span of his long life. He did not often publicly refer to his issues with rage, but a few years after he attacked McKnight, he did just that. In a sermon he gave in Ogden in early 1879, he told the congregation that he was well aware that among self-anointed "good deliberate brethren," JFS was dismissed as "hot blooded" and "only a boy." He took that occasion to put his critics on notice that he acted as directed by "the spirit of God," and if his unwillingness to "swap jack-knives with the devil" by being polite ruffled some feathers, it was something they would just have to deal with.[93]

10 Mission President in England, Losing the Lion

In a sermon delivered in January 1879, Joseph F. Smith expressed a desire to "burrow in the sacred precincts of my home, and ... to dwell forever in the society and hearts of my family and no more go out from them."[1] But that was not to be. In late 1873 he was once again called upon to leave home.[2]

At the October 1873 general conference, JFS was called to go to Europe. It would prove to be one of the most difficult assignments of his life, and one in which he would take little pleasure. JFS apparently had no idea this assignment was coming, and it isn't clear if he immediately understood that he was not simply being called to go to Europe, but to preside over the British mission. As president, he would not only be responsible for the church in Britain, but would also oversee the presidents of the other missions in Europe. JFS wrote almost nothing about this new calling in his journal, noting only his call and, in November, his having been set apart as mission president.[3]

If JFS felt any trepidation about the new assignment, he did not show it. At least not at first. But just before his departure, he visited his half brother John and requested another patriarchal blessing.[4] John's blessing indicated that an angel sent from God had been protecting and watching over JFS from the time of his birth, and that this angel had "preserved [his] life many times" and had delivered him out of the "hands of [his] enemies." John promised that the angel would continue to protect him, and that he would even "converse" with him as with a "familiar friend." JFS would need all of this help because, John warned, "the ungodly shall seek to take thy life." But the blessing forecasted he would "perform [his] mission in honor and return in safety," and that he would live to see "the coming of the Savior." John concluded the blessing by admonishing JFS to "be at rest in thy mind, for all shall be well with you."[5]

After completing his preparations, JFS left for New York, without any of his wives or children, on 28 February 1874. In contrast to his 1860 trip, JFS was able to go by rail the entire way, something he found convenient but also slightly disorienting. As the train swept across the vast, flat midsection of the country, he complained in his journal that he was "travelling figuratively in the dark as I cannot learn the names of any of the towns along the track, and only occasionally can find out where we are."[6]

JFS also availed himself of new communications technology. On his previous mission, he had to wait weeks to send letters to his family and receive their replies while he was on the trail; this time he telegraphed them at every stop, allowing them to follow his journey in real time. After brief stops in Chicago and Pittsburgh, which JFS judged to be "the blackest and dingiest place I have ever seen," he arrived in New York.[7] The entire journey had taken only four days. In 1860, it had taken almost three months.

JFS had always enjoyed himself in New York City, and he made a point of visiting one of his favorite attractions, the Barnum Museum. His brother-in-law, Joseph Richards, lived in the city and no doubt helped to ease any homesickness that JFS was feeling. A medical student at the time, Richards took JFS to see the anatomical lab where he was dissecting cadavers. JFS stood agog as Richards "showed us what he was dissecting, handling matters as you would handle dough for biscuits, not even caring to keep his coat sleeves from the carrion."[8]

JFS then took the opportunity to travel by rail to Washington, DC, to visit George Q. Cannon. Although JFS had long admired Orson Pratt from a distance, he looked up to Cannon from a place of personal intimacy forged by their common connection to Hawaii and JFS's service as a missionary under Cannon in Britain in the 1860s. Cannon had been serving since 1872 as a non-voting Utah territorial delegate. JFS enjoyed the sights of the city, which he found charming, convenient, and pleasantly cheap. His visit culminated in a brief trip to the White House, where JFS "shook hands with U.S. Grant."[9]

Despite the animosity that he and many other LDS leaders expressed toward the U.S. government and its Mormon policies, JFS did not record a single negative remark during his time in Washington, even though his visits to the White House, Supreme Court, and the House of Representatives would have provided such an opportunity. This is illustrative of the deeply ambiguous feelings that JFS had about the United States. On the one hand, he believed deeply in the principles of liberty that the nation espoused, but he despised that, at least in the case of the Mormons, those freedoms were often honored more in the breach than in the observance. When he returned to the legislative chambers as president of the LDS Church in 1904, his trip would prove far less enjoyable.

JFS returned to New York, and after hiding five dollars in Joseph Richards's house because he knew that he wouldn't accept it, he set sail on the steamship *Idaho* on 10 March 1874. He spent his time onboard playing chess and checkers, reading a book about Christopher Columbus, and conversing with members of the crew. Disturbing dreams interfered with his sleep, however. In one nightmare, "it was night time. I found a patch of corn, between the house and the barn, on fire. Julina helped me put out the fire, and Mamie and Donnie stood at the east door looking on. the rest of the folks were asleep. When I awoke I was itching terribly, and felt restless."[10] Dreams of fire threatening his family revealed JFS's deepest fears about leaving the family he had worked so hard to house and provide for thousands of miles behind, but eventually the horrific nightmares passed.

On 21 March 1874, JFS found himself back in Liverpool. In 1871, George Reynolds—an English convert who had returned to his homeland as an assistant to the mission president—had written to JFS reporting that the British mission office at 42 Islington was as "black and dingy as ever," but the inside of the building was "more dilapidated" than when he had last been there. JFS soon discovered that Reynolds had not been exaggerating. The entire neighborhood seemed to have declined. He observed orphans begging beneath his window, and the once quiet streets were now plagued with such "drunken rowdeyism and noise" that he sometimes had trouble sleeping.[11] At one point, a gang of thieves robbed JFS, an event that he recorded dramatically in his journal. "For the first time in my life," he wrote, "I was robbed. No man can know my mortification, shame and chagrin."[12]

Reynolds had warned JFS that decades of emigration had skimmed "the cream of the mission" and ensured that the "zealous, the persevering, the indefatigable [and] the energetic laborers have journeyed westward."[13] The number of LDS converts had gone from around 42,000 between 1840 and 1850, to 14,000 between 1860 and 1870, when more than 10,000 British Mormons emigrated to Utah.[14] JFS was facing a situation in which fewer converts were being added than ever before, and the number of seasoned Mormons leaving for Utah was nearly equal to the number of baptisms. "Our experience of today," JFS wrote of missionary service in Britain, "is not what it might have been 20 years ago. We are now gleaning the fields after the harvest is gathered."[15]

After taking a few hours to re-familiarize himself with the office and settle into his rooms, JFS wasted little time getting to work. This was his first opportunity to truly lead. He would function, in essence, as the president of the LDS Church in Europe, directing all ecclesiastical affairs as well as the ongoing logistical complexities of emigration. Additionally, he would become the editor of the *Millennial Star*, which was arguably the most important LDS periodical at the time. Unlike previous mission presidents, who had relied on people like George Reynolds to see to the day-to-day business, JFS took over emigration, publication, and tithing personally, all of which would present major challenges during his tenure.

JFS seemed particularly disappointed with the state of the church in northwest England. In fact, the Liverpool conference, which for decades had been the breadbasket of Mormon conversions, baptized fewer people than emigrated in 1872–1873.[16] The church in Preston, made famous by Heber C. Kimball's missionary exploits in the 1830s, had grown "cold, almost stiff ... [filled] with hard-shelled, conniving, whiffling, complaining, worthless members."[17] Tithing remained a perennial problem in Britain and, indeed, much of Europe. European Mormons typically wanted to save all of their money, which usually was not much, to cover the costs of emigration. This meant that many of them failed to pay tithing, which, in turn, left the church increasingly impoverished. The day after his arrival, JFS attended the daytime and evening meetings of the Liverpool branch, where he was immediately "struck with the fewness of attendants, most of whom, in the evening were" not even members of the LDS Church.[18]

It was not uncommon for curious members of the public to outnumber Mormons at their meetings; JFS attended one meeting in London with 600 people in attendance, only thirty of whom were Mormons. Although Mormonism had increased its potency as a curiosity, the religious fervor that had prevailed among the English in the 1850s and 1860s was waning, partially due to an increase in overall income and family stability that characterized the late Victorian period (the scene in the neighborhood around the British mission office at 42 Islington notwithstanding). Mormonism, at least as JFS saw it, was attracting the dregs of British society. The members of the church, he wrote, "drag out a hand to mouth existence ... some of them little better than our degraded Indians." He continued by noting that "only the faithless and worthless remain, the energetic and faithful having gathered out to Zion."[19]

JFS left proselytizing to the missionaries under him while he turned his attention to emigration. It fell to him to arrange for a shipping company to carry each season's emigrants. LDS emigration promised a high volume of ticket sales, so there was no shortage of companies vying for the church's business. JFS regularly met with company representatives to discuss special rates and inspect the vessels that would carry the migrating saints. In his letters home, JFS expressed a great deal of self-doubt about his capacity to deal with representatives of massive corporations. "What troubles me most," he wrote to Sarah in April 1874, "is the thought of meeting lots of emigration agents.... I hope the Lord will give me wisdom to properly manage this important part of my labors."[20]

By June 1874, emigration business was causing JFS "considerable anxiety, worry and labor" and left him feeling "good for nothing"; it was here, more than in any other aspect of his mission presidency, that he felt his "want of experience, and lack of education and business knowledge." He lamented, "It was not my fault that I did not go to school, I would have been glad of the chance. I had to go to the seared ground, to the canyon, to dig, plough, harrow, reap and harvest food for the belly."[21] Rarely was JFS so frank about his own shortcomings and so petulant and self-pitying about their perceived causes.

Emigration problems also aroused JFS's characteristic hot temper, especially when he found himself dealing, repeatedly, with profiteers hoping to enrich themselves from the movement of Mormons from Europe to Utah. "I am surprised," he fumed in January 1875, "that anyone should think of entering into business for the purpose of making money, the profits of which to be wrung out of the wretchedly poor and helpless creatures that we are sending off from here."[22] He was especially mortified that an advertisement for such a scheme appeared in the *Millennial Star*, giving it the appearance of church approval.

166   Chapter 10

JFS was not above bending the rules in order to save the emigrating saints some money. In a guide to emigration policies that he prepared for the 1874 season, he advised that "when children are small at the ages of 10, 11, 12, 13, 14, and sometimes even older (when small)," they can be passed off as younger in order to get a lower fare. JFS noted that the carrier "has never shown any disposition to enquire after real ages," but he instructed that four-year-old children trying to pass as infants "should be dressed and carried to pass the Gov. Doctor." He justified this process of "cutting down" on the basis that the savings "figure up to a large amount during one season."[23]

Anxiety and Family Separation

JFS's letters home during his second British mission open a window on two other important areas of his personality that are otherwise inaccessible—namely, his almost pathological anxiety about the safety of his children and his highly idealized and specific view of how a family should work. His experiences away from home during this mission differed from all of his previous experiences. This was his first prolonged absence since he entered plural marriage and became a father, and he found the adjustment difficult. "One thing I am convinced of," he wrote to Sarah, "I think too much of home," something that caused him to see himself as "a veritable old granny, a <u>he granny</u>, the worst kind of granny."[24]

This was not the only time JFS raised the subject of his perceived lack of masculinity in the context of his home life. On another occasion, he wrote to Sarah that "I am better adapted to fill the maternal, instead of the paternal side of the house. I am sure my anxiety is as great, and my sympathy and forethought as keen and lively, even to weakness, in behalf of my children, as any woman I ever saw."[25] JFS overtly viewed these traits as feminine and as weaknesses, but he never tried to blunt the intensity of his tender feelings toward his children. He admitted to friends that, during his mission, his "greatest trial is my separation from [my children]."[26] At times, the separation anxiety threatened to consume JFS, and he could "scarcely subdue [his] feelings.[27]

We get some sense of the intensity of JFS's longing for home from the evocative imagery he used to describe it. His homesickness, he lamented, "sometimes comes over me like a consuming flame, and then, but for the stern obligations of duty, I would expunge the Atlantic Ocean and annihilate distance and time that separates me from [the children] and never again leave them beyond my own vigilant care."[28] This overt emotional connection to his children sets JFS apart from many other church leaders, including Brigham Young and Wilford Woodruff, whose writings suggest a greater degree of detachment from the sentimental areas of home life. It is also stands in clear contrast to his more public tough-guy persona.

Interestingly, both sides could lead JFS to violence. The maternal element of his personality could be drawn out by children, and sometimes women, especially if he felt that his loved ones were being harmed. As in the case of him defending his sister, Martha, from the schoolteacher, JFS was capable of lashing out in defensive or retributive violence. Even as a more mature man, he swore that "if harm should come to one of my children by the hand of the living, I should not ask God for vengeance, [mine] would be swift and terrible."[29]

Part of the problem for JFS was that he remembered everything he had ever heard or read about a child being killed or injured, and he maintained an ever-growing index of all the possible things that could go wrong. He pleaded with his wives to "take care of the children" because all of the alarming stories "in the papers of sickness, and death among children, so many accidents by drowning, poisoning, kniving, and maiming" were keeping him in a state of "constant dread of some terrible calamity."[30] In his letters, JFS warned his wives repeatedly about four specific dangers: disease, drowning, lye, and fire. Other sundry dangers occasionally surfaced as well, such as "axes or hatchets or sharp knives with which [the children might] hurt themselves or each other," and allowing the children "to breathe the dust of carpets while sweeping."[31]

JFS's most pervasive fear was of disease, and he refused requests for the children to attend any large gatherings because of "whooping coughs, fevers, etc."[32] Furthermore, he cautioned his wives against allowing visitors into the home for fear of contamination. Drowning also featured prominently on his list of fears. In a letter to Sarah, he wrote, "I have cautioned you about leaving tubs standing about with water in them. I repeat, do not suffer yourself nor anyone else to leave a tub or deep vessel or barrel with water in it where it is possible for any—mark you any of the children to reach it." He also vividly imagined his children consuming lye, and wrote that he would not be able to "feel easy in my mind unless I know the deadly stuff is banished from under my roof." JFS even cast the dangers of lye in moral terms, writing that "its insidious venom [is] always working its evil in secret and in the moment least expected or looked for."[33]

The danger of fire often preyed on JFS's mind while away from home, especially because of his own experiences with destructive fires. His belongings were destroyed by fire during his first mission to Hawaii, his barn burned down, and his aunt Mercy Thompson lost eight tons of hay to a fire caused by "children and matches." "I saw not long ago a notice in the paper of the roof of St. Marks School House taking fire from sparks," he wrote, adding that "he thought of my own chimneys, and trembled." He repeatedly cautioned his wives, reminding them that "In the summer the children will be dressed in calico—keep them from playing with, or in any way exposing themselves to fire."[34]

JFS wanted constant reassurance that nothing at home had gone horribly wrong, and he instructed Julina, Edna, and Sarah to always include specifics about

168   Chapter 10

the health of the children in their letters. If the wives delayed writing, or if the mail encountered delays en route, JFS would become extremely agitated. "Not having received a letter from home this week," he wrote in 1875, "I am greatly concerned about the children."[35] On another occasion he wrote to Julina that he had been "looking four days for a letter from ... one of you but none has come. I hope nothing is wrong ... that the children are well." Toward the end of the letter he expressed a sense of "dread lest something should be the matter at home, seeing I have received no letter from any of you this week."[36]

When these inevitable gaps in correspondence occurred, he imagined horrific things happening. Even a letter mentioning something as benign as a cold could set off JFS's "evil imaginations." He once read such a letter just before going to sleep and woke terrified from a nightmare in which his son Hyrum had died.[37] To ease his mind, he prayed to God for revelation about the state of his children and tried to interpret his dreams to find answers.

Perhaps the clearest example of JFS's anxiety came in May 1875, when one of the missionaries working in the office received a letter stating that "Brother Joseph F.'s little Alvin is sick with the chickenpox, his name on our altar to be prayed for." This proved almost too much for JFS to handle. He immediately wrote to Edna, Alvin's mother, demanding to know the state of his son's health. "I cannot tell my feelings," he wrote. After hearing the news, he felt completely drained. "If I had been struck with lightning I could not have been much more exhausted." And while he attempted to "recover [his] composure," he kept asking himself, "Why have I not received my accustomed letters this week?!" JFS also flashed his anger, asking Edna, "Why don't you write or get someone to do so every day if he is sick!" "Do not," he warned, "keep me in suspense about my children."[38]

Reporting the incident to Sarah two days later, he wrote that his "fearful imagination rose up like a whirlwind and almost carried me off my feet! and although the Lord manifested through his spirit that all was right, a dream I had had, and the failure of getting my usual letters from home kept me in a boiling fever of anguish, hope and doubt."[39] Before he finally found out that Alvin was fine, JFS suffered from nightmares, one of which caused him to "awake crying and sobbing."[40]

JFS also hated when any of his wives, and it was usually Sarah, left to visit her parents. To keep his mind at ease, he had to be able to visualize his family at home. "I can always see you at home, but not in some strange place," he wrote to Sarah, adding, "I am never so comfortable as when I am under the impression that you are all at home, safe and well."[41] JFS was self-conscious about all of these anxious feelings, calling them "weaknesses," and in one letter he warned Sarah to keep them secret because although "some think me stoic, I am a child."[42]

JFS despised weakness, especially in men, and he remained tremendously strong even into old age. In 1875, he could hold twenty-five-pound weights straight out from his body without so much as a "tremor," and, more impressively, he could "skin a cat, go over and pull myself up to a horizontal bar seven times without much effort."[43] This physical prowess may have provided JFS with a sense of security in the world, but it did nothing to alleviate the panic he felt when his imagination ran wild, and he must have found the contrast between his bodily strength and apparent emotional fragility troubling.

All of this anxiety also manifested itself in JFS's ongoing efforts to understand and accept death. He faced, with great trepidation, the prospect of losing Mercy Thompson, his mother's sister, who was his last connection with his mother's family. "I often think of you," he wrote on 5 February 1875 after learning of her declining health. He assured her that he prayed daily for her "preservation" and her presence in his life "for many years to come." But, he added, "I cannot shut my eyes to the fact that we are all rapidly hastening to the end of our mortal cares, and notwithstanding all we might wish or anticipate or hope or do to the contrary, one by one we are passing away."[44]

JFS had written to Mercy's daughter, Mary Jane, the day before, expressing his difficulty in accepting that Mercy "is getting old. I see her in my mind, 10, 15, or 20 years ago and oh! How I wish she had a lease of as many years to come." As with so many things, however, just beneath the surface of his worry over Mercy were thoughts of his own mother. His letter to Mary Jane shifted dramatically from the subject of Mercy's health to a multipage recitation of Mary Fielding Smith's virtues. "What would I give today to have my mother under my roof, that I might honor her with my love and truth, for the pure example of her life, her faith, her endurance and integrity that I might try to emulate but can never hope to equal." His mother was, he concluded, "almost superhuman."[45]

By nesting this expansive tribute to his mother within the broader issue of his aunt's ill health and age, JFS signaled that Mercy, the last living link to the mother he idolized, was far more to him than just a beloved aunt. Mercy was for JFS, ironically perhaps, what he was for so many who saw him as the living symbol of his father and uncle. With Mercy's health failing, he now felt that death was not only taking his friends and family, but devouring his own past.

George A. Smith, JFS's mentor and surrogate father, provided additional cause for concern. In June and July of 1875, George had several close brushes with death. On 29 July, JFS awoke at 1 a.m. to the sound of someone ringing the bell at 42 Islington. It was a cable, short on information but long on implication, ordering George A. Smith's son, John Henry, who was serving a mission in England, to return to Utah immediately. JFS immediately dressed and walked a mile to the nearest general post office, where he sent a telegram to John Henry, who was serving in Birmingham. By the time he got back from the post office, it was nearly 4 a.m. and JFS was a nervous wreck.[46]

Later that day he wrote to Mercy about the incident, telling her that he had been "worrying since midnight about Pres. Geo. A. Smith. . . . I cannot allow myself to think he is going to leave us yet."[47] JFS told John Henry that "no greater calamity could befall God's People than . . . the death of your father."[48] A few days later, he got word that George A. was well, and in early September he expressed hope that the "monster's icy hand will be stayed now for awhile," at least long enough for him to see George A. again.[49] Sadly, the icy hand had not been stayed for long. It had come for George A. Smith in August.

The day after the worrisome cable arrived, JFS responded to a letter that he had received from William Cluff three months earlier informing him of the death of "our dear old friend Bishop Wilde." Thinking that George A. might be dying, JFS felt inclined to reflect on the subject of mortality. "My recollections of [Wilde]," he wrote to Cluff, "go back to boyhood in the Sugar House Ward," a period of almost mythological beauty in JFS's memory. The death of Wilde was, again, more than just a personal loss; it was evidence that JFS's connections with his past were "passing away." He told Cluff that "the last 15 months since my absence from home has been fraught with more mortality from among the ranks of the true and faithful than ever, to my recollection, before. Death has been busy and has claimed his share."[50]

In a letter to Edna, JFS took an almost personal umbrage to the "appalling number of deaths since I left home." It was only natural, of course, that as he moved toward early middle age, more and more of the people from his parents' generation would meet with timely deaths. For JFS, however, the prospect of losing Mercy Thompson and George A. Smith was almost like losing his parents all over again. In fact, when he received word that George A. had in fact died, he lamented that "his was the only true fatherly love I ever fully realized."[51]

While difficult, the loss of his older relatives was for JFS far less fraught than the untimely deaths of children and young parents. Even as he struggled under the crushing administrative load of being mission president, JFS wrote often to the parents and widows of the recently deceased to offer comfort and counsel, but it is clear, in retrospect, that he was also trying to figure things out for himself. In 1875, he wrote a lengthy letter to Henry Richards, who had recently lost a son. "The change we call death," JFS wrote, was but a "transition from mortality to immortality, from death unto life!" For the righteous, death "is regarded as a release from suffering and pain," and the door to a place of "rest from the burdens of mortality," where there will be "a happy reunion, a joyous meeting of father, mother, son, daughter, husband and wife, parents and children." Those whose family relationships were fixed as a "nail in a sure place," he assured the grieving man, could expect to live with their families in "the glorious court of Father's mansion."[52]

JFS's letter to Richards represents the two chief ways in which he managed the notion of death. First, he redefined it as a doorway from the shadowy, painful world of mortality to the real "life" that lies beyond—casting mortal life as a kind of illusion, but the afterlife as absolutely real. Second, he very specifically imagines heaven as a place where families are reunited. In another letter written in the same period, JFS added another wrinkle. JFS wrote to a friend that after death the righteous may expect to be among not only family members but also "the martyred

Prophet, Hyrum, Heber [Kimball], Willard [Richards], Jedediah [Grant], Parley [Pratt], and all the noble and glorious" servants of God.[53]

At the center of JFS's attempts to tame death was his understanding of the temple. As he wrote to one grieving widow, "the blessings sealed in the House of the Lord now shine out from the dark clouds of affliction in majestic splendor, healing the wounded and broken heart, filling the soul with joy and gladness and making tolerable the short remainder of this [life]."[54] Modern Mormons take for granted the linked ideas of eternal families, temples, and the presence of the righteous dead in heaven, but they came together in the form that they currently exist due in large measure to JFS's influence.

Over the years, JFS would continue to reflect on death and the afterlife, culminating in his 1918 "Vision of the Redemption of the Dead," which provides scriptural grounds for both the belief in heaven as a family home and the idea that deceased church leaders play a prominent role on the "other side of the veil."[55] It also includes a further elaboration on the role of temples in the redemption of the dead. But in the 1870s, these ideas remained only semi-articulated and somewhat theoretical.

Although JFS expressed supreme confidence in his letter to Richards, just days later, when L. John Nuttall, a missionary who also worked in the mission office, received word that one of his children had died, JFS confessed that "he would not be able to bear so sad an affliction" and remain on his mission.[56] Sadly, JFS would have many more challenges that tested his faith in his own view of death, especially as he lost more children. With each loss, his concepts of death as an end to illusion and heaven as a family affair would come into sharper focus.

Although attempting to construct psychological profiles of figures from the past is generally an unproductive method for biographers, the basic psychology on display in JFS's writing merits comment. His default position was to assume, without evidence or complete information, that something horrible had happened or was going to happen to his children. This tremendous anxiety over his children may also have been related to the deaths of his parents, the twin traumas of his childhood.

JFS viewed his children as both objects of and sources for unconditional love. As he phrased it, "O! Who will love me as my children will? I am selfish."[57] Understanding what his children represented for him—namely, ultimate safety and transcendent love—helps us better comprehend the engine of his anxiety and the wellspring of his profound grief. Anxiety as severe as what JFS suffered in relation to his children generally functions as a means of trying to create an illusion of control via the expenditure of emotional energy. The internal logic of someone with severe anxiety suggests that assuming the worst and worrying as hard as one can will somehow prevent the worst from happening or, at the very least, minimize the psychological and emotional trauma inflicted should the feared events occur. Whatever else one might conclude, it is clear that JFS suffered tremendous anxiety

172   Chapter 10

when separated from his family, particularly his children, and it is reasonable to trace this anxiety response back to the severe traumas that JFS suffered as a child.

Understanding JFS's anxiety also helps us to understand another issue that his letters home reveal: his idealized dream of family life. JFS invested himself almost totally in the creation and maintenance of a family because, despite his high church position and the heavy workload it required, his "interests, hopes, and heart all center on my family."[58] Of course, JFS had very little exposure to any sort of organized family life as a child and adolescent, a lack that exerted at least two significant forces on him. First, it led him to believe that any problems he had could have been avoided if he had not been denied a normal family life, and, second, in the absence of any model of how real family life is lived, it allowed him to construct an ideal unbound by reality.

JFS attempted to achieve this ideal throughout his life, and he offered hints of it in his letters home from Britain in 1874–1875. In a letter to Sarah, he wrote a mini-manifesto on the subject: "Home should be the dearest place on earth, at least to children. To this end it should be made pleasant and attractive, and love should be there, never absent. I wish it was possible to observe a perfect system with [children], a time for everything, to play, to practice, work, study, take meals, everything in a systematic manner."[59]

The late Victorian mores that JFS borrowed to create his ideal family type would eventually inform some of the policies that he made as president of the LDS Church. This is especially evident in his idea that "Home should be a temple, a sanctuary, an altar of righteousness, a symbol of heaven!"[60] Linking the home with the temple has very specific connotations for Latter-day Saints, for whom temples are the most sacred spaces on earth.

Even as JFS was laying out his plan for how a family should operate, he did so knowing that his own family was struggling with a variety of issues, particularly his adopted son, Edward. Now a young adolescent and the only one of his children old enough to cause serious trouble, Edward had developed a rebellious streak that manifested immediately upon JFS's departure from Utah. Julina, who had assumed the role of his mother, reported that Edward had taken a pistol from the house and had begun roaming the streets with similarly armed young men looking for trouble. He was staying out all night, leading Julina eventually to lock him out. He had dropped out of school but had been leaving the house every day anyway. Only when she went looking for him at the school did Julina discover that he went there only to incite other youngsters to leave with him. Eventually he ran away, but not far. After sleeping in neighbors' wagons for a few days, he finally returned and apologized for his behavior.[61]

JFS's wives were also having problems getting along with each other, and even fought with JFS via transatlantic mail. While the letters contain abundant expressions of love and concern, they also show signs of stress. One of the earliest conflicts arose over a suggestion that George Q. Cannon made to JFS when he was in Washington, DC. Cannon told him that he should bring one of his wives to England to keep him company, but he left it up to JFS to decide which of the three it should be. JFS was leaning toward bringing Sarah.

When Julina got wind of this, she wrote a scathing letter rejecting the logistical argument he tried to offer as an explanation for his choice. "You would _rather_ have her go," Julina wrote, pointing out that "you know as well as I do that my baby is older than hers and not so much trouble and that I have not anything in the world to keep me at home. You might as well say 'it is Sarah I want.'"[62] Julina recognized the harsh tone of the letter and instructed JFS to burn it after reading, an order that he obviously ignored. In the end, none of the wives joined him on that trip, but tensions at home continued to run high even after that situation was resolved.

Sarah was often on the outs with Edna and Julina, which is hardly surprising since they were sisters, not only sister wives. Julina had also taken on the role of dignified matriarch. Sarah was the youngest, both in terms of age and time in the family. Edna, for her part, was most similar to JFS in temperament, which sometimes led to fireworks. In one letter he described himself to Edna as "the most disagreeable of men," prone "to find fault or grumble or to be dissatisfied with as many things as I can," before reminding her that "our patience is of the same width of cloth, and cut off at the same end."[63]

Most disagreements, at least those that merited inclusion in the letters, were minor, but JFS could be blunt to the point of cruelty in his rebukes. Sarah wrote to JFS complaining about a satchel he had sent as a gift, and he responded with furious sarcasm: "Your _grumbling_ little letter … is before me, how pleased I am to get such pleasant acknowledgments for my endeavors to please and gratify you." He told Sarah that while he forgave her for her insolence, she needed to "be a woman and not a girl or a child."[64]

Fighting over gifts often proved a problem. JFS could rarely send three of the same item, so he had to guess which wife would like which gifts. At one point, he figuratively threw up his hands in frustration, writing, "I can't serve you all just alike in this matter," adding that he would "rather give [the gifts] away or even see them burnt up" than have to deal with the negative feelings the gifts caused at home.[65] When Edna indicated that she planned to attend a "Sabbath school" course, JFS decried it as "nonsense" that would take her away from their children, and he pointedly reminded her of what he thought her first priority should be. "I think your little ones are quite a sufficient task at present," he wrote, especially since "I know you could not attend properly to the children, or rather child, when I was at home, and I do not see how you can now."[66]

JFS often complained when his wives did not write, when they did not write enough, or when what they wrote was unsatisfactory. The content, spelling, and even the dating of letters all came under scrutiny. Sarah's habit of leaving her letters undated drove the meticulous JFS nearly mad with irritation and confusion because letters mailed days or weeks apart sometimes arrived simultaneously, leaving him to

174   Chapter 10

puzzle over the order in which they ought to be read. Edna's propensity to include gossip and "unpleasant memories" of "pitiable creatures" prompted JFS to complain that the seventeen-cent postage had been wasted. When Julina and Sarah failed to write a letter to go along with one that Edna sent, JFS informed Edna that he was going to withhold letters from the other two until they showed him some consideration.[67]

JFS's wives continued to work full-time to support their families. Julina and Edna worked at the Endowment House kitchen, something that JFS wanted Sarah to do as well. When she resisted, JFS told her he would not force her to do anything "against her will."[68] Sarah also stayed out later than JFS felt appropriate, and he was not shy about letting her know. She also occasionally took her children away for extended periods, and JFS seemed to take it as a personal insult. "Is your home so unattractive that you want change? Are you better off away than at home? More comfortable? The children more healthy better cared for or safer?"[69]

Sometimes the wives tattled on one another. Julina once indicated to JFS that while she would never neglect her children and allow them to cry unimpeded, such could not be said for Sarah and Edna. "There has been considerable crying in the house since you left," she informed him, "but it has not been from my children."[70] Edna wrote to JFS that even though Sarah's excuse for not wanting to work at the Endowment House was that she did not want to neglect her children, she let her little ones "screem from morning till night." According to Edna, Sarah said she "didn't care" if the baby cried, and Edna, in turn, declared that if JFS was there, he would "thrash" her. The ever-spirited Sarah simply said, "I expect he would" and then carried on with her work.[71]

The letters exchanged between JFS and his wives show something of the deeply complex nature of plural marriage. JFS's three wives courted his favor, sometimes at the expense of the other two, and they all wanted to be seen as the best mother in the family. But for all of this, they worked together well most of the time. Caring for their children, doing household chores, and maintaining the property required strenuous, constant labor, and they did it with very little money. At this point, most of what they had to eat came from the Tithing Office.

A Homesick Mission President

JFS found no respite from his family worries in his work as mission president and repeatedly expressed his desire to leave England the entire time he was there. Except for his belief that God required such service from him, he would have happily "let the world go down to ruin" rather than be away from his family.[72] He also generally disliked office work, which he found confining and frustrating, and he did not have as many opportunities to interact with people on a day-to-day basis as he had during his previous mission to Britain. He rose at six each morning and did not get to bed until 10:45 p.m. at the earliest, and often much later. His days were spent sitting at a desk. "I have been writing all day," he complained to Julina. "I have scarcely been to the door, much less been out and my shoulder aches and I am tired of writing." He was growing weary of "smoky, sooty, dark, dingy, drunken, degraded Liverpool," where he found himself chained to a desk, "answering correspondents, writing for the *Star*, writing to the brethren, writing" from Monday to Saturday.[73]

Although most of the letters that JFS wrote for work concerned banal mission business, he did occasionally hold forth on subjects that had nothing to do with ecclesiastical work, and those letters offer valuable insights into JFS's worldview. For example, he wrote a lengthy, and somewhat angry, letter to William Staines about people who think that wealth is the same thing as freedom. By this time, JFS had largely given up on his youthful dreams of a well-heeled lifestyle, so he turned his relative poverty into a virtue. "When I can't get [something I want]," he wrote, "I can't get it and I try to content myself without it, for I have no rich relatives to fall back upon." He would rather walk than borrow money for train fare because this rendered him "free, independent, unbeholden to anyone." He speculated that "little contentment and liberty are found in riches."[74]

JFS would never have occasion to test that theory, but it sheds some light on his resentment of wealthy people, which is itself something of a puzzle. Although never wealthy, JFS was in fact much less well off than many of his contemporaries in the church hierarchy, who generally shared the political and economic views of the American upper classes. And despite being resentful of the treatment his impoverished mother endured at the hands of those upon whom she relied for support, he despised unionized labor and the redistribution of wealth via taxation. JFS viewed unions, and strikes in particular, as "combinations" akin to the wicked secret societies that undermined civilizations in the Book of Mormon and stood as an affront to the Zionic ideal.[75]

When he learned that his nephews were on strike from their jobs on the railroad in Utah, JFS dashed off a letter of reprimand calling their actions "most deplorable" and decrying the "evil tendencies" that led to union action. "Strikes," JFS warned, "have always been injurious to the employed, much more so than to employers," adding that every employee had the right to quit, but not the right to "dictate terms to their employer." After a lengthy recitation of the economic, political, and social evils of strikes, JFS concluded the letter by informing his nephews that "there are greater reasons why you should not join with strikers—your religion teaches you better. The word of God is against combinations." "Read the Book of Mormon," he concluded pointedly, "and reflect."[76]

This apparent contradiction between JFS's financial status and his support for the managerial classes over the workers may have its roots in JFS's Yankee Protestant devotion to the morality of work, and also in his peculiar position as a man of considerable power but severely limited means. In this way he was not unlike Britain's landed gentry whose titles lived on as atavistic traces of the wealth they

176 Chapter 10

once enjoyed, but who identified in sociological terms much more strongly with the rich than with the poor.

The day after writing his letter about the chains of wealth, JFS held forth on a very different subject. He revealed to his old Hawaiian mission friend John Cain that he had never forgotten his Anglo-American identity, and that it manifested in his political preferences. "As regards my faith in the principles of the Constitution," he wrote, "I am thoroughly American, but in the practical results to the governed, I am thoroughly English."[77] It is not exactly clear what JFS meant by this, but it is a helpful reminder, again, of his complexity. He was fathered by a New England–born Yankee and raised by an English mother, and he found ways to honor both sides of his ancestry.

English ancestry notwithstanding, JFS had reached his breaking point as mission president and wanted to go home. For most of his time in Britain, JFS could get no response to his letters to headquarters. In the summer of 1875, scarcely two months before he left to return to Utah, he complained, "I have never received a word from President Young since I left home, but little more from President Wells, and still little more from President Smith."[78]

Young had good reasons for his lack of contact. In 1874–1875 he directed a great deal of energy to reviving the Order of Enoch and attempting to create consecrated communities throughout Utah. Young's health had also begun a steep decline. He walked with difficulty and had to undergo the indignity of catheterization to relieve problems caused by an enlarged prostate. If this were not enough, one of his plural wives, Ann Eliza Webb, had initiated divorce proceedings and was enjoying the celebrity status earned by public appearances as a former member of Young's "harem."[79]

None of this made JFS any less tolerant of Young's long silences, which had proved simultaneously puzzling and frustrating, and also placed him in a difficult position when it came to requests from subordinate mission presidents that required input from headquarters. When the mission president in Germany repeatedly requested permission to publish the Doctrine and Covenants in German, JFS had eventually to respond, somewhat sheepishly, that "I have not heard a word from the First Presidency respecting the publication."[80] His requests for missionaries also proved a source of deep frustration. "I send for 12 or 14 experienced elders as the mission needs that kind of men, and I get <u>26</u> nearly all of whom are inexperienced boys and superannuated old men."[81] JFS's previous missionary experiences had not prepared him for conditions like this. He wanted to go home.

JFS was not the only person who wanted him to leave Britain. Back in Utah, the man whom JFS had replaced as mission president, the apostle Albert Carrington, was not happy about the arrangement and wanted to return to England as mission president as soon as possible. A Vermonter and a graduate of Dartmouth College, Carrington had joined the church in 1841, served as the editor of the *Deseret News*, and was called to the Quorum of the Twelve in 1870. Although JFS's junior in the Quorum, Carrington was part of Young's inner circle, and his apparent erudition gave him an inordinate amount of sway at church headquarters. JFS never expressed much affection for Carrington, and even made a point of noting in his journal that Carrington "dropped some tobacco out of his pocket while dressing" in his temple robes at a prayer circle meeting.[82]

In late 1874, JFS began receiving letters from friends concerned about his health. Puzzled by the onslaught of unwarranted concern, he eventually traced the rumors back to Carrington when George Gibbs wrote that he "was very sorry to learn, thro' Bro. Carrington, that your health is not good."[83] In a letter to Samuel Smith, JFS sarcastically noted that "it did not appear from whence Bro. Carrington got the intelligence" and assured Samuel that "my health has never been better."[84]

While Carrington was spreading rumors about JFS's failing health, he also busied himself writing to other European mission presidents offering advice and counsel, and even assigning missionaries to fields of labor, as if he were still in charge of the European mission. "Elders come here," JFS noted incredulously, "with special private and unauthorized instructions from C[arrington] and I must disregard my own judgment or his, and yet I am held responsible for all results."[85] He was furious after a missionary named Peter Sinclair informed him that Carrington had assigned him to the Orkney Islands. "There is something in the above sentence," JFS responded, that is "not quite clear to my mind."[86]

Clarity came soon enough. One of the European mission presidents wrote to JFS to express confusion about conflicting instructions he had received. One set came from JFS, and the other from Carrington. JFS did not try to hide his feelings about the interference any longer, replying that only one set of directives was ever legitimate—those coming from the president of the European mission—and further revealing that "Carrington has never recognized me as the President of the European Mission only in the second or third degree, or rather as directly subordinate to himself, in consequence of his inordinate desire to occupy the position himself, to which he is most welcome so far as I am concerned."[87]

The most important thing about the entire Carrington affair is that it prompted JFS to state, repeatedly, just how little he cared for the job and how desperate he was to return to Utah. By the late summer of 1875, he was showing signs of acute depression. In addition to everything else on his mind, the weather that summer came in cold and rainy and stayed that way. JFS had never been enamored with English weather, but the "dark, gloomy, comfortless" skies that summer were "enough to give old Nick [Satan] the blues."[88]

If all that were not enough, a sudden plague of lovesickness swept through the mission, with the main problem being that missionaries were falling in love with the maids. In an August letter to Julina, JFS said he could not stand to hear about "another going stark mad over some love or courting matters."[89] Then he received word that his barn had burned down, and his home, where his wives and children were sleeping, only narrowly escaped the same fate.[90] It was almost more than JFS could bear. "My temper," he wrote to Edna, "is of rather a bluish cast ... inclining toward that condition in women when it becomes necessary to 'have a good cry.'"[91] This period of depression led him to reflect, rather deeply, on his own weaknesses, and he opened up to Sarah, confiding that "if I had taken my own course through life it would have been the downhill path," and admitting that although he was struggling to "climb the hill of true and manly progress," his progress was "slow," his efforts "weak," and he was "much in need of help!"[92]

As usual, the main source of frustration for JFS was his anger, which may have cooled but still flared at times. Only his bone-deep dedication to his faith, and to what he believed to be the call of God, would induce JFS to remain in a place he did not want to be, where at least one other powerful figure did not want him to be, and where he was isolated from his wives and children.

If it had not been for Carrington's lobbying, JFS probably would have remained in England longer than he did. In May 1875, Brigham Young and George Q. Cannon had visited his wives and told them that JFS ought to remain there for at least four years.[93] But rumors were spreading, most certainly from Carrington, that JFS would likely be released from his position that summer or fall, a prospect that obviously thrilled him. But JFS was loath to surrender the position to Carrington, whom he suspected would be his replacement. When word reached JFS that "it is rumored that bro. Carrington will be called this spring to release [him]," he immediately concluded that this was not a wise move. In a letter to Sarah, he wrote, "Elder Woodruff would do more good in this position" than Carrington.[94]

JFS did not keep his thoughts about Carrington within the family circle. Instead, he lobbied George A. Smith to install Woodruff instead. In the last letter that JFS would ever receive from his beloved friend and mentor, George A. gently upbraided him, reminding him that "Woodruff is sixty-eight years old, and has endured almost incredible mental and physical labors during his life. We can hardly expect him to go on a mission to England."[95] But JFS refused to let the matter go. He wrote back that while he realized that "Woodruff has passed through many narrow escapes, and has seen hard service, he will work wherever he is [anyway], but no harder here than at home." The mission needed Woodruff's "life and energy," something that JFS admitted he could not muster himself.[96] He frankly noted in his journal that he did "not think Elder Carrington is the man for this mission," insisting that "Woodruff is the man the mission needs."[97]

Carrington was only seven years younger than Woodruff, so the argument about age seemed weak, and JFS knew it. The truth was that Brigham Young wanted Carrington in England, and that was going to happen regardless of JFS's misgivings. What no one knew at the time was that Carrington had been involved in an adulterous relationship with a young woman in England since his first stint there as mission president. Although rumors and allegations with sufficient credibility had prompted Young to question him on the matter, Carrington denied it, and Young let the matter drop.[98]

The next news JFS heard about George A. Smith was a cable from Utah informing him that his closest confidant in the Mormon leadership, his surrogate father, had died. Although only fifty-eight years old, George had been morbidly obese for decades, and his health had been failing in recent years, but his death still came as a crushing shock to JFS. He paid tribute to George in his journal:

> The People loved him as they did President Young, or as they did the Prophet Joseph Smith. No man ever possessed more supremely the love, and confidence of the entire Church. He never preached a false doctrine, nor to my knowledge ever made a mistake in his whole public career, neither religiously nor politically. His whole great Soul was centered in the Kingdom of God, and his most valuable life was spent in the interests of the people. The world has lost a bright light, and an honest man, The Saints a wise and faithful counselor, a Prophet, Seer and Revelator, and as true a friend as Christ the Lord. As for myself, I feel as though he were my own father, and my greatest Earthly benefactor.[99]

George A. Smith's death shook JFS in profound ways. For days after receiving the news, he sat alone in his office at 42 Islington, so paralyzed with grief and "a sense of loneliness akin to horror" that he could not even complete a notice for the *Star* about the death. He cried openly, frankly admitting that "I am no stoic when my heart is burdened ... tears are a relief, and I welcome them."[100] He spent hours staring at the lithograph of Salt Lake City that hung on the office wall, imagining the "mournful cortege" making its way through the city to the cemetery. JFS felt adrift and afraid. He confided to Sarah that "I feel as though I need his fatherly care, his friendly counsel, his cheering advice." JFS had lost his one true intimate among the leaders of the church and again felt cast back onto his own resources to make his way. Always sensitive to the issue of his own masculinity, he paid George the highest tribute he could give when he wrote, "If I am not a man, it is not because he did not try to make me one."[101] Even fifteen years later, JFS maintained his deep feelings for this uncle. In 1890, he sent a letter to Bathsheba Smith, writing that "no man ever lived, except my own father, for whom I have a deeper affection that for ... George A. Smith."[102]

Not only was the death an emotional blow to the entire church, and to JFS personally, but JFS sensed something sinister in its timing, which came just as "all hell was let loose to war against the Priesthood."[103] He saw the death of George A. Smith as part of a larger trial for the church, one that seemed to never end. "There are ravening wolves after the blood of thine anointed," JFS wrote in an open letter to God.[104] George A.'s death also drew out in JFS an unusual longing for someone still in his thirties. "I feel as though one by one the ties of earth are being severed, and not very slowly," he wrote to David McKenzie, the day after George A.'s death, "and soon the greater attractions will be behind the veil."[105]

180 Chapter 10

On 21 August 1875, JFS received word from Brigham Young that, owing to JFS's supposed ill health, he was being released from his duties as president of the European mission so that he could "recruit [his] health amid your family and friends in Utah."[106] His replacement, of course, would be Albert Carrington. Although JFS weakly protested that his health had never been better, his heart was no longer in it. On 6 September, he confided in his journal, writing, "I am not sorry that this is likely to be my last Sabbath in Liverpool." The loss of George A. Smith had proved to be the final blow, the last bad moment in a mission of nearly continuous anxiety, disappointment, and frustration. JFS welcomed the opportunity to leave, and he greeted his release with more relief than he had ever before experienced.[107]

On 15 September 1875, JFS—bowed and, to a great degree, humbled—"bid farewell to old England, perhaps for the last time." It would not, of course, be the last time, because although he firmly believed that he was "more useful at home than abroad," Young did not agree. JFS did not know it, but he would be back in Britain in less than two years.

In the fall of 1875, JFS settled back into his life in Salt Lake City. After a brief stop at Brigham Young's office, he was finally reunited with his beloved wives and children. However, he found their appearance slightly shocking, describing them in his journal as looking "as poor and thin as weasles."[108] But it did not take long before the sentimental haze that had hovered around JFS while away from home yielded to the considerable demands of his daily routine of family and church responsibilities. In a moment of candor, he wrote to a friend that "my mission was a rest for me, compared with the labors I now have to perform here."[109] Still, he found the "mountain breezes ... of our beautiful city" even "more congenial and pleasant" than when he left.[110]

JFS found that the general level of spiritual zeal among the Mormons in Utah had undergone a "decided improvement" during his years away, despite being "vigorously assailed ... by the whole force of the powers of darkness."[111] He did not use such language about the powers of darkness figuratively. Like most Mormons at that time, JFS believed strongly that he was living in the end times, and that he was in the middle of a cosmic struggle between good and evil that would end with the imminent return of Christ to the earth. Thus, nearly every difficulty that he faced he attributed to "his Satanic majesty's ... determined efforts against the work of God." The intensity of the "opposition" to Mormonism served as evidence for JFS that Satan was engaged "in the final desperate struggle to maintain his supremacy" over the world.[112] That struggle between Satan and Christ was playing out, at least as JFS saw it, on all stages of human endeavor, most noticeably in politics and economics.

Economically, things were not as good as they might have been if the "perfidious judges and carpetbaggers and their lying sheet" had not "effectually frightened away capital, and made times dull and money scarce."[113] The deeply entrenched relationship between religion, politics, and economics in Utah, to which JFS referred, formed the basis for his next assignment as a general authority. In December, he accompanied Brigham Young and John Taylor to Davis County, just north of Salt Lake. According to Young, the "Priesthood" in Farmington wanted a "president" to take charge of their "material and spiritual interests."[114] Young, on the spot, gave the assignment to JFS, so in addition to his regular work at the Endowment House and the Historian's Office, he now had to regularly travel to Davis County, where he served, for all practical purposes, as the stake president.

In addition to his ecclesiastical duties, JFS devoted a great deal of energy to fixing problems with the economy in Davis County. When he arrived, the county had the usual mercantile, which was performing fairly well, but several small cooperatives were failing, including a tannery, a shoe shop, and an outlet for "surplus stock."[115] The ward at Kaysville was in the midst of a squabble over the local bishop's management of the community grist mill, and similar divisions threatened to break out if the local businesses continued on their downward slopes. In an attempt to remedy the situation, JFS gathered all of these businesses together under the name Davis County Cooperative Company. He served as president, and the bishops of the local wards in the county served as directors. In short order, the tannery and shoe shop got back on their feet, with JFS spearheading investment efforts that yielded the considerable sum of $600. Additionally, JFS experimented successfully with dry farming in the county and, at the direction of Young, planted an acre of tobacco.[116]

The mid-1870s brought a surprising and unwelcome possibility into JFS's life when he nearly ended up serving as church patriarch. His half brother John, with whom he had always had a somewhat strained relationship, had never embraced his role as patriarch with the zeal that Brigham Young expected. John was by nature a retiring and shy man, an introvert who preferred to stay out of the spotlight and who had little confidence in his own capacities as a public speaker or representative of the church. The same insecurities that he had expressed to JFS twenty years earlier continued to bedevil him. On top of that, although he had two wives, John seemed unenthusiastic when it came to plural marriage. Add to that his relaxed approach to the Word of Wisdom, and the scene was set for conflict.

Young simply could not stand John. At the general conference in April 1873, JFS felt stung when Young refused to present John's name during the sustaining of church authorities.[117] During the October 1875 general conference, a combined meeting of the Quorum of the Twelve and the First Presidency met and voted to release John and replace him with JFS. JFS intervened, probably for reasons of both family loyalty and self-interest. According to Wilford Woodruff, the brothers met with Young, and JFS "pled vary hard to try John another six month to see if he would magnify his calling any better than he had done in the past."[118]

Eight years later, JFS told a meeting of the School of the Prophets that "John had not lived his religion" because "he smoked and, though having two wives, he lived entirely with one." JFS encouraged the other members of the school to

182 Chapter 10

work with John and help him "become a man."[119] Following his typical pattern, JFS equated religiosity with masculinity, something that his fifty-one-year-old brother probably did not appreciate. In any case, John survived the close scrape with his calling intact, but JFS would struggle with his complex feelings toward his brother until John's death in 1911.

As JFS settled into a routine of work, both at the Salt Lake City Endowment House and the Historian's Office and in Davis County, he wasted no time expanding his family. All three of his wives gave birth in 1876. In July, Julina had a baby boy named after his father. He was known as Joseph Fielding Smith, and he became president of the LDS Church in 1970. Another son, born to Sarah, was named Heber John Smith. Edna gave birth in December to Alfred Jason Smith. He now had nine living children.

Later that year JFS mourned the loss of his half sister, Sarah Smith Griffin. Only thirteen months older than him, Sarah was the last child born to Hyrum Smith and Jerusha Barden. She and JFS had never been particularly close, but when she died just weeks after giving birth to a daughter in November 1876, JFS took the child in and determined to raise her as his own. Sadly, the baby died two months later.[120] Then, in March 1877, after an illness of six weeks, JFS's son Heber died at the age of five months.[121] Alfred passed away just a little over a year later, in April 1878. The loss of his sister and the three babies shattered JFS, but with each passing year, his family continued to be an anchor that made it easier for him to continue in the face of such tragedy. Although he would never grow accustomed to losing loved ones, at least he had a growing number of loved ones remaining to comfort him.

In October 1876, JFS had been called to return to Liverpool to serve as president of the European mission the following spring. In April he attended the public dedication of the St. George Temple and spoke for over an hour. The last time a temple had been dedicated, in Nauvoo in 1846, JFS was seven years old and preparing to flee to an unknown wilderness. Now, not yet forty, he witnessed a temple dedication in a much different setting. The Mormons, under Brigham Young's aggressive leadership, had created an empire that stretched from San Bernardino, California, to northern Utah. They had managed to stave off the U.S. Army and had continued to practice plural marriage largely unmolested despite legislative action against it. What JFS did not know as he sat in the St. George Temple was that the next decade would be one of the most challenging the church would ever face.

For reasons that were not recorded, JFS had decided to take Sarah and four-year-old Joseph Richards to England with him. When they left, Julina found the parting difficult, particularly because little Joseph Fielding was suffering from a terrible sore throat. Dealing with a fussy child must have underscored her trepidation at having to oversee the operation of a massive household that now had 50 percent fewer adults to help shoulder the load. She faced the prospect of being without her husband and sister-wife, for what she thought would be four or five years, with faith. "I will look to the Lord for help," she wrote in her journal, "and believe he will help missionary's wives and children that are left at home, as well as the missionary, wife, and child that are absent."[122]

Julina's faith was rewarded, and in late May, JFS arrived in Liverpool with Sarah and Joseph Richards in tow. Sarah and Richards, as they called the little boy, had suffered considerably from seasickness, which JFS "could not help laughing at them about." Richards, desperately wanting to prove himself to his father, "would go to the table with [JFS] every time, and when he would get so sick he could not sit up and eat, he would … finish his meal" prostrate on the chair next to his father. JFS could not have been prouder of this demonstration of grit and recorded with satisfaction that his son behaved as a "little man."[123] Even a four-year-old could sense what it would take to impress JFS.

Back at the 42 Islington office, JFS found himself staving off homesickness again. Even with Sarah and Richards to keep him company, he found that he had to work hard to ensure that his "heart was hardened and the thoughts trained and disciplined in the school of duty and stern reality."[124] When the Lambson sisters did not write with the regularity that JFS desired, he chastised Julina because he had written to her "twice as much as you did to me."[125] Edna, knowing JFS's neediness in this regard, had seized the opportunity to take a passive aggressive swipe at her husband, informing him that, because he had "company," he "must not expect to hear so often" from her.[126]

When not attending to his family, JFS's efforts were focused on a special project that Brigham Young had given him and wanted put first on his list of priorities: moving the headquarters of the British mission from Liverpool to London. For some reason, Young believed that London's climate was healthier than Liverpool's, "especially for Americans." But beyond this, he recognized that the church in northern England had essentially stopped growing. In London and its environs, new congregations were being added, and church meetings were well attended. In Liverpool, by contrast, "the most zealous efforts to obtain congregations of any size have no effect upon the people."[127]

Young gave JFS a lengthy list of requirements for the potential new office. It had to be cheap, but in a good neighborhood. It had to be close to ports and railways, but not subject to worldly influences. It needed to be centrally located among the local church branches, but it had to function as an office, a printing and binding location, and a house. Young thought this would be an easy thing to arrange given what he believed to be London's real estate situation.[128]

Ever dutiful, JFS traveled to London to investigate. Of course, he immediately confirmed what he already suspected: the cheap buildings were not in good neighborhoods—especially not a building of the size that Young required—and neither were ports and railway depots. There was simply no way to meet all, or even most, of Young's requirements. In July, JFS wrote a detailed report about the prospects of the move to London. Without being too pointed about the general impossibility

184   Chapter 10

of the task, he simply listed the rents and conditions in the various neighborhoods, pointing out that no one location had everything Young wanted.[129]

JFS also volunteered two reasons for staying in Liverpool. First, he argued that it was far superior for Mormons to emigrate through Liverpool's port. London would not do, and therefore they would have to maintain an office in Liverpool anyway to handle emigration matters. Second, he pointed out that the church's printing press was in no condition to be moved from Liverpool to London. At the risk of overselling his point, JFS speculated that the press could not even be sold as anything but scrap iron, and a new press would have to be purchased for the proposed London office.[130]

Besides scouting around London, JFS's work as mission president followed the same rhythms as it had during his previous tenure. He involved himself heavily in the production of the *Millennial Star* and spent a good deal of time on emigration matters. JFS also found himself once again in the position of having to deal with missionaries and the general problem of staffing that bedeviled all LDS missions. In the nineteenth century, the duration of a proselytizing mission depended largely on personal circumstances. Most men did not apply for mission service as they do today. Instead, bishops and stake presidents submitted names of potential missionaries to church headquarters, which would extend an official call. The vast majority of missionaries during this period were married men with children, so how much time they spent on the mission depended in part on how well their families got on without them. JFS, for example, received a letter from Brigham Young requesting that a missionary laboring in Switzerland be released and sent back to Utah "because his wife is in poor health and his family is in straightened circumstances."[131]

JFS regularly handled requests from missionaries to return home for various reasons, some of which he found more convincing than others. As a general rule, he did not want any missionary who did not want to be there. Most of the men serving in the missions worked hard and kept their noses clean. The ones who made it into the historical record usually did not. In 1877, for instance, JFS dealt with one missionary who was charged with receiving stolen goods, and several who became "entangled" to various degrees with local women. "It is wrong," JFS counseled one man, "for any Elder, while on a mission, to form any alliance with women. They are not here for that purpose, and they have no business to entangle themselves by making vows or covenants of marriage." JFS viewed any unauthorized plural marriage as adultery, and "adultery is DEATH!"[132] Of these and other troublesome missionaries, JFS wrote that "sometimes men do no good on missions, or more harm than good," and in such cases, "they should be released at once as the cause will be better served with them at home."[133]

Over the summer of 1877, JFS heard from Brigham Young with unusual frequency. Young wrote long, chatty letters about the progress of the church in areas of Utah outside of Salt Lake, the problems that missionaries were facing in Mexico, and the progress of the three temples under construction in Salt Lake, Logan, and Manti. He also told JFS to lean harder on the members of the church in his mission to provide funds specifically for building a temple. On 15 August 1877, JFS read a letter from Young declaring that his "health is excellent," but it was the last letter Young would ever send to JFS.[134] At 7:45 a.m. on 30 August, JFS received a cable informing him that Young had died of "inflammation of the bowels superinduced by cholera morbus." Although "stunned with amazement and grief at the most unexpected sad news," JFS did not suffer anything close to the depression that had overwhelmed him almost exactly two years earlier when George A. Smith died.[135]

JFS and Young never had a particularly close relationship, but JFS's admiration for Young was considerable. Although technically a member of the First Presidency since 1866, JFS had rarely functioned as a counselor to Young. In fact, the two apparently had something of a falling out in 1876, when Young wanted to appoint his wayward son, John, to replace George A. Smith in the First Presidency. JFS had told Young that if he had to have one of his sons, it should be Brigham Jr., who at the very least gave the impression of religious devotion. Not surprisingly, Young ignored JFS.[136]

After Young's death, JFS fretted that a schism might develop over the question of succession, but all he could do from across the ocean was hope that "the spirit of peace and unbroken union brood over the councils of the Priesthood." Still, JFS noted that the Mormon people had come a long way since they lost their last prophet. "Unlike his predecessor, Joseph Smith, [Young] did not die by violence in the midst of enemies, but in peace in the house of his family."[137]

Young's death also put the spotlight on one of JFS's interesting idiosyncrasies. He believed strongly in premonitions, but he often didn't mention them until after the fact. In this case, JFS claimed in a letter to Edna that a few days before Young's death, he "had an impression that some great event was about to happen" but assumed that it meant "Queen Victoria would die soon." "It seems the whispering of the Spirit is correct," he reflected, "tho' I missed the name."[138]

Young's death also signaled the end of JFS's mission. He and Orson Pratt, who had come to England to oversee publication of a new edition of the Doctrine and Covenants, received word from church headquarters on 2 September 1877 that they were expected back at once. JFS dutifully packed up Sarah and their son and headed west, arriving in Utah in early October.

New Leader, Old Challenges

The majority of Mormons in Utah thought that the October 1877 general conference would include the installation of a new church president. In fact, the settlements buzzed with speculation about what would happen. Upon Young's death, the First Presidency was dissolved, and John Taylor, as president of the Quorum of the Twelve, became the highest-ranking ecclesiastical figure. Given the various other tasks at hand, Taylor apparently did not want to introduce another potential source of contention by pushing to reorganize the First Presidency. This did not stop members of the Twelve from expressing their opinions on the matter. Franklin D. Richards took many members of the Quorum by surprise, suggesting that JFS be presented for a sustaining vote as Young's successor. Unsurprisingly, "the apostles did not accept this and there was some time before there was perfect union so that the Presidency could be organized."[139]

George Q. Cannon spoke frankly to the public on the topic at the general conference. He knew, he said, that the people were expecting the announcement of Young's replacement, but "The Lord has not revealed [the identity of the new president] to us, and until he shall require this [reorganization] at our hands, we shall not do it." "You can wait," he told them, "for the voice of the Lord . . . [and until then] cease engaging in vain and foolish ideas upon these subjects."[140] And with that, the matter was closed.

Once he was back in Utah, JFS found himself in an unsettled position. His return had occasioned a brutal attack from the *Salt Lake Tribune* that described him as an "insensate bigot" and the "most intemperate fanatic in the whole multitudinous priesthood." The *Tribune* had gotten hold of Levira's 1867 affidavit and used JFS's treatment of his "neglected and shamefully abused first wife" as evidence of his "brutal instincts."[141]

As embarrassing as this must have been, JFS had larger problems with which to struggle. He remained president of the European mission, which meant that he had to conduct all mission business via transatlantic mail. In October 1877, he sent a letter to Charles Nibley at the Liverpool office, writing that "so far brother Taylor holds me to my post and for the present I would like you to send me a transcript of monthly and quarterly reports that I may keep track of matters."[142]

Despite Nibley's eager and able assistance, the lion's share of the work fell to JFS. Well into 1878, he still did not know if he would be released or required to return to England and resume his mission, although he made it clear that he would prefer to remain home; Richards, for his part, wanted to return and finish his mission in England even though JFS "wished [I] could say definitely that I thought it was" over.[143]

In the meantime, JFS still had to account for the progress of things in the mission, and Taylor showed a particular interest in the low levels of tithing coming in from Britain. JFS explained the disappointing numbers by blaming it on the return to Utah of several "prominent" missionaries.[144] Britain was in poor shape indeed if the ebb and flow of a relatively small missionary corps could have a measurable impact on tithing receipts, but the situation in Utah was little better, as JFS found out during his next assignment.

In addition to JFS's work as mission president, Taylor appointed him to a committee whose task was to audit the estate of Brigham Young. It was difficult to tell which parts of Young's estate belonged to him, and which belonged to the church. Although this had also happened in the wake of Joseph Smith's death, both the reasons for it and the scale of it were different in Young's case. The Morrill Act of 1862 dictated that no religious or charitable organization in any American territorial holding could possess real estate valued at or above $50,000.[145]

The easiest way around this was simply to deed any real estate above that limit to Brigham Young. All of this was, of course, a sham. The government could not seize the assets because, on paper, Young owned them. When he died, this presented a complex problem. Even acknowledging the obvious ruse, it was not completely clear what should be considered, by the church, Young's personal holdings and thus liable to be distributed to his heirs, and what should be transferred to the next church president.

The auditing committee, chaired by Wilford Woodruff, also included the apostle Erastus Snow, and they did their best to tease apart the situation and come to an equitable resolution. In April 1878, the committee issued its findings. Their report stated that the bulk of Young's estate, around $700,000, could not rightly be transferred to his heirs because it belonged to the church.[146] Not surprisingly, Young's many heirs found this hard to swallow and initiated legal proceedings to keep the church from claiming such a large part of the estate.

Although the situation eventually was settled through skillful negotiations between Woodruff and Young's family, JFS was appalled at what the audit revealed. Young, it turned out, had been rather free with church funds. While JFS was begging the Tithing Office for potatoes, Young's heirs were "importunate and eager for their shares" of the remnants of Young's luxurious lifestyle. Meanwhile, the church was facing financial problems. "We are in the narrows financially," JFS wrote, and, being too loyal to Young's memory to state his disgust explicitly, he merely noted that "while it is not my province to blame anyone for this condition of things, I cannot altogether close my eyes to the belief that it might have been different."[147]

JFS found other tasks more enjoyable. In 1877–1878, he worked on two projects with his intellectual mentor, Orson Pratt. Pratt had replaced George A. Smith as church historian, and JFS had returned to employment at the Historian's Office in 1877. In late 1877, JFS and Pratt produced a report drawing John Taylor's attention to "certain discrepancies, disagreements, errors, omissions, etc., in different editions of the Book of Mormon and other Church publications." The report focused on two main sources of disagreement: conflicts between the first and third American editions of the Book of Mormon, and disagreement in various early sources about the identity of the angel who visited Joseph Smith in 1823 and revealed to him the location of the gold plates.[148]

In their comparison of the editions of the Book of Mormon, Pratt and JFS identified more than thirty points of disagreement, most of which consisted of single words or short phrases. The question of the angel's identity was more problematic. Although the official position, as published in the Doctrine and Covenants, was

188   Chapter 10

that the angel's name was Moroni, several early manuscripts as well as an article from the Nauvoo-era newspaper *Times and Seasons*, identified the angel as Nephi. Pratt and JFS concluded that, in both cases, the errors were scribal errors or printer's mistakes. They recommended that "a very careful and judicious revision … be made of the whole" Book of Mormon so that a "more correct edition may be published … so that it may serve as the standard edition" of the book. As for the confusion about Nephi and Moroni, the two historians concluded that Moroni was the correct name, and that this information ought to be "published for general information at as early a date" as possible.[149]

Just a few years later, JFS continued his efforts to locate and pin down solid historical footings for knowledge that had been taken for granted for decades. In early 1882, he wrote to Addison Everett, saying that he had heard from Eliza R. Snow, who might "have some information, not generally known or understood, relative to the time and place at which Peter, James, and John conferred the Melchisedec [*sic*] Priesthood upon Joseph and Oliver." Everett responded with an account that, to this day, remains part of the canonical explanation of the event. According to Everett, Joseph Smith and Oliver Cowdery had been on trial in Pennsylvania on the charges of being "false prophets," but even though the judge dismissed the charges, a violent mob awaited the men outside of the courthouse. Their attorney aided their escape through a back window, after which the two men wandered all night through a swampy forest. At dawn, exhausted, they collapsed, and just at that moment, three heavenly messengers appeared and conferred upon Smith and Cowdery the Melchizedek Priesthood.[150] JFS promptly responded, thanking Everett for the information and promising to check his account with the known movements of Joseph Smith.[151]

These may seem like rather unremarkable tasks, but they reveal something significant about both JFS and the development of Mormonism as a religious tradition. Here, again, JFS was involved with an effort to systematize Mormonism, to iron out the historical wrinkles just as he had tried to do with the theological ones. The urge toward systematization is a common phase through which most historically persistent religious traditions pass. Religions reach a point at which, in order to survive as an organization, they must take the messy and often contradictory ideas left by the charismatic leaders of the first generation and arrange them into a uniform, rational system of thought that can be more readily transmitted and taught to those without firsthand experience with the founding generation. JFS was deeply involved in this process for his entire life, partially because of his position in the second generation of church leaders, and partly because of his personal predilection for order.

The second project for the Historian's Office called for Pratt and JFS to travel east to gather information about Mormon history and note the condition of historical sites. Pratt, who initiated the trip, saw it as an opportunity to speak to any still-living witnesses to the early events of church history who never made the journey to

Utah. The report, written in JFS's hand and bearing the marks of his thinking and writing style, stated that Independence, Missouri, the land pronounced by Joseph Smith to be the future site of the New Jerusalem from which Christ would reign, was in poor condition. Unsurprisingly, JFS did not cast a charitable eye on the state in which he was born. All the trees that had once been there were gone, and the ground was "parched and dusty." The land was generally overgrown, and farms were "almost universally small, old, and dilapidated presenting the appearance of unthrift and decay." All of this, JFS concluded, was "unmistakably the result of indolence."[152]

The scenery may have left something to be desired, but JFS and Pratt found interesting conversation partners, including William McLellin, a member of the original Quorum of Twelve Apostles called in 1835. After a bitter falling out with Joseph Smith, he was excommunicated from the church in the spring of 1838, but he remained in Missouri for the rest of his life. He welcomed Pratt and JFS warmly and provided them with an extensive tour of important sites in the Independence area, as well as a lengthy interview giving his firsthand perspective on the events of the 1830s. JFS found McLellin "eccentric and opinionated" and his belief that Joseph Smith was a prophet who eventually fell out of favor with God repugnant. Although he provided them with useful information, JFS was convinced that McLellin's "spiritual life had died, and his growth ceased at the time of his apostasy from the church."[153]

Leaving Independence, JFS and Pratt traveled to Richmond, Missouri, where they met with David Whitmer, who at that time was the last of the Three Witnesses to the Book of Mormon still living. JFS found Whitmer "well preserved" for a man of seventy-three years, and the owner of a "conscientious, honest heart." They peppered him with questions: Did he know when Peter, James, and John visited Joseph Smith? What were the date and time of his experience with the gold plates? Where did Oliver Cowdery die? Did he actually see an angel? Did he know when the sealed portion of the Book of Mormon would be "brought forth"? And, finally, the question that they most wanted an answer to: "Have you, in your possession, the original manuscript of the Book of Mormon?" What Whitmer actually possessed was a copy (usually called the printer's manuscript) of the original manuscript that was used to publish the Book of Mormon. And what did he plan to do with it when he died? He didn't know, but it was clear that he did not intend for it to ever end up in Utah.[154]

Pratt tried every avenue he could to get Whitmer to relinquish the manuscript, but to no avail. The Whitmers believed that it had "apotropaic" qualities and viewed the object as "a source of protection to the place or house in which it might be kept." Furthermore, the Book of Mormon, Whitmer told them, was to go to "all the world." JFS read a subtle criticism in that remark and tartly replied, "Yes, and we have sent that book to the Danes, the Swedes, the Spanish, the Italians, the French, the Germans, the Welsh, and to the Islands of the sea." The book had even been translated into "Hindoostani," and all by the LDS Church, the "Brighamites" whom Whitmer so despised. "You see, Whitmer," JFS concluded, "the church has

190   Chapter 10

not been idle."[155] As with McLellin, JFS struggled while talking to Whitmer to keep his conflicting emotions in check. Both men simultaneously mesmerized and infuriated him; they were living artifacts of a dying past that meant everything to JFS, and yet they had ultimately rejected Joseph Smith, Brigham Young, and polygamy.

JFS's feelings were far less mixed when he and Pratt arrived at Far West, Missouri, and stopped by the home of Jacob Whitmer, David's nephew. JFS asked for lodgings, which were refused as soon as his identity became clear, and then he asked if the man knew where any of the Smiths had lived. JFS told Jacob that he had been born in Far West, and that he would be obliged to see his birthplace for the first time as an adult. Whitmer then began to talk about where "Joe Smith" might have lived.

Although he did not know it, Whitmer was edging breathtakingly close to danger. All of his life, JFS despised hearing anyone referred to as Joe. He even castigated his own daughter for referring to her husband by that name, claiming that the nickname "seems to cast a slight on the whole line of Joseph's reaching back to him who was sold into Egypt." The name Joseph was so sacred, he wrote, that his sense of honor "would not permit me to abbreviate it even if it were borne by my worst enemy."[156] Hearing Whitmer use the dreaded name in his presence was more than JFS could stand. Having finally reached his breaking point, he rather pointedly remarked upon Whitmer's lack of respect. JFS managed to avoid fisticuffs, but furiously concluded that Jacob Whitmer was "contemptible and low," a man awash in the foul brew of "bigotry and disrespect."[157]

After inspecting the abandoned temple site at Far West, JFS and Pratt traveled to Illinois, where they enjoyed a friendly visit with Joseph Smith's youngest sister, Lucy. They also attended, and preached polygamy, at an RLDS meeting before heading to Kirtland. There they toured the temple, which was in use as an RLDS meetinghouse, and although JFS remarked upon the poor condition of the building's interior, he was happy to see that the external walls seemed sturdy.

After touring Kirtland and environs, JFS and Pratt decided to continue east to Palmyra. Neither of them had ever been there, and they spent their entire visit exploring the Hill Cumorah. The two observed "seven good sized trees" growing on the west side of the hill, toward the north end, about two-thirds of the way to the top. Among the trees, they found "a distinct impression," which they concluded "must have been the very spot from whence the plates were taken ... in 1827."[158] JFS found the experience deeply moving because of both his religious and family connections to the place. Curiously, the two men did not make any effort to locate the "sacred grove" or the Smith family's farm during this trip. More than twenty years would pass before JFS returned to Palmyra, but when he did, he would make a point of visiting the sacred grove, which had, by that time, become much more prominent in LDS historical narratives than it was in 1878.

The men ended their tour in New York City, where Pratt embarked for England to finish his publication of the scriptures that had been cut short by Brigham Young's death. JFS returned to Utah, where things seemed a bit bleak.

In a December 1877 letter to friends in England, JFS described a grim economic picture in Utah. Winter had brought a flood of "tramps" to Salt Lake "begging for grub and lodgings," land prices were falling, individual Mormons were going deep into debt, and home industries were failing. JFS also found the materialism of many Mormons repugnant and dangerous. He said it was the "extravagance, the vain desire to imitate the fashions and follies of the world," together with a seemingly unquenchable "desire for money or gain," that had brought the Mormons "to this verge of ruin." JFS also lamented that "our rail roads and coal mines are all gone out of our hands," leaving the Mormons "at the hands of the Union Pacific Railroad, a soulless, merciless corporation."[159]

Corporations were indeed riding high in the late 1870s on a tide of increasing capital based on high savings rates and the absence of the regulatory welfare state that would tame laissez-faire capitalism in the 1880s and 1890s.[160] For JFS, the rise of sinister corporations could be explained simply: "evil has done it."[161] He "reprehended the silliness of those who follow after fashions," not only because of their worldliness, but also because of their tendency to lag "a long way behind" the trends.[162]

Of course, the causes of the economic troubles in Utah stemmed from far more complex sources than JFS identified. Part of the problem was the intractable boom and bust nature of the nineteenth-century American economy. If the Mormons had ever been isolated from these cycles, by the late 1870s they most certainly were not. Home industries had failed not because of religious indifference, as JFS implied, but because superior products could be purchased much more cheaply from other sources. JFS found this excuse wanting and publicly castigated the Mormons for allowing home industries to dwindle just because they "were more expensive." Relying on cheaper imported goods, JFS warned, would leave the saints "dependent upon Babylon." When the Mormons finally woke up and started to take the "best interest of Zion" seriously, then they would "be proud to wear home made clothes" even though "it costs us more" than "to wear the stuffed, starched, glossed and glittering shoddy of the world."[163]

Ironically, one of JFS's own letters illustrates the problems of home industry. Not long after JFS returned from England, he ordered a rug from a local Mormon artisan. Shortly after placing the rug in his home, he wrote to the manufacturer and complained that while he did not mind paying more for a rug to support home manufacture, he found the quality of the rug questionable. He expected it to be "more substantial" and "more durable" than it apparently was. Instead, he said, "It feels slazy"—that is, of low quality.[164]

One of the most pronounced features of JFS's worldview was his proclivity to assign simple, morally inflected causes to complex social, economic, and political problems. This did not represent a lack of intellect; JFS was arguably among the most intelligent church leaders of his day. But it does reflect his need to index his experiences and observations according to a deeply, almost cosmically, dualistic

192   Chapter 10

paradigm. From his earliest days, JFS had interpreted everything according to an absolutely intransigent belief that God and the devil were fighting a war, and he was in the middle of it. He saw things in black and white, with very few gray areas. The LDS Church and its leaders were God's proxies in this war, and anyone or anything that challenged either of those was nothing more than a weapon wielded by Satan. There was no such thing as a nonreligious issue to JFS.

In a sermon in January 1879, JFS mocked the proposal put forward by some that the church should give "a portion of our municipal offices to some of our outside friends." With searing sarcasm, JFS wrote that

> we came to this desert, desolate, gathered and made American citizens. Now we certainly ought to be most liberal and divide the few meagre offices that are left that are of a local character among our enemies. That is a splendid idea.... And then perhaps it might be well to elect some of our Methodist ministers to be bishops in our Church.

He reminded his listeners that "when we were mixed up with the world if we enjoyed any rights it was because our enemies could not help it."[165] Now that the demographic tables had turned, JFS believed it would be folly to allow the church's "enemies" any quarter, political or otherwise.

JFS explained the broader principle behind such sentiments to the assembled congregation at the April 1879 general conference: "I have never yet found anyone who draws the dividing line between our spiritual and temporal interests, nor do I expect to."[166] It was the duty of each Latter-day Saint to adopt a holistic view of life and understand that the so-called temporal issues with which the saints struggled were indeed part of the process of building up the kingdom of God. This would have important implications for his eventual leadership of the church. It would fall to JFS to reconcile the church's desire to become "American" with the need for an independent Kingdom of God, a task for which he was not ideally suited.

JFS's path to leadership was not clear after Brigham Young's death. John Taylor delayed the reorganization of the First Presidency for three years, but in the fall of 1880, the apostles had a series of discussions about creating a fully functional First Presidency. Significant disagreement surfaced when Taylor broached the subject at a meeting at the Endowment House on 6 October 1880. JFS wrote in his journal that the proposal "Was not well received," least of all by him; in fact, he was "astounded" at the prospect. The members of the Quorum spoke freely on the matter in meetings held over the next couple of days. Some of the men felt that creating a new First Presidency would require a revelation from God. When one of them asked Taylor if he had received such a divine communication, he "declined to answer."[167]

Orson Pratt chided the others for even asking such a question, pointing out that they "already had the Lord's mind on this," and then quoting the relevant portions of the Doctrine and Covenants.[168] While Taylor may have taken heart from Pratt's support, his good feeling melted when Pratt suggested that, given the advanced age of many members of the Quorum, a younger man ought to be advanced to the presidency. Pratt almost certainly had JFS in mind, but Wilford Woodruff objected, arguing that Taylor, as senior apostle, ought to be church president. Woodruff, as the next senior apostle, and with one eye on the future, had his own reasons for advocating a process that advanced the senior apostle to the presidency.

JFS was not persuaded by any of the arguments. He did not feel that the creation of a new First Presidency was "very important or necessary."[169] Things seemed to be going relatively smoothly, with the Mormon people seemingly content under the leadership of the Twelve. Changing this up would, he thought, invite unnecessary conflict, especially between the First Presidency and the Twelve.

George Q. Cannon, a tireless champion of his uncle John Taylor, claimed that Brigham Young had designated Taylor as his successor, something other members of the group found unlikely given Young's dislike for Taylor. Daniel Wells frankly told Cannon that no one could ever have heard Young say that because Young "never thought" that Taylor should succeed him. Despite the palpable tension on the subject, Taylor was insistent. One by one, opponents fell into line behind him. On 9 October, between sessions of the general conference, Wilford Woodruff nominated Taylor to be president of the church, and the apostles unanimously, if somewhat begrudgingly, agreed.[170]

Along with JFS, Taylor chose his nephew George Q. as one of his counselors, a natural choice given their close relationship. Taylor chose JFS, it seems, for two reasons. First, as discussed above, the two had deep ties and got along reasonably well. Second, Taylor knew that Pratt, and probably others, thought that JFS should have been considered as Young's replacement. Exactly the same issue would arise when Woodruff organized the First Presidency after Taylor's death. JFS's name always found its way into the discussion, so Taylor may have been induced to add him as a counselor to mollify Pratt.[171]

Once the decision was made, the leadership presented a united front to the church membership. Church leaders announced the decision first to the priesthood holders at the conference. The overwhelming support for Taylor among the saints deeply impressed Woodruff, who described it as being like "the rushing of many waters—there is power in it."[172]

The First Presidency under Taylor's leadership was quite different than it was under Young. Taylor did not add endless counselors, instead limiting the First Presidency to three and relying heavily on his two counselors. For the first time, JFS would have genuine opportunities to shape church doctrine and policy. He would do so for nearly four more decades, but the magnitude of the moment did not seem to register. The day that Woodruff felt rushing waters, JFS recorded a single sentence: "I paid Z.C.M.I. $6 on Julina's carpet."[173]

Taylor called Cannon and JFS together and spoke with "considerable plainness" of the need for absolute unity in the First Presidency.[174] Differences had to

194   Chapter 10

be aired, discussed, and resolved. Divided, the First Presidency could find itself weakened and in a subordinate position to the Quorum of the Twelve, some of whom remained privately opposed to Taylor's presidency.

From 1880 until 1885, JFS continued to work at the Endowment House, traveled widely within the growing Mormon culture region, and attended regular meetings of the First Presidency at Taylor's office or his residence at the Gardo House. Occasionally, the routine was broken by unusual visitors. JFS, who worked alone at the office whenever Cannon and Taylor traveled to the southern settlements, once received a young man named John Seamount who told him that he had received a revelation from God, and that he had been forbidden to eat until he walked from Provo to Salt Lake City and delivered it to the First Presidency. JFS conversed with his visitor and found nothing noticeably awry with the conversation or his demeanor, but he sensed an "evil influence" afflicting Seamount's mind. Something about the troubled young man touched JFS. He could not help but feel "sympathy for so apparently promising a young man" and concluded that something must have happened in his life to "give the Adversary power over him." JFS's concern led him to ask Abraham O. Smoot, president of the Provo stake, to notify the leaders in Seamount's ward of the young man's difficulty so they could "guide his mind into the proper channels."[175]

Just as JFS's brutal beating of McKnight illustrated some of the worst facets of his personality, his treatment of John Seamount illuminates some of his best. JFS's capacity for empathy and compassion was both unusually large and difficult to reach. While one situation might evoke rage, another might elicit deeply felt concern and action. As mentioned earlier, children and young people, especially troubled young Mormon men, plucked most handily at JFS's heartstrings.

In 1884, JFS arranged for his nephew, Martha Ann's son Hyrum Harris, to be called on a mission to Hawaii around the same time that JFS was preparing to leave for the islands himself. Harris's family situation was less than ideal, and his alcoholic father treated his mother poorly. Hyrum had shown little interest in religion, but two weeks before he was scheduled to leave for his mission, JFS wrote to Harris's bishop with a few requests. First, the bishop should find members of the ward willing to pay for Harris's mission if possible. Second, he wanted the bishop to "call [Hyrum] to you, show him the right way, confer on him, or put him in the way to receive the Priesthood."[176]

JFS's interest in Hyrum did not stem only from his avuncular relationship. He saw a lot of himself in the young man, who at that time was "very much in the same condition of mind and other circumstances that I was in myself some 30 years ago when I started on my first mission." That mission call, JFS believed, "was the starting point of my life on the road of paramount duty and happiness," and he hoped "for the same good results for my nephew."[177] When he felt someone needed protection, JFS could hardly be stopped from providing it.

In some cases, however, JFS was powerless to protect those he loved the most. In the summer of 1878, Sarah gave birth to a baby girl named Rhoda. Following a pattern that had become miserably familiar, she lived just eleven months. JFS held Rhoda in his arms as she slipped away. He spent the next day procuring yet another tiny coffin and fifty pounds of ice in which to pack the body so that she could be preserved against the brutal July heat long enough to be sketched and memorialized. JFS expressed utter frustration at the loss of another of his precious children. "Why in the name of reason," he asked in his journal, "can we not preserve the lives of our children?"[178]

Less than a year after Rhoda's death, Sarah had another child, Minerva, followed in 1882 by Alice and in 1884 by Willard. Julina had two boys in the space of two and a half years: David, who was born in May 1879, and George, who joined the family in October 1881. They were joined by a sister, named after her mother, in 1884. Edna followed the same pattern, first giving birth to a girl named Edna in October 1879, followed by a boy named Albert in September 1881. Albert died one month shy of his second birthday, losing his struggle with the "grim monster of death." JFS described it as "one of the sorest trials of my life," second only to the death of his firstborn child years earlier.[179]

In some ways, JFS looked at the deaths of his children as a form of rebirth into the heaven that he believed awaited them. A poem he composed three years after Albert's death provides some insight into the depth of pain it inflicted, as well as revealing, once again, JFS's concept of heaven as a place for families to reunite for eternity.

> Gone to join his noble kindred
> In their bright and happy home,
> Gone where mortal ills are ended
> And no death can ever come.
>
> Where his sweet angelic spirit
> Bright as pure celestial light
> Sped, his blessings to inherit
> Whence from earth he took his flight
>
> O! Our Albert how we loved him!
> Swelled our hearts with ample joy
> Now on earth we e'er shall miss him
> Miss our pretty infant boy[180]

But no matter what JFS did, deaths kept coming. Another son, Robert, born in November 1883, did not live to see his fourth birthday. JFS, once again consumed

196   Chapter 10

by grief, identified his feelings as both infantile and feminine, lamenting, "I am on these matters childish ... and weaker than a woman."[181] The wounds gnawed at him, mounting as they did year after year. He continued to find an outlet in poetry. On the sixth anniversary of Rhoda's death, JFS sent a poem to Sarah, concluding the effort with this stanza:

> Our sad separation e'er long will be ended
> And then O! how gladly we'll hasten to thee.
> Our Rhoda and Heber and Ella and Alfred
> And Mercy and Albert, so happy and free.[182]

JFS's family life during these years was one continuous cycle composed in equal measure of joy and grief. As always, he relied on his religious views to sustain him, comforting himself with the belief that his children died pure in God's eyes. He even went so far as to suggest that he would rather they "should die in childhood, while innocent, than to live to deny the faith. I would go to my grave happier childless than leaving posterity who would prove unworthy of my martyred father's name and cause."[183] Although it was easier to think such things when time had blunted a bit the searing pain occasioned by the loss of a child, JFS's deep convictions never deserted him, even in moments of extreme distress, and remained to enhance the exquisite joy of welcoming new children to his family.

In May 1883, JFS purchased forty acres of farmland southwest of Salt Lake City, and he would need everything this ground could yield because he married his two final wives during this period.[184] Alice Kimball, a striking twenty-five-year-old divorcée, married JFS in December 1883. Like JFS, she was descended from Mormon royalty. She was born in 1858 to Heber C. Kimball and had been married at a young age to David Rich, son of the apostle Charles C. Rich. They had three children: Alice, born in 1877, and Charles and Heber, twins born in 1881. David Rich, an alcoholic, would abandon the family for weeks at a time and eventually ended up robbing Zion's Mercantile Bank, brutally beating the cashier with an iron rod before escaping. He was apprehended in a brothel, where police found him in bed with a prostitute, counting the money he had stolen. He served a sentence in the Utah Territorial Penitentiary for his escapade.[185]

John Taylor then canceled Alice's temple sealing and steered her toward JFS, who adopted her three children. Apparently his other wives were not consulted, which resulted in some initial tension. In January 1884, one month after marrying Alice, JFS was sealed to his fifth and final wife, John Taylor's eighteen-year-old niece, Mary Taylor Schwartz.[186]

Back in October 1881, when JFS's mentor Orson Pratt passed away, JFS sat at the bedside, pencil and pad in hand, waiting to record any last words, in perfect late Victorian fashion. Just before he died, Pratt instructed JFS to write this epitaph to be engraved on his headstone: "My body sleeps but a moment. But my testimony lives, and shall endure forever."[187] JFS heartily endorsed the simple message; indeed, he continued to invest every ounce of his energy to ensure that his own testimony of the LDS Church would endure forever. This, however, would prove exquisitely challenging. Everything JFS had worked to build over the past two decades, both personally and as a leader of the LDS Church, would be the very things he would have to battle to save for the next two.

11 | Exile

On 29 August 1888, Joseph F. Smith sat down and recorded a caustic note in his letterpress copybook. "This book was laid aside four years ago today ... from which date until now I have been in exile."[1] The toll of those four years on JFS were significant. Unlike previous absences from home and family, this was not in the service of a mission from his God. He had been driven from his home, forced to hide and act, as he saw it, like a coward in the face of an all-out blitz by the U.S. government to dismantle LDS control of Utah Territory. The issue that the government used to force the capitulation of the Mormons was, of course, polygamy. If JFS had been told on the day he went into exile in 1884 that the church would publicly renounce the practice of plural marriage six years later, he would not have believed it. By the time he sat down to explain the four-year gap in his letterpress copybook, the possibility that polygamy could be forcibly ended must have seemed much more likely.

"The nineteenth-century state," argues historian Jurgen Osterhammel, "was a reforming state," driven to change by the fear of the mere "perception of national backwardness."[2] The last quarter of the nineteenth century saw reform movements rise in the United States against a wide array of issues, but none was more pressing than Mormon polygamy. With slavery abolished, polygamy and the still-mysterious theocracy occupying much of the American West became symbols of backwardness that needed eradication. There were economic reasons too: Mormon Utah could hinder the shipment of goods across the continent. In the world of muscular capitalism, that was simply not acceptable. Thus, for reasons both economic and political, the U.S. government had finally decided to do away with the Mormon theocracy and its hideous but remarkably intransigent dedication to polygamy.

The U.S. government had been attempting to stamp out both polygamy and theocracy since the 1850s, when Republicans famously lumped Mormon polygamy in with slavery as the "twin relics of barbarism."[3] On this point, almost everyone in the country could agree. For the dominant evangelical Protestants, it was a gross affront to decency; for federal politicians with an eye on America's reputation abroad, it was an embarrassing stain on its claim to civilization; and for the new

Exile   199

capitalist class that depended on trouble-free cross-continental shipping lines, it was dreadfully inconvenient and risky. It is a testament to Mormon resilience and dedication to what they believed were God-given commandments that they managed to stave off government efforts to break them for decades.

The attacks had come in waves, but until the 1880s, they had little effect. The first move that the federal government made to exert control over Mormon theocracy and polygamy was the Morrill Act of 1862, which attacked Mormon power in Utah in three ways. First, it made "bigamy" illegal, but to prove bigamy, there had to be direct evidence of a second marriage. Naturally, the participants in the marriages had little reason to cooperate. Second, it capped the amount of real estate that a religious organization in a U.S. territory could own at $50,000. We have already seen, in the case of Brigham Young, how the Mormons got around the $50,000 cap by transferring all property above that amount to the personal holding of the church president.

Finally, it disincorporated the LDS Church. The last provision had no real effect. Compounding the general weakness of the Morrill Act was the control that the LDS Church had over certain parts of the judicial system, especially the power to empanel juries. Even if a Mormon ended up on trial, it was difficult to wring a guilty verdict out of a Mormon jury. In an attempt to fix this, Congress passed the Poland Act. Despite all of the energy expended, polygamy continued to flourish, but that changed with the Reynolds case, which took nearly fifteen years to reach the end of all possible appeals.

JFS watched the early efforts to eradicate polygamy with a mixture of fury and contempt. He reserved his most vicious criticisms for the federally appointed judges of the Utah Territorial Supreme Court. The first substantive notice that JFS paid to the federal attack on polygamy was in April 1863, when he learned that a large meeting had been held at the tabernacle during which various resolutions declared the governor and the justices incompetent, and requested that President Abraham Lincoln remove them.[4] In 1870, when a bill introduced by Illinois Republican Shelby Cullom aimed at stricter enforcement of the Morrill Act was working its way through Congress, JFS observed that "Congress has as much right to compel the Catholic minister to have a wife, as to prohibit the Mormon minister from having more than one."[5]

In general, JFS did not say very much about legal principles or legislation. He focused his anger over the anti-polygamy legislation on individual representatives of the government. He felt very strongly about certain territorial judges. President Ulysses S. Grant had appointed James B. McKean, a Civil War veteran and former member of Congress from New York, as chief justice of the Utah Territorial Supreme Court. McKean arrived in Utah with, he believed, mandates from the U.S. president, as well as from the Almighty, to end polygamy and the Mormon stranglehold on Utah Territory. It did not take long before JFS formed an opinion of the man. When McKean was recalled to Washington in 1875, JFS

200   Chapter 11

"greatly rejoiced" at his "political decapitation" and hoped that he would "never . . . return unless to the penitentiary or gallows!"[6]

JFS and the rest of the Mormon leadership felt absolutely confident that plural marriage was protected under the free exercise clause of the First Amendment to the U.S. Constitution, and that the U.S. Supreme Court would be fairer in judging the matter than the legislatures or the territorial judges. In the fall of 1874, George Q. Cannon was arrested on charges of polygamy. Through secret negotiations with William Carey, the federal prosecutor assigned to Utah, church leaders agreed to provide someone for a "test case" if Carey would drop the charges against Cannon and other church leaders. A test case would involve the prosecution of a polygamist Mormon who would admit to his practice in open court, essentially agreeing to conviction, so that the decision could be appealed to the U.S. Supreme Court, which would, in turn, decide on the constitutionality of the 1862 Morrill Act.

George Reynolds, a British convert who was a friend of Cannon's and a newly married polygamist, was suggested for the test case. Cannon encountered Reynolds on South Temple Street in Salt Lake and casually informed him that a test case deal had been reached and that "it had been decided to present [his] name before the grand jury." Reynolds accepted this as a religious duty. "I was asked to step to the front," he wrote, and "I willingly complied and afforded the prosecution such information with regard to my marriages . . . as I thought could prove the facts desired."[7] After a two-day trial, Reynolds was found guilty. In a surprise move, the Utah Territorial Supreme Court overturned the conviction on the grounds of flaws in the jury selection process. Reynolds was granted a new trial, and even though he actively fought the prosecution, the evidence he had previously provided sealed his fate. This time the territorial court upheld his conviction.

The case then proceeded, more quickly than church leaders had hoped, to the U.S. Supreme Court. In November 1878, the justices listened to two days of argument. The court was initially divided and voted informally 5-4 to uphold the conviction. Eventually, however, all of the justices fell in line with the majority and issued a unanimous decision on 6 January 1879. Chief Justice Morrison Waite argued in his decision that although plural marriage was motivated by religious conviction, the free exercise clause of the First Amendment was not absolute. Citing Thomas Jefferson, Waite concluded that First Amendment protections do not extend to "overt acts against peace and good order." Polygamy, he stated, represented a "subversion of good order" sufficient to move it beyond the shield of the First Amendment.[8]

On the day that the Supreme Court issued its decision in the Reynolds case, JFS was at the home of a friend, William Cooley. That evening, another guest cut his own throat at the dinner table, covering everything in blood. JFS said little about either event, noting them in his journal without comment.[9] His silence notwithstanding, one cannot help but wonder if he saw something portentous in the coincidence. The man survived the suicide attempt, but bore the ropey scar for the rest of his days. JFS did not know it yet, but the Reynolds case would not kill the church. It would not even kill polygamy. But it would draw blood, and it would most certainly leave a scar.

Church president John Taylor agreed to an interview on 1 January with O. J. Hollister, who was both a representative of the IRS in Utah and a correspondent for the *New York Tribune*. Although it was a lengthy interview, Taylor's remarks had a simple point: the U.S. Supreme Court had put the desire to destroy the Mormons above their loyalty to the Constitution. The United States was thus no better than the government of France that persecuted the Huguenots or the English who punished the nonconformist Puritans. After quoting the First Amendment, Taylor told Hollister that the government "will allow us to think—what an unspeakable privilege that is—but they will not allow us the free exercise of that faith which the Constitution guarantees. Here is the injustice and the manifest breach of faith." Despite counterarguments from Hollister, Taylor remained unshakeable in his belief that "Congress has . . . placed us in antagonism to what we term an unconstitutional law, and it now becomes a question of whether we should obey God or man."[10]

Taylor's rhetoric was not quite as confrontational as it first appears. He knew that it had not come to such a stark juncture just yet. In fact, he and nearly all of the other interested church members knew that declaring the Morrill Act constitutional would not make it any easier to prosecute. Reynolds's conviction could not have occurred without the evidence that he voluntarily provided. Taylor knew that if the U.S. government was serious about getting rid of polygamy, they would have to restructure existing laws to make polygamy easier to prove without the cooperation of the accused. He also knew that this would take time, and church leaders were confident that any such efforts would likely fail, just as they had in the past.

Instead of backing away from polygamy, Taylor became increasingly aggressive in ensuring that all church leaders accepted and practiced it. In 1882, he issued a revelation purporting to be the word of God to his prophet. In addition to directing that two men, George Teasdale and Heber J. Grant, be added to the Quorum of the Twelve, the revelation also promised the Mormons that if they

> put their houses in order according to the law of God, and attend to the various duties and responsibilities associate therewith . . . you shall be my people and I shall be your God; and your enemies shall not have dominion over you, for I will preserve you and confound them saith the Lord; and they shall not have power or dominion over you.[11]

The revelation also indicated that Seymour B. Young should be appointed to the presidency of the Seventy "if he received the law of celestial [plural] marriage."[12] George Q. Cannon addressed the leaders who had assembled to hear the revelation read, informing them that any stake president who did not currently practice plural marriage had the choice to either "obey this law or resign their positions."[13]

202   Chapter 11

No doubt those revelatory words rang in JFS's ears in the spring of 1884, when, even knowing that federal marshals were actively attempting to serve him with "subpoenas ... in polygamy cases," he believed that the renewed effort to "make the most of the anti-polygamy laws" would fail just as their "predecessors have failed." He predicted little more than a "grand fizzle."[14] On this point, they underestimated the resolve of the American people. By October, JFS had reason to reconsider his opinion; the October general conference came and went while JFS stayed locked in his house three blocks west of the tabernacle. "My confinement," he wrote, was intended to shelter him from the "F.O.H.'s [Federal Office Holders'] Inquisition," which he was "indisposed towards." He correctly observed that the "inquisition has an itching desire to interview ... myself ... on some inquisitorial matters."[15]

JFS would eventually have to go a lot farther than his house to escape the "inquisition," but even as anti-polygamy action began heating up in earnest, he continued to hold fast to two key beliefs. The first was that polygamy was a commandment of God, a requirement for exaltation in the highest degree of glory in the afterlife. He had expressed this opinion publicly in 1878, when some church leaders had apparently discussed retreating from the practice of polygamy. "Some of the saints ... believe that a man with one wife, sealed to him by the authority of the Priesthood for time and eternity will receive an exaltation as great and glorious ... as he possibly could with more than one," JFS observed incredulously. "I want here to enter my solemn protest against this idea, for I know it is false."[16]

JFS expressed this view in private six years later in a response to a question from a man in Cache County, in northern Utah. The man reported that his ward was being painfully divided between those who believed that exaltation was the reward of anyone "married celestially (that is, in the temple or Endowment House)," regardless of the number of wives involved, and those who felt that "only those who marry a plurality of wives will receive a celestial exaltation." He was writing to JFS rather than a lower-ranking leader because, he wrote, "nothing but 'Thus saith the Lord' will satisfy them."[17]

These were no mere theological trifles. The question of whether plural marriage was a requirement, especially in the face of increasing legal risks, was a matter of grave significance to many Mormons. JFS based his answer on a close parsing of a foundational scriptural text—in this case, the first four verses of the "revelation on marriage," which is now Doctrine and Covenants section 132. He specifically rejected the idea that "celestial marriage" was the same thing as "eternal marriage" or monogamous marriage performed in the temple or Endowment House. Joseph Smith, JFS argued, had enquired of God regarding why the ancient patriarchs had many wives; the issue of eternal marriage "was not the question." It was the "plurality of wives ... and the restoration of that principle and doctrine" that was the "only question, the 'eternity' of the marriage covenant being only an essential, integral part of the 'law.'" Quoting the revelation, JFS wrote that "no man can reject this covenant and be permitted to enter my glory.'" "Plurality," JFS concluded, "is the 'new and everlasting covenant.'"[18] The church's interpretation of this scripture would, of necessity, be reversed in coming decades, but in 1884, JFS clearly believed that polygamy was not optional, and he grounded that belief in what he viewed as an unimpeachable reading of the revelatory text.

JFS's belief in the necessity of polygamy was not merely theoretical. In 1885, just nine days after the death of his twenty-year-old daughter Netta, James Henry Martineau stood next to JFS as the latter prepared to leave on a train. Standing on the platform, Martineau worked up the courage to offer "to give President Smith our Netta." JFS responded eagerly, "and said he had wished for it, but hesitated to ask me for her, but as he already had two of my sisters, would be very glad to have her also."[19]

Modern sensibilities may recoil at the language of property exchange that pervades this incident, and the larger practice of which it is illustrative. But looking beyond that provides an important insight into just how powerfully polygamy shaped JFS's experiences and thinking. At the funeral of a deceased young woman, JFS's thoughts turned immediately toward her single state and the blessings that this would preclude her from claiming. She had left mortality, as had Martineau's sisters, without entering into the "new and everlasting covenant" of plural marriage. There can be no question that JFS believed absolutely in both an afterlife and in the centrality of polygamy in determining the nature of that afterlife. For him, plural marriage was not only at the center of life, it was literally larger than life.

The second, related belief JFS held was that the laws of "the world" could never abrogate the higher law of God. In the spring of 1884, he had more reason than ever to believe in the church's ability to endure and overcome. He wrote to an inquiring journalist in April that the entire legal machinery of the United States could not produce "over 8 indictments ... against polygamists."[20] At the very least, he believed that Congress was so distracted by the presidential race between Grover Cleveland and James Blaine that the "Mormon question" would be "pushed out of sight."[21]

In May, he traveled with Taylor, Cannon, and others to Logan, where they dedicated the magnificent new temple. The Logan Temple stood like a dual-towered, crenelated fortress on the eastern bench of Cache Valley. It embodied the attitude the Mormons had adopted in the 1870s and 1880s in the face of "gentile" hostility: solid, unflinching, seemingly immovable—built to stand in the shadow of persecution. Even the total cost of the building had to be kept secret for fear that the knowledge would "sharpen the efforts of our enemies."[22] At the dedication services, JFS told the assembled "saints" that the temple and its rituals and covenants were worth "far above anything upon the earth, of greater worth than the whole earth."[23] God, he was certain, would not let the assembled forces of his enemies destroy it.

JFS was sailing headlong into a crushing storm, yet he remained confident that it was the government's wave that would break, leaving "the old ship Zion" tossed but upright. In public, JFS appealed, as always, to scripture to give shape to his rhetoric. "The Lord has revealed that we do not have to break the laws of the land

204 Chapter 11

to keep His laws," he said, referring to a revelation Joseph Smith dictated in August 1831.[24] The meaning of this scripture, to JFS at least, could not be clearer: when the laws of God and man conflict, God's people keep God's laws until the laws of man come back into harmony with revealed truth. This reading of the text demanded a belief in a system in which divine and governmental laws *could not* be in conflict; therefore, if such a conflict appeared to exist, one side of the law *could not* truly be considered law.

The tortuous and ultimately untenable position of the revelation had its roots in the early Missouri conflicts, the ending of which JFS would have occasion to revisit when it came time to see how one makes sense of God's apparent defeat. In the mid-1880s, however, he remained convinced that God's law would ultimately triumph, although he exhibited hints of frustration at God's timing. The Mormons' day would come, he wrote, and it "will be a glorious one when it comes, for it seems to be long deferred."[25] Delayed it might have been, but even in 1889, just one year before the Woodruff Manifesto, JFS assured Joseph Smith III that "neither of us will live to see [plural marriage] destroyed, tho' we live to the age of a tree."[26] Nothing could shake his trust that God would deliver the church "from the malice, vituperation, slander, bigotry, hatred and machinations of all her enemies."[27]

JFS also continued his efforts to promulgate a systematized Mormonism. When he toured Mormon settlements in southern Utah, Colorado, and Arizona in the summer of 1883, he repeatedly spoke of how "this world is ignorant of what they call Mormonism." But it seems it was not only "this world" that did not understand Mormonism; he sometimes "Explained what Mormonism is" to his Mormon audiences.[28] The following summer he embarked on a similar tour and again noted that he spent his time explaining to the Mormons what Mormonism is. In a notebook that he took on that trip, JFS listed several points of doctrine with accompanying scriptural references that, together with other statements, sermons, and letters, provide us with a picture of how he defined Mormonism.

The bedrock principle in JFS's definition of Mormonism was obedience. "Obedience is the first law of heaven," he explained. JFS clearly meant to convey the idea of obedience to God's will as expressed by the leaders of the church. Twelve years later, in 1896, he reiterated and clarified his thoughts about obedience. "It is frequently said that order is the first law of heaven," JFS told a stake conference audience in Provo. "But," he added, "order in the church is the result of obedience ... [thus] obedience is the first law of heaven."[29] In 1897, JFS instructed his missionary son Hyrum that "there is nothing like order, which is the result of obedience to rules and discipline."[30] By 1909, his attitude toward obedience had not shifted. "There can never be order in heaven or on earth without obedience ... to law and submission, which is but another mode of expression for obedience to <u>constituted authority</u>."[31]

JFS firmly believed that Mormon orthodoxy had to include a belief in Joseph Smith's calling as a prophet, the divinity of the Book of Mormon, and the literal conferral upon Joseph Smith of priesthood keys by various angelic beings. Those keys were what gave, first, the Quorum of the Twelve, then Brigham Young, then John Taylor, and so on the authority to speak and act for God. Hence, obedience, to JFS, meant adherence to the voice of God's servants on earth.

Second, JFS propounded the belief in eternal family relationships with the corollary beliefs in temple sealings and plural marriage. In his 1884 travel notebook, JFS listed a series of references to the necessity of plural marriage followed immediately by scriptures from John 11, 12, and 20 that suggest Mary and Martha participated in the sacred anointing ritual that Mormons performed in temples between husbands and wives.[32] JFS and many other early church leaders believed and taught that Joseph Smith had restored this practice based not solely on practices from the Hebrew Bible but also from references in the New Testament that could only be deciphered with the help of Joseph Smith's revelations. Plural marriage, JFS believed, was a practice in which Jesus himself engaged.

JFS's 1884 notes also reflect his strong conviction that persecution was both a badge of honor and a test from God. Adherence to the principle of plural marriage, the centerpiece of "the great work and mission of Prophet Joseph Smith," had led the Mormons to "inherit all the bitter persecutions and malignity which followed the Martyr and his faithful brethren." He included in his list of references part of a revelation Joseph Smith received in 1833. "In the day of their peace they esteemed lightly my counsel," the revelation reads, "but in the day of their trouble, of necessity, they feel after me."[33]

Apparently, JFS connected this scripture with a revelation from 1834 that promises the Mormons will eventually find deliverance if they are obedient under all circumstances, because God has "sent forth to destroy and lay waste mine enemies; and not many years hence they shall not be left to pollute mine heritage and to blaspheme my name."[34] JFS thus viewed the tension between Mormonism and every other religious, philosophical, and political system as an inherent feature of Mormonism itself, to be eased only when the other systems eventually were either destroyed or converted.

JFS felt strongly that Mormons ought to resist assimilation into the broader "gentile" culture wherever possible. They had largely failed to avoid economic entanglements with the broader culture, but JFS continued to resist in other ways. Public education, an engine of assimilation that would vex and divide both the Jews and the Catholics in America throughout the nineteenth century, worried him. "We should not trust our children to be educated by the gentiles," JFS told an audience in early 1884.[35] Later that year, he remarked, "We are at sea when we have to bring in [gentile] teachers to settle our difficulties."[36] This emphasis on in-group/out-group dynamics, so vitally important to Mormon identity, is on prominent display in JFS's remarks about education. For him, Mormonism remained an outpost of God's righteousness surrounded by enemies.

Mormonism, as JFS explained it in the 1880s, was a religion anchored in a belief that Joseph Smith's reception and transmission of priesthood authority provided

206 Chapter 11

an orderly basis for the implementation of the religion practiced by Jesus Christ. This religion centered on the key doctrine of eternal families and the key practice of plural marriage, all of which must, by divine design, be carried out under constant persecution. Understanding JFS's religious worldview in the 1880s—in tandem with an acknowledgment of his strong impulse to create in the minds of believers a systematic, shared Mormon worldview that matched his own—is key to appreciating his attitude toward the U.S. government before the Woodruff Manifesto and the massive challenge he faced in remaking the Mormon worldview in the decades following Utah statehood. His expertise at routinization grounded in scriptural eisegesis was as much a strength during his later years as his intransigence concerning the defining traits of Mormons proved to be a weakness.

JFS, it turns out, was wrong to believe that the federal laws were "impotent." By upholding the Morrill Act, the Supreme Court signaled that plural marriage did not enjoy First Amendment protections. All that the government needed to do now was to craft legislation with the teeth that the Morrill Act lacked. In 1882, the problem of proving bigamy was solved when the Congress passed the Edmunds Act, which substituted the term "polygamy" for "bigamy" and introduced another crime: "unlawful cohabitation." To prove unlawful cohabitation, prosecutors needed only to demonstrate that a married man "cohabited" with a woman who was not his wife. This was a misdemeanor, but the Edmunds Act allowed polygamy and cohabitation to be presented as a joint indictment. Furthermore, the act required potential jurors to affirm that they not only were not polygamists, but also that they did not accept the principle of plural marriage. Finally, under the Edmunds Act, anyone practicing polygamy or unlawful cohabitation could neither vote nor hold public office.

The landscape had now permanently changed. There would be no more space for legal subterfuge or passive resistance. By the fall of 1888, 500 Mormons had been convicted and sent to prison for polygamy, with hundreds more to follow. The members of the First Presidency were not among them because they all went underground. The piece of anti-polygamy weaponry that essentially broke the back of Mormon polygamy was the Edmunds-Tucker Act of 1887, which disenfranchised Mormon women, ended the Perpetual Emigration Fund, ruled that all church holdings over $50,000 were to be placed in federal receivership, and prevented children of polygamous marriages from inheriting estates.[37] For the first time, women could be compelled to testify against their husbands in these matters, which resulted in Mormon women also facing prison time.

"The Raid" is what Mormons came to call this final legislative assault on polygamy. From the vantage of hindsight, the dismantling of plural marriage and the Mormon theo-democracy of which it stood as the most potent symbol, was inevitable. From the point of view of the U.S. government, the Mormons posed the same types of problems that Native Americans did. Historian Steven Hahn has argued that the federal government viewed the American West in colonial terms, and, as with any colonial power, the subalterns would have to undergo cultural "reconstruction" for the broader empire to function. Assimilation of varied cultural expressions into the broader capitalist, Protestant, material-oriented consumer culture of the American mainstream would require "detribalization." The goal was to shift the primary self-identity of members of minority groups from their "tribe" to "America."

Detribalization, Hahn argues, in its most generic sense, requires the severance of the connection between the individual and the "land base and communal practices that sustained tribal culture." While the Mormons viewed the attack on polygamy as a satanic assault on the kingdom of God, the U.S. government saw it as an attempt to break the "tribal identity" of Mormonism by shearing away the practice that was both their most distinctive trait and the one most at odds with the American cultural ideal. Hahn views the federal approach to Mormonism as a hybrid of the methods used for subduing Native American independence and the punitive measures used to "punish rebel leaders and reconstruct the rebellious South" after the Civil War. In the 1880s, this resulted in a combination of "land confiscation, taxation, disfranchisement, loyalty oaths, and criminal prosecutions" aimed, not at the eradication of Mormonism per se, but at the integration of Mormons into the American mainstream.[38]

The raid on Mormonism in Utah resulted in profound social and cultural dislocation. For JFS, it carried heavy personal and religious consequences. He found that his old enemy, that white-hot temper, was rising and "needed breeching."[39] JFS, John Taylor, and George Q. Cannon knew by the fall of 1884 that they could easily end up in prison. The history of their own movement had taught them that though God would eventually deliver them from their enemies, he could very well let them cool their heels in prison before he did so. But because they remained absolutely committed to living as polygamists and to administering the affairs of the church, they would have to stay out of the penitentiary. Seeing no other option, they decided to go into self-imposed exile, which they called "the underground."[40]

For Taylor, going underground meant moving among various safe houses in the vicinity of Salt Lake. At first, JFS thought he could hide out in outlying areas of the Mormon culture region, but in October 1884, Taylor requested that he take a mission to northern Utah, which he dutifully did.[41] JFS, however, presented a special problem: his role in performing and recording sealings in the Endowment House made him particularly appealing to the federal marshals.[42] Not only could they prosecute him under the Edmunds Act, but they could also pressure him to provide testimonial and documentary evidence for hundreds of polygamous marriages. JFS's underground hideaway would have to be far away from Utah Territory.

Around this time, things began to vanish from the Church Historian's Office and other places where sensitive documents might be located. According to Franklin Richards's journal entries from November 1887, by the time the receiver, Frank Dyer, took over and inventoried the Tithing Office, the Historian's Office, the

208   Chapter 11

Gardo House, and the President's Office, most of the documents he wanted to see had been secreted away, and so had the people who created them.[43]

According to a letter that JFS wrote in December 1884, Taylor became "very worked up" about the possibility of his arrest and "determined that a few [leaders] shall 'skin out.'"[44] JFS also received a letter from Cannon, in Hawaiian, telling him that he needed "to go the Islands for a season" with one of his wives.[45] JFS then informed Edward Partridge, president of the Hawaiian mission, that he could expect JFS, Julina, and one of their children to arrive in Hawaii in January 1885. JFS did not seem to mind the assignment, noting that "winter is coming on apace, and I would like a tropical climate."[46] He would be safe from imprisonment there, but he would also be isolated from church headquarters and, once again, from most of his family. Only Julina and their youngest child would accompany him.

JFS was no longer leaving just babies behind, however. His older children were mature enough to feel the absence of their father. On 18 December 1884, JFS gathered his entire family together under cover of darkness and pronounced a father's blessing on each child, as well as a blessing on each of the wives. After bidding tearful goodbyes, JFS, Julina, and their infant daughter, Julina Clarissa, bundled into a sleigh and drove off. The three made their way to California, then on to Hawaii aboard the steamship *Mariposa*. They docked in Honolulu on 9 February. The next day, Partridge got word that a group of visitors were on their way to the mission headquarters at the Laie plantation. Expecting a man named Joseph Speight, Partridge was shocked to open the door and find JFS standing there with Julina and a baby.[47]

Hiding Out in Hawaii

When JFS arrived in Hawaii in February 1885, he had no idea how long he would have to remain in exile. That same month he was formally indicted on the charge of unlawful cohabitation, which meant he was liable for arrest and imprisonment in Utah. The previous December, his half brother John had reached out to offer support and encouragement. "Have no fear," he wrote, "the God of our father will go with you, that you will go in peace, and in due time return in safety."[48] JFS guessed that "in due time" would be at least three years, and "if the Lord permits me to return all will be well." By July, he was starting to fear that he "might never come home again."[49] But as he had done so often in the past, JFS found solace in work and reconciled himself to both exile and the deep uncertainty he felt about his future.

On his first Sunday at Laie, JFS spoke to the congregation in Hawaiian, much to their delight. Remarkably, he had maintained his fluency since first learning the language in the mid-1850s. A choir welcomed JFS with a new song, composed in Hawaiian specifically for him.[50] Shortly after arriving, he oversaw the installation of a new mission president, Enoch Farr. JFS held no official position but made himself available to help without being too overbearing. He did, however, assert his views in a few areas. First, having seen firsthand how poor record-keeping in the missions could create headaches for the leaders at headquarters, he instructed Farr to remedy the "unsatisfactory manner in which the mission accounts were kept" and insisted that he provide accurate statistical and financial reports.[51]

JFS also set up a theological school for the missionaries and church members living in Laie. He wrote the curriculum himself, and it reflected his belief that a coherent and systematic theological basis was an absolute necessity. He taught incoming missionaries the method of doctrinal interpretation, innovation, and uniformity that he developed during the 1870s. On one occasion, he taught a class on the truthfulness of the Book of Mormon, identifying and attempting to debunk criticisms of the text.

Frederick Beesley, a missionary who arrived at Laie in 1886, provides a striking example of JFS's method in action. During a lesson on the Book of Mormon, JFS pointed out, in harmony with the text, that Jesus taught the same material to the Nephites that he taught in Palestine, and that these same truths were taught to the lost tribes of Israel and, from there, "to all the world." With that scriptural warrant, JFS argued that Jesus must have visited "the Mohammadans, the Buddhists, the Chinese and the Japanese." Therefore, he said, it stood to reason that

> the personages whom these people revered as Mohammad, Buddha or Confucius were really one and the same as Jesus Christ, and that he appeared to these different nations in succession immediately after his appearance to the Nephites—statements of historians to the contrary notwithstanding.[52]

This incident clearly illustrates JFS's method of doctrinal reasoning and innovation, and indicates his trust in scripture over secular knowledge, an inclination that became increasingly important to him during his presidency.

One of the last foundations that JFS established in Hawaii was a course on the Hawaiian language for the missionaries that he created and taught himself. He also busied himself with a variety of ecclesiastical tasks and manual labor. Every six months, Mormons from all over Hawaii gathered in Laie for mission conferences. JFS always spoke at these gatherings, in both Hawaiian and English, and usually at least once each Sunday. He also held special meetings during which he doled out advice to the missionaries preparing to go out and proselytize among the Hawaiians. According to Frederick Beesley, JFS warned them that "the natives should not be treated too familiarly, else they will take advantage and shirk their labor." He also cautioned them to "guard against" any "undue familiarity" with Hawaiian women, "as it is likely to lead ... from the path of rectitude and bring shame and dishonor besides dragging [the offender] down to hell."[53]

The old tropes of native laziness and lasciviousness were still alive and well, but JFS also drew upon a much more familiar figure as a warning against sexual misconduct. Before one group of missionaries departed Laie, he reminded them of

Albert Carrington, whom he "deprecated in the most impressive terms," as a way of warning the missionaries of the wide-ranging impact that sexual sin could have, not only on the individual, but also on the church.[54] In addition to these ecclesiastical duties, JFS also helped on construction projects and assisted with the livestock, all while keeping up his First Presidency correspondence with Taylor and Cannon.

While JFS was finding ways to keep busy, Julina was working herself nearly to death. Even with the help of two young Hawaiian women, she could barely keep up with the meals, the washing, and other duties that seemed to devolve upon her. The Hawaiian women, unfamiliar with the stove imported from the United States, tended to leave it burning at full heat all the time, ruining two stoves in short order.[55] Julina needed a stove because it fell to her to make lunch each day for the workers at the sugar mill, and often dinner as well. She also had to mend clothes and make shirts, pants, and temple garments for JFS and others at the plantation. On top of the endless chores, the climate disagreed with her, her baby was often sick, and she desperately missed home. As early as the fall of 1885, JFS was looking in vain for a way to get Julina home. "I cannot consent for her to go without counsel of the proper authorities," he wrote to Sarah, adding that all he could do was to "keep hoping and praying for the way to open for her to return."[56]

After nearly a year of endless work in a place to which she could not seem to adjust, Julina poured out her frustration, or at least as much as she allowed herself to acknowledge, in her journal. She wrote, "Little did I think that I would have been separated from my children for so long," adding with a sad rhetorical flourish, "When, oh! When can we go home?"[57] As if she was not uncomfortable and busy enough, Julina became pregnant in the late summer of 1885. On 21 April 1886, she gave birth to Elias Wesley Smith. A few weeks later she noted that she and JFS had been married for twenty years. Now with two nursing babies to care for, Julina convinced JFS to send for their fourteen-year-old daughter, Donnette. Much to Julina's relief, Donnette arrived on 31 October 1886. She quickly found herself put to work studying Hawaiian and teaching "five white children" in Sunday school in addition to helping care for the baby.[58]

Although JFS had escaped the reach of federal law enforcement, his wives could not, and officials remained convinced that he had secreted away incriminating records from the Endowment House. In March 1885, JFS learned that marshals had searched the home shared by Sarah and Edna, tearing it apart looking for records of plural marriages and sending a strong message by displacing some of his family members. When he heard of the search, JFS could scarcely contain his rage. With a trembling hand he wrote to Sarah:

> I would give all I am worth and borrow to the extent of my credit to be
> at home in possession of my liberty and power to execute my judgement
> or rather Gods judgement upon the damned villains who have expelled

my wives and little innocents from their homes in the dead of winter to become a charge upon the benevolence and charity of our friends. If I could curse them until the elements were white-hot and their miserable carcasses were consumed to ashes it would not do justice to my feelings.

On the emotional scale, rage fell only slightly ahead of guilt. His own safety served only to intensify his feelings of anger and helplessness as he saw his family suffer the consequences of his actions. "I would naturally and purposely rather serve six month in the Pen," he wrote, "than to have you and my little Pets tossed about and exposed to the dreaded vicissitudes of winter."[59]

JFS struggled to help his children understand the reasons for such stressful times. To his fourteen-year-old daughter Nonie, guessing at the questions in her mind, he wrote, "What evil has your papa done, or your Mamma, or any of my children? Have we wronged anybody?" The answer to these questions, of course, was "No, no, my darling, you know we have not." JFS explained that all of the suffering was unjust and that "our enemies would deprive me of my family, turn your Mamma out in the street, and brand her as a fallen-wicked woman and me as a libertine and a villain." The letter's tone then turned extremely dark. It must have been unnerving and alarming for Nonie to learn that the suffering of their family led JFS to "feel, as though death would be a sweet morsel. If I could but die in the defense of my wives and my children."[60] JFS obviously believed that his children needed to be educated in the realities of life as he understood it: the world was a wicked place, filled with enemies; death was preferable to capitulation; and loyalty to religious principle could bear no compromise.

JFS was spared the fate of Cannon, Lorenzo Snow, and hundreds of others who found themselves serving time in the territorial prison east of Salt Lake City. For these men, prison became a symbol of religious devotion. Their belief that unjust persecution had led them to "the pen" solidified their sense of religious peculiarity, specialness, and chosenness. Some inmates performed the priesthood ritual of dedication of their cells, something normally reserved for homes, churches, temples, and graves. The flood of new inmates required multiple expansions of the prison facilities. Non-Mormons incredulously looked on as inmates, having served their terms, "were met at the prison doors by brass bands and a procession with banners, escorted to their homes to be toasted, extolled, and feasted as if it were the conclusion of some brilliant and honorable achievement."[61]

JFS and the Nature of Americanism

Until the early twentieth century, JFS demonstrated what might be termed a theory of constitutional restorationism. He believed that the United States had been founded through the inspiration of God, but that the corruption of the state and the slothfulness of the Latter-day Saints had converged to produce the current crisis. It would fall to the Latter-day Saints to purify themselves and then "rescue from oblivion" the "original principles of the Constitution," an act that JFS saw as coterminous with the establishment of the United States as "the land of Zion."[62] JFS argued that it was, in fact, his bone-deep "Americanness," rather than his Mormonism, that had led to his conflict with the U.S. government. "I love this country for it is the land of my birth," he wrote. "My fathers for five generations were American born and I inherited independence and a love for freedom from them." JFS was astonished that the nation that represented liberty was doing all it could to make him "a serf to the dictum of an ignorant popular clamor."[63] This idea was not original to JFS. In fact, he had told his wife Mary that Joseph Smith believed that "this people would rescue the Constitution."[64] But JFS's expressions demonstrate his capacity and propensity to connect abstract theological concepts with fine-grained, gritty, messy lived realities.

In addition to the drama generated by the raids both at home and abroad, the lived complexities of plural marriage continued unabated. While still in Hawaii, JFS wrote an article for the *Deseret News* in which he attempted to refute the common belief that Mormon plural marriage was rooted in lust. "Men can generally gratify this passion as they do their appetite for tobacco and liquor," JFS wrote. They can "simply buy what they want . . . taking care not to purchase more than their lust requires." Plural marriage, by contrast, involves "buying" a great deal more than sexual satisfaction, including "all of the obligations, duties, labors, and expenses of maintaining large families. It is absurd to suppose that men would assume all these consequences simply to gratify lust."[65]

JFS's article stemmed from his personal experience with the realities of polygamy. His most recent marriages had disrupted the well-established dynamic between JFS, Julina, Edna, and Sarah. Mary and Alice did not live under the same roof as the others, and they had not shared the early experiences that had bound the first three wives together emotionally. Alice, in particular, found it difficult to join the sisterly community. She repeatedly, and rather morosely, reported to JFS that every time she stopped at Julina's house, she was always entertaining "company" and had little time for her. There is no mistaking the tone of hurt and isolation in Alice's letters to JFS as she contrasts her lonely life with that of Julina's. In April 1887 she wrote, "I cannot help feeling that my life had not as many comforts in it" as Julina's did.[66] In another letter, she wrote that she hated having to hide her status as JFS's wife: "It would be so nice if I could throw off my mask and not play a part."[67]

When JFS left for Hawaii in 1884, he had been married to Alice and Mary for barely a year. The two women could not have been more different. Alice was living an impoverished life with her children from her first marriage. Although she was the daughter of Heber C. Kimball, one of the great heroes of Mormonism, her parents' deaths had left her largely disconnected from the interior world of Mormon elites. She was twenty-six when JFS fled to Hawaii, but her relatively difficult life had aged her beyond her years. "I have had trials in every shape it seems to me," she reflected early in her marriage to JFS, noting that while she had "always tried to look on the bright side, the bright side looks awful dark sometimes."[68] She had even rented out a room in her small house to try to make ends meet.

Mary, by contrast, lived first in the Gardo House and then in the dormitory at Brigham Young Academy in Provo. In the Gardo House, the mansion her uncle John Taylor intended for use as his official residence, she enjoyed the services of household staff and security guards. Nineteen and childless when JFS went into hiding, Mary lived in comfort and ease. Her mother lived with her, and even continued to set her bedtime. John Taylor cautioned her, before marrying, that JFS would "not let her have her way" as she had become accustomed to.[69]

Clearly, the second generation of JFS's wives did not mesh well with the first, but this conflict can only be glimpsed obliquely in the documentary record. In 1887, a few years after the two became sister wives, Alice felt confused and sad that Mary "dislike[s] me so very much" despite their having exchanged fewer "than a dozen words in my life."[70] However, during JFS's exile, the women would have had very little contact with each other, especially since they had to keep their marriages a secret. Mary continued her education, and by 1886 she had earned licenses in obstetrics and nursing. During JFS's absence, she also served as president of the Fourteenth Ward Retrenchment Association.[71]

Mary and Alice had not been named in the original indictment against JFS, and he needed to keep federal officials from becoming aware of their existence, which would expose them to legal difficulties.[72] Adding to the difficulty was Mary's youth and beauty. Untrammeled by the vicissitudes of life, her letters betray a dewy optimism and naiveté. Whereas Mary would write JFS letters with bubbly quotes in Spanish and schoolgirl expressions of endless devotion, Alice wrote to her secret, absentee husband that she often wondered "if men are capable of feeling the real love for their wives that wives do for their husbands." Her conclusion? "No."[73]

In March 1887, JFS finally arranged for Julina to return home with little Julina, baby Wesley, and Donnette. He also sent for Mary to come and keep him company, and apparently instructed her to leave without informing her sister wives, a decision that led to some serious domestic tension. Julina complained that Mary's parents were being loose-lipped about the move, increasing the danger of exposing JFS's whereabouts.[74] In truth, however, by 1887 his location was no secret, and the real source of Julina's, Sarah's, and Edna's ire was Mary. After word leaked out that she was to join JFS in Hawaii, a confrontation erupted between Mary and Edna in which "Sarah expected to see Edna slap [Mary] in the face." Julina placed the blame on Mary, who "manifested a spirit . . . that has not left a favorable impression with me," but she saved some scolding for JFS. "It hurt me," Julina wrote to JFS,

214   Chapter 11

"that you sent for [Mary] . . . and said nothing to the rest of us about it. That is not like you."[75] In the end, Mary made the voyage, but by the time she arrived, JFS's time in Hawaii had drawn to a close, and they had to return to Utah.

JFS viewed his years in exile in Hawaii as tainted and unpleasant. "They never knew my heart," JFS wrote of the people with him during that period, "for I was not myself. I was a prisoner and this fact cast a shadow over me. Besides, I found there a spirit that was not congenial to me . . . which placed me in antagonisms from the effects of which I never did get clear."[76] As always, though, he felt an internal struggle whenever he thought about Hawaii. "There is something very natural and homelike to me in the thought of living" there, he wrote, hastening to add that "the thought is perhaps more pleasant than the reality."[77]

In January 1886, JFS wrote to John Taylor and George Q. Cannon from his tropical exile asserting that a compromise on plural marriage was simply unthinkable. He rejected outright the argument that abandoning plural marriage would bring Mormon "troubles to an end." The merciless attacks by the "enemies of God," he pointed out, had driven the Mormons to and fro long before any public announcement of plural marriage had been made. The principle and the practice of polygamy, he wrote, were "beyond the domain of compromise" and could no more easily be surrendered than could belief in "the atonement [of Christ], or repentance, or baptism, or the resurrection of the dead."[78]

Just two years later, the situation had changed so dramatically that JFS had to admit that the end of Mormon plural marriage was a real possibility. In May 1888, he informed his cousin John Henry Smith that "if the enemy prevent [the continued practice of plural marriage] let God require it at the hands of the enemy and visit his wrath, judgment, and indignation on those who shall hinder the work."[79]

Polygamy, Politics, and Statehood

Greatly compounding the difficulties caused by polygamy was the instability within the upper echelons of church leadership. John Taylor's health was failing, the apostles could not agree on any compromise on polygamy, and they were even divided about who Taylor's successor would be. In May 1887, George Q. Cannon wrote to JFS informing him that William Cluff had been dispatched to Hawaii with instructions to accompany him back to Salt Lake immediately. To ensure his safe travel, Cannon had kept the news of JFS's recall secret, limiting the information to only six individuals.[80]

Taylor's health had been declining since January; each passing day he had less energy and an increasingly foggy brain. "His mind is affected to some extent by his sickness," Cannon wrote, explaining that "he cannot listen to details nor grasp them." Cannon was struggling under "the responsibility which rested upon us as the First Presidency of the Church and especially so as Bro. Joseph F. Smith is absent and President Taylor's health is in the condition that it is."[81] Taylor was in hiding, with Cannon, at an isolated house in Kaysville. Cannon dutifully attended to him, but Taylor rarely moved except from his bed to a nearby rocking chair. At times he did not recognize his wives when they came to see him. In his few lucid moments, he insisted that Cannon keep his condition a secret, even from his own family. However, some of the apostles knew because they had witnessed the scene firsthand. Wilford Woodruff ignored Taylor's demand for secrecy and sent a hastily scrawled message to JFS. "Strictly private," the note read, "for your own eye alone." Woodruff painted a vivid and distressing portrait of Taylor as a "dying man" who "cannot breathe" and whose limbs had grown "swollen and purple." He closed the note by imploring JFS to "burn this up and let it remain in your breast."[82]

In a farewell sermon to the Latter-day Saints at Laie, JFS hinted at the trouble he knew awaited him back on the mainland. He said he was sad to leave, but that he felt glad to return and "bear persecution."[83] On 18 July 1887, JFS arrived at the house in Kaysville, and Cannon nearly broke down from an overwhelming sense of relief. For more than two years, he and Taylor had done the work of three, and for months Cannon had carried the entire load himself. He took JFS in to see Taylor. The bedridden president may not have recognized JFS, but Cannon thought that he "might have."[84] JFS, for his part, was shocked and dismayed to see Taylor in such grave condition.

JFS and Cannon began immediately tending to First Presidency business. One week after JFS's first visit to the hideout, he and Cannon were there to hear the appeal of a case decided by the Parowan high council when they were summoned to Taylor's room. It was clear to everyone that he was fading fast. At 7:55 p.m., JFS watched John Taylor die.[85] The man who had been with JFS's father and witnessed the murders at Carthage jail slipped away peacefully, taking with him another of the dwindling associations that connected JFS with his father. JFS experienced this moment, like so many others, as part of the great web that had as its center the murder of Hyrum Smith. "The Great Martyr," JFS wrote, referring to Taylor, "breathed his last. Thus what the deadly bullets of the Carthage assassins failed to do 43 years ago ... the malignant persecutions of their successors have accomplished."[86]

JFS had come home to a quorum divided once again over the question of succession and the perennial problem of plural marriage. The next few years would force the Mormon leadership to decide how to best be Mormon in America—and who should lead them. JFS's skills, especially his ability to find scriptural justifications for doctrinal and practical changes, and his capacious grasp of sacred texts would ensure his voice an important, even central, place in the chambers of leadership.

Although Cannon had been doing much of the work of the First Presidency, he was not particularly popular among some in the Quorum of the Twelve. Heber J. Grant, a junior apostle, bore a particularly strong animus toward him, as did Moses Thatcher. Grant "found a good deal of fault with the way [Cannon] had treated his brethren, with many of his official acts" and the "way [he] had acted in the fall of his son, John Q." (John Cannon fell from grace in 1886 when he publicly confessed to an adulterous affair with a woman named Annie Wells.)[87]

Grant also strongly suspected that Cannon's vaunting ambition, to which "there is no limit," would lead him to make a play for the presidency once Taylor died. Such a move would be a departure from the preceding successions, in which the most senior apostle had taken over.[88] Grant impudently asked Wilford Woodruff, the most senior apostle after Taylor, to "point me to any revelation that states that this [the idea that the most senior apostle succeeds the presidency] must be the case."[89] Woodruff responded to Grant in writing, informing him, without pointing to the requested revelation, that "the President of the Apostles must be made President of the Church in case of the death of our president."[90] Grant did not challenge this publicly, but privately he felt "very strongly impressed that Joseph F. Smith will be the successor to John Taylor."[91] He also felt, incorrectly, that Cannon disliked JFS and that he had sent him into exile not to escape prosecution, but because he viewed him as some sort of threat.

Just days after returning to Utah from Hawaii, JFS was back at work, finding out where trouble was brewing and doling out assignments. Franklin D. Richards received a note from JFS instructing him to "adjust some difficulties in Emery County."[92] Soon JFS found himself trying to plan Taylor's funeral.

Figure 1. Joseph F. Smith in 1911. Courtesy LDS Church Archives (LDS Church History Library).

Figure 2. Joseph F. Smith at age nineteen, shortly after his return from his first mission to Hawaii. Courtesy LDS Church Archives (LDS Church History Library).

Figure 3. Joseph F. Smith and his half brother John Smith. Although the relationship was often strained, Joseph repeatedly fought to keep John from being ousted from his position as church patriarch. Courtesy LDS Church Archives (LDS Church History Library).

Figure 4. Joseph F. Smith and his son Joseph Fielding Smith Jr. They would become the only father and son to both serve as LDS Church president. Courtesy LDS Church Archives (LDS Church History Library).

Figure 5. Joseph F. Smith during his first mission to Britain in 1861. Courtesy LDS Church Archives (LDS Church History Library).

Figure 6. Joseph F. Smith on his final trip to Hawaii in 1915. Courtesy LDS Church Archives (LDS Church History Library).

Figure 7. Joseph F. Smith in 1874 during his first stint as president of the European mission. This photograph was taken shortly after his violent encounter with James McKnight. Courtesy LDS Church Archives (LDS Church History Library).

Figure 8. Joseph F. Smith and the two other members of the First Presidency, John R. Winder and Anthon H. Lund, in the presidency's outer office, ca. 1905. Courtesy LDS Church Archives (LDS Church History Library).

Figure 9. The Joseph F. Smith family in 1904. This photo shows all five of his plural wives and most of his children. Courtesy LDS Church Archives (LDS Church History Library).

12 | "We were unsettled as a Quorum"

Joseph F. Smith's first meeting with the Quorum of the Twelve took place on 3 August 1887. Wilford Woodruff, the senior apostle, opened the meeting by reminding the others that he was the only one among them who had received the endowment ritual under the hands of Joseph Smith and heard with his own ears Smith's "final charge" in which he told the apostles that the authority to run the affairs of the church devolved upon them after his death. Woodruff, nonconfrontational by nature, told the group that he had no desire to reorganize the First Presidency. As they had in 1880, the group discussed the various pros and cons of creating a First Presidency. JFS's thinking on this had evolved in the intervening years. Although he had opposed a reorganization in 1880, by 1887 he had come to believe that it was not only right, but essential. "The Church," he told the group, was "not fully organized until we had a First Presidency," but he did not wish to rush the matter if the other members of the quorum had reservations. Daniel Wells went even further, insisting that "the 12 Apostles were in no sense a presiding council."[1] Wells moved that the First Presidency be reorganized. No one else agreed. This gave Grant the opportunity to attack George Q. Cannon.

Grant brought up his issues with Cannon, and soon it became apparent that instead of having a discussion about the potential First Presidency, Cannon was going to have to convince the other apostles to let him back into their quorum. JFS watched the meeting unfold, remarking only that the group was clearly "unsettled" and that any discussion of reorganizing the First Presidency had to wait until they sorted out the question of Cannon's position. Cannon tried to defend himself against a host of accusations dealing with, among other things, the conduct of his children and his handling of church mining interests.

Since 1881, John Taylor had been advancing the interests of a mining company in Utah's Tintic Mining District. He used church funds to invest in the Bullion, Beck, and Champion Mining Company, and had used profits from the company as a "special contingency fund" intended solely for the president of the church. Taylor left instructions that when he died, the shares should be placed in Cannon's

218   Chapter 12

name.[2] The stock had initially been accepted by Taylor as a result, he claimed, of a revelation from God indicating that the stock would help "redeem Zion." Grant, in particular, felt that Cannon had taken advantage of his family relationship with Taylor to personally enrich himself with the mining stock.[3]

JFS felt torn. Grant looked to him as a mentor and role model, and JFS did not wish to alienate him. On the other hand, his bond with Cannon went back to their shared experience as missionaries in Hawaii in the 1850s, and was cemented further by Cannon's own mentoring of JFS during his mission to Britain in the 1860s. JFS clearly did not side with Grant on the matter of Cannon's son. In fact, JFS went out of his way to express his "kind and merciful feelings" toward John Q. Cannon, even as Grant excoriated him.[4]

JFS had less charitable feelings, however, toward George Q. Cannon's brother Angus. As part of the effort to shield church holdings by dispersing them among private individuals, Angus had taken control of a piece of property known as the Barn Lot, located just west of the Lion House. He had refused to return the property, even though JFS told him in "plain talk" that the land had only been deeded to Cannon to protect it from government seizure.[5] Notwithstanding his ongoing contention with Angus, at the meeting JFS told Grant that he felt "sick" at the way George Cannon was being treated and that the accusations should have been brought up privately rather than in the forum of a quorum meeting.[6] The meeting ended without any resolution, and it would be years before the Cannon question was satisfactorily settled.

The Carrington Scandal

The quorum had issues other than polygamy and the First Presidency to attend to, including one that led to further disagreement. In August 1887, Woodruff informed the other church leaders that he had received several requests for rebaptism from a disgraced former apostle, Albert Carrington.[7] JFS had been in Hawaii when Carrington was excommunicated for adultery, and he had missed the meeting at which Carrington made the rather shocking decision to defend himself by claiming that his crime was not adultery because he had not "spilled his seed in the woman."[8]

JFS knew all about the case, however. After learning the details, he wrote to John Taylor from Hawaii that Carrington, "while wearing the garb of an apostle and minister of Christ," had proven himself to be not only an adulterer and a hypocrite, but a "defiled, corrupt, abominable, hideous monster in the sight of God."[9] The intervening years had not softened JFS's attitude, and he forcefully expressed his incredulity at Carrington's shameless attempt to be readmitted. While some of the apostles suggested that they could spare a little mercy for Carrington and agree to his rebaptism, JFS was having none of it. Carrington had committed "a cool, premediated, deliberate, and oft-repeated crime against other men's wives while in cold blood and in daily connection with the Priesthood in sacred places." Not only that, he was "a man of culture and intelligence, and under the New and Everlasting covenant of marriage; a man of age and experience with grown up sons and daughters. An Apostle!"[10]

When considered in the aggregate, the circumstances led JFS to the conclusion that Carrington had committed "the unpardonable sin." From the days of Joseph Smith, Mormons have believed that everyone will eventually inherit a "kingdom of glory" except for those "sons of Perdition" who have committed "the unpardonable sin," identified in the Doctrine and Covenants as "denying the Holy Ghost." While vaguely defined, the contours of the unpardonable sin had generally been accepted as a complete rejection of Christ after one had attained a "perfect knowledge" of his reality.

Sexual sin, while always serious, was not typically coupled with the unpardonable sin. In fact, no one has ever been tried by an LDS ecclesiastical court for committing the unpardonable sin. But JFS argued that Carrington's "heinous crimes" coupled with the high leadership post that he had held met the bar for being cast into "outer darkness," the place prepared for the sons of perdition. In what was becoming something of a trademark, JFS moved with alacrity between theological innovation to ecclesiastical bureaucracy when he observed that the question should not even have come up because it was not the business of the Quorum of the Twelve to approve rebaptism: that was a task for Carrington's local bishop.

JFS's charge against Carrington met with near-unanimous objections from the other apostles. Even those who did not want to see Carrington rebaptized could not accept JFS's unusual reading of scripture. JFS replied that if this was not a case of the unpardonable sin, he had no idea what would be. However, his personal animus toward Carrington, something which he had always denied but clearly held since the 1870s, probably fueled some of the vitriol he expressed. A more important factor was JFS's deep abhorrence of sexual misconduct.

Church leaders over the years had held a surprisingly wide array of opinions about just how sexual sin should be treated. During the 1850s, it was not uncommon for an open confession of adultery to be granted immediate forgiveness. JFS did not hew to that more liberal view, favoring disciplinary action, especially for adultery, and most especially for adultery committed by persons married in the temple. "Among the saints 'murder will out,'" he wrote to a nephew, reminding him that "adultery is the most deadly sin."[11] In an 1890 letter, JFS added "chastity" to the ancient Pauline trifecta of "faith, hope, and charity."[12] JFS's hard line on this issue would eventually become codified and accepted by the church to such a degree that, within Mormonism, "immorality" refers only to sexual misconduct. The meeting ground to a halt, and Woodruff moved off the topic, promising to revisit it later. In late October 1887, Woodruff took advantage of JFS's absence from a meeting of the quorum to propose Carrington's rebaptism, and all present sustained the action.[13]

220   Chapter 12

Tending to Church Business

JFS spent part of the fall of 1887 hobbled not only by a broken quorum, but also by a broken ankle. In spite of both, he remained actively engaged in church business. Because the leadership had been scattered and in hiding for so long, a fair amount of business needed to be reviewed or audited. The state of Zion's Bank, the ZCMI, the construction of the temples in Manti and Salt Lake, the condition and usefulness of the Gardo House, questions about the state constitutional convention, the issue of whether the Presiding Bishop's Office should shift to a cash-based model for the collection of tithing, the establishment of and maintenance of colonies in Mexico, and many other matters demanded attention.

In mid-August, JFS had revealed to the apostles that some non-Mormon political contacts had been cultivated in Washington. These contacts requested that their information be limited to only two or three leaders within the church. Woodruff, Cannon, and JFS formed the committee that would handle these "confidential matters," and they appropriated $100,000 to fund their activities "in interest of the statehood question."[14]

Many of the issues JFS had to address proved contentious. He found himself at odds with Woodruff and Cannon on the issue of stipends for the apostles. Cannon and Woodruff suggested that the more senior apostles be given annual stipends of $3,000, while junior members would draw $2,000. Apparently, during Taylor's administration, the apostles worked directly with the church president to determine how much they should draw. Taylor had authorized JFS to take $3,600 annually, and he strenuously objected to taking a $600 pay cut. Cannon pressed hard to keep the limit at $3,000, and JFS could not overcome his insistence. To avoid further schism in the quorum, however, it was agreed that all of the apostles should be granted an equal amount, regardless of seniority.[15]

Although Woodruff had not yet reorganized the First Presidency, he treated JFS and a few others in the quorum as de facto counselors, meeting with them regularly outside of the normal quorum context to solicit advice. JFS and Woodruff also began regularly attending plays at the Salt Lake theater together.

Despite the endless meetings and side conferences that had taken up almost all of JFS's time in the fall of 1887, the year closed the way it had begun, with the Mormon leadership at an apparent impasse. As Woodruff noted in his journal on 31 December,

> The prisons are filled with Elders of Israel Because they will not abandon their wives & Children. It will be all right with the Saints of God if they will ownly commit Adultry fornication & whoredom as the Gentile Christians do and not Marry their women. But the whole Christian world seem to be persecuting the Saints of God and seeking their destruction.[16]

JFS, of course, shared Woodruff's frustration with the hypocrisy of federal officials who imprisoned polygamists but themselves kept mistresses and took advantage of the growing number of prostitutes in Salt Lake City.

Notwithstanding their indignation, by early 1888 Woodruff and JFS almost certainly knew that to get statehood for Utah, they had to convince the federal government that polygamy was not being extended but was, in fact, declining. The implication, of course, was that the practice would be allowed to die out on its own, and Mormon leaders would do nothing to inhibit this natural declension. JFS accepted, at least in theory, the idea that plural marriage could be curtailed, but he could not accept the possibility of a deal that required him to abandon all of his wives except for Julina. The best they could hope for was a plan that would allow them to continue to care for and support their plural wives, even if no new marriages were contracted.

In early 1888, Woodruff concluded that he needed a forceful, smart, dedicated, and trustworthy representative in Washington to oversee the ongoing efforts to work out a deal for Utah statehood and try to ensure that an equitable deal could be reached. On 2 February, Woodruff announced at a meeting of the apostles that JFS was to oversee political negotiations, and he had power to decide the wisest "mode of procedure." The rest of the apostles "approved heartily."[17]

Woodruff's decision to send JFS signaled his supreme confidence in JFS's ability to deftly handle himself in the world of Washington politics, to meet the major figures of American politics on an equal intellectual footing, and to represent the LDS Church as a civilized, sane, and, most importantly, American institution.[18] Although JFS's official calling involved presiding over the entire church in the "Eastern states," the primary reason for sending him to Washington was to supervise "political matters, and to control and supervise all financial transactions connected therewith, and to give counsel and manage everything pertaining to the labors of those ... selected ... to assist in bringing the claims of Utah to be admitted into the United States."[19]

Driving Woodruff's decision to send JFS to Washington was the First Presidency's utter lack of confidence in John W. Young. A son of Brigham Young who had only a passing interest in Mormonism, John W. had convinced many church leaders that his connections in the East could be of use to the church. But he had already spent years meeting a wide variety of political leaders and spending a great deal of money to little effect. JFS had long been suspicious of Young anyway, initially because he found "the manner of his treatment of his wives" dishonorable. He also ridiculed John Young's incompetence and his seemingly endless need for more money from church headquarters. After Young wrote to the leaders arguing that prospects for statehood in 1889 looked good, JFS jokingly described Young's plan as an effort to "buy up Congress and the U.S. for $2,000,000—or so much thereof as might not be needed for John W. himself in the promotion of his little scheme of building several railroads from Alaska to Yucatan."[20]

222   Chapter 12

In January 1888, John W. Young asked for another $10,000, which the First Presidency sent "reluctantly" along with a pointed reminder that they had all agreed that Young would only request money if he could provide information relative to the "direction in which you expected to spend it." "Upon none of these points," the letter continued, "have we received any information."[21] Even as JFS was making his way to Washington, Young demanded $25,000 more, causing Woodruff to inform JFS that Young needed to be sent packing, and soon. "He has embarrassed us," Woodruff wrote, noting that "our [non-Mormon] friends can do better."[22]

JFS Goes to Washington

When JFS arrived in Washington, DC, he found Young's behavior infuriating. In March and April 1888, he sent letters to Woodruff, Cannon, his wives, and several other people detailing Young's extravagance with the church's money. He complained that he would have no more money troubles if he had been given some of what Young had spent. JFS became obsessed with Young's purchases, and in a letter to Sarah, he noted they included "$40 for a single cut-glass pitcher, $175 for a small porcelain ornament, $13 for a little mantlepiece adornment, $150 for an opera box for one week! $5.00 for a puppy, and carriages and a darkey in a livery to drive" him around.[23]

In April JFS wrote to Woodruff and Cannon that "in every move and act," Young "has sought to build up only himself; and he has used every dollar he has handled, and your influence to boot, for that purpose." Young had no interest in statehood for Utah, JFS continued, but "railroads, ranches, and banking" consumed him. He judged Young's entire time as the church's representative in Washington a "sickly and imbecile" performance, "with sham, show, and fraud for the background." Young argued, not incorrectly, that lobbying in Washington was expensive, and the more well-heeled a lobbyist appeared to be, the stronger his influence. JFS rejected this explanation and was so outraged that he suggested that Young be brought before the First Presidency and Quorum of the Twelve to defend his standing in the church.[24]

Young may indeed have been profligate in his spending, but the situation also revealed JFS's persistent political naiveté. "Friendship purchased with money is a rope of sand," he philosophized, "which crumbles at the touch when the money abates." JFS suggested that true friends to the cause could only be made by enlightening them "with stubborn facts" that would make it difficult to withdraw support at a later time.[25] JFS's quaint trust in facts as self-evident political realities would not survive the 1890s. He would find out by his own experience that, in national politics, a rope of sand was not the worst thing with which to be bound. And by the time he faced the Reed Smoot controversy, he had fully embraced the practicality of sandy ropes and tangled webs.

As he had in England nearly thirty years earlier, JFS began his work in Washington with a trip to the tailor. In this case, he turned to the well-known New York tailor John Byrne, who supplied him with a "black, diagonal Prince Albert coat and vest and cass pants" for the considerable sum of forty-five dollars.[26] JFS, Woodruff, Cannon, and all the other leaders agreed that appearances mattered, even if they thought that John W. Young had taken this notion to extremes.

One of JFS's main tasks during the months he spent in the East was to run a public relations campaign designed to convince the American people, via the popular press, that Mormon leaders were serious about making changes to polygamy. Against significant odds, the church made decent inroads on this point. Much to JFS's dismay, however, some church leaders decided to use the April 1888 general conference to voice their disgust with any move toward statehood that would impede the practice of plural marriage. JFS wrote, in a tone of confusion and irritation, that "remarks on polygamy at conference are reported in several New York papers in proof" of the determination of the church to continue and extend polygamy. "Very damaging to our cause. We understood such remarks were discouraged." Sermons by Seymour Young and Rudger Clawson, in particular, seemed to "stir up a regular hornet's nest of abuse against Utah."[27]

Woodruff, who remained in hiding and did not attend the conference, assured JFS that he had left explicit instructions with Lorenzo Snow, the ranking apostle in attendance, "that if anyone attempted to speak about polygamy, to throw his hat at him."[28] However rankled JFS may have been at the uproar over the sermons, he confessed to Seymour Young that his absence from the conference was "a good thing in view of the fact that I might have done so much more and worse."[29] Although they braced for a congressional backlash, none followed. "Strange to say," JFS wrote a month later, "it made little perceivable influence on Congress."[30]

The tension between JFS's personal and ecclesiastical roles would never be greater than in the years immediately preceding Woodruff's 1890 Manifesto. As an apostle and a member of the First Presidency, JFS knew that refusing to compromise on polygamy would leave Utah in a perpetual state of "territorial vassalage," governed by "whoremasters, drunkards, and gamblers," men who were not Utah's "leaders ... but aliens in all that term implies."[31] The federal government granted territories far less autonomy than states, and in the case of Utah, it was clear that the federal government intended to aggressively curtail the civil rights of Mormons in ways that it could not do if Utah were a state. All of the anti-polygamy legislation of the 1880s, for example, applied only to territories, not to states. Likewise, Mormon control of the judicial, legislative, and executive branches would be a foregone conclusion if Utah could become a state. JFS and the other church leaders could move about openly if statehood were achieved. Mormon independence therefore depended on making, at the very least, a fundamental compromise on what JFS believed was the Mormons' most important practice.

The LDS Church's contacts in Washington indicated that if Utah had any hope of being admitted in 1889, they "must issue some kind of a manifesto as to our future course, acknowledging the supremacy of the government." By the summer

224   Chapter 12

of 1889, Mormon leaders had "succumbed to, if we have not accepted in good faith, the situation," and JFS hoped that the fact that they had "ceased to proclaim against submission, ceased to oppose by public speech the [anti-polygamy] laws and to advocate defiance of it" would be enough to satisfy the opponents to Utah's statehood bid. But he knew it would likely require far more. Although JFS recoiled at the dilemma, he was practical enough to recognize that "if we are going to concede any more [we should] do it now and claim the prestige of it, or never yield anymore and become still further Martyrs to the cause. To be consistent and prudent we should do one thing or the other."[32]

In any case, JFS's opinion of the United States had fallen to a new low. On 4 July 1888, he wrote that "the celebration is going on [and] we catch the distant strains of the bands occasionally, and hear the sound of the drum, but the voice of liberty is hushed and the freedom of our homes in this boasted 'land of the free' and the brave, is a thing of the past and a dream of the future."[33]

JFS generally disliked the political intrigue that went hand-in-hand with the statehood issue. He felt that, on the whole, Woodruff and the others were pushing too hard with too little divine guidance. They were in danger of forgetting the relationship between "cause and effect on the question of Mormonism." The cause, he argued, is God's will, and any effect that stems from any other source, however well motivated, is doomed to failure. JFS feared the "arrogance and conceit" that would lead anyone to say, "Is not this beautiful Zion which I have built!" Now was the time, he insisted, for revelation, not for "the labyrinths of arguments pro and con." JFS expected to see "startling things when God shall move the earth and the elements for his cause, but only if the Mormons had the patience to "wait and see." He also hated the fact that the church was in the position of negotiating with the Democrats, whom he described as a "most treacherous and unreliable stick to lean upon." He pointedly argued that the church's "efforts should be directed to the other party [Republicans], and our reliance should be on God and the justice of our cause."[34] JFS found himself in conflict with the opinion of most of the other church leaders, who, he believed, ought to be trusting in God first and then, if necessary, in Republicans.

JFS found his time in Washington as difficult personally as it was politically. Characteristically, he worked like "a beaver day and night," and, equally characteristically, he complained about it. "I am the only drone in the hive," JFS complained to Woodruff, noting his late hours, early rising, and endless paperwork.[35] He was also receiving less mail from home than he thought was warranted and frostily informed Edna, "I would like to hear from you when you feel the kindly emotions of your heart evolving from their hidden springs, down in the deep recesses of your nature."[36] But when letters did come, they often fanned the flames of JFS's smoldering anxieties into full-blown conflagrations of panic. When he learned that one of the children had fallen ill with scarlet fever, he fell into a deep state of worry, obsessing about which of his children would be most susceptible to catching it next.

During this period, JFS could barely function under the burden of his fear. "I am," he admitted, "almost useless when anything ails the children."[37]

In 1888, JFS found himself on the cusp of the type of change that both animates and rearranges religious traditions. Religions that persist over time always find ways to adapt and change in response to, and in conversation with, cultural imperatives, but since they also claim to be the owners of truth, the need to change must be reconciled with the self-perception of eternal changelessness. JFS and other leaders had spent decades not only defending plural marriage, but describing it as a requirement for the highest exaltation in the afterlife. To reverse course must have seemed like a disastrous capitulation, but JFS knew that something had to change. He never fully embraced this approach, although he acknowledged that the right course for the church was to use "tongue or pen for good," even if he still longed to "meet the Devil at his gate [rather than] beat around the bush."[38]

JFS eventually came to view the less-militant approach to the controversy with the federal government simply as a change in tactics, not strategy. He refused to "compromise with the Devil," but he had little objection to "halt, and plan, and maneuver to defeat the full purpose of the foe."[39] On several occasions in 1888, JFS argued that a precedent existed by which such maneuvers could be executed without appearing to violate the commandments of God. He expressed his opinion that the precedent of "suspension" existed in the church both in the case of the United Order and the construction of the temple in Jackson County, and he saw no reason that it could not be applied to polygamy.

In both previous cases, JFS argued, God had commanded that certain things should be carried out, then suspended, but did not rescind, the commanded actions. In the case of the United Order, the suspension stemmed from the weaknesses of the people, and in the case of the temple, it was the fierce opposition of the Missourians that led to the suspension. JFS never expected Brigham Young's attempts to revive the United Order to succeed because "the Lord suspended, through Joseph, that principle because the people and the conditions were not ready for it," and "the suspension has [not] been removed." He also frankly admitted that he did not "believe that the Temple will be built in Jackson Co. during the life of any of the generation when the Revelation was given [because] the Lord has suspended that revelation." JFS did not necessarily want to go down this road. If he had his way, he told a meeting of the First Presidency and the Twelve in December 1888, the church would "take a stand right here and never yield another point." However, if need be, they could "come out and say we will not in the future carry out the commands of God [relating to polygamy] because we are prevented by our enemies."[40] This had not been a popular view with Woodruff. Only after the official change was made in 1890 did JFS's views about suspension find enough traction to be useful in bringing previous teachings and pronouncements in line with the new cultural reality. But that was still more than a year away.

226   Chapter 12

Back to Utah

Woodruff recalled JFS to Utah after only a few months, and by early 1889, it was clear that Utah would again be denied statehood. But that wasn't the only bad news. The disfranchisement of Mormon women and polygamists had resulted in the election of a Salt Lake City government that was not controlled by Mormons, which is, of course, exactly the sort of outcome that statehood would have precluded. In the waning days of 1889, church leaders called for a churchwide day of fasting and prayer to call for God's help in saving the church from its enemies. The First Presidency chose to hold the fast on 23 December as a way of marking the birthday of Joseph Smith.

During a meeting in early December, the First Presidency met with the apostles to discuss what to tell the church at large about the purpose of the fast. As the meeting progressed, JFS's mood grew dark, and he told a story that left a deep impression on many of his fellow leaders. Some years earlier, he told them, he had been traveling near Carthage, Illinois, where Joseph and Hyrum Smith were murdered. On that trip, he encountered a man who claimed that he had arrived at the jail just five minutes after the murders. Without revealing his identity, JFS asked how the man felt about the deaths of the Smith brothers. The man paused before answering, during which time JFS clutched and opened a pocket knife, ready, he said, to strike the man "to the heart" if he approved of the killings. Fortunately for all involved, the man said he always thought that the act was "damned cold-blooded murder."[41]

JFS had been prompted to tell the story by George Q. Cannon, who said that he had made an oath in the Nauvoo Temple to avenge the blood of Joseph Smith. This had also become an issue in Utah's battle for statehood. It was a violent relic of a different time, something that would not fit in the world the Mormon leaders wanted to enter. In his instructions to the Mormons about the fast, Cannon wrote that they should "not condemn our enemies but leave them in the hands of God; we should, however, pray for our own sins to be forgiven, and ask that the hearts of the nation's rulers might be softened towards our people."[42]

JFS apparently disagreed. His hostility toward his enemies was particularly sharp in late 1889. In August, his three-year-old son, John Schwartz Smith, had died, and he laid the blame for the child's death squarely at the feet of the anti-polygamy crusade. The boy, JFS wrote, "fell a victim to the cruelty and exposures inflicted upon his mother during the infamous rade [sic]."[43] Abraham H. Cannon recalled in his journal that the day after the child's death, the Quorum of the Twelve and the First Presidency had dressed in their holy temple robes and held a prayer circle. Each man prayed in turn, and when JFS gave voice to his prayer, he asked God to strike the anti-polygamist attorney Robert Baskin "blind, deaf and dumb unless he would repent of his wickedness."[44]

In late 1889, apostles had begun traveling to different wards in the area to read parts of a revelation that Woodruff claimed came to him in November after his legal counsel encouraged him to make some conciliatory moves regarding plural marriage. The revelation instructed the church to make no "further pledges" about abandoning polygamy, and to leave their "enemies" in the hands of the Lord, who would soon visit the nation with stern judgments if they would not cease to persecute the Mormons.[45] The revelation was strident and defiant, and the audiences to whom it was read received it with "great joy."[46] Woodruff's revelatory vehemence, Cannon's softer approach, and JFS's more strident one had the intended effect. In early 1890, the Supreme Court upheld the constitutionality of the Idaho Test Oath, designed to keep anyone who believed in plural marriage from voting, on the grounds that polygamy represented a moral danger to men and women.[47]

13 | An Emerging Gospel Scholar, Iosepa, and the Manifesto

Joseph F. Smith continued to refine his methods for creating a systematic and internally coherent Mormonism that ensured doctrinal continuity between the Old Testament, the New Testament, the Book of Mormon, Joseph Smith's revelations, and current church practices. He fielded doctrinal questions frequently, even while underground and in exile. Many of the questions came from people wanting to understand how LDS teachings and practices, especially the temple rituals and plural marriage, fit within the broader context of the Judeo-Christian scriptural tradition. In one particularly lengthy response, JFS's grasp of scripture, Mormon revelation, and innovative logic are all quite impressive. In a twelve-page answer to a one-line question—"Did they baptize for the dead in Solomon's Temple, or in the succeeding one before and up to the Savior's time?"—JFS made the case that scriptures in both the Old and New Testaments indicate that the temple endowment, eternal sealings, and plural marriage were all part of ancient Jewish and Christian temple worship.[1]

JFS began his disquisition with a revelation received by Joseph Smith in January 1841 (Doctrine and Covenants 124) that God's people were "always commanded" to build temples, and he described the various functions of a true temple. He then worked backward through the Book of Mormon and New Testament, arguing

> That the apostles [at the time of Christ] fully understood the principle of baptism for the remission of sins, that they were taught the redemption of the dead, and that they knew the doctrine of baptism for the dead, and understood the sealing ordinance for time and eternity is indisputable and sure.

JFS was equally sure about his assertion that Christ himself practiced all of the ordinances of Mormonism, including polygamy. He then moved even father back in time, to the days of Solomon, concluding that "it is not questioned that the Endowment from which 'freemasonry' has developed was a part of the ceremonies of Solomon's Temple" and had been practiced by "Moses and the Prophets."[2]

228

An Emerging Gospel Scholar, Iosepa, and the Manifesto   229

When his old friend Susa Young Gates had a question about the nature of the Holy Ghost, JFS provided another detailed and logically designed explanation based on his reading of scripture as well as his own reasoning to explain the difference between the Holy Ghost and the Holy Spirit. Since Mormon scripture is not clear on the differences, JFS saw another opportunity to make all of the pieces of a doctrinal puzzle fit together through a combination of his facility with scripture and his creative, religion-making genius.[3] He excelled in scriptural knowledge and fluency, and in his eagerness to deploy them, he was quickly becoming Mormonism's great theological systematizer, the first since Parley Pratt.

People who did not know JFS well often perceived him as arrogant and even bullying, but his self-perception was quite different. Both publicly and in private, he signaled a deep and persistent self-doubt. In 1891, for example, he told a congregation that he had not yet mastered faith and repentance, and did not expect to before he died. "I am still trying," he admitted, "to bring myself into subjection to ... God."[4] And, like everyone else, JFS fretted about his appearance. He sat for a portrait in 1893 and later complained to the photographer that he was "a little disappointed in the front view. There is an unfavorable expression about the mouth. With me it is no doubt a clear case of a natural dislike of an exact picture rather than a likeness." People, he wrote, "like to be flattered" by a portrait, and this could hardly be done in his case when the camera captured reality.[5] Whether this deprecation functioned as compensation for JFS's often aggressive expressions of opinion or it was the other way around, it is impossible to say. What is undeniable is that the opposing tendencies created a pronounced turbidity of mind and heart. As he observed his fiftieth birthday in 1888, JFS was still plagued by insecurities that had dogged him all of his life. He pleaded with his best friend, Charles Nibley, to "regard me rather for what I would be than for what I am." And what he was, at least in his own mind, was "childlike and dependent," and riddled with weaknesses and faults that seemed to be exacerbated when people "exalted [him] above [his] status."[6]

The depth of JFS's friendship with Nibley allowed him to express his insecurities unselfconsciously, and indeed the degree of emotional intimacy between the two men was rivaled only by the bond JFS had with his wives. His circle of intimates had always remained small, but he expressed disappointment that no one outside of his immediate family had remembered to wish him happy birthday, a fact that does seem somewhat unusual given his status and celebrity in Utah. Although this was probably an indication of how distant he could be, and the lack of intimate friendships between him and other church leaders, JFS interpreted it as more evidence that his presence in the world was largely unwelcome by all except his own family.

He also had difficulty accepting compliments, even from close friends, and was quick to see insults disguised as pleasant observations. When Nibley expressed admiration for his writing skills, calling his letters a form of "poetry," JFS responded that he thought the comments "a little <u>thick</u>, if not sarcastic," adding, "I always

230   Chapter 13

knew I could not write."[7] In a letter to Susa Young Gates he wrote, "If there is anything I hate—with zeal it is flattery."[8]

Iosepa

During all the tumult surrounding the issues of statehood and polygamy, JFS took time from his schedule of political work in Washington, DC, to write to church president Wilford Woodruff, imploring him to help the Hawaiian Latter-day Saints in any way possible. Concerned that they would "suffer at the hands of sharpers or lack for employment and means of support," JFS wanted to make it clear that they "are apt to receive but slim attentions from any quarter" despite their "keen sense of friendship and brotherly love." He reminded the Woodruff that the Hawaiians, despite their serious cultural problems, were members of the "House of Lehi" and thus the responsibility of the church. Moreover, he wrote, "they are human and have souls to save."[9] In October 1890, he wrote to Marriner W. Merrill, president of the Logan Temple, authorizing him to perform the second anointing ritual on a Hawaiian couple, who were to be "adopted to the Prophet Joseph Smith."[10] JFS could not have bestowed higher honors.

Despite encouragement from church leaders for the Hawaiian Latter-day Saints to remain on the islands and build up the church there, many of them migrated to Utah. "They come to Utah," JFS explained in an 1888 letter to Woodruff, "believing it to be the gathering place for the Saints—the Zion of the latter days—and while they are ignorant of our language and customs and will appear awkward and dependent somewhat at first, they are naturally bright."[11] The Hawaiians were so eager to participate in the sealing and endowment rituals of the temple, they had begun performing them, without authorization, in Hawaii. While JFS found their zeal admirable, he advised the mission president that "a strong effort should be made to enlighten them [and teach them that] baptisms for the dead, endowments, sealings, and adoptions must be done in Temples."[12]

Generally reluctant to offer unsolicited advice to his ecclesiastical superiors, JFS could not help but do so in the case of the migrating Hawaiians because "I have spent so much of my life among them that I feel deeply interested in their welfare." Although some Mormons were already helping the Hawaiian migrants in an unofficial capacity, JFS suggested to Woodruff that such men would put forth "greater zeal in their behalf if his labors were under the sanction, approval, or other recognition of the Brethren." He urged Woodruff to officially appoint someone to provide the "wide direction and employment they need."[13]

The Hawaiian migrants were the first ethnic group to settle as Mormons in Utah in substantial numbers. The general racism of whites in Utah in general, Mormon or not, clashed with the ideal of the gathering to Zion. Hawaiian Mormons

An Emerging Gospel Scholar, Iosepa, and the Manifesto 231

found themselves less than welcome in hotels, restaurants, and rental properties. To make things easier for them, the church created a joint-stock company, the Iosepa Agriculture and Stock Company, to serve as a gathering place for the Hawaiian Mormons. In May 1889, Woodruff appointed William Cluff, H. H. Cluff, and F. A. Mitchell, three men familiar with Hawaii and its culture, to begin looking for a suitable location for the Hawaiian colony.[14] The committee ended up choosing a site in Skull Valley, in the desert west of Tooele. The settlement was called Iosepa, Hawaiian for "Joseph," in honor of JFS and, probably, Joseph Smith Jr.

Although it was his idea, JFS soon started having reservations about the project. The leaders of the colony seemed to feel no pressing need to communicate with church headquarters for extended periods of time, and when they did, the news was often depressing. Rumors swirled that leprosy and other serious, and contagious, ailments had broken out in the colony. Although he had ample evidence that white Mormons were no strangers to vices of all kinds, JFS had long felt that Hawaiian culture tilted individuals toward sin, and he feared the effects of recreating that culture in Utah. "I feel somewhat uneasy in my mind about so many of our Hawaiian brethren coming along at once," he wrote to William King, the Hawaiian mission president, indicating that unless the church could find a way to strip the newcomers of their cultural baggage, "we may have trouble."[15] Despite his misgivings, JFS recognized that "the long experience I have had upon those islands and the intimate acquaintance I formed with that people in the days of my childhood and youth [had given him] a particular warmth of friendship in my heart towards them which I could not overcome if I would."[16]

In the late summer of 1890, the three members of the First Presidency traveled to Iosepa and engaged in a performance of ritual exchange. The white Mormons paraded in with a procession led by a wagon full of sagebrush, representing Utah as it was, followed by a wagon filled with corn, oats, barley, and fruit representing Utah as it is. No doubt this unusual display was meant to encourage the Hawaiians on two levels: first, to make them feel better about the harsh surroundings in which they had been settled by pointing out that all of Utah had once been like that, and second, to suggest that only through disciplined labor would they be able to reap the bountiful harvest. The Hawaiians, for their part, cooked meat underground in the traditional fashion, demonstrating that their way of doing things worked just as well in the dusty Utah ground as it did in the rich Hawaiian soil.

The didactic parade of produce was also unnecessary: the colony had a booming agricultural yield just waiting to be harvested: 155 acres of "small grain," 250 tons of stacked hay with more to come, a corn crop "equal to that of the Missouri river bottoms," as well as pumpkin, squash, melons, turnips, and mangle wurzel that JFS judged "unsurpassed."[17] They also had a large number of livestock and a fishery. But JFS mused that this bounty may have been helped more than a little by the whites who ran the colony. Too many of the Hawaiians, he wrote, "were given to drink and

232 Chapter 13

general worthlessness," and "great patience and charity are needed to get along with those people."[18] However, he was certain that if they "work and allow their labor to be wisely directed," prosperity would likely follow.[19]

After the procession and ritual exchange, Woodruff dedicated the colony of Iosepa to God, a prayer that JFS translated into Hawaiian. JFS then offered a second, and different, dedicatory prayer in Hawaiian. The ambivalence that the leaders felt about the settlement also manifested itself in the choice of Harvey H. Cluff, a haole, or non-Hawaiian, to preside at Iosepa.[20] Cluff was given "full authority to administer in all spiritual affairs . . . as a presiding elder in their midst."[21] Similarly, rather than place Iosepa under the direction of the Tooele stake, as it would have been if it had been settled by whites, it was decided that Cluff would report directly to the First Presidency.

This story of JFS and the Hawaiian Latter-day Saints is riddled with irony. He clearly felt deeply connected with them and acknowledged their good qualities, and although he believed they were prone to sin, they were much more likely than non-Mormon whites to confess their sins. "They are not," he wrote to a nephew serving a mission among the Hawaiians, "so much behind some other nations who boast a higher civilization."[22] But JFS also considered them part of a racial continuum that placed whites, especially Mormon whites, at the top, Hawaiians in the middle, and Native Americans at the bottom. As he wrote to Woodruff, the Hawaiians would prove "equal if not much better citizens and members of the church than any of the native Lamanites for whom we [white church leaders] have done and are still doing so much."[23]

One of the most striking ironies is that the Mormon leaders in Utah were in the process of imposing a colonial structure on the Hawaiian migrants at the same moment that they were trying everything in their power to throw off the quasi-colonial yoke of territorial status. What is more, the Mormons had the same fears about Hawaiians that the broader American culture had about white Mormons: contagion and cultural rot. Even the undeniably fantastic agricultural achievements of the colony's first year could only have come, as far as JFS was concerned, because of the wise direction of the colonial overseers. The irony, it would seem, was lost on all involved.

Back to the Underground

JFS remained in hiding from 1888 through 1890 because the risk of arrest still loomed large. He traveled only at night and spent the rest of his time locked away indoors. By 1890, the strain of being underground began to show. He could no longer freely spend time with his wives and children, who had been separated and forced to live as single mothers much of the time. JFS shared the same fate as many church leaders. In the late 1880s, most polygamist men lived separately from their wives, and the wives themselves went into hiding to avoid being called to court to testify against their husbands. In June 1890, JFS wrote a letter to his older sister, Jerusha, with whom he had never been close and had not been in contact with since 1885. "I am still living," he wrote, and "altho' invisible to the public I have not forgotten kindred ties."[24]

The question of just how this untenable situation would end remained unsettled well into the spring of 1890. Although Woodruff had officially stopped giving permission for new plural marriages in April 1889, the First Presidency had not reached a decision regarding the future of the practice. In fact, they were sending decidedly mixed signals. Woodruff had authorized several plural marriages even after his stated 1889 ban, yet there was a rumor that Cannon had issued "extermination orders" calling for polygamists to be disfellowshipped (one step short of excommunication). A decision depended on the outcome of two Supreme Court cases. The first decision, in *Davis v. Beason*, came down in February 1890. This was the decision that upheld the Idaho test oath and set the stage for disenfranchising anyone who expressed sympathy for the practice of plural marriage. In response, JFS began advising men to begin thinking about the possibility that their wives and families might have to live under separate roofs permanently. Polygamist Mormons, he wrote, needed to protect "themselves against any inimical movements [on the part of the government]" and not delay because "changes sometimes come suddenly and violently."[25] The second case, decided in May 1890, was the *Late Corporation of the Church of Jesus Christ of Latter Day Saints v. U.S.* The court's decision upheld the portion of the Edmunds-Tucker Act providing for seizure of church property.

Even after the two Supreme Court decisions came down against the church, however, some confusion remained. For example, when Charles Nibley wrote to JFS in the summer of 1890 asking about the possibility of him taking a plural wife, JFS's response reflected both his commitment to the concept of plural marriage and his increasing doubts about its future. Under normal circumstances, JFS wrote, the marriage would go forward, but he pointed out the official line that called for an "absolute prohibition" on new plural marriages in the United States. "Under existing circumstances," he wrote, Nibley would have to "leave well enough alone ... pass it by, dismiss the subject." JFS wrote that nothing short of a command directly from God could induce him to take another plural wife, and that no one who had "fulfilled the law" of plural marriage should be adding wives at such an uncertain time.[26]

In May 1890, just after the Supreme Court announced its decision, JFS quashed the republication of one of Brigham Young's sermons in the *Young Women's Journal.* In his letter to the editor, Brigham Young's daughter Susa Young Gates, he held that the sermon's mention of a "political kingdom of God" was "impolitic" and ought not to be published. He assured her that although "the day will come when the truth may and will be told, and the world will have to endure it ... that time seems not to be just now." JFS did not like it, but he accepted that, for the moment, "silence is

234   Chapter 13

all that is required." After all, he wrote, "while we are under the claws of the great American eagle, there is no use of teasing it by plucking its tailfeathers."[27]

Late in the summer, the First Presidency visited Mormon settlements in Colorado. On 17 August 1890, Woodruff, Cannon, and Smith spoke to a congregation about "politics and family matters." Woodruff—who had previously rejected JFS's analogy between the suspension of the commandment to build the temple in Jackson County and the possible suspension of plural marriage—now seemed to embrace it. He told the assembled Mormons that "God did not and never will hold us responsible for building the temple in Jackson County until he opens the way." "God," he told them "would hold the nation responsible for hindering his work." Curiously, no transcript exists of the sermon, and neither Cannon nor Woodruff mentioned the subject in their journals. JFS, however, on one slim page of a pocket calendar, hastily made note of Woodruff's analogy, which, of course, was actually JFS's idea.[28] Cannon angered some men in the audience when he informed them that the time had come to disperse their families, just as church leaders had been doing for some time. The next day, Cannon met with disgruntled Mormons who argued that maintaining multiple households presented an impossible financial burden. Cannon, taken aback, simply explained that he was offering advice, not commandments. But it was good advice, and timely.

On 1 September 1890, the First Presidency met to discuss a troubling new development. The Utah Commission, it seemed, had turned its attention toward the church's four temples "so as to get some claim upon them."[29] The government suggested that because the Mormons used their temples for plural marriages, and because the buildings were private rather than open for public worship, they could potentially be seized. Woodruff found this possibility deeply ominous. The nearly completed Salt Lake Temple and the temples in Manti, Logan, and St. George not only represented the pinnacle of Mormon religious expression, but were also the products of decades of toil and money. To surrender them would be unthinkable.

With the fate of the temples weighing heavily on their minds, the members of the First Presidency traveled to San Francisco, where they sought advice from several legal experts regarding the upcoming Supreme Court session. Cannon, who took the lead during this trip, wanted to know if the government was likely to take the action authorized in May of seizing church property and assets. Facilitating their meetings in San Francisco was Col. Isaac Trumbo. A non-Mormon born to a Mormon mother, Trumbo greatly admired the LDS Church and lobbied tirelessly on its behalf among California's political elite. Among those Trumbo arranged for the First Presidency to meet was Morris Estee, a Republican politician and prominent attorney. He offered the frank assessment that the Mormons had to face reality. They could not expect "65 millions of people to come to your standard," and they needed to accept the fact that the time had arrived to "make some announcement concerning polygamy and the laying of it aside."[30]

Soon after returning from California, Charles Penrose and Franklin Richards, who were monitoring developments in Washington met with the First Presidency to discuss the Utah Commission's report accusing the church of continuing to authorize and perform plural marriages in Utah, including at least forty-five such marriages since June 1889. Although the allegations were largely true, Cannon thought that there "should be a square denial, and I remarked that perhaps no better chance had been offered to us to officially, as leaders of the church, make public our views concerning the doctrine and the law that had been enacted."[31]

The report, which had been provided to the *Salt Lake Tribune*, would have sweeping consequences. If allowed to stand unchallenged, it would effectively dissolve the goodwill that the church had managed to build up among influential members of government. It showed the church acting in bad faith, something that would confirm the worst suspicions of those who opposed Utah statehood, and raise questions even among those who supported it. Woodruff then issued what became known to history as the Manifesto.[32]

The Manifesto

The Manifesto was exactly what Estee had recommended. It claimed, falsely, that no new plural marriages had been authorized since 1889. It announced that no such marriages would be authorized or performed. Woodruff announced his intention to "submit to those laws" that had been "enacted by Congress forbidding plural marriage." He also claimed that no church leader had, since 1889, taught or encouraged the practice of plural marriage. He concluded by offering "advice" to the church membership not to contract any illegal marriages. The First Presidency hoped this would be sufficient to keep their property, especially their temples, from government seizure.[33]

As soon as the Manifesto was published in the *Deseret News*, JFS sent a copy to Isaac Trumbo in California, pleading with him to share it widely, especially among the many "friends" of the Mormons who remained "unfamiliar with the facts," and to vouch for the honesty of the piece.[34] In his journal, Woodruff simply noted that "I have arrived at a point in the History of my life as the President of the Church of Jesus Christ of Latter Day Saints where I am under the necessity of acting for the Temporal Salvation of the Church.[35]"

Many of the apostles saw the Manifesto as nothing more than public acknowledgement of what had been internal church policy for more than a year. Franklin Richards adopted JFS's argument about historical precedence for the suspension of commandments, but John Henry Smith found that particular argument repugnant. In fact, he said that "if we as a people had taken the heroic stand and maintained all of the principles of faith" that had been "suspended," then "our troubles would

236   Chapter 13

have been over by this time."[36] Nevertheless, the Quorum of the Twelve approved the statement, and it was read to the assembled Mormons at the church's general conference on 6 October 1890.

Two days later, JFS wrote to Trumbo that the "conference is now over. The 'child is born' and I hope it will rapidly grow to good proportions and fulfill all our hopes." He noted that Judge Charles Zane had already "announced his readiness to admit 'Mormons' to citizenship."[37] In November 1889, Judge Anderson of the U.S. Third Circuit had ruled that Mormon immigrant "aliens" could not be admitted to citizenship, but if the Manifesto was sufficient to change Zane's mind on the matter, then higher courts would likely agree with him.

Although the tone of JFS's letter to Trumbo was optimistic, it remained to be seen just how far the Manifesto would go in moving Utah toward statehood. L. John Nuttall believed that the effects could be profound. In January 1891, he wrote to JFS from Washington that the Manifesto "will have more effect than all which can be said by outsiders in our behalf, however friendly they may be towards us."[38] It clearly had as its intended audience the powerful outsiders, but the reaction of the Mormons themselves also had to be considered. JFS knew that even though the voting on the issue at conference was recorded as unanimous, in reality it came as an unpleasant shock to many rank-and-file Mormons.

Before the news broke, JFS wrote to Sarah, then hiding in Nephi, Utah, south of Provo. "Tomorrow you may hear some news that will no doubt startle some folks," he wrote cryptically. But he reassured her that she need not be troubled by it, and that "only those who could and would not, and now can't . . . will be affected by it." JFS predicted that those who "growl and find fault and censure" the church leadership would be those who had failed to do their duty. He was already anticipating resistance to the move and framing it as a sifting process. "Those who have done their whole duty," he wrote, would have no need to criticize or object.[39]

JFS's aspersions were grossly unfair to the many faithful polygamists who reacted with horror to the announcement. The news blindsided B. H. Roberts, one of the seven presidents of the Seventy, who read the Manifesto in a train car. The more he thought about the document, the less he liked it. He grew angry as he thought about his imprisonment and exile, about the sacrifices he and his wives had made to sustain it. "Our community had endured every kind of reproach from the world for the sake of it," he wrote, "and this was to be the end?" Roberts pronounced the Manifesto a "cowardly proceeding," and when it was presented for a sustaining vote in general conference, he refused to raise his arm.[40] Many shared Roberts's feelings, and although he eventually came to accept the Manifesto, others did not, and JFS would have ugly encounters with faithful friends over it.

The Manifesto did not bring JFS any immediate relief from exile and its various challenges. Still wanted by law enforcement officers, he found that "while my duties are many, I am compelled to more cautiously and carefully perform them."[41]

He walked the streets of Salt Lake only at night, and even then he made a modest effort at disguise by tucking his beard into his coat. JFS could not even find a way to attend meetings of the Cooperative Wagon and Machine Corporation until he asked if the meetings could be brought to him.[42] A similar situation arose regarding meetings of Zion's Bank, and he responded incredulously to an invitation to attend a board meeting at the bank: "of course it will not be convenient at that place."[43] This hardship was relatively easy to bear because, as JFS admitted, he paid "but little attention [to] business matters" because "they are not my life."[44]

JFS paid significantly more attention to his family, although he still lived separately from his wives and saw them infrequently. This led to some fraught domestic situations. In 1891, his twenty-year-old daughter Leonora found herself the object of romantic attention from a young man named Joseph Nelson. JFS had heard rumors that Nelson had been showing up at Sarah's residence with increasing frequency. When he asked Sarah about Nelson's visits, she said, probably less than honestly, that she had no idea what was going on.

In May, JFS received a letter from Nelson requesting his permission to marry Leonora. Although he usually did not respond to correspondence very promptly during this period, he wrote back to Nelson the very day that the letter arrived. Clearly furious, JFS demanded to know "by what right you have paid your respects to my daughter with a view to matrimony, without first consulting, or asking permission of her parents to do so?" JFS felt insulted that his "right to be consulted" on this matter had been abridged in transgression of the laws of reason, propriety, "common courtesy," "Church custom," "the order of the Priesthood," "ancient scripture," and "modern practice." JFS told Nelson that he intended to exercise his veto power over his daughter's desire to marry on three conditions: the suitor was not a Mormon, the suitor was a Mormon but lacking in zeal, or the suitor sought "the affections of one of them without her parents' permission and approval." JFS's feathers had been ruffled, no doubt, by Nelson's breach of etiquette, but later in the letter, he reveals the underlying cause for his reaction. "I am in no hurry for any one of my daughters to assume the responsibilities of married life," he wrote, adding, probably wishfully, that "not one of them is in any haste to do so." Leonora, he pointed out to Nelson, "is young and has no need to hasten from her parental roof."[45]

JFS had perhaps forgotten than he himself had "hastened from the parental roof" not one but four women who, at the time of their marriages, were younger than Leonora was in 1891. Leonora's mother, Sarah, married JFS when she was only eighteen. In the most time-honored parental tradition, the deeds of the parents could not be used as precedent to justify the wishes of their children. But this also speaks to JFS's desire to spare his daughter, for as long as possible, the toil and misery that he had seen his wives endure. The fact that the courtship had been carried out in one of his homes, under his wife's nose, but without his knowledge, increased his frustration with life underground.

JFS Faces "Gentile" Materialism in Zion

One of the things that JFS had in common with millions of other Americans was a persistent personal struggle with money. After the Civil War, the engines of capitalism had driven a wedge between the rich and poor that divided them more starkly than ever before in American history. In 1890, 9 percent of Americans controlled 71 percent of the wealth, and 27 percent of those belonged to the top 1 percent. At the same time, capitalism gave rise to a type of consumerism that nineteenth-century sociologist Thorstein Veblen dubbed "conspicuous consumption." Discussing Veblen's ideas, Rebecca Edwards argued that money could be made if "merchants and advertisers ... [could make] it their specific goal to entice people to buy products they did not need." Storefront window displays became a stage where needs were created and nurtured. "The pain of poverty," Edwards argued, "was made all the keener by lavish displays" in stores and catalogues.[46]

During this period, Christmas became the centerpiece of American consumerism, "a celebration of material abundance, marked by trees, stockings, and gifts."[47] In 1874, Macy's department store in New York City introduced its "famous display window," imitated by stores small and large across the country. This context helps us understand one of JFS's most moving published articles, a Christmas reminiscence that began as a letter to one of his sons but eventually found its way into the *Deseret News*.

In the letter, JFS remembered Christmas as a time when he felt loved in the midst of his "God-given mamas, and our precious chicks," but lacked even "a dollar in cash with which to buy one thing for Christmas." All around him, the spirit of conspicuous consumption seemed to taunt him.

> I saw many reveling in luxuries, with means to lavish on their every *want*, which were far greater than their needs—riding in buggies, on prancing horses, enjoying their leisure while I—we all—were on foot and, of necessity, tugging away with all our mights to keep body and soul together. Under these spiritless conditions, one day just before Christmas ... I walked up and down Main Street, looking into the shop windows ... and then slunk out of sight of humanity and sat down and wept like a child.[48]

Even Utah, which sought to hold itself apart from the soulless capitalism and greed of nineteenth-century America through attempts at communal living and home manufacture, could not immunize itself against the changing tide of American consumerism, and JFS never forgot how painful and humiliating it was.

JFS did, at least, have some support from the church, unlike B. H. Roberts, one of the seven presidents of the Seventy, who visited the First Presidency late in 1890, hat in hand. Roberts had written to Woodruff, Cannon, and Smith some weeks earlier asking for $600 but had received no response. At the meeting, he again asked

An Emerging Gospel Scholar, Iosepa, and the Manifesto 239

for the money, and then inquired whether he could expect to be compensated in the future, or whether he should start looking for other sources of income rather than working full-time on church business. The First Presidency then agreed to give Roberts the requested amount and "released [him] to look after [his] own affairs." Roberts concluded that he would get "no assistance from the Church" for the foreseeable future.[49]

JFS may not have been particularly sympathetic to Roberts, who at least had the funds to disperse his family underground. Many church leaders followed this course, sending wives and children to live in remote areas in New Mexico and Colorado, beyond the reach of the dreaded subpoenas. But JFS wrote to his mother's sister Mercy Thompson that "I cannot hide them on the underground" because "they are so many and so small." This meant that his families had to contend with the continuing attention of federal officials. "My family is too numerous to scatter them beyond the reach of the meddlers without I sold my homesteads to get the money to do it," he complained. Without divine intervention, JFS believed, he would be "doomed to remain in hiding for some time to come."[50]

Meanwhile, Mormons languishing in the penitentiary had grown sufficiently frustrated with the conditions, and with the failure of church leaders to alleviate them, to start threatening those leaders. In 1891, an imprisoned polygamist named Hans Jesperson sent word to church headquarters that unless "something is done for him immediately," he would reveal to the federal authorities the name of the man who performed his most recent polygamous marriage. That marriage had been performed in the Endowment House "just before it was demolished" in November 1889, which was during the moratorium on plural marriage that Woodruff described in the Manifesto. The sealer was liable to two years in the penitentiary and a staggering $1,000 fine, and whatever goodwill the Manifesto had engendered could be dashed if Jesperson and others went public. Church leaders immediately visited Jesperson and took every avenue available to help his cause and keep him quiet.[51]

As November 1890 waned, JFS passed another birthday alone and in hiding. He took the opportunity to write to Mercy Thompson to thank her for a gift she sent. As the closest remaining link to his mother, Mercy's attention moved JFS deeply. "The remembrance of 52 years ago," JFS wrote, "must awaken peculiar thoughts in your mind." He expressed his happiness that his aged aunt would "not again have to pass through a repetition of the scenes of those times," even as he was living a life in hiding—a faint echo of the bloody past.[52]

Not all his birthday reflections were so somber. JFS had always prided himself on his physical fitness, and he boasted to his friend Charles Nibley that even at fifty-two, he could "still crack my heels twice in one jump ... [and] do the 'double shuffle,' and the 'pigeon wing,'" albeit "not with as little wind as I used to." He delighted in the many "evidences of undeparted youth" that remained with him, but wondered if they passed by his wives unnoticed. "One thing is sure," he wrote to Nibley with

240   Chapter 13

a wink, "I manage some way to keep them pretty well employed when I am not too far away."[53] JFS may have been in hiding and his families separated, but he managed to spend enough time with his wives to father four children in 1890 and another in 1891. Four more daughters and a son joined his family, with each wife contributing one child to the group.

Outsiders liked to imagine that Mormon polygamy was a sexual playground, but JFS could not have been more straitlaced in matters of sexuality. In the 1890s, he continued to emphasize chastity and took every opportunity he could to make it a central moral facet of Mormonism, as he had done since the 1870s. Like most American Christians at the time, JFS strongly believed that illicit sexual activity, especially masturbation, could lead to a wide variety of mental and physical ailments. He viewed it as an evil to be avoided at all costs. In the late nineteenth century, the British and American medical communities began to embrace circumcision as a preventative for masturbation. This represented, according to one historian, the most surprising of "Victorian bodily management practices."[54]

JFS found this notion so compelling that in March 1896 he arranged to have seven of his sons, ranging in age from seven to twenty-three, circumcised by his brother-in-law, Dr. Joseph Richards. "The Lord, through Moses, commanded [circumcision] for a wise purpose," JFS wrote to his son Hyrum, and although he never directly indicated, at least in writing, what that purpose was, he strongly hinted at it when he observed that "one thing is sure—there are no insane Jews." In his son Buddy's case, JFS believed surgical intervention was urgent. He confided to Hyrum that Buddy "needs to be circumcised badly."[55]

Even though JFS was willing to subject his sons to what must have been a painful ordeal to keep them from "polluting" themselves, he struggled with how to warn the young people of the church of the dangers of sexual vices. He supervised the publication of the *Young Women's Journal*, and in that capacity he was shocked by the frankness of a proposed article that crossed his desk in December 1890. In a letter to the journal's editor, Susa Young Gates, JFS wrote that the article, bearing the cryptic title "Secret Impurities the Cause of Intense Suffering," was "very crude" and "might do some harm." He agreed that the "pernicious habit referred to" in the article was a "vile, life destroying, unnatural crime," but he insisted that broaching the subject "in <u>print</u>" was completely inappropriate and tended to produce an effect "more <u>suggestive</u> than <u>corrective</u>." Rather than publish an article on the subject, JFS suggested that the best course to combat this "evil" was "for the parents to live in the confidence of their children and vice versa, and the children may learn from their parents."[56]

JFS's aggressive denunciation of youthful sexual experimentation coupled with his insistence that the subject be kept private and addressed only between parents and children set the stage for secrecy and shame. How likely would other parents be to frankly address such an issue if JFS could not even bring himself to use the word "masturbation" in a private letter on the subject? He repeatedly fought any effort on the part of the church to address sexuality publicly. Masturbation, birth control, and other matters were deemed evil, but discussion remained taboo. In this regard, Mormonism did not differ substantially from American Catholic and Protestant attitudes of the time. The irony, of course, is that JFS was among the most sexually active religious leaders in the United States and among the most conservative on sexual issues, a conservatism that he managed to embed within institutional Mormonism.

JFS's influence on the church's approach to sexuality was profound, deep, and durable. When the church did finally produce, in the 1960s, materials that spoke to such things as masturbation, the moral issue remained wedded to discredited, spurious, late Victorian "scientific" ideas linking masturbation with emotional problems and identifying it as a gateway to homosexuality. Bruce R. McConkie's writings in *Mormon Doctrine* and Spencer Kimball's in *The Miracle of Forgiveness*, which continue to influence official Mormon attitudes toward sexuality, have their roots in JFS's own preferences for the treatment of the subject.[57]

JFS also took other steps that would shape Mormon ideas of morality. In the early 1890s, he began to advocate a move away from Brigham Young's policy of sending young men on missions as a way to reform them—a policy from which JFS benefitted greatly. There had been some discussion of sending Hyrum Kimball, a son of Heber C. Kimball, on a mission to try to temper his rowdy ways. But in a letter to Solomon Kimball, JFS declared, "The day has passed for men to stand [on anything] except upon their own merits. No man is fit to go on a mission unless he is exemplary in his own life." He noted that "a man may be ignorant, but he can learn and the mission field is a good school," but potential missionaries must "reform themselves" before going on mission and attempting to "reform others."[58]

JFS expressed similar sentiments at a conference in the fall of 1894. "It is a sad reflection on the youth of Zion," he remarked, "that there should be a single young man in Israel who ... would have to undergo radical changes in himself." But such radical changes were now requirements because JFS was disgusted at "the idea of calling a young man to go out to preach the gospel who needs to be preached to, and to reform!" Under the rules he favored—that is, sending out only those who "are exemplary in every way [and] pure minded and faithful"—JFS himself probably would not have qualified to serve his first mission in Hawaii.[59] Nevertheless, his emphasis on the importance of a high moral standard for potential missionaries remains a central tenet of LDS practice.

In the spring of 1891, JFS began taking steps to get out from under his 1885 indictment. Trumbo, one of the church's chief political contacts in California, inquired of Assistant U.S. Attorney John Zane about the best course of action. Zane suggested that JFS write and sign a document in which he should "say that he intended to obey and uphold the laws of the United States and would encourage others to do the same." JFS immediately did so and submitted his official petition for amnesty on 22 June 1891. On 10 September, President Benjamin Harrison

242   Chapter 13

signed his amnesty papers. For the first time in nearly seven years, JFS could live his life in the open again.[60]

The End of Exile

The news of his amnesty came in time for JFS to speak at the general conference, the first time in more than seven years that the three members of the First Presidency had been together in public. When JFS mounted the podium in the tabernacle, the audience of 10,000 was "silent as the tomb."[61] He spoke for forty-five minutes, making sure to thank "President Harrison and my friends for my release from exile." JFS made a point to praise the United States as a "glorious country," and, as he promised to do in his application for amnesty, he urged his listeners to be good citizens and obey the law. His appearance surprised some in the congregation, and JFS admitted that he looked substantially grayer than when last seen at the pulpit. He also noted that there were many there who did not know him, something that he had never before experienced.[62]

After years in hiding and the apparent capitulation of the church to the government's demands, JFS felt obliged to respond to what he assumed was an unspoken accusation of cowardice. "It is not an exhibition of manhood for men to disobey the words of God and the righteous counsels of His chosen servants," he declared. But "there was no cowardice in a man obeying at all times righteous counsel when it came from the Presidency of the church," he protested; in fact, "it was manly to hearken to such counsel." According to Abraham Cannon, JFS took this opportunity to bear "powerful testimony to the truth, and promising all that they might receive a similar testimony by rendering obedience to the commandments of God" as given through the First Presidency.[63]

JFS was sculpting the contours of Mormon culture in this address, decoupling masculinity from righteous resistance to the tyranny of an oppressive state, and marrying it instead to obedience to an increasingly assimilated church. Thus manliness did not flow from devotion to a set of fixed principles, but rather from obedience to leaders who could change principles as circumstances might demand, and then expect "manly" acceptance of any change.[64]

To understand the importance of this rhetoric to the adaptation of the LDS Church, it's important to understand the stakes of abandoning a foundational practice in the evolution of a religion. Historian Jonathan Z. Smith has argued that the religious systems that emerged from the ancient Near East, commonly called the Judeo-Christian traditions, have as a foundational belief that "the meaning of life is rooted in an encompassing cosmic order in which man, society, and the gods all participate."[65] Within this cosmic order, "the chief responsibility of priests ... is to attune human order to the divine order." Humans, in turn, are responsible for "harmonizing with the great rhythms of cosmic order and destiny."

In times of crisis, Smith notes, practitioners of these faiths relied on the eternal principles, the only things in the cosmos that are "real, having been established by the gods."[66]

The Manifesto presented a problem of cosmic scale because it appeared as if the "priests" had performed their function in reverse, bringing the divine order into line with human order, and exacerbating the crisis by apparently erasing the eternal truth of plural marriage. This, in turn, would leave Mormons confused about the source of the "great rhythms of cosmic order" described by Jonathan Z. Smith. The church, primarily through the work of JFS, solved both problems. The rhetoric of masculinity as obedience and the idea of suspension of doctrine, both of which JFS pioneered, demonstrate his intuitive grasp of the complex interaction of religion and culture. To frame it within Jonathan Z. Smith's schema, we could say that JFS reordered the Mormon cosmos at a time of crisis by reclaiming the power of the priest and broadening it to include the possibility of divinely sanctioned suspension of laws as an alternate way of framing submission to a non-divine authority, and focusing the attention of rank-and-file Mormons on the priestly leaders rather than on their own senses to determine the "rhythms of cosmic order."

As a result, the prophetic leadership had never before in Mormon history been so strong, so immune to internal challenge, as it was in the years after the Manifesto, even during the presidency of Brigham Young. Obviously, JFS would not have been thinking in these terms, but it is equally clear that he was a gifted religious innovator, served well by his constant desire to create a coherent Mormonism out of the doctrinal pieces that lay scattered around the late nineteenth-century Mormon landscape. No one else in Mormon history has ever equaled JFS in his capacity to systematize faith.

14 | The Ever-Tightening Knot of Utah Politics

Plural marriage was not the only obstacle to statehood for Utah. For decades, the LDS Church had dominated the territorial legislature and city and county political offices through its own People's Party. Standing against the People's Party was the Liberal Party. Like everything else in Utah, political identities flowed from religious ones. Every election was another battle in the "Mormon/Gentile" war. The People's Party presented a problem primarily because it mingled church and state in a way that many non-Mormons found troubling. Church leaders chose the electoral slates for the People's Party, or offered themselves as candidates, and Mormons duly voted for them. The territorial legislature and local governments thus functioned as church assignments, but church leaders recognized that this would have to change if Utah were to become a state.

By the 1890s, the national political scene was dominated by the Republicans and Democrats, with the Republicans ascendant after 1896. The problem for church leaders was more practical than political. If they expected to be admitted to the Union, the Mormons would not only have to leave their People's Party behind, they would have to distance themselves from identity politics in general. It would not do if all Mormons in Utah flocked to only one of the major parties. When given the option, most Mormons in the early 1890s favored the Democratic Party, but in an ironic effort to appear less politically powerful, the church, in essence, divided members more or less evenly between the Democrats and the Republicans.

In the 1890s, Joseph F. Smith underwent a major shift in his attitude toward party politics, from abject abhorrence to indifference and, finally, to zealous partisanship. The underlying cause of this shift, of course, was religion, and it reflected the broader movement of Mormons from being a quasi-ethnic outsider group to a more integrated part of American culture. We have already had occasion to witness JFS's damning indictment of politicians springing from his experiences in Washington, DC, in 1887 and 1888. In October 1890, just after the Manifesto was published, JFS confided in Charles Nibley that politicians were soulless, cowardly, sickening men who had as their "prime purpose in life ... power, money, women, and wine." Neither Republicans nor Democrats, he argued, had any convictions beyond the desire to win elections. As for his own political leanings, JFS preferred "not to be too pronounced … as to political affiliations." But this was no mere abstention based on the morally repellant nature of politics; JFS believed affiliation should be kept quiet and secretly flexible so as to increase "the margin to trade upon" within the "narrow and more than less degrading" world of party politics.[1] In this, JFS was in line with Wilford Woodruff and most members of the Quorum of the Twelve.

In April 1890, Woodruff had called a meeting during which "the advisability of the Saints uniting with either the Republicans or Democrats in politics was considered." A discussion ensued, but Woodruff concluded that the church "should hold ourselves aloof from both parties." The message of the church toward political parties, the group decided, ought to be "we are now out of politics, but you gentlemen bring forth your best men, and we will vote for those who best suit us."[2] At that time JFS's prime interest, and that of the church, was to maintain viable connections with both parties as a means of negotiating. He still viewed the church as an entity that stood outside of the American political establishment, an entity generally unified politically against non-Mormons and only selectively supportive of the party most likely to help the church.

JFS Becomes a Republican

By 1895, JFS's views had completely changed. He had become one of the most prominent church leaders to strongly affiliate with a party and to take an active role in promoting it. As he did with everything in his life, when JFS decided he was a Republican, he did so with tremendous zeal. His evolution in political philosophy mirrored the larger shift of Mormonism from being an organization whose members could be assumed to share a general distaste for American politics and believe that American political interests typically militated against Mormon interests. By the end of the 1890s, Mormons had come to believe that so-called Mormon interests were more personally than communally determined. Attitudes, for example, toward income tax, labor unions, or even war were no longer drawn exclusively from the well of communal Mormon identity directed from the top down, but rather from personal application of what the individual believed to be the most salient principles of Mormonism. To the degree that either major party represented an individual's view of morality, that party took its place next to Mormonism as part of an individual's identity. Mormons were no longer a single political "we." They could now be Mormon Democrats or Mormon Republicans in a sense that would have previously been incoherent.

The ground had first begun to shift after an election in early 1891 in Ogden, a railroad town dominated by non-Mormons, with politically like-minded Mormons and gentiles split along party rather than religious lines. Calling themselves

246   Chapter 14

the Citizens Party, this mixed group challenged the Liberal Party and narrowly won most of the municipal races. Although it was a spontaneous event, Woodruff and some of the other leaders saw it as proof of the principle that Mormons could diversify politically without shaking their loyalty to the faith. Cannon, however, remained unsure. He argued that all inclinations toward political division should be ignored, but where "Saints are in the minority in any Stake, and outsiders invite them to unite with them as they did in Ogden, then the matter could be considered."[3] JFS, however, seized the momentum and suggested not only that the church officially authorize and encourage the Mormons in Ogden to divide along party lines, but that the *Ogden Standard* newspaper be designated a "Republican" paper to complement the Democratic-leaning *Salt Lake City Herald*.[4] This marked a significant change. For decades, newspapers in Utah had functioned, by and large, as Mormon or anti-Mormon propaganda machines. Making the newspapers political rather than religious in their advocacy was a significant bellwether of things to come.

In 1891, the Utah Commission highlighted the change in its annual report to the secretary of the interior with a tone of optimistic skepticism. "This departure from established methods," the commission reported, "was hailed by some as the end that had long been looked for, while others looked upon it as a ruse through which the leaders of the Mormon Church were seeking statehood, well knowing that their large majority would control the State thus formed." The commission did not say which side it came down on, but did suggest that any "step in the direction of educating people to think for themselves politically will tend to loosen the bonds in which they have in the past been held by the Church." The commission concluded, "It will do no harm to wait and see what this sudden conversion will bring about."[5]

Others were unwilling to adopt the wait-and-see attitude advocated by the commission. Many non-Mormons in Utah thought that the church would simply direct Mormons to vote in an ad hoc manner, even within the new political divisions; thus, the objection that the church violated the separation of church and state remained. In August 1891, Woodruff and Cannon answered a series of questions posed to them by the *Salt Lake Times*. The *Times* had struck a deal with church leaders in early 1891 to provide a friendly counterpoint to the *Tribune* in return for financial support from the church.[6] The *Times* was the perfect platform to use because it was not owned or edited by Mormons and so appeared neutral, but it was in fact partially subsidized by the church, ensuring friendly treatment. Woodruff and Cannon wanted to go on record to assure everyone in Utah that the church hierarchy would not attempt to influence elections. They asserted that "however much appearances may have indicated that we have favored the union of church and state ... there is no real disposition among the people of our church to unite church and state." The new "order of things," they contended, would not involve church direction of individual Mormon votes.[7]

Unfortunately, the newly restyled political arrangements led the First Presidency and the Quorum of the Twelve into a nasty public dispute. The roots of the conflict went back to 1888, when Apostle Moses Thatcher had urged church leaders to abandon the People's Party in favor of the Democratic Party. Thatcher was ahead of his time in his belief that Mormons and gentiles could be political allies in Utah. The church eventually followed Thatcher's proposal, but unfortunately for him, the most powerful church leaders favored the Republican Party. JFS had been objecting to the Democrats on religious grounds as early as 1886. In a letter to John Taylor and George Q. Cannon, he wrote that the Democratic Party had as its secret motto "Let Zion be Defiled!" "There is no longer any doubt," he elaborated, that the "present [Democratic] administration [is] guilty of the determination to destroy the Kingdom of God from the face of the earth."[8]

Although Thatcher's political vision was doomed from the start, he demonstrated remarkable courage and tenacity, for which he paid dearly. He was furious when Republicans swept into local office in Logan in an election in early 1892. The demographics suggested that most Mormons in Logan preferred to vote Democrat, so Thatcher was convinced that the First Presidency, all of whom leaned Republican, had influenced the vote by signaling church support for the Republicans. Woodruff and JFS met with Thatcher and other Democratic leaders and denied any wrongdoing. There is some evidence, however, that Cannon (who was in Washington, DC, at the time of that meeting) did, in fact, use his influence to sway the election—and JFS had been even more deeply involved.

In early February 1891, JFS had written to N. C. Edlefsen, a Republican political operative in Logan, regarding the number of registered voters on both sides. "You give the total registered at 867, Rep 344, Dem 250, Neutral 139," he wrote. "Now are the 139 really neutral? And can we depend on a fair share of that number when it comes to voting?" The real problem came in his instruction that "some good work ought to be done in a prudent way among" the neutral voters. Not only was Edlefsen a prominent Republican, he also served as a counselor in the Logan Temple presidency, further blurring the lines between his loyalty to JFS as a politician and as a leader of the church. JFS told Edlefsen that he could not come to Logan "just prior to the city election [because] it might be distorted into treason against the government by our ungracious, irrational opponents." "Besides," he continued, "Moses [Thatcher] is not there, and the howlers would arouse sympathy by the cry of 'foul play'" and "raise the cry of 'Church influence.'"[9] JFS thus correctly forecasted Thatcher's reaction. The outrage naturally cast some doubt over the sincerity of Woodruff and Cannon in their *Times* interview from 1891.

The response to the Logan election paled in comparison to the firestorm that erupted in May 1892 when Moses Thatcher addressed the Territorial Democratic Convention. In a speech that he later claimed had been incorrectly represented, Thatcher purportedly said that "Lucifer and those who rebelled with him were acting upon a Republican theory of government."[10] When John Henry Smith brought the matter up with the First Presidency, Woodruff concluded that Thatcher had "exceeded the bounds of propriety, as an Apostle, in using arguments to [that]

248   Chapter 14

effect," and he believed a public response was called for.[11] With the help of Frank Cannon, JFS and John Henry Smith prepared a response to Thatcher's remarks. B. H. Roberts, a Democrat and a general authority, thought the published response was "cruel and unjust in the extreme." After he and Thatcher teamed up to speak at Democratic events around Utah, JFS gave a sermon in which he claimed that certain general authorities were going rogue. He later asserted that he was not referring to Thatcher and Roberts, but that is not how most people watching the drama saw it.

In the fall of 1892, members of the Quorum of the Twelve began warning Roberts that JFS was displeased with "the course [he] was taking in politics," especially in some of the political editorials he had written. Eventually, Roberts and Thatcher found themselves face to face with JFS and some members of the Twelve who made it clear that political activity on any significant scale needed to be directed through the First Presidency. Roberts was not particularly happy about the situation but acquiesced. Thatcher did not. Although the initial scuffle with Thatcher quickly blew over, it was only the opening salvo in a war that would eventually end with his dismissal from the quorum.

Both JFS and John Henry Smith continued to act in defiance of the assurances given by Cannon and Woodruff in the *Times* interview. John Henry was an unapologetic campaigner for the Republican Party. In a meeting in July 1891, he explained that he felt called by God to campaign for Republicans. He feared that the division into parties would end with a Mormon rush to the Democrats, thus defeating the purpose of the division. JFS also spoke up in favor of Republican activism. "I do not know a single Democrat who is helping us," he said, though he knew many Republicans who were doing so. Moreover, he applauded John Henry for proving for all to see that "a man could be a Republican and still be a Saint. I wish more of the apostles belonged to this party and would sign the roll."[12]

Cannon confided in his diary that he was relieved that JFS "spoke at length and with considerable force upon the political situation" because he was afraid other church leaders might have assumed that only Cannon, among the First Presidency, held such views.[13] Among church leaders and prominent leaders in the former People's Party, Democrats abounded. Franklin S. Richards, Heber J. Grant, Franklin D. Richards, B. H. Roberts, Charles Penrose, and John Winder had all declared allegiance to the Democrats.[14] The few Republicans, however, were well placed and not above using their church offices for political recruitment.

In January 1892, JFS toured the settlements in northern Utah and southern Idaho. At a meeting in Franklin, Idaho, he delivered a fifty-minute sermon without a whiff of political content. Following the general meeting, JFS instructed bishops from the area to see that their congregations were divided along party lines, but then he promoted the Republican agenda. He told them, "As soon as the Republican party is sure that there is strong representation of Mormons who are Republicans they will restore to us our rights" to vote. He closed by expressing his "hope that a goodly number of the people would become Republicans."[15] It would have taken an obtuse observer, indeed, to see that behavior as politically neutral.

JFS did, at times, try to maintain the façade of keeping his church and his political roles separate. For example, he wrote to John C. Graham, publisher of Provo's Republican newspaper, the *Daily Inquirer*, requesting that the editor avoid applying "the words 'President,' and 'Apostle,' and 'Bishop,' to such of us as may be favored with those titles, when you speak of us in your Paper on political matters. Substitute 'Hon.' Or 'Judge' or some such title instead."[16] Of course this would make no difference. Who in the territory did not know that John Henry Smith and JFS were apostles? But JFS felt that it was an important technicality.

Sometimes JFS simply could not help himself and veered into open political stumping in ecclesiastical settings. At a stake conference in Logan, he set up his political speech by telling his audience, "I am not a politician." It was true, he said, that church leaders had apparently made a change when they instructed church members to choose between the Democrats or the Republicans. Previously, he said, when members had been instructed to vote as a bloc, it was simply a matter of "self-protection." Now the world had changed, and "our only self-preservation and safety" was to divide. The motives for bloc voting and division were the same: preservation of the church. JFS assured the audience that they were free to choose between the Democrats and the Republicans, but that the Mormons should "be about equally divided" between the two parties. Some brave soul in the congregation then shouted, "Yes, because you're a Republican!"[17]

Everyone knew that most Mormons, left to their own devices, would naturally gravitate toward the Democrats. It was, after all, the Republicans who had called polygamy the twin of slavery and a "relic of barbarism," and Republicans who had administered anti-polygamy legislation. But JFS wanted Utah to become a state, and he was betting that the Republicans would be better for the Mormons. Convincing them would not be so easy. For JFS to say that he hoped for equal division meant that he wanted many more Mormon Republicans than would likely appear naturally. "There has been an impression entertained by some Latter-day Saints that it was necessary to be a Democrat to be a good Latter-day Saint," he said, adding, "I do not think so at all." To the heckler, JFS admitted, "I am a Republican." Then he said something that provides an important insight into why he leaned that way: "I came through a Republican line of ancestors. I cannot help it. I do not know that I am particularly responsible." In Nauvoo, he said, "Joseph the Prophet voted for Mr. Harrison, a Whig in those days ... [a party that] subsequently [became] Republican." The ties of the Smith family to the Whigs had clearly left a deep impression on JFS. In fact, he pressed, "if we should all combine to vote for a Republican president, we would not be very far wrong."[18]

JFS also believed, based on the Republican treatment of the South after the Civil War, that Republicans could be trusted to grant amnesty for polygamists and give them aid in integrating Utah into the Union. What JFS wanted his audience to know, he concluded, is that one could be a good Mormon and good Republican or a good Democrat. In private, however, he held a different view. He blamed Democrats for "slavery, disintegration [of the Union], rebellion, violence, mobocracy and misrule," and he opined that the Democratic Party was "founded on a theory opposed to Divine rule and has never risen even to the standard of intelligent human wisdom, much less that of inspiration."[19]

It wasn't long before JFS came to view any sign of affinity with the Democrats as traitorous. In October 1895, after Bathsheba Smith was quoted in the *Deseret News* saying vaguely complimentary things about the state Democratic convention, JFS fired off an inquisitorial and paranoid missive demanding to know if "the statement expressed is your own, freely and voluntarily expressed," and requesting her response "in writing over your own signature so what you say cannot be distorted nor misunderstood."[20]

In 1891, only four months before his speech in Logan, he had written to a friend that although "a good Latter-day Saint may be a good Republican, a good Latter-day Saint must of necessity be a poor Democrat." Not satisfied with the severity of that observation, JFS went further, concluding that "a good Dem cannot be a thoroughly good Mormon. It would be contrary to his principles. Good Republicans have the courage of their convictions. A Dem? Never!"[21] But however reckless JFS may have been in his political machinations, he at least knew better than to broadcast his real feelings to a room full of Mormon Democrats.

The key to statehood, JFS believed, was to convince the Republicans in Washington that Utah could be counted on to emerge as a Republican state. The GOP was gun-shy after the admission of Colorado, which, as a territory, had appeared to be Republican but turned out to be a Democratic state. "The Republicans," JFS wrote, "supposing we are Democratic, object to our admission." But he believed that if the Republicans could be convinced, via Republican victories in city and county elections, that "Utah had a chance to become Republican, they would not hesitate a moment" to support admission.[22]

If JFS could help the Republicans win in Utah, he had no scruples about doing so. In 1892, he personally wrote to stake presidents and other local LDS leaders "from Idaho to St. George" to raise money for the *Ogden Standard*. JFS pitched the newspaper as "one of the strongest friends of Utah, to her people and her interests." Mormons would obviously assume that to mean that the paper was pro-Mormon. "It is important," he wrote, "to see your name among its stockholders."[23] The *Standard* was a staunchly Republican newspaper, which was the reason for JFS's interest in it, but he clearly applied ecclesiastical pressure to raise money for it.

JFS always tried to paint his partisanship as concern for the general condition of the state. "This is not partisan," he insisted, but rather about "the welfare of Utah."[24] All he wanted, he wrote to a Republican operative in Provo, was "freedom, peace and union for our beloved Utah." Although it had been "strongly impregnated with Democratic leaven, for these many years," the result had been nothing but persecution. "Utah has been trodden under foot, and disowned and discarded by both of the great political parties," he observed, "but now, when the leaven of true Republicanism is beginning to work, light breaks through the mist of darkness heretofore impenetrable and final release from political bondage looms up under the strong protective aegis of the G.O.P."[25]

By 1892, prominent church leaders and members were openly taking sides and trying to conduct a relatively civil debate. Charles Penrose, editor of the *Deseret News* and one of JFS's future counselors in the First Presidency, published a pamphlet, "Plain Talk," in which he argued that the Democratic Party represented the best fit for Mormons. Not willing to let this go uncontested, JFS published his own pamphlet, a sixteen-page refutation of Penrose titled "Another Plain Talk."[26] This pamphlet, although somewhat rambling, provides the clearest window into why JFS felt so strongly attached to the Republicans. He argued, as he had before, that in the early years of the church, the Whigs had always been friendlier to the Mormons than the Democrats. Furthermore, it was the Whigs who created Utah Territory, whereas Democrat James Buchanan had tried to use the U.S. Army to destroy it. JFS also took a personal jab at Penrose, suggesting that he might have better understood that particular situation if he had been in Utah in 1858, sharing "the hardships and privations of those days," rather than in the safer environs of Great Britain. Setting that aside, JFS argued, it was the Democrats who had repeatedly blocked Utah's admission to the Union, viewing Utah as a "fly in the Democratic ointment."

JFS's attempt to portray the Republicans as loyal and courageous and the Democrats as untrustworthy cowards was, however, somewhat tortuous. The Republicans had always been upfront about their feelings toward polygamy and never pretended to be friends of Utah while it was being openly practiced. The Democrats, JFS said, should have been friendlier to Utah because so many Mormons leaned that way, but they only pretended to be less hostile than the Republicans and repeatedly stabbed Utah in the back. JFS argued that if the Republicans had thought of the Mormons in Utah as their friends, they never would have treated them the way the Democrats had: "Whatever faults the Republican party might have, cowardice is not one of them. It stands by its friends." He portrayed the Democrats, by contrast, as a study in "insincerity and hollowness." The G.O.P., although once hostile, "has changed its attitude toward Utah. It seeks out friendship." JFS viewed the Republicans as the party of courage and loyalty, and for him there were no higher virtues. As to the party's economic policies, Penrose objected to the protectionist tariff favored by the Republicans, but JFS countered by pointing out that the great push for "home manufacture" in Utah was nothing more nor less than protectionism designed to insulate the Mormon economy from that of the gentile world—one more piece of evidence, in JFS's mind, that Mormons had always been crypto-Republicans, at least philosophically.

According to Anthon Lund, political tensions eventually escalated to the point that JFS and Thatcher could barely attend meetings together.[27] Lund wrote in his

252   Chapter 14

journal that in the spring of 1893, Woodruff, Cannon, and JFS told the apostles that Thatcher's "opposition to the First Presidency" in political matters was exerting a "hurtful influence ... upon the people," and they had also singled out B. H. Roberts and Charles Penrose, both Democrats, for using "their priesthood position to influence the people." According to Lund, Thatcher again apologized and promised to conform to the new rules of political discourse. JFS instructed the other members of the Twelve that all three men should "be labored with and made to see the error of their ways."[28]

As the dedication of the Salt Lake Temple drew near, JFS and the other members of the First Presidency took advantage of the political divisions to keep the Quorum of the Twelve from increasing its ecclesiastical power. On 22 March 1893, Woodruff, Cannon, and JFS attended a meeting of the Twelve at which they "desired to know from all present whether or not they considered they had a right to dictate to us the policy we should pursue in politics, as well as in all other things, temporal or spiritual."[29] Not surprisingly, all of the apostles, including Thatcher, agreed that the First Presidency had the right to dictate to everyone, including the apostles, in any and all matters. According to Lund, JFS felt sufficiently satisfied with Thatcher's reply that he visited him that night, laying his hands on Thatcher's head to bless him even as he vomited blood.[30]

Finishing the Salt Lake Temple

The deep divisions among the Quorum of the Twelve and between them and the First Presidency on a wide range of theological, political, and economic issues threatened to cast a pall over the most important religious event of the 1890s: the completion and dedication of the Salt Lake Temple. For forty years, the walls had been slowly emerging from the foundation until the temple was ready for the placement of its capstone.

On 6 April 1892, a bright spring day, tens of thousands of Mormons converged on Temple Square to witness the capstone ceremony. Several days earlier, to make room for the crowds, Cannon had ordered that several buildings south of the temple be razed and replaced with a viewing platform.[31] It took a full forty-five minutes for the various priesthood quorums to assemble at the square.

JFS opened the ceremonies with a prayer, and Woodruff lowered the capstone, which contained a list of past and present church leaders, scriptures, and pictures of previous church presidents and the current members of the First Presidency. Unable to mount the scaffolding, Woodruff lowered the capstone using an electrical switch. Lorenzo Snow had earlier led the crowd of 40,000 in the sacred Hosanna shout. The entire crowd then offered a stirring rendition of "The Spirit of God Like a Fire Is Burning," a hymn written for and sung at the dedication of the Kirtland

Temple.[32] Despite the contention among church leaders, all of them shared the deep emotions that accompanied that moment.

The temple, however, was only completed on the outside. Inside, there were no furnishings, no decorative woodwork, no lathing, nearly nothing at all. Woodruff challenged the Mormons to finish the temple in time to dedicate it on 6 April 1893, the fortieth anniversary of Brigham Young's dedication of the cornerstone. Although Woodruff's announcement appeared spontaneous, the idea to complete the temple by 1893 had been discussed at a general priesthood meeting in early October 1891. At that time, a decision was made to begin collecting donations from church members. The First Presidency estimated that it would cost no less than $100,000 to complete the temple.[33]

This appeal for money was nothing new; between 1853 and 1887, just over $2 million, or about $75,000 per year, had been collected from church members for construction costs. But money for finishing the interior had to be collected quickly and systematically.[34] The First Presidency assigned fundraising quotas to each stake. "The allotments to the stakes have been placed as low as possible," they wrote to a stake president in Heber City, "and it is absolutely necessary that each stake make up its full amount." The First Presidency expected at least half of the assigned amount by 15 December 1892 and the balance by 1 March 1893.[35] The goals were met and exceeded.

As money came in from the stakes, Woodruff appointed JFS to head a committee along with Lorenzo Snow and Abraham H. Cannon to oversee completion of the temple prior to dedication. JFS captured the urgency of the work when he described the purpose of the committee as "the pushing of the work on the Temple."[36] Members of the committee visited the workers at the temple in mid-April 1892, informing them of the need to rush the work, "requesting all to use their best endeavors to crowd the work ahead, and to refrain from evil conversation, discussion of politics, etc., as well as to cease the use of intoxicants, while at work on this sacred edifice." The committee members also visited the stakes, encouraging them to set aside a "temple day" on which "each man, woman and child [would] devote the income which he or she receives or a sum equal to his or her earnings [for that day] for the work of completing the Salt Lake Temple," and they regularly spoke to congregations encouraging them to generously support the temple fund "that it may be speedily completed."[37]

For nearly a year, JFS visited the temple three or more times a week, checking on the progress and providing motivation and guidance. In January 1893, George Q. Cannon felt nervous enough about the pace of work that he summoned "the contractors and foremen of the various departments in the temple" to a meeting of the First Presidency, "impressing upon them the seriousness of the responsibility that rested upon us as the First Presidency, in view of the pledge that had been given that the Temple should be completed for dedication on the 6th of April."[38] Cannon

254 Chapter 14

thought the meeting went well and felt confident in the progress. JFS was far less sanguine.

One problem that arose involved the men who had been sent to Paris at church expense to train as painters so that they could paint murals for some of the temple's rooms. When they met with JFS in January, they demanded $17,000 (nearly $500,000 in today's money) for the work. According to Lund, JFS, nonplussed, called the amount "unreasonable and outrageous." The artists protested that their bid was only one-third the going rate, but JFS felt that given the funding they had received from the church for their artistic education, the discount was not nearly deep enough. He told the artists to think about the issue and return with a better offer.[39]

Not until the font was installed in mid-February 1893 did JFS finally feel comfortable telling Woodruff that the temple would be ready for dedication in April. It would come down to the wire, but the dedication would go forward on 6 April. In a letter to Mary Gatewood, JFS wrote that even though his committee work on the temple had "kept me so busy I have had no time," he had found that completion of the temple was bringing out the best in almost everyone. "I never saw a better spirit manifested by our people generally than is visible on every hand respecting this Temple," he wrote. "Everybody seems not only willing, but anxious to do all they can to forward the work," a fact made more remarkable by the help coming from "some half-Mormons and occasionally an outsider."[40] One non-Mormon man from Montana gave the church $100 toward the temple after he had a dream about it, an event that JFS felt demonstrated the degree to which "the Lord has softened the hearts of the gentiles," who just "three years ago [sought] to take possession of our temples and turn them into a U.S. barracks."[41]

Many members of the church, having either experienced or heard of the amazing supernatural phenomena reported during the dedication of the Kirtland Temple in 1836, began to wonder if similar events might occur at the dedication of the Salt Lake Temple. JFS fielded this question many times in the months leading up to the event. In a sermon in March 1893, he tried to manage expectations by explaining that he would be more than satisfied, and in fact expected, to "hear the whisperings of the still, small, voice that the Lord is there by His Spirit." As to the expectation some people held that angels, or even Christ, might appear, JFS said that he did not consider himself worthy to "witness such an event." However, he continued, if any in the audience arrive at the temple "with greater faith than mine, with greater perfection, with greater purity of heart, with greater power ... and can see the Father and the Son sitting on the throne ... God be praised," but, he continued, "I am about as well prepared as the rest of you."[42] JFS clearly sought to prepare the saints to experience subtler events than those reported in 1836.

Despite his cautious attitude toward potential spiritual experiences, the dedication of the temple represented one of the spiritual high points of JFS's life, and 6 April remains a day of great significance for Latter-day Saints. It is the day upon which the church was formally organized in 1830, and, according to LDS teaching, it is the exact date of Jesus Christ's birth. In 1893, that day was cold, raw, and stormy, but the weather, interpreted by some as evidence that Satan wanted to use nature to stop the dedication, did not dampen the Mormons' wild enthusiasm.

The dedication services consisted of thirty-one separate sessions held between 6 and 24 April 1893. At each session, the dedicatory prayer was read and sermons delivered. At the first session, JFS took the stand "weeping like a child" and, in a rare public display of emotion, said, "Brethren and sisters, how can I help shedding tears in this Holy place, for we are in the presence of God."[43] Gone was the anxiety he had expressed in a sermon the month before about the Mormons having taken too long to build the temple: "I believe that the energy and push that has been exerted this last year, if it had been distributed over two or three years about thirty years ago, would in that time have completed the building, and we would have had it all these past years to use." In his opinion, the work of building the temple had been "neglected" for decades, and it remained an open question "whether the Lord will blame us for being so long about this work."[44] But what mattered most, JFS said at the dedication, was that the temple had finally been finished. This held great symbolic weight for him. Despite decades of "persecution," isolation, governmental attack, hard summers and harder winters, the temple rose. To JFS, it was almost as if the hardships had fertilized the soil from which grew the mighty granite "mountain of the Lord."[45]

JFS had always taken temple work extremely seriously. When work needed to be done for deceased relatives, or when individuals petitioned JFS to be sealed or adopted into Hyrum Smith's family, he usually saw to the matter personally. For example, in May 1891, traveling at night to avoid arrest, JFS had arrived at the Logan Temple at midnight and remained there for three days "in the interests of some aged and infirm persons who wanted some work done which made my presence necessary."[46] Such trips were not unusual for JFS, despite the weight of First Presidency business, so the completion of the Salt Lake Temple was important for him practically as well as symbolically.

Woodruff and Cannon were generally pleased with the Salt Lake Temple dedication, but they expressed shock at the character of some of the people who attended. JFS must have felt some sense of satisfaction given Woodruff's decision to oppose his recommendation that only temple-worthy members be admitted. The First Presidency blamed local authorities, accusing them of insufficient scrutiny. "There were numbers who gained admission to these services whose lives had, for many years, been inconsistent with their calling as Saints," they wrote to bishops in the region. They admitted that these people met the requirements laid out for admission in that they were members of the church and "fellowship had not been withdrawn from them," but they returned the lists of names to the local wards, tersely informing the bishops that "it now becomes the duty of the local authorities . . . to see that all such assume the responsibility of their profession" as members

256   Chapter 14

of the church. The letter strongly suggested that a good many of these people be given "no further opportunity ... to repeat the course they took to gain admission to the Temple services."[47] JFS included Moses Thatcher in this group, telling a high council in Logan that Thatcher "was admitted to the dedication of the Temple by the skin of his teeth"—and certainly against JFS's wishes.[48]

On this issue, as on many others, JFS again found himself alone among the First Presidency. Cannon and Woodruff had a tight bond, just as Cannon had enjoyed with Taylor, but JFS remained something of an outsider. Woodruff leaned heavily on Cannon, especially as his health declined. Just two days before the first dedicatory session, Cannon had to remind Woodruff that someone would have to be assigned to preside over the temple. Woodruff drew a blank when asked for his pick, stating only that it should be one of the apostles. Cannon suggested Lorenzo Snow, president of the Quorum of the Twelve. Cannon recorded in his journal that "President Woodruff was much pleased with the suggestion and thanked the Lord for it. He said he relied a great deal on me in these things, that I had a great many revelations and was his counselor, and he wished me to freely make suggestions."[49]

In the fall of 1893, while JFS was in Chicago, he lost his beloved aunt Mercy Thompson, whose death he had been dreading since the 1870s. On 20 September he attended her funeral. In a letter to John Henry Smith a week later, he described her "as a true-born Latter-day Saint."[50] Mercy had lived an exceptionally long life, eighty-six years and three months, and this seemed to soften the blow a bit for JFS. Because she was the last living connection he had to his mother, Mercy had always functioned in his mind as something of a sacred symbol. By 1893, however, JFS was in a far more stable position to deal with the loss of another mooring to the past. Part of that stemmed from the pleasure he took in his adult children. They were marrying in the faith and serving missions. The fears that he had harbored about their dedication to the church slowly faded as he witnessed their willingness to maintain their childhood faith in Mormon principles as they grew into adulthood.

The Political Manifesto

By 1893, the Manifesto and the division of Mormons between the Republican and Democratic Parties had begun to yield political gains. That year a joint resolution of Congress returned the church's property (a process completed in the summer of 1896 when the church reclaimed title to all properties that had been in receivership). In the fall of 1893, Utah's delegate to Congress, Democrat Joseph Rawlins, submitted a bill for Utah statehood. Signed by President Cleveland on 16 July 1894, the statehood bill authorized Utah to draft a constitution that had to "guarantee religious freedom, prohibit plural marriage, and to renounce any claim to federal and Indian lands within its borders."[51]

The Ever-Tightening Knot of Utah Politics   257

In the fall of 1895, the first elections to federal office were held in Utah. JFS's work had paid off, and Republicans were elected to most of the major offices. Utah, at long last, was a state. However, there was still one political matter that plagued church leaders. The Quorum of the Twelve was continuing to have difficulty with Apostle Moses Thatcher, who had been afflicted with severe digestive ailments since at least 1890 and had apparently become addicted to the opiates given to him for pain management. He rarely attended meetings of the quorum, but openly disagreed with decisions they made.

Matters came to a head in the spring of 1896. The First Presidency decided to pull back on overt political involvement and produced a document, known as the political manifesto, decreeing that no high church officer could run for political office without permission from the First Presidency. JFS was surprised when the document met with some resistance. After press reports suggested that the purpose of the political manifesto was to limit church members' political freedoms, JFS traveled to Cache Valley, home of Moses Thatcher, one of the most prominent opponents of the document, and delivered an indignant sermon. Any intimation that the document took away liberty, he said, must be coming from those who "have not confidence in the Church," especially those who lacked faith in "the authorities of the church."[52]

JFS often employed this rhetorical technique of casting dissent over a single principle as complete opposition to the church. This had the intended effect of inducing faithful Mormons to stifle their disagreement lest they be viewed as complete apostates. JFS then made what can be charitably viewed as an argument based on a sliver of a technicality. The church, JFS declared, had never "sought to dominate the state." He said, "I deny that the church and state have been married in Utah," and he angrily argued that "the church and state have never been married in Utah. They need no divorcement. They have never been married!" To any observer of life in nineteenth-century Utah, such claims must have sounded absurd and probably vaguely insulting. JFS based this dubious argument on the fact that no law had ever been passed in Utah "uniting the church and the state.""There is no man ... in the world," he continued, "that will place a finger upon a law that has been passed by the church that is calculated to dominate the state."[53]

On one level, of course, this is true: there was no law of the kind that one would have found in seventeenth-century Massachusetts, for example, that formally united church and state. However, the very structure of JFS's language betrays the reality he attempted to deny. He said "the church" had not passed laws. How could it? What he meant was that the Mormon legislators could have passed such a law, but they chose not to. Why would they choose not to? Because they did not need to. For most of the nineteenth-century, Mormon leaders chose the slates of candidates for city, county, and territorial legislatures, and church members voted accordingly. They chose the slates because they wanted to control the policies. Most of those elected to political office were also the ecclesiastical leaders of the communities.

258   Chapter 14

JFS's anger at the reaction to the political manifesto was misplaced, and it led him to engage in a shocking act of obfuscation. There is no question that JFS was the member of the hierarchy most interested in using the political manifesto to consolidate the power of the First Presidency. He announced publicly in April 1896 that the document "applies not only to those who signed their names to it, but to every officer and member of the Church."[54] JFS intended to include under the umbrella of those requiring First Presidency permission to run for office not only church leaders, but all church members.

JFS immediately faced harsh criticism from Mormons and non-Mormons alike. The *Salt Lake Tribune* called his address "astounding" and "un-American."[55] John Henry Smith felt that JFS went too far and could "cause trouble for our people everywhere."[56] JFS found the reaction risible. "I spoke at the Provo conference a week ago," he wrote to his son Hyrum, "and it proved a veritable long-pole which served to stir up the parrot and monkey show."[57] To his wife Mary, he complained that "it is getting dangerous now for me to speak in public, as every word is watched and if possible warped into meaning sedition." He ultimately faulted "his Satanic Majesty" for the uproar, concluding that "the devil must be dreadfully mad about it."[58]

JFS's overriding interest in creating and maintaining doctrinal and hierarchical order within the church was rooted deep in his own experience. In his mind, dissent and disorder had led directly to his father's death, and the chaotic aftermath had splintered the church and put him at bitter odds with his own cousins. Doctrinal disorder had contributed to sharp schisms among leaders during JFS's early years in the hierarchy. Most recently, lack of coherence and order had led to the fighting that nearly destroyed Cannon in the aftermath of Taylor's death. As John W. Taylor and Matthias Cowley would learn by bitter experience, JFS held the principle of "obedience to order" inviolable. The refusal to recognize and defer to an ordered hierarchy brought about what JFS called the "curse of disobedience," which always resulted in the "downfall and disintegration of the people."[59]

Against this backdrop, it is easier to understand JFS's strident application of the political manifesto and his reaction to Thatcher's open dissent.[60] The document was to be read and voted on at the general conference on 6 April 1896. Thatcher was in Salt Lake but unable to attend the various meetings because of his ill health, so Woodruff dispatched Lorenzo Snow and Brigham Young Jr. to his house to ask him to sign the document. Cannon assumed, perhaps naively, "that Brother Thatcher, seeing the names of his fellow servants, would sign it without any question."[61] But Thatcher was not swayed by peer pressure. After some consideration, he refused to sign, and presented Young and Snow with a letter explaining his reasoning. That afternoon, Woodruff did not permit Thatcher's name to be presented for a sustaining vote along with the other members of the quorum. JFS felt the action was taken "none too soon." The crux of the matter was in the need for a renewed emphasis on "the proper regard for, and recognition of, the rights of

The Ever-Tightening Knot of Utah Politics   259

Presidency by high officials."[62] JFS argued that even though public opinion seemed to be against the move, "we could not do otherwise. We were united [and] he alone stood against us! That was enough."[63]

Woodruff and JFS felt particularly insulted by Thatcher's attitude, and on 19 November 1896, the Quorum of the Twelve unanimously voted to drop the still recalcitrant Thatcher, announcing the decision to the church at large at the next general conference.[64] JFS lost no sleep over the action. "He has not been in fellowship nor sympathy with the Twelve since the death of John Taylor," he observed, adding that he had always felt that Thatcher "has been a greatly overestimated man."[65] He had no qualms about setting things right by endorsing the decision to rid the leading councils of the church of a problematic, individualistic Democrat.

15 | Politics, Economics, and Polygamy Collide

Joseph F. Smith's life in the 1890s was probably more stressful than his life underground had been. Economic challenges compounded the political and religious stresses that accompanied the bid for statehood. In 1893 the United States entered one of the worst periods of economic depression in its history. That April, U.S. gold reserves dipped below $100 million. A weakening dollar panicked investors at home and overseas, crop prices were in freefall, and local banks collapsed. A quarter of all railroad capitalization was wiped out through bankruptcies.[1] Utah's economy was crushed, and, with it, the church's financial stability.

JFS informed Charles Nibley that it was the worst financial situation the church had faced "since 1857 and that time our fears of Johnstons Army and the hard times were only as flea bites in comparison to our fears of financial . . . hard times now."[2] Wilford Woodruff sent George Q. Cannon to England to try to borrow money. Woodruff then fell ill again, so the entire weight of the economic disaster fell squarely on JFS in the summer of 1893. JFS sent Cannon an urgent telegram in June saying that "times are desperate here, and growing worse, we must have help soon."[3] Heber J. Grant was supposed to have gone with Cannon to England, but he decided to go only as far as New York, where he used his business contacts to try to secure loans for the church. Although he did eventually secure loans, at an extremely high interest rate, the task proved difficult.

Tithing had also stopped coming in. It shocked JFS to learn that by July 1893, "the tithing offices of all stakes" had been totally depleted. The church could not pay its bills, which meant JFS did not get paid. Even the Tiffany stained-glass windows in the new temple had not been paid off yet. JFS drafted a circular and sent it out to stake presidents ordering them to sell off "cheap for cash" any livestock, produce, or real estate they had "and send the same to us at once."[4]

Soon the crisis began to impact the missionary force. Throughout the Utah period, it was not uncommon for men called on missions to request extra time to put their affairs in order, or ask to be excused from missionary service because of personal, financial, or family issues. But by the fall of 1894, JFS, who served on the church's missionary committee, noticed that, more often than not, potential missionaries could not respond to calls issued by the church because of their financial situation. JFS even began preaching "the Word of Wisdom" on economic grounds. "If the members of this church were to abstain one year from the use of tobacco, intoxicating drinks, and tea and coffee," he told one congregation, "there would remain in this country enough money to pay every debt owed by the people [because] the money expended for these goods is not kept in this territory."[5]

JFS's personal finances were also in shambles. In 1892, Mary had moved to Franklin, in southern Idaho, where she set up a house and lived with her children along with other "exiled" plural wives. He sent her as much money as he could, but warned her that help might be hard to come by in the future. He had to cut Edna's and Alice's monthly "allowances" in half, and Julina and Sarah had to make do with "much less than that," so JFS's wives had to turn to the tithing storehouse for meat and other foodstuffs. To ensure that his family did not incur any debt, JFS wrote to the management at ZCMI instructing them that if any of his wives' accounts showed a balance at the end of the month, then "their credit must be stopped." As he explained to Mary, his situation was grave: "my taxes are more than ever this year and dividends have stopped, and every man is called on to help the church by paying up their tithes and offerings and where possible to loan money to it."[6]

JFS always keenly desired connection with family members no matter how distant, geographically or emotionally, they were. "Somehow," he wrote to his cousin Ina, "I have a warm place in my feelings for my kindred, no matter how they feel for me."[7] However, JFS lacked sufficient emotional literacy to express his feelings without a compelling reason. Given such a reason, he could be remarkably empathetic, even toward his estranged ex-wife, Levira, or his most fierce filial rivals, the sons of Joseph Smith Jr.

In December 1891, JFS learned from his cousin Mary that Levira had died some three years earlier in St. Louis. Despite the ugliness of the later years of their marriage, their bond as Smith cousins remained, if only in JFS's mind. Even two years after hearing news of her death, he continued to seek answers. In 1893, he fired off a staccato list of questions to Mary about her: "I would like to know how L. came to go to St. Louis, with whom stayed while there, what were her means of living, and her course of life, when and where she died and of what cause."[8]

Similarly, in 1896, after JFS read in the *Saints Herald* that Joseph Smith III's wife Bertha had died in a tragic accident, he immediately set aside the strident feelings for his cousin that he had carried for decades and wrote a short letter of condolence. "Altho' far removed from each other by almost every interest and hope in life; and unalterably fixed in our opposite views on many points," JFS wrote, "you and your children deserve, and have, my heart-felt sympathy." He told his cousin that he knew from experience that only "the silent and gentle mercies of time and truth" would see him through his "sad hours of bereavement."[9] After a visit from Alexander Smith in 1893, JFS concluded, as he had after his altercations

262   Chapter 15

with his uncle James Fielding thirty years earlier, that "when kinsfolk cannot agree on religion, or anything else, the wisest thing to do is to agree to disagree, and stop fighting and provoking each other."[10]

The State of JFS's Family as the Century Turned

JFS's family continued to grow in numbers, and the children also grew in maturity. JFS did not always find this an easy thing to accept. In 1891 his sons Hyrum, Joseph Richards, and Alvin were working at ZCMI; Joseph Fielding was working for the bank; and his daughter Donnette graduated from the teaching program at LDS College. While JFS admired his sons' work ethic, he would have preferred that they attend school.[11] Against his will and deepest wishes, he had observed his children from a distance for most of the 1880s and early 1890s. Surreptitious nighttime visits, letters, and church functions were JFS's only interactions with his children during this period. Although the depth of his love cannot be questioned, the degree of his emotional intimacy with some of the children was undoubtedly weak. By the end of 1891, JFS had twenty-seven living children ranging in age from four months to thirty-three years. In February 1897, he became a grandfather for the first time, meaning that he had children who were younger than his grandchildren.[12]

The timing of JFS's life was such that the most labor-intensive parts of parenthood coincided with the most demanding and disruptive period of his career in church leadership. Julina's oldest son, Joseph F. Smith Jr., frankly observed that "during the years when a boy needs the counsel of his father the most, I had no father."[13] Absent he may have been, but he paid close attention to the welfare of his children nonetheless. In 1896, when his son Hyrum was on a mission in northern England, JFS penned a letter to him that revealed his encyclopedic memory of the various injuries the children had suffered over the years. "I recall your broken arm," he wrote, as well as "Buddy's broken foot, Joseph's broken leg, Willard's and Ina's broken arms, Willard's injured back, etc."[14] His anxiety about the children's health and his soul-deep fear of their deaths led him to keep close tabs, even from a distance. As his sons began to leave on missions, JFS changed his attitude about missionaries and money. He had repeatedly expressed displeasure with parents who sent money to missionaries in the field, believing that they should be able to get by without the extra help. He was not so parsimonious when it came to his own missionary sons.

In the years preceding the admission of Utah into the Union, JFS had to face changes not only in the facts of his life, but also in the symbolic arrangement of his world. Until the mid-1890s, he maintained a worldview framed by his belief in an imminent apocalypse, the utter corruption of the world, the importance of building a physical kingdom where the people of God could gather, and Mormons, at least white Mormons living in the American West, as a monolithic "us" standing against a "them" defined by their desire to see God's work destroyed. There had always been a gap between this worldview and reality as JFS experienced it, but the gap was widening at an alarming pace in the 1890s, and he would need to restructure some of the fundamental beliefs undergirding his worldview.

At first glance, this appears to be a typical case of cultural transformation via cultural intercourse. Even though the Mormons had for decades attempted to live separately from "the world," they needed things that the dreaded world produced. To "gather the elect from the four quarters of the earth," they had to use gentile ships. To proclaim their gospel in print, they employed the presses of the wicked. To communicate, they relied on postal services and telegraph lines outside of their control. The Mormons in Utah had always been connected with the world by a thousand tendrils. Although pioneer-era Mormons certainly believed that they had removed themselves from the world, they retained the bedrock values of that world. If we consider, for example, those traits that JFS considered virtuous, we see clear antecedents in the broader American culture. Belief in the righteousness of hard work, manliness, and physical courage; the necessity of creating a civilization in the wilderness; the superiority of people; the need for political parties; the importance of capitalism (with its obsession with industriousness and accumulation of personal wealth); the rhetorical power of religious intolerance; the importance of using political power to moral ends—all of these were convictions shared by the majority of Americans in the nineteenth century. Except for the practice of polygamy—a vivid marker of difference and alienation—much of what made Mormons "peculiar" was a matter of rhetorical emphasis. JFS and others loved to speak about how different they were from the gentiles, but the fact that the decline of polygamy from 1890 to about 1910 was all that stood in the way of Mormonism's relatively rapid merger with American culture is suggestive. JFS, and the type of Mormonism of which he was a symbol, had been more rather than less American all the time.

Culture is a slippery concept and difficult to define, but by any definition, there can be no doubt that nineteenth-century Mormon culture was enmeshed with American culture in so many ways that except for the practice of polygamy, the two would have been all but indistinguishable. In his appeal for amnesty in 1891, JFS did his best to make that very point. "My fathers for five generations were American born and loyal to the colonies [against the British] and to the government of the United States," he proudly declared, adding that he had "always sought to emulate their examples of loyalty to my country." He wrote that he was a Republican, had supported Lincoln in 1864, and believed that the U.S. Constitution was "divinely inspired."[15]

There is a tendency to think of Mormonism as undergoing an Americanization process during this period, but a careful consideration of the evidence suggests that no such process was necessary. In fact, Mormons had been Americanizing immigrants even as they Mormonized them since the 1830s. But for JFS, the greatest challenge was acknowledging that the dream of a truly separate Mormon people

264   Chapter 15

would not come in his lifetime. The way he came to terms with this new reality in the early twentieth century was to make the case that Mormons were Americans by every important measure. "A bond of sympathy unites, and should unite all American commonwealths," JFS wrote, a bond based on "race of origin, consanguinity, tradition, aims and aspirations." The vast majority of Mormons, JFS pointed out, came from the same English and northern European "common stock" as the rest of white America. The story of the "settlement and founding" of Utah, therefore, "is to a great extent the history of the settlement and foundation of" all of the states, both culturally and biologically. Perhaps most telling of all is the way that JFS began to recast the well-worn tale of his childhood. "When I was ten years old," he wrote in 1905, "I crossed the desolate plains and bleak mountains with my widowed mother and other homeless people, settling in this Salt Lake Valley." The struggles he faced were now "the fast fading reminiscences of the *American* pioneer." JFS slowly reimagined his story of trauma, loss, and victimized alienation from his American roots to one that placed him squarely in the broader story of American pioneering, settlement, and the "building of empire."[16]

Looking back from the vantage point of the early twentieth century, JFS erased the rupture between Mormons and Americans. "The feelings of pure and unalloyed loyalty to our government, which were deep seated in the hearts of the Mormon people [in 1846], are still part and parcel of our very being now," he wrote to Theodore Roosevelt, concluding that it "could not be otherwise, for the simple reason that as a community, we are an integral part of the nation itself."[17] In a sermon at the April 1907 general conference, he reminded the world that most of the founding generation of Mormon leaders "were descendants of the Pilgrims and Puritans [tracing] their lineage to the founders and first defenders of the nation." It was an undeniable fact, JFS continued, that Mormonism is "the most distinctively American church."[18]

In 1904, at the height of the controversy about Reed Smoot's eligibility for the Senate as a Mormon, JFS commissioned Susa Young Gates to write an article giving the world a behind-the-scenes look at JFS and his wives. In that article, Gates went to great lengths to link JFS, and Mormonism, with "old New England," a culture with a long history of serving as the sentimentalized, and even caricatured, image of what it was to be American. She described JFS's home and office, and other early Utah architecture, as reflective of "New England tastes and memories." Julina Smith is painted as "a generous type of that thrifty womanhood which filled New England farmhouses for the first centuries of American civilization." JFS's "diet and regime is inherited New England routine." His wife Sarah "is a daughter of a skillful New England physician." His son Hyrum is "puritanical in his genuine asceticisms." His wife Alice comes from "the well-known New England Kimballs."[19] Her point is all but impossible to miss.

By 1909, JFS's intellectual evolution on the relationship between Mormonism and America had solidified. The "constitutional restorationism" that dominated his thought for the whole of the nineteenth century—his belief that America was divinely founded but in a state of political apostasy that could only be righted by Mormon dominance—had been modified. He no longer emphasized the differences between Mormons and Americans, but stressed that to be Mormon in the United States was to be American—and not just American, but American of the white, Anglo-Saxon, Puritan-descended variety. "Neither in mental attitude nor in conduct have we been disloyal to the government under whose guarantee of religious freedom our Church was founded," he wrote to the former governor of Idaho. "The Book of Mormon proclaims America to be the land of Zion, a land dedicated to righteousness and liberty," JFS declared, shifting from his earlier emphasis on the need for Mormon-led cosmic interference to right America's wrongs to a declaration that America, as it currently existed, demonstrated significant features of righteousness.[20]

Terry Eagleton, a scholar of cultural phenomena, delineates the practical and symbolic aspects of culture. Practical culture consists of things as they are lived day to day. Symbolic culture is composed of ideals and values as they are expressed in the abstract. Eagleton's work on the tension between the symbolic and practical aspects of a culture sheds some light on the changes in Mormon culture that JFS observed in the last two and half decades of his life. Over time, Eagleton writes, "social facts begin to come adrift from cultural values, a process that involves new kinds of freedom as well as new forms of hardship."[21]

The chief social fact faced by JFS, and Mormonism at large, in the 1890s was that polygamy had to die. The main hardship posed by this fact had to do with rationalizing change. Historically persistent religions must change constantly to maintain their place within the larger cultural web of which they are always a part. Religions that claim exclusive access to ultimate truth coupled with a belief in an unchanging God must come up with creative ways to disguise, defend, minimize, or explain major changes. We have already seen the chief mechanism used by Mormons in the nineteenth century to accomplish this. We may call it "ideal suspension."

If we look closely at JFS's writing during the late 1890s, we see glimpses of how this process was beginning to take shape in his own mind. His children, born in polygamy, would not be able to practice it, but the suspension of the practice did not invalidate the principle. JFS made this clear in a letter to his missionary son Hyrum in 1896.

> My children cannot deny the divine law of marriage through which they have been given life and being. My son, I tell you and God is my witness, that the Revelation on Plural Marriage came from God through the Prophet Joseph Smith and there is no more holy, more sacred principle ever been revealed to man! It is for the fullness of my glory saith God. And no man to whom it is revealed can reject it <u>from his heart</u> without condemnation.[22]

266   Chapter 15

This is a notable departure from JFS's rhetoric of the 1880s, in which he pronounced doom upon anyone who rejected the practice of polygamy. By 1896, condemnation fell only upon those who rejected emotional allegiance to the principle rather than its practice.

With the death of Orson Pratt in 1881, space opened up for JFS to solidify his reputation as one of the great doctrinal scholars in the LDS Church. People continued to write to him for answers to questions about theology, scripture, and doctrine. One correspondent was church leader Francis M. Lyman, who wrote to JFS in 1895 after listening to one of his sermons to tell him that it was "the choicest doctrinal discourses I have listened to."[23] Occasionally, however, JFS found his ideas challenged. Lyman, for example, objected to his teaching that the ancient apostle Peter did not receive "the Gift of the Holy Ghost" before he denied Christ.

JFS had written to Lyman in the hope of gaining a doctrinal ally because in February 1895, Woodruff, Cannon, and nearly all of the apostles said they disagreed with JFS about Peter and the Holy Ghost. JFS's basic contention was that "the power and the gift of the Holy Ghost are two different things," an idea that his fellow leaders found unconvincing, calling it a "very fine distinction." JFS persisted in his view, which, it should be noted, is the official position of the church on the subject today.[24] The following year, Joseph Hyde, the son of Apostle Orson Hyde, wrote effusively to JFS that he "frequently made the assertion that Joseph F. Smith leads the world on doctrines of salvation."[25]

One of the reasons for JFS's reputation as an expert on LDS doctrine was his friendship with Susa Young Gates. He had first become acquainted with Gates during his exile in Hawaii, where she and her husband, Jacob, were serving as missionaries. They bonded over the loss of children that they both experienced there. Gates, the vivacious and assertive daughter of Brigham Young, developed very strong feelings for JFS, and he treated her like a sister. From early on in their friendship, Gates made a habit of posing difficult and/or controversial doctrinal questions to JFS, and she was not afraid to press him if she found his answer unsatisfactory. In 1888, for example, during one of the most stressful periods of JFS's life up to that point, he took the time to answer a letter she wrote about women and the priesthood. JFS wrote that the "woman does share the honors and glories of her husband, but not his priesthood." Gates wrote back asking, rather pointedly, "What are those honors, what are the privileges?"[26]

In the 1890s, Gates frequently wrote to JFS asking questions with less barb, the answers to which she would publish in the *Young Woman's Journal*. This set a precedent that would later be followed by Joseph F. Smith Jr. in a column for the *Improvement Era*. Their exchanges are important not only for the questions JFS chose to answer, but also because of those he did not. He insisted on final editorial approval over any journalistic use to which his answers might be put, but he was generally frank in his replies. In an 1891 letter, Gates asked JFS a series of questions ranging from which doctors to use to alcohol and tithing. She asked, "Are the saints justified in

Politics, Economics, and Polygamy Collide   267

calling in physicians or surgeons not of our faith?" JFS preferred to avoid physicians of any faith, but he informed Gates that while one should go to a Mormon practitioner if possible, "it would be folly and bigotry not to avail oneself of such needed skillful help" regardless of religious persuasion.[27] This is the first instance that I have found in which JFS recognizes and articulates the notion that Mormon avoidance of gentiles on religious grounds could be considered bigotry. That is a small phrase, but potent in its implications. Although Mormons had been in contact with "others" even during the apparently isolated early years in Utah, it was only in the 1890s that JFS began to recognize that the world he inhabited was not, and could never be, sterilized of outside influence. He was adjusting to the modern, multilayered culture described by Eagleton as "different peoples living in different ways in the same place."[28]

Gates next asked about the propriety of keeping whiskey for medicinal purposes. JFS replied that it was probably all right, but ought not to be "bragged about." She asked a similar question about beer, and he declared beer was relatively harmless as long as it was home brewed. Those two questions indicate the resurgence of "the Word of Wisdom" as a test of Mormon orthodoxy. At this point, JFS emphasized small amounts privately consumed. He would eventually take a much stronger stance.[29]

Finally, Gates posed a question about tithing. JFS refused to answer it. "I hope someday to comply with your request for something on that subject," he wrote apologetically, but he simply could not at present because he had yet to "receive the spirit of it." "Perhaps," he added optimistically, "it will come upon me soon."[30]

An important element in JFS's epistemological repertoire remained his reliance on the supernatural power of the Holy Ghost to provide pieces to the doctrinal puzzles that scripture study and natural mental faculties could not, including one time when he fielded questions from church members about some of the more intricate logistical features of family sealings. He explained that until 1894, Mormons were not only sealed in temples to members of their family, but they could also be adopted—that is, they could have their family grafted into the family of another, usually prominent, Mormon. JFS received many requests from people who wished to be adopted into his father's family, as well as into his uncle Joseph's family.

JFS's letters to his son Hyrum while he was on a mission evinced the same pattern. In letter after letter, Hyrum posed questions, and JFS provided lengthy, detailed, and characteristically systematic answers, showcasing his ongoing desire to fashion a coherent doctrinal architecture for Mormonism. Perhaps the most famous story about Hyrum and JFS's correspondence during this period involves the change of the church's "fast day" from the first Thursday of the month to the first Sunday of the month. In the traditional telling of the story, Hyrum wrote to his father from northern England, concerned that miners and other local workers had to miss work, and thus forfeit needed pay, to attend the meeting on Thursday. JFS, consulting with the First Presidency, convinced Woodruff to change fast day to Sunday churchwide.

268   Chapter 15

The documents suggest a slightly different story, however. When Hyrum asked about moving the fast day from Thursday to Sunday, JFS noted that since at least 1877, "the first Sunday in each month [had already] been set apart in foreign lands and in all the mission fields" so as to avoid "interfering with their employment." Apparently, saints in the British Isles had decided on their own to fast on Thursday "in order to be in unison with the Church in Zion." At this point, JFS proposed to the First Presidency that Zion and, strangely enough, England be brought into harmony with the practice already well established in the vast majority of foreign missions.[31] Ironically, in the same letter JFS betrayed his obsession with order when he pointed out to Hyrum, apropos of nothing, that "if there is one thing that Mamma [Edna] lacks, it is a [sense of] order and system."[32]

A Year of Sadness

Although Hyrum's mission went smoothly, JFS was about to enter one of the most difficult years of his life. Two primary sources of worry and grief plagued JFS during this period. The first was the near-death of his wife Sarah. Around Christmas of 1897, she developed typhoid fever. Though typhoid was frequently fatal within weeks, Sarah survived the acute stage but remained dangerously ill for months. In September 1898, she was still lingering, "her very life trembling in the balance day to day."[33] Sarah's illness required JFS to employ a skilled nurse as well as a "hired girl" for months at considerable expense.[34]

In March 1898, JFS had lost yet another child. In a letter to Mary and Donnette, he wrote that the "most trying ordeals of sickness" began with Sarah's typhoid fever, followed by the same illness befalling Alice, and then Emily, Rachel, and finally Ruth contracted scarlet fever. On 11 March 1898, four-year-old Ruth, JFS's daughter with Edna, "commenced with scarlet fever." Two days later, he reported that she was doing "as well as we could expect."[35] But four days after that, she was dead. As JFS approached his sixtieth birthday, he faced yet another tiny grave, the ninth such hole into which he had buried a baby and his tears, but not his faith.

No matter how many times JFS endured this same scene, he never grew callous or cold toward it. It still crushed him, leaving him to remark that the loss of his child "seems impossible," while struggling with the knowledge that it was "all too true." He could not even collect himself enough to put pen to paper to notify his sister Martha for several days. "I should have written you sooner," JFS confessed when he finally found the strength to send her a message, "but my poor heart has been in the icy chamber with the cherished lovely form of my darling babe!"[36] "We feel keenly the loss of our precious little pet," he wrote a week after Ruth's death. And, as he did with each of the children he lost, he remembered her as the one he wanted the least to lose. "There is no other one of our little ones who could possibly be missed more than our precocious and most interesting little Ruthie."[37]

JFS venerated his deceased children, elevating them in his memory to the extent that he believed that they represented "by far the brightest souls committed to my care." These souls were never far from his thoughts. Just a few days before he turned sixty, JFS gathered nearly all of his family members together to have a portrait taken and then have dinner together. Eleven descendants were absent, but JFS expressed delight in the "forty-four strong" who surrounded him, as well as the nine other children "on the other side of the veil," bound to him by "kindred ties stronger than death."[38]

In April 1898, Joseph F. Smith Jr. married Louie Shurtliff. JFS, of course, took great joy in performing the sealing ceremony in the Salt Lake Temple. The newlyweds moved into a room in JFS's main home in Salt Lake City, but even though he was happy to have them so close, it aroused in him a sense of financial inadequacy. JFS feared that the "cozy" accommodations must seem to his new daughter-in-law "a great let-down from the palatial mansion of [her] parents."[39] Louie's father, Lewis, was three years older than JFS, and his parents had joined the church during the Kirtland period. He was a political and religious fixture in Weber County, north of Salt Lake, and at the time of Louie and JFS Jr.'s marriage, he was serving as a state senator. Despite the prestige of his church office, JFS winced at the thought that his daughter-in-law might feel she had married down.

Less than a year later, Joseph Richards Smith (called Buddy) and JFS Jr. were called to serve in the same mission that their brother Hyrum had recently returned from. JFS had arranged for both of them to be called to the British Isles, where he had spent so many years. It is a stroke of good fortune for historians that both sons served missions simultaneously because we are left with a documentary record in the form of letters that clearly demonstrate how JFS handled each of them.

The day that Buddy and JFS Jr. left Salt Lake for Philadelphia, where they would catch a steamer to England, JFS dictated a letter of introduction for them to hand to their mission president. He went out of his way to assure the president that he expected no special treatment for his sons, but he did want him to know that "this is the first time these boys have ever been from home," and, while under JFS's care, "they have always been good boys."[40] His expectation, he wrote, was for them to "be faithful while abroad." The subtext of the letter is clear: since they have always been good at home, if these boys fall into trouble, it will probably be because of poor leadership abroad.

Buddy left home without his overcoat and spent most of the two-week voyage across the Atlantic being seasick, but JFS Jr. remained upright, something that JFS believed demonstrated true manliness (apparently forgetting leaning over the sides of ships on his own adventures). When the two arrived in England, they wrote to their parents. JFS wrote to JFS Jr. of his disappointment in "the spirit of Buddy's letters," in which he "seemed to look at everything from the very hardest point of view and did not breathe at all a contented spirit." He blamed this on Buddy's "fears and timidity," two traits that JFS could never abide in a man. That he felt free to share this with JFS Jr. suggests that even though Buddy was the older of the two, JFS looked on the younger brother as the natural leader. He offered no critique whatsoever of JFS Jr., only sharing with him news from home and, of course, his "great disappointment" in Buddy.[41]

On the same day, JFS penned a stern letter to Buddy, chastising him for depressing his mother, Sarah, who was already "feeble." "She was in tears nearly all day," JFS scolded, "and looked very sad." "Joseph F. [wrote] very cheerfully and in an excellent spirit," JFS chided, adding, "I wish the same could be said for you." He ended the letter with warnings that bordered on threats. "Never again write to Mamma in the strain of your last letter," JFS instructed. "If you feel that way and feel that you must say it, write to me but not to Mamma." Just to make sure that Buddy knew where JFS stood on the importance of this mission, he ended the letter by informing him that "nothing could give me greater sorrow ... than for you to fail! You must not fail! And you will not."[42]

In his next letter, JFS continued to warn Buddy of the high stakes of his mission by invoking the memory of Hyrum Smith and Willard Richards. "Both your grandfathers were martyrs for the truth ... and the blood of Joseph Smith flows in your veins, and no man of that blood can afford to go back on him!" In letter after letter, JFS expressed his hope that Buddy was "finally" getting "the spirit of your mission," and he took every opportunity to teach him how various principles of the gospel could be traced to specific scriptural passages. However, when Buddy attempted to engage his father with doctrinal questions, things often went sideways. JFS tried to answer some questions Buddy had about the Holy Ghost and other subjects, but expressed his disappointment that Buddy would "express doubts and uncertainty or any perplexity of mind in relation to these things" given that "all these things seem so plain and so simple to one who has received the spirit of truth which is born of repentance and obedience to the laws of God." Buddy made a major mistake when he referred to the "Lectures on Faith" as a "jumbled up mess." JFS was shocked that his son could "speak so flippantly about ... a matter that should be held most sacred to you."[43]

In JFS Jr., his father saw a more fully developed man. "I like your spirit," JFS wrote, and "I have faith in your integrity, and I have pleasure and satisfaction in you."[44] During these years, he tutored young Joseph in the art of doctrinal expression. After being in the mission field a few months, JFS Jr. wrote to his father asking that he mention to two of JFS's younger sons "some passages of scripture in relation to sprinkling" that they should "investigate preparatory to their going on a mission." JFS saw this as an opportunity for his doctrinally inclined son to do some writing of his own. "I would suggest," JFS responded, "that ... you write to the boys and expound to them some of those passages which the elders have to meet among the sectarian churchmen." JFS hoped that "in that way you may awaken an interest in the boys that they would not otherwise feel."[45] JFS also enlisted JFS Jr.'s help in "relieving the stress upon Buddy's mind about such trifling matters" as polygamy.[46]

He also expressed his frustration with Buddy to JFS Jr., writing, "I love him as I love you," but it seemed that Buddy simply could not seem to "feel the true spirit of his mission, and this grieves me."[47]

Buddy may have lacked his father's knack for systematic doctrinal exposition, but he certainly inherited JFS's refusal to take criticism lying down. Rather than accept his father's criticism of his lack of understanding, he asked JFS why he should "marvel" that his son had questions. After all, Buddy wrote, men of greater years, more experience, and better education were "equally at sea." Furthermore, Buddy sharply replied to his father's defense of the Lectures on Faith by arguing that no one had the right to decide if the lectures were a "jumble" except for the individual reader. JFS responded in a similarly pointed tone, informing Buddy that anyone with any common sense at all would marvel "that my son who grew up with so many opportunities, should not have known how to answer certain simple questions." JFS rebuked Buddy for being "the only one of my sons [who has] asked [me] questions apparently for the purpose of argument." Be careful, JFS warned, not "to mistake argument for reason."[48]

It appears that Buddy had a gift for getting under JFS's skin, partially because he was writing letters to various other people, including Lorenzo Snow, which his father found embarrassing. JFS's famous temper trembled on the verge of exploding as he asked Buddy if his heart bore "true allegiance to me and my cause." JFS doubted it given the "spirit of your letters in answer to your call to go on a mission, which fell like lead upon my soul." Oh, and by the way, JFS jabbed, "why do you correspond with a worthless creature like B.F.K. Jr, in the spirit and words which you have done?"[49]

Buddy was probably surprised to learn that his father had obtained a copy of the letter, which JFS helpfully offered to send to Buddy as proof. Its contents are lost to history, but whatever it was that Buddy wrote, JFS "wished it could be effaced forever from my memory and that your pen hand never written it." Buddy, it seems, had somehow managed to criticize James Talmage, B. H. Roberts, and his own father in a single letter. He apparently felt that Talmage and Roberts lacked humility, to which JFS responded that Buddy had provided "unmistakable evidence that . . . it is my son who needs humility and the love of God in his heart."[50]

JFS sent a copy of Buddy's objectionable letter to JFS Jr. with a handwritten postscript: "I want you to see how Buddy has written. I think you [already] saw his [apparently insolent] letter to Prest. Snow in answer to his call for a mission. Keep this to yourself."[51] It is difficult to know why JFS would involve JFS Jr. by secretly providing copies of Buddy's correspondence, but whatever the motive, the fact that he did is strong evidence that he felt closer to JFS Jr. and considered him an ally to be cultivated.

Even as his oldest children were making their own way in the world, JFS continued to welcome new babies to the family. He had two sons born in 1900, one to Alice and one to Mary, and it was Mary who delivered JFS's youngest child, Royal,

272   Chapter 15

in 1906. These births had to be kept quiet because there was an investigator "hot on our track and we do not know at what moment he may spring his trap upon us."[52] Fathering children with plural wives was illegal, and the authorities had proven their disinclination to turn a blind eye when Angus Cannon, president of the Salt Lake stake, was convicted after the birth of a child in 1899.

The Work Intensifies

As the children grew up and left home, JFS entered a stage of life that for most men would be a period of retirement. Given the structure of advancement in the LDS hierarchy, however, he knew that he would never retire. There was no question that he would die in office, but just which office remained to be seen.

In the fall of 1898, events conspired to move JFS one step closer to the highest office in the church. In August, Woodruff, though aged and chronically ill, had traveled to northern California with Cannon. All seemed well as the party visited with old friends such as Isaac Trumbo and went on various expeditions by sea and land. To JFS's great shock, he received a telegram from Cannon on 1 September 1898 informing him that Woodruff was gravely ill, "not sensible," and not expected to survive. The next morning another telegram arrived, confirming the previous day's prognosis. Woodruff had died in his sleep. Cannon tersely instructed JFS to "notify [Woodruff's] family."[53] He did so, and then undertook to notify the scattered members of the Quorum of the Twelve, instructing them via telegram that Woodruff's death required their return to Salt Lake.[54]

On 3 September 1898, JFS noted in a letter that he, along with other general authorities and members of Woodruff's family, would travel the next day by train from Salt Lake to Ogden to meet "the remains of our beloved President."[55] For the third time since JFS had become a member of the First Presidency, a church president had died. Although he had not been particularly close to Woodruff on a personal level, he had held him in great esteem and marveled at his apparently inexhaustible energy directed toward the establishment of Zion over the course of many decades. Years later, JFS revealed another reason for his admiration of Woodruff. In 1916, he suggested that one of his grandsons be named Wilford because it was Woodruff "alone among the leading authorities of the Church [who] repeatedly pronounced the prediction, openly and in private, that I would someday stand before the Church in the position occupied, in the beginning, by the Prophet Joseph Smith."[56]

In the days following Woodruff's death, JFS found it difficult to concentrate on the various pressing business matters brought to his attention. The "sorrowful exigencies resulting from [his] sudden death" had left him with "scarcely time or heart to engage in any other matters."[57] Funeral arrangements came together quickly, and on 8 September 1898, the tabernacle was bedecked in flowers, and under a sign reading "Being Dead Yet Speaketh" rested Woodruff's casket, a plain wooden affair made of native wood, just as he had requested. JFS spoke for about thirty minutes. This was the first time that he had been able to attend the funeral of a church president since the death of Joseph Smith in 1844. His sermon moved quickly beyond a tribute to Woodruff's life and labors to paint a vast picture of the Latter-day Saints as a besieged people, surrounded on all sides by those whose "infidel tongues" slandered the greatest men who ever lived. JFS paid Woodruff the highest compliment when he compared him to Joseph Smith, saying both men had been "misunderstood by the world." Woodruff, he proclaimed, was like Joseph and Hyrum Smith in another way, being "made of the material of which martyrs are made" and, despite having died of natural causes, proving himself willing to die for the cause, "never qualing in the face of danger, no matter who of his associates may have proved themselves traitors."[58] The sermon revealed JFS's continuing belief that "the world's" hatred for the Mormons and their leaders was intractable. The remaining years of his life would give him no reason to change those views.

For the first time in LDS history, the transfer of power from the deceased president to his successor occurred quickly and without difficulty. In fact, it was such an unusually rapid transition that the *Deseret Evening News* felt obliged to explain the move rather than simply report it. According to the article, the Quorum of the Twelve had met to discuss "important business of a financial character," and it became clear during the meeting that a "trustee-in-trust for the Church" had to be appointed "in order that the business might be transacted."[59] Almost as an afterthought, it seemed, the group concluded that the most efficient way to take care of this would be to reorganize the First Presidency.

There was little reason to suspect such a relatively smooth transition. Snow, a seventy-seven-year-old Ohio native, had joined the LDS Church in 1836. Brigham Young admitted him to the Quorum of the Twelve in 1849, and he had served nearly a year in the Utah Territorial Penitentiary during the anti-polygamy raids of the late 1880s. He had been serving as president of the Quorum of the Twelve during Woodruff's church presidency, and as president of the Salt Lake Temple since its dedication in 1893. Snow had a reputation as a relatively conciliatory presence in the Mormon hierarchy, not prone to bluster, ego, or rage. He did, however, have a tense relationship with one powerful individual that suggested the possibility of problems.

The main obstacle to a reorganization of the First Presidency in 1898 was a familiar one: George Q. Cannon. Although the crippling economic circumstances of the early 1890s had eased somewhat, the church remained deeply in debt, for which Snow blamed Cannon. Furthermore, Snow and many of the other apostles resented the First Presidency's meddling in what Snow believed to be affairs well within the Twelve's sphere of authority. They all knew that Woodruff had relied heavily on Cannon, especially in his final years, and this had led to significant jealousies. In the summer of 1898, just months before Woodruff's death, Snow

274   Chapter 15

unleashed a "stormy" tirade in a meeting in which he accused Cannon of "not trust-ing the Twelve" and "nearly ruining the credit of the church with schemes that have failed."[60]

Cannon was not without his defenders in the Twelve, however. John Henry Smith, family relationships notwithstanding, told the Twelve that, in his estima-tion, JFS was "a plain, blunt man ... lacking in cunning and the ability to shape things to suit his opinions," and with Woodruff in ever-worsening health, it had fallen to Cannon to get things done. He noted that Cannon was "one of the most gifted of men ... a writer, a diplomat," but he was not superhuman. In John Henry Smith's view, Cannon acted imprudently only because he was the "one [functioning] member of the First Presidency," and the extraordinary demands placed on Can-non had outstripped even his many gifts.[61] It is little surprise that when Woodruff died, and Snow faced the responsibility of leading the church, he seemed to feel a pressing need to cultivate order and unity among the church leaders that exceeded his distaste for Cannon's financial activities.

On 9 September 1898, Snow met with Cannon and JFS to get a sense of what issues the First Presidency had been dealing with. At that time, the members of the First Presidency shared very little of their business with the apostles, who were seen primarily as ministers rather than administrators. Although Snow did not suggest reorganizing the First Presidency, he clearly signaled his intention to "not allow such scenes, if he could prevent them, as had occurred at previous times, say, for instance, after the death of President Taylor."[62] Obviously, he planned to organize the First Presidency and make sure that Cannon was not subject to the same type of attacks he had endured previously.

For his part, Cannon felt enormous relief at the prospect of being "delivered from such scenes and conversations [of] fault-finding, censure or condemnation" that he had endured before. Perhaps fearing that Snow might lose his nerve when the entire quorum met later, Cannon argued that two cardinal principles ought to be adopted to regulate affairs between the First Presidency and the Quorum of the Twelve. First, it was "not the province of the Twelve Apostles to call the First Presidency to account and to pronounce censure or condemnation upon them," and, second, "no one of the First Presidency should be selected and blamed or censured apart from the others; that what we had done we had done unitedly and we had stood together."[63]

Although clearly self-serving, Cannon's "fundamental principles" established a more stable relationship between the two quorums by asserting the basic pri-macy of the First Presidency and by creating a unified front against criticism from any member of the Twelve. This represented a fundamental shift in the way the quorums did business, and when they all met together a few days later, the stage was set for a smooth transition. Although the Twelve had not been notified of any impending plans for reorganization, some of them seemed to know it was coming. When Brigham Young Jr. saw JFS moving his desk out of the office he had occupied as second counselor, he "suggested that it might be a little too quick. He might need it."[64] He was prophetic on both counts.

At the 13 September 1898 meeting, several of the apostles pushed to immediately reorganize the First Presidency. After all of them had either voiced their approval or remained silent, Snow told them that he had felt very depressed, almost discouraged, in thinking of the load that rested upon him, so he had gone before the Lord, clothed in his temple robes, to seek the mind of the Lord. He said that in answer to his prayer, God had revealed to him how the First Presidency should be organized and who his counselors should be.[65]

Although that story is the more dramatic, Snow also told a much different one. In 1892, he said, Woodruff had pulled him aside after a brush with death and told him that when he died, Snow must immediately reorganize the First Presidency. Regardless of what actually prompted Snow, the result was the same: JFS and Cannon took their places again as counselors to the church president.[66]

Soon after the installation of the new First Presidency, JFS wrote a letter to Cannon, saying,

> I gratefully appreciate the assistance you have rendered me throughout my life. I recall the many things you have done for me, dating back to my first mission in England from 1860 to 1863, and the numberless acts of love and kindness I have received at your hands ever since. I thank you, President Cannon, with all my heart for all these precious memories of your brotherly—nay—<u>fatherly</u> kindness toward me.[67]

Cannon was moved to tears by the letter of support and the demonstration of JFS's loyalty to those who showed him kindness. He remained one of the few mentors that JFS had in the church hierarchy, and he expressed pleasure at being able to continue serving closely with him.

The vacancy created by Woodruff's death gave Snow his first opportunity to call a man to the apostleship. Speculation raced through the city about who would get the nod. The *Salt Lake Herald* reported that Snow was "ambitious to have his son, Le Roi chosen."[68] The *Salt Lake Tribune* noted that such an ambition "was only natural since each of the presidents of the Mormon church, save Joseph Smith, is represented by a son in the quorum."[69] Brigham Young Jr., in a slight breach of etiquette, tested the *Herald*'s theory by openly suggesting that one of Snow's sons ought to be called to fill the vacancy. JFS "took [him] to task for such an unwise suggestion [because] it put President Snow in a very embarrassing position."[70]

It is difficult to understand why JFS would have reacted this way given the fact that he would place two of his sons in the Quorum of the Twelve during his own presidency. It probably transgressed his philosophy of communication within the church hierarchy, especially if he suspected Young or others had spoken to the media. JFS hated it when church affairs leaked. He vigilantly policed the leading

276   Chapter 15

quorums to ensure that information was handled on a need-to-know basis, even among the apostles. Anthony Ivins discovered as much when he brought up a sensitive issue with fellow apostle Francis Lyman. When JFS found out, he was furious that Ivins had not "made his communication ... to the man who holds the keys of authority [Lorenzo Snow]." "In these troubled times," JFS chastened Ivins, matters "should be kept as nearly as possible within the smallest limits of publicity." He told Ivins that his "motto is and has always been to protect to the uttermost in my power the rights and secrets of my friends and the friends of the Kingdom of God."[71]

If that is the sort of reaction JFS had to information shared between two apostles, it goes without saying that his opinion about an apostle influencing, or being influenced by, the media would have been strongly negative. In any case, Snow already had a candidate in mind. When he proposed forty-one-year-old Rudger Clawson, all of the members of the Twelve knew about him. Clawson had been the missionary companion of Joseph Standing, and the two were together in Georgia in the summer of 1879 when they were attacked by a group of armed men. The mob fired on the missionaries, mortally wounding Standing but leaving Clawson untouched.

Snow had become friendly with Clawson when both men were serving time in the territorial penitentiary. Clawson served an unusually long sentence, just over three years, for polygamy, and Snow arranged for him to be called as president of the Box Elder stake in northern Utah. Snow had kept a close eye on Clawson's administration of the stake and was sufficiently impressed to make him his first choice to fill the vacancy in the Twelve. Both the First Presidency and the Quorum of the Twelve were now fully staffed and functional.

At the October conference in which Snow was presented to the body of the church and sustained as church president, JFS stressed three major themes: authority, order, and the sacredness of work—especially manual labor. God, he said, had provided the people with "officers in the Church [that they] may be guarded from the evils of the world." One of the evils that JFS had in mind was the voluntary scattering of Latter-day Saints. The Mormons had come to the "valley of the mountains" to "live and to die" in a community of believers whom God intended to "associate with each other." This community, JFS continued, was of divine design, "the pattern He has given us," and he chafed at the growing tendency for Mormons to separate their spiritual lives from their temporal lives.[72]

As the nineteenth century drew to a close, many Mormons were less interested in taking direction from church leaders on such issues as where to live or how to earn a living. For JFS, this threatened to sunder the footings of God's work: "The Lord Almighty has gathered us out of the nations of the earth and called us to the tops of these mountains" for "temporal and spiritual salvation." He foresaw people becoming a "law unto [themselves]," living in "contention and disorder," if they started down the slippery slope of deciding which church edicts to follow

Politics, Economics, and Polygamy Collide   277

and which to ignore. He held that it was "essential" that "every man holding a standing in the Church ... if he wants to move ... obtain a recommendation from the bishop of the ward in which he lives" as to where he might move, with the only acceptable options being places where "he can find members of the Church."[73]

JFS found it astonishing that Latter-day Saints failed to understand that the only reason settlement in Utah was possible at all was because of the sacred community itself. All of the irrigation canals in the world could not have removed "the curse of sterility [that] was upon the soil when we came to this valley." It was God who had "removed the curse" and made the land "fruitful." Dismantling the community would lead not only to a return to barren soil, but also "apostasy and darkness, dissension and division." In 1901 he told the Latter-day Saints that "if you want new homes and new locations, consult the authorities before you act." Scattering would only result in the Mormons becoming "like the rest of the sectarian world, and that will not do."[74]

There was another reason why JFS discouraged movement. As he explained to one individual who asked permission to start an LDS colony in Guatemala, "our people remaining at home and jealously owning and occupying the lands within our reach" was the only way to avoid "courting a repetition of the evils and misfortunes" of the past. "This is emphatically a gathering dispensation," JFS continued, and whatever "blessings we have ... developed through closely and rigidly adhering to the spirit of this wise policy that were devised for our protection by the Lord Himself."[75] To highlight the seriousness of this concept, the First Presidency wrote that "only saints living in a gathered condition, that is, in a ward and stake are recommended for temple work."[76]

No sooner had Snow been installed than speculation started buzzing among JFS's family and friends about the likelihood that he would soon be in that position himself. We do not know what his private thoughts on that matter were, but he was plainly disturbed when someone broached the subject with him directly. After Lucy Kimball Smith, one of Joseph Smith Jr.'s plural wives from the Nauvoo period, made the mistake of suggesting that JFS was bound to occupy the office first held by his uncle, he told her, "Keep it to yourself" and warned her against "even suggesting the same to me in the future." JFS refused to offer his own thoughts, citing his willingness to "abide the will of the Lord" on the matter.[77] However, some uncertainty hovered over just how to discern divine will on the issue.

By this point, the precedent that the most senior of the apostles would become church president was firmly set. There remained, however, disagreement about how to determine seniority. Over the years, three different ways of measuring seniority had held sway: age, time in the Quorum of the Twelve, and time as an apostle. The first of these had been rejected decades before Snow took office, but the other two remained in play. This was no trivial matter in 1898 because Snow and Cannon, the two most senior apostles by all measures, were quite old. After them came JFS and Brigham Young Jr. Young had been ordained an apostle earlier than JFS, but he was

278   Chapter 15

not admitted into the quorum until after JFS. Everyone knew that, in all likelihood, resolving the problem of seniority would need to be addressed definitively in the relatively near future. Snow made his position clear in a private meeting with JFS and Cannon in late March 1900. JFS recorded in his journal that Snow "favored and practically decided that Brigham ranked next to me in the council of Apostles."[78]

Snow presented the issue at a meeting of the First Presidency and the Quorum of the Twelve just before the April 1900 general conference. Despite having already made up his mind, he asked for input from each man present, and according to the minutes of the meeting, "all were agreed that the seniority should be based on the time the brethren were admitted to the quorum and not from the date of ordination."[79] JFS was circumspect in his response, noting simply that "this important ruling settles a long unsettled point, and is most timely."[80] Young, however well he hid it during the meeting, was crushed. In his personal journal, Young recorded that his father had told him in no uncertain terms that seniority in the quorum was to be based on date of ordination, that "my name had been given to him [to be ordained an apostle] by revelation," and that his "place in the quorum [would be determined] by that ordination."[81] This decision would prove life-changing for both men.

In March 1899, JFS felt ready to begin his public ministry in support of Snow's agenda, which was to increase tithing receipts to alleviate the church's $115,000 debt. In May, Snow and JFS led a large entourage through the settlements from Salt Lake to St. George to preach on the subject of tithing. For the eighty-six-year-old Snow, this was a major undertaking. In twelve days, the party traveled over 700 miles and held twenty-four meetings, with Snow delivering no fewer than twenty-six sermons on tithing. In St. George, as elsewhere, he declared it "the will of the Lord" that the members of the church begin paying a full tithe. It was here, however, that Snow made one of the most famous statements of his life when he told the settlers that the drought currently strangling them nearly to death could only be abated by faithfully paying tithes. The Mormons paid their tithing, and the rains came in August.[82]

Back in Salt Lake, Snow told a meeting of the Deseret stake that God required a full tithing of his people in order to "sanctify" and "secure" their lands. In both the April and October conferences of 1899, JFS gave lengthy and impassioned sermons on the necessity of "observing the law of tithing." In keeping with his long-held belief that "obedience is the first law of heaven," JFS linked tithing to the more general principle of obedience to gospel law as promulgated by church authorities. JFS, the other members of the First Presidency, and the Twelve preached tithing at stake conferences up and down the Mormon culture region.

In early July 1899, the First Presidency held a solemn assembly in the Salt Lake Temple for all general authorities, stake presidents, and bishops of the church. The audience crowded into the celestial and terrestrial rooms of the temple to hear what Snow described as a twofold message: "to get those who attend the meeting to pay a full tithing, and through them, to get those over whom they preside to do the same." Snow and most of the other speakers approached the tithing issue from a practical point of view. If the saints paid their tithing as they ought to be doing, the church would have a surplus. If they failed to pay, Snow prophesied, "we shall have repetition of scenes of Missouri and Illinois." It simply would not do to "dicker with the Lord" on the subject.[83]

JFS argued that tithing was more than just a practical way of raising revenue for the church. It was a binding commandment of God, and to ignore it would bring condemnation. "The books," he suggested, "should record not only what we do, but what we ought to have done and did not do." Furthermore, "the poor of a ward—widows and orphans—all should pay their tithing."[84] JFS firmly believed that, far too often, the blessings of tithing were withheld from the poor by well-meaning church leaders who discouraged them from tithing on their already vanishingly small store of food or money.

JFS's approach to tithing is illustrative of how his unique worldview shaped his views on every issue that came before him, and how so many of his adult feelings were anchored deeply in his childhood. "My mother was a widow," JFS reminded the congregation at the April 1900 general conference, "with a large family to provide for." She once rummaged through the "potato pit" and selected the best of the slim crop, loading them onto a wagon which JFS drove to the Tithing Office. When they arrived at the steps, a tithing clerk met them and had the temerity to suggest that it was a "shame" that she had to pay tithing. Mary told the clerk that he should be "ashamed" at his effort to "deny me a blessing." JFS's anger at this memory was evident as he icily told the congregation that "the first two letters of the name of that tithing clerk was William Thompson." As he often did when recalling his mother, JFS could not resist pointing out how poorly she had been treated by the church. "You may turn to the records of the Church from the beginning unto the day of her death and you will find that she never received a farthing from the Church to help her," JFS exclaimed, despite the fact that "she paid thousands of dollars in wheat, potatoes, corn, vegetables, and meat."[85]

Before long, JFS's sermon had shifted from a talk on the blessings of tithing to a full-blown rant on the unyielding righteousness of his mother in the face of an exploitative and indifferent hierarchy. He picked up speed as he continued the sermon, saying that "the tithes of her sheep and cattle, the tenth pound of her butter, her tenth chicken, a tenth of her eggs, the tenth pig, the tenth calf, the tenth colt—a tenth of everything she raised was paid." She "prospered," he said, in spite of the church and because of her obedience.[86]

Tithing, JFS believed, was not primarily a revenue-generating endeavor. It was not about money, and it was not even about sacrifice. Like everything else asked of church members, tithing was just another test of obedience, "the first law of heaven," and he married his obsession with obedience to his lifelong feeling that the "widows and orphans" of the church were all too often being conspired against.

280   Chapter 15

It is not a surprise, then, that the centerpiece of many of JFS's sermons on tithing was a story about his mother and her fight against a male trying to deny her the blessings of obedience, one of the signs of God's true church. Among those things that distinguished "Mormonism from the religions of the world," JFS said, was that "you must not only believe, but you must obey."[87]

In 1900, JFS had another opportunity to travel abroad. In a situation not terribly unlike the one necessitating his mission to Hawaii in 1864, he was given the job of trying to stop something that a church president had started. Earlier that year, Benjamin Cluff Jr. secured permission from Snow to set off on an expedition through Central and South America "to explore Book of Mormon lands." Cluff, a Provo native who was educated at the University of Michigan, was serving as president of Brigham Young University at the time of the expedition. He saw himself as part of the tradition of explorers who had, since the early nineteenth century, been mapping rivers and cutting through jungles in search of "lost" civilizations. Unlike earlier explorations motivated by colonialism, these newer expeditions were intended as academic expeditions. Explorers had been scouring Central and South America for evidence of earlier civilizations and collecting samples of the flora and fauna of different regions. These trips often paid off in spectacular ways, as would be the case a decade after Cluff's expedition, when Hiram Bingham rediscovered the ruins of Machu Picchu in the highlands of Peru.

Cluff wanted to connect the emerging archaeological evidence of civilizations such as the Maya and the Olmec to the peoples described in the Book of Mormon. The expedition consisted mostly of students from Brigham Young Academy. Cluff had earlier approached JFS about sending one of his sons along, but he politely declined, citing financial difficulties and other factors.[88] He was more forthcoming in a letter to JFS Jr. in which he admitted that "I have not quite got the spirit of [the expedition]."[89] The upshot of it was that Cluff would have to do without any of JFS's boys.

The plan was to make their way through southern Utah and Arizona, and then into Mexico. Along the way, members of the expedition would perform missionary duties as opportunities presented themselves. Trouble began brewing, however, when the group reached Thatcher, Arizona. Before the group left Utah, JFS had granted permission for Cluff to take a plural wife. (Despite the prohibition on plural marriages declared in the 1890 Manifesto, a small number of marriages continued to be authorized and contracted.) After they got to Thatcher, Cluff instructed the expedition members to remain there while he traveled across the Mexican border to the Mormon colony of Juárez so he could court Florence Reynolds.

Heber J. Grant met the expedition and found the situation appalling. When he returned to Salt Lake, he told the Quorum of the Twelve and the First Presidency that the church had made a mistake giving its imprimatur to the expedition, the members of which were not only behaving badly, but were "utterly incapable" of safely executing such a demanding journey. Grant believed the group would not get very far into Mexico before they were robbed or worse.[90] Cannon and Snow found Grant's report sufficiently alarming that they contacted Snow, who had been ill and absent from the meeting. Snow concurred that something ought to be done and soon settled on sending JFS to Mexico to meet the expedition, withdraw church approval, and attempt to convince Cluff to cancel the trip.

JFS and his wife Edna arrived in Juárez on 31 July 1900. Anthony Ivins, president of the local stake, met JFS and his party at the train station, and JFS informed him about the reason for his visit. After he strongly encouraged Cluff to abandon the expedition and return to Utah, however, Cluff refused to "give up his cherished scheme of exploring the south, although I told him we thought it would be well for him to do so." After reading a letter from JFS to the First Presidency and the Twelve about the situation, Cannon and Grant were furious at Cluff's impudence. They could not believe that he would dare disregard a request from a member of the First Presidency.[91]

It was only at this meeting that Cannon learned what JFS and Snow already knew: that part of the reason for the expedition involved Cluff taking a plural wife. The woman in question was one of Cluff's former students at Brigham Young Academy, and members of the expedition claimed that Cluff disappeared for long periods to spend time with her. Cannon was shocked, telling the group that if he had known about the marriage plans, he would never have voted to support the expedition. The meeting ended with a decision to send a telegram to JFS and tell him to insist on the return of the expedition, but "if they proceed they must assume all responsibility."[92]

After JFS read the telegram to Cluff, Ivins, and other leaders at Juárez, Cluff was unmoved. He told JFS that he "greatly desired to go forward" because to return would ruin his reputation as both a scholar and a Mormon. Unable to persuade him, JFS assured all of those who wished to return—and that was most of them—that they did so with an "honorable release."[93] This incident is somewhat puzzling, given JFS's typically strong reaction to impertinence. His apparent reluctance to come down harder may be due to the close ties that he enjoyed with the Cluff family. Both Cluff's father and Cluff himself had served missions in Hawaii, and Cluff's uncle presided at the Iosepa colony. Whatever the reason, JFS took no action against Cluff, who continued on.

The Death of Cannon

On 23 March 1901, JFS stood in the Fourteenth Ward Meetinghouse and spoke over the body of William H. Folsom. Folsom joined the church in 1842 and had worked as an architect on the Nauvoo and Manti Temples and many other buildings in Utah. JFS's funeral sermon focused on two of his favorite themes: persecution and martyrdom. After fleeing Nauvoo, Folsom and his family lived in the

282   Chapter 15

hamlet of Farmington on the Des Moines River, where they eked out a living selling clothespins and horse nets. The locals did not like the Mormons who had settled in their community, and one day they captured Folsom and attempted to hang him while repeatedly trying to get him to "confess" to being a Mormon. After two false starts, they succeeded in hoisting him by the neck and left him hanging over an awning. A passerby saw him, apparently with his tongue sticking out, and hurriedly cut him down. The story captivated JFS, with its melding of violence and religion. He felt it bore repeating at the funeral, describing it as a "crucial test of faith."[94]

In early 1901, shortly after his seventy-fourth birthday, Cannon visited his beloved Hawaiian Islands for what would be the last time. Although apparently healthy during the trip, soon after returning home he started showing signs of failing health. In mid-February, he stopped attending meetings of the First Presidency. That month, one of his wives wrote to her son that, despite her best efforts, she could no longer "hide from her heart" Cannon's weakness. March brought a case of influenza. In a move reminiscent of Wilford Woodruff's last months, Cannon decided to travel to California in the hope of rallying his spirits and his health. Only a few weeks after he arrived there, Cannon went into a rapid decline. JFS wrote to JFS Jr. describing Cannon as "very ill," but he expressed hope that the "faith and prayers of the people [that] ascend daily in his behalf" would save him. Perhaps because of Cannon's recent battle with influenza, JFS anxiously advised both JFS Jr. and Buddy to "be vaccinated ... in the most approved way." He told them that such a vaccination "saved me from the disease when I was in England."[95]

JFS's progressive stance on vaccination is somewhat curious given his aversion to doctors and the hotly contested nature of vaccines in the early twentieth century. Many members of the Quorum of the Twelve not only opposed vaccination, but saw in it an evil conspiracy. Brigham Young Jr. believed that "Gentile doctors [are] trying to force Babylon into the people and some of them are willing to disease the blood of our children." Besides, he confided in his journal, this was a matter of faith since "God alone can avert the contagious diseases and calamities ... and we must make him our friend and protector."[96] Ordinarily, JFS would have been sympathetic to that kind of thinking, but his personal experience in England had been sufficiently powerful to move his thinking forward.

Although JFS's sons escaped the flu, the prayers offered in Cannon's behalf did not seem to be helping. On 7 April 1901, JFS wrote what would be his last letter to the man who had tutored him in his life's work for so very many years. I "grieve for your sufferings," JFS wrote, and he grew emotional as he reflected on Cannon's "wise and fatherly watch care over me from the days of my youth" up to that very hour. "I would gladly go to the ends of the earth to do you good, if it were in my power."[97] Sadly, it was not. Four days later, JFS correctly predicted in a letter to Buddy that "long before this reaches you, he will have taken a turn for the better or his earthly career will be terminated."[98] The next day, 12 April 1901, JFS received word that the man whom he had four decades earlier called an example of "true nobility [and] real, unfeigned greatness" had died.

Snow, who like Woodruff had relied heavily on Cannon, took the loss hard. He holed up in the Beehive House, where he "gave orders that he was not to be disturbed, as he did not care to discuss the sad event in his present state of mind."[99] The loss brought on a spell of ill health, precluding Snow from attending Cannon's funeral, so JFS presided. He told the congregation that when he was left "fatherless and motherless before reaching manhood," Cannon had gone out of his way to be a father to him.[100] After paying further homage to "the wisest man I have ever known," JFS did what he almost always did at the funeral of a tried and true Mormon, the very thing that Brigham Young had done at the funeral of JFS's mother nearly half a century earlier: he admonished Cannon's descendants to do as their father had done. "There is no salvation for you except to walk in the footsteps of your illustrious sire."[101]

On the way to the cemetery, the driver of the carriage in which JFS was riding lost control at the corner of South Temple and M Streets when the horses spooked and plunged off the road, smashing the back wheels to splinters. A more superstitious man might have seen that as an ominous sign, but JFS dusted himself off and stepped into another carriage.[102]

Only twelve days after JFS presided over Cannon's funeral, death once again reached in and took one of his children from the family circle. Shortly after arriving at his office, he received word that seventeen-year-old Alice, Sarah's daughter, was not long for this world. Although heartbreaking, the death of an older child was somewhat easier for JFS to deal with than the deaths of the very young. He held the funeral at Sarah's house, where he wept through sermons and musical performances, and then buried Alice on a gentle slope in the Salt Lake City cemetery.[103]

Barely two weeks passed before JFS found himself at yet another funeral. This time he spoke over the body of Alonzo Raleigh.[104] Raleigh had lived in Nauvoo before migrating west in 1848, and he had served as a justice of the peace, city alderman, and, for decades, as the bishop of the Salt Lake Nineteenth Ward.[105] JFS could not have escaped the oppressive sense accompanying the unstoppable fading away of the church's first generation of leaders, but as he aged, he grew increasingly philosophical about death. His vision of a family-based heaven intensified as he saw so many friends and relatives die. "By and by we shall all get through with the affairs of mortality," he wrote to a friend whose mother had just died, "and the pleasure and joy of meeting, no more to part, with those whom we honor and love will be beyond the power of man to express."[106]

There is a notable uptick in the volume of JFS's official correspondence beginning in the late summer of 1901. He was handling business that had previously fallen to Cannon, and Snow's energy was beginning to flag. JFS corresponded with mission presidents, missionaries, people who needed funds for some project or

284   Chapter 15

another, representatives of safety pin companies, and even the occasional would-be prophet.

One of the perennial tensions within Mormonism centers on the question of revelation. Joseph Smith had, in the earliest period of his ministry, preached that revelation was available to anyone who honestly sought to know the mind of God. The immediate problem, of course, is that some sort of structure had to be imposed if any organized movement were to survive. The solution, worked out in the early 1830s with the Hiram Page incident, among others, was the idea that revelation was hierarchical—that is, one could receive a revelation only about things for which one had responsibility. For example, a man could receive a revelation about his family, but not for the ward he lived in; that would be the purview of the bishop. The bishop could receive revelation for his ward, but not for his stake, and so on, up to the president, who could receive revelation for the entire church.

Although JFS never overcame his temper, he managed, especially in his later years, to develop a level of compassion that offset his anger. He may even have gained a degree of self-awareness. In May 1901, he stood before a congregation in Kamas, Utah, and warned them, "When anger takes hold of a person, he is not safe." Then, getting unusually specific, he warned that "under such influence . . . husbands commit acts of violence that will be stamped upon their brows throughout all their lives."[107] JFS again turned to the subject of marriage in a letter to his son Heber. Marriage, he wrote, will bring nothing but "breakers, storms, and tempests" unless a husband and wife "have temperaments congenial to each other and each a disposition to bear with the other's weaknesses."[108] Whether or not he was thinking of Levira and their failed marriage as he wrote those words, JFS clearly felt privately chastened over his earlier behavior and had apparently cultivated some genuine humility over the decades.

In the late summer of 1901, after completing their ecclesiastical work, JFS and John Henry Smith traveled to the Teton Valley on the Idaho-Wyoming border to establish a new stake. They headed first to Jackson Hole, Wyoming, and then to Yellowstone National Park, JFS's first visit there. During the trip, JFS was shocked by the news that President William McKinley had been assassinated in New York. He told a reporter for the *Deseret News* that he was "unable to do justice to his feelings over the national tragedy."[109] In a letter to McKinley's successor, Theodore Roosevelt, JFS professed that he held McKinley in "the highest possible personal regard and admired him as a statesman."[110]

JFS organized memorial services for the fallen president in the Idaho towns of Chester, Parker, and Rexburg before returning to Salt Lake to prepare for the October 1901 general conference.[111] As the conference got underway and JFS prepared to read the names of the general authorities for a sustaining vote, Snow told him to read his own name as first counselor and Rudger Clawson's as second counselor. Just days later, Snow fell ill and could not attend the 10 October meeting of the First Presidency and the Twelve. During that meeting, JFS received two messages informing him that Snow was on the verge of death. The apostles headed en masse to the Beehive House, where Snow remained "conscious but uncommunicative." As the assembled group watched, Snow slipped away at 3:35 p.m.[112]

Although generally not easily shaken, JFS immediately felt the weight of the world on his shoulders. As he stood over the body of his only senior in the church hierarchy, he was "appalled" because he "fully expected [Snow] to tarry with us until at least a few undertakings should be completed and accomplished." His feelings, he later recalled, were "better imagined than described."[113] The previous April, JFS had spoken at Snow's eighty-eighth birthday celebration, stating, likely with more hope than conviction, that although he was more than twenty years his senior, in reality Snow was "younger both mentally and physically."[114] None of that mattered now.

16 | Presiding High Priest, 1901–1918

Less than a month before Lorenzo Snow died, another man had ascended to high office by dint of a death. Forty-two-year-old Theodore Roosevelt became president of the United States after an assassin's bullet ended the life of William McKinley. Roosevelt reached the apex of the American political pyramid through political machinations, wartime heroics, inherited money, a wide-ranging and powerful intellect, a penchant for self-promotion, and, perhaps his most celebrated quality, sheer grit. Roosevelt had successfully created and marketed an image for himself, and the TR brand served him well.

Joseph F. Smith shared some traits with Roosevelt. Both linked masculinity with violence and physical prowess, and both loved the American West and the various opportunities it provided to indulge in a rugged existence. Both had family connections to thank, in part, for the upward course of their careers. They also shared boundless curiosity, acerbic wit, and intelligence far beyond most of their peers. When Edmund Morris described Roosevelt's internal self as one of "conflict between belligerence and civilized restraint, between animal brutality and human decency, between pessimism and optimism," and as a man operating in a state of containment, "like a volcano sheathed in hardened lava," he could as easily have been describing JFS.[1] Perhaps most importantly, the two men assumed their respective presidencies to face constituencies rife with tensions; they were called to govern at a time demanding great decisions, when the identities of church and nation required a reforging sufficient to face the realities of a new century.

Roosevelt was now leading a nation that could be transformed into an empire, a place where both the industrial and the pastoral poor were growing increasingly agitated by the accumulation of wealth in the hands of a tiny few, where more people from more places were demanding a voice in the political and economic culture of the nation. He led a nation in which religious freedom flourished as it had nowhere else on earth, but where a Protestant coalition still formed the core of the nation's conscience. It was also a nation that killed its presidents at an alarming rate.

Presiding High Priest, 1901–1918   287

JFS's challenges were no less monumental. In some ways, the last seventeen years of his life were among the most frustrating he had ever experienced. He turned sixty-three in 1901, and his health and stamina were not what they once were. In December 1902 he wrote to his son Alvin that the effects of a lifetime of "over work" had begun taking their toll on "the machinery of the body," and that while he had healed from many injuries over the years, they "always remain a reparation, which is never as good as new!"[2] He found the work of presiding over the church increasingly taxing. Moreover, in these years he was obliged to do be involved with the two things he liked least: national politics and big business.

Much has already been written about the three major events in JFS's presidency: the controversy over the Utah-Idaho Sugar Company, the Reed Smoot hearings, and JFS's vision concerning the redemption of the dead. All three events demonstrate the close relationship between Mormonism and American culture, and the first two indicate how little trust most Americans had in Mormons. JFS also faced some of the harshest public criticism of any LDS president since Brigham Young. The *Salt Lake Tribune*, among others, lampooned him mercilessly over his testimony in the Smoot hearings. This ridicule wounded JFS deeply and was compounded by the fact that Frank J. Cannon, a son of George Q. Cannon, left the church and became one of his most vocal critics. As late as 1888, JFS had expressed his belief that Frank Cannon would recognize his "mistakes and errors" and return to the fold, but the press onslaught of the first decade of the twentieth century changed that. For the rest of his life, JFS referred to his former associate as "Furious Judas Cannon." [3]

The increased scrutiny generated by the Smoot hearings forced JFS to deal with the ongoing problem of plural marriage. In fact, one of the most pressing issues in the middle years of his presidency was the need to make sense of Woodruff's 1890 Manifesto. The Manifesto, and the subsequent scaling back of plural marriage, had certainly achieved the desired end when Utah attained statehood in 1896, but it remained for JFS to decide if the church really meant it. In 1901, many Mormons—and probably even more non-Mormons—had their doubts. After all, church leaders had spent most of the previous fifty years preaching the theological centrality of polygamy to Mormonism, with JFS's voice being among the loudest and most voluble. He would have to decide how to accommodate his certainty that the practice of polygamy was vanishing with his equally certain belief that Mormonism could not abandon belief in the principle. After his public humiliation in front of the Smoot committee in 1904, JFS issued a second manifesto on plural marriage. This inaugurated an internal crackdown on church authorities who continued to practice plural marriage, which ultimately resulted in two apostles, one of whom was the son of John Taylor, being dropped from the Quorum of the Twelve.

With the death of Snow, the church lost its last convert president. JFS had watched as legend after legend died off: Joseph and Hyrum Smith, Heber Kimball, George A. Smith, Brigham Young, Wilford Woodruff, John Taylor, George Q.

288   Chapter 16

Cannon, and finally Lorenzo Snow. JFS represented a new generation. He was, quite literally, the first and the last. He was born into the church and represented the first generation of leaders who never knew life outside of Mormonism. He was also the first man to become president after being a member of the First Presidency. But he was the last church president to have seen the face and heard the voice of Joseph Smith, even if only as a very small child.

JFS was always fixated on the "blood of the martyrs," both that which was spilled at Carthage and the remnant that flowed through his veins. He was acutely aware that he was the last remaining link, by blood and personal experience, to the founder of Mormonism. He also felt like the loneliest person on earth. Francis Lyman, an apostle who was presiding over the British mission at the time of Snow's death, sent a letter to JFS immediately upon hearing the news. "We are sorry for you," he wrote, and, seeking to console JFS and to wipe away "the burning tears you are shedding," Lyman reminded JFS that "you have at your back 12 apostles who love you and ... without a quiver of suspicion. In their faith and love of God and you, there is not an unsound spot."[4]

JFS desperately needed such reassurance and support. No matter how difficult the trials he had faced in his life, there had always been someone to look to, to seek out, to lean on. Not now. Not when he needed it most. For the first time in his life, he alone became the face, voice, and heart of Mormonism, the final authority who had to "merit [not only] the confidence and love of our people, [but] the respect of all men." JFS, without hyperbole, wrote that he was "astonished ... at how very weak I am ... how dependent ... how <u>much I need</u> the help of God and my brethren." Despite his self-doubt and trepidation, JFS trusted in the relationship that he had built with his God over the course of his long life. He trusted that the God who, he believed, had healed his mother's oxen on the plains; had heard his desperate, boyish pleadings as he struggled in distant Hawaii; had gifted him with dozens of beautiful children; had comforted him when some of those children were called back; and had preserved JFS's life more times than he could count—he trusted that this God would find a way to use JFS "in His own great work."[5]

When Roosevelt had the U.S. presidency dropped on him unexpectedly, JFS took a moment to send him a letter. "We realize that upon your shoulders has fallen great responsibility, but we fully believe, under the blessings of divine Providence, you will be able to acquit yourself in that way that shall best subserve the interests of your countrymen."[6] Just a month later, the words JFS had written to Roosevelt could have served as a prayer for himself.

There was no question that JFS would move immediately to reorganize the First Presidency. On 16 October 1901, before the Quorum of the Twelve had even voted on the issue, JFS told John Henry Smith that he intended to call John R. Winder and Anthon H. Lund as his counselors. The next day, JFS walked with Apostle Anthon Lund to the meeting of the Twelve and informed him that he intended to organize the presidency. At the meeting, JFS told the group that "it was urgent that some action be taken with reference to the reorganization of the First Presidency."[7] The assembled apostles agreed and unanimously voted to reconstitute the First Presidency with JFS as president and trustee-in-trust of the church, and as president of the Salt Lake Temple.

JFS quickly made two moves to strengthen the influence of his family in the church hierarchy. First, he brought his half brother John, who had been serving as church patriarch since Brigham Young's administration, into his inner circle. In an unprecedented act, JFS insisted that John be the one to set him apart as president of the church, a task ordinarily performed by the new president of the Quorum of the Twelve. He also began inviting John to participate in meetings of the First Presidency and the Twelve from that point on. This must have been somewhat surprising to the other church leaders since JFS and John had drifted apart in the 1890s. "Neither of us darkens the other's door," he wrote in 1895, and "his children and my children are perfect strangers to each other."[8] Whatever the tension had been between them, JFS's accession to the presidency brought them into close contact once again.

The second thing JFS did to strengthen his family's standing was to propose that his oldest son, Hyrum, be called to fill the vacancy in the Quorum of the Twelve created by Snow's death. Eight days after becoming president, JFS formally nominated Hyrum, "as it is my privilege so to do."[9] John Henry Smith cautioned that such a move would no doubt provide fodder for critics of the church who would pounce on the overt nepotism, but JFS dismissed the issue, reminding everyone that enemies would always find something to complain about. John's concern notwithstanding, the apostles voted unanimously to admit twenty-nine-year-old Hyrum Mack Smith to the Quorum of the Twelve.[10]

JFS was the last president of the LDS Church to call sons to the apostleship. He held strong views about the importance of having the Smith family represented in the highest councils of the church; he believed that there was something special, almost supernaturally powerful, in having the blood of Joseph and Hyrum coursing through his veins and those of his descendants. While Joseph Smith's sons had been handed the leadership of the RLDS Church, JFS had watched as Hyrum's descendants were, by and large, ignored in Utah. Even though he had served in the First Presidency, and John as church patriarch, JFS felt that both of them had always been outsiders. This was especially true of John, who had been kept so far from the circles of power under all previous church presidents that he was nearly invisible. JFS even had to persuade Brigham Young to keep John as patriarch when Young wanted him gone.

Even as a member of the First Presidency, JFS had always been the odd man out. Cannon had been the confidant and chief advisor to Taylor, Woodruff, and Snow. He shared rooms, and sometimes beds, with the church presidents he served. When there was a trip to be made, JFS had often been left in Salt Lake to handle the office business, but when he did go along, he typically found his own lodgings.

Also, even if JFS was available, Snow would put off making decisions if Cannon was out of town. JFS later told Lund that he had never felt any sense of connection with Snow, who "constantly kept [me] at arm's length."[11]

Although it may have appeared that JFS was an insider's insider, he certainly never felt that way. Whatever else he had in mind when he assumed the presidency, JFS was determined to reassert the Smith influence that he felt had been intentionally diminished within the church since his father's death. He had always felt that, in the last days of Nauvoo, church leaders "abused" his mother, the faithful woman who accepted Young's authority, at the same time they fawned over Emma Smith, a woman whom JFS viewed as a lying harridan with blood on her hands. With the renewed influence of John Smith, the appointment of Hyrum to the quorum, and the coming appointment of JFS Jr. in 1910, JFS was redressing some long-held grievances.

In December 1901, Brigham Young Jr. wrote JFS a letter which either demonstrates that Young shared JFS's view on this subject or, at the very least, that he recognized how important this was to JFS. On December 22, the day before Joseph Smith's birthday, which usually saw commemorations in Utah, Young wrote that he was "a little disturbed as I have been about a certain matter in relation to your father's memory. The Prophet and Patriarch are indivisible in my mind." To him, it seemed only fair that they should "dwell together in the hearts of the people forever and in our acts in all gatherings and celebrations foster this idea."[12] JFS could not have agreed more.

JFS's selection of Winder and Lund as counselors also carried symbolic importance. He had flanked himself with a polygamist and a monogamist, a businessman and an educator, an Englishman and a Dane—converts both. JFS had reached outside of the Quorum of the Twelve to call Winder, who became his first counselor. Winder had been serving as a counselor in the presiding bishopric since 1889, and before that he had enjoyed a successful career as a businessman and investor. Born in England in 1821, Winder emigrated to Utah in 1853. A polygamist, he had assisted Woodruff in drafting the Manifesto in 1890. In addition to other positive attributes, Winder was known as a fiscal conservative, a pleasant contrast to the controversial Cannon. JFS had kept an eye on Winder for nearly a decade. He had been deeply impressed with his tireless efforts to prepare, under JFS's direction, the Salt Lake Temple for dedication in 1892–1893. Winder's willingness to "work from morning till night, then go home and dream about" the work made him a man JFS could entrust with difficult tasks, knowing they would be done correctly and on time.[13]

Lund joined the church in his native Denmark at the age of twelve in 1856. In 1862 he arrived in Utah and settled near Manti. Lund served as president of the Scandinavian and, later, the European missions when JFS's son Hyrum served as a missionary there, and also as president of the Manti Temple. During this time, Lund was heavily involved in education in Utah Territory as well as in the church.

He had served as an apostle since 1889. Lund did not practice plural marriage, making him something of a novelty among church leaders.

On 31 October 1901, the new First Presidency visited Charles Savage's photo studio to sit for an official portrait. JFS, wearing the glasses he now required all the time resting astride a nose so prominent that it reached almost to his mouth, still displayed the broad shoulders, long, thick arms, and piercing eyes he was known for. Under his double-breasted jacket, however, it was becoming more difficult to conceal the slight thickening around the middle, and his almost completely gray hair and beard marked him as a man not only of many years but also hard experience. A slight drooping of the brow gave his face a quality of resignation, but it was offset by the defiant set of his jaw. Despite the signs of age, JFS appeared healthy, even vigorous, as autumn moved rapidly toward winter.

Mormonism and American Religion during JFS's Presidency

Since the earliest days of Mormonism, the faith had always maintained a sectarian edge. The founding question of Mormonism, after all, was concerned with which church was right. Joseph Smith lived in the world created by the Second Great Awakening, and his religious turmoil was the natural outgrowth of the turbidity of the era.[14] Methodist, Presbyterian, and Baptist itinerant revivalists worked together to get people to accept Christ, but they then moved on, leaving the local churches to fight over the newly converted souls. Joseph Smith's question was implicitly smaller in scope than it appeared. He wanted to know which church, among the newly dominant evangelical groups, was the right one. The answer he claimed to receive from God was that all the churches in the world were in a state of apostasy, and had been ever since the death of the first generation of Christian leaders in the second century.

Over the course of the nineteenth century, the American religious landscape evolved and changed just as Mormonism did. Although Protestant denominations remained culturally dominant, they fractured over slavery in the mid-nineteenth century and began to separate internally over the question of reform. By the time JFS's church presidency began, Mormons and their Protestant sectarian "enemies" had come to parallel conclusions on issues like temperance, Sabbatarianism, and the social evils of prostitution and gambling.

One of the great ironies of American religious history is that Mormonism, which became a deeply conservative movement, initially shared many ideas with the progressive movement known as the "social gospel." The social gospel grew out of Protestant concerns that the nation, which they viewed as fundamentally Christian, was in a state of moral decay. The goal of the social gospellers was to save the nation through civic action. They sought to map their beliefs about the evils of capitalism, poverty, drunkenness, prostitution, slavery, and many other ills onto the legal structures of the nation. The "central goal was to create a righteous

292   Chapter 16

society that could approximate a heavenly kingdom on earth."[15] They believed that social and legal reform would bring about national righteousness and, eventually, the Second Coming of Christ. Of course, Mormons had held similar beliefs for decades. Their goal was the creation of a Zionic community to which the righteous could flee when the destruction accompanying the Second Advent occurred.

JFS found himself in agreement with many of the social gospel's moral tenets and simultaneously repulsed by the "apostate" denominations that preached them. His struggle with the social gospel is emblematic of the larger struggle that formed the basis of his entire presidency: once launched on the course of Americanization—with its growing belief in pluralism, the idealization of the (monogamist) nuclear family, and increasing imperial ambitions—how could the distinctiveness of Mormonism be preserved? How could Mormons cooperate and be fully a part of a nation that JFS had believed for decades was in apostasy and which he had repeatedly declared was run by Satan himself? How could Mormonism claim exclusive title to truth in the American national context? Could, and should, Mormons find a way to pursue both their long-standing project of establishing Zion and the broader project of American nationalism that they had so long rejected?

Nothing symbolizes this struggle more potently than the sight of JFS in front of the Smoot committee in Washington, DC. There he sat, a man who for years had rejected American culture and blamed it for allowing, and even causing, persecutions to rage against him personally and his religion generally, the child of a murdered religious leader, wearing a button on his lapel with a picture of his dead father on it, answering questions posed by men for whom JFS had deep contempt—all in the service of allowing a Mormon apostle to become a U.S. senator, part of the fabric of the very culture that JFS blamed not only for the persecution of his people, but also for his own orphaned state.

One of the ways that JFS managed such agonizing internal conflict was to intensify his lifelong obsession with order. As we have seen, JFS worked for decades to fashion an internally consistent Mormon theological and liturgical landscape; during his presidency he was finally in a position to formally institutionalize these ideas. By 1901, his quest for uniformity and coherence was informed not only by his theological leanings, which had been the driving force behind his efforts since the late 1870s, but also by the new imperative to become less conspicuous on the American cultural landscape. Much to his chagrin, the cost of statehood was far higher than simply suspending the practice of polygamy. He now had to tolerate federal interference in Mormon business affairs. For decades, Mormons in Utah had more or less shaped their economy without legal interference, but this changed during the first decades of the twentieth century. JFS believed it was no one's business how Mormons made money, but he had to cede the regulation of Mormon business interests to the federal government.

Although the church's October 1901 general conference had only recently concluded, JFS called for a special conference to be convened on 10 November at which he would be presented to the body of the church for a sustaining vote. In his first sermon as president of the church, JFS spent most of his time talking about succession in the church and justifying the speed with which he had reorganized the First Presidency. His rhetorical approach contained elements of his broader concern with order. He believed that there existed a divine order to everything, including how the church was to be governed, and that "we have not always carried out strictly the Order of the Priesthood, we have varied from it to some extent." He argued that although his way of doing things appeared to be out of step with historical precedent, he had in fact discovered and fully instituted, for the first time in church history, the true order of things as God intended them to be.[16]

JFS's apologia began with a recitation of the events surrounding the death of Joseph Smith and moved on through the passing of Lorenzo Snow. In the case of the former, JFS said, the "organization [of the First Presidency] might have been effected within twenty-four hours after the death of the Prophet Joseph Smith," and the mistaken choice to run "the government of the church with twelve men at the head was not only cumbersome, but was not fully perfect in the order of the Holy Priesthood as established by the Lord." When Young died, Taylor "followed ... the example of his predecessor," and when Taylor died, "Woodruff hesitated and allowed time to pass before the Presidency was again organized." Lorenzo Snow acted in the proper haste, JFS argued, and instructed JFS to do the same. Thus JFS stood before the assembled Latter-day Saints and proclaimed that his succession to the presidency was done "in strict accordance with the pattern the Lord has established in His Church." JFS had found "the exact channel and course that the Lord has marked out for us to pursue," and he intended to "adhere strictly to the order He has established."[17]

Before the conference began, on the morning of 10 November 1901, JFS had privately broached a discussion with members of the Quorum of the Twelve about the propriety of presenting the patriarch to the church for a sustaining vote after the First Presidency and before the Twelve.[18] The apostles objected, naturally, to the symbolic suggestion that the patriarch, John Smith, outranked them. JFS did not press the matter any further in private, although he did make his position known to the public during the special conference.

Conforming to his long-established pattern of anchoring his doctrinal ideas and policies in carefully culled scriptural citations, he read from section 124 of the Doctrine and Covenants, which states, "First, I give unto you Hyrum Smith, to be a Patriarch unto you, to hold sealing blessings of my Church, even the Holy Spirit of promise." JFS told the congregation that "it may be considered strange that the Lord should give first of all the Patriarch; yet I do not know any law, any revelation or any commandment from God to the contrary." Again, he noted that this was another case in which the divine "order has not been strictly followed from the day we came into these valleys until now," but he did not intend to "make any change at present."[19]

Chapter 16

JFS was clearly seeking to elevate the office of church patriarch, at least in part because it was a hereditary office promised by revelation to the descendants of Hyrum Smith. Increasing the hierarchical stature of that office would ensure an ongoing Smith presence in the highest leadership circles in perpetuity. JFS was never able to work his will in this regard as fully as he wished, but there can be no doubt about his desire to do so.

Not everyone was impressed with JFS's moves on this front. J. Golden Kimball, the notoriously profane and tactless son of Heber C. Kimball, who was not only a brother-in-law to JFS but also a member of the First Council of Seventy, was particularly miffed. Kimball mocked "the appointment of the boy Apostle," referring to Hyrum M. Smith's call to the Twelve, but he reserved his hotter scorn for JFS himself. How dare he "publicly arraign and criticize men that are his superiors in every way," Kimball wondered, when so doing would "not add one cubit to [JFS's] strength or height."[20]

JFS concluded the conference by reminding the church that with the death of Lorenzo Snow, there remained only two "apostles [JFS and Brigham Young Jr.] who had the privilege and honor of being acquainted with the Prophet [Joseph Smith] during his lifetime"—and only one who both knew him and in whose veins the blood of the prophet coursed.[21]

The next seventeen years were filled with unprecedented challenges that JFS, as the public face of the LDS Church and as a relatively heavy-handed administrator, would have to face. As president of the church he occupied an unsheltered place at a time when governmental scrutiny was as high as it had ever been, and when church leaders could no longer go into exile in the hope that the storms would blow over. He faced the gale, and, as we have come to expect from him, he hardly even flinched.

In late 1901 and early 1902, however, the major events of JFS's presidency remained years in the future. His early presidential years were filled with minutiae that would stun modern Mormons. Heber J. Grant found the situation astonishing. Rather than delegating "little details," JFS insisted on reading "every little letter about every trivial thing." Grant thought this was a "waste of a great deal of valuable time."[22] JFS seemed congenitally incapable of delegating to anyone beyond the First Presidency. The last time he had spent so much time chained to a desk was in the miserable summer of 1874. In a monumental act of understatement, he told a mission president in 1902 that it "required very close attention on the part of the Presidency to pick up the ins and outs and get well in hand the business, temporal and ecclesiastical, of the church."[23] And in 1903, he wrote, "My duties keep me constantly engaged during the working hours of the day, and often far into the hours of the night," and he lamented that "the only moments I have for myself are moments purloined from the hour of meals or sleep."[24]

JFS personally dealt with mission presidents who had questions about doctrine or wayward missionaries, and bishops who had complaints about ward matters.

As president of the church, he personally responded to hundreds of letters that, by modern standards, should never have even crossed his desk. He dealt with people unhappy with the dividends they received from various co-ops, people wanting to be sealed to Hyrum or Joseph Smith, requests for divorce, requests for autographed photos, questions about the proper wearing of the temple garment, and the occasional letter claiming to have information relevant to the long-awaited return to Missouri.[25]

By the early twentieth century, these sorts of ideas were increasingly unwelcome and tended to come from people on the fringes of Mormonism. JFS developed a sardonic approach to letters like that. One example is representative of them all. In early 1902, a church member wrote to JFS claiming to have important information "as to how Zion is to be redeemed, and the wisdom of the wise set at naught." JFS responded that he did not "think it would be proper for me to put you to the trouble of imparting to me that knowledge," not least of all because "the time of myself and associates is already fully occupied in things which more immediately concern us."[26]

"Some of the most foolish queries imaginable are coming in from all quarters," JFS complained, including whether Joseph and Hyrum Smith had been resurrected since their bones could not be found. JFS assured his correspondent that "their remains were left in … Nauvoo where, in all probability, their ashes still remain." JFS also found himself in the position of having to quash a rumor circulating widely that he had told a congregation in Idaho that he had seen "the Savior face to face and shook hands with him and saw the nail prints in his hands." JFS stated unequivocally that he "never made any such statement" and that people would do well not to "attribute their fancies" to him.[27]

Other problems brought to JFS's attention were of a personal nature. For example, the wife of a son of the late apostle Franklin D. Richards came to the office with a two-month-old baby. That something untoward had occurred was obvious since the woman's husband had been gone for well over a year. To JFS's horror, the woman initially claimed that her own brother was the child's father. She then changed her story and claimed to have been "seduced" by an unnamed young man. They expected JFS to "tell them what to do." He insisted that they break the news to the husband and "prosecute the guilty party."[28]

A man in Maryland wrote to ask if a woman who had undergone an abortion could be forgiven. JFS responded that, while such an act was indeed "murder" and that "for such a sin she cannot be forgiven in this life," after suffering whatever punishments God sought to inflict, she might in the next life get a "fresh start."[29]

JFS heard from one bishop seeking guidance about what to do with young people who committed fornication but then repented. JFS determined that rebaptism was required, even if no excommunication had taken place. Another bishop inquired about the rebaptism of a woman excommunicated for adultery. JFS authorized the rebaptism, but also required the rebaptism of the husband on the ground

296   Chapter 16

that he "lived with his wife after having been informed of her fallen condition" and had thus become polluted by a sexually "fallen woman."[30]

JFS's strong opinions about sexual morality only intensified as polygamy receded. One of the major arguments that nineteenth-century Mormon leaders deployed in support of polygamy was that it served as a stable outlet for male sexual desires. Prostitution, adultery, and other debauchery were the fate of a society that did not require its males to pay for their sexual satisfaction with marital commitment. When JFS looked at his sons and daughters, he saw people who would have to live sexual lives completely alien to his own experience. He was naturally concerned that the moral decay he had attributed to monogamy would come home to roost among the new generation of Mormon monogamists.

In a 1912 letter to the Parowan stake presidency, JFS wrote that with the introduction of anti-polygamy legislation decades before, "it became very apparent that the then-changed conditions confronting us were going to work out great evil amongst our community, especially among our young people."[31] JFS's views on the issues of sexuality in marriage, both polygamous and monogamous, are made clear in a letter he wrote to a Massachusetts physician in early 1905. Dr. Frank Bellings was writing a book about the "morality and ethics" of various religious and cultural groups, and he had sent JFS a list of frank questions. Impressed with Bellings's objective and respectful posture toward Mormonism, JFS responded with equally, and surprisingly, frank answers.

He first made it clear that the church

> has formulated no special rules governing the [sexual] association of married people, although it can be stated positively that there is a widespread sentiment, a profound conviction, in the Mormon mind, that during the periods of gestation and lactation the wife and mother should be free from sexual cohabitation; such a course being conducive, not only to her health, but to the welfare of her offspring.

JFS used this to segue into a discussion of polygamy, a system which "took cognizance of these things, and sought to meet every emergency." By "emergency," of course, he meant the sexual needs of a man whose wife was pregnant or nursing. In a polygamous marriage, no woman, the argument went, would have to bear the burden of her husband's sexual demands alone. JFS wrote that this division of sexual labor "was the purpose—one purpose at least—for which it was instituted."[32] Without it, JFS believed, both men and women would have more difficult burdens to bear, and he worried about the effects.

JFS's solution was to tighten his already strict view of sexual morality. One of the points of contention during the discussions about Albert Carrington's possible rebaptism (after being excommunicated for adultery) was that previous presidents had been flexible on the subject of sexual morality, even when it came to unchaste missionaries. Until 1907, mission presidents had a great deal of latitude in how to handle missionaries who fell into sexual sin, although they usually consulted the First Presidency. Not infrequently, the missionary was allowed to continue to serve if he or she demonstrated genuine repentance. In 1907, JFS scrapped this policy, replacing it with a far stricter one. Any missionary guilty of fornication or adultery was to be excommunicated by the mission president and sent home "no matter what the circumstances might be."[33] Even a missionary confessing to sexual misbehavior that occurred before his or her call was to be immediately sent home to be dealt with by the bishop who had sent the missionary out.

Throughout his presidency, JFS continued to refine and sharpen the framework for doctrinal elaboration he had developed as early as the 1880s, placing heavier emphasis on the importance of the words of the living prophet. One example will stand for the many we could examine. In 1902, JFS read a book by church member Solomon Stephens entitled *The Philosophy of the Earth and of Man*.[34] In the book, Stephens promoted, among other things, Brigham Young's teachings about Adam being the father of Jesus Christ—and therefore God. Known as the Adam-God doctrine, the concept had never gained much traction among church members, and JFS had always rejected it outright. Stephens went a step further than Young had, arguing that Adam was both Christ and God.

JFS wrote to Stephens, accusing him of taking statements from both Young and Joseph Smith out of context to make his speculative case. More important than JFS's specific response to Stephens's theological opinions, however, was that he set forth the sources of what constituted official church doctrine even more clearly than he had done in the past: the things taught "in sacred and holy places" (meaning the temple endowment), the "utterances of the earthly founder of our faith, the great prophet, seer and revelator to whom Jesus Christ ... made known the truth for the guidance of his people," and those things "contained within the lids of the books recognized and accepted by us as doctrinal standards of the church." Everything, JFS continued, had to be measured against these sources, and "while many things may be true that are not in these books, the fact remains that what is not in them and has not been accepted in General Conference, is not Church doctrine and should not be taught." As for any potential "new" ideas, JFS insisted that such things would come "through the proper channel, His mouth-piece to the church"—meaning, of course, the church president—rather than through "lesser authorities." Doctrinal speculation, he continued, has "nothing to do with [the] present duties of [other] Latter-day Saints."[35] In response to a different theological question from Lillie Golsan, JFS categorically proclaimed that "not even a revelation from God should be taught to this people until it has first been approved by the presiding authority—the one through whom the Lord makes known his will." No idea, teaching, or revelation, "however true," can be "inculcated until proper permission is given."[36]

In these letters we have striking examples of JFS's ongoing effort to create a coherent doctrinal core for Mormonism and to tie the explication and elaboration

298   Chapter 16

of that doctrine to the hierarchy. As in previous decades, JFS wrote of scripture as if the ideas expressed within are self-explanatory and require no interpretation. But, of course, no text speaks for itself, and the unspoken key to JFS's system is that it is the prerogative of the church president to both receive revelation and provide the correct interpretation of earlier revelations accepted as scripture. In response to a question about whether people assigned to the telestial kingdom "required baptism," JFS literally included his official interpretation in the text itself. As he often did in such cases, he prefaced his explanation by pointing out how obvious the answer was. Rhetorically, this provides a powerful incentive for a reader to accept JFS's subsequent interpretation based on the reader's desire to not miss the obvious. In this particular instance, JFS wrote that "the matter is made exceedingly plain in the Book of Doctrine and Covenants," from which he then quoted verses 81–86. However, at two crucial junctures in the text, JFS added his own parenthetical interpretations: "'These are they who received not the gospel of Christ, neither the testimony of Jesus. (Therefore they were not baptized.) These are they who deny not the Holy Spirit. (Because they never received it.)'"[37]

JFS also applied this approach to a question about a passage in the New Testament. In this case, a member of the church inquired what Christ meant when he said "upon this rock will I build my church," a passage that had been theologically problematic since at least the time of the Protestant Reformation. Catholics generally believe that "the rock" was Peter, who, of course, they accept as the first pope. Protestants, again speaking broadly, take this passage to mean that Christ was referring to himself. JFS rejected both readings as "supremely ridiculous," claiming that the "Church of Christ was and is built upon the rock of revelation." Once again, JFS supplied an annotated version of the text reflecting his interpretation: "'and upon this rock (revelation from the Father in heaven) I will build my Church.' The words 'and I say unto thee that thou art Peter' were spoken to emphasize the great principle of Revelation from God."[38]

It is debatable whether JFS's interpretation of those verses is obvious or not, or whether alternate readings are "supremely ridiculous." But what was no longer debatable was whether the president of the church had the final word on scriptural interpretation or not. For JFS, true doctrine was found in the scriptures, and the scriptures meant whatever he said they did. He did express some concern that people had the impression that he intended to "stifle thought and free speech ... or to brand as 'false doctrine' any and every mystery of the kingdom." Nevertheless, he insisted that any doctrine not "clearly and fully defined in the revealed word of God" should not be "promulgated." JFS's emphasis on theological and doctrinal coherence and uniformity required that he scuttle discussion "upon abstruse themes, these partly-revealed principles, respecting which there are such wide differences of belief."[39]

JFS's new emphasis stood in stark contrast to the more freewheeling theological world of mid-nineteenth-century Mormonism, in which apostles openly challenged church presidents on doctrinal interpretations as a matter of course. The genius of JFS's doctrinal system is that it provides not only coherence, but also a veneer of stability that masks its flexibility—something that is essential for the successful adaptation and growth of any religious system. Although the consensus among Mormons is that this type of doctrine codification came to full flower under the direction of JFS Jr. and his son-in-law Bruce R. McConkie, it is perfectly plain that they modeled their approach on the one developed by JFS.[40]

JFS personally responded to dozens of letters of a more banal nature. He wrote to the givers of the many gifts he received, including a spoon bearing the likeness of Joseph Smith. He thanked another donor for the "cheese and kindness." As if the fates were conspiring to him keep frustrated, if not humble, JFS found out the hard way that his new position held no sway with the U.S. Postal Service. He was shocked when the post office refused to take his check to purchase a money order, something that caused him to be delinquent in a payment to a company in Kentucky. "I never carry money with me," JFS somewhat sadly pointed out, begging the creditor's forgiveness for the tardiness of his payment.[41]

JFS took the time to send his sister Martha, always in his thoughts and perpetually struggling to keep her head above water, ten dollars for a Christmas turkey and said he wished he could send more. He also arranged a "monthly remittance" for the "widows of the prophets and apostles and Presidents of the church" consisting of part cash and part tithing scrip. He actively corresponded with shareholders in the Consolidated Wagon and Machine Company in his executive capacity and fielded repeated requests for employment.

JFS found the requests for work particularly frustrating, not only because he had to turn them down, but because he could not understand why they were coming to him. "I am besieged from all quarters for employment," he wrote in 1902, "as if people supposed that I am in possession of the magic wand which I only need to wave to open the door of remunerative employment." "My special duties," he continued, "are ecclesiastical rather than temporal and I am not engaged directly in any business affording employment to men."[42] There could scarcely be a clearer statement of JFS's discomfort with the non-ecclesiastical elements that necessarily devolved upon the president of the church. But he should not have been as surprised as he appeared to be. After all, he was among the most vociferous advocates that there was no appreciable difference between temporal and spiritual matters, but once the full load of that hybrid philosophy rested on his shoulders, he seemed to reconsider the wisdom of it.

In his correspondence during the first years of his presidency, JFS repeatedly referred to the incredible strain under which he struggled, but there were rare moments of comic relief. One such moment came when a man JFS had known in England in the 1870s sent him a newspaper clipping that profiled a reverend named H. Clay Trumbull. The accompanying photograph of Trumbull, however, was actually a picture of JFS. The mystery of how his image ended up mislabeled in an East Coast newspaper was never solved, but it is safe to say that neither JFS nor the Reverend Trumbull found the mistake flattering.[43]

JFS also received dozens of invitations to attend civic events, celebrations, stake conferences, and so forth, and he accepted as many as he could. He spoke frequently to the Young Men's and Young Women's Mutual Improvement Association (YMMIA/YWMIA). In 1903, he gave his first major address to the Relief Society, outlining his vision for that group. One of the first significant vacancies that JFS had to fill when he became church president was that of the General Relief Society president. Zina Young, the previous president, had died in August 1901, and Snow had never named a successor. JFS chose Bathsheba Smith, the widow of George A. Smith and the aunt of JFS's wives Julina and Edna. The apostles accepted his choice, but only on the condition that "younger women" be called as counselors to the seventy-nine-year-old Bathsheba.[44]

JFS did not always enjoy a perfectly harmonious relationship with the Relief Society, but he had certainly come a long way since his 1869 speech in which he openly questioned the usefulness of an auxiliary that would draw women out of the home. In fact, in 1903 he told the assembled women that he did "esteem this Society organized as it was by the Prophet Joseph Smith, one of the most important auxiliary organizations in the church." Perhaps some of his change in attitude can be attributed to the fact that he could now tie the Relief Society directly back to Joseph Smith rather than having to acknowledge that its resurgence in the late 1860s came because of Brigham Young. JFS also probably saw the proliferation of organizations for women during this period as a source of competition for the interests of LDS women. Since the late nineteenth century, organizations founded by women on the national and local levels had been meeting for purposes that ranged from reading clubs to major political reform movements.[45]

JFS often expressed his opinion that men should not join fraternal organizations because it sapped time and resources that ought to be spent in service to the church, so it is not unreasonable to suppose that he held similar views about sororal organizations. Whatever the reason, JFS as church president presented a global vision for the Relief Society in which "the wisdom and influence" of the "mothers and daughters" of Zion would "extend throughout the nation and from continent to continent." What did JFS see as the primary forms that this influence would take? "Charity to the poor, the sick, the afflicted, and the fatherless" topped his list of important duties. Furthermore, and somewhat surprisingly, he saw it as the duty of the society "to assist all you can in giving the daughters of Zion a proper education." The theme that tied all of the responsibilities together was the maintenance of the family unit. It was their job to teach families about the "relations which should exist between husband and wife, between parents and children, and between children themselves."[46]

Despite JFS's newfound enthusiasm, he believed that the sphere of the Relief Society's influence extended over women and children, but there it stopped.

Relief Society sisters could "assist the wife to be wise and prudent, the mother how to manage her children and household affairs … and the children to appreciate the sacred ties that bind them to their parents," but they must never forget that they were "subject always to the Authority of the Holy Priesthood." In the course of the relatively short sermon he gave to the Relief Society in 1903, JFS mentioned no fewer than three times that it had been founded by Joseph Smith. To no one's surprise, he never so much as whispered the name of the society's founding president, Emma Smith.[47] When Bathsheba Smith died in 1910, JFS replaced her with Emmeline B. Wells, and in a move that echoed on the distaff side what had been going on in the priesthood hierarchy, Wells's new counselors were very close to JFS. The first counselor was his daughter Clarissa and the second counselor was his wife Julina.

The overall effect of the demands of the church presidency was that JFS was overwhelmed. "I am constantly under strain to meet my ever recurring duties and have scarcely a moment to devote to my own affairs, or to the necessities of my family."[48] He found himself unable to spend any significant time with his exponentially expanding family, which by 1903 had grown to include thirteen grandchildren. On one of the rare occasions when he escaped the city for some time on Salt Lake, he returned with a vicious sunburn that did nothing to make his time in the office more enjoyable.[49]

During the early years of his presidency, JFS also began to display an uncharacteristic testiness when his children asked him for money or other support. "It would seem," he wrote to his son Edward, "that it has come to the point with me where it is necessary for everybody to look after himself."[50] He complained, rather dramatically, to one correspondent that he "runs long hours [but] how long I can endure it remains to be seen."[51] The demands on his time were such that "it has been almost impossible to get time for personal correspondence."[52] When he did get around to writing personal letters, it was usually only after the office staff had left. By this point, he was in the habit of dictating letters, which were then typed up by his secretaries. When he worked late on private and personal correspondence, he wrote in his own hand.

Many of these handwritten letters were to his children, who were doing a great variety of things. JFS always enjoyed corresponding with his children on missions, and in the first years of his presidency he took great pleasure in corresponding with his son Coulson, who was serving as a missionary in Hawaii. But the anxiety that had plagued him so severely when he was away from home sometimes flared up when he thought about his missionary children, particularly Coulson. JFS, apparently worried that his son lacked sufficient masculinity, hoped the mission would "develop what manhood there is in him."[53] When word reached JFS and Coulson's mother, Alice, that the young man was suffering from a swollen leg, both parents wrote to Coulson's mission president, and JFS wrote to Coulson, chastising him for keeping his ailment a secret and admonishing him to write to the mission president "stating to him your <u>true</u> condition."[54] Most of the time, however, the letters were not quite so dramatic or alarming. More often, these letters just put JFS in a pensive mood. However difficult and trying his early years in the islands had been, there had been a simplicity in his life there that must have been terribly appealing to him as the burdens of the presidency and age exacted their due.

"I read your letters with interest," JFS wrote to Coulson, adding that his greatest hope was that his son was "progressing favorably in the language." "Do not stop short of mastering it," he admonished, "so that you can make yourself clearly understood to the natives on any and all subjects." JFS, who had always prided himself on his facility with the Hawaiian language, sheepishly admitted that although he had written to Coulson in Hawaiian, he found the task unusually difficult. He could manage nothing better than "broken language." Time, like a thief in the night, would not leave even this untouched. As JFS sat alone in the semidarkness of his office, stroking his gray beard as he always did when lost in thought, he concluded his letter to Coulson by repeating the admonition he had repeated to himself countless times over the years, and which he would need to hear again soon: "Be a man, in the truest and broadest sense of the term, and never flinch from the right."[55]

In early 1902, JFS had declared, either out of desperate hope or sheer psychological denial, that "the ecclesiastical position occupied by me places me beyond the pale of politics."[56] In 1898, Utah Democrat B. H. Roberts was elected to the U.S. House of Representatives. Although nearly a decade had passed since the 1890 Manifesto, many Americans remained suspicious of Mormonism and its ongoing relationship with polygamy. The House refused to seat Roberts on the grounds that he was a practicing polygamist. The impetus for this opposition came in part from Presbyterians in Utah led by the Princeton-educated pastor of Salt Lake's First Presbyterian Church, William Paden.

A committee of nine congressmen launched an investigation into the matter. Lorenzo Snow and other church leaders recognized that if the federal government objected to the presence of practicing polygamists in elected or appointed positions, the church's influence in national politics would be greatly eroded. The renewed aggression aimed at polygamists whose marriages predated the Manifesto worried church leaders.

In order to assuage the concerns of the congressional committee, and the antipolygamy crusaders putting pressure on its members, the church launched an internal investigation to get a sense of just how many polygamists were living in Utah and how old they were. The demographic information did not come in soon enough to help with the Roberts case, but JFS began reviewing the data in 1902. According to that data, there had been about 2,500 polygamist families in Utah in 1890, a number that had dropped to fewer than 900 by 1902 due to death, divorce, and individuals moving out of Utah Territory. The report concluded that, in addition to the dramatic drop in the number of polygamist families, those men who were engaged in the practice were, overwhelmingly, of an "advanced age."[57]

Utah Senator Kearns had asked for this information to combat yet another proposed constitutional amendment on plural marriage. The message that the church wanted to get across was that polygamy, with no new marriages being performed, would die out on its own within a couple of decades. But this position raised an uncomfortable question, one that would be put to JFS in the most public manner possible: Was it true that no more plural marriages were being authorized and contracted by church leaders? The answer, of course, was no. Since 1890, plural marriages had continued to be authorized and performed, especially in Mexico. JFS had given tacit approval to one such marriage in 1892 and possibly participated in the post-Manifesto plural marriage of Abraham Cannon in 1896.

Between 1898 and 1901, JFS personally authorized several of these marriages, occasionally in direct opposition to Lorenzo Snow's wishes. Snow had tried to clamp down not only on plural marriages, but also on cohabitation. He wanted to ensure that no polygamist men would have more children with their plural wives. In a meeting of the presidency and the Twelve in late 1899, Snow ordered that "brethren must not have children born to them by their wives here in Utah."[58] JFS obviously disregarded the admonition, as he had three children born in Utah after this meeting.[59]

The question remained open and was only revisited when occasional waves of anti-polygamy sentiment arose, such as with the Roberts and Smoot cases. In the statement prepared and signed by JFS protesting any anti-polygamy amendment in 1902, he cited the statistics of declining numbers of living polygamists, and asserted again the false claim that "[plural] marriages have entirely ceased," a statement he endorsed "most emphatically and without any reservation." But he also defended the rights of pre-Manifesto polygamists to associate with, and provide for, their families.

> There are still some persons living who, having contracted plural marriages many years ago, under a covenant and contract which they regard as binding for all eternity, cannot conscientiously view those relationships as dissolved, nor cast aside the women and children dependent upon them.[60]

In April 1900, Snow called Reed Smoot, the son of the prominent Provo civic and church leader Abraham Smoot, to fill a vacancy in the Quorum of the Twelve. Reed's business acumen and political ambition helped him gather not only money but also ecclesiastical attention. Smoot had his eye on the U.S. Senate and wanted to run in 1901, but Snow would not allow it because he had already promised church support to Republican Thomas Kearns, a non-Mormon mining magnate. Kearns handily won a four-year term and headed to Washington in 1901. The ending of the Roberts debacle and the fizzling out of interest in the polygamy amendment led JFS to prematurely breathe a sigh of relief.

The respite would not last for long. JFS did not share Snow's political interest in Kearns, so once Snow was out of the picture, Kearns no longer had his most

304   Chapter 16

important political patron. When Kearns paid him a visit, JFS made it clear to the senator that he, as president of the church, had no interest in supporting a gentile candidate when a perfectly good Mormon one was available. Although JFS made it clear that Smoot was the candidate he wanted in Washington, his rebuff of the senator would bear bitter fruit in the coming years after Kearns purchased the *Salt Lake Tribune* and began using it as a vehicle for punishing JFS for his unfriendliness.

When Paden and other opponents of polygamy got wind of Smoot's campaign for the Senate, the controversy once again sprang to life. In late November 1902, a reporter named Copp from the Associated Press met with the First Presidency "to obtain from President Smith a statement from him in regard to certain charges made by the ministers of Utah to the effect that polygamous marriages were being solemnized again." JFS agreed to answer questions as long as they were submitted, and answered, in writing. Copp went right to the heart of the matter with his first question: "Does the church solemnize or permit plural marriages?" JFS's answer was, by any measure, a lie. "Certainly not," he responded, seeming to bristle at the impertinence of the question. "The church does not perform or sanction or authorize marriage in any form that is contrary to the laws of the land."[61] He may have been trying to use very specific language regarding "the laws of the land" to answer the question with regard only to the United States. JFS knew that marriages had been and continued to be performed in Mexico, but he went on to blame enemies of the church who conflated new plural marriages with the ongoing support of plural families.

In private, JFS insisted that the church could not and would not require men who had previously entered into plural marriages to end their support of their families, and that the Manifesto never intended that it should. Shortly after it was presented, Woodruff addressed this subject explicitly: "This manifesto only refers to future marriages, and does not affect past conditions. I did not, could not and would not promise that you would desert your wives and children. This you cannot do in honor."[62]

As historian D. Michael Quinn has demonstrated, however, between 1890 and 1904, church leaders took a dizzying array of public and private positions on the matter. JFS made comments in private that did not comport with statements he made in public, sometimes under oath. Given the contradictory statements, JFS's actions bear more weight than his words.[63] Those actions, especially the siring of multiple children after the Manifesto, indicate that JFS supported cohabitation for previously married polygamists. He found that the censuses of polygamists in the United States carried out by the church in 1890, 1899, and 1902 came in handy in his interview with Copp. He reported that between deaths, migration to Mexico and Canada, and divorces, the original number of polygamists in 1890 had been reduced by "63%, leaving then only 897, the great majority of whom were of advanced age." JFS assured Copp and, he hoped, his readers by saying, as he had before, that "the number of polygamous families will soon be reduced to zero."[64] Nobody—probably not even JFS—believed that. Certainly the U.S. Senate found it hard to swallow when it came time for Smoot to take his seat.

JFS's evasive response to Copp foreshadowed his performance before the Smoot committee. In fact, Copp moved to the topic of Smoot next when told, "It is widely asserted that Apostle Reed Smoot ought not to be elected United States Senator, because he is a high Church dignitary, and his Church position is compared to that of a cardinal or archbishop in other ecclesiastical bodies," and then asked, "How do you regard this objection?" By invoking Catholicism, a culture that in 1902 was still perceived as alien by many Americans, Copp broached an issue that was broader than polygamy. Just as Catholics took orders from the pope, a Mormon apostle-senator would, many feared, be a puppet for the LDS Church leadership. JFS responded by arguing that the office of apostle did not closely parallel that of an archbishop or cardinal because LDS apostles were not financially supported by the church and continued to engage in various professions while serving.

JFS was technically correct in this argument, although he intentionally exaggerated the independence of apostles. He made one other statement, however, that was untrue. Addressing an unspoken question, JFS asserted that "it is not true that he has been put forward by the church as a candidate for public office." It's possible to quibble over what JFS meant by the phrase "put forward," but the truth is that the First Presidency made it known that they endorsed Smoot's candidacy. It was widely understood that the church and the Utah gentiles would "take turns" when it came to senatorial elections. Smoot had wanted to run in 1900, but opposition from none other than Theodore Roosevelt shut it down. The next cycle belonged to Smoot, and the First Presidency backed him. Before he left Utah for Washington, Smoot received a priesthood blessing from JFS to send him on his way.[65]

The Smoot Controversy

In January 1903, the Republican-controlled Utah legislature elected Smoot as U.S. senator by a 43 to 16 margin. One of the first indications that Smoot's election would prove problematic came in January 1903, when Senator Kearns informed John Henry Smith, who in turn reported to the First Presidency, that Smoot would likely "not be permitted to take his seat in the U.S. Senate even if elected by the Utah Legislature, for the reason that to permit an Apostle to sit in the Senate would have a bad effect, and perhaps prevent Roosevelt's re-election."[66]

Roosevelt himself suggested that an apostle-senator would be an unwelcome addition to government, a statement that Rudger Clawson, and JFS, saw as "an unwarrantable interference on the part of the president and deserves to be treated with cold indifference (as doubtless it will be)."[67] Local papers in Utah—except for the *Deseret News*, of course—published article after article condemning

306   Chapter 16

the church's "power play." The intensity of the panic was indeed striking, but it was largely contained to Utah. Local overreaction was one thing, but no one knew what would happen when Smoot actually got to Washington.

Soon after Smoot arrived, he sent JFS a telegram indicating that "Leilich's polygamy charge prevents oath. Excited public and the press against our interests."[68] Senator J. C. Burrows and the leader of the Methodist missions in Utah, John Leilich, had filed separate petitions of protest arguing that Smoot should not be permitted to be take the senatorial oath because the First Presidency and the apostles held "supreme authority in all things temporal and spiritual," including "political dictation" and "belief in polygamy and polygamous cohabitation." Furthermore, Smoot, as an LDS apostle, "sought not only [to] connive at violation of, but protect and honor violators of the laws against polygamy and polygamous cohabitation."[69]

JFS responded aggressively at first, suggesting that charges of libel ought to be brought against Leilich. Although that never came about, he believed that "Lielich's false statement will prove boomerang on ministers' association," and he advised Smoot to "keep cool, say little, keep facts prominent. There have been no plural marriages by the church since the manifesto, therefore there are no records of them."[70] What he meant, of course, is that since there were no records of the post-Manifesto marriages, they could not be proven; therefore, as far as the law was concerned, they never happened.

On 5 March 1903, Smoot sent a triumphant telegram notifying JFS that he had been "sworn in without objection. Great applause. Public sentiment is favorable." He cautioned JFS to ensure moderation in the church's periodicals to avoid unnecessarily inflaming opposition again, but he concluded that "nine chances to one will [we] hear no more of it."[71] But they would hear more of it. Much more.

As late as May 1903, JFS still believed that not much would come of the opposition to Smoot. He was amused at how the "Sectarian howlers are very much moved in wrath.... How they chatter, how they rage!" he wrote to Charles Nibley. "Is it true 'whosever the gods would destroy they first make mad?'" he asked lightheartedly. "If so, the ministers are doomed!"[72] Later, JFS noted gleefully that after the recent Methodist conference in Salt Lake, during "which they had to unload the usual quantity of anti-Mormon venom," Leilich found himself "relieved of his Utah charge and relegated to Scranton, Pa."[73]

By the summer, Presbyterian leaders in Utah had joined forces with "some of the Women's Leagues and Societies in an active campaign [to accomplish] the unseating of Senator Reed Smoot." Although representatives from various organizations apparently hired private detectives to find evidence of post-Manifesto plural marriages, a grand jury failed to return a bill of indictment. JFS gloated that this should "cause them some reflections before continuing their efforts." He had some reason to believe that resistance to Smoot on the national stage might be nominal.[74]

In 1904, JFS was elated to be invited to attend the Louisiana Purchase Exposition (informally called the World's Fair). He traveled by private railcar to St. Louis, where President Roosevelt and a host of other dignitaries spoke over the course of the three-day opening ceremony. JFS spent time with various dignitaries who, to his apparent surprise, treated him without any evident prejudice or condescension. JFS had dealt with people all over the world, but almost always in a sectarian capacity in which he viewed others as enemies or, at the very least, rivals. At the Louisiana Purchase Exposition, JFS was accepted as a man of importance to the nation.

JFS doubtless read more victory into this development than was warranted, but there is evidence that he may have suspected at least some degree of continued scrutiny on the Smoot matter. Throughout 1903, JFS had become increasingly circumspect in his correspondence with regard to plural marriage. He made a point of telling friends, in writing, that no plural marriages had been authorized or performed by the church since 1890. To his friend Samuel Woolley, then president of the Hawaiian mission, JFS wrote that no church leader could possibly be in legal danger "for there have been no plural marriages in this judicial district since the issuance of the manifesto."[75] JFS, of course, knew this to be untrue. Why would he include such a statement in his letter to Woolley? While we can never know with certainty, it is possible that he foresaw the possibility of having his official correspondence scrutinized in legal proceedings and therefore seeded the letterpress books with denials. In any event, there were more frustrating cases in which men attempted to take plural wives by falsely claiming to have been given permission from JFS. JFS wrote to one of these men in Hawaiian to obscure the content of the letter. He warned him that he had seen a copy of a letter the man had circulated indicating JFS's complicity, and that if he did not recant, he was in danger of being tried for his membership. To enter new plural marriages, JFS wrote, "ia mea he hewa" [is a sin].[76]

By early 1904, matters had reached the point that JFS was required to testify in Washington. In January, he wrote to Smoot that "since it pleases our 'friends the enemy' to insist on an investigation of Mormonism, we are altogether willing." After all, he wrote, somewhat sarcastically, "we are pleased to have another opportunity of presenting the doctrines of the church ... before the world. This we have been striving to do for the last seventy years." JFS's aggressive tone foreshadowed his testimony at the forthcoming hearings: "Don't shrink from the issue," he admonished Smoot, "tell them to come ahead." JFS's attitude probably exacerbated an already explosive situation. Smoot believed that if he could keep the investigation focused on his own life as a monogamist and a well-known independent thinker among Mormons, the prosecutor, R. W. Tayler, and the Senate Committee on Privileges and Elections would have little ammunition. JFS, however, insisted in the same letter that the committee launch a "full and complete investigation of our religion in all its phases."[77]

While the committee would have done this anyway, JFS's open invitation hampered Smoot's attempt to blunt the investigation. He telegrammed JFS asking if

308   Chapter 16

he would prefer testifying before a traveling subcommittee in Utah or travel to Washington. JFS replied that it was "immaterial," but that he would just as soon travel to Washington.[78] Unfortunately, JFS's journals from this period are either nonexistent or unavailable to scholars, so we cannot know his private reaction to this summons. One thing is certain: JFS had no fear of the lawmakers he would face in Washington, and he was far more intelligent, wily, and cunning than they could possibly have imagined.

Although JFS had few people to turn to for advice or inspiration, by sheer coincidence he received a letter in December 1903 from Gabriel Huntsman. Huntsman had been a handcart pioneer and a bodyguard for John Taylor in the 1850s. JFS admired handcart pioneers above all others, and this particular one he respected even more than most.[79] Having lost track of Huntsman, he had assumed that he, along with so many of the pioneer generation, had died. The letter gave JFS new energy and a renewed sense of purpose. Reviewing all of the sacrifices and hardships Huntsman endured, JFS proclaimed,

> if I admire a man, it is the man who grasps a good thing and stays by it. Who starts on the right path and never quits it. Who never goes back on his people nor his principles and who would, if need be, die for his friends and the truth! Who cannot afford to quit when the goal of our hopes is just within our reach.[80]

It is difficult to read JFS's words outside of the context of the upcoming Smoot hearings. He knew, of course, what he would be asked about, and he knew that he would do everything in his power to convince the committee that Mormons were loyal Americans and that polygamy was a thing of the past. The latter would require some measure of obfuscation, if not outright lying. But JFS had a flexible concept of honesty. In 1885, he explained to Heber J. Grant that his "rule is not to remember what I want to forget."[81] And in 1909 he advised his son Elias Wesley, "Even the truth should not be said at all times ... it is not lying, nor deceitful ... to withhold from speaking unpleasant truths." He also reminded him to live by the maxim that one should "never attempt the difficult task of telling all you know."[82]

At this point in his life, JFS was facing some unpleasant, or at least uncomfortable, truths about himself. On one hand, he remained deeply committed to the particular character of nineteenth-century Mormonism, with its insularity, its aggressive rejection of gentile culture, its ideals of self-sufficiency and chosenness, and its loyalty to the teachings of Joseph Smith. Could he go back on that? On the other hand, his heart burned with the desire to see Mormonism, broadly conceived, succeed in becoming recognized and respected as a significant force in the nation and in the world. He knew, of course, that Mormonism would never receive recognition and respect without changes to some of its more infamous practices.

JFS arrived on 2 March 1904 for the Smoot hearings with a far less generous attitude than the one he expressed a few months earlier, when he said that he welcomed the chance to give the church more exposure. In fact, JFS had no intention of giving an inch to Robert W. Tayler, the committee's attorney. JFS began resisting immediately, insisting on "affirming" rather than "swearing" to tell the truth. Then Tayler asked if JFS and "the apostles" held the titles of "prophets, seers, and revelators," to which JFS replied, "They are sustained as such." Tayler, sensing some evasion, pressed for a more direct answer. "I want to know if they do not hold that title now." JFS retorted, "If they are sustained they must have that title."[83]

The only reason JFS could have had for not answering the initial question with a "yes" was that he did not feel like being helpful. He gave a similar performance when asked about the "standards of authority in the church." "Do you mean the books?" JFS asked blandly, and then proceeded to name them: the Bible, the Book of Mormon, the Doctrine and Covenants, and the Pearl of Great Price. Tayler asked if that represented a comprehensive list of authoritative books. "They are the only books that I know of that have been accepted by the church," JFS replied, as if there could possibly be some of which he did not know.[84]

Tayler then led JFS through a series of questions in which he summarized the events of the coming forth of the Book of Mormon. JFS agreed with his characterization, but when Tayler later made reference to this exchange by asking whether "the Book of Mormon came in to existence in the manner you have described," JFS corrected him, saying, "Which *you* have already described." Tayler soon found himself tangled up by JFS's stubborn refusal to give a simple answer to any question. His frustrating replies led Tayler through a lengthy and tortuous discussion of the nature of the copyright to James Talmage's *Articles of Faith*, a topic that Tayler did not want to waste time on. On and on this went. When Tayler asked if JFS knew who owned the *Deseret News*, he replied that he "knows who owns the building that it is in." After several more questions and various incursions by the very confused committee chairman, JFS admitted that he "presumed he knew that the church owned it."[85] If Tayler thought he faced an easy mark, he knew by this point that he was mistaken.

The Smoot hearings have received considerable attention from scholars, most recently from historian Kathleen Flake. Her insightful and thorough treatment of the complex issues surrounding Smith's testimony and the general impact that the hearings had on the relationships among the church, mainstream Protestantism, and American government is the best work on the subject.[86] However, my interest in the hearings is limited here to their impact on JFS's life, so a brief summary of the basic themes, outcomes, and fallout of the hearings, followed by a discussion of how these issues relate to JFS on a personal level, will suffice.

First, controversy erupted within the church over JFS's statement that he had received "no revelation" other than a confirming witness of the "truthfulness" of

Mormonism.[87] Second, and closely related to the first, was concern on the part of many Mormons about the general nature of his testimony. JFS had been known for decades for his bracing, if not abrasive, frankness, but in the Smoot transcripts, he appeared as a man with something to hide and a propensity for aggressive obfuscation. JFS received almost immediate pushback from church members on these issues. On 20 March 1904, he received a letter from O. C. Wixom, a Mormon in Canada who found it impossible to believe that JFS had not simply answered "yes" to Tayler's question about JFS being a "prophet, seer, and revelator."[88] JFS responded that the "synical prosecutor" was a "fool" who, if JFS had answered the question in the simple affirmative, would have accused him of "blasphemy." Whether Tayler intended to do so is irrelevant because JFS thought he would and so crafted his response based on that assumption. He further justified his testimonial style by citing the example of Jesus in the New Testament, who, when asked if he were the Christ, replied, "Thou has said." "Why," JFS asked, incensed, "did He not answer 'I am'?"[89]

Aside from providing some insight into his reasoning, JFS's reply to Wixom is also an example of how he reacted to criticism on the issue. In the space of a single page, JFS repeatedly intimated that the writer was either not a member of the church or was a stupid and impudent one. "If you are a member of the church in good standing," JFS jabbed, "you should have known yourself whether the office I hold is entitled to the spirit of revelation and prophecy or not." In other words, he maintained the bizarre position that a faithful member of the church would already know that JFS was a prophet, seer, and revelator, so it did not matter how JFS answered the question. JFS ended the fiery missive by reiterating his "surprise at your question" before closing by expressing his doubt that the author was "even a Mormon."[90]

The truth is that JFS was honestly perplexed by the entire Smoot circus—all of this outrage over "a handful of honest old men [who they want to keep] from living in the status of plural families, which they had long before the law prohibiting the same." Why, he wondered in a 9 April 1904 letter to Smoot, is it such a national priority to deprive these elderly men from "feeding, clothing, and educating [their families] until their short span of life is run and they may go down into their graves" secure in the knowledge that they "abode true" to their responsibilities? If the "National Salons" insist on making a point to "punish and insult and degrade this little handful of men who are rapidly passing away ... historians will laugh at their folly and write them down ASSES in the broadest sense."[91]

JFS was at least as furious over the allegations of church control over political affairs. Immediately upon returning, he had written to Smoot, still smoldering with rage over the accusations. "This is a false cry that has come down from the old Territorial days through the lineage of the now defunct 'Liberal Party,'" he wrote, referring to the political party that stood opposed to the Mormon People's Party before the political realignments of the 1890s. If the LDS Church controlled politics in Utah, JFS asked, how could one explain the presence and relative success of such an "immoral" political organization? If the Mormon leadership did control politics, he continued, why were there so many "saloons, gambling halls, and brothels" in Utah? These were things that the Liberal Party had agitated for in their effort to "break down the moral influence of the Mormon Church and people."[92] JFS claimed not to understand how the politicians in Washington could look at Utah's checkered moral quality and still believe that the LDS Church leaders called the shots. "I am misjudged," he declared in a 5 January 1905 letter to William Glasmann. "I am falsely charged with power and deeds I am innocent of!"[93]

There is no doubt that JFS resented being questioned so relentlessly at the Smoot hearing, especially by men whom he believed to be his moral inferiors. *Harper's Weekly* published a photograph of him that spoke volumes. JFS appears to have his jaw clenched and his eyes slightly narrowed and looking sideways, and his mouth in a sneer that, although hidden, made an unnatural slope of his thicket of facial hair. *Harper's* reported that JFS had poor "control over his temper," a judgment reached on the basis of his curt answers.[94] Had they been more familiar with JFS, they might have known that by limiting himself to obfuscation and the occasional snappish response, he was exerting an extraordinary level of self-control. He may not have been happy, but he was not confused.

In private, JFS rejected the stated premises of the hearings. The furor was not about Smoot, and it was not about polygamy. He grew tired of the argument that Smoot should resign. "If Reed Smoot is the cause of all of our trouble," he asked, "why do they not say that he is also the cause of Fred Dubois's opposition to our people in Idaho?" Others claimed that "the cause of all our troubles and persecutions was plural marriage," to which JFS said, "We knew all the time that it was not the cause." JFS expressed frustration at the inability of so many Mormons to see "the real causes: 1st it is the world against Zion, and 2nd, the disappointment of ambitious politicians and office-seekers in failing to get Church influence to boost them into official positions" (by whom he primarily meant Thomas Kearns).[95]

But the second cause was incidental anyway, from JFS's point of view. "The world against Zion" was a contest that would last until Jesus returned and ended it once and for all. The actors changed, but the play remained the same. Whatever else JFS may or may not have been, it is indisputable that his primary orientation to everything—including politics, economics, and sex—was grounded in his religiously binary worldview. He was not motivated by money or power, although he certainly would have liked more of the former and sometimes used too much of the latter. This is why the questions about his fitness as a "revelator and seer" knocked him off balance. It was the only question that the committee asked of him that he also asked of himself. More than a decade later, this issue still stuck in JFS's craw.

Lund argued that because so many church members were beginning "to doubt the sincerity ... of President Smith before the investigating committee," JFS would have to make a public statement to both the church and the world that plural

312   Chapter 16

marriage was finished for good.[96] Discussion of such a pronouncement began as soon as JFS returned from testifying. Franklin S. Richards was "very urgent that something be said" at the upcoming general conference about JFS's testimony. On 4 April, the available apostles and the First Presidency met and "discussed the wisdom of saying something to pacify the country." Rudger Clawson and Abraham Woodruff both strongly objected. Woodruff argued from emotion, objecting to any statement "against the principle which had given him birth and which would tend to obliterate it."[97] Lund, who was neither born into polygamy nor a polygamist himself, had become a voice to which JFS always listened and his position prevailed.

"We are living in peculiar times," JFS told the congregation at the April 1904 general conference. "I am going to present a matter to you that is unusual," he continued, "and I do it because of a conviction which I feel that it is a proper thing for me to do." Knowing that reading the statement might diminish him in the eyes of church members, he wanted it clearly understood that he was not responding to pressures, either external or internal. This was his own doing.

"Inasmuch as there are numerous reports in circulation," the statement began, echoing the first line of Joseph Smith's written history, which begins with the phrase "owing to the many reports which have been put in circulation by evil-disposed and designing persons."[98] Intentional or not, the similarity is striking. Both JFS and his uncle framed their explanatory statements as corrections. JFS continued by stating that no plural marriages had been "solemnized with the sanction, consent, or knowledge of the church of Jesus Christ of Latter-day Saints" since 1890.[99]

Was this a lie? It certainly gave the impression that no authorized plural marriages had been contracted, and, of course, that was the impression JFS intended it to have. But that is not exactly what it *said*. The statement gave anthropomorphic qualities to the church that it could not possibly have. A church cannot sanction anything. Humans acting in an official capacity within the organization must do that. JFS did not deny that plural marriages had occurred after the Manifesto, neither did he deny that church leaders approved of them. He did not lie, but his statement was intentionally deceptive and therefore dishonest. However, it was the next part of the statement that carried the more important implications for JFS and the church:

> I hereby announce that all such marriages are prohibited, and if any officer or member of the church shall assume to solemnize or enter into any such marriage he will be deemed in transgression against the church and will be liable to be dealt with, according to the rules and regulations thereof, and excommunicated therefrom.[100]

In this JFS did not equivocate or obfuscate.

Still, confusion persisted among many Latter-day Saints about plural marriage as a principle and a practice. Certainly, the church, and JFS himself, had a history of being double-tongued on the subject of polygamy, and some of the apostles disapproved of JFS's newfound forthrightness. Abraham O. Woodruff was so irate about "the Second Manifesto" that, just weeks after it was issued, "he offered himself to May Eldredge to be her husband."[101] Woodruff's attempt was stymied by the young woman's mother, and Woodruff himself was silenced by the grave when he succumbed to smallpox in August.

Finally, JFS had to do what Woodruff did not. He had to apply the ecclesiastical powers of disfellowshipping and excommunication to publicly discipline church leaders and members who refused to comply with the 1904 declaration. Most importantly, this meant that two members of the Quorum of the Twelve, Matthias Cowley and John W. Taylor, would be dropped from the quorum and disciplined. They had not yet appeared before the committee, but JFS promised to remedy that.

When he first got back to Utah from Washington, JFS made a half-hearted effort to locate the two men. In early April, he wrote to Smoot that he had not "heard even one word" from either of them despite "having written and telegraphed in various directions for them." He suspected that Taylor was in Canada and Cowley was touring the "Northwestern States Mission." JFS, rather laconically, guessed that "they will turn up somewhere ere long." Besides, he mused, he ought to let "the imperious Czar hunt up his own witnesses!"[102]

As the months wore on, however, and the pressure on Smoot continued to grow, Taylor and Cowley were running out of time. Most members of the Quorum of the Twelve wanted them to resign. Others thought that Smoot should resign instead and spare the church any further exposure. Heber J. Grant, in particular, went to great lengths to intervene with JFS on their behalf. In January 1906, he wrote to him, pleading "from the bottom of my heart for my brethren—even if Reed has to resign if that would do any good in their case." Grant felt indebted to Taylor for a blessing that he had pronounced promising a resurgence in his financial condition; a blessing which did indeed come to pass. Grant also argued that he had been counseled by Brigham Young Jr. to take a plural wife after the Manifesto and had intended to do so, but encountered logistical problems. "It is circumstances that have prevented me from being guilty," he wrote, adding that Taylor and Cowley "have done no more than I had intended to do."[103] JFS was thus forced to choose between getting rid of Cowley and Taylor, thereby quelling the national irritation with apparent Mormon recalcitrance, or throwing Smoot under the proverbial bus by dropping him from the quorum, thus bringing an end to the apostle-senator conundrum.

Religions vanish or thrive on such decisions. Although not without significant difficulty, JFS ultimately decided to set his deeply held personal beliefs aside and act in what he thought—correctly, it turned out—would be in the best long-term interests of Mormonism. However, it took a long time for him to make a move. Six months after he had solicited letters of resignation from Cowley and Taylor,

314   Chapter 16

he decided that he had to accept them. At the April 1906 general conference, JFS announced that the two had been dismissed from the quorum. Grant then lobbied JFS to appoint Anthony Ivins, president of the only LDS stake in Mexico, as a replacement. Given Ivins's close association with post-Manifesto plural marriages in Mexico, JFS felt that it was an inopportune moment to elevate him to such a prominent position.[104] He opted instead for George F. Richards, the brother of JFS's wife Sarah.

The replacement of Taylor and Cowley did not put a stop to JFS's problems with plural marriage. The issue was complex not only theologically and historically, but also because it was a matter involving family devotion. The question of whether plural marriages could be authorized cropped up periodically for years. In fact, plural marriages continued to be performed, although likely without JFS's knowledge.

In 1910, a rash of reports of new plural marriages emerged. In response, JFS prepared a circular to be sent from the First Presidency to all stake presidencies. It included the entire 1904 statement (the Second Manifesto) and continued by reporting that "in the face of this action, emphasized repeatedly in private and public by us we now find that some person or persons have assumed authority to solemnize plural marriage." The First Presidency formally requested stake presidents "to instruct each Bishop in your Stake to carry out the provisions of the foregoing resolution by dealing with the offenders" through excommunication. "No one," the circular continued, "has been authorized to solemnize plural marriages and [anyone] who advises, counsels, or entices any person to contract a plural marriage renders himself liable to excommunication." The intransigence with which this was met in some quarters resulted in the circular being reissued in 1914.[105]

Matthias Cowley, a former member of the Quorum of the Twelve, was apparently one of those talking about loopholes and official doublespeak. Although he had been dropped from the quorum in 1906, he had retained his church membership and the office of apostle. In May 1911, the apostles, with input from the First Presidency, summoned Cowley to defend his continued support, and possible performances, of plural marriages. Cowley frankly told the assembled leaders that he had taken JFS's previous statements as "bluffs for the world and not taking any authority already given." He did, however, admit that he had been mistaken and agreed to leave plural marriage alone in the future. In a somewhat unusual decision, the apostles decided to allow Cowley to maintain his church membership, but they stripped him of the authority to "officiate in any office of the Priesthood" (although he still held it). This sanction was not lifted until 1936. John W. Taylor did not fare so well. Brought back along with Cowley, he showed no remorse or contrition, and was excommunicated.[106]

Even these moves were not enough to stop the performance of illicit marriages. In 1914, in response to rumors that he was personally looking the other way when it came to new plural marriages, JFS once again sent out the 1910 memo. At this point, his motive for moving against plural marriage was far less ambivalent. Previously, of course, he had been loath to do anything that even hinted at a renunciation of what he believed was a sacred principle. But once he had decided on and issued sincere edicts on the matter, the moral principle shifted from compliance with external pressure, which could be justifiably ignored under certain circumstances, to obedience to prophetic authority, which must be absolute.

JFS's famous axiom that "obedience is the first law of heaven" became the engine that drove him to end plural marriages in the church once and for all. He had been clear about this in the 1910 circular. "After the church had spoken thus plainly [in 1904], we took it for granted that none of its members would be found disobeying its voice," yet, to his astonishment, he found "men professing membership in the church disregard[ing] the command of the church."[107]

Even after this statement, JFS received letters asking if he really meant what he said. He found such inquiries as insulting as they were astonishing. "You must consider me capable of giving counsel in private entirely contradictory to my public utterances," he replied to one man, telling him in no uncertain terms that he had never "in word or act given any man a right to form such an opinion of me." Again, JFS focused tightly on obedience in his response, reiterating that no one has the "privilege to act for himself in opposition to the laws and rules of the church. Such a course would be subversive to good order and discipline." As far as JFS was concerned, the question of plural marriage had been settled in the U.S. courts, and "the book of Doctrine and Covenants tells us to obey the law." Any attempt to practice plural marriage therefore represented "a disposition to satisfy self at the risk of endangering the whole membership of the church."[108]

In a brilliant doctrinal shift, JFS was now coloring what had once been a sign of selfless loyalty as badge of selfishness, subversiveness, and rank disobedience. When he learned that one of the people performing plural marriages in 1914 was his old friend John W. Woolley, he summoned him to his office. When pressed, Woolley admitted that he had, in fact, performed such ceremonies in the temple. JFS responded by crying tears of rage and exclaiming, "You betrayed me!"[109] JFS found Woolley's behavior repugnant, in large measure, because he viewed disobedience as a personal affront. The ongoing problem of plural marriage became much easier to handle after JFS framed it as an obedience issue, and it was this reframing, more than anything else, that drove plural marriage out of the LDS Church.

17 | The Complexities of Religion in a New Century

The national spotlight of the Smoot hearings allowed Joseph F. Smith to view Mormonism from the point of view of modern Americans. The concern expressed from many quarters about the theocratic nature of Mormonism, which manifested as the elision of church and state in the Mormon corridor at all levels of government, gave JFS some pause. In December 1904, several newspapers, from Washington, DC, to Utah, published testimony from the Smoot hearings from a man named Birdsall who told of how the church had involved itself in a land dispute between his daughter and another party. The ecclesiastical court ruled against Cora Birdsall, a decision upheld by JFS, and she was subsequently excommunicated. The *Washington Post* reported that the young woman suffered severe physical and emotional distress from the situation and nearly "lost her mind."[1]

Of course, thousands of such cases had been heard by ecclesiastical courts in Utah since 1847, but in the context of the new century, it struck many as a strange arrangement indeed. According to the *Salt Lake Tribune*, evidence that the "church intruded its alleged authority into such a case must have been a clinching proof to the minds of the committee that the charge of dominance sought by the church in all affairs of its people" was true.[2] Antagonistic as the *Tribune* was, in this case JFS apparently agreed with its assessment. He went so far as to direct a high council court in Paris, Idaho, that was adjudicating a land dispute to "dismiss the case before you" and direct the litigants to seek redress "in a [civil] court of competent jurisdiction." JFS did not conceal the reason for this admonition, writing that it was made "in view of the investigation now being held in Washington."[3] (In 1907, JFS would speak in Manti, in central Utah, about "the folly of litigation whether in civil or ecclesiastical courts.")[4]

On 11 January 1905, JFS sent Smoot copies of seven letters written to various church members instructing them "that complaints involving questions of legal rights should not be tried by our Church tribunals but referred to courts of competent jurisdiction." The cases reached as far back as 1895, and JFS hoped that this admittedly thin evidence would convince some members of the committee that the church was relinquishing its grip on civil matters.[5]

While the scrutiny of the Smoot hearings forced church authority to recede in some areas, JFS simultaneously strengthened the position of the First Presidency in areas deemed strictly "religious." In early 1905, he noted that the First Council of Seventy had never provided the First Presidency with a report of its financial dealings. He directed that such a report be made using information about income and disbursements collected as far back as possible, and that every year going forward, a "detailed" annual report should be submitted. JFS also ordered regular audits of the council's books. He gave similar instructions to the Relief Society, the Sunday School Union, the Young Men's and Young Women's Mutual Improvement Associations, and the Primary.[6]

With the shift away from the involvement of local bishops in civil affairs, they, like the members of the First Presidency, ended up with increased religious responsibilities. JFS instructed the bishops that the days when "the president of the church felt constrained to deal with" locally committed transgressions in "a drastic way" were over. Such things were now "to be dealt with by the local authorities according to their merits."[7] This marked a significant departure in practice from previous years, during which people regularly approached the church president, on their own or at the direction of local leaders, to confess sins and seek instruction about repentance. Although the change had begun under Snow, it did not emerge as policy until JFS's administration.[8]

If the first few years of JFS's presidency taught him anything, it was that the president of the church should do nothing that could be appropriately done by someone else. The office of bishop, going all the way back to the 1830s, had been established to oversee the operation of the United Order. After that failed, they were responsible primarily for temporal issues that arose within the boundaries of their wards. After the Smoot hearings, bishops no longer needed to spend time settling legal disputes and therefore became perfect candidates to take over some of the more clearly spiritual tasks.

When he first got back from Washington, JFS seemed to give himself high marks for his tactical work before the committee. And, as he had counseled a shaken and distressed Smoot, Mormons had been subjected to far worse. "Do not worry, do not get alarmed," he told him. Having endured the "Edmunds-Tucker raids . . . the reign of judicial terror in the then Territory, the wholesale imprisonment of hundreds of the best men in all Utah [with its] segregation, outlawry and tyranny . . . Johnston's Army, our abandonment of homes . . . back to Nauvoo, to Independence, to Far West and to Kirtland," JFS wrote that he felt "somewhat inured to the spirit of the times." There had never been and, in his mind, would never be a place where Mormonism did not suffer at the hands of some form of "persecution and mobocracy." "The Devil is not dead nor yet altogether bound," he wrote, "but he is having a hard time."[9]

318   Chapter 17

As 1904 drew to a close, the devil was not the only one having a hard time. Sitting near the Christmas tree that dark December, JFS had never felt so exhausted and burdened in his life. "I am this day sixty-six years and one month old," he reflected in a letter to his cousin Jesse N. Smith, "and I sometimes wonder if I shall be permitted to reach my 70th anniversary. The pressure from all sides upon my strength, seemingly increasing as the months roll by, is about all I know how to bear."[10]

In early January 1905, JFS wrote a letter of thanks for a gift from his old friend Junius Wells, the designer of the Joseph Smith Birthplace Monument. As he sat marveling at Wells's delicate gift, a statuette of Joseph Smith resting precariously in his thick fingers, JFS began to weep. It was, he recalled, "the most choice gift I ever received." JFS said that he "gazed upon it [and] saw in it a resemblance and likeness to him I love as my kinsman, and as the chosen instrument in God's hands."[11] The small statue veritably exploded with emotional and symbolic significance for him. JFS had never felt closer to his uncle, nor further from his help. He now knew something of what it meant to be *the* prophet, the authority of last resort, the hero and the villain. Even his father, Hyrum, had never been in this position.

After his Smoot testimony, a wider public than JFS knew even existed found many things to criticize about him. Most of it he ignored, but one thing from his testimony continued to haunt him. When JFS told the committee that he had received only "one revelation," he had meant it, but he also knew that it was not up to him to decide when revelations would come, or in what form. "I yearn for wisdom and light," he wrote to his friend Ben Rich, but he was at the mercy of divine will. "If I never had more than 'one revelation' in my life, I want to live so that God may speak to me when HE WILLS," but he wanted to remain focused on his worthiness to "comprehend and obey the many revelations already given through the prophets and servants of God."[12]

In this letter JFS set forth what would become the model for prophetic church governance in the twentieth century. His obsession with creating a coherent and orderly Mormonism that smoothly integrated theology, liturgy, and doctrine made him the perfect person to put forward this new order.[13] From this point on, LDS leaders increasingly viewed prophetic revelation in a broad sense that allowed for the occasional dramatic word from on high, but which emphasized the spirit-led interpretation and application of earlier revelations to current crises and questions.

The Smoot hearings, which finally ended for good in 1907, reinvigorated the antagonistic spirit of the *Salt Lake Tribune*. Not since the days of Brigham Young had the *Tribune* been so fiercely critical of one man as it was of JFS after 1904. There are many reasons for this, but the most conspicuous were linked to individual personalities. After Thomas Kearns, the senator who had forged a working relationship with Lorenzo Snow but was unceremoniously snubbed by JFS, ended up losing his seat in the Senate, he purchased the *Tribune* and took aim at JFS. Among his most valuable employees was Frank J. Cannon. A son of George Q.

The Complexities of Religion in a New Century   319

Cannon, Frank had previously held the Senate seat later held by Kearns. Cannon, a Republican, made powerful enemies in Utah when he voted for a bill that would have raised tariffs on sugar. Sugar production was a major enterprise in Utah, and the LDS Church was heavily involved in it. In 1901, Frank Cannon lost support of the LDS hierarchy as well as his reelection bid. He emerged as one of the most vocal and vicious critics of the LDS Church generally, and of JFS in particular.

To say that JFS grew to hate Frank Cannon is not overstating the case. Dubbing him "Furious Judas," JFS concluded that "no viler creature than he ever engaged the use of his serpent, poisonous tongue against the church." He could scarcely conceive how George Q. could have sired such a man, a "drunken, dishonest" wretch who "for years has been a cunning frequenter of brothels and dens of infamy."[14] JFS admitted that the "terrible venom spewed forth" by young Cannon, the "wicked son of a noble sire," was "at least unexpected, if not new, in the history of the church."[15] Due to his father's influence, Frank had been "shielded" from ecclesiastical consequences "for too long," but JFS insisted that "now the cord is cut that bound him as with a spider's web to us, and it remains to be seen what further use the devil has for him." JFS managed a spiteful pity for the man who had turned against "his only friends on earth."[16]

For the rest of his life, JFS would consider Frank Cannon a villain of the deepest dye, a pathetic coward who defamed his father's legacy with every rancid word he spoke. Still, JFS admired Cannon's facility with language, despite the evil purposes to which he put it, and wished that he had someone with such skill at his disposal. "It has often seemed to me lamentable," he wrote to Junius Wells, "that we do not have more incisive writers ... who possess the ability and disposition ... to handle in scathing terms the malicious creatures who are so atrocious in their denunciation of the Latter-day Saints."[17]

For the better part of 1906 and 1907, JFS and other church leaders endured the distractions brought on by the chronic flare-ups of the Smoot investigation. In the fall of 1906, JFS was charged with unlawful cohabitation, a charge he could hardly deny given the birth dates of some of his children with Mary. JFS refused to "give them the chance" to foist upon him the indignity of a public arrest and instead "appeared in court by my attorney." The judge released JFS on his own recognizance and postponed sentencing until after the upcoming elections. After enduring relentless accusations of dishonesty, and worse, JFS found it deeply gratifying that the court "knew my word was good and that I would not run away. They think I am not the running kind."[18] Once the elections were over, JFS returned to court. Somehow the case ended up before a relatively friendly judge who fined JFS $300.

On 20 February 1907, JFS finally got word that the full Senate had voted to admit Smoot, 42 to 27, bringing an end to what Anthon Lund referred to as "four years of great anxiety."[19] On 27 February 1907, JFS dictated a lengthy letter to

Smoot and expressed the somewhat naïve wish "that now, since the schemers and plotters who have so persistently sought to ride into political power at the expense of the Mormon Church, have so utterly failed ... that the doors of Congress will be for all time closed against all such men."[20]

18 | From Salt Lake to Sharon

Adding to the drama of the early years of Joseph F. Smith's administration was his ongoing conflict with Joseph Smith III. The decades-long rift between JFS and his cousin had never mended, although some moments were more tense than others. February 1904 marked Hyrum Smith's 104th birthday, and JFS held a reception to mark the occasion. He invited Joseph Smith III, but he sent his son Frederick in his stead. Although more than 200 relatives showed up, JFS kept a close eye on young Frederick, guessing he was "about thirty years of age." In a letter to Edward A. Smith, JFS wrote that he had decided it best not to mar the occasion by raising "the differences of our views on religion" with his guest.[1] But if he was hoping that fences might be mended, he would be sorely disappointed.

Joseph Smith III and the rest of the RLDS contingent had sought to take advantage of the chaos caused by the Smoot hearings, and some of their missionaries had used JFS's testimony in their efforts to gain converts. In several community meetings in 1905 and 1906, RLDS missionaries preached that JFS had promised the Smoot committee that he would "abandon" his plural families. When news of this reached JFS, he reacted to the "slander and abuse" not only by castigating the "so-called elders of the so-called Reorganized Church" but also by noting his disappointment that "any person professing to have any knowledge of the Gospel of Jesus Christ should stoop to heed, much less be swayed by" such deplorable wickedness.[2]

JFS had already made moves to seize the legacy of Joseph Smith once and for all. In the fall of 1905, he and a party of family and friends traveled east to sites of historic importance to the church. The first stop was Sharon, Vermont, where JFS dedicated a monument. Kathleen Flake has offered a compelling argument that JFS's trip to the "cradle of the restoration" marked an increased emphasis on Joseph Smith and "the First Vision" that was designed to blunt the dislocative effects of abandoning polygamy.[3] While I take no issue with that interpretation, there may be another dimension that Flake did not mention.

321

322   Chapter 18

A secondary message of the trip to Vermont may have been aimed at JFS's cousins, especially now that polygamy had been renounced. The obelisk at Sharon was not only a tribute to the thirty-eight and a half years of Joseph Smith's life, but also a flag of ownership, planted as part of the symbolic colonization of sites that would eventually include the Smith homes in the Palmyra area; the Sacred Grove, where Smith claimed to have seen Christ and God the Father; the Hill Cumorah, where Moroni's famed gold plates were unearthed; and the Peter Whitmer farm, where the Church of Christ was organized in 1830.

Atop the Hill Cumorah, JFS offered a stirring prayer and attempted to locate the site where the gold plates had been deposited. On the way back to Utah, the group stopped at the one site still held by the "reorganites"—the Kirtland Temple.[4] It would be 100 years before the LDS Church found a significant historical foothold there. JFS would doubtless be chagrined to know that the former RLDS Church, now the Community of Christ, still owns and operates that temple.

In October 1905, Joseph Smith III and his son Frederick showed up at the general conference, and the presence of the two RLDS representatives was not coincidental. They strongly objected to JFS's plans to purchase and dominate the early restoration sites. In their view, the imposition of a "Brighamite" narrative of Mormon history onto the sacred landscapes of Joseph Smith's early years was a grave insult to his legacy. Joseph F. Smith Jr., who had become his father's part-time secretary and confidant, believed that Joseph Smith III was seeking to capitalize on the confusion and pressure of the Smoot hearings to poach church members.

It is impossible to judge their motives, but the RLDS missionaries certainly became unusually visible in Utah during this period. JFS was also convinced that thy were working to undermine LDS work in foreign mission fields, especially Hawaii. In a 1908 letter to Samuel Woolley, he wrote that he was "convinced that the attempt to besmirch the good name of the church and the reputation of those in charge of the Hawaiian mission, had its origin at the headquarters of the Reorganized Church in Honolulu."[5] The protests against the LDS efforts in Vermont and New York, amplified in Utah through the *Salt Lake Tribune*, only hardened JFS's resolve. He had no interest in sparing the feelings of his cousins and their church. "Our people are in poor business to give aid to the 'Reorganites,'" he mused. "They are a bad lot."[6]

JFS's relationship with another relative also became increasingly rocky. One of his longest-lasting and most interesting relationships was with his cousin Ina Coolbrith, the daughter of Don Carlos Smith. He had spent time with her on his way to and from Hawaii in his youth, and continued to correspond with her for the rest of his life. Unlike the children of Joseph Smith, Ina rejected not only Mormonism, but organized religion in general. She had forged a notable career as a writer, artist, and socialite, and became California's first poet laureate.

JFS and Ina shared a clear attraction and affinity, but they often differed bitterly over religious issues. Ina thought her mother had been treated poorly by the church, and she also felt that it championed backward thinking and oppressive social practices. From time to time, JFS heard from Mormons who resided near Ina in northern California's Bay Area. Joseph Robinson, a mission president in California, wrote to JFS in late 1907 about his hopes that Ina might move to Utah and embrace the faith her parents had held so dear. "To be candid," JFS replied ominously, "I cannot feel very hopeful of such results." He added,

> Ina's whole life, since her girlhood and more particularly since the death of her mother, seems to have been aimed at the hope and ambition of becoming popular with the world.... She has foolishly cast from herself the substance in the vain attempt of grasping the shadow, I pity her.[7]

In 1908, JFS, seeking to escape the incessant criticism of the pressure cooker in Salt Lake City, informed Robinson that he was heading to southern California and would like to spend some time at a "seaside resort." JFS asked him to find such a resort and ensure that no press found out about his presence in Los Angeles. The trip took JFS's party through the Bay Area, where they stopped briefly. George Albert Smith, the son of John Henry Smith and a future president of the church, said he had heard that Ina was virtually penniless as a result of the 1906 earthquake. When he mentioned that she might like to accompany JFS's party to Los Angeles for a few days of leisure, JFS told George not to waste his time.[8]

Despite the warning, and without JFS's knowledge, George and his wife paid Ina a visit. JFS knew nothing about it until he returned to Salt Lake. Ina, irate, sent JFS a scathing letter, reprimanding him for the continual intrusions on her privacy. Missionaries and local church members—"strangers to me!"—apparently showed up regularly on her doorstep. George Smith's visit pushed her over the edge, and she vented her considerable frustration on JFS. In July 1908, she wrote a letter addressed to JFS's half brother John, which she instructed him to share with JFS. Now that she had attained fame, she wrote, her long-lost relatives were showing interest in her. She lashed out at the insularity and "backwardness" of Mormonism and insinuated that JFS had no idea how poorly regarded Mormonism was outside of Utah.[9] The letter not only badly missed the mark in terms of the motives of the kindly and gentle George Albert Smith, it left JFS agog at the rude and condescending tone (to say nothing of Ina's apparent obliviousness when it came to how much JFS knew about how the "outside world" viewed Mormonism).

Although Ina had insisted that no further contact be made, JFS wrote to her anyway. On 29 December 1908, he took his pen in hand to write her "a few lines," even "with the certainty of incurring [her] displeasure." Those "few lines" are among the most pointed JFS ever wrote. The letter opens a clear window into JFS's frustration in the middle of his presidential years: "We know what 'the world' is, I presume, quite as well as you do, but we have chosen another mode and course to cope with it than that which you have chosen. It remains to be seen who will conquer without cringing or cowardice."[10]

324   Chapter 18

Ina was also mistaken about JFS's insularity. Beginning with his trip to Europe in 1906, he undertook an international travel schedule unprecedented for a man in his position. He was the first sitting church president to tour Europe and Hawaii, and he made multiple trips to Canada. He also announced temples in Hawaii and Canada, the first to be planned for construction outside of the traditional Mormon culture region. JFS would not live to see either of the temples dedicated, but he is widely credited with bringing an international dimension to Mormonism.

During JFS's years as a missionary and mission president, one of his primary responsibilities had been to encourage and facilitate the movement of Mormon converts from their countries of origin to Utah. There were a variety of reasons for this. In the 1830s, the aim of "gathering" Mormons into a physical location was protection against the calamities that would befall the world immediately before the return of Christ. By the 1840s, Joseph Smith was teaching that the righteous had to be gathered to participate in temple rites. In the early Utah period, more practical reasons were added. Making the desert "blossom as the rose" required a great many hands and an even greater number of hours. However, in the middle years of JFS's presidency, he found himself discouraging emigration every chance he got. For example, in 1907, when Heber J. Grant asked if he should compensate a woman who helped translate the Book of Mormon into Armenian by paying for her to emigrate to Utah, JFS told him, "pay her. Do not emigrate or induce her to emigrate."[11]

JFS also faced a problem with reverse migration, especially in Switzerland. Disaffected Mormons who had been to Utah and attended the temple but had fallen away had returned to their native land, where they began preaching against Mormonism. JFS indicated that "previous presidencies" had probably been too

> particular ... in administering second anointings [in] that they drew the line between faithful members of the church who died without gathering and faithful members who gathered and remained faithful afterwards, leaving the faithful people who died in a scattered condition to be dealt with by the authorities on the other side of the veil.[12]

JFS's international trips began as a means to get out from under the increasingly heavy burdens he faced at home. His friend and confidant Charles Nibley invited JFS and Edna on a three-month tour of Europe in the summer of 1906. Nibley, who had amassed a considerable fortune by then, paid for the entire voyage. The group spent time touring the missions in Britain, France, Germany, Holland, and Belgium. Although the official reason for the trip was church business—and, in fact, JFS held dozens of meetings across the continent—the primary goal for JFS seemed to be escape.

It was a joy for JFS to visit, once again, the scenes of his experiences in Europe in the 1860s and 1870s, joys made sweeter by the improved modes of transportation and lodging. After landing back in New York, the party revisited the new Joseph Smith monument in Vermont, the "old Smith homestead" in New York, the Hill Cumorah, and the "grove where the first childhood prayer of the Prophet Joseph Smith was offered up." JFS reported that standing on this ground evoked "serious thought and peculiar feelings" in him. He found it "pleasing and inspiring to visit the haunts of that great and good man [Joseph Smith]."[13]

JFS had less kind things to say about his visit to Kirtland, which he passed through on his way back to Salt Lake. He described it as a "scattered little village" standing "nearly deserted" where "many years ago a prosperous, thrifty people dwelt in somewhat large numbers." This was not simply a commentary on demographic declension, however; JFS was implying that the wasteland Kirtland had become was a result of the desecration of the its temple. Speaking of the RLDS Church, JFS claimed that "those who possess [the temple] now comprehend little of the objects and purpose for which the temples of God are built." The principle of temple-building, he continued, "is rejected by those who are today in possession of the building." Although JFS concluded that it no longer mattered, because "today we have no use for it," it still rankled him that "the manner in which [the RLDS] came in possession of [the temple] is exceedingly questionable."[14]

Bleaker still was the next stop on the itinerary. Despite having made numerous trips across the Midwest and visiting Nauvoo, Illinois, JFS had always avoided visiting the Carthage jail. The murders of his father and uncle there on 27 June 1844, events known collectively as "the Martyrdom," still loomed large in Mormon memory. We have seen how crucial this event was in JFS's own self-conception, representing in some sense the birth of his personality, and it was perhaps the elaborate, monstrous grandiosity of the memory of their martyrdom that kept JFS away from Carthage for so long. Still, he "had a desire to see that place ... to see the spot where the blood ... was shed." He immediately regretted it. Speaking to the assembled Mormons at the October 1906 general conference, JFS was circumspect and vague, saying only that he would "not attempt to express to you in the least degree how I felt on that ground." All he would say is that he "did not remain there long."[15]

Charles Nibley later shared more details of the Carthage jail visit. He revealed that when JFS was shown a dark stain on the floor and was told that it was the blood of his father, he began to weep uncontrollably and collapsed on the floor. Eventually, JFS composed himself enough to tell Nibley that he wanted to leave: "I despise this place. It harrows up my feelings to come here."[16] This account, though dramatic, was shared years after the events and is secondhand. If true, it would explain JFS's reticence to publicly discuss the details of his visit. In any case, the group quickly moved on to Nauvoo, where JFS experienced "great delight and pleasure" while visiting these "ancient, and now almost obliterated" scenes from his childhood.[17]

Nibley left a lengthy reminiscence of his travels with JFS, published after JFS's death. He described how they often passed the time together talking and playing

326   Chapter 18

checkers. JFS had grown quite skilled at the game while playing with crew members of the vessels he had sailed on years before. Nibley found that he could beat JFS only about one in every four games. He also noted with some amusement JFS's competitive streak. Nibley remembered that if JFS

> had beaten me two or three times in succession and I would make a wrong move and instantly draw the checker back he would say nothing about it, but if on the other hand I should happen to have beaten him and then make a move to draw any checker back that I could see had been wrongly moved, he would yell out, "No you don't! You leave it right there."[18]

At times, the conversations turned to weightier matters. One evening, Nibley and JFS were leaning on the railing of the ship's deck, chatting and looking out at the Atlantic Ocean illuminated under a full moon. Nibley, showing a remarkable mixture of courage and familiarity, suggested that allowing Reed Smoot to take a seat in the Senate would be a mistake. He "ventured to suggest to [JFS] that it would be a wise and prudent thing for Senator Smoot to stay at home." At this, JFS exploded, slamming his fist into the ship's railing. He turned to Nibley and said, "If I have ever had the inspiration of the spirit of the Lord given to me forcefully and clearly it has been on this one point concerning Reed Smoot, and that is, instead of his being retired, he should be continued in the United States Senate!" Nibley duly, and prudently, "withdrew [his] opposition."[19]

Nibley was an emotional and financial booster of JFS for decades, and their friendship has garnered its own share of attention from scholars. Not long after their European trip, JFS found an opportunity to move his "best earthly friend" into the hierarchy. In late 1907, presiding bishop William Preston's mental and physical health seemed to be failing. JFS released him and summoned Nibley to come to his office. He did not extend a calling to Nibley as much as he issued an edict. JFS told him that the church needed a presiding bishop, and it was going to be him. According to Nibley, after he accepted the new position, JFS "took me in his arms and kissed me and wept tears of joy as he hugged me and blessed me, as he only can do."[20]

JFS did not allow Nibley to choose his own counselors. Rather, he insisted that one of Preston's counselors, O. P. Miller, be carried over as first counselor, and he appointed his own son David A. Smith as second counselor. JFS clearly felt the need to surround himself with people he trusted and, if possible, people to whom he was related. This is not surprising, especially given the isolation and suspicion that the Smoot affair imposed on him.[21]

With Nibley as presiding bishop, JFS had an official reason to take him along on more international trips. In early 1909, a party including JFS, Julina, and Nibley set out for Hawaii—JFS's fifth such trip. When the group stopped briefly in Sacramento, JFS was the object of a "celebrity sighting." He noticed a group of women taking "special notice" of him, attention that made him uncomfortable. When they finally approached him, JFS was relieved to learn that one of the women had a Mormon relative, and she wondered if JFS would provide "just a word" that could be relayed to the elderly woman. "Take my blessing to your dear old grandmother," JFS said, then reboarded the train.[22] For all of his intensity and infamous temper, JFS was at heart an extrovert who loved to meet and speak with people.

The party proceeded to San Francisco, where they spent the night. Before boarding their ship, JFS and Julina paid a visit to Ina Coolbrith. Probably desiring to smooth out the tensions brought about by the visit three years before, JFS called on her at home. What he saw there shocked him, but he seemed to feel a vague schadenfreude at the condition of his stubbornly "apostate" cousin. She lived, he wrote, in a "poor little home ... two rooms, poorly furnished." But the shabby state of the house was exceeded by Ina's physical condition. JFS recorded in frank, if uncharitable, detail his cousin's appearance. "She has grown fleshy and coarse," he noted, not retaining "one bit of the sweetness of her girl-hood. She is completely changed for the worse." Ina said she would have known JFS anywhere because he had "retained [his] natural appearance." "I could not say so much for her," he lamented.[23] JFS left no record of his conversation with her, but it was probably short and pleasant. He often tried to avoid face-to-face confrontation with his Smith relatives if he could, preferring to quarrel with them via letter.

In any case, JFS soon found himself worrying about his own physical condition. The seas were extremely rough even before the ship got out of San Francisco Bay. JFS, who prided himself on his professed resistance to seasickness, admitted that as he watched his fellow sailors "casting up accounts," he "did not feel at all comfortable myself," although he "stuck it out." The next morning, his "arms, shoulders and back" were "lame and sore [from] trying to keep from being thrown out of my berth." The following day, JFS decided to show his courage in the face of the storm and planted himself in a deck chair tied to the ship's railing. Suddenly the ship pitched up, and the chair broke loose from its moorings and, along with JFS, rocketed across the deck to the opposite railing, resulting in some nasty bruises and sore ribs. Despite the vicissitudes of the wild ride, JFS's competitive streak surfaced when he noted that Nibley was unable to leave his cabin for days, while JFS was up riding deck chairs. He did allow, however, that he "did not crave for food."[24]

The rest of the journey to Hawaii passed without incident. JFS spent the days reading a book about Francis Drake (which he dismissed as "fairy tales"), writing letters, sending telegrams, beating Nibley at checkers, and taking notes on the other ships that came into view. On 26 February 1909, the ship arrived at Honolulu, where JFS and his friends were greeted by "elders and native saints" who, as tradition dictated, covered JFS with leis.

What happened next has gone down in JFS lore thanks to Nibley's published reminiscences, but his depiction seems at odds with JFS's account of the incident in his journal. According to Nibley, he "noticed a poor old blind woman, loitering under the weight of about ninety years, being led in [with] a few choice bananas in her hand." The elderly woman began shouting "Iosepa! Iosepa!" and JFS "instantly" ran to her, "hugged her and kissed her over and over again, patting her on the head saying . . . 'my dear old Mamma.'" In Nibley's version, JFS then turned to him "with tears streaming down his cheeks" and said, "Charlie, she nursed me when I was a boy, sick and without anyone to care for me. She took me in and was a mother to me."[25] JFS's account of the same event, written the day it happened, consisted of a single sentence. "My old friend 'Ma'—widow of Manuhii came with bananas tho' she is totally blind."[26] He made no other mention of the incident in his writings. Nibley did tend to sentimentalize JFS after his death, and this appears to be another such instance.

After being welcomed back to Hawaii, JFS traveled to the mission home, where he addressed a packed house. Speaking first in Hawaiian, then in English, JFS recalled "the god-like character and labors of Joseph Smith" and emphasized his "intimate" connection with Mormonism's founding prophet. In addition to attending meetings, JFS did some sightseeing and shopping, at one point purchasing a Hawaiian/English dictionary and a history of Hawaii, all the while lamenting the "thick and fierce" swarms of mosquitos, which he "fought savagely." JFS's daughters and some of the other women enjoyed playing in the surf—at least that was what JFS guessed based on the "screams, yells, and laughter" he could hear.[27]

Late in the afternoon of 2 March 1909, JFS arrived at the plantation at Laie, the site of his exile more than twenty years earlier. His daughters embarrassed him by arriving late to the morning prayer meeting, but his feelings were soothed by a horseback ride through the plantation. For most of his stay, JFS conducted regular church business, keeping in touch with leaders in Utah and answering questions they forwarded to him. One such question involved a couple who had "procured an abortion" before they joined the church. They wondered if they could ever be forgiven. JFS responded in the affirmative.[28]

JFS soon sought refuge from the traveling headquarters on the plantation and sailed to the island of Hawaii. His favorite event of the trip was a hike by lantern light to the top of Kilauea. JFS stared down in awe at the "red and white-hot seething, surging, boiling cauldron" of the volcano. It was, he concluded, a "stupendous display of nature's secret forces operating below."[29] When the group returned to Laie, JFS received a cable informing him that the wife of one of the missionaries there had died. The cable requested that JFS "break the news gently." Disliking potentially emotional personal encounters, he "got Julina to break the news to him" while JFS "wrote a letter expressing [his] sympathies and condolence."[30]

After another couple of weeks spent visiting church members, administering priesthood blessings, and delivering sermons, JFS boarded the ship for home on 24 March 1909. In the only sentimental journal entry of the entire trip, he recorded his thoughts as he watched "the familiar lines of Oahu till they disappeared from view." "I felt a little homesick," he admitted, then asked himself, "Shall I ever see them again? Or is this the last time?"[31] It would not be. He visited Hawaii again in 1915, 1916, and 1917.

JFS and the Cartoonists

Although the Smoot hearings ended in 1907, they left a permanent mark on JFS. His natural sense of mild paranoia was amplified, and he became incredibly sensitive to the ridicule his public remarks would bring. During the Smoot affair, he had suffered relentless and often vicious criticism from the *Salt Lake Tribune*. From 1904 through 1907, scarcely a day went by without a scathing article or cartoon, or both, showing up in the paper's pages, aimed squarely at JFS. The *Tribune* accused him of everything from sexual debauchery to sedition to stupidity. "Smith is notoriously an ignoramus," one editorial observed, not a prophet at all, but "a money-grabbing earthly man. And a mighty gross one at that." Every sermon he gave became fodder for the overall argument that JFS was standing in the way of everything good that might come to Utah. "Every advancement of the commonwealth in public schools, in great public institutions of learning, in churches, in fraternities, in mining and smelting, have been made against his will and against his work," the *Tribune* declared in one of its milder editorials.[32]

The *Tribune* played to the growing non-Mormon population in Utah in an effort to further the political interests of the American Party by presenting JFS as a cruel autocrat who would not hesitate to use the power of the government to drive non-Mormons from the state.

> If Joseph F. Smith had his way, there would not be a Gentile in Utah.... If JFS would not sell a foot of land to an outsider and if he would not lend aid to one, then necessarily that is his idea of community life; and if his plan could prevail, there wouldn't be a place in Utah upon which a Gentile could set his foot and call it home.[33]

JFS attempted to dispute these assertions by pointing out that his sermon singled out "enemies" rather than "gentiles," but that only provided further grist for the mill. When JFS publicly expressed love for his fellow man, the *Tribune* howled at his claim to "the personal possession of the milk of human kindness in large gobs." The truth, the *Tribune* claimed, was that "any man [who] shall have the temerity to oppose Smith will arouse a very fiend of malevolence." JFS, the editorial asserted, was a man of "pure maliciousness."[34]

The sermon that JFS gave to open the October 1907 general conference was deemed by the *Tribune* as one of "puerility and senseless bigotry," given by a man who could "more appropriately consort with scorpions and tarantulas than with the man of average human courtesy."[35] In public, JFS put on a brave face. "I do not

330   Chapter 18

care for and don't want to pay any heed to the ridiculous nonsense, the foolish twaddle, and the imperious slurs that are being cast against me," he told a gathering of Mormons in 1906. The "wicked hearts and perverted minds" from whence these attacks originated were best ignored, he said, counseling his listeners not to "allow yourselves to be troubled over these things in the least."[36] In private, however, signs of stress from the unrelenting criticism were beginning to show. The editorials were bad enough, but JFS found the cartoons almost unbearable. Always easily embarrassed, he saw the cartoons lampooning him as almost obscene.

In the early twentieth century, political cartoons were as common as late-night talk show jokes about public figures are today. They represented an integral part of civic and cultural discourse, and no public personality was spared. Still, JFS found the illustrations so odious and offensive, that he approached the Salt Lake Commercial Club about the issue in 1907. Commercial clubs were a standard feature in many cities during the Progressive era, and they served to protect local economic interests. The Salt Lake Commercial Club had been formed in 1901–1902.

In 1907, JFS attempted to enlist the club's help in curtailing the cartoons in the *Tribune*. He argued that such humiliating representations of such a prominent member of the community would terrify tourists and discourage economic development. Naturally, the *Tribune* had a field day with this. "Joseph F. Smith wants the Commercial Club to make his personal annoyance its chief concern!" the *Tribune* mocked.

> What is the matter with him? Is he any better than Teddy Roosevelt or Wm Jennings Bryan? Is he any worse than Johann Most or Jack the Ripper? All men who come before the public either in good or bad light, are subject to the cartoonist's pencil.

According to the editorial, JFS's appeal to the Commercial Club was just more evidence of the *Tribune*'s long-standing assertion that he thought he was above the law, entitled to special treatment and abject deference.

> This individual—the chief lawbreaker of his generation—tries to make his community regard him with a peculiar sanctity, and being too brutally willful in wrong-doing to retreat and permit this State to have peace, he crawls to the commercial organizations of the community and begs them, in the name of business interests here, to protect him from the public exposure of his own infamies.

The *Tribune* had no intention of curtailing "the truth being told about [JFS], both in language and in picture." But they did have one piece of advice: "let him stop his infamies and then the cartooning will stop."[37]

JFS found that he could do nothing about the free press, an irony made maddeningly more intense by the fact that much of the ridicule centered on his purportedly iron-fisted rule of Utah. He was beside himself with rage at the situation. Eventually, however, he learned that the less he said, the better. In early 1908, the newly formed Utah Association of Life Underwriters asked JFS to address its annual convention. He was a natural choice since the church, at the urging of Heber J. Grant and in direct opposition to the policies of Brigham Young, had become involved in the life insurance business. "It would not be an act of wisdom on my part to appear before the public as a speaker in a gathering of that description," JFS replied cryptically, adding, "I am positive from the temper of the times that my consenting to appear would prove to be a trap into which my enemies would be delighted to see me fall."[38]

JFS had an interesting relationship with the word "enemies." All of his life, he had tended to see the world as a hostile place, and his working assumption was that a stranger was an enemy until he or she could prove otherwise. The intensity of the criticism he faced as church president did nothing but reinforce this proclivity. However, he began increasingly to see his enemies as enemies of God rather than rivals.

The nature of JFS's enemies grew in scope as his life went on. In the early days, Cornelius Lott represented the brutality of a world indifferent, and even hostile, to widows and orphans. Walter Murray Gibson stood in for all those who would challenge ecclesiastical authority and turn the system to their own advantage. Hecklers and scoffers in the mission field represented the general indifference of the world to the messengers of God. McKnight was the symbol of challenges to JFS's masculinity, challenges to be met with brute force. Carrington was the poster child for hypocrisy in high places. But by 1907, there was not an enemy JFS could find that was not symbolic of the great cosmic battle between good and evil. In the minds of thousands of people, and in his own mind, JFS literally represented God on earth, all of his anger was righteous, and all of his enemies represented the devil himself. As for the *Tribune*, by the end of 1907, JFS could wearily report simply that "The 'Trib" is as wicked and against me as ever."[39]

Events in late 1907 and early 1908 brought abundant reasons for JFS to forget about the *Tribune* for a time. In December, his daughter Leonora, known as Nonie, suffered a stillbirth, and complications followed. Although she was traumatized and weak, the doctors assured JFS that she was on the road to recovery. With this assurance, he traveled to Cache Valley on church business. At the train station on his return home, he was "met with the shocking, death-laden message that our darling Nonie, one of the brightest jewels in my crown of life, had passed away!"[40] Nonie left behind a husband and five young children.

This loss hit JFS unusually hard. He had, of course, lost many children over the years, with each loss bringing the same crushing grief, but he would typically put his

332   Chapter 18

head down and bury himself in work right away. For some reason, this loss, "one of the severest blows I ever felt," left JFS totally flattened, "stunned beyond measure."[41] He found some comfort, however, in his now-familiar view of a family-based heaven where his daughter would be met with "the open arms and loving embrace of my own sweet mother . . . and hosts of kindred beyond this vale of tears."[42]

JFS had a particularly difficult time moving on with his usual routine after Nonie's death. "I think I have never felt more keenly the terrible shock of parting with any of my beloved ones than I have this time," JFS wrote to his friend Richard Lyman. Grasping for an explanation, he ventured a guess that "it may be on account of my advanced age."[43] Age no doubt contributed to the depth of JFS's grief, but other factors compounded his sorrow, including his motherless grandchildren. JFS had never before lost a child who left children behind, so seeing Nonie's children suffer the loss of their mother no doubt reopened his own ancient wounds from his father's murder. Nonie's death was also the first that JFS had suffered as church president.

Although earlier deaths in JFS's family had elicited sympathy from his inner circle, Nonie's death brought forth a flood of condolence messages that streamed into his office for months. And every time one of those letters came in, JFS responded by detailing the circumstances of his daughter's death. He relived his grief over and over, a process that must have left him emotionally anchored to the trauma in a way that he had not previously experienced. Perhaps that was because his emotional resilience had been badly damaged by the demands of his work and the public humiliations in the local press. Whatever the reasons, JFS entered 1908 in a deep depression.

A few years earlier, he had begun to celebrate the birthday of his father in an effort to replicate the widespread celebrations of Joseph Smith's birthday. But on 9 February 1908, JFS was in no mood to celebrate, noting glumly that "today is the 180th anniversary of the birth of my martyred father, Hyrum Smith. There will be no celebration or family gathering in honor of the day."[44] He was also growing unusually snappish in his interactions. In March, he accidentally mixed up letters, sending one meant for his son to his daughter, and vice versa. When he learned that the family had found the incident mildly amusing, JFS icily commented, "[I was] pleased to know I had been the cause for them to have a good laugh. If they wrote as many letters as I do in the same time, I might have cause to think it was 'funny' too."[45]

JFS grew pensive in his depression. "Time seems precious," he wrote to his daughter Emma in March 1908, "and time is flitting by on swifter than feathered wing, and what will we have, by and by, to show for it?" Thoughts of the upcoming general conference further darkened his mood. "Just a month until General Conference. I dread the responsibility and cares of conference."[46]

Even though his present situation was growing increasingly stressful, JFS's memories of the past sometimes brightened his mood. Any contact with Samuel Adams, one of his few remaining childhood companions, always sparked nostalgia.

When Adams sent JFS a photograph of himself, he wistfully replied that the photo "carried me back to the early days of youth and boyhood, when all was simple, natural life, and peace and good will pervaded the quiet, industrious and happy homes and neighbors of our very own people."[47]

Apart from the particular losses JFS suffered during these years, it is clear from his description of both his current environment and the idealized memory of the world of his youth that he was uncomfortable with some features of modernity. Urbanization, automobiles, sugar refineries, smelters, railroads, electricity, and countless other technological wonders left JFS feeling off balance, dislocated. The air he breathed was polluted, and the quiet world of his youth had been destroyed by the noise of machines ranging from giant rail engines to the incessant ringing of his office telephone. All of this made him feel the years weighing heavily on his shoulders.

"Well, Samuel," he wrote, "we neither of us are quite so young, nor quite so active as we were some 54 or 55 years ago, near old Canyon Creek ... and the Log Schoolhouse," invoking once again the iconic log school that loomed so large in his memory. "How times have changed!" he lamented. "How many of the dear old friends, the boys and girls of 1853, have long since passed over the 'dark river'— to the bright beyond!" Worse still, "those few who remain are scattered over the land," a diaspora that symbolized for JFS the dilution of Mormon identity.[48]

JFS's memories of the past, particularly of his early, formative years in Utah, served as a palimpsest for him throughout his life. But his memories shifted in tone and tint according to the circumstances that evoked them. For example, the year 1853 was, of course, not as kind to JFS as the recollections evoked by Samuel Adams's photograph. When he needed energy and righteous anger, he remembered those years as oppressive, unfair, tragic, and dark. But when he felt despair at his current life in a "grimy, smutty, dusty, dirty world" in which peace and happiness were hard to obtain, and even harder to keep, what he needed more than anything was a comforting memory.[49]

During an earlier dark time, when JFS was in Washington working for Utah statehood during the era of the anti-polygamy raids, he had written a letter to Adams in which he listed all of the things that did not exist in Utah in the early 1850s.

No enemies within a thousand miles, no vain and foolish pride, no grasping avarice, no eager reaching out for Babylon ... no gambling halls, no thieves, no houses of ill repute, no male or female prostitutes, no land jumpers or petty-fogging shysters ... no multitude of Ishmaelitish gentiles eager to devour our substance and pounce upon our inheritances, no murderers, infanticides, abortionists, no saloons.[50]

The world of the past, as he described in his letters to Adams, was one of simplicity, pristine nature, peace, friendliness, quiet, happiness, and life surrounded by "our very own people"—the absolute opposite of the life he lived during his presidency. Even though JFS had counseled his friend Marion "not to dwell on the past, nor lament the present, but look hopefully into the future," in the midst of his own depression, he was finding it increasingly difficult to follow his own advice.[51]

Just when it seemed as though things could get no bleaker, JFS absorbed another tragedy. In early 1908, Louie, the wife of JFS Jr., grew alarmingly ill. As with Nonie, the case involved complications from pregnancy. Louie was admitted to the hospital after growing thin and weak from constant vomiting and underwent an operation (which JFS refused to name), but despite an initially positive prognosis, she died on 30 March. "Louie ... died this morning. I have no time nor heart for words," he wrote to Wesley Smith.[52] To Edna and Emma Smith, he wrote, "Three months ago we buried our darling Nonie and now our Darling Louie is called away. Two better girls I never knew. My burden of grief for our temporal loss, seems almost all I can bear."[53]

JFS's depression, deepened by this new loss, dragged on. Five months later, he was still unable to find his way out of it. In another letter to Wesley, he wrote that looking at his grandchildren, those "darling little motherless babies," undid him. At this point JFS came as close as he ever would to asking, "Why me?" "How many thousands," he wondered, "could better have been spared than our precious Nonie and Laurie!"[54]

As JFS struggled under the various burdens of family tragedy, age, and the presidency, his health began to suffer. Frequent colds and minor back issues had troubled him since the 1860s but rarely impeded his work. By 1908, however, he was suffering from frequent, severe attacks of sciatica and lumbago. In a letter written in June 1910, he referred to his ailments collectively as his "grim tormentor."[55] Later that summer, an attack of sciatica that lasted into the early fall confined him to bed. Of all the illnesses and dangers he had experienced in his long and adventurous life, this was the first time he had been bedridden for any significant amount of time.

Over the years, JFS had often found himself in bed during the colder weather of winter and early spring with "la grippe," a term that referred to influenza or, more commonly, a severe cold with flulike symptoms. Seeking a healthier climate, he began to take advantage of his contacts at the various railroads to make frequent trips to Los Angeles, usually in the early months of the year. Initially, he stayed with Joseph Robinson, president of the California mission, but as his visits to southern California grew longer and more frequent, JFS concluded that it would be cheaper and more convenient to buy a house.

In 1913, the church decided to build a ten-room home on Brentwood Terrace in Santa Monica for $7,500.[56] For the final four or five years of JFS's life, Deseret Santa Monica, as it was known, served for weeks at a time as the headquarters of the church. Southern California not only offered JFS a milder winter, but also far less stress than he faced in Salt Lake. In California, he was anonymous, and he took full advantage of his ability to move around unrecognized. He visited the beach, auto races, alligator farms, amusement parks, and other attractions. He was almost always accompanied by some of his children and grandchildren, and his personal account books indicate that he cast off his natural parsimony when it came to buying souvenirs for his grandchildren.[57]

JFS relied heavily on his son David, a counselor to the presiding bishopric, to handle his affairs in Utah while he was away. Kindly and solicitous of his father's needs, David often encouraged him to extend his stays in California. In May 1916, he convinced JFS to remain in Santa Monica long enough for Charles Nibley to visit and "show you how to play golf." David and Nibley both believed that golf would do him "a great deal of good." JFS initially resisted, remarking that he was not "under any pledge to play golf" and teasingly bosting that if he did decide to play, he had no doubt that Nibley would "come out at the end of the game about as he does with me at checkers."[58]

Nibley did, indeed, introduce JFS to golf, who at the age of seventy-seven took up the sport with an enthusiasm that outstripped his skill. He enjoyed the exercise and the chance it gave him to spend time with Nibley outdoors. However, the serene setting of the golf course at the Brentwood Country Club was not enough to keep JFS's temper completely at bay. On one occasion, after "topping" his shot twice in a row, a deeply frustrated JFS swung with all of his might, knocking the ball about 100 feet beyond the hole and into a ditch. When David asked why he had done such a thing, JFS replied with a growl, "I was mad at it!"[59]

Once he was back in Salt Lake, JFS remained busy in all of the usual ways. Visitors, correspondence, and visits to church units took up most of his time. His position as church president also came with chairmanships and memberships of various businesses, and although he took virtually no interest in their operation, he was obliged to attend a wide array of their meetings. The income he made from these positions was barely enough to keep him afloat, a fact made all the more rankling by the widespread opinion that he was a man of considerable means. "I am not made of money as some people suppose," he wrote in a letter in 1910.[60]

JFS had always maintained a deep ambivalence toward people of wealth, Charles Nibley and Heber J. Grant being exceptions. At times he seemed to simultaneously wish success and failure on Utah's economy and the monied individuals whose fortunes rose and fell with it. In late 1909, JFS demonstrated this ambivalence when he wrote that "the building craze in this city is ... phenomenal," and it appeared that "Salt Lake City is to grow to be one of the great cities ... quickly." "It would be a great surprise," he continued with barely restrained glee, "if the bottom of the boom should give way and let all their extravagant hopes fall through!"[61] JFS's perennial money problems were not a reflection of the hours he worked. He rarely got to bed before midnight, a fact that he pointed out in nearly every letter he wrote.

Occasionally, larger issues surfaced that demanded JFS's attention. In 1910, his counselor John Winder died of pneumonia. JFS advanced Lund to first counselor and selected his cousin John Henry Smith to take Lund's place as second counselor.

JFS recognized that John Henry had skills that he lacked, particularly when it came to dealing with people who held differing opinions. As JFS explained it, "John Henry could meet and shake hands with the damndest scoundrel unhung," something he could not do. He simply was "not big enough" to do so. Such people, he added, should "keep out of his way."[62] Recognizing his own shortcomings, JFS found men who could complement him in the presidency.

The selection of John Henry as second counselor left a vacancy in the Quorum of the Twelve, which JFS unabashedly filled with another of his sons, JFS Jr., who is known to history as Joseph Fielding Smith. He had already been working as an assistant to his father for several years. JFS had recognized his son's tremendous capacity for scriptural and doctrinal mastery early on. He had also trained him in the art of doctrinal innovation, which JFS himself developed under the influence of Orson Pratt. For years, JFS had privately counseled with his namesake on doctrinal questions that came before him, as well as on manuscripts written by mission presidents to be published and used in their proselytizing efforts.

By April 1901, JFS had three sons in the hierarchy. Hyrum, who was not only an apostle but also president of the European mission, JFS Jr., and David. To critics, this was nothing more than rank nepotism, a naked power grab. However, JFS's reasons for packing the hierarchy with his sons were more complex than that and have their roots in his veneration of his own father. Throughout his life, JFS lived with the memory of his father as an exalted human being, chosen by God to fulfill a special mission. In January 1841, when he was just over two years old, his uncle Joseph published a revelation in which Hyrum was promised that "whoever he blesses will be blessed, whoever he curses shall be cursed; that whatsoever he shall bind on earth shall be bound in heaven." He was also promised that "his name shall be had in honorable remembrance from generation to generation forever."[63]

For those who do not believe that Joseph Smith spoke the very mind of God, these promises hold very little meaning. For believers—and there was no more committed believer than JFS—these words came from God himself. He believed that his father was favored of God, known and called by name by the creator of heaven and earth. He believed that his father was so important to the work of God that the name "Hyrum Smith" would be esteemed for all eternity. It is little wonder that JFS felt so acutely his duty as a son of this spiritual giant—a duty that included raising a righteous posterity that would help fulfill these prophecies. JFS was more than a son; he saw himself as the divinely called guardian and caretaker of a sacred prophetic bloodline. He certainly convinced many of his descendants that their blood was preternaturally unique and therefore justifiably included abundantly in the LDS hierarchy.

The family rhetoric coming from JFS and continuing with his posterity focuses on the concept of blood. This belief has been expressed most recently by M. Russell Ballard, a great-grandson of JFS through Hyrum M. Smith's line who was called as an LDS apostle in 1984. Ballard has frequently spoken of the "believing blood that flows through [his] veins." On one occasion, he said that every Latter-day Saint needs to be grateful for "the believing blood that flowed in the veins of the Smith family." At a symposium honoring JFS held at Brigham Young University, Ballard gave the keynote address, in which he once again focused on the need to understand the nature of "the faithful, believing blood that flowed through [JFS's] veins," and the fact that "this believing blood of the Smiths and the Macks flowed through the veins of their children."[64]

Although the idea of "believing blood" has been used in LDS discourse to refer to those scattered members of the "House of Israel" who joined the LDS Church, within JFS's family culture, it carried an additional, and far more specific, meaning. So dedicated was JFS to the idea of believing blood that he tailored a common saying to better fit with his ideas: "*good* blood," he wrote to his cousin Ina Coolbrith, "is thicker than water."[65]

Parental Struggles

JFS was always quick to sing the praises of his all-but-perfect children to anyone who would listen, but one does get an occasional glimpse behind the curtain. Those brief flashes indicate that JFS struggled with the same issues as any other parent. In 1917, he requested that his son David access the church tithing records and report how much tithing each of his children had paid the previous year. He then compared those figures with what he knew about their sources of income. He was especially displeased to learn that Coulson and Buddy were not paying anything.[66] He also expressed concern about the company his children kept, occasionally chastised one or another of them for being rude to one of his wives, and chided them for spending too much money. His younger children seemed especially prone to money problems while on missions, and JFS finally had to "serve notice that I will NOT pay any more debts!" He also loved to tell them that "no one ever sent me a dollar when I was on my missions, and I've been on a <u>few</u>!"[67]

One interesting shift in JFS's rhetoric about the importance of frugality for missionaries occurred when he became church president. In the past, he had tried to instill frugality in his sons, and that is where his concern stopped, but after he became president, JFS saw missionary spending as a threat to the entire Mormon economy. When his son Franklin told him that missionaries serving with him regularly received thirty dollars a month from home, JFS was astonished, and not a little disturbed. "What a terrible drain this must be on their poor parents who have to furnish them the money," he wrote, then expanded his dystopian fantasy of ruination to include all of Mormon country: imagine the outcome if "all the Elders, numbering nearly 2,000 were to require thirty dollars a month for their expenses!"[68]

The expanded scope of JFS's thinking on the issue of frugality did not spill over into every area in which his children strayed. His son Calvin and a few of his

338   Chapter 18

friends once obtained access to the church's only automobile, took it for a joyride, and damaged it. JFS's reaction was surprisingly restrained, especially compared to his response when he found out that Buddy, who at that point was thirty-six years old, was neglecting his church duties. As he often did when dealing with prickly matters involving relatives, JFS decided in that case to engage Buddy in writing, even though they were within "speaking distance." Before JFS got into specifics, he set an ominous tone, referring to the "evil" that Buddy was involved in as "already serious and may soon be still more so."

With foreboding preliminaries out of the way, JFS finally explained that his letter was prompted by a report from "the presiding officers of the Quorum of Seventies," of which Buddy was a member. They had essentially told him that Buddy was not coming to the Sunday meetings of his quorum, no matter how often they reminded him to do so, instead taking the opportunity to recreate in the canyons on Sundays. JFS pulled out all the rhetorical stops, reminding Buddy that he was old and close to death, that he had been plagued by "wicked men [who] raged against me as they raged against the Prophet Joseph, and as they raged against the son of God," that he had endured "cruel laws" and "constant espionage upon my freedom," and that he had "spent [his] life in the service of the church, labored in poverty, without purse or scrip." JFS played his favorite card, of course, when he reminded Buddy, "I have had to fight my own battles in this world, without the counsel or assistance of Father or mother," and inherited little other than "the enemies of my father." All of this, JFS wrote, "I can endure better than to see my children turn their backs upon me, by parting their way from my own."[69]

The pressure that JFS applied to his children is nowhere more clearly on display than in this May 1909 letter to his son Buddy. It raises the question of why he felt compelled to be so heavy-handed in such matters. Part of it, obviously, is that he was a true believer in Mormonism and wanted his children to make choices that would lead to their exaltation. But there does seem to be something more basic, almost instinctive, about JFS's response. If anything is crystal clear in the story of JFS's life, it is his lifelong attempt to create as an adult the family that was taken from him as a child. It is not veering too closely toward historical-psychological malpractice to note that children who suffer trauma often have difficulty forming healthy boundaries in later life. They tend to have difficulty sensing where they, as a person, end, and where others begin.

The letter to Buddy, as well as the extreme separation anxiety that plagued JFS when he was away from his children, also indicates that he saw his children as extensions of himself, and that his core identity, his most important persona, could be literally dissolved by his children's choices. That makes sense when one considers the importance that an eternally intact family had for JFS. It probably was not hyperbole when he said that it would be easier to endure being orphaned than to undergo the trauma of one his children rejecting Mormonism. For JFS, such events would have been nearly identical in terms of their emotional impact.

This is why he always portrayed the moral standing of his children in absolute and unrealistic terms. Even in the letter to Buddy, he wrote that he did not believe that he would "indulge a single wicked thought. I am sure you are too pure and too good and too noble and upright for that."[70] JFS needed to believe this: he absolutely had to maintain this fantasy, and that led him to micromanage his children.

JFS could be very difficult to please, and his children must have found his fathering deeply frustrating at times. If a child complained, JFS demanded a better attitude, but even when a child said what they thought JFS wanted to hear, they sometimes got criticized for that as well. Wesley, serving a mission in Hawaii, wrote a letter, clearly calculated to please his father, in which he claimed to be "perfectly satisfied and contented" and committed to "try hard to do my duty all the time." His area of labor "could not have been better," he wrote, adding that he was "happy all the time." JFS responded by quoting the lengthy, upbeat section of the letter and "congratulating" Wesley "on possessing the feeling expressed therein," but admonishing him not to use such language "lest some one will think that you are either parading your virtue or merely talking to hide a suspected desire to the effect that your mission could not end too soon to suit you."[71]

This was a pattern with JFS, not an isolated incident. Franklin received a strikingly similar letter from his father. "In your long letter of five pages . . . you express many very excellent thoughts, in which I heartily concur," JFS wrote. But he then brought the hammer down on his son's "verbiage and superfluity . . . repetition [and] verbosity," and admonished him to "learn to understand the King's English, both in writing and in speaking."[72]

Despite his perfectionistic parenting, JFS's deep devotion to his wives and children could never be questioned. In March 1915, Sarah died after a short bout of the flu. He described it as "the hardest blow dealt me in married life."[73] But it is telling that he mourned Sarah more for her role as a mother than as a wife. JFS had spent his entire life trying to recreate the family that fate had stolen from him. He never expressed this more clearly than in a letter he wrote to his cousin Ina after Sarah's death. Although her passing did not cripple him in the same way that the deaths of his children had, it clearly touched a very old emotional nerve. His first thought was of the "motherless family" that she left behind. Even though there were "others to mother them," he wrote, "there can be but <u>one real</u> mother!" How much mothering these children still needed, considering that they were all adults, is an open question. But because JFS lost his own mother as a child, he tended to infantilize others who had to endure such a loss. He wrote that he was heartbroken to lose this "most beloved mother, wife, companion, and friend," putting mother first in the line of social identities.[74]

It is also interesting that JFS referred to each of his wives as "Mamma." As he explained immediately after Sarah's death, "I love each of my Mammas—the mothers of my children. They are all Darling Mammas to me!"[75] On several occasions he described the great hierarchy of human beings with his mother at the top and his "Mammas" just below her. Aside from his own personal history, JFS probably related to his wives primarily as mothers because of the way polygamy sculpted its practitioners' emotional landscapes. In JFS's case, his wives lived, for the most part, separately, and sometimes not even in the same state. This meant that he had to devote what little nonworking time he had to the development of emotional intimacy with five individual wives. They, in turn, formed far stronger emotional ties with their children than with JFS. Idealizing the mother-child relationship as he did, JFS based his love for his wives on the strength of the love they showed to their children.

Although he is not generally remembered as a sickly president, JFS's health continued to decline as his presidency wore on. By mid-1916, he required twice-daily massages on his hip and lower back to stifle the pain from sciatica and lumbago.[76] JFS maintained his wariness of doctors, and he angered his personal physician, A. S. Vincent, by informing him that walking around a golf course was both more effective and less expensive than the good doctor's treatments.[77]

In addition to the old complaints of back problems and respiratory infections, JFS's eyesight was growing worse, and he found reading "long letters written on cards" difficult. He began to tire easily and need more assistance at the office and at home than he ever had before. "I cannot get through my work as quickly as I did in my younger days," he complained in a letter to Hyrum in 1916. He continued to work until one or two in the morning on a regular basis, after which he lay in bed "thinking of things I ought to do, which were not done for lack of time and strength, mental and physical." Too proud to ask for respite, he silently resented that "no one seems to realize that I am approaching my 78th year," that they ignored the fact that he had lived a "strenuous life since 7½ years of age," and that "everybody seems to expect" that he could carry the load of a much younger man. JFS imagined that if he could "shift a little more of my responsibility upon others, I might hold my own a little better."[78]

JFS must shoulder much of the blame for his predicament. He had, for decades, cultivated a reputation of tirelessness and virility, and it would have taken a brave soul indeed to suggest that he might not be up to tasks both assigned and assumed. Still, the fact that he could admit, even privately, that he was not what he once was physically, a dimension of life that had been so central to his self-image all of his days, indicates the rapidly accumulating toll of his hard years. His increasingly frequent trips to Santa Monica created a vicious cycle of exhaustion: he sought relief there from his work, but when he returned, he found that he had to dig out from under three weeks' or a month's worth of correspondence. This led to more late nights, worse health, and a desire to return to California. His sons Hyrum, Joseph F., and David A. made efforts to assist their father in these last years of his life, but it was his son Wesley, more than anyone else, upon whom JFS came to rely.

Adding to JFS's burden during this period was his son Coulson's ongoing struggle with alcohol. Coulson apparently had trouble holding down a job, in part because of his drinking. In 1916, Francis Lyman Jr., Coulson's father-in-law, disclosed to JFS that Coulson had "been under the influence of liquor since his change of employment." JFS described this as a "stunner" and, not trusting himself to keep his temper in check, sent David to confront his brother about the allegations. Coulson confirmed that he had, indeed, been drinking. JFS reported the situation to Coulson's mother, Alice, then in Cincinnati.[79] Her response, which is no longer extant because JFS claimed he burned it, apparently accused him of being "disappointed" in her children and "offering a stone" when she had asked for bread.[80]

Some of this tension was the result of Coulson's parentage: JFS had adopted him and his twin brother when he married Alice, and she likely harbored insecurities about the place of the twins in her husband's heart. JFS responded in a fiercely self-defensive tone, claiming to find her letter "astonishing" and arguing that "never in my life have I ever said an unkind word to ... Coulson," even though he admitted to being "deeply hurt" by his behavior. As he so often did, JFS suggested that his children were fortunate to have parents available to provide love, even if was of the tough variety. "I have many times longed for a father and mother," he reminded Alice, "but neither will come to me." In closing, he warned Alice that "it might be well for you to keep calm when you write to me."[81]

Just when JFS thought things could not get any worse, the Republicans in Utah took a beating in the 1916 elections. He could scarcely contain his shock that the "Democratic two-faced infidel" William King had defeated the incumbent Republican, and future Supreme Court justice, George Sutherland. JFS expressed bewilderment at the gullibility of Americans in general, and Utahns in particular, to buy Woodrow Wilson's claim that he had "kept us out of war." That slogan, he wrote, was the "silliest of silly things" given Wilson's various military adventures in Mexico and along the southern border of the United States. "Consistency," JFS observed acidly, "is a jewel!"[82]

Ascending toward Modern Mormonism

Despite the many significant challenges that JFS faced personally and professionally during his presidency, he presided over one of the most successful periods of growth in LDS Church history. Membership nearly doubled, from 283,765 when Lorenzo Snow died to 567,530 by the end of 1918. JFS selected, dedicated, and announced sites for two temples, one in Canada and another in Hawaii at the plantation at Laie. The site for the Cardston Alberta Temple was dedicated in the summer of 1913 while JFS was there attending a stake conference.

An important site of Mormon colonization for decades, Cardston was home to a sizeable population of Mormons, and JFS's decision to build a temple there grew out of his cherished belief in the importance of the sealing ordinances performed within the temples. He had grown frustrated with having to watch young people

342   Chapter 18

who otherwise would have married in a temple for eternity have to settle for civil marriages simply because they could not afford to travel to one of the temples in Utah. He worried that even those who could save the money to come to Utah might not have any left with which to start a family. "By and by," he told the audience at the October 1916 general conference, "we will have a temple up there, and [people] will not be compelled to waste all their substance to come to a temple here."[83]

JFS decided in 1915 to build a temple in Hawaii for the same reason. Always cognizant of significant historical dates, JFS noted to his traveling companions on 1 June that it was the anniversary of Brigham Young's birthday, which had always been important to him. He immediately followed that observation by telling Reed Smoot and Charles Nibley, "I feel impressed to dedicate this ground for the erection of a temple to God, for a place where the peoples of the Pacific can come and do their temple work." JFS had not broached this idea even with his counselors in the First Presidency, "but if you [Smoot and Nibley] think there would be no objection to it, I think now is the time." Of course, as Smoot recorded in his journal, no objection was lodged, and JFS performed the ritual of dedication that evening.[84]

Although Smoot does not mention it, JFS must have informed Samuel Woolley, the president of the Hawaiian mission, of his decision during the visit. Shortly after his return, JFS wrote to Woolley in August 1915, under the heading "<u>Private</u>," that "the matter of building a sacred place at Laie was presented to the Council [of the First Presidency and Quorum of the Twelve] last Thursday ... and was joyfully accepted."[85] He admonished Woolley to keep the news to himself. JFS made the formal public announcement in October.

As with so many other things that JFS did as church president, the decision to build temples abroad represented concrete action resulting from decisions made by earlier administrations. The decision to reverse course on bringing converts from abroad to the Mormon culture region dated back at least to the 1890s. JFS's decision to establish temples in Hawaii and Canada confirmed the intention of Mormon leaders to export their religion rather than import converts.

By 1907, the church had regained solid economic footing, partially due to the increased emphasis on tithing and the sale of church bonds. In early 1910, JFS reported that the church had "witnessed the high-water mark ... in the receipt and accumulation of cash tithing." With just over "the seven unit mark," the church had never been in possession of such vast cash assets.[86] According to JFS, by 1914 the church had paid down the million-dollar debt it carried in 1901. The church's financial recovery allowed for meetinghouses to be built in a wide variety of overseas locations, primarily in Europe and the Pacific. JFS wrote, "We have bought more meeting houses in Great Britain, and in Scandinavia, and in the islands of the sea ... than the church ever owned before, all put together." And it was not just meetinghouses. "In New Zealand we have built a forty thousand dollar college," JFS proclaimed, "and we are sending elders there at the expense of the church to teach school to the Māori people." Church members in these areas had, for decades, met in rented spaces in less-than-ideal conditions. As with the temples in Hawaii and Canada, JFS saw a symbolic statement in the construction of these buildings. Regarding the new LDS buildings abroad, he said, "The world is beginning to think that these Mormons have come here to stay."[87]

In 1913, JFS reluctantly approved plans for a headquarters building in Salt Lake City that would house offices for the First Presidency, the apostles, the presiding bishopric, and other leaders.[88] Now known as the church administration building, the structure was expensive, and JFS had to constantly be convinced, usually by his son David, that the expenditure was worthwhile.

Two years earlier, JFS had again been forced to appoint new church officers. In October 1911 his cousin, friend, and counselor John Henry Smith died. The next month, his half brother John, who had labored so long in JFS's shadow as patriarch to the church, developed pneumonia and died within a week of the first symptoms. JFS lamented these deaths, naturally, but he was always able to quickly adjust to the loss of aged men. He accepted these blows as part of the natural cycle of life, and he feted the lives of both men. However, replacements were required.

JFS chose Charles Penrose, with whom he had worked in Washington on statehood efforts in the late 1880s, as his second counselor. Penrose, a member of the Quorum of the Twelve, had most recently served as president of the European mission. He was also a writer, editor, and an occasional teacher at Brigham Young Academy, and he had helped Wilford Woodruff prepare the 1890 Manifesto. Penrose was in many ways very similar to John Winder, and JFS chose him for the same reasons; both had slightly different political leanings than JFS had (Penrose was a Democrat), both were known to be fiscally conservative, and both had records of long-standing, nondramatic church service.

Replacing John Smith would be more problematic. The office of presiding patriarch (or patriarch to the church) was established in the 1830s as a lineal office to be held by a direct descendant of Hyrum Smith. The general assumption was that John's oldest son, Hyrum F., would be called to replace his father. But Hyrum had a few problems. Like his father, he had a troubled relationship with the Word of Wisdom. Given the renewed emphasis on the prohibition of alcohol and tobacco that the Word of Wisdom was enjoying at the time, JFS could not appoint Hyrum F. without answering some very difficult questions. His chances were not helped by his recent separation from his wife.

JFS made it clear to the Quorum of the Twelve that Hyrum F. was not eligible, but he left them to locate a suitable replacement for John. The only restriction they faced was that they had to choose a worthy, direct descendant of John Smith. The apostles selected Hyrum F.'s son Hyrum G., and he assumed office in May 1912.[89] When JFS presented Hyrum G.'s name to the church's membership for a sustaining vote, he went out of his way to compare the new patriarch to both his father and grandfather. "[He] has been a clean, pure, intelligent boy," he explained, pointing out with particular emphasis that he had "never been addicted to any

344   Chapter 18

habits that he had to abstain from to be in harmony with the principles of the gospel."[90]

The LDS Church's increasingly prominent profile attracted attention from a variety of corners. Almost as soon as the church had paid its debts, it became the victim of an ill-conceived blackmail attempt. A young German convert, Gisbert Bossard, had surreptitiously entered the Salt Lake Temple in the summer of 1911 when it was closed for cleaning and took more than sixty low-quality photographs of the various rooms. The photos ended up in the hands of an entrepreneur named Max Florence, who took them to New York City. In September, he sent eight of the photos to JFS, along with a letter offering the church the opportunity to purchase the photos and threatening, if they declined, to sell them in the lively market of "postal card bureaus, magazines and a great many others."[91]

The threat of an exposé was a bit strange, since, as the *Deseret News* pointed out, hundreds of people had toured the temple during the open house period, and the church itself had published detailed descriptions of the rooms. James Talmage hit upon the idea of preempting whatever minor threat the photos posed by publishing an official collection of high-quality, church-produced photos of the temple's interior. JFS readily embraced the idea and commissioned Talmage to write what would become the LDS classic *The House of the Lord: A Study of Sanctuaries Ancient and Modern*.[92]

The Bossard affair, although an abject failure as a blackmail scheme, demonstrates the church's increasing legal and organizational sophistication. It was now able to deploy skilled lawyers, to say nothing of Smoot himself, to investigate copyright and other issues that the church could use to respond to the threat. Smoot's caution to JFS about hastily replying to the letter may have been an indication of his sophistication and his belief that the church could use the power of the legal system, rather than the angry rhetoric of persecution, to address the problem.

The painful experience of putting an end to plural marriage had taught JFS some important lessons about concession that his younger self would have rejected. At his seventy-sixth birthday party in 1914, he told the group that truth must be embraced and defended even if "the heavens fall, and the stars tremble." But sometimes, he said, stating the obvious truth about polygamy, one must "yield to what is apparently inevitable, that seems to come in contrast ... with that which we know to be right." JFS concluded that when one is left with no option other than "yielding and suffering" under the imposition of laws that contradict divine truth, it tends to develop within one's soul "a good deal of mellowness of spirit, mildness and softness of spirit, and some humility perhaps." He admitted to his assembled friends and family that he needed such softening. "Frequently, in the course of my experiences in life," he confessed, "I have been a little bit severe ... quick to express my displeasure. And I can recall ... circumstances in which I gave offense ... caused injury and hurt ... to members of the church. I felt very sorry for it."[93] "The truest heroism," he wrote to his sister Martha in 1909, "is that of a Saint, who meekly bows to the inevitable."[94]

From Salt Lake to Sharon   345

These expressions reveal a very different JFS than the JFS of decades past. In December 1914, JFS published a sermon in *Liahona: The Elders' Journal* suggesting his growing capacity for introspection and self-understanding. "Our first enemy," he observed, "we will find within ourselves." The first task of any man or woman seeking holiness, he continued, was to "overcome that enemy first, and bring ourselves into subjection to the will of the Father."[95] That was a battle that JFS knew well through long and painful experience.

JFS Faces a World at War

As war clouds gathered over Europe in 1914, JFS had to wrangle with his level of devotion to the United States. Given his memories of past persecutions, there was no chance he would give an unqualified antiwar declaration; he was no pacifist. However, he deplored national aggression. At a meeting in the Salt Lake Temple in the fall of 1914, he "prophesied ... that this terrible European War will not end till those who have brought it on are humiliated in the dust."[96]

World War I coaxed from JFS a latent apocalyptic streak. Although he had never been a hair-trigger apocalypticist in the style of Wilford Woodruff, when he got word in 1916 that his son Hyrum, then serving as president of the European mission, was dodging bombs being dropped over Liverpool by German zeppelins, he looked for understanding in the religious worldview of his youth. JFS was appalled that Germany would undertake such "wicked destruction of property and the taking of defenseless lives." "No such thing has ever been known," JFS observed incorrectly, "in any so-called civilized country before." He believed that this war represented something different and felt that Germany was "possessed" by what he called "the spirit of murder, the shedding of blood." JFS could reach only one conclusion as he puzzled over this butchery: "these are days of trouble and calamity which have been spoken of the prophets and it behooves all men to repent and to turn to the Lord before ... destruction overtakes them."[97]

As late as 1916, JFS did not believe that the United States would become seriously involved in World War I. That was not an uncommon opinion among Americans at the time, but what is interesting is how JFS couched his description of the situation in scriptural terms, and how he seemed to use the term "Zion" in a slightly different way than he had in years past. He noted that "the unifying republics of the Western Hemisphere, and the move looking to general preparedness as a means of defense against invasion, are in line with what has been foreshadowed." At this point, JFS divided the world up between the "Gentile nations," by which he apparently meant the nations of Europe, and "Zion," a term that he was now applying to the United States, not just to the Latter-day Saints. "The Gentile nations will yet look upon the land of Zion with jealous eyes," JFS predicted, "because of her gold and silver ... and will hesitate in their councils to come up to battle against

346   Chapter 18

her because her inhabitants will be regarded as terrible ... against whom they will not be able to stand." Europe, which JFS referred to as "the Gentile world," would suffer "in the extreme sense of the word," but "there will be rejoicing in Israel, whose day is dawning, and who is soon to come in remembrance before the Lord."[98]

It is sometimes difficult, when examining the tumultuous years of JFS presidency, to see through the politics and the business and the general turbidity of the era to the beating heart of religion that drove JFS's life. In his reflections on World War I, his religious side fully materialized in ways that were both traditional and innovative. One key innovation is his identification of America as Zion. Although this idea goes back to the Book of Mormon and was used to a certain extent during the 1840s, it had largely fallen out of rhetorical favor during the nineteenth-century Utah period. JFS was expressing a vision of world events influenced by his reading of Joseph Smith's revelation about the Civil War, verses 3 and 6 of which he believed applied to World War I, coupled with an increasingly irenic relationship between the Mormon and American identities of church members.

JFS's reluctance to join in full-voiced American religious opposition to World War I reflected his deep ambivalence toward progressivism in general. Obviously, Mormon attitudes toward sex and the increasing emphasis on the Word of Wisdom's ban on alcohol, along with JFS's hatred of card playing and spiritualism, all created common ground with progressives in the United States, particularly Protestants. But several problems kept JFS from embracing the antiwar movement.

First, JFS's unshakeable belief that Mormonism was God's unique vehicle for the revelation of truth made cooperation difficult, even under ideal circumstances. The church, as JFS understood it, had to remain independent of other groups, even when it agreed with them on moral principles. He had always envisioned Mormonism as a lone voice calling out truth from the wilderness, so he viewed cooperation with other people of other religions as a potential dilution of Mormonism's identity as "the only true Church." He claimed that progressives were taking their religious ideas from Mormonism anyway. "We are becoming better known by the intelligent, reading, thinking, travelling, broader-minded people of our own land," he wrote to his son Hyrum, noting the contrast with the many years in which Joseph Smith, "one of the greatest of all the prophets[,] has been held without honor." It was therefore no coincidence that progressive religionists agreed with the church on so many issues since "already many of the great truths revealed through [Joseph Smith] are forcing themselves into the minds and compelling the convictions of the foremost thinkers of the age." Although they would certainly never give credit to Mormonism as "the source of their convictions ... they cannot conceal the fact."[99] For JFS, progressive religious principles were nothing more than Mormon teachings wrapped in a mantle of mainstream American Protestantism.

The second reason that JFS was wary of religious progressives was that they had led the cultural campaigns against polygamy. From the days of the 1880s raids all the way to the Smoot hearings and beyond, American religious progressives viewed

Mormonism as an affront to decency, a sexist prison for women, and a threat to the Christian moral order that they believed formed the foundation of American civilization. As Michael McGerr, a historian of Progressivism observed, "The progressives tended to wrap their worries about a host of problems in a consuming fear for the fate of the home." Mormons did the same thing, but JFS's concept of the "ideal" home remained essentially polygamic. This fact made it all but impossible for Protestant progressives and Mormons to come together, despite sharing a hatred of "card playing, horse racing, Sabbath breaking, pornography, dance halls, [and] contraception." Finally, progressives "unequivocally welcomed government interference in private life."[100] This was a touchy subject for JFS. He certainly had no objection to using his own influence to legislate morality in Utah, but it was this very trait of progressivism, this legislative nosiness, that had brought JFS so much personal anguish over the collapse of polygamy.

The issue of Prohibition also illuminates the complex relationship between JFS and religious progressives in the United States. The temperance movement blamed drunkenness for a host of social ills and called for the prohibition of alcohol. By the early 1900s, progressive temperance activists wielded significant influence in many state legislatures and Congress. By 1909, Georgia, Alabama, Oklahoma, Mississippi, North Carolina, Tennessee, and Kansas were totally "dry" thanks to the activism of people like Carry A. Nation. Given JFS's vocal opposition to alcohol and "saloon culture," one might expect him to support Prohibition efforts. But Reed Smoot convinced JFS that the only way for the church to maintain political dominance via the Republican Party in Utah was to support the so-called "local option." This approach to the management of alcohol required localities, usually counties, to determine whether they would be "wet" or "dry." Smoot warned in 1909 that if the church supported statewide prohibition of alcohol, the American Party (formed by Thomas Kearns in the aftermath of Smoot's election to the Senate) would gain greater traction in areas where the non-LDS population was growing, especially in Salt Lake and the railroad town of Ogden.[101]

The Prohibition question placed JFS in an excruciatingly difficult position. His age and declining health compounded the problem. On one hand, Grant represented a chorus of voices calling for JFS to take the moral stand most completely in line with Mormon teachings, regardless of the political consequences. Smoot, by contrast, represented yet another group that worked to impress JFS with the importance of maintaining LDS political influence in Utah, even if it required some degree of compromise. Smoot lobbied JFS incessantly on this subject. In February 1909, when JFS left for a trip to Hawaii, Smoot assumed that he was trying to "get away from the Prohibition fight."[102] This is unlikely the only reason JFS left, given that the trip cost between $700 and $800, which he said "came close to 'washing me ashore' so to speak."[103]

Setting aside Smoot's arrogant belief that his pet issue was the only thing on JFS's mind when he traveled to Hawaii in 1909, he was correct in sensing that the

348   Chapter 18

Prohibition debate placed a tremendous strain on him. Neither side was happy about the noncommittal stance JFS had tried to adopt. Non-Mormon Republicans with business interests in the liquor industry demanded to know why the church was throwing its weight behind Prohibition. JFS claimed innocence in the matter. "Heber J. Grant is a member of the Anti-Saloon league," JFS wrote to one angry Republican, "[but] for those acts the church is not responsible." Although it was obvious that the church had always been "strongly in favor of temperance," JFS hoped "to be spared the annoyance of being dragged into public notoriety over this question, as I earnestly desire to keep entirely aloof from it."[104]

In a letter written a few days later, JFS emphasized that "from the beginning of this movement [Prohibition] I have strenuously endeavored to keep myself absolutely apart and aloof from participation on either side and I am determined to remain so."[105] Smoot, however, eventually won JFS over, and the church was instrumental in keeping Prohibition from becoming law in Utah in 1909. JFS consistently opposed further attempts to pass comprehensive Prohibition legislation in Utah for the rest of life.

Without access to JFS's journals for this period, we are left to guess about his personal feelings on Prohibition. In some respects, the issue was part of the church's increasingly intimate dance with modernity that had been ongoing since at least the completion of the transcontinental railroad in 1869. Two forces existed within Mormonism. One sought to more fully integrate Mormonism with American culture through the adaptation of some Mormon practices in the face of political and cultural realities. The other force was reactionary, deeply conservative, and, to borrow a categorical term from religious studies, fundamentalist. JFS, like most Mormons, found himself moved by both forces depending on the particular issue at hand. On Prohibition, JFS took the modernist stance and rejected the fundamentalist position of Grant and others.

On other matters, however, JFS was an unyielding reactionary. Unlike the urgent political or economic pressures from without, Mormon doctrine and ritual yielded to his efforts to create order and coherence. Historian Jonathan Stapley, one of the foremost experts on Mormon ritual, correctly observes that JFS also "wielded tremendous influence over the patterns, forms, and rituals of Church life and that influence generally took the form of imposing uniformity, simplicity, and permanence on to a wide variety of Mormon ritual practices." Stapley specifically looked at rituals of baptism for health, which JFS did away with; baby blessings, which JFS simplified; and female participation in healing rituals, which JFS supported but left outside of the realm of codified ritual, thus ensuring its demise as members of the church came to rely heavily on published ritual handbooks from which the female healings had been omitted.[106]

The development of the temple garment is another classic example of JFS in fundamentalist mode. When Joseph Smith introduced the temple endowment in Nauvoo, part of the ritual involved the initiate being clothed in an undergarment that, when properly marked with sacred symbols, became a powerful "apotropaic" object, meaning one designed to avert evil. Endowed Mormons were instructed to wear the undergarment day and night until death. Joseph Smith apparently experimented with different styles until he settled on a union-suit design featuring long legs and sleeves, a collar, and string ties up the front. By the early 1900s, however, the garment began to pose practical problems, especially for women.

As skirts and dresses shortened to the point that portions of the lower legs were visible, women began to wear hosiery—nearly impossible to combine with the garment. When women began slightly modifying the garment to accommodate the changing styles, rumblings among church members about the troubles they had wearing "modern fashions" reached JFS's ears. He believed, however, that the design of the garment had been given by revelation from God to Joseph Smith. He did not know about the experimentation that Smith engaged in as he designed it.

In 1906, JFS penned a strongly worded editorial in the *Improvement Era* stating unequivocally that "the Lord has given unto us garments of the holy priesthood ... and yet there are those who mutilate them in order that we may follow the foolish, vain and (permit me to say) indecent practices of the world." This would simply not do. Faithful Latter-day Saints were expected to "hold these things that God has given unto them sacred and unchanged and unaltered from the very pattern in which God gave them." Failure to do so was "to break a covenant and so commit a grievous sin."[107]

During his presidency, JFS produced two major theological proclamations codifying doctrine that had evolved throughout the nineteenth century, one on the origin of man and the other on God the Father and Jesus Christ. In 1909, Charles Darwin and his theories of organic evolution were much talked about because it was the 100th anniversary of Darwin's birth. JFS, naturally, rejected Darwin's theories, or at least the popular versions of them that most Americans knew about. He rejected the notion that humans have any lineage between Adam, a fully human male, and God. God created Adam and Eve, placed them in the Garden of Eden, and the rest was, to JFS, literal history. Darwin's ideas, coupled with the constellation of notions governing biblical studies known as "higher criticism" (emanating from Germany), posed a serious threat to the dominant literalist view of the Bible. Julius Wellhausen, a German scholar, introduced the documentary hypothesis, which argued that the first five books of the Hebrew Bible were not written by Moses, as tradition insisted, but by four separate redactors far removed in time from the events they described.

JFS was so troubled by these ideas that he commissioned Orson F. Whitney to draft a proclamation outlining the LDS Church's views on the subject. Whitney, a grandson of Heber C. Kimball, and therefore JFS's nephew by marriage, had served as an assistant church historian since 1899, and an apostle since 1906. In October 1909, the First Presidency read Whitney's first draft of the proclamation, but they were not satisfied. He showed them a second draft shortly thereafter,

350   Chapter 18

to which JFS made a few alterations and then authorized for publication. The short document made the case that human beings are "the direct and lineal off-spring of Deity [and that] God Himself is an exalted man, perfected, enthroned, and supreme." But the proclamation also signaled the church's rejection of higher criticism by insisting that Adam, Moses, the brother of Jared, and other figures mentioned in scripture were historical persons, and that Moses was the author of the Torah. The final product was published as "The Origin of Man" in the church publication *Improvement Era*, with authorship attributed to the First Presidency.[108]

In 1910, three professors at Brigham Young University were investigated by a committee appointed by the First Presidency on suspicion of teaching organic evolution and approaching the Bible through the paradigm of higher criticism. By this point, JFS was expressing in private his belief that there was an unbridgeable gap between "the doctrine of Christ and fictitious science."[109] Publicly, he took a slightly more nuanced stance. In 1911, after months of meetings and discussions, the three professors were fired. JFS defended this action in an editorial in the *Improvement Era*. The problem, as he framed it, was not one of content, but of epistemological dominance. He had always championed the idea that Mormonism welcomed truth from whatever source it came. But truth for JFS could only be determined through a comparison between any scientific discovery and revealed truth. And, as we have seen, by "revealed truth," JFS meant official interpretation of scripture. The professors, he wrote, believed that a conflict between science and scripture had to be resolved by an appeal to science. "The church," he wrote, by contrast, "holds to the definite authority of divine revelation which must be the standard." Science was unstable, he wrote, and "changed from age to age," but "divine revelation ... must abide forever."[110]

This stance is in perfect accord with the concept of doctrinal formation that JFS developed in the 1870s and 1880s, well before science presented any specific challenge. The key to JFS's doctrinal thinking was always vested in the ability of the church president to control scriptural interpretation in such a way as to emphasize stability by insisting on the obviousness and unchangeability of doctrine, especially during periods when scriptural interpretations were changing the most. So while he claimed to welcome all truth with joy, if it contradicted the traditional, literalist reading of scripture, then it was not truth. Such an epistemological model was required to maintain the internal consistency and doctrinal order that JFS sought to create within Mormonism, and it was this pressing need for order and coherence, in other words sociological conservatism rather than theological conservatism, that led JFS to guide the church down a deeply conservative channel both theologically and sociologically.

A similar document, designed to clarify LDS Church doctrine concerning the relationship between God the Father and Jesus Christ, was written at JFS's behest in 1916, although "establish" is a more accurate term than "clarify" for what the document did. In a letter to his son Hyrum, JFS wrote that he felt forced to produce a statement "to settle the questions arising on the subject in the ministry of the Elders and in the Priesthood meetings."[111] This was part of JFS's decades-long effort to silence doctrinal debate at all levels of the church. He still regularly responded personally, and not altogether patiently, to letters asking him to settle questions arising in priesthood and Sunday school classes. To one such inquiry regarding Adam-God and the question of multiple mortal probations, JFS asserted that "such questions [that cannot] be settled by accepted revelations should not be raised, either in a priesthood meeting or any other assembly."[112]

To lay the debates about God and Christ to rest, JFS chose James Talmage to write the text, and he approved it wholeheartedly. In many ways, "The Father and the Son: A Doctrinal Exposition" bears the marks of a classic JFS doctrinal innovation. It takes an issue that is, in fact, scripturally unclear—in this case, how the Son can be called the Father and still be a separate being—and presents an interpretation that makes it seem completely obvious and non-contradictory. Thus the interpretation is presented not as interpretation, but as nothing more than a correct reading of the relevant texts.

The significance of "The Father and the Son" is not in the rather banal doctrinal points it makes, but in the way that it further highlights the increasing importance of hierarchical control of official doctrine within Mormonism. The contrast with the way things worked in the nineteenth century could not be starker. The Pratt brothers and other theologians wrote and published under their own names, and they often challenged the church president's view of doctrinal concepts. JFS, by contrast, cultivated faithful intellectuals like Whitney, Talmage, and John A. Widtsoe who shared his epistemological orientation, and then brought them into the hierarchy. There they were expected to put their minds to work in the service of JFS's agenda and to forgo personal credit for their writing, allowing it to be subsumed under the cope of the First Presidency.

19 | Dusk

The year 1917 was one of the most peaceful of Joseph F. Smith's presidency. He made a trip to Hawaii, which would be his last, and inspected the temple being built on the site of the old plantation at Laie. In July, he headed for Deseret Santa Monica, where he did his best to stay away from work and to engage in "golf therapy." When he returned to Salt Lake, he spent fewer hours in the office, relying on his counselors, Lund and Penrose, to pick up the slack.

One notable difference in JFS was that his patience with visitors was beginning to wear thin in a way that it had not in previous years. According to Lund, one family who had an audience with him claimed that their house was "full of evil spirits," which they had seen. JFS apparently had heard enough ghost stories and "got out of patience with the ideas presented." He told the father to use his priesthood to "drive them out" and sent the family off with a reminder that only unrepentant sinners had anything to fear from demons.[1]

By October 1917, JFS's health was again poor, and he retreated to Santa Monica. This time the California air did little for him, and he was back in Utah to celebrate his seventy-ninth birthday in November. He was finding it increasingly difficult to sit through meetings and frequently had to leave early and rest at home. During another visit to California in early December, a fire broke out in the Logan Temple, causing significant damage. Although kept abreast of the situation, JFS left it to Lund and Penrose to investigate and begin rebuilding.

Against the counsel of family members, JFS insisted on hitting the links, but once on the green, he began to suffer from heart palpitations and dizziness so severe that he could barely stand. Unsurprisingly, JFS shook off the hands that reached out to steady him and obstinately pressed on to the next hole. He later explained that he simply could not face the "shame" of abandoning the course "after he had reached the green."[2] But JFS's independence and sheer will could only put off the inevitable for so long. Just after Christmas, JFS collapsed at the Beehive House and had a catheter inserted to aid with bladder problems, possibly caused by an enlarged prostate.

In January 1918, Hyrum M. Smith—a favorite son, an apostle, and one of the great lights of JFS's life—died suddenly of complications from a burst appendix. The entire church was in shock, but no one more than the seventy-nine-year-old president of the church. This was the thirteenth and final child JFS would bury. At times, there is a dark, poetic symmetry in history: two dead Hyrum Smiths; two traumas too deep to heal. The deaths of his father and son, both taken before their time, framed JFS's life. The death of his father signaled the dawn of his life in much the same way that the death of his son signaled its dusk.

Accompanied by Lund and Penrose, JFS went to view Hyrum's body for the last time. According to Lund, he "broke down and groaned." It was, he observed, "a very bad scene."[3] At the Salt Lake City Cemetery, George Albert Smith dedicated the grave. JFS looked on silently as the snow gently blanketed the earth. This was the one loss from which he would never recover.

JFS sought refuge at Deseret Santa Monica, where he wore his grief like a mask. Over the next two months, his bladder problems intensified. His doctor also reported that JFS's "heart [is] not doing well" and complained that he was resisting medical care, tending to "put it off" if he could get away with it. "Insist upon rest," the doctor said.[4] Perhaps because of such warnings, Edna and others of the "folks at home" castigated David for writing to JFS so frequently on matters of church business.[5] JFS, still fiercely independent, resented such interference, reassuring David that regardless of "what Aunt Edna or anybody else says about your writing to me," the only reason he should stop writing would be if "I suggest it myself."[6]

Although in frequent contact with David, JFS had little contact with the other members of the First Presidency, but they had grown accustomed to working without his input. He did not work another full day until the end of March. He returned to Salt Lake just in time to learn of a major offensive launched by the Germans against the British in the ongoing European bloodbath. Coming so close on the heels of his own son's death, the news of the staggering casualties in Europe resonated deeply with JFS. In April, for the first time on record, he attended a temple meeting of the First Presidency and the Quorum of the Twelve without clothing himself in the sacred priesthood robes. He was simply too weak.

In May, JFS suffered a minor stroke that forced him to use a cane, but by then he seldom went to the office. On 27 June 1918, he managed to attend and briefly speak at the dedication ceremony of the monument built in the Salt Lake Cemetery to his father's memory. JFS spent the rest of the summer and early fall at home, attended by a full-time nurse, as well as his sons David and Joseph. What little business he conducted, he did in his dressing gown, describing himself as "wobbly."[7] As the summer wore on, JFS's appetite vanished, and Lund sadly reported that "what [food] he takes is just forced down."[8]

It was around this point, according to David, that JFS "made up his mind ... that his work was finished and that he was ready to join those of his family and loved ones who have gone before."[9] Grant felt that JFS's punishing work ethic had finally

354   Chapter 19

caught up with him. "When I was 24 I broke down from over work," Grant wrote Reed Smoot in 1918. "I collapsed utterly and for 20 days I had to have assistance to rise up in bed, but I only worked a single month as [JFS] has been doing for 38 years." JFS's apparently bottomless reserve of energy was down to the dregs by late August. Grant wrote that he "seemed to lack the vitality and the spirit to hang on to life," and frequently "frightened" him by "saying things [indicating] he was more than willing to say goodbye."[10] Once or twice, he appeared close enough to death that family members living in distant areas were asked to hurry home.[11]

Fear about JFS's fragile condition led his family to keep bad news from him. In late September, Hyrum's widow, Ida, died from complications in childbirth. The family feared the news would literally kill JFS, so they did not tell him. One day, some of the family took JFS out for a ride in the car, and he asked to be taken to Ida's house so he could see his new grandchild. The family "pretended not to understand just what he wanted and got him home." JFS persisted in requesting that he be permitted to perform the ordinance of naming and blessing the baby, so the family arranged for the child to be brought to the Beehive House, where JFS performed the ritual with a great show of emotion. They still did not tell him about Ida's death, a fact that led Grant to observe that the family had better not "delay much longer telling him of Ida's death for fear that he might hear it from some other source."[12] When JFS finally was told, he was silent.

By this time, he had full-time medical supervision, and the doctors insisted that he be left alone and not troubled by visitors. Grant, president of the Quorum of the Twelve, went weeks without seeing JFS despite efforts to get an audience.[13] This enforced loneliness could not have helped JFS's state of mind, and it did nothing to inspire optimism in the leaders who were being kept away.

JFS's decline was significant enough to spark off a minor succession debate between the apostles and the presiding patriarch. When JFS had increased the symbolic importance of the office of presiding patriarch in 1901, some of the apostles, including John Henry Smith, had worried that it might lead to complications over succession when JFS died. Hyrum G. Smith, John's successor, told Grant and JFS Jr. that it was his opinion that he would become "the presiding authority in the church" upon JFS's death. Grant stifled any potential debate by producing a letter written by Wilford Woodruff in 1887 indicating that the president of the Quorum of the Twelve should succeed to the presidency of the church upon the death of the president barring "a direct revelation from the Lord" to the contrary.[14] The apostles brought the issue to Lund, but decided that they would not tell JFS about the controversy because of his health.

Although he had no appetite and was wasting away, JFS was not ready to be written off just yet. He informed the church authorities that he would attend the October 1918 general conference. With this as a goal, he seemed to rally. As the October conference got underway, JFS appeared frail and wispy in the pulpit. His once powerful voice quavered, and his feet shook as he steadied himself.[15]

He wasted no time in addressing his health. "As most of you know," he said as soon as he reached the podium, "I have been undergoing a siege of very serious illness for the last five months." JFS went on to give an unusual opening address in which he hinted to the congregation that he had much more to tell them than he had strength with which to tell it.

"I have not lived alone these five months," JFS told them. Although stricken in body during that time, he had "dwelt in the spirit of prayer, of supplication, of faith, and of determination." Just what he had been supplicating his God for he did not say. He did, however, tell his audience that he "had my communion with the Spirit of the Lord continuously." This communion had borne spiritual fruit, but JFS decided to "postpone until some future time . . . my attempt to tell" his listeners what was on his mind. That time, of course, never came. What JFS did tell them, however, was that they should be very careful about "stories of revelations that are being circulated around [by] persons who have no authority." When God wanted to speak to his people, JFS reminded them, the message would be clear and would come from the president of the LDS Church. There is no need, he assured them, to "be hunting after revelations from Tom, Dick, and Harry all over the world."[16]

JFS's final conference included, perhaps inevitably, a minor controversy over plural marriage. Charles Penrose gave a sermon in which he strongly denounced those men who had entered into plural marriages after 1890 as "rebels and traitors."[17] Many in the audience could scarcely believe what they were hearing. Joseph Robinson, president of the California mission, fumed in his seat, especially since this was coming from a man who, Robinson believed, had "taken another man's wife" as a plural bride "after 1890."[18]

Perhaps sensing the reaction from the crowd, JFS took the podium and endorsed Penrose's condemnation of post-Manifesto marriages. "I want to say to this congregation and to the world," he proclaimed in the strongest voice he could muster, "that never at any time since my presidency of the church has any plural marriage been performed with my sanction or knowledge, or with the consent of the church." They could "put down in your notebook," he said, that any plural marriages contracted since 1901 were "null and void . . . and are not marriages."[19]

Since many in the room knew that JFS had authorized several such marriages, the entire performance was baffling. Many of the church leaders also knew that JFS had secretly sent Penrose to take charge of the European mission in 1906 because he was "marked . . . as subject for arrest and prosecution on the charge of unlawful cohabitation."[20] Robinson, unable to let go of his anger, brought the issue up with Apostles Anthony Ivins and Heber J. Grant several days later. Ivins, who had been heavily involved in post-Manifesto marriages in Mexico, shared Robinson's confusion but indicated it was nothing new. "I want to tell you frankly brother Robinson," Ivins confided, "President Smith's position in the matter has always been an enigma to me."[21]

Still unable to settle his mind, Robinson managed to get an audience with JFS a few days later. He told him of his and others' reactions to the Penrose talk. If it

356   Chapter 19

bothered him so much, JFS asked, then "why didn't Tony [Ivins] stand up [in conference] for what he knows has been done?" Although somewhat puzzled by JFS's strange suggestion that Ivins should have publicly called a member of the First Presidency, and indeed JFS himself, a liar and a hypocrite at general conference, Robinson asked if it might be possible to keep Penrose's sermon from being published in any of the church periodicals. To his surprise, JFS agreed, observing that it was "bad enough to print it in our conference report." JFS ended the meeting by expressing his hope that Penrose's talk would not do any lasting emotional damage to Robinson or his wives, the second and third of whom he had married in 1901. Until the very end of his life, JFS apparently could not reconcile the conflicting imperatives that plural marriage and its cessation forced upon him.[22] The final words he spoke to the church membership before his death seem to sum up the problem he faced regarding this elusive reconciliation: "time will not permit."[23]

At the meeting of the First Presidency and the apostles on 31 October 1918, JFS Jr. came bearing a typed document that he wished to read to the assembled group. It was, he said, a revelation JFS had received on 3 October and which he had dictated to his son sometime in the latter half of the month. Anthon Lund described the revelation in his journal as a vision in which JFS "saw the spirits in Paradise and he also saw that Jesus organized a number of brethren to go and preach to the spirits in prison but did not go himself. It was an interesting document and the Apostles accepted it as true and from God."[24]

This lengthy revelation came to JFS as he had been reading the New Testament and "pondering" over material in the third chapter of 1 Peter that describes Christ's mission to the spirits of the dead. He was puzzled over how Christ could have accomplished so much in the brief time between his death and his resurrection. The revelation explained that Christ did not do the work personally, but rather "organized" spirits to go forth and teach repentance to the wicked spirits. When they had been converted and repented, they could claim the blessings of the temple, provided earthly proxies had performed the ordinances for them. But that was not all the revelation contained. It also described a heaven in which JFS saw his own relatives and other important figures from scriptural history, from Adam and Eve all the way to Wilford Woodruff. Curiously, there is no mention of Lorenzo Snow.

In early November, Susa Young Gates visited JFS at the Beehive House. From his bed, he read the revelation to her. "He tells of his view of Eternity," she marveled in her journal, including scenes of "the Savior when He visited the spirits in prison, how His servants minister to them; he was the Prophet [Joseph Smith] and all his associate Brethren laboring in prison houses," and, most importantly to Gates, "Mother Eve and her noble daughters engaged in the same holy cause!" She identified three key contributions of the revelation. First, it was evidence that the "heavens are still opened!" Second, it depicted a spirit world in which women played an essential role. Finally, and, to her mind, "above all," the revelation came at a time when "temple work and workers need such encouragement."[25]

Dusk   357

Gates's observations concerning the significance of the document were remarkably astute. In this revelation, JFS had distilled a lifetime of concerns and ideas. He had never ceased to be rankled by the humiliating line of questioning regarding revelation in front of the Smoot committee. There he sat, a prophet with no prophecy, a revelator with no revelations. During his months of confinement in 1918, it seems likely that he spent a great deal of time appealing to God for a revelation that he could give to his people. And when that revelation came, it contained the ideas that had so long been percolating in JFS's mind and heart: a home-centered heaven where mothers hold prominent place, coupled with a fully articulated rationale for proxy temple work. Since Joseph Smith had introduced the concept in the 1840s, it had struggled to find a champion, someone who possessed a passion for the work of the temple as well as a capacity for doctrinal thinking that could place proxy temple work within the larger whole of Mormon belief and practice. JFS did both.

Scholars who have examined the roots of this revelation have pointed to World War I and the death of JFS's son Hyrum M. Smith as its primary catalysts. Certainly, both events focused JFS on the question of death and the afterlife in an urgent way. Of course, he also had in mind his own impending death. The revelation was as much his own personal vision of the life he was about to enter as it was anything else. But the ideas, as we have seen, were old ones. JFS did not require World War I or Hyrum's demise to put him in mind of death. It had stalked him his entire life. JFS's mind was a machine that produced order, coherence, and theological, doctrinal, and ritual complementarity. As early as 1875, he committed to writing the material that would emerge in more dramatic form in the 1918 revelation.

Mormons believe that revelation requires the use of the mind; a kind of mental and spiritual reaching out toward God is necessary for the divine to communicate. For Joseph Smith, this usually resulted in a revelation that could be dictated immediately. JFS did not receive this revelation on 3 October 1918, as he claimed. That was simply the moment when the vessel was full. JFS had been receiving this revelation, on behalf of his people, drop by excruciating drop, since the moment his father died.

JFS's final illness, a respiratory infection, took hold in early November 1918. He turned eighty on 13 November. At that point he was being treated with morphine, and his consciousness was oscillating unpredictably. On 18 November, Heber J. Grant—the president of the Quorum of the Twelve and, by tradition, the next in line for the presidency—visited JFS. "A great responsibility is coming to you," JFS managed to whisper, and he counseled Grant to "always remember that the Lord is greater than men and he makes no mistake in those he chooses to lead his Church." Later that evening, Grant returned, accompanied this time by Lund and three of JFS's sons. JFS fixed his nearly black eyes on them and requested that they give him a priesthood blessing. "Brethren," he said as they went to place their hands on his head, "pray that I may be released." It was the first time in his life that

JFS had ever asked to be released from anything. Lund reluctantly obliged, praying, "Lord, if Prest. Smith's mission is finished, release him from his suffering."[26] JFS lost consciousness soon after, and several hours later, at 4:50 a.m. on 19 November 1918, he died.

Julina saw to it that JFS was dressed in his temple robes and laid out for a private viewing in the Beehive House. The family had decided that no public funeral service would be held because of an outbreak of Spanish flu then ravaging the country. Those who came to see his body were uniformly impressed with the look of "dignity" he wore in death. Emmeline B. Wells, president of the General Relief Society, was "greatly grieved" at the sight of JFS, "very grand and beautiful in his lovely robes."[27] "How glorious and kingly he looked," wrote Susa Young Gates, "he was the greatest and noblest man I ever knew except my father." Despite being told to stay away, crowds of people surrounded the Beehive House. "The poor and obscure folks," Gates noted in her finest patrician tone, "just crowded in begging just to look at his face."[28]

JFS's funeral was a small affair, after which he was buried near his children in the Salt Lake City Cemetery. He was not alone. On the day of his burial, the "hosts of the dead" laid low by influenza were so great that the cemetery sexton had to hire extra gravediggers.

Afterword

In 1996, the Church of Jesus Christ of Latter-day Saints instituted a curricular change for adult priesthood and Relief Society meetings. The new course was developed from a series of manuals based on the teachings of previous church presidents. These manuals are useful examples of how the church desires each of its presidents to be remembered. There is a great deal of repetition, with most of the manuals containing sections on the Book of Mormon, Joseph Smith, temple work, following church leaders, treating people with kindness, sexual purity, and so forth. The Joseph F. Smith manual follows these patterns, but there are several statements that are jarring to anyone who has studied JFS's life in detail.

JFS was the subject of study in 2000 and 2001. While the compilers of the manual cannot be faulted for claiming that the famous story about JFS being "late but clean" occurred in Hawaii—after all, they were quoting JFS's misremembrance of an event that had actually occurred in England more than a decade later than he claimed—other inclusions are puzzling, assuming the church committee that compiled the book had access to JFS's papers.

In a chapter titled "The Wrongful Road of Abuse," the editors of the manual state that JFS was "a tender and gentle man who expressed sorrow at any kind of abuse. He understood that violence would beget violence, and his own life was an honest expression of compassion and patience, warmth and understanding." Further, they wrote, "violence ... was unthinkable to him." This is a puzzling statement to make about anyone, let alone a man who admitted to beating his first wife and severely beating his neighbor, with no recorded remorse for either act surviving for us to see.

Why include such a strong, almost ridiculous claim? Naturally, the LDS Church, in an insider publication designed to build faith rather than historical knowledge, would not be expected to include all of the details of JFS's violent past. But they did not simply ignore the problems, emphasizing his legitimate tender side. Rather, they chose to proactively and absolutely preclude any possible discussion of what was, arguably, JFS's best-known trait among Latter-day Saints during his lifetime. In many ways, this part of the manual—which, notably, makes claims that JFS never made himself—is the photographic negative of the Scott Kenney piece "Before the Beard" discussed in the introduction to this book.

While some readers may dismiss the manual's misrepresentation of JFS, it raises important questions about historical figures and the roles that their memories play long after their deaths. What is JFS to us now? Is he an elastic figure to be used to further agendas that have little use for a full picture of the man? I suggest in the strongest possible terms that using individuals from past eras as mascots for our own propagandist purposes does terrible violence to the truth.

Fortunately, not all treatments of JFS are as disturbing. Just as in his life, JFS in death has occupied a unique place among LDS leaders. In many accounts, he is portrayed as a particularly brave man, as attested by the endless retellings of his alleged "true blue through and through" encounter, but also as a man with an astonishingly tender heart, evidenced by the frequent evocation of his reactions to the deaths of his young children. And, of course, he is best known among LDS Church members for "The Vision of the Redemption of the Dead," which is currently section 138 of the Doctrine and Covenants and the scriptural foundation for much of the doctrine around LDS temple work for the dead.

At the October 2018 general conference, Apostle M. Russell Ballard delivered a sermon commemorating the 100th anniversary of JFS's "Vision of the Redemption of the Dead." Ballard was the perfect choice to give this talk since he is a great-grandson of JFS. Apart from the devotional content of Ballard's remarks, they stand as a testament to the persistence of two of JFS's most important accomplishments; namely, his development of the idea of a family heaven, and the presence of a Hyrum Smith descendant in the upper echelons of LDS Church leadership. From the time of the church's organization in 1830 until the time of this writing (2022), Hyrum Smith or one of his descendants has been in either the First Presidency or the Quorum of the Twelve for all but twenty-six years. JFS and JFS Jr. remain the only father and son to serve as church presidents, something that would no doubt have pleased JFS.

Over the years, attempts have been made to present a kinder, gentler version of JFS by focusing on the more tender elements of his personality. Such efforts are as damaging to his memory as those that focus exclusively on his more brutish traits. The truth is that JFS was a living coincidence of opposites. He was caring and cruel, abusive and adoring, sentimental and scathing, intelligent and ignorant, deeply spiritual and terrifyingly violent. Anyone who neglects these conflicting traits cannot do justice to the man who endured so much trauma and experienced, and embodied, so much of the American experience in the second half of the nineteenth century. It is my hope that this volume has done justice to the full scope of JFS's life, thought, and experiences.

Notes

INTRODUCTION

1. JFS to E. W. Tullidge, 29 June 1876, JFS Papers, MS 1325, box 30, folder 2, LDS Church History Library.
2. Joseph Fielding Smith, *The Life of Joseph F. Smith* (Salt Lake City: Deseret News, 1938).
3. Francis M. Gibbons, *Joseph F. Smith: Patriarch and Preacher, Prophet of God* (Salt Lake City: Deseret Book, 1984).
4. Scott G. Kenney, "Before the Beard: Trials of the Young Joseph F. Smith," *Sunstone* 20 (November 2001): 20–42.
5. Oleg V. Khlevniuk, *Stalin: A New Biography of a Dictator* (New Haven: Yale University Press, 2015), x.
6. Craig K. Manscill et al., eds. *Joseph F. Smith: Reflections on the Man and His Times* (Salt Lake City: Deseret Book, 2013).

CHAPTER I

1. For information on William Laud and his "Eleven Years of Tyranny," see Hugh Trevor-Roper, *Archbishop Laud* (New York: Phoenix Press, 2001). For a discussion of Robert Smith, see Richard Lyman Bushman, *Joseph Smith: Rough Stone Rolling* (New York: Knopf, 2005), 14.
2. Lavina Fielding Anderson, "Lucy Mack Smith," in *United by Faith: The Joseph Sr. and Lucy Mack Smith Family*, ed. Kyle R. Walker (American Fork, UT: Covenant Communications, 2006), 42.
3. Mark L. McConkie, "Joseph Smith Sr.," in Walker, *United by Faith*, 11–12.
4. Simply put, Arminianism is a theology that teaches, in contrast to Calvinism, that Christ's atonement in not limited to a predestined elect; rather, it is unlimited, but depends upon the acceptance of Christ as one's personal savior.
5. Bushman, *Joseph Smith*, 23.
6. Bushman, *Joseph Smith*, 26.
7. It is well known at this point that Joseph Smith provided multiple accounts of his theophany. These accounts differ on certain details, including how many divine beings were present and exactly what the beings said. The version referred to above is from an 1838 account, which is now included in LDS scripture as part of the Pearl of Great Price.

362   *Notes to Pages 7–13*

8. Ronald K. Esplin, "Hyrum Smith," in Walker, *United by Faith*, 124–26.

9. Jonathan Rodell, *A Rise of Methodism: A Study of Bedfordshire* (Rochester, NY: Bodell and Brewer, 2014).

10. Mary Fielding to Joseph Fielding, 18 March 1833, Mary Fielding Smith Collection, MS 2779, box 1, folder 3, LDS Church History Library.

11. Samuel W. Taylor, *The Last Pioneer: John Taylor, a Mormon Prophet* (Salt Lake City: Signature Books, 1999), 14–27.

12. Terryl L. Givens and Matthew J. Grow, *Parley P. Pratt: The Apostle Paul of Mormonism* (New York: Oxford University Press, 2011), 83.

13. Mercy Rachel Thompson, Centennial Letter to Posterity, 1880, MS 2737, box 1, folder 6, LDS Church History Library.

14. Mary Fielding to Mercy Fielding, 8 July 1837, Mary Fielding Smith Collection, MS 2779, box 1, folder 3, LDS Church History Library.

15. Mary Fielding to Mercy Fielding, ca. August–September 1837, Mary Fielding Smith Collection, MS 2779, box 1, folder 3, LDS Church History Library.

16. Mary Fielding to Mercy Fielding Thompson, 8 July 1837, Mary Fielding Smith Collection, LDS Church History Library.

17. Samuel Smith to Hyrum Smith, 13 October 1837, Hyrum Smith Papers, MS 14305, LDS Church History Library.

18. "Obituary," *The Elder's Journal of the Church of Latter Day Saints* 1:1, 10.

19. Mary Fielding to Unknown Suitor, 1832, "never to enter into the important and responsible situation of Step Mother." Quoted in Jay A. Parry, "Called to Drink the Bitter Cup," in *Women of Faith in the Latter Days*, ed. Richard Turley and Brittany Chapman, vol. 2, *1821–1845* (Salt Lake City: Deseret Book, 2012).

20. Mary Fielding Smith to Hyrum Smith, 14 September 1842, Mary Fielding Smith Collection, MS 2779, box 1, folder 3, LDS Church History Library.

21. Jon Meacham, *American Lion: Andrew Jackson in the White House* (New York: Random House, 2008), xix.

22. H. W. Brands, *Andrew Jackson: His Life and Times* (New York: Anchor Books, 2005), x.

23. Richard E. Ellis, "The Market Revolution and the Transformation of American Politics, 1801–1837," in *The Market Revolution in America: Social, Political, and Religious Expressions, 1800–1880*, ed. Melvyn Stokes and Stephen Conway (Charlottesville: University of Virginia Press, 1996), 159.

24. Christopher Clark, "The Consequences of the Market Revolution in the American North," in Stokes and Conway, *The Market Revolution in America*, 37.

25. Jon Butler, *Awash in a Sea of Faith: Christianizing the American People* (New Haven: Yale University Press, 1990).

26. Katie Oxx, *The Nativist Movement in America: Religious Conflict in the Nineteenth Century* (New York: Routledge, 2013), 54.

27. Quotes from the *Southern Times*, *Richmond Whig*, and *National Gazette* are from David Grimsted, *American Mobbing, 1828–1861: Toward Civil War* (New York: Oxford University Press, 2003), 3.

28. Michael Lind, *Land of Promise: An Economic History of the United States* (New York: Harper, 2012), 116.

29. For a detailed discussion of the Kirtland Safety Society and its collapse, see Mark Lyman Stake, *Hearken, O Ye People: The Historical Setting of Joseph Smith's Ohio Revelations* (Salt Lake City: Greg Kofford Books, 2009), 463–519.

Notes to Pages 13–18 363

30. See Ronald K. Esplin, "Joseph Smith and the Kirtland Crisis," in *Joseph Smith: The Prophet and Seer*, ed. Richard Holzapfel and Kent P. Jackson (Salt Lake City: Deseret Book, 2010), 261–90. The term "general authorities" refers to leaders in the LDS Church who are above the level of stake president, which is the highest level of local leadership.

31. Revelation given 20 July 1831; a manuscript image is reproduced in *The Joseph Smith Papers: Revelations and Translations, Manuscript Revelation Books*, by Robin Scott Jensen, Robert J. Woodford, and Steven C. Harper (Salt Lake City: Church Historian's Press, 2009), 159–60.

32. See Alexander L. Baugh, "The Haun's Mill Massacre and the Extermination Order of Missouri Governor Lilburn W. Boggs," *Mormon Historical Studies* 10, no. 1 (Spring 2009): 22–31.

33. Joseph Smith Papers Project (JSPP), *Histories*, 1:513.

34. Bushman, *Joseph Smith*, 362.

35. Bushman, *Joseph Smith*, 372.

36. For general information about the Mormon War, see Leland H. Gentry and Todd M. Compton, *Fire and Sword: A History of the Latter-day Saints in Northern Missouri, 1836–1839* (Salt Lake City: Greg Kofford Books, 2011).

37. Hyrum Smith, affidavit, published in *Times and Seasons*, 1 July 1843, 254.

38. Mercy Rachel Thompson, Centennial Letter, 1880, MS 2737, box 1, folder 6, LDS Church History Library.

39. Caroline Frances Angell Davis Holbrook, "A Sketch of the Life and Experiences of Caroline Frances Angell Davis Holbrook (1825–1908)," microfilm of typescript, MS 20168, folder 2, LDS Church History Library. I am indebted to Jonathan Stapley for bringing this document to my attention. Also available at https://doctrineandconvenantscentral.org/history/caroline-frances-angell-davis -holbrook/.

40. Elder Edward Stevenson, *Reminiscences of Joseph, the Prophet and the Coming Forth of the Book of Mormon* (1893; Createspace Independent Publishing Platform, 2017), 41.

41. Alexander L. Baugh, "Was Joseph F. Smith Blessed by His Father Hyrum Smith in Liberty Jail?," *Mormon Historical Studies* 4, no. 3 (Spring 2003): 104.

42. Mary Fielding Smith to Hyrum Smith, 11 April 1839, Mary Fielding Smith Collection, MS 2779, box 1, folder 2, LDS Church History Library.

43. Mary Fielding Smith to Hyrum Smith, 11 April 1839, Mary Fielding Smith Collection, MS 2779, box 1, folder 2, LDS Church History Library.

44. Mary Fielding Smith to Joseph Fielding, 1841, Mary Fielding Smith Collection, MS 2779, box 1, folder 2, LDS Church History Library.

45. Don Carlos Smith to Joseph Smith and Hyrum Smith, 6 March 1839, in Joseph Smith, *History of the Church* (Salt Lake City: Deseret Book, 19991), 3:273–74.

46. Joseph Fielding to Mary Fielding Smith, 2 October 1837, Mary Fielding Smith Collection, MS 2779, box 1, folder 5, LDS Church History Library.

47. James Fielding to Joseph Fielding, 27 August 1838, Joseph Fielding Correspondence, 1838–1839, MS 749, box 1, LDS Church History Library.

48. James Fielding to Joseph Fielding, 15 September 1838, Joseph Fielding Correspondence, 1838–1839, MS 749, box 1, LDS Church History Library.

49. "Jos. F. Smith's Journal commencing 13 Nov. 1838," box 1, folder 1, LDS Church History Library.

364   *Notes to Pages 19–24*

CHAPTER 2

1. Thomas A. Tweed, *Crossing and Dwelling: A Theory of Religion* (Cambridge: Harvard University Press, 2006), 62.
2. Tweed, *Crossing and Dwelling*, 62.
3. JFS, journal entry, ca. 1890, "Jos. F. Smith's Journal commencing 13 Nov. 1838," box 1, folder 1, LDS Church History Library.
4. JSPP, *Revelations and Translations*, 1:633.
5. Patriarchal Blessing of Alma Owens, copy in author's possession.
6. Joseph Fielding Smith, *The Life of Joseph F. Smith* (Salt Lake City: Deseret News Press, 1938), 60.
7. Glen M. Leonard, *Nauvoo: A Place of Peace, A People of Promise* (Salt Lake City: Deseret Book, 2002), 60.
8. Wilford Woodruff, journal entry of 18 May 1839, *The Wilford Woodruff Journal*, ed. Dan Vogel (Salt Lake City: Benchmark Books, 2020), 1:237.
9. Woodruff, journal entry of 18 May 1839, Vogel, *Wilford Woodruff Journal*, 1:237.
10. James B. Allen and Glen M. Leonard, *The Story of the Latter-day Saints* (Salt Lake City: Deseret Book, 1992), 156.
11. JSPP, *Histories*, 1:514.
12. For a detailed history of the town, see Leonard, *Nauvoo*.
13. By Joseph Smith's time, the "diffusionist" or "degeneration" theory described here was well-established among Christian historians and theologians. See, for example, George Faber, *Origin of Pagan Idolatry Ascertained from Historical Testimony and Circumstantial Evidence* (New York: F and C Rivingtons, 1816).
14. Doctrine and Covenants, 128:18.
15. This document is currently section 132 of the current LDS Doctrine and Covenants, which was produced in July 1843.
16. Bushman, *Joseph Smith*, 496.
17. Bushman, *Joseph Smith*, 491.
18. Linda King Newell and Valeen Tippetts Avery, *Mormon Enigma: Emma Hale Smith* (Urbana: University of Illinois Press, 1994), 255.
19. Todd Compton, *In Sacred Loneliness: The Plural Wives of Joseph Smith* (Salt Lake City: Signature Books, 1997), 714.
20. Leonard, *Nauvoo*, 218–19.
21. Bushman, *Joseph Smith*, 491.
22. Bushman, *Joseph Smith*, 496.
23. Roger D. Launius, *Joseph Smith III: Pragmatic Prophet* (Urbana: University of Illinois Press, 1988), 132.
24. Devery S. Anderson and Gary J. Bergera, eds., *Joseph Smith's Quorum of the Anointed, 1842–1845: A Documentary History* (Salt Lake City: Signature Books, 2005).
25. Joseph F. Smith, "Boyhood Recollections of President Joseph F. Smith," *Utah Genealogical and Historical Magazine* 7, no. 2 (April 1916): 56.
26. David John Buerger, *Mysteries of Godliness: A History of Mormon Temple Worship* (Salt Lake City: Signature Books, 1994), 40.
27. Jonathan A. Stapley, "Women and Mormon Authority," in *Women and Mormonism: Historical and Contemporary Perspectives*, ed. Kate Holbrook and Matthew Burton Bowman (Salt Lake City: University of Utah Press, 2016).
28. Bushman, *Joseph Smith*, 497.

Notes to Pages 24–34   365

29. Mercy Fielding Thompson, Autobiography, 1880, MS 4580, LDS Church History Library.
30. Anderson and Bergera, *Joseph Smith's Quorum of the Anointed*, 26–27.
31. Joseph F. Smith, "Testimony," *Improvement Era* (August 1906): 308–10.
32. Bushman, *Joseph Smith*, 495.
33. Martha Ann Smith Harris, Autobiography, ca. 1920, MS 22299, LDS Church History Library.
34. Smith, "Boyhood Recollections," 57.
35. Richard P. Harris, "Martha Ann Smith," *Relief Society Magazine* 11 (1921): 11.
36. Smith, "Boyhood Recollections," 57.
37. Bushman, *Joseph Smith*, 406–7.
38. Mary Fielding Smith to Hyrum Smith, Mary Fielding Smith Collection, MS 2779, box 1, folder 2, LDS Church History Library.
39. Bushman, *Joseph Smith*, 217.
40. Bushman, *Joseph Smith*, 405.
41. For the complex history of the office of "Patriarch of the Church," see Irene M. Bates and E. Gary Smith, *Lost Legacy: The Mormon Office of Presiding Patriarch* (Urbana: University of Illinois Press, 1996).
42. This revelation was received by Joseph Smith on 19 January 1841, and the quoted material is now found in Doctrine and Covenants, 124:94.
43. Smith, "Boyhood Recollections," 54.
44. Marvin S. Hill, "Mormon Religion in Nauvoo: Some Reflections," *Utah Historical Quarterly* 44 (Spring 1976): 174.
45. Leonard, *Nauvoo*, 202.
46. Laub, Reminiscences and Journal, 1845, MS 9628, folder 1, LDS Church History Library.
47. Laub, Reminiscences and Journal, 1845, MS 9628, folder 1, LDS Church History Library.
48. Leonard, *Nauvoo*, 218–19.
49. Smith, "Boyhood Recollections," 55.
50. Steven Mintz, *Huck's Raft: A History of American Childhood* (Cambridge, MA: Belknap, 2006), 83.
51. Smith, "Boyhood Recollections," 55.
52. Smith, "Boyhood Recollections," 57.
53. Smith, "Boyhood Recollections," 56.

CHAPTER 3

1. Joseph Smith, "The King Follett Discourse: The Being and Kind of Being God Is; The Immortality of the Intelligence of Man," sermon on 7 April 1844, in Smith, *History of the Church*, 6:302–17.
2. In Vogel, *Woodruff Journals*, 24 March 1844, 1:620–21.
3. *Nauvoo Expositor*, 7 June 1844, 1.
4. Dallin H. Oaks "The Suppression of the *Nauvoo Expositor*," *Utah Law Review* 9 (Winter 1965): 862–903.
5. Oaks, "Suppression of the *Nauvoo Expositor*," 875.
6. Autobiography of Joseph Grafton Hovey, 1812–1868, MS, L. Tom Perry Special Collections, Brigham Young University, Provo, UT.

Notes to Pages 35–42

7. Dallin H. Oaks and Marvin S. Hill, *Carthage Conspiracy: The Trial of the Accused Assassins of Joseph Smith* (Urbana: University of Illinois Press, 1975), xii.
8. Oaks, "Suppression of the *Nauvoo Expositor*," 862–903.
9. Bushman, *Joseph Smith*, 546.
10. Bushman, *Joseph Smith*, 543.
11. Bushman, *Joseph Smith*, 545–46.
12. Bushman, *Joseph Smith*, 551–52.
13. There are many places to read about the events in the Carthage jail. The most accessible and balanced is Bushman, *Joseph Smith*, 549–50.
14. Bushman, *Joseph Smith*, 550.
15. JFS, sermon given 15 December 1915, Salt Lake City, JFS Papers, box 38, folder 27, LDS Church History Library.
16. Quoted in Brian Q. Cannon, "'Long Shall His Blood … Stain Illinois': Carthage Jail in Mormon Memory," *Mormon Historical Studies* 10, no. 1 (Spring 2009): 7.
17. John Turner, *Brigham Young: Pioneer Prophet* (Cambridge, MA: Harvard University Press, 2014), 108.
18. In Vogel, *Woodruff Journals*, 11 July 1844, 1:651.
19. "State of Feeling at Nauvoo," *New York Daily Tribune*, 9 July 1844.
20. "Cold Blooded Murder of Joe Smith and Other Mormon Leader," *Indiana State Sentinel*, 11 July 1844.
21. B. W. Richmond, "The Prophet's Death," *Deseret News*, 27 November 1875.
22. Joseph Fielding Smith, *The Life of Joseph F. Smith* (Salt Lake City: Deseret Book, 1938).
23. Lucy Walker statement, quoted in Stanley B. Kimball, *Heber C. Kimball: Mormon Patriarch and Pioneer* (Urbana: University of Illinois Press, 1981), 123.
24. JFS, journal entry, ca. 1890, "Jos. F. Smith's Journal commencing 13 Nov. 1838," box 1, folder 1, LDS Church History Library.
25. JFS to Solomon Kimball, 4 October 1889, JFS Papers, box 31, folder 3, LDS Church History Library.
26. Devery S. Anderson and Gary J. Bergera, eds., *The Nauvoo Endowment Companies, 1845–1846: A Documentary History* (Salt Lake City: Signature Books, 2005), 497.
27. Ronald W. Walker, "Six Days in August: Brigham Young and the Succession Crisis of 1844," in *A Firm Foundation: Church Organization and Administration*, ed. David J. Whittaker and Arnold K. Garr (Salt Lake City: Deseret Book, 2011).
28. Walker, "Six Days in August."
29. Walker, "Six Days in August."
30. For a detailed discussion of many of these groups, see Newell G. Bringhurst and John Hamer, eds., *Scattering the Saints: Schism Within Mormonism* (Independence, MO: John Whitmer Books, 2007).
31. Turner, *Brigham Young*, 123.
32. Brigham Young to Amos Fielding, 9 August 1845, CR 1234, box 16, folder 3, Brigham Young Office Files, LDS Church History Library.
33. Turner, *Brigham Young*, 119.
34. Bathsheba W. Smith, Autobiography, MS 391, LDS Church History Library.
35. For a comprehensive record of these rituals, see Anderson and Bergera, *Joseph Smith's Quorum of the Anointed*, ix–xlii.
36. For a comprehensive exploration of the long-standing tensions between Young and Emma Smith, see Linda King Newell and Valeen Tippetts Avery, *Mormon*

Enigma: Emma Hale Smith (Urbana: University of Illinois Press, 1994). See, especially, chap. 14, "The Lion and the Lady."

37. James B. Allen and Glen M. Leonard, *The Story of the Latter-day Saints* (Salt Lake City: Deseret Book, 1992), 245–46.

38. Joseph Fielding, journal entry, 18 February 1846, in "'They Might Have Known That He was Not a Fallen Prophet': The Nauvoo Journal of Joseph Fielding," ed. Andrew Ehat, *BYU Studies Quarterly* 19, no. 2 (April 1979): 133–66.

39. A clipping of the notice announcing Mary Smith's intent to hold the auction is found in JFS Papers, box 47, folder 3, LDS Church History Library.

40. Quoted in Sarah Harris Passey, "History of Martha Ann Smith Harris," unpublished manuscript, copy in author's possession.

41. Jurgen Osterhammel, *The Transformation of the World: A Global History of the Nineteenth Century* (Princeton, NJ: Princeton University Press, 2015), 108.

42. Bushman, *Joseph Smith*, 545–46.

43. Osterhammel, *Transformation of the World*, 108.

44. The idea of America as a promised land that would not be overtaken by enemies as long as they remained faithful to the God of their understanding is grounded in the narrative of the Book of Mormon.

45. Parley P. Pratt, January 1841, George A. Smith Collection, box 7, folder 5, LDS Church History Library.

46. Quote from 19 July 1840, as recorded by Martha Jane Knowlton Coray, Joseph Smith Papers, March 10, 1844, LDS Church History Library.

47. Parley P. Pratt, Willard Richards, John Taylor, and W. W. Phelps, "To the Saints Abroad," *Times and Seasons*, 15 July 1844.

48. Quoted in Breck England, *The Life and Thought of Orson Pratt* (Salt Lake City: University of Utah Press, 1985), 113.

CHAPTER 4

1. Osterhammel, *Transformation of the World*, 154.

2. John D. Unruh Jr., *The Plains Across: The Overland Emigrants and the Trans-Mississippi West, 1840–60* (Lincoln: University of Nebraska Press, 1993).

3. Mintz, *Huck's Raft*, 151.

4. Emmeline B. Wells, quoted in Carol Cornwall Madsen, *Journey to Zion: Voices from the Mormon Trail* (Salt Lake City: Deseret Book, 1997).

5. Mary and JFS traveled the last leg of the journey to Winter Quarters with Thomas Bullock, whose journal records their arrival date. Will Bagley, ed., *The Pioneer Camp of the Saints: The 1846 and 1847 Mormon Trail Journals of Thomas Bullock* (Logan: Utah State University Press, 2001), 99.

6. Richard E. Bennett, *Mormons at the Missouri: Winter Quarters, 1846–1852* (Norman: University of Oklahoma Press, 1987).

7. Andrew F. Ehat, ed., "'They Might Have Known That He Was Not a Fallen Prophet': The Nauvoo Journal of Joseph Fielding," *BYU Studies Quarterly* 19, no. 2 (April 1979): 133–66.

8. JFS, journal entry, ca. 1890, "Jos. F. Smith's Journal commencing 13 Nov. 1838," box 1, folder 1, LDS Church History Library.

9. Bennett, *Mormons at the Missouri*, 141.

10. Quoted in *The Journals of John D. Lee, 1846–47*, ed. Charles Kelly (Salt Lake City: Western Printing, 1938), 129.

368   *Notes to Pages 50–58*

11. Church of Jesus Christ, https://history.churchofjesuschrist.org/chd/organization/pioneer-company/daniel-spencerperrigrine-sessions-company-1847?lang=eng, accessed 3 November 2022.

12. Joseph F. Smith, "Boyhood Recollections of President Joseph F. Smith," *Utah Genealogical and Historical Magazine* 7, no. 2 (April 1916): 60.

13. JFS, journal entry, ca. 1890, "Jos. F. Smith's Journal commencing 13 Nov. 1838," box 1, folder 1, LDS Church History Library.

14. Ehat, "'They Might Have Known That He was Not a Fallen Prophet.'"

15. JFS, journal entry, ca. 1890, "Jos. F. Smith's Journal commencing 13 Nov. 1838," box 1, folder 1, LDS Church History Library. All of the excerpts regarding Lott are drawn from this source.

16. JFS, journal entry, ca. 1890, "Jos. F. Smith's Journal commencing 13 Nov. 1838," LDS Church History Library; and Joseph F. Smith, "Recollections of a Prophet," in "Memorial Services in Honor of the Prophet Joseph Smith's Birthday, Held in the Sixteenth Ward Meeting House, December 23, 1894," in *Collected Discourses*, ed. Brian H. Stuy (Burbank, CA: B.H.S., 1987–1992), 5:28.

17. Daniel Davis, "Overland Travels," LDS History. http://history.lds.org/overlandtravels.

18. JFS, journal entry, ca. 1890, "Jos. F. Smith's Journal commencing 13 Nov. 1838," LDS Church History Library.

19. JFS, journal entry, ca. 1890, "Jos. F. Smith's Journal commencing 13 Nov. 1838," LDS Church History Library.

20. This story is well known, not least of all because it has been taught to LDS children for generations. Space precludes a comprehensive list of all of the articles, lesson manuals, and so forth in which the story has appeared, but this one should suffice: https://www.churchofjesuschrist.org/study/friend/1993/07/mary-fielding-smith-mother-in-israel?lang=eng, accessed 3 November 2022.

21. JFS, journal entry, ca. 1890, "Jos. F. Smith's Journal commencing 13 Nov. 1838," LDS Church History Library.

22. John Smith, "Autobiography of John Smith, Patriarch to the Church of Jesus Christ of Latter-day Saints, 1885," LDS Church History Library.

23. JFS, journal entry, ca. 1890, "Jos. F. Smith's Journal commencing 13 Nov. 1838," LDS Church History Library.

24. JFS to John Smith, 30 January 1861, MS 2681, Joseph F. Smith Letters to John Smith, LDS Church History Library.

25. Joseph F. Smith, "Recollections of a Prophet," in "Memorial Services in Honor of the Prophet Joseph Smith's Birthday, Held in the Sixteenth Ward Meeting House, December 23, 1894," in Stuy, *Collected Discourses*, 5:28.

26. Richard Slotkin, *The Fatal Environment: The Myth of the Frontier in the Age of Industrialization* (Norman: University of Oklahoma Press, 1985), 124.

27. Slotkin, *Fatal Environment*, 276.

28. The finest treatment of American overland migration is John D. Unruh Jr., *The Plains Across: The Overland Emigrants and the Trans-Mississippi West* (Urbana: University of Illinois Press, 1979).

29. Stanley B. Kimball and Violet T. Kimball, *Villages on Wheels: A Social History of the Gathering to Zion* (Draper, UT: Greg Kofford Books, 2011), 103.

30. Elliott West, *Growing Up With the Country: Childhood on the Far Western Frontier* (Albuquerque: University of New Mexico Press, 1989), 7.

31. West, *Growing Up*, 26.

Notes to Pages 59–64   369

32. West, *Growing Up*, 21.

33. West, *Growing Up*, 102.

34. Thomas G. Alexander, *Utah: The Right Place*, 2nd rev. ed. (Salt Lake City: Gibbs-Smith, 2007), 99.

35. JFS to James E. Talmage, 28 October 1909, Joseph F. Smith Papers, box 35, folder 1, LDS Church History Library.

36. JFS to James E. Talmage, 28 October 1909, Joseph F. Smith Papers, box 35, folder 1, LDS Church History Library.

37. Martha Ann Smith Harris, Centennial Letter, LDS Church History Library.

38. All quotes from the funeral of Mary Fielding Smith come from LaJean Caruth's 26 May 2010 transcription of "Funeral of Mary Fielding Smith," 23 September 1852, CR 100 317, box 1, folder 44, LDS Church History Library.

39. Heber J. Grant Journal, 5 April 1900, D. Michael Quinn Collection, WA MSS S-2692, Beinecke Rare Book and Manuscript Library, Yale University.

40. JFS to Solomon Kimball, 23 September 1889, quoted in Kenney, "Before the Beard," 37n19.

41. JFS to Adenath Grover, 5 September 1912, Joseph F. Smith Papers, box 35, folder 2, LDS Church History Library.

42. John Smith to JFS, 31 January 1856, Joseph F. Smith Papers, box 8, folder 26, LDS Church History Library.

43. John Smith to JFS, 31 January 1856, Joseph F. Smith Papers, box 8, folder 26, LDS Church History Library.

44. Agnes Pickett to Joseph F. Smith, 21 January 1853, Joseph F. Smith Papers, box 8, folder 26, LDS Church History Library.

45. "Patriarchal Blessing of Joseph F. Smith," 25 June 1852, MSS SC 585, L. Tom Perry Special Collections, Harold B. Lee Library, Brigham Young University.

46. Nathaniel R. Ricks, "The Triumphs of the Young Joseph Smith," in *Joseph F. Smith: Reflections on the Man and His Times*, ed. Craig K. Manscill et al. (Salt Lake City: Deseret Book, 2013), 39.

47. Joseph F. Smith to Agnes and Josephine Smith, 5 July 1857, Joseph F. Smith Correspondence, 1854–1918, MS 18119, LDS Church History Library.

48. Joseph F. Smith, autobiographical entry in "The Twelve Apostles," in *The Historical Record* (May 1887): 184.

49. JFS to Samuel L. Adams, 11 May 1888. This letter was reproduced as a typescript by Joseph Fielding McConkie in an unpublished collection entitled "Truth and Courage: The Letters of Joseph F. Smith." The original of this letter, according to McConkie, exists in a letterpress copybook that was "among the personal effects" of Joseph F. Smith Jr. McConkie does not provide an indication of the location of this book, and it is not listed in any collection at the LDS Church History Library; however, there is a copy of McConkie's typescript of the letters in the archives under the title "Truth and Courage: The Joseph F. Smith Letters," M270.1, S6534st, LDS Church History Library.

50. JFS to Samuel Adams, 20 September 1907, JFS Papers, box 34, folder 3, LDS Church History Library.

51. JFS to Samuel L. Adams, 11 May 1888, JFS Papers, box 34, folder 3, LDS Church History Library.

52. JFS to Robert Barratt, 9 March 1875, JFS Papers, box 30, folder 1, LDS Church History Library.

Notes to Pages 64–72

53. JFS to Samuel L. Adams, 11 May 1888, JFS Papers, box 34, folder 3, LDS Church History Library.

54. *Reminiscences of Charles W. Nibley* (Salt Lake City: privately published, 1934).

55. B. F. Cummings, Jr., "Shining Lights," in *The Contributor* 16, no. 3 (January 1895): 174.

56. Nibley, *Reminiscences.*

57. JFS to James Clove, 11 June 1896. M270.1, S6534st, LDS Church History Library.

58. JFS to George Q. Cannon, 8 May 1888, MS 27013, box 1, LDS Church History Library.

59. Oscar Lyons to George A. Smith, 20 June 1865, George A. Smith Collection, MS 1322, box 6, folder 17, LDS Church History Library.

60. JFS to Samuel L. Adams, 11 May 1888, JFS Papers, box 34, folder 3, LDS Church History Library.

CHAPTER 5

1. JFS to Ina Coolbrith, 20 April 1918, Joseph F. Smith Correspondence, 1854–1918, MS 18119, LDS Church History Library.

2. JFS to Ina Coolbrith, 20 April 1918, Joseph F. Smith Correspondence, 1854–1918, MS 18119, LDS Church History Library.

3. JFS to Samuel Russell, 31 January 1913, Joseph F. Smith Papers, box 35, folder 2, LDS Church History Library.

4. JFS to Ina Coolbrith, 20 April 1918, Joseph F. Smith Correspondence, 1854–1918, MS 18119, LDS Church History Library.

5. JFS to Ina Coolbrith, 20 April 1918, Joseph F. Smith Correspondence, 1854–1918, MS 18119, LDS Church History Library.

6. Young, *Memoirs*, 274–75.

7. James Bradley, *The Imperial Cruise: A Secret History of Empire* (Boston: Back Bay Books, 2010), 150.

8. Sally Engle Merry, "Law, Culture, and Cultural Appropriation," in *Yale Journal of Law and the Humanities* 10, no. 2 (1998): 578.

9. James L. Haley, *Captive Paradise: A History of Hawaii* (New York: St. Martin's, 2014), 163.

10. Merry, "Law, Culture, and Cultural Appropriation," 587.

11. Jonathan Kay Kamakawiwo'ole Osorio, *Dismembering Lahui: A History of the Hawaiian Nation to 1887* (Honolulu: University of Hawaii Press, 2002), 11.

12. Haley, *Captive Paradise*, 48.

13. Haley, *Captive Paradise*, 46.

14. Osorio, *Dismembering Lahui*, 12.

15. Haley, *Captive Paradise*, 57–58.

16. Laurie F. Maffly-Kipp, "Assembling Bodies and Souls: Missionary Practices on the Pacific Frontier," in *Practicing Protestants: Histories of Christian Life in America 1630–1965*, ed. Laurie F. Maffly-Kipp, Leigh E. Schmidt, and Mark Valeri (Baltimore: Johns Hopkins University Press, 2006), 54–55.

17. Jennifer Thigpen, *Island Queens and Mission Wives: How Gender and Empire Remade Hawaii's Pacific World* (Chapel Hill: University of North Carolina Press, 2014), 102.

18. Maffly-Kipp, "Assembling Bodies and Souls," 68.

19. Maffly-Kipp, "Assembling Bodies and Souls," 68.

Notes to Pages 72–76   371

20. Chad M. Orton, ed., *The Journals of George Q. Cannon: Hawaiian Mission, 1850–1854* (Salt Lake City: Deseret Book, 2014), xxxix.

21. R. Lanier Britsch, *Moramona: The Mormons in Hawaii* (Laie, HI: Institute for Polynesian Studies, 1989), 14.

22. Orton, *Journals of George Q. Cannon*, entry for 27 December 1850, 40.

23. Philip B. Lewis to Brigham Young, 16 March 1853, Hawaiian Mission Manuscript History and Historical Reports, 1850–1867, LR 3695, box 1, folder 2, LDS Church History Library.

24. Britsch, *Moramona*, 25–35.

25. JFS to Samuel L. Adams, 11 May 1888, LDS Church History Library.

26. JFS to Martha Smith Harris, 9 June 1855, Joseph F. Smith Letters to Martha Ann Harris, Letters: 1855–1857, MS 9577, folder 1, LDS Church History Library.

27. Joseph F. Smith, "My Missions," *Deseret News*, 21 December 1901, 57.

28. JFS to H. Harrison Millward, 16 May 1908, Joseph F. Smith Papers, box 34, folder 3, LDS Church History Library. This letter is important because JFS reflects on how Honolulu had changed on each of his three major tours there (1854, 1864, 1885).

29. Silas Smith Journal, May 1854–June 1855, MS 18803, LDS Church History Library.

30. Reddin A. Allred to Robert Campbell, 2 January 1854. Published in *Deseret News*, 27 April 1854.

31. Silas Smith Journal, May 1854–June 1855, MS 18803, LDS Church History Library.

32. Reddin A. Allred to Robert Campbell, 2 January 1854. Published in *Deseret News*, 27 April 1854.

33. JFS to Martha Ann Smith, 17 October 1854, Carole Call King Collection, MS 16763, box 1, folder 1, LDS Church History Library.

34. JFS to Martha Ann Harris Smith, 1 November 1854, Carole Call King Collection, MS 16763, box 1, folder 2, LDS Church History Library.

35. JFS's mission assignments in Hawaii were as follows: Hamakua, Kula, and Honolulu on the island of Maui, September 1854–April 1856; Hilo and Kohala on the island of Hawaii, April 1856–April 1857; Molokai, April–June 1857; Lanai and Maui, July–September 1857. For a precise and detailed chronology see Ricks, *My Candid Opinion*, ix.

36. Joseph F. Smith to George A. Smith, 20 October 1854, George A. Smith Papers, LDS Church History Library.

37. John Smith to JFS, 30 April 1856, Joseph F. Smith Papers, box 8, folder 26, LDS Church History Library.

38. Joseph F. Smith, Sermon, *LDS General Conference Report*, April 1900, 41.

39. JFS to Elias Wesley Smith, 10 May 1908, Joseph F. Smith Papers, box 34, folder 3, LDS Church History Library.

40. Francis A. Hammond to Brigham Young, 15 April 1855, Brigham Young Incoming Correspondence, 1839–1877, CR 1234 1, box 24, folder 3, LDS Church History Library.

41. JFS to George A. Smith, 19 March 1855, Joseph F. Smith Papers, box 46, folder 1, LDS Church History Library.

42. John T. Caine to James Ferguson, 14 April 1855, quoted in Smith, *The Life*.

43. Mary Jane Woodger, "The Ten Pioneering Missionaries of the Sandwich Islands, 1850–1854," in *Go Ye Into All the World: The Growth and Development of Mormon Missionary Work*, ed. Fred E. Woods and Reid L. Neilson (Provo, UT: Brigham Young University Religious Studies Center, 2012), 223–24.

372   *Notes to Pages 76–82*

44. JFS Journal, 5 May 1857, JFS Papers, box 1, folder 15, LDS Church History Library.
45. Entry for 11 January 1855, Silas Smith Journal, May 1854–June 1855, MS 18803, LDS Church History Library.
46. JFS to Elias Smith, 14 April 1857, MS 3728, LDS Church History Library.
47. John R. Young to Brigham Young, 18 November 1856, Brigham Young Incoming Correspondence, 1839–1877, CR 1234 1, box 25, folder 9, LDS Church History Library.
48. Entry for 21 March 1855, Silas Smith Journal, May 1854–June 1855, MS 18803, LDS Church History Library.
49. JFS to Martha Smith Harris, 9 June 1855, Joseph F. Smith Letters to Martha Ann Harris, Letters: 1855–1857, MS 9577, folder 1, LDS Church History Library.
50. John Smith to Joseph F. Smith, 31 May 1856, Joseph F. Smith Papers, box 8, folder 26, LDS Church History Library.
51. John Smith to Joseph F. Smith, 20 April 1856, Joseph F. Smith Papers, box 8, folder 26, LDS Church History Library.
52. John Smith to JFS, 31 July 1856, Joseph F. Smith Papers, box 8, folder 26, LDS Church History Library.
53. JFS Journal, 15 June 1856, JFS Papers, box 1, folder 15, LDS Church History Library.
54. JFS Journal, 15 June 1856, JFS Papers, box 1, folder 15, LDS Church History Library.
55. JFS Journal, 27 July 1856, JFS Papers, box 1, folder 15, LDS Church History Library.
56. JFS to Martha Smith Harris, 23 November 1855, Joseph F. Smith Letters to Martha Ann Harris, Letters: 1855–1857, MS 9577, folder 1, LDS Church History Library.
57. This is included as an addendum to the Silas Smith Journal, May 1854–June 1855, MS 18803, LDS Church History Library.
58. JFS Journal, 16 August 1857, JFS Papers, box 1, folder 15, LDS Church History Library.
59. JFS to John R. Young, 27 August 1915, Joseph F. Smith Papers, box 36, folder 1, LDS Church History Library.
60. JFS Journal, 25 June 1856, JFS Papers, box 1, folder 15, LDS Church History Library.
61. JFS Journal, 6 May 1856, JFS Papers, box 1, folder 15, LDS Church History Library.
62. Entry for 26 January 1855, Silas Smith Journal, May 1854–June 1855, MS 18803, LDS Church History Library.
63. John Smith to JFS, 31 January 1856, Joseph F. Smith Papers, box 8, folder 26, LDS Church History Library.
64. JFS Journal, 18 April 1857, JFS Papers, box 1, folder 15, LDS Church History Library.
65. Hawaiian Mission Manuscript History and Historical Reports, 1850–1867, LR 3695, box 1, folder 2, LDS Church History Library.
66. JFS Journal, 22 January 1856, JFS Papers, box 1, folder 15, LDS Church History Library.
67. Jeffrey Tobin, "Savages, the Poor, and the Discourse of Hawaiian Infanticide," *Journal of the Polynesian Society* 106, no. 1 (1997): 67–68.
68. JFS Journal, 22 January 1856, JFS Papers, box 1, folder 15, LDS Church History Library.
69. Ricks, "Triumphs," 45.
70. JFS to Martha Smith Harris, 17 April 1857, Joseph F. Smith Letters to Martha Ann Harris, Letters: 1855–1857, MS 9577, folder 1, LDS Church History Library.

Notes to Pages 82–85   373

71. JFS Journal, 19 June 1856, JFS Papers, box 1, folder 15, LDS Church History Library.

72. JFS Journal, 4 July 1856, Joseph F. Smith Papers, box 36, folder 1, LDS Church History Library.

73. JFS to Mary Jane Gee, 20 April 1857, MS 1325, box 36, folder 1, LDS Church History Library.

74. JFS Journal, 4 July 1856, Joseph F. Smith Papers, box 36, folder 1, LDS Church History Library.

75. JFS Journal, 22 April 1857, JFS Papers, box 1, folder 15, LDS Church History Library.

76. JFS Journal, 5 May 1857, JFS Papers, box 1, folder 15, LDS Church History Library.

77. JFS to Martha Smith Harris, 17 April 1857, Joseph F. Smith Letters to Martha Ann Harris, Letters: 1855–1857, MS 9577, folder 1, LDS Church History Library.

78. JFS Journal, 6 May 1857, JFS Papers, box 1, folder 15, LDS Church History Library.

79. "Home Items," *Deseret News*, 17 July 1867, 1.

80. "Sabbath Meetings," *Deseret News*, 15 December 1869, 11.

81. Rufus Anderson to Sandwich Islands Mission, 10 April 1846, quoted in Haley, *Captive Paradise*, 168.

82. Entry for 15 December 1854, Silas Smith Journal, May 1854–June 1855, MS 18803, LDS Church History Library.

83. JFS to Mary Jane Gee, 20 April 1857, Joseph F. Smith Papers, box 36, folder 1, LDS Church History Library.

84. Henry W. Bigler to William Farrer, 28 February 1853, original in L. Tom Perry Special Collections, Brigham Young University, quoted in Woodger, "Pioneering Missionaries," 223.

85. George A. Smith to Joseph F. Smith, 14 July 1864, CR 100:38, Historian's Office Letterpress Copybooks, vol. 2: 1859–1869, LDS Church History Library.

86. George Q. Cannon to Brigham Young, 14 March 1854. Copy included in Hawaiian Manuscript History and Historical Reports, 1850–1867, LR 3695, box 1, folder 2, LDS Church History Library, 25. The letter was also reprinted in the *Deseret News*, 27 April 1854.

87. "Nathan Tanner Letter of Authority," copied in Hawaiian Manuscript History and Historical Reports, 1850–1867, LR 3695, box 1, folder 2, LDS Church History Library, 28.

88. For a comprehensive discussion of the efforts to find a gathering place for Hawaiian Mormons, see Fred E. Woods, "The Palawai Pioneers on the Island of Lanai: The First Hawaiian Latter-day Saint Gathering Place, 1854–1864," *Mormon Historical Studies* (Fall 2004): 3–35.

89. JFS, "A Report of My Mission," 24 February 1858, JFS Papers, box 32, folder 2, LDS Church History Library.

90. JFS, "A Report of My Mission," 24 February 1858, JFS Papers, box 32, folder 2, LDS Church History Library.

91. JFS to Albert J. Harris, 17 June 1891, JFS Papers, box 32, folder 2, LDS Church History Library.

92. JFS to Martha Smith Harris, month illegible, 1855, Joseph F. Smith Letters to Martha Ann Harris, Letters: 1855–1857, MS 9577, folder 1, LDS Church History Library.

93. JFS to Martha Smith Harris, 9 June 1855, Joseph F. Smith Letters to Martha Ann Harris, Letters: 1855–1857, MS 9577, folder 1, LDS Church History Library.

374   *Notes to Pages 86–90*

94. JFS to Martha Smith Harris, 17 April 1857, Joseph F. Smith Letters to Martha Ann Harris, Letters: 1855–1857, MS 9577, folder 1, LDS Church History Library.

95. See, for example, JFS's journal entry for 25 May 1857; JFS Papers, box 1, folder 15, LDS Church History Library.

96. JFS Journal, 5 May 1856, JFS Papers, box 1, folder 15, LDS Church History Library.

97. For a slightly different reading of this document, as well as the dream featuring Brigham Young, see Ricks, "Triumphs," 46.

98. JFS Journal, 25 December 1856, JFS Papers, box 1, folder 15, LDS Church History Library.

99. JFS to H. W. Naisbitt, 10 December 1877, JFS Papers, box 30, folder 3, LDS Church History Library.

100. JFS Journal, 25 December 1856, JFS Papers, box 1, folder 15, LDS Church History Library.

101. JFS Journal, 25 December 1856, JFS Papers, box 1, folder 15, LDS Church History Library.

102. JFS Journal, 24 July 1856, JFS Papers, box 1, folder 15, LDS Church History Library.

103. JFS Journal, 5 July 1856, JFS Papers, box 1, folder 15, LDS Church History Library.

104. JFS Journal, 8 April 1856, JFS Papers, box 1, folder 15, LDS Church History Library.

105. JFS Journal, 29 May 1856, JFS Papers, box 1, folder 15, LDS Church History Library.

106. JFS Journal, 20 July 1857, JFS Papers, box 1, folder 15, LDS Church History Library.

107. JFS Journal, 24 May and 26 May, 1856, JFS Papers, box 1, folder 15, LDS Church History Library.

108. JFS Journal, 2 June 1857, JFS Papers, box 1, folder 15, LDS Church History Library.

109. He mentions this practice in his journal entry for 27 June 1857, JFS Papers, box 1, folder 15, LDS Church History Library.

110. JFS Journal, 30 July 1856, JFS Papers, box 1, folder 15, LDS Church History Library.

111. Ina Coolbrith to JFS, 19 March 1857, Joseph F. Smith Correspondence, MS 18119, LDS Church History Library.

112. JFS to Ina Coolbrith, 5 July 1857, Joseph F. Smith Correspondence, MS 18119, LDS Church History Library.

113. JFS to Martha Smith Harris, 9 June 1855, Joseph F. Smith Letters to Martha Ann Harris, Letters: 1855–1857, MS 9577, folder 1, LDS Church History Library.

114. JFS to Ina Coolbrith, 5 July 1857, Joseph F. Smith Correspondence, MS 18119, LDS Church History Library.

115. JFS to Ina Coolbrith, 22 July 1857, Joseph F. Smith Correspondence, MS 18119, LDS Church History Library.

116. This is not the first time that JFS's family ignored letters from Agnes Smith and her family. In a letter that Agnes wrote to JFS in 1853 upon hearing of the death of Mary Fielding Smith, Agnes seemed genuinely wounded that "we have not heard one word from you [even though] we have written three times." Agnes Smith Pickett to JFS, 21 January 1853, Joseph F. Smith Papers, box 8, folder 26, LDS Church History Library.

117. Agnes Smith Pickett to JFS, 21 January 1853, Joseph F. Smith Papers, box 8, folder 26, LDS Church History Library.

118. JFS Journal, 1 September 1857, JFS Papers, box 1, folder 15, LDS Church History Library. It is worth noting that this is one of several instances in which JFS expresses fear about expressing his emotions.

Notes to Pages 90–94 375

119. JFS to Ina Coolbrith, 1857, 1 September 1857, Joseph F. Smith Correspondence, MS 18119, LDS Church History Library.

120. JFS to Ina Coolbrith, 1 September 1857, Joseph F. Smith Correspondence, MS 18119, LDS Church History Library. Nathaniel Ricks argues that this letter provides strong evidence of JFS's eager and able defense of the LDS faith. Ricks, "Triumphs," 43.

121. JFS Journal, 15 December 1856, JFS Papers, box 1, folder 15, LDS Church History Library.

122. JFS Journal, 20 July 1856, JFS Papers, box 1, folder 15, LDS Church History Library.

123. JFS Journal, 8 September 1856, JFS Papers, box 1, folder 15, LDS Church History Library.

124. JFS Journal, 18 June 1857, JFS Papers, box 1, folder 15, LDS Church History Library.

125. JFS Journal, 6 September 1857, JFS Papers, box 1, folder 15, LDS Church History Library.

126. JFS Journal, 11 September 1857, JFS Papers, box 1, folder 15, LDS Church History Library.

127. JFS Journal, 29 September 1857, JFS Papers, box 1, folder 15, LDS Church History Library.

128. JFS Journal, 6 October 1857, JFS Papers, box 1, folder 15, LDS Church History Library.

129. JFS Journal, 7 October 1857, JFS Papers, box 1, folder 15, LDS Church History Library.

130. JFS Journal, 14 October 1857, JFS Papers, box 1, folder 15, LDS Church History Library. JFS believed that Joseph Smith taught that people of African descent had been cursed because they were descended from Cain as well as Ham, who, according to JFS, tried "to castrate his father, Noah." Quoted in Lyman, *Insights*, 315. In recent years, scholars have demonstrated that while Joseph Smith's ideas about the curse of Cain are somewhat muddled, the policy of banning people of African descent from holding the priesthood and participating in LDS temple rites was instituted by Brigham Young. Even the official website of the LDS Church has admitted this, reversing many decades of teachings. See https://www.churchofjesuschrist.org/study/manual/gospel-topics-essays/race-and-the-priesthood?lang=eng.

131. JFS Journal, 3 October 1857, JSF Papers, box 1, folder 15, LDS Church History Library.

132. These details are drawn from Joseph F. Smith, "A Report of My Mission," 24 February 1858, JFS Papers, box 1, folder 20, LDS Church History Library.

CHAPTER 6

1. On home industries and the Brigham Young Express and Carrying Company, see Thomas G. Alexander and James B. Allen, *Mormons and Gentiles: A History of Salt Lake City* (Boulder, Colorado: Pruett, 1984), 60–62.

2. John Smith to JFS, 3 November 1856, Joseph F. Smith Papers, box 8, folder 26, LDS Church History Library.

3. David Roberts, *Devil's Gate: Brigham Young and the Great Mormon Handcart Tragedy* (New York: Simon and Schuster, 2008).

4. Ronald W. Walker, Richard E. Turley, and Glen M. Leonard, *Massacre at Mountain Meadows* (New York: Oxford University Press, 2011). For an argument that Young

376   *Notes to Pages 94–100*

did order the massacre, see Will Bagley, *Blood of the Prophets: Brigham Young and the Massacre at Mountain Meadows* (Norman: University of Oklahoma Press, 2002).

5. Brigham Young to George A. Smith, 26 January 1857, George A. Smith Collection, MS 1322, box 5, folder 13, LDS Church History Library.

6. Gene A. Sessions, *Mormon Thunder: A Documentary History of Jedediah Morgan Grant* (Draper, UT: Kofford Books, 2008), 277.

7. John Smith to JFS, 4 November 1856, Joseph F. Smith Papers, box 8, folder 26, LDS Church History Library.

8. The term "rebellion" is contested and tends to track with how sympathetic one is to the Mormon cause. The Mormons in Utah did not see their actions as rebellious, but the U.S. government did.

9. Robert V. Hine and John Mack Faragher, *The American West: A New Interpretative History* (New Haven: Yale University Press, 2000), 369.

10. John Smith to JFS, 3 August 1857, Joseph F. Smith Papers, box 8, folder 26, LDS Church History Library.

11. For a concise description of the major events of the Utah War, see Turner, *Brigham Young*, 276–300.

12. Joseph F. Smith, "My Missions," *Deseret Evening News*, 21 December 1901, 57.

13. JFS to Martha Smith Harris, 20 May 1858, Joseph F. Smith Letters to Martha Ann Harris, Letters: 1858–1877, MS 9577, folder 2, LDS Church History Library.

14. Turner, *Brigham Young*, 111.

15. JFS to Levira Smith, 26 February 1859, JFS Papers, box 6, folder 3, LDS Church History Library.

16. Scott G. Kenney, "Before the Beard: Trials of the Young Joseph F. Smith," *Sunstone* 20 (November 2001): 29.

17. JFS to Martha Ann Smith Harris, 14 July 1857, Carole Call King Collection, MS 1673, box 1, folder 4, LDS Church History Library.

18. JFS to Martha Ann Smith Harris, 25 July 1857, Carole Call King Collection, MS 1673, Box 1, folder 4, LDS Church History Library.

19. JFS to Samuel Adams, 20 September 1907, JFS Papers, box 34, folder 3, LDS Church History Library.

20. "The New High Council," *Deseret News*, 19 October 1859, 4.

21. JFS to Levira Smith, 14 May 1860, JFS Papers, box 6, folder 2, LDS Church History Library.

22. Levira Smith to JFS, 16 June 1860, JFS Papers, box 6, folder 2, LDS Church History Library.

23. In a 1902 article, posthumously republished to a wide readership in a collection of JFS's writings, he warned that consulting astrologers, mediums, and the like "derive their power from the devil. . . . Unless they reprent, they will be destroyed." Joseph Fielding Smith Jr., comp., *Gospel Doctrine: Selections from the Sermons and Writings of Joseph F. Smith* (Salt Lake City: Deseret News Press), 1919, 472–73.

24. JFS Journal, undated entry, probably August 1860, JFS Papers, box 1, folder 9, LDS Church History Library.

25. JFS to Levira Smith, 23 August 1860, JFS Papers, box 6, folder 3, LDS Church History Library.

26. JFS Journal, undated entry, probably August 1860, JFS Papers, box 1, folder 9, LDS Church History Library.

Notes to Pages 100–108   377

27. JFS to Levira Smith, 13 July 1860, JFS Papers, box 6, folder 2, LDS Church History Library.

CHAPTER 7

1. JFS to Levira Smith, 29 July 1860, JFS Papers, box 6, folder 2, LDS Church History Library.
2. JFS Journal, 27 July and 3 August 1860, JFS Papers, box 1, folder 11, LDS Church History Library.
3. Robert Tombs, *The English and Their History* (New York: Knopf, 2015), 477.
4. Ruth Goodman, *How to Be a Victorian: A Dawn to Dusk Guide to Victorian Life* (New York: W. W. Norton, 2013), 54.
5. JFS to Levira Smith, 29 July 1860, JFS Papers, box 6, folder 2, LDS Church History Library.
6. JFS Journal, 28 July 1860, JFS Papers, box 1, folder 11, LDS Church History Library.
7. Osterhammel, *Transformation of the World*, 86–87.
8. JFS Journal, 10 August 1862, JFS Papers, box 1, folder 15, LDS Church History Library.
9. Malcolm R. Thorp, "Early Mormon Confrontations with Sectarianism, 1837–40," in *Mormons in Early Victorian Britain*, ed. Richard L. Jensen and Malcolm R. Thorp (Salt Lake City: University of Utah Press, 1989), 49.
10. Simon Jenkins, *A Short History of England* (New York: Public Affairs, 2011), 201.
11. Simon Gunn, "Urbanization," in *A Companion to Nineteenth-Century Britain*, ed. Chris Williams (London: Blackwell, 2004), 238.
12. Tombs, *The English and Their History*, 487.
13. Sven Beckert, *Empire of Cotton: A Global History* (New York: Knopf, 2014), 200.
14. Tombs, *The English and Their History*, 466.
15. JFS to Levira Smith, 22 September 1861, JFS Papers, box 6, folder 5, LDS Church History Library.
16. *Millennial Star* 20:25, 9 January 1858.
17. Amasa Lyman to George A. Smith, 7 August 1860, in "Journal History of the British Mission," LR 1140 2, box 10 folder 3, LDS Church History Library.
18. "Arrival of Missionaries from Utah," *Millennial Star* 22:33, 18 August 1860, 524.
19. J. G. Bigler, "Correspondence," *Millennial Star* 24:42, 18 October 1862, 668.
20. William Cluff to JFS, 21 November 1862, JFS Papers, box 9, folder 15, LDS Church History Library.
21. William Cluff to JFS, 11 November 1862, JFS Papers, box 9, folder 15, LDS Church History Library.
22. JFS to Levira Smith, 27 December 1860, JFS Papers, box 6, folder 3, LDS Church History Library.
23. JFS Journal, 28 July 1860, JFS Papers, box 1, folder 11, LDS Church History Library.
24. Formally known as Kingston-Upon-Hull, the city is located on the northeast coast of England at the confluence of the River Hull and the Humber estuary.
25. Patricia Pulham, "The Arts," in *A Companion to Nineteenth-Century Britain*, ed. Chris Williams (London: Blackwell, 2004), 451.
26. JFS Journal, 3 August 1860, JFS Papers, box 1, folder 11, LDS Church History Library.
27. JFS Journal, 7 September 1860, JFS Papers, box 1, folder 11, LDS Church History Library.

28. JFS Journal, 5 September 1860, JFS Papers, box 1, folder 11, LDS Church History Library.

29. I am counting only those visits to the theater that JFS recorded in his journals between 1860 and 1863. He may have attended more often than he recorded.

30. JFS Journal, 28 August 1860, JFS Papers, box 1, folder 11, LDS Church History Library. Although now an obscure figure, Wallet was sufficiently well known in his life to publish an autobiography popular enough to demand three editions. See *The Public Life of W. F. Wallet, the Queen's Jester* (London: Bemrose and Sons, 1880).

31. JFS Journal, 27 August 1860, JFS Papers, box 1, folder 11, LDS Church History Library.

32. JFS to William Cluff, 22 September 1860, JFS Papers, box 9, folder 10, LDS Church History Library.

33. JFS to Hyrum M. Smith, 18 May 1896, MS 27013, box 2, LDS Church History Library.

34. JFS Journal, 31 December 1860, JFS Papers, box 1, folder 11, LDS Church History Library.

35. JFS Journal, 5 January 1861, JFS Papers, box 1, folder 11, LDS Church History Library.

36. Amasa Lyman, Charles C. Rich, and George Q. Cannon to Joseph F. Smith, Letter of Appointment, 27 December 1860, box 9, folder 10, LDS Church History Library.

37. As of 2023, an Area Seventy is a hierarchical office that occupies the space between the general authorities of the LDS Church (who are full-time employees) and stake presidents (who are the highest-ranking lay members of the church).

38. JFS to Levira Smith, JFS Papers, box 6, folder 4, LDS Church History Library.

39. A. N. Wilson, *The Victorians* (New York: W. W. Norton, 2003), 351.

40. Colin Matthew, *The Short Oxford History of the British Isles: The Nineteenth Century* (New York: Oxford University Press, 2000), 87.

41. JFS to Levira Smith, 24 October 1861, JFS Papers, box 6, folder 5, LDS Church History Library.

42. JFS notes that his first English buggy ride occurred on 5 January 1863. JFS Journal, 5 January 1863, JFS Papers, box 1, folder 11, LDS Church History Library.

43. For example, he walked eighteen miles on 7 February 1861, the same distance on 21 February 1862, and seventeen miles on 4 June 1861. Although examples are prolific in his journals, see entries for 9 August, 4 September, 16 September, 17 November, and 19 November 1860; 8 January, 7 February, and 4 June 1861; and 21 February 1862 for specific references to the significant distances he walked. JFS Journal, JFS Papers, box 1, folder 11, LDS Church History Library.

44. JFS to Levira Smith, 16 June 1861, JFS Papers, box 6, folder 4, LDS Church History Library.

45. JFS to Levira Smith, 22 September 1861, JFS Papers, box 6, folder 5, LDS Church History Library.

46. See, for example, entries for 7 and 11 October 1860; 19 March and 7 April 1861. JFS Journal, JFS Papers, box 1, folder 11, LDS Church History Library.

47. JFS Journal, 13 January 1861, JFS Papers, box 1, folder 11, LDS Church History Library.

48. JFS Journal, 20–22 April 1861, JFS Papers, box 1, folder 11, LDS Church History Library.

49. JFS Journal, 6 February 1861, JFS Papers, box 1, folder 11, LDS Church History Library.
50. JFS's notes on a sermon by Charles C. Rich, JFS Journal, 6 January 1862, JFS Papers, box 1, folder 11, LDS Church History Library.
51. JFS to Levira Smith, 8 October 1861, JFS Papers, box 6, folder 5, LDS Church History Library.
52. JFS Journal, 17 February 1861, JFS Papers, box 1, folder 11, LDS Church History Library.
53. JFS Journal, 7 November 1861, JFS Papers, box 1, folder 11, LDS Church History Library.
54. For a case of adultery, see JFS Journal, 5 March 1861; for child abuse, see JFS Journal, 28 October 1861; JFS Papers, box 1, folder 11, LDS Church History Library.
55. JFS Journal, 3 October 1860, JFS Papers, box 1, folder 11, LDS Church History Library.
56. JFS Journal, 1 September 1860, JFS Papers, box 1, folder 11, LDS Church History Library.
57. JFS to FAHF Mitchell, 20 September 1860, JFS Papers, box 9, folder 10, LDS Church History Library.
58. JFS to Levira Smith, 16 October 1862, JFS Papers, box 6, folder 6, LDS Church History Library.
59. JFS Journal, 6 October 1860, JFS Papers, box 1, folder 11, LDS Church History Library.
60. JFS Journal, 7 October 1860, JFS Papers, box 1, folder 11, LDS Church History Library.
61. JFS Journal, 20 October 1861, JFS Papers, box 1, folder 11, LDS Church History Library.
62. JFS Journal, 20 October 1862, JFS Papers, box 1, folder 11, LDS Church History Library.
63. JFS Journal, 23 January 1863, JFS Papers, box 1, folder 11, LDS Church History Library.
64. Glossolalia is mentioned on 8 September 1860 and 26 February 1863. JFS Journal, JFS Papers, box 6, folder 3, LDS Church History Library.
65. JFS to Levira Smith, 17 May 1861, JFS Papers, box 6, folder 4, LDS Church History Library.
66. JFS to Levira Smith, 8 July 1862, JFS Papers, box 6, folder 6, LDS Church History Library.
67. JFS Journal, 30 June 1861, JFS Papers, box 1, folder 11, LDS Church History Library.
68. JFS Journal, 17 January 1863, JFS Papers, box 1, folder 11, LDS Church History Library.
69. JFS Journal, 19 August 1862, JFS Papers, box 1, folder 11, LDS Church History Library.
70. JFS Journal, 27 January 1862, JFS Papers, box 1, folder 11, LDS Church History Library.
71. JFS Journal, 23 July 1862, JFS Papers, box 1, folder 11, LDS Church History Library.
72. George Q. Cannon to JFS, 7 February 1863, JFS Papers, box 1, folder 11, LDS Church History Library.
73. JFS to Junius F. Wells, 30 November 1875, JFS Papers, box 30 folder 2, LDS Church History Library.

74. George Q. Cannon to JFS, 7 February 1863, JFS Papers, box 1, folder 11, LDS Church History Library.

75. JFS to Levira Smith, 16 October 1862, JFS Papers, box 6, folder 6, LDS Church History Library.

76. JFS Journal, 5 March 1862, JFS Papers, box 1, folder 11, LDS Church History Library.

77. JFS to C. Fred Schade, 6 September 1910, box 35, folder 9, LDS Church History Library.

78. JFS to Levira Smith, 5 July 1861, JFS Papers, box 6, folder 5, LDS Church History Library.

79. JFS to Levira Smith, 8 July 1862, JFS Papers, box 6, folder 6, LDS Church History Library.

80. JFS to Levira Smith, 29 June 1861, JFS Papers, box 6, folder 4, LDS Church History Library.

81. JFS to Levira Smith, 16 October 1862, JFS Papers, box 6, folder 6, LDS Church History Library.

82. JFS to Robert Barratt, 9 March 1875, JFS Papers, box 30, folder 1, LDS Church History Library.

83. JFS to Levira Smith, 17 June 1861, JFS Papers, box 6, folder 4, LDS Church History Library.

84. JFS to Levira Smith, 14 November 1862, JFS Papers, box 6, folder 6, LDS Church History Library.

85. JFS to Levira Smith, 22 April 1861, JFS Papers, box 6, folder 4, LDS Church History Library.

86. JFS to Levira Smith, 22 April 1861.

87. JFS to Levira Smith, 22 April 1861.

88. This equation of manliness and moral virtue never left JFS. In 1902, while serving as church president, he admonished the high priests in Manti, Utah, to avoid saloons, alcohol, and sabbath breaking and instead to "be men!"—by which he meant, they should be "exemplary in their conduct." Manti Stake Conference, 15 November 1902, North Sanpete Stake Historical Record, 1900–1906, LR 8046 11, vol. 2, LDS Church History Library.

89. JFS to Levira Smith, 22 April 1861, JFS Papers, box 6, folder 4, LDS Church History Library.

90. JFS to Levira Smith, 15 July 1860, JFS Papers, box 6, folder 4, LDS Church History Library.

91. Levira Smith to JFS, 14 August 1860, JFS Papers, box 6, folder 3, LDS Church History Library.

92. Levira Smith to JFS, 9 December 1860, JFS Papers, box 6, folder 3, LDS Church History Library.

93. Levira Smith to JFS, 9 December 1860, JFS Papers, box 6, folder 3, LDS Church History Library.

94. Levira Smith to JFS, 9 December 1860.

95. JFS to Levira Smith, 19 January 1861, JFS Papers, box 6, folder 4, LDS Church History Library.

96. Although JFS's temper had been widely known since at least 1850, see the note below concerning his fight with McKnight, as well as multiple other incidents, including the domestic violence that Levira reported in the 1860s.

97. JFS to Levira Smith, 3 August 1861, JFS Papers, box 6, folder 6, LDS Church History Library.

98. Levira Smith to JFS, 14 August 1860, JFS Papers, box 6, folder 3, LDS Church History Library.

99. Levira Smith to JFS, 4 November 1860, JFS Papers, box 6, folder 3, LDS Church History Library.

100. JFS Journal, 6 November 1860, JFS Papers, box 1, folder 11, LDS Church History Library.

101. JFS to Levira Smith, 6 December 1862, JFS Papers, box 6, folder 6, LDS Church History Library.

102. JFS to Levira Smith, 8 July 1862, JFS Papers, box 6, folder 6, LDS Church History Library.

103. JFS to Levira Smith, 8 July 1862, JFS Papers, box 6, folder 6, LDS Church History Library.

104. JFS to Levira Smith, 2 November 1860, JFS Papers, box 6, folder 3, LDS Church History Library.

105. JFS to Levira Smith, 27 December 1860, JFS Papers, box 6, folder 3, LDS Church History Library.

106. JFS Journal, 12 December 1860, JFS Papers, box 1, folder 11, LDS Church History Library. For his clandestine trip to the circus, see JFS Journal, 2 May 1861, JFS Papers, box 1, folder 11, LDS Church History Library.

107. JFS to Levira Smith, 19 January 1861, JFS Papers, box 6, folder 4, LDS Church History Library.

108. Levira Smith to JFS, 3 November 1861, JFS Papers, box 6, folder 5, LDS Church History Library.

109. Levira Smith to JFS, 23 July 1860, JFS Papers, box 6, folder 2, LDS Church History Library.

110. JFS to Levira Smith, 14 May 1862, JFS Papers, box 6, folder 6, LDS Church History Library.

111. JFS to Levira Smith, 4 June 1862, JFS Papers, box 6, folder 6, LDS Church History Library.

112. Zina D. H. Young to JFS, 27 February 1862. The original letter is missing, but JFS copied it into this journal on 9 April 1862. JFS Papers, box 1, folder 11, LDS Church History Library.

113. JFS to Levira Smith, 8 July 1862, JFS Papers, box 6, folder 6, LDS Church History Library.

114. JFS to Brigham Young, 12 April 1862, CR 1234/1, box 42, folder 10, LDS Church History Library. In this box of correspondence, there are two sets of JFS letters; this comes from the first set, labeled "Joseph F. Smith, 1862, 1864."

115. JFS to Levira Smith, 11 December 1862, JFS Papers, box 6, folder 6, LDS Church History Library.

116. JFS Journal, 24 July 1862, JFS Papers, box 1, folder 11, LDS Church History Library.

117. JFS Journal, 13 November 1861, JFS Papers, box 1, folder 11, LDS Church History Library.

118. JFS Journal, 13 November 1860, JFS Papers, box 1, folder 11, LDS Church History Library.

119. JFS to S. M. Wright, 1 August 1911, JFS Papers, box 35, folder 1, LDS Church History Library.

382   *Notes to Pages 123–128*

120. JFS to Mary Jane Thompson, 4 February 1875, JFS Papers, box 30, folder 1, LDS Church History Library.
121. Levira Smith to JFS, 4 November 1860, JFS Papers, box 6, folder 3, LDS Church History Library.
122. JFS to George A. Smith, 22 August 1860, George A. Smith Papers, MS 1322, box 5, folder 22, LDS Church History Library.
123. George A. Smith to JFS, 11 October 1860, CR 100:38, Historian's Office Letterpress Copybooks, vol. 1: 1854–1861, LDS Church History Library.
124. JFS to John Smith, December 1860, MS 2681, Joseph F. Smith Letters to John Smith, LDS Church History Library.
125. JFS to John Smith, 28 June 1861, MS 2681, Joseph F. Smith Letters to John Smith, LDS Church History Library.
126. JFS to John Smith, 30 January 1861, MS 2681, Joseph F. Smith Letters to John Smith, LDS Church History Library.
127. JFS to John Smith, 30 January 1861, MS 2681, Joseph F. Smith Letters to John Smith, LDS Church History Library.
128. JFS to John Smith, 30 January 1861, MS 2681, Joseph F. Smith Letters to John Smith, LDS Church History Library.
129. Levira Smith to JFS, 12 August 1862, JFS Papers, box 6, folder 6, LDS Church History Library.
130. William Cluff to JFS, 30 June 1862, JFS Papers, box 9, folder 15, LDS Church History Library.
131. Entry for 19 March 1862, in *The Office Journal of President Brigham Young, Book D, 1858–1863*, ed. Fred C. Collier (Hanna, UT: Collier's, 2006), 362.
132. Entry for 3 December 1860, in Collier, *Office Journal of President Brigham Young, Book D*, 175.
133. George A. Smith to JFS, 17 January 1861, CR 100:38, Historian's Office Letterpress Copybooks, vol. 1: 1854–1861, LDS Church History Library.
134. JFS Journal, 23 April 1862, JFS Papers, box 1, folder 11, LDS Church History Library.
135. JFS Journal, 24 April 1862, JFS Papers, box 1, folder 11, LDS Church History Library.
136. JFS Journal, 23 April 1862, JFS Papers, box 1, folder 11, LDS Church History Library.
137. JFS Journal, 23 April 1862, JFS Papers, box 1, folder 11, LDS Church History Library.
138. George Q. Cannon to JFS, 19 March 1863, JFS Papers, box 1, folder 11, LDS Church History Library.
139. JFS to Levira Smith, 14 June 1863, JFS Papers, box 6, folder 7, LDS Church History Library.
140. Kevin Folkman, "Letters from JFS to His Adopted Son Edward Arthur Smith," in *Joseph F. Smith: Reflections on the Man and His Times*, ed. Craig K. Manscill et al. (Salt Lake City: Deseret Book, 2013), 115.

CHAPTER 8

1. JFS Journal, 29 July 1863, JFS Papers, box 1, folder 11, LDS Church History Library.
2. JFS Journal, 29 July 1863, JFS Papers, box 1, folder 11, LDS Church History Library.

Notes to Pages 128–135   383

3. JFS Journal, 29 July 1863, JFS Papers, box 1, folder 11, LDS Church History Library.

4. JFS Memoranda Notebook, October 1863–November 1871, JFS Papers, box 5, folder 4, LDS Church History Library.

5. JFS to George Q. Cannon, 4 May 1864, Historian's Office Journal History of the Church, vol. 61, CR 100 137, LDS Church History Library.

6. JFS Journal, 24 January 1864, JFS Papers, box 1, folder 11, LDS Church History Library.

7. Jacob Adler and Robert Kamins, *The Fantastic Life of Walter Murray Gibson: Hawaii's Minister of Everything* (Honolulu: University of Hawaii Press, 1986), 112.

8. Woodruff Journal, 11 January 1860, Wilford Woodruff Journals and Papers, 1828–1898; Wilford Woodruff Journals, 1833–1898; Wilford Woodruff Journals, 1860 January–1865 October, LDS Church History Library.

9. Woodruff Journal, 16 January 1860, Wilford Woodruff Journals and Papers, 1828–1898, LDS Church History Library.

10. Woodruff Journal, 22 January 1860, Wilford Woodruff Journals and Papers, 1828–1898, LDS Church History Library.

11. Woodruff Journal, 7 March 1860, Wilford Woodruff Journals and Papers, 1828–1898, LDS Church History Library.

12. Woodruff Journal, 16 January 1860, Wilford Woodruff Journals and Papers, 1828–1898, LDS Church History Library. Although the meeting took place in November 1859, Woodruff reports it in detail in his January 1860 journal.

13. "New York 'Sun' and Captain Gibson," *Deseret News*, 23 December 1868, 5.

14. Woodruff Journal, 25 April 1860, Wilford Woodruff Journals and Papers, 1828–1898, LDS Church History Library.

15. Adler and Kamins, *Fantastic Life of Walter Murray Gibson*, chaps. 4 and 5.

16. JFS to Franklin W. Young, 25 April 1900, JFS Papers, box 33, folder 3, LDS Church History Library.

17. In Vogel, *Woodruff Journals*, 29 February 1864, 3:581.

18. "A Blessing upon Joseph F. Smith, given in the President's Office in Great Salt Lake City, Feb. 29, 1864, under the hands of the First Presidency," JFS Papers, box 50, folder 21, LDS Church History Library.

19. Ina Coolbrith to JFS, 30 May 1864, JFS Papers, box 9, folder 24, LDS Church History Library.

20. JFS to Levira Smith, 20 March 1864, JFS Papers, box 6, folder 8, LDS Church History Library.

21. JFS to Levira Smith, 28 May 1864, JFS Papers, box 6, folder 8, LDS Church History Library.

22. JFS to Levira Smith, 28 May 1864, JFS Papers, box 6, folder 8, LDS Church History Library.

23. JFS to George Q. Cannon, 4 May 1864, Historian's Office Journal History of the Church, vol. 61, CR 100 137, LDS Church History Library.

24. JFS to W. W. Cluff, 10 November 1900, JFS Papers, box 33, folder 3, LDS Church History Library.

25. Alma L. Smith, Letter to the Editor, *Deseret News*, 19 August 1869, 1.

26. JFS to Samuel H. B. Smith, 14 September 1864, MS 4672, Joseph F. Smith, Letters, 1864–1875, box 1, folder 1, LDS Church History Library.

27. Derinda Kimball to Levira Smith, 19 March 1865, JFS Papers, box 6, folder 9, LDS Church History Library.

384   *Notes to Pages 135–137*

28. Dr. C. White to Mrs. Smith, 5 May 1865, JFS Papers, box 6, folder 9, LDS Church History Library. Also Derinda Smith to JFS, 19 March 1865, JFS Papers, box 6, folder 9, LDS Church History Library.

29. Derinda Kimball to Levira Smith, 28 July 1865, JFS Papers, box 6, folder 9, LDS Church History Library.

30. Entry for 18 December 1864, Church Historian's Office Journal, 1844–1879, CR 100 1, box 4, vol. 28, LDS Church History Library.

31. Entry for 22 January 1865, Church Historian's Office Journal, 1844–1879, CR 100 1, box 4, vol. 28, LDS Church History Library.

32. Woodruff Journal, 22 January 1865, Wilford Woodruff Journals and Papers, 1828–1898, LDS Church History Library.

33. Woodruff Journal, 22 January 1865, Wilford Woodruff Journals and Papers, 1828–1898, LDS Church History Library.

34. Entry for 19 February 1865, Church Historian's Office Journal, 1844–1879, CR 100 1, box 4, vol. 28, LDS Church History Library.

35. The endowment is a ritual depicting the journey of human beings from their premortal state through the fall into the degraded "telestial" or mortal world, and then, if they prove faithful to church covenants and teachings, their eventual return to the divine presence.

    "Sealing" is a term introduced by Joseph Smith to describe a number of rituals, all of which have as their purpose the uniting, or sealing, of individuals together for eternity. In modern Mormonism, the term primarily refers to the marriage between a man and a woman, and the sealing of children to parents. In JFS's day, it also included polygamous sealings of multiple women to one man, as well as the sealing of individuals to prominent Mormon families. This last practice was known as the Law of Adoption and was discontinued in 1894 at the direction of church president Wilford Woodruff.

36. Levira Smith to JFS, 24 January 1865, JFS Papers, box 6, folder 9, LDS Church History Library.

37. Levira Smith to JFS, 24 January 1865, JFS Papers, box 6, folder 9, LDS Church History Library.

38. Derinda Kimball to Levira Smith, 28 July 1865, JFS Papers, box 6, folder 13, LDS Church History Library. This letter was written to the mother of JFS's wife, whose name was also Levira Smith.

39. Ina Coolbrith to JFS, 30 January 1865, JFS Correspondence, MS 11819, LDS Church History Library.

40. C. White to JFS, 5 May 1865, JFS Papers, box 6, folder 12, LDS Church History Library.

41. JFS to C. White, 23 May 1865, JFS Papers, box 6, folder 12, LDS Church History Library.

42. JFS to C. White, 23 May 1865, JFS Papers, box 6, folder 12, LDS Church History Library.

43. JFS Journal, 27 January 1872, JFS Papers, box 3, folder 2, LDS Church History Library. JFS had a lifelong suspicion of doctors as well as medicine. In 1868, he castigated a group of women at a meeting of the Relief Society for relying on "quack medicines" instead of on "the ordinances of the gospel" to cure sick children. "Meeting of 16th Ward Relief Society, 3 July 1869," reported in *Deseret News*, 14 July 1869, 2.

44. JFS to Levira Smith, 14 March 1865, JFS Papers, box 6, folder 10, LDS Church History Library.
45. Levira Smith to JFS, 16 June 1865, JFS Papers, box 6, folder 12, LDS Church History Library.
46. Levira Smith to JFS, n.d. (but it was written after 21 May 1865 and received by JFS on 4 June 1865), JFS Papers, box 6, folder 12, LDS Church History Library.
47. JFS to Levira Smith, 14 March 1865, JFS Papers, box 6, folder 10, LDS Church History Library.
48. Levira Smith to JFS, 23 April 1865, JFS Papers, box 6, folder 11, LDS Church History Library.
49. Levira Smith to JFS, n.d. (but it was written between 3 and 15 June 1865), JFS Papers, box 6, folder 12, LDS Church History Library.
50. Levira Smith to JFS, 16 June 1865, JFS Papers, box 6, folder 12, LDS Church History Library.
51. Levira Smith to JFS, 21 July 1865, JFS Papers, box 6, folder 12, LDS Church History Library.
52. JFS to Samuel H. B. Smith, 13 January 1865, MS 4672, Joseph F. Smith, Letters, 1864–1875, box 1, folder 1, LDS Church History Library.
53. Levira Smith to JFS, 21 July 1865, JFS Papers, box 6, folder 13, LDS Church History Library.
54. JFS to Samuel H. B. Smith, 13 June 1865, MS 4672, Joseph F. Smith, Letters, 1864–1875, box 1, folder 1, LDS Church History Library.
55. Quoted in Joseph Fielding Smith, *The Life of Joseph F. Smith* (Salt Lake City: Deseret News Press, 1938), 231.
56. Julina Lambson, "Autobiography," in *The Descendants of Joseph F. Smith, 1838–1918*, comp. Joseph F. Smith Family Genealogical Committee (Provo, UT: J. Grant Stevenson, 1976), n.p.
57. Entry for 5 May 1866, Church Historian's Office Journal, 1844–1879, CR 100 1, box 4, vol. 28, LDS Church History Library.
58. JFS to J. D. M. Crockwell, 28 January 1868, JFS Papers, box 10, folder 3, LDS Church History Library.
59. Edith Smith Patrick, "How Joseph F. Smith Chose His Wives," in Smith, *The Descendants of Joseph F. Smith*, n.p.
60. Smith, *The Life of Joseph F. Smith*.
61. JFS to Levira Smith, 18 July 1867, JFS Papers, box 6, folder 15, LDS Church History Library.
62. Levira Smith to JFS, 17 July 1867, JFS Papers, box 6, folder 15, LDS Church History Library.
63. Levira Smith to Brigham Young, 12 August 1867, Incoming Correspondence, Brigham Young Collection, CR 1234 1, box 66, folder 23, LDS Church History Library. For some reason, Kenney ("Before the Beard") claims that this letter is undated.
64. Levira Smith to Brigham Young, 12 August 1867, Incoming Correspondence, Brigham Young Collection, CR 1234 1, box 66, folder 23, LDS Church History Library.
65. JFS to Brigham Young, 25 August 1867, Incoming Correspondence, Brigham Young Collection, CR 1234 1, box 66, folder 23, LDS Church History Library.
66. "Adulterer Shot," *Deseret News*, 2 May 1877.

386   *Notes to Pages 142–147*

67. JFS to Brigham Young, 25 August 1867, Incoming Correspondence, Brigham Young Collection, CR 1234 1, box 66, folder 23, LDS Church History Library.

68. Reva B. Siegel, "'The Rule of Love': Wife Beating as Prerogative and Privacy," Faculty Scholarship Series Paper 1092 (New Haven: Yale University Press, 1996), 2123.

69. JFS to Brigham Young, 25 August 1867, Incoming Correspondence, Brigham Young Collection, CR 1234 1, box 66, folder 23, LDS Church History Library.

70. JFS to Samuel Roskelly, 25 May 1891, JFS Papers, box 32, folder 2, LDS Church History Library.

71. Smith, *Life of Joseph F. Smith*, 241.

72. JFS Journal, 16 June 1871, JFS Papers, box 2, folder 9, LDS Church History Library.

73. JFS to B. R. Watts, 12 August 1875, JFS Papers, box 30, folder 2, LDS Church History Library.

74. JFS to John M. Mahuka, 10 April 1909, JFS Papers, box 34, folder 3, LDS Church History Library.

CHAPTER 9

1. For a discussion of the significance of the prayer circle, see D. Michael Quinn, "Latter-day Saint Prayer Circles," *BYU Studies* 19, no. 1 (1979): 79–105.

2. Entry for 1 July 1866, Historian's Office Journal History of the Church, CR 100 137, vol. 66, LDS Church History Library.

3. Although JFS was ordained to the priesthood office of apostle at the time he was put into the First Presidency, he did not become a member of the Quorum of the Twelve Apostles until 1867. In the nineteenth century, it was common practice to ordain men, and sometimes boys, to the apostleship without adding them to the Quorum. The reason for this is that, unlike the First Presidency, which can have extra counselors, the Quorum may not have more than twelve active members at any given time. JFS was sustained as a member of the Quorum in October 1867 to fill the vacancy created by the excommunication of Amasa M. Lyman.

4. Roger D. Launius, *Joseph Smith III: Pragmatic Prophet* (Urbana: University of Illinois Press, 1988), 224–25.

5. Joseph F. Smith, "Which Religion Is Best?," sermon given 17 February 1867, *Journal of Discourses* 11:291–305.

6. Sarah Ellen Richards, "Autobiography," in *The Descendants of Joseph F. Smith, 1838–1918*, comp. Joseph F. Smith Family Genealogical Committee (Provo, UT: J. Grant Stevenson, 1976), n.p.

7. Turner, *Brigham Young*, 102.

8. Alexander, *Utah*, 153.

9. "Meeting of the 16th Ward Relief Society, 3 July 1869," reported in *Deseret News*, 14 July 1869, 2.

10. Martha Sonntag Bradley, *ZCMI: America's First Department Store* (Salt Lake City: ZCMI, 1991), 50.

11. In Vogel, *Woodruff Journals*, 31 January 1868, 4:103.

12. In Vogel, *Woodruff Journals*, 10 February 1868, 4:104.

13. "Co-Operative Wholesale Store," *Deseret News*, 14 October 1868, 4.

14. "Items," *Deseret News*, 4 November 1868, 8.

15. Sarah Ellen Richards, "Autobiography," in *The Descendants of Joseph F. Smith, 1838–1918*.

16. "Home Items," *Deseret News*, 14 October 1868, 4.

Notes to Pages 147–153   387

17. "Home Items," *Deseret News*, 14 October 1868, 4.

18. In Vogel, *Woodruff Journals*, 8–11 October 1868, 4:133.

19. In Vogel, *Woodruff Journals*, 6 October 1868, 4:132.

20. At the time, church leaders had yet to completely resolve some of the problems of seniority in the Quorum that had troubled them for years. The main unresolved matter in 1868 was whether one's seniority should be determined by the date of ordination as an apostle or by the date of entry into the Quorum. By the former measure, Brigham Young Jr. was JFS's senior, but by the latter, JFS came out on top. Eventually, the group decided that seniority would be calculated by date of entry to the Quorum. Had the decision gone the other way, JFS may never have become church president.

21. JFS's children who preceded him in death included Sara Ellen (1869), Mary Josephine (1870), Heber John (1877), Alfred Jason (6 April 1878), Rhoda Ann (1879), Albert Jesse (1883), Robert (1886), John Schwartz (1889), Ruth (1898), Alice (1901), Leonora (1907), Zina (1915), and Hyrum Mack (1918).

22. Heber J. Richards to JFS, 15 March 1869, JFS Papers, box 10, folder 4, LDS Church History Library.

23. JFS Journal, 5 June 1870, JFS Papers, box 2, folder 6, LDS Church History Library.

24. JFS Journal, 6 June 1870, JFS Papers, box 2, folder 6, LDS Church History Library.

25. JFS Journal, 6 June 1870, JFS Papers, box 2, folder 6, LDS Church History Library.

26. JFS to Bathsheba W. Smith, 4 September 1875, JFS Papers, box 30, folder 2, LDS Church History Library.

27. Joseph E. Robinson Journal, 29 March 1903, Joseph E. Robinson Papers, MS 7686, box 1, folder 5, LDS Church History Library.

28. JFS notes the nature and cost of the coffin in his journal entry of 6 June 1870, JFS Papers, box 2, folder 5, LDS Church History Library.

29. 21 July 1929. Julina L. Smith Journal, Julina L. Smith Papers, 1870–1933, MS 4364, LDS Church History Library.

30. JFS Journal, 19 October 1870, JFS Papers, box 2, folder 6, LDS Church History Library.

31. JFS to E. Wesley Smith, 30 March 1908, JFS Papers, box 34, folder 3, LDS Church History Library.

32. JFS to Adele Jones, 2 April 1908, JFS Papers, box 34, folder 3, LDS Church History Library.

33. Abraham H. Cannon Journal, 18 December 1890, quoted in Jonathan L. Stapley, "Adoptive Sealing Ritual in Mormonism," *Journal of Mormon History* 37, no. 3 (Summer 2011): 105.

34. In Vogel, *Woodruff Journals*, 17 July 1869, 4:168.

35. Valeen Tippetts Avery, *From Mission to Madness: The Last Son of the Mormon Prophet* (Urbana: University of Illinois Press, 1998), 96.

36. JFS to Orson Pratt, 19 July 1875, JFS Papers, box 30, folder 2, LDS Church History Library.

37. JFS to Sarah Ellen Richards Smith, 13 September 1869, MS 2574, box 1, folder 1, LDS Church History Library.

38. JFS Journal, 28 August 1870, JFS Papers, box 2, folder 7, LDS Church History Library.

39. JFS to Deseret News, 20 August 1869, in *Deseret News*, 1 September 1869, 12.

40. JFS to Junius F. Wells, 30 November 1875, JFS Papers, box 30, folder 2, LDS Church History Library.

41. JFS to A. J. Davis, 15 February 1893, JFS Papers, box 32, folder 3, LDS Church History Library.
42. JFS to George A. Smith, 11 July 1872, JFS Papers, box 10, folder 8, LDS Church History Library.
43. George A. Smith to JFS, 17 July 1872, JFS Papers, box 10, folder 8, LDS Church History Library.
44. "Last Testimony of Sister Emma," *The Saints Herald*, 1 October 1879, 1.
45. Joseph F. Smith, "Joseph the Seer's Plural Marriages and His Wife Emma's Consent Thereto," *Deseret News*, 22 October 1879, 13.
46. "Home Items," *Deseret News*, 14 December 1865, 4.
47. J. C. Reed, "Personnel of the Lower House of the Utah Legislative Assembly," *Deseret News*, 26 February 1868, 8.
48. "Our City Council and the Public," *Salt Lake Tribune*, 2 August 1872, 2.
49. "The Conference," *Salt Lake Tribune*, 5 October 1882, 2.
50. "Elder Joseph F. Smith," *Salt Lake Tribune*, 28 September 1873, 4.
51. JFS Journal, 29 October 1870, JFS Papers, box 2, folder 6, LDS Church History Library.
52. JFS Journal, 31 October 1870, JFS Papers, box 2, folder 6, LDS Church History Library.
53. "Fortieth Annual Conference," *Deseret News*, 13 April 1870, 5.
54. JFS to Charles W. Nibley, 14 November 1890, JFS Papers, box 32, folder 1, LDS Church History Library.
55. "The Circus," *Salt Lake Tribune*, 6 April 1880, 4.
56. Card Journal, 6 October 1896, 363.
57. Most of JFS's journal for the summer of 1871 is concerned with these issues, which were repeated at nearly every stop that was made. For example, see JFS Journal, 15 July 1871, JFS Papers, box 1, folder 11, LDS Church History Library.
58. JFS Journal, 15 July 1871, JFS Papers, box 1, folder 11, LDS Church History Library.
59. JFS Journal, 18 July 1871, JFS Papers, box 1, folder 11, LDS Church History Library.
60. JFS Journal, 18 July 1871, JFS Papers, box 1, folder 11, LDS Church History Library.
61. "President Young's Trip North," *Deseret News*, 2 September 1868, 3.
62. JFS Journal, 21 July 1871, JFS Papers, box 1, folder 11, LDS Church History Library.
63. JFS Journal, 23 July 1871, JFS Papers, box 1, folder 11, LDS Church History Library.
64. JFS Journal, 1 January 1871, JFS Papers, box 2, folder 8, LDS Church History Library.
65. JFS to Susa Y. Gates, 9 August 1890, JFS Papers, box 32, folder 1, LDS Church History Library.
66. JFS to Susa Y. Gates, 16 May 1890, JFS Papers, box 32, folder 1, LDS Church History Library.
67. JFS Journal, 31 June 1871, JFS Papers, box 1, folder 11, LDS Church History Library.
68. Smith, *Life of Joseph F. Smith*, 231.
69. Joseph F. Smith, "Discourse," *Deseret News*, 6 February 1867, 3.
70. JFS Journal, 5 May 1870, JFS Papers, box 2, folder 6, LDS Church History Library.
71. JFS Journal, 19 June 1870, JFS Papers, box 2, folder 6, LDS Church History Library.
72. JFS Journal, 17 July 1870, JFS Papers, box 2, folder 6, LDS Church History Library.
73. JFS Journal, 5 May 1870, JFS Papers, box 2, folder 6, LDS Church History Library.
74. JFS Journal, 15 May 1870, JFS Papers, box 2, folder 6, LDS Church History Library.

Notes to Pages 159–163   389

75. JFS Journal, 11 June 1870, JFS Papers, box 2, folder 6, LDS Church History Library.

76. JFS Journal, 17 July 1870, JFS Papers, box 2, folder 6, LDS Church History Library.

77. JFS Journal, 19 June 1870, JFS Papers, box 2, folder 6, LDS Church History Library.

78. JFS Journal, 17 July 1870, JFS Papers, box 2, folder 6, LDS Church History Library.

79. JFS to Orson Pratt, 19 July 1875, JFS Papers, box 30, folder 2, LDS Church History Library.

80. JFS Journal, 3 November 1875, JFS Papers, box 3, folder 8, LDS Church History Library.

81. Martha Smith to JFS, LDS Church History Library.

82. JFS Journal, 1 January 1873, JFS Papers, box 3, folder 3, LDS Church History Library.

83. JFS Journal, 7 January 1873, JFS Papers, box 3, folder 3, LDS Church History Library.

84. JFS Journal, 7 January 1873, JFS Papers, box 3, folder 3, LDS Church History Library.

85. James McKnight to JFS, 25 January 1874, JFS Papers, box 10, folder 15, LDS Church History Library.

86. James McKnight to JFS, 25 January 1874, JFS Papers, box 10, folder 15, LDS Church History Library.

87. JFS Journal, 30 January 1874, JFS Papers, box 3, folder 8, LDS Church History Library.

88. JFS Journal, 21 January 1874, JFS Papers, box 3, folder 8, LDS Church History Library.

89. JFS to Edna Lambson Smith, 27 July 1875, JFS Papers, box 30, folder 2, LDS Church History Library.

90. James McKnight to Julina Lambson Smith, 22 March 1875, JFS Papers, box 30, folder 2, LDS Church History Library.

91. JFS Journal, 3 November 1875, JFS Papers, box 3, folder 8, LDS Church History Library.

92. James McKnight to Joseph McKnight, 26 July 1906, James McKnight Papers, MS 18504, box 1, folder 2, LDS Church History Library.

93. Joseph F. Smith, Untitled Sermon, 20 January 1879, JFS Papers, box 78, folder 5, LDS Church History Library.

CHAPTER 10

1. JFS, Untitled Sermon, 20 January 1879, JFS Papers, box 78, folder 5, LDS Church History Library.

2. JFS to Edna Lambson Smith, 21 January 1875, JFS Papers, box 30, folder 1, LDS Church History Library.

3. "Setting apart" is the term for a brief ritual in which a person called to a specific position within the church has hands laid on their head and is given the authority to act in this calling.

4. In the nineteenth century, individuals often received multiple patriarchal blessings.

5. Patriarchal Blessing given to JFS by Patriarch John Smith, 25 February 1874, JFS Papers, box 47, folder 34, LDS Church History Library.

6. JFS Journal, 3 March 1874, JFS Papers, box 3, folder 3, LDS Church History Library.

Notes to Pages 163–167

7. JFS Journal, 4 March 1874, JFS Papers, box 3, folder 3, LDS Church History Library.

8. JFS to Sarah Ellen Richards Smith, 6 March 1874, Sarah Ellen Richards Smith Collection, MS 2574, box 1, folder 2, LDS Church History Library.

9. JFS Journal, 7 March 1874, JFS Papers, box 3, folder 3, LDS Church History Library.

10. JFS Journal, 12 March 1874, JFS Papers, box 3, folder 3, LDS Church History Library.

11. JFS Journal, 7 June 1874, JFS Papers, box 3, folder 8, LDS Church History Library.

12. JFS Journal, 15 May 1874, JFS Papers, box 3, folder 3, LDS Church History Library.

13. George Reynolds to JFS, 21 July 1871, George Reynolds Letterpress Copybooks, MS 13759, box 1, folder 1, LDS Church History Library.

14. Bloxham et al., *Truth Will Prevail*, 214.

15. JFS to John R. Young, 18 February 1878, JFS Papers, box 30, folder 3, LDS Church History Library.

16. John Neff to Albert Carrington, 17 October 1873, Journal History of the British Mission, LR 1140 2, box 10, folder 3, LDS Church History Library.

17. JFS to George Reynolds, 20 August 1875, JFS Papers, box 30, folder 2, LDS Church History Library.

18. JFS to George Reynolds, 20 August 1875, JFS Papers, box 30, folder 2, LDS Church History Library.

19. JFS to George Reynolds, 20 August 1875, JFS Papers, box 30, folder 2, LDS Church History Library.

20. JFS to Sarah Ellen Richards Smith, 9 April 1874, Sarah Ellen Richards Smith Collection, MS 2574, box 1 folder 2, LDS Church History Library.

21. JFS to Sarah Ellen Richards Smith, 25 June 1874, Sarah Ellen Richards Smith Collection, MS 2574, box 1 folder 3, LDS Church History Library.

22. JFS to William C. Staines, 7 January 1875, JFS Papers, box 30, folder 1, LDS Church History Library.

23. JFS, "Instructions Regarding Emigration Procedures, 1873–1874," JFS Papers, box 5, folder 8, LDS Church History Library.

24. JFS to Sarah Ellen Richards Smith, 22 July 1874, Sarah Ellen Richards Smith Collection, MS 2574, box 1, folder 4, LDS Church History Library.

25. JFS to Sarah Ellen Richards Smith, 10 September 1874, Sarah Ellen Richards Smith Collection, MS 2574, box 1 folder 5, LDS Church History Library.

26. JFS to William Burton, 31 July 1875, JFS Papers, box 30, folder 2, LDS Church History Library.

27. JFS to Julina Lambson Smith, 10 August 1875, JFS Papers, box 30, folder 2, LDS Church History Library.

28. JFS to Julina Lambson Smith, 10 August 1875, JFS Papers, box 30, folder 2, LDS Church History Library.

29. JFS to Sarah Ellen Richards Smith, 1 April 1874, Sarah Ellen Richards Smith Collection, MS 2574, box 1, folder 2, LDS Church History Library.

30. JFS to Julina Lambson Smith, 10 August 1875, JFS Papers, box 30, folder 2, LDS Church History Library.

31. JFS to Sarah Ellen Richards Smith, 21 January 1875, JFS Papers, box 30, folder 1, LDS Church History Library. On the dangers of carpet dust, see JFS to Julina Lambson Smith, 10 August 1875, JFS Papers, box 30, folder 2, LDS Church History Library.

32. JFS to Sarah Ellen Richards Smith, 22 September 1874, Sarah Ellen Richards Smith Collection, MS 2574, box 1 folder 5, LDS Church History Library.

33. JFS to Sarah Ellen Richards Smith, 11 May 1874, Sarah Ellen Richards Smith Collection, MS 2574, box 1 folder 2, LDS Church History Library.

34. See Rogers, *Diaries of L. John Nuttall*, entry for 19 September 1879, 28.

35. JFS to Julina Lambson Smith, Edna Lambson Smith, and Sarah Ellen Richards Smith, 11 May 1875, JFS Papers, box 30, folder 1, LDS Church History Library.

36. JFS to Julina Lambson Smith, 2 February 1875, JFS Papers, box 30, folder 1, LDS Church History Library.

37. JFS to Edna Lambson Smith, 26 January 1875, JFS Papers, box 30, folder 1, LDS Church History Library.

38. JFS to Edna Lambson Smith, 11 May 1875, JFS Papers, box 30, folder 1, LDS Church History Library.

39. JFS to Sarah Ellen Richards Smith, 13 May 1875, JFS Papers, box 30, folder 1, LDS Church History Library.

40. JFS to Edna Lambson Smith, 11 May 1875, JFS Papers, box 30, folder 1, LDS Church History Library.

41. JFS to Sarah Ellen Richards Smith, 1 May 1875, JFS Papers, box 30, folder 1, LDS Church History Library.

42. JFS to Sarah Ellen Richards Smith, 7 August 1875, Sarah Ellen Richards Smith Collection, MS 2574, box 1, folder 12, LDS Church History Library.

43. JFS to Edna Lambson Smith, 2 February 1875, JFS Papers, box 30, folder 1, LDS Church History Library. "Skinning the cat" is a gymnastics move requiring significant upper-body strength and agility in which an individual grasps a bar, then brings their feet up and between the arms and then back down.

44. JFS to Mercy Thompson, 5 February 1875, JFS Papers, box 30, folder 1, LDS Church History Library.

45. JFS to Mary Jane Thompson, 4 February 1875, JFS Papers, box 30, folder 1, LDS Church History Library.

46. JFS narrates these events in a letter to his wives. JFS to "Dear Girls," 29 July 1875, JFS Papers, box 30, folder 2, LDS Church History Library.

47. JFS to Mercy Thompson, 29 July 1875, JFS Papers, box 30, folder 2, LDS Church History Library.

48. JFS to John Henry Smith, 16 June 1875, John Henry Smith Journals, LDS Church History Library.

49. JFS to Edna Lambson Smith, 4 September 1875, JFS Papers, box 30, folder 2, LDS Church History Library.

50. JFS to William Cluff, 31 July 1875, JFS Papers, box 30, folder 2, LDS Church History Library.

51. JFS to Bathsheba W. Smith, 4 September 1875, JFS Papers, box 30, folder 2, LDS Church History Library.

52. JFS to Henry Richards, 28 January 1875, JFS Papers, box 30, folder 1, LDS Church History Library.

53. JFS to F. M. Lyman, 3 September 1875, JFS Papers, box 30, folder 2, LDS Church History Library.

54. JFS to Bathsheba W. Smith, 4 September 1875, JFS Papers, box 30, folder 2, LDS Church History Library.

55. See Doctrine and Covenants 138.

56. JFS to Julina Lambson Smith, 2 February 1875, JFS Papers, box 30, folder 1, LDS Church History Library.
57. JFS to Edna Lambson Smith, 29 April 1875, JFS Papers, box 30, folder 1, LDS Church History Library.
58. JFS to Sarah Ellen Richards Smith, 27 July 1875, Sarah Ellen Richards Smith Collection, MS 2574, box 1, folder 11, LDS Church History Library.
59. JFS to Sarah Ellen Richards Smith, 1 May 1874, Sarah Ellen Richards Smith Collection, MS 2574, box 1, folder 10, LDS Church History Library.
60. JFS to Edna Lambson Smith, 10 August 1875, JFS Papers, box 30, folder 2, LDS Church History Library.
61. JFS to Julina Lambson Smith, 24 June 1874, JFS Papers, box 7, folder 3, LDS Church History Library.
62. JFS to Julina Lambson Smith, 24 June 1874, JFS Papers, box 7, folder 3, LDS Church History Library.
63. JFS to Edna Lambson Smith, 21 January 1875, JFS Papers, box 30, folder 1, LDS Church History Library.
64. JFS to Sarah Ellen Richards Smith, 13 April 1875, Sarah Ellen Richards Smith Collection, MS 2574, box 1, folder 9, LDS Church History Library.
65. JFS to Julina Lambson Smith, 27 July 1875, JFS Papers, box 30, folder 2, LDS Church History Library.
66. JFS to Edna Lambson Smith, 26 January 1875, JFS Papers, box 30, folder 1, LDS Church History Library.
67. JFS to Edna Lambson Smith, 3 August 1875, JFS Papers, box 30, folder 2, LDS Church History Library.
68. JFS to Sarah Ellen Richards Smith, 1 May 1874, Sarah Ellen Richards Smith Collection, MS 2574, box 1 folder 10, LDS Church History Library.
69. JFS to Sarah Ellen Richards Smith, 1 May 1874, Sarah Ellen Richards Smith Collection, MS 2574, box 1 folder 10, LDS Church History Library.
70. Julina Lambson Smith to JFS, 21 July 1874, JFS Papers, box 30, folder 1, LDS Church History Library.
71. Edna Lambson Smith to JFS, 15 February 1875, JFS Papers, box 30, folder 1, LDS Church History Library.
72. JFS to Julina Lambson Smith, 26 June 1875, JFS Papers, box 30, folder 1, LDS Church History Library.
73. JFS to Julina Lambson Smith, 26 June 1875, JFS Papers, box 30, folder 1, LDS Church History Library.
74. JFS to William Staines, 20 August 1875, JFS Papers, box 30, folder 2, LDS Church History Library.
75. JFS to Hyrum, Frank, and John Harris, 26 September 1890, JFS Papers, box 32, folder 1, LDS Church History Library.
76. JFS to Hyrum, Frank, and John Harris, 26 September 1890, JFS Papers, box 32, folder 1, LDS Church History Library.
77. JFS to John T. Caine, 21 August 1875, JFS Papers, box 30, folder 2, LDS Church History Library.
78. JFS Journal, 21 July 1877, JFS Papers, box 3, folder 3, LDS Church History Library.
79. For details on Young's various challenges during 1874–1875, see Turner, *Brigham Young*, 373–407.

Notes to Pages 176–179   393

80. JFS to J. Stucki, 28 July 1875, JFS Papers, box 30, folder 2, LDS Church History Library.

81. JFS to Sarah Ellen Richards Smith, 22 June 1875, Sarah Ellen Richards Smith Collection, MS 2574, box 1, folder 10, LDS Church History Library.

82. JFS Journal, 30 April 1871, JFS Papers, box 2, folder 9, LDS Church History Library.

83. George F. Gibbs to JFS, 22 December 1874, JFS Papers, box 10, folder 13, LDS Church History Library.

84. JFS to Samuel H. B. Smith, 14 January 1874, JFS Papers, box 30, folder 1, LDS Church History Library.

85. JFS to Sarah Ellen Richards Smith, 22 June 1875, Sarah Ellen Richards Smith Collection, MS 2574, box 1, folder 10, LDS Church History Library.

86. JFS to Peter Sinclair, 14 January 1875, JFS Papers, box 30, folder 1, LDS Church History Library.

87. JFS to C. G. Larsen, 6 February 1875, JFS Papers, box 30, folder 1, LDS Church History Library.

88. JFS to Sarah Ellen Richards Smith, 20 July 1875, JFS Papers, box 30, folder 2, LDS Church History Library.

89. JFS to Julina Lambson Smith, 7 August 1875, JFS Papers, box 30, folder 2, LDS Church History Library.

90. Sarah Ellen Richards Smith to JFS, 13 June 1875; Sarah Ellen Richards Smith to JFS, 30 May 1875, Sarah Ellen Richards Smith Collection, MS 2574, box 1, folder 29, LDS Church History Library.

91. JFS to Edna Lambson Smith, 7 August 1875, JFS Papers, box 30, folder 2, LDS Church History Library.

92. JFS to Sarah Ellen Richards Smith, 27 July 1875, JFS Papers, box 30, folder 2, LDS Church History Library.

93. Sarah Ellen Richards Smith to JFS, 30 May 1875, Sarah Ellen Richards Smith Collection, MS 2574, box 1, folder 29, LDS Church History Library.

94. JFS to Sarah Ellen Richards Smith, 22 April 1875, Sarah Ellen Richards Smith Collection, MS 2574, box 1, folder 9, LDS Church History Library.

95. George A. Smith to JFS, 13 July 1875, JFS Papers, box 11, folder 21, LDS Church History Library.

96. JFS to George A. Smith, 17 August 1875, JFS Papers, box 30, folder 2, LDS Church History Library.

97. JFS Journal, 6 September 1875, JFS Papers, box 3, folder 8, LDS Church History Library.

98. JFS Journal, 2 September 1875, JFS Papers, box 3, folder 8, LDS Church History Library.

99. JFS Journal, 2 September 1875, JFS Papers, box 3, folder 8, LDS Church History Library.

100. JFS to Sarah Ellen Richards Smith, 4 September 1875, box 30, folder 2, LDS Church History Library.

101. JFS to Sarah Ellen Richards Smith, 4 September 1875, box 30, folder 2, LDS Church History Library.

102. JFS to Bathsheba W. Smith, JFS Papers, box 32, folder 1, LDS Church History Library.

394   *Notes to Pages 179–183*

103. JFS Journal, 5 September 1875, JFS Papers, box 3, folder 8, LDS Church History Library.
104. JFS Journal, 5 September 1875, JFS Papers, box 3, folder 8, LDS Church History Library.
105. JFS to David McKenzie, 3 September 1875, JFS Papers, box 30, folder 2, LDS Church History Library.
106. Brigham Young to JFS, 21 August 1875, CR 1234/1, Letterbook 13, LDS Church History Library.
107. JFS Journal, 6 September 1875, JFS Papers, box 3, folder 8, LDS Church History Library.
108. JFS Journal, 1 October 1875, JFS Papers, box 3, folder 8, LDS Church History Library.
109. JFS to J. U. Stucki, 12 November 1875, JFS Papers, box 30, folder 2, LDS Church History Library.
110. JFS to William Binder, 12 November 1875, JFS Papers, box 30, folder 2, LDS Church History Library.
111. JFS to J. H. Clementshaw, 12 November 1875, JFS Papers, box 30, folder 2, LDS Church History Library.
112. JFS to Alma L. Smith, 21 December 1875, JFS Papers, box 30, folder 2, LDS Church History Library.
113. JFS to J. H. Clementshaw, 12 November 1875, JFS Papers, box 30, folder 2, LDS Church History Library.
114. JFS to J. H. Clementshaw, 12 November 1875, JFS Papers, box 30, folder 2, LDS Church History Library.
115. JFS to Brigham Young, 7 January 1877, CR 1234/1, box 42, folder 12, LDS Church History Library.
116. JFS to Brigham Young, 7 January 1877, CR 1234/1, box 42, folder 12, LDS Church History Library.
117. JFS Journal, 7 April 1873, JFS Papers, box 3, folder 3, LDS Church History Library.
118. In Vogel, *Woodruff Journals*, 9 October 1875, 4:424.
119. These quotes from the School of the Prophets meeting are drawn from Bates and Smith, *Lost Legacy* (Urbana: University of Illinois Press, 1996), 134–35.
120. JFS to Joseph Smith III, 17 January 1877, JFS Papers, box 30, folder 2, LDS Church History Library.
121. JFS to Ward Pack, 11 March 1877, JFS Papers, box 30, folder 2, LDS Church History Library.
122. Julina Lambson Smith Journal, 8 January 1877, Julina Lambson Smith Papers, MS 4364, box 1, folder 1, LDS Church History Library.
123. JFS to Rhoda Richards, 11 June 1877, JFS Papers, box 30, folder 3, LDS Church History Library.
124. JFS to Julina Lambson Smith, 16 June 1877, JFS Papers, box 30, folder 3, LDS Church History Library.
125. JFS to Julina Lambson Smith, 16 June 1877, JFS Papers, box 30, folder 3, LDS Church History Library.
126. JFS to Edna Lambson Smith, 23 June 1877, JFS Papers, box 30, folder 3, LDS Church History Library.
127. Brigham Young to JFS, 11 May 1877, JFS Papers, box 12, folder 10, LDS Church History Library.

128. Brigham Young to JFS, 11 May 1877, JFS Papers, box 12, folder 10, LDS Church History Library.

129. JFS to Brigham Young, 20 July 1877, Brigham Young Incoming Correspondence, CR 1234/1, box 42, folder 12, LDS Church History Library.

130. JFS to Brigham Young, 20 July 1877, Brigham Young Incoming Correspondence, CR 1234/1, box 42, folder 12, LDS Church History Library.

131. Brigham Young to JFS, 6 June 1877, JFS Papers, box 12, folder 10, LDS Church History Library.

132. JFS to P. J. Lammans, 9 June 1877, JFS Papers, box 30, folder 3, LDS Church History Library.

133. JFS to O. N. Liljienquist, 16 June 1877, JFS Papers, box 30, folder 3, LDS Church History Library.

134. Brigham Young to JFS, 17 July 1877, JFS Papers, box 12, folder 10, LDS Church History Library.

135. Cablegram from LDS Church Headquarters to J. F. Smith, 30 August 1877, LDS Church History Library.

136. Turner, *Brigham Young*, 385.

137. JFS to Julina Lambson Smith, 1 September 1877, JFS Papers, box 30, folder 3, LDS Church History Library.

138. JFS to Edna Lambson Smith, 1 September 1877, JFS Papers, box 30, folder 3, LDS Church History Library.

139. The accuracy of this statement remains in question. It was made by Richards more than twenty years after the 1898 discussion of organizing the First Presidency after the death of Wilford Woodruff. Heber J. Grant Journal, 4 October 1898, typescript in D. Michael Quinn Papers, WA MSS S-2692, Beinecke Rare Book and Manuscript Library, Yale University.

140. George Q. Cannon, Untitled Discourse, 8 October 1877, *Journal of Discourses* 19:237.

141. "The Returned Apostles," *Salt Lake Tribune*, 30 September 1877, 2.

142. JFS to Charles Nibley, 30 October 1877, JFS Papers, box 30, folder 3, LDS Church History Library.

143. JFS to Stephen L. Richards, 19 November 1877, JFS Papers, box 30, folder 3, LDS Church History Library.

144. JFS to Charles Nibley, 6 December 1877, JFS Papers, box 30, folder 2, LDS Church History Library.

145. Edwin Brown Firmage and Richard Collin Mangrum, *Zion in the Courts: A Legal History of the Church of Jesus Christ of Latter-day Saints* (Urbana: University of Illinois Press, 1988), 131.

146. Alexander, *Wilford Woodruff*, 233.

147. JFS to Charles Nibley, 6 December 1877, JFS Papers, box 30, folder 2, LDS Church History Library.

148. Orson Pratt and JFS, Report to John Taylor, 18 December 1877, Historian's Office Correspondence Files, 1856–1926, CR 100/394, box 1, folder 31, LDS Church History Library.

149. Orson Pratt and JFS, Report to John Taylor, 18 December 1877, Historian's Office Correspondence Files, 1856–1926, CR 100/394, box 1, folder 31, LDS Church History Library.

150. Addison Everett to JFS, 12 January 1882, JFS Papers, box 30, folder 4, LDS Church History Library.

Notes to Pages 188–194

151. JFS to Addison Everett, 29 January 1882, JFS Papers, box 30, folder 4, LDS Church History Library.

152. For a fuller exploration of this trip, see Reid L. Neilson and Mitchell I. Schaefer, "Excavating Early Mormon History: The 1878 History Fact-Finding Mission of Apostles JFS and Orson Pratt," in Manscill et al., *Joseph F. Smith*.

153. Neilson and Schaefer, "Excavating Early Mormon History."

154. Neilson and Schaefer, "Excavating Early Mormon History."

155. Neilson and Schaefer, "Excavating Early Mormon History."

156. JFS to Julina Clarissa Smith, 6 January 1909, JFS Papers, box 35, folder 1, LDS Church History Library.

157. JFS to Julina Clarissa Smith, 6 January 1909, JFS Papers, box 35, folder 1, LDS Church History Library.

158. JFS to Edith Smith and Emily Smith, 16 July 1916, JFS Papers, box 36, folder 1, LDS Church History Library.

159. JFS to H. W. Naisbitt, 1 December 1877, JFS Papers, box 30, folder 3, LDS Church History Library.

160. Jackson Lears, *Rebirth of a Nation: The Making of Modern America, 1877–1920* (New York: Harper Perennial, 2009), 87.

161. JFS to H. W. Naisbitt, 21 November 1877, JFS Papers, box 30, folder 3, LDS Church History Library.

162. "Home Items," *Deseret News*, 10 July 1867, 1.

163. JFS, Untitled Discourse, 8 April 1879, *Journal of Discourses* 20:347.

164. JFS to rug manufacturer, JFS Papers, box 78, folder 5, LDS Church History Library.

165. JFS, Untitled Sermon, 20 January 1879, JFS Papers, box 78, folder 5, LDS Church History Library.

166. JFS, Discourse, April 1879 general conference, *Journal of Discourses* 20:210.

167. JFS Journal, 6 October 1880, JFS Papers, box 4, folder 3, LDS Church History Library.

168. The account of the meetings comes from Moses Thatcher Journal, 6–9 October 1880, Moses Thatcher Papers, 1866–1923 (COLL MSS 22), Utah State University, Special Collections and Archives Department.

169. JFS Journal, 6 October 1880, JFS Papers, box 4, folder 3, LDS Church History Library.

170. Moses Thatcher Journal, 6–9 October 1880, Moses Thatcher Papers, 1866–1923 (COLL MSS 22), Utah State University, Special Collections and Archives Department.

171. Moses Thatcher Journal, 6–9 October 1880, Moses Thatcher Papers, 1866–1923 (COLL MSS 22), Utah State University, Special Collections and Archives Department.

172. Wilford Woodruff, Untitled Discourse, 10 October 1880, *Journal of Discourses* 21:316.

173. JFS Journal, 10 October 1880, JFS Papers, box 4, folder 1, LDS Church History Library.

174. George Q. Cannon Journal, 30 September 1882, Church Historian's Press, https://www.churchhistorianspress.org/george-q-cannon/1880s/1889/09-1889?lang=eng.

175. JFS to Abraham O. Smoot, 18 November 1881, JFS Papers, box 3, folder 11, LDS Church History Library.

Notes to Pages 194–201   397

176. JFS to J. P. R. Johnson, 12 October 1884, JFS Papers, box 31, folder 3, LDS Church History Library.

177. JFS to J. P. R. Johnson, 12 October 1884, JFS Papers, box 31, folder 3, LDS Church History Library.

178. JFS Journal, 6–8 July 1879, JFS Papers, box 31, folder 2, LDS Church History Library.

179. Quoted from an untitled poem that JFS composed on 26 May 1885, Julina Lambson Smith Papers, MS 4364, box 1, folder 4, LDS Church History Library.

180. JFS, untitled poem, composed 26 May 1885, Julina Lambson Smith Papers, MS 4364, box 1, folder 4, LDS Church History Library.

181. JFS, untitled poem, composed 26 May 1885, Julina Lambson Smith Papers, MS 4364, box 1, folder 4, LDS Church History Library.

182. JFS to Sarah Ellen Richards Smith, 12 June 1885, Sarah Ellen Richards Smith Collection, MS 2574, box 1, folder 16, LDS Church History Library.

183. JFS to Lucy Smith Kimball, 23 November 1883, JFS Papers, box 31, folder 3, LDS Church History Library.

184. Land Description and Map, 1883, JFS Papers, box 44, folder 10, LDS Church History Library.

185. "Bold Robbery!," *Salt Lake Herald*, 11 July 1883.

186. Richard N. Holzapfel and R. Q. Shupe, *Joseph F. Smith: Portrait of a Prophet* (Salt Lake City: Deseret Book, 2000), 67.

187. JFS to Milando Pratt, 26 May 1891, JFS Papers, box 32, folder 2, LDS Church History Library.

CHAPTER 11

1. JFS annotation, 29 August 1888, JFS Papers, box 31, folder 4, LDS Church History Library.

2. Osterhammel, *Transformation of the World*, 625–27.

3. Digital History, https://www.digitalhistory.uh.edu/disp_textbook.cfm?smtID=3&psid=4028, accessed 3 May 2021.

4. JFS Journal, 6 April 1863, JFS Papers, box 1, folder 11, LDS Church History Library.

5. JFS Journal, 15 January 1870, JFS Papers, box 2, folder 6, LDS Church History Library.

6. JFS to Sarah Ellen Richards Smith, 8 April 1875, Sarah Ellen Richards Smith Collection, MS 2574, box 1, folder 8, LDS Church History Library.

7. George Reynolds Journal, 16 October 1874, in Bruce A. Van Orden, *Prisoner for Conscience Sake: The Life of George Reynolds* (Salt Lake City: Deseret Book, 1992), 61.

8. Edwin B. Firmage and R. Collin Mangrum, *Zion in the Courts: A Legal History of the Church of Jesus Christ of Latter-day Saints, 1830–1900* (Urbana: University of Illinois Press, 1987), 154.

9. JFS Journal, 6 January 1879, JFS Papers, box 2, folder 6, LDS Church History Library.

10. O. J. Hollister, "The Supreme Court Decision in the Reynolds Case: An Interview Between President John Taylor and O.J. Hollister, Esq. Salt Lake City, Utah, January 18th 1879," *New York Tribune*, 18 January 1879.

11. "Revelation Given Through President John Taylor, Salt Lake City, 13 October 1882," typescript in Susa Young Gates Papers, 1870–1933, MS 2692, box 48, folder 20, LDS Church History Library.

Notes to Pages 201–205

12. George Q. Cannon Journal, 13 October 1882, Church Historian's Press, https://www.churchhistorianspress.org/george-q-cannon/1880s/1882/10-1882?lang=eng.

13. George Q. Cannon Journal, 14 October 1882, Church Historian's Press, https://www.churchhistorianspress.org/george-q-cannon/1880s/1882/10-1882?lang=eng.

14. JFS to Charles W. Nibley, 27 May 1884; JFS to John Henry Smith, 25 May 1884, JFS Papers, box 31, folder 3, LDS Church History Library.

15. JFS to Jesse N. Smith, 12 October 1884, JFS Papers, box 31, folder 3, LDS Church History Library.

16. JFS Sermon, 7 July 1878, published in *Journal of Discourses* 20:28.

17. Henry Stokes to JFS, 1 January 1884, JFS Papers, box 12, folder 20, LDS Church History Library.

18. JFS to Henry Stokes, 25 May 1884, JFS Papers, box 31, folder 3, LDS Church History Library.

19. James Henry Martineau Journal, 18 January 1885, MS 18300, LDS Church History Library.

20. JFS to T. W. Curtis, 22 April 1884, JFS Papers, box 31, folder 4, LDS Church History Library.

21. JFS to Helaman Pratt, 13 June 1884, JFS Papers, box 31, folder 4, LDS Church History Library.

22. Franklin D. Richards Journal, 15 May 1884, Richards Family Collection, 1837–1961, MS 1215, box 3, vol. 33, LDS Church History Library.

23. Nolan P. Olsen, *Logan Temple: The First 100 Years* (Providence, UT: Watkins and Sons, 1978), 140.

24. Charles Ora Card Journal, 9 April 1882, MSS 1543, Charles Ora Card Collection, L. Tom Perry Special Collections, Harold B. Lee Library, Brigham Young University. The revelation to which JFS referred is currently Doctrine and Covenants section 58.

25. JFS to Edward Partridge, 11 December 1884, JFS Papers, box 31, folder 3, LDS Church History Library.

26. JFS to Joseph Smith III, 3 May 1889, JFS Papers, box 31, folder 3, LDS Church History Library.

27. JFS to William Smith, 12 July 1884, JFS Papers, box 31, folder 3, LDS Church History Library.

28. Minutes of San Luis (Arizona) Stake Conference, 9–10 June 1883, CR 100 589, Historian's Office and Reports (Local Units) 1840–1886, LDS Church History Library.

29. JFS Sermon, 19 April 1896, in *Thy Servants Speak*, ed. Jason Hansen (Salt Lake City: 3rd Day, 2012), 200.

30. JFS to Hyrum M. Smith, 18 February 1897, JFS Papers, box 31, folder 3, LDS Church History Library.

31. JFS to Elias Wesley Smith, 17 June 1909, JFS Papers, box 34, folder 1, LDS Church History Library.

32. JFS Notebook, 1884, JFS Papers, box 5, folder 9, LDS Church History Library.

33. Doctrine and Covenants, 101:7–8.

34. Joseph Fielding Smith, in his biography of his father, claimed that JFS wrote these scriptural references in the journal of a young woman who asked him for some inspirational thoughts. This is a puzzling assertion since they are recorded in JFS's own notebook, which also contains a list of expenditures incurred during his trip, tithing collected, a list of people he knew who had died since 1859, and several

Notes to Pages 205–210   399

notes wishing him well in his travels. The most reasonable explanation is that JFS recorded these references for his own use. JFS Notebook, n.d. [1884], JFS Papers, box 5, folder 9, LDS Church History Library.

35. Charles Ora Card Journal, 3 February 1884, MSS 1543, Charles Ora Card Collection, L. Tom Perry Special Collections, Harold B. Lee Library, Brigham Young University.

36. Charles Ora Card Journal, 17 May 1884, Charles Ora Card Collection, L. Tom Perry Special Collections, Harold B. Lee Library, Brigham Young University.

37. Richard S. Van Wagoner, *Mormon Polygamy: A History* (Salt Lake City: Signature Books, 1989), 121.

38. Steven Hahn, *A Nation Without Borders: The United States and Its World in an Age of Civil Wars, 1830–1910* (New York: Viking, 2016), 389.

39. JFS to John Henry Smith, 17 December 1884, JFS Papers, box 31, folder 3, LDS Church History Library.

40. Sarah Barringer Gordon, *The Mormon Question: Polygamy and Constitutional Conflict in Nineteenth-Century America* (Chapel Hill: University of North Carolina Press, 2002), 158.

41. JFS to John Taylor, 14 October 1884, First Presidency (John Taylor) Correspondence, CR 1 180, box 11, folder 19, LDS Church History Library.

42. Mrs. G.S.R., "Lifting the Veil," *Salt Lake Tribune*, 5 October 1879, 3.

43. Franklin D. Richards Journal, 5–15 November 1887, Richards Family Collection, 1837–1961, MS 1215, box 4, vol. 36, LDS Church History Library.

44. JFS to John Henry Smith, 12 December 1884, JFS Papers, box 31, folder 3, LDS Church History Library.

45. George Q. Cannon Journal, 1 December 1884, Church Historian's Press, https://www.churchhistorianspress.org/george-q-cannon.

46. JFS to Edward Partridge, 11 December 1884, JFS Papers, box 31, folder 3, LDS Church History Library.

47. Edward Partridge Journal, 8 February 1885, MS 17670. LDS Church History Library. "Joseph Speight" was one of several aliases used by JFS during his time "on the underground."

48. John Smith to JFS, 12 December 1884, JFS Papers, box 8, folder 29, LDS Church History Library.

49. JFS to Sarah Ellen Richards Smith, 23 July 1885, Sarah Ellen Richards Smith Collection, MS 2574, box 1, folder 15, LDS Church History Library.

50. Edward Partridge Journal, 15 February 1885, MS 17670, LDS Church History Library.

51. Edward Partridge Journal, 1, 12, and 17 February 1885, MS 17670, LDS Church History Library.

52. Frederick Beesley Journal, 20 December 1886, MS 1674, LDS Church History Library.

53. Frederick Beesley Journal, 23 December 1886, MS 1674, LDS Church History Library.

54. Frederick Beesley Journal, 3 January 1887, MS 1674, LDS Church History Library.

55. JFS to William Pack, 25 November 1890, JFS Papers, box 32, folder 1, LDS Church History Library.

56. JFS to Sarah Ellen Richards Smith, 23 September 1885, Sarah Ellen Richards Smith Collection, MS 2574, box 1, folder 17, LDS Church History Library.

57. Julina Lambson Smith Journal, 6 and 29 January 1886, Julina Lambson Smith Papers, MS 4364, LDS Church History Library.

58. Donnette Smith to Sarah Ellen Richards Smith, 27 November 1886, Sarah Ellen Richards Smith Collection, MS 2574, box 2, folder 7, LDS Church History Library.

59. JFS to Sarah Ellen Richards Smith, 11 March 1885, Sarah Ellen Richards Smith Collection, MS 2574, box 1, folder 17, LDS Church History Library.

60. JFS to Leonora Smith, 2 June 1885, Sarah Ellen Richards Smith Collection, MS 2574, box 2, folder 4, LDS Church History Library.

61. Unnamed federal official, quoted in Dean L. May, *Utah: A People's History* (Salt Lake City: University of Utah Press, 1987), 122.

62. JFS to John Taylor and George Q. Cannon, 30 September 1886, First Presidency (John Taylor) Correspondence, 1877–1887, CR 1 180, box 18, folder 6, LDS Church History Library.

63. JFS to John T. Caine, 5 July 1888, MS 27013, box 1, LDS Church History Library.

64. Mary Schwartz Smith to JFS, 6 September 1886, JFS Papers, box 8, folder 8, LDS Church History Library.

65. Joseph F. Smith, "The Mormon Question," *Deseret News*, 10 March 1886, 121.

66. Alice Ann Kimball Smith to JFS, 10 April 1887, JFS Papers, box 8, folder 1, LDS Church History Library.

67. Alice Ann Kimball Smith to JFS, 12 March 1887, JFS Papers, box 8, folder 1, LDS Church History Library.

68. Alice Ann Kimball Smith to JFS, 25 November 1884, JFS Papers, box 8, folder 1, LDS Church History Library.

69. Mary Schwartz Smith to JFS, 4 January 1886, JFS Papers, box 8, folder 8, LDS Church History Library.

70. Alice Ann Kimball Smith to JFS, 10 April 1887, JFS Papers, box 8, folder 1, LDS Church History Library.

71. "Biographical Sketch of Mary Taylor Schwartz," in Joseph F. Smith Family Genealogical Committee, *The Descendants of Joseph F. Smith*, 138.

72. The original indictment against JFS is in the JFS Papers, box 47, folder 8, LDS Church History Library.

73. Alice Ann Kimball Smith to JFS, 10 April 1887, JFS Papers, box 8, folder 1, LDS Church History Library.

74. Julina Lambson Smith to JFS, 8 July 1887, JFS Papers, box 7, folder 9, LDS Church History Library.

75. Julina Lambson Smith to JFS, 8 July 1887, JFS Papers, box 7, folder 9, LDS Church History Library.

76. JFS to Joseph H. Dean, 5 April 1888, MS 27013, box 1, LDS Church History Library.

77. JFS to William King, 21 April 1888, MS 27013, box 1, LDS Church History Library.

78. JFS to John Taylor and George Q. Cannon, 7 January 1886, First Presidency (John Taylor) Correspondence, 1877–1887, CR 1 180, box 18, folder 6, LDS Church History Library.

79. JFS to John Henry Smith, 9 May 1888, MS 27013, box 1, LDS Church History Library.

80. George Q. Cannon to JFS, 26 May 1887, JFS Papers, box 31, folder 3, LDS Church History Library.

Notes to Pages 215–219 401

81. George Q. Cannon Journal, 13 June 1887, Church Historian's Press, http://www
.churchhistorianspress.org/george-q-cannon.

82. Wilford Woodruff to JFS, n.d., probably early summer 1887, JFS Papers, box 14,
folder 5, LDS Church History Library.

83. Entry for 25 June 1887, Hawaiian Mission Manuscript History and Historical
Reports, 1850–1867, LR 3695, box 1, folder 2, LDS Church History Library.

84. George Q. Cannon Journal, 25 July 1887, Church Historian's Press, http://www
.churchhistorianspress.org/george-q-cannon.

85. George Q. Cannon Journal, 25 July 1887, Church Historian's Press, http://www
.churchhistorianspress.org/george-q-cannon.

86. Quoted in Francis M. Gibbons, *Joseph F. Smith: Patriarch and Preacher, Prophet of
God* (Salt Lake City: Deseret Book, 1984), 157.

87. Heber J. Grant to JFS, 27 February 1887, JFS Papers, box 14, folder 5, LDS Church
History Library.

88. Heber J. Grant Journal, 4 July 1887, D. Michael Quinn Collection, WA MSS
S-2692, Beinecke Rare Book and Manuscript Library, Yale University.

89. Heber J. Grant Journal, 5 April 1887, D. Michael Quinn Collection, WA MSS
S-2692, Beinecke Rare Book and Manuscript Library, Yale University.

90. Heber J. Grant Journal, 5 April 1887, D. Michael Quinn Collection, WA MSS
S-2692, Beinecke Rare Book and Manuscript Library, Yale University.

91. Heber J. Grant Journal, 23–24 June 1887, D. Michael Quinn Collection, WA MSS
S-2692, Beinecke Rare Book and Manuscript Library, Yale University.

92. Franklin D. Richards Journal, 20 July 1887, Richards Family Collection, 1837–1961,
MS 1215, box 3, vol. 33, LDS Church History Library.

CHAPTER 12

1. Franklin D. Richards Journal, 3 August 1887, Richards Family Collection, 1837–
1961, MS 1215, box 3, vol. 33, LDS Church History Library.

2. Bitton, *George Q. Cannon*, 286.

3. See R. Jean Addams, "The Bullion, Beck, and Champion Mining Company and the
Redemption of Zion," *Journal of Mormon History* 40, no. 2 (2014): 159–234.

4. JFS to George Q. Cannon, 18 April 1888, JFS Papers, box 15, folder 3, LDS Church
History Library.

5. Rogers, *Nuttall Diaries*, 23 September 1889, 375.

6. Heber J. Grant Journal, 3 August 1887, D. Michael Quinn Collection, WA MSS
S-2692, Beinecke Rare Book and Manuscript Library, Yale University.

7. Heber J. Grant Journal, 12 August 1887, Quinn Collection, WA MSS S-2692,
Beinecke Library, Yale University.

8. Heber J. Grant Journal, 6 November 1885, D. Michael Quinn Collection, WA MSS
S-2692, Beinecke Rare Book and Manuscript Library, Yale University.

9. JFS to John Taylor and George Q. Cannon, 7 January 1886, First Presidency (John
Taylor) Correspondence, 1877–1887, CR 1 180, box 18, folder 6, LDS Church History Library.

10. JFS to Francis M. Lyman, 10 May 1888, MS 27013, box 1, LDS Church History
Library.

11. JFS to Albert J. Davis, 17 June 1891, JFS Papers, box 32, folder 2, LDS Church History Library.

12. JFS to Susa Y. Gates, 9 August 1890, JFS Papers, box 32, folder 1, LDS Church History Library.

13. Franklin D. Richards Journal, 31 October 1887, Richards Family Collection, 1837–1961, MS 1215, box 3, vol. 33, LDS Church History Library.

14. Franklin D. Richards Journal, 13 August 1887.

15. Heber J. Grant Journal, 8 September 1887, D. Michael Quinn Collection, WA MSS S-2692, Beinecke Rare Book and Manuscript Library, Yale University.

16. Vogel, *Woodruff Journals*, 31 December 1887, 5:413

17. Franklin D. Richards Journal, 2 February 1888, Richards Family Collection, 1837–1961, MS 1215, box 3, vol. 33, LDS Church History Library.

18. Vogel, *Woodruff Journals*, 2 February 1888, 5:418

19. JFS Letter of Appointment, 10 February 1888, JFS Papers, box 47, folder 19, LDS Church History Library.

20. JFS to Heber J. Grant, 30 March 1886, Grant Papers, box 34, folder 5, LDS Church History Library.

21. First Presidency to John W. Young, 17 January 1888, John W. Young Papers, typescript in D. Michael Quinn Papers, WA MSS S-2692, Beinecke Rare Book and Manuscript Library, Yale University.

22. Wilford Woodruff, telegram to "Jason Mack" (pseudonym for JFS), 18 February 1888, typescript in D. Michael Quinn Papers, WA MSS S-2692, Beinecke Rare Book and Manuscript Library, Yale University.

23. JFS to Sarah Richards Smith, 17 March 1888, MS 27013, box 1, LDS Church History Library.

24. JFS to Wilford Woodruff and George Q. Cannon, 17 April 1888, MS 27013, box 1, LDS Church History Library.

25. JFS to John Henry Smith, 9 May 1888, MS 27013, box 1, LDS Church History Library.

26. John J. Byrne to JFS, 19 March 1888, JFS Papers, box 15, folder 1, LDS Church History Library.

27. JFS to Edwin Davis, 22 April, 1888, MS 27013, box 1, LDS Church History Library.

28. Both statements are quoted in Edward Leo Lyman, *Political Deliverance: The Mormon Quest for Utah Statehood* (Urbana: University of Illinois Press, 1986), 90–91.

29. JFS to Seymour B. Young, 23 April 1888, MS 27013, box 1, LDS Church History Library.

30. JFS to Francis M. Lyman, 10 May 1888, MS 27013, box 1, LDS Church History Library.

31. JFS to Jacob F. Gates, 12 June 1889, JFS Papers, box 3, folder 1, LDS Church History Library.

32. JFS to Jacob F. Gates, 12 June 1889, 12 June 1889, JFS Papers, box 3, folder 1, LDS Church History Library.

33. JFS to Daniel H. Wells, 4 July 1888, MS 27013, box 1, LDS Church History Library.

34. JFS to Charles W. Nibley, 13 December 1888, JFS Papers, box 31, folder 44, LDS Church History Library.

35. Heber J. Grant Journal, 9 April 1893, D. Michael Quinn Collection, WA MSS S-2692, Beinecke Rare Book and Manuscript Library, Yale University.

36. JFS to Edna Lambson Smith, 17 April 1888, MS 27013, box 1, LDS Church History Library.

Notes to Pages 225–230   403

37. JFS to Julina Lambson Smith, 1 April 1888, MS 27013, box 1, LDS Church History Library.
38. JFS to Joseph A. Harris, 6 April 1888, MS 27013, box 1, LDS Church History Library.
39. JFS to John Henry Smith, 9 May 1888, John Henry Smith Papers, box 7, in George A. Smith Family Papers, MS 0036, Special Collections, J. Willard Marriott Library, University of Utah.
40. Heber J. Grant Journal, 20 December 1888, D. Michael Quinn Collection, WA MSS S-2692, Beinecke Rare Book and Manuscript Library, Yale University.
41. Abraham H. Cannon Journal, 6 December 1889, in *Candid Insights of a Mormon Apostle: The Diaries of Abraham H. Cannon, 1889–1895*, ed. Edward Leo Lyman (Salt Lake City: Signature Books, 2010), 35.
42. Abraham H. Cannon Journal, 22–23 December 1889, in Lyman, *Candid Insights*, 39–40.
43. JFS to Ben E. Rich, 20 December 1910, JFS Papers, box 35, folder 1, LDS Church History Library.
44. Abraham H. Cannon Journal, 22–23 December 1889, in Lyman, *Candid Insights*, 39–40.
45. In Vogel, *Woodruff Journals*, 24 November 1889, 5:506–7.
46. Franklin D. Richards Journal, 23 December 1889, Richards Family Collection, 1837–1961, MS 1215, box 4, vol. 38, LDS Church History Library.
47. Firmage and Mangrum, *Zion in the Courts*, 234–35.

CHAPTER 13
1. JFS to James Hetfield, 28 May 1891, JFS Papers, box 32, folder 3, LDS Church History Library.
2. JFS to James Hetfield, 28 May 1891, JFS Papers, box 32, folder 3, LDS Church History Library.
3. JFS to Susa Young Gates, 8 January 1889, JFS Papers, box 31, folder 44, LDS Church History Library.
4. JFS Sermon, 1 November 1891, Logan, UT, in Hansen, *Thy Servants Speak*, 28.
5. JFS to Thomas Gess, 12 August 1893; JFS to Charles W. Nibley, 28 May 1891, JFS Papers, box 32, folder 3, LDS Church History Library.
6. JFS to Charles Nibley, 28 May 1890, JFS Papers, box 32, folder 1, LDS Church History Library.
7. JFS to Charles Nibley, 13 December 1888, JFS Papers, box 31, folder 44, LDS Church History Library.
8. JFS to Susa Young Gates, 8 January 1889, JFS Papers, box 31, folder 44, LDS Church History Library.
9. JFS to Wilford Woodruff, 19 May 1888, First Presidency General Authority Correspondence, CR 1/176, box 2: Joseph F. Smith, 1888, LDS Church History Library.
10. JFS to Marriner W. Merrill, 20 October 1890, JFS Papers, box 32, folder 1, LDS Church History Library.
11. JFS to Wilford Woodruff, 19 May 1888, MS 27013, box 1, LDS Church History Library.
12. JFS to William Pack, 25 November 1890, JFS Papers, box 32, folder 1, LDS Church History Library.

404   *Notes to Pages 230–236*

13. JFS to Wilford Woodruff, 19 May 1888, MS 27013, box 1, LDS Church History Library.

14. Vogel, *Woodruff Journals*, 16 May 1889, 5:481.

15. JFS to William King, 17 March 1890, JFS Papers, box 32, folder 1, LDS Church History Library.

16. JFS to Alice M. Smith, 13 September 1899, JFS Papers, box 33, folder 2, LDS Church History Library.

17. JFS to Albert J. Davis, 17 June 1891, JFS Papers, box 32, folder 2, LDS Church History Library.

18. JFS to Albert J. Davis, 17 June 1891, JFS Papers, box 32, folder 2, LDS Church History Library.

19. JFS to William Pack, 9 August 1890, JFS Papers, box 32, folder 1, LDS Church History Library.

20. George Q. Cannon Journal, 15 August 1889, Church Historian's Press, https://www.churchhistorianspress.org/george-q-cannon.

21. Wilford Woodruff, George Q. Cannon, and JFS to Harvey H. Cluff, 17 October 1892, in James R. Clark, *Messages of the First Presidency* (Salt Lake City: Deseret Book, 1965), 3:240.

22. JFS to Albert J. Davis, 17 June 1891, JFS Papers, box 32, folder 2, LDS Church History Library.

23. JFS to Wilford Woodruff, 19 May 1888, First Presidency General Authority Correspondence, CR 1/176, box 2: Joseph F. Smith, 1888, LDS Church History Library.

24. JFS to Jerusha Pierce, 11 June 1890, JFS Papers, box 32, folder 1, LDS Church History Library.

25. JFS to John Henry Smith, 20 March 1890, JFS Papers, box 32, folder 1, LDS Church History Library.

26. JFS to Charles W. Nibley, 18 July 1890, JFS Papers, LDS Church History Library.

27. JFS to Susa Young Gates, 21 May 1890, JFS Papers, box 32, folder 1, LDS Church History Library.

28. JFS Notebook, "Notes on a Meeting in Manassas, Colorado, 17 August 1890," JFS Papers, LDS Church History Library.

29. George Q. Cannon Journal, 1 September 1890, Church Historian's Press, https://www.churchhistorianspress.org/george-q-cannon.

30. George Q. Cannon Journal, 12 September 1890, Church Historian's Press, https://www.churchhistorianspress.org/george-q-cannon.

31. George Q. Cannon Journal, 22 September 1890, Church Historian's Press, https://www.churchhistorianspress.org/george-q-cannon.

32. Thomas G. Alexander, *Things in Heaven and Earth: The Life and Times of Wilford Woodruff, a Mormon Prophet* (Salt Lake City: Signature Books, 1991), 257–58.

33. Alexander, *Things in Heaven and Earth*, 258.

34. JFS to Isaac Trumbo, 30 September 1890, JFS Papers, box 30, folder 2, LDS Church History Library.

35. Vogel, *Woodruff Journals*, 25 September 1890, 5:541.

36. Grant Journal, 29–30 September 1890, D. Michael Quinn Papers, WA MSS S-2692, Beinecke Rare Book and Manuscript Library, Yale University.

37. JFS to Isaac Trumbo, 8 October 1890, JFS Papers, box 32, folder 1, LDS Church History Library.

Notes to Pages 236–242   405

38. L. John Nuttall to JFS, 19 January 1891, JFS Papers, box 32, folder 2, LDS Church History Library.
39. JFS to Sarah Ellen Richards Smith, 24 September 1890, JFS Papers, box 32, folder 1, LDS Church History Library.
40. In *History's Apprentice: The Diaries of B. H. Roberts, 1880–1898*, ed. John Sillito (Salt Lake City: Signature Books, 2004), 225.
41. JFS to Charles Nielsen, 24 October 1890, JFS Papers, box 32, folder 1, LDS Church History Library.
42. JFS to Rulon Wells, 14 November 1890, JFS Papers, box 32, folder 1, LDS Church History Library.
43. JFS to Heber M. Wells, 13 October 1890, JFS Papers, box 32, folder 1, LDS Church History Library.
44. JFS to Charles W. Nibley, 28 October 1890, JFS Papers, box 32, folder 1, LDS Church History Library.
45. JFS to Joseph Nelson, 27 May 1891, JFS Papers, box 32, folder 2, LDS Church History Library.
46. Rebecca Edwards, *New Spirits: America in the Gilded Age* (New York: Oxford University Press, 2006), 89.
47. Edwards, *New Spirits*, 91.
48. This story is well-known among Latter-day Saints. The most accessible version of it is in Laura F. Willes, *Christmas with the Prophets* (Salt Lake City: Deseret Book, 2010), 63–64.
49. Sillito, *History's Apprentice*, 209.
50. JFS to Mercy F. Thompson, 18 November 1890, JFS Papers, box 32, folder 1, LDS Church History Library.
51. Abraham H. Cannon Journal, 9 April 1891, in Lyman, *Candid Insights*, 203.
52. JFS to Mercy Thompson, 18 November 1890, JFS Papers, box 32, folder 1, LDS Church History Library.
53. JFS to Charles W. Nibley, 14 November 1890, JFS Papers, box 32, folder 1, LDS Church History Library.
54. Robert Darby, *A Surgical Temptation: The Demonization of the Foreskin and the Rise of Circumcision in Britain* (Chicago: University of Chicago Press, 2005), 7.
55. JFS to Hyrum M. Smith, 28 March 1896, MS 27013, box 2, LDS Church History Library.
56. JFS to Susa Young Gates, 9 December 1890, JFS Papers, box 32, folder 1, LDS Church History Library.
57. Bruce R. McConkie, *Mormon Doctrine* (Salt Lake City: Deseret Book, 1958); Spencer W. Kimball, *The Miracle of Forgiveness* (Salt Lake City: Deseret Book, 1969).
58. JFS to Solomon Kimball, 12 June 1891, JFS Papers, box 32, folder 2, LDS Church History Library.
59. JFS Sermon, 5 October 1894, in Hansen, *Thy Servants Speak*, vol. 4, 136–37.
60. All of the documents relating to Joseph F. Smith's amnesty, including the Trumbo letter, are found in Amnesty Papers, 1891–1892, JFS Papers, box 45, folder 3, LDS Church History Library.
61. "The Mormon Conference," *Salt Lake Tribune*, 5 October 1891.
62. "The Mormon Conference," *Salt Lake Tribune*, 5 October 1891.
63. A. H. Cannon Journal, 4 October 1891, quoted in Lyman, *Candid Insights*, 256.
64. "General Conference," *Deseret Evening News*, 5 October 1891.

406   *Notes to Pages 242–250*

65. Jonathan Z. Smith, *Map Is Not Territory: Studies in the History of Religion* (Chicago: University of Chicago Press, 1978), 133.

66. Smith, *Map Is Not Territory*, 161.

CHAPTER 14

1. JFS to Charles W. Nibley, 28 October 1890, JFS Papers, box 32, folder 1, LDS Church History Library.

2. Abraham H. Cannon Journal, 5 April 1890, in Lyman, *Candid Insights*, 80.

3. Abraham H. Cannon Journal, 7 April 1891, in Lyman, *Candid Insights*, 202.

4. Accounts of this meetings are found in the Nuttall Journal, 19 February 1891, and the Grant Journal of the same date, LDS Church History Library.

5. *Report of the Utah Commission to the Secretary of the Interior* (Washington, DC: Government Printing Office, 1891), 5–6.

6. George Q. Cannon Journal, 22 January 1891, Church Historian's Press, https://www.churchhistorianspress.org/george-q-cannon.

7. "Heads of the Church," *Salt Lake Times*, 6 June 1891.

8. JFS to John Taylor and George Q. Cannon, 2 March 1886, First Presidency (John Taylor) Correspondence, 1877–1887, CR 1 180, box 18, folder 6, LDS Church History Library.

9. JFS to N. C. Edlefsen, 22 February 1891, JFS Papers, box 32, folder 2, LDS Church History Library.

10. George Q. Cannon Journal, 20 May 1892, Church Historian's Press, https://www.churchhistorianspress.org/george-q-cannon.

11. George Q. Cannon Journal, 20 May 1892, Church Historian's Press, https://www.churchhistorianspress.org/george-q-cannon.

12. Abraham H. Cannon Journal, 9 July 1891, in Lyman, *Candid Insights*, 231.

13. George Q. Cannon Journal, 9 July 1891, Church Historian's Press, https://www.churchhistorianspress.org/george-q-cannon.

14. Alexander, *Utah*, 202.

15. Abraham H. Cannon Journal, 23 October 1892, in Lyman, *Candid Insights*, 365.

16. JFS to John C. Graham, 23 January 1892, JFS Papers, box 32, folder 2, LDS Church History Library.

17. JFS sermon delivered at Cache stake quarterly conference, 2 November 1891, in Hansen, *Thy Servants Speak*, 4:377–79.

18. JFS sermon delivered at Cache stake quarterly conference, 2 November 1891, in Hansen, *Thy Servants Speak*, 4:377–79.

19. JFS to Langley A. Bailey, 24 September 1895, MS 27013, box 1, LDS Church History Library.

20. JFS to Bathsheba W. Smith, 24 October 1895, MS 27013, box 1. Bathsheba Smith's brief comments appeared in the *Deseret News*, 22 October 1895, 5.

21. JFS to N. C. Edlefsen, 14 July 1891, JFS Papers, box 32, folder 2, LDS Church History Library.

22. JFS to William Budge, 19 December 1892, JFS Papers, box 32, folder 3, LDS Church History Library.

23. JFS to William Budge, 19 December 1892, JFS Papers, box 32, folder 3, LDS Church History Library.

24. JFS to N. C. Edlefsen, 22 February 1891, JFS Papers, box 32, folder 2, LDS Church History Library.

Notes to Pages 251–256   407

25. JFS to John C. Graham, 23 January 1892, JFS Papers, box 32, folder 2, LDS Church History Library.

26. Joseph F. Smith, *Another Plain Talk* (Salt Lake City: Republican Central Committee, 1892).

27. Anthon H. Lund Journal, 13 January 1893, Anthon H. Lund Papers, MS 1256, LDS Church History Library.

28. Anthon H. Lund Journal, 23 March 1893, Anthon H. Lund Papers, MS 1256, LDS Church History Library.

29. Abraham H. Cannon Journal, 22 March 1893, in Lyman, *Candid Insights*, 381.

30. Anthon H. Lund Journal, 23 March 1893, Anthon H. Lund Papers, MS 1256, LDS Church History Library.

31. George Q. Cannon Journal, 6 April 1892, Church Historian's Press, https://www .churchhistorianspress.org/george-q-cannon.

32. Abraham H. Cannon Journal, 6 April 1892, in Lyman, *Candid Insights*, 322.

33. Circular letter from Wilford Woodruff, George Q. Cannon, and Joseph F. Smith to Bishops, 16 October 1892, in James R. Clark, *Messages of the First Presidency* (Salt Lake City: Deseret Book, 1965), 3:237.

34. Wallace Alan Raynor, *The Everlasting Spires: A Story of the Salt Lake Temple* (Salt Lake City: Deseret Book, 1965), 56.

35. Wilford Woodruff, George Q. Cannon, and Joseph F. Smith to Abraham Hatch, 16 October 1892, in Clark, *Messages of the First Presidency*, 3:237.

36. JFS to A. J. Davis, 15 February 1893, JFS Papers, box 32, folder 3, LDS Church History Library.

37. Abraham H. Cannon Journal, 15, 17 and 24 April 1892, in Lyman, *Candid Insights*, 328–29.

38. George Q. Cannon Journal, 3 January 1893, Church Historian's Press, https://www .churchhistorianspress.org/george-q-cannon.

39. Anthon H. Lund Journal, 13 January 1893, Anthon H. Lund Papers, LDS Church History Library.

40. JFS to Mary Gatewood, 5 March 1893, JFS Papers, box 32, folder 3, LDS Church History Library.

41. JFS to A. J. Davis, 15 February 1893, JFS Papers, box 32, folder 3, LDS Church History Library.

42. JFS Sermon, Salt Lake stake conference, 4 March 1893, in Hansen, *Thy Servants Speak*, vol. 4, 95–96.

43. Charles Ora Card Journal, 6 April 1893, MSS 1543, Charles Ora Card Collection, L. Tom Perry Special Collections, Harold B. Lee Library, Brigham Young University.

44. JFS Sermon, Salt Lake stake conference, 4 March 1893, published in Hansen, *Thy Servants Speak*, vol. 4, 95–96.

45. John Henry Smith Journal, 23 April 1896, in *Church, State and Politics: The Diaries of John Henry Smith*, ed. Jean Bickmore White (Salt Lake City: Signature Books, 1990).

46. JFS to Charles W. Nibley, 28 May 1891, JFS Papers, box 32, folder 2, LDS Church History Library.

47. Wilford Woodruff, George Q. Cannon, and Joseph F. Smith to Stake Presidents, 9 May 1893, published in Clark, *Messages of the First Presidency*, 3:245–46.

48. JFS to Orson Smith, 20 May 1896, MS 27013, box 2, LDS Church History Library.

408   *Notes to Pages 256–262*

49. George Q. Cannon Journal, 4 April 1893, Church Historian's Press, https://www.churchhistorianspress.org/george-q-cannon.
50. JFS to John Henry Smith, 27 September 1893, JFS Papers, box 32, folder 3, LDS Church History Library.
51. Alexander, *Utah*, 204–5.
52. "Joseph F. Smith's Speech," *Salt Lake Tribune*, 22 April 1896.
53. JFS Sermon, Logan, UT, 3 May 1896, in Hansen, *Thy Servants Speak*, vol. 4, 210–11.
54. "Joseph F. Smith's Speech," *Salt Lake Tribune*, 22 April 1896.
55. "Joseph F. Smith's Speech," *Salt Lake Tribune*, 22 April 1896.
56. John Henry Smith Journal, 23 April 1896, in White, *Church, State and Politics: The Diaries of John Henry Smith*.
57. JFS to Hyrum M. Smith, 27 April 1896, MS 27013, box 2, LDS Church History Library.
58. JFS to Mary Schwartz Smith, 22 April 1896, MS 27013, box 1, LDS Church History Library.
59. JFS Sermon, Salt Lake City, 6 October 1899, in Hansen, *Thy Servants Speak*, vol. 4, 302.
60. Kenneth W. Godfrey, "Moses Thatcher in the Dock: His Trials, the Aftermath, and His Last Days," *Journal of Mormon History* 24, no. 1 (1998): 54–88.
61. George Q. Cannon Journal, 6 April 1896, Church Historian's Press, https://www.churchhistorianspress.org/george-q-cannon.
62. JFS to John E. Booth, 10 April 1896, MS 27013, box 2, LDS Church History Library.
63. JFS to Julina Lambson, 8 April 1896, MS 27013, box 2, LDS Church History Library.
64. Church of Jesus Christ of Latter-day Saints, *The Thatcher Episode: A Concise Statement of the Facts of the Case* (Salt Lake City: Deseret News, 1896), 18–19.
65. Heber J. Grant Journal, 8 July 1896, D. Michael Quinn Collection, WA MSS S-2692, Beinecke Rare Book and Manuscript Library, Yale University.

CHAPTER 15

1. Ronald Seavoy, *An Economic History of the United States From 1607 to the Present* (New York: Routledge, 2006), 195.
2. JFS to Charles W. Nibley, 30 June 1893, JFS Papers, box 32, folder 3, LDS Church History Library.
3. Telegram, JFS to Heber J. Grant, 18 June 1896, JFS Papers, LDS Church Archives.
4. JFS to Heber J. Grant, 30 June 1893, JFS Papers, box 32, folder 3, LDS Church History Library.
5. JFS Sermon, 5 October 1894, in Hansen, *Thy Servants Speak*, vol. 4, 136–37.
6. JFS to Mary Schwartz Smith, 16 August 1893, JFS Papers, box 32, folder 3, LDS Church History Library.
7. JFS to Ina D. Smith [Coolbrith], 15 October 1890, JFS Papers, box 32, folder 1, LDS Church History Library.
8. JFS to Mary Gatewood, 5 March 1893, JFS Papers, box 32, folder 3, LDS Church History Library.
9. JFS to Joseph Smith III, 7 November 1896, JFS Papers, box 33, folder 1, LDS Church History Library.
10. JFS to Mary Gatewood, 5 March 1893, JFS Papers, box 32, folder 3, LDS Church History Library.

Notes to Pages 262–268 409

11. JFS to Albert J. Davis, 17 June 1891, JFS Papers, box 32, folder 2, LDS Church History Library.

12. Anthon H. Lund Journal, 27 February 1897, Anthon H. Lund Papers, LDS Church History Library.

13. Quoted in Francis M. Gibbons, *Joseph Fielding Smith: Gospel Scholar, Prophet of God* (Salt Lake City: Deseret Book, 1992), 15–16.

14. JFS to Hyrum M. Smith, 4 September 1896, JFS Papers, box 33, folder 1, LDS Church History Library.

15. JFS to President Benjamin Harrison, 22 June 1891, JFS Papers, box 45, folder 3, LDS Church History Library. An unknown individual advised JFS to remove his declaration of loyalty to the Republicans from his final draft of the petition because it appeared as if he was seeking to curry partisan favor with Harrison. JFS followed the advice.

16. JFS to J. E. Taylor, 9 February 1905, JFS Papers, box 34, folder 1, LDS Church History Library.

17. JFS to Reed Smoot, 27 February 1907, JFS Papers, box 34, folder 2, LDS Church History Library.

18. JFS Sermon, April 1907 general conference, in Hansen, *Thy Servants Speak*, 26:493–94.

19. Susa Young Gates, "The President of the Mormon Church at Home," 1904, typescript in Susa Young Gates Papers, MS 7692, box 102, folder 5, LDS Church History Library.

20. JFS to W. J. McConnell, 4 January 1908, JFS Papers, LDS Church History Library.

21. Terry Eagleton, *Culture* (New Haven: Yale University Press, 2016), 7.

22. JFS to Hyrum M. Smith, 31 October 1896, JFS Papers, box 33, folder 1, LDS Church History Library.

23. Francis M. Lyman to Joseph F. Smith, 1 March 1895, JFS Papers, box 19, folder 24, LDS Church History Library.

24. Abraham H. Cannon Journal, 22 February 1895, in Lyman, *Candid Insights*, 620.

25. Joseph Hyde to Joseph F. Smith, 5 May 1896; Francis M. Lyman to Joseph F. Smith, 1 March 1895, JFS Papers, box 19, folder 24, LDS Church History Library.

26. JFS to Susa Young Gates, 7 July 1888, Susa Young Gates Papers, MS 7692, box 46, folder 30, LDS Church History Library.

27. JFS to Susa Young Gates, 29 May 1891, JFS Papers, box 32, folder 2, LDS Church History Library.

28. Eagleton, *Culture*, 13.

29. JFS to Susa Young Gates, 29 May 1891, JFS Papers, box 32, folder 2, LDS Church History Library.

30. JFS to Susa Young Gates, 29 May 1891, JFS Papers, box 32, folder 2, LDS Church History Library.

31. JFS to Hyrum M. Smith, 31 October 1896, JFS Papers, box 33, folder 1, LDS Church History Library.

32. JFS to Hyrum M. Smith, 31 October 1896, JFS Papers, box 33, folder 1, LDS Church History Library.

33. Lucy Kimball Smith to Joseph F. Smith, 27 September 1898, JFS Papers, box 33, folder 2, LDS Church History Library.

34. JFS to David A. Smith, 28 September 1898, JFS Papers, box 33, folder 2, LDS Church History Library.

410   *Notes to Pages 268–274*

35. JFS to Mary and Donnette Smith, 13 March 1898, JFS Papers, box 33, folder 1, LDS Church History Library.

36. JFS to Martha Ann Harris Smith, 19 March 1898, Carole Call King Collection, MS 16763, box 1, folder 74, LDS Church History Library.

37. JFS to Mary and Donnette Smith, 24 March 1898, JFS Papers, box 33, folder 1, LDS Church History Library.

38. JFS to Andrew Jenson, 16 November 1898, JFS Papers, box 33, folder 2, LDS Church History Library.

39. JFS to David A. Smith, 4 May 1898, JFS Papers, box 33, folder 2, LDS Church History Library.

40. JFS to Platte D. Lyman, 13 May 1899, JFS Papers, box 33, folder 2, LDS Church History Library.

41. JFS to Joseph F. Smith Jr., 20 June 1899, JFS Papers, box 33, folder 2, LDS Church History Library.

42. JFS to Joseph R. Smith, 20 June 1899.

43. JFS to Joseph R. Smith, 13 September 1899, JFS Papers, box 33, folder 2, LDS Church History Library.

44. JFS to Joseph F. Smith Jr., 8 August 1899, JFS Papers, box 33, folder 2, LDS Church History Library.

45. JFS to Joseph F. Smith Jr., 20 July 1899, JFS Papers, box 33, folder 2, LDS Church History Library.

46. JFS to Joseph F. Smith Jr., 2 September 1899, JFS Papers, box 33, folder 2, LDS Church History Library.

47. JFS to Joseph F. Smith Jr., 18 October 1899, JFS Papers, box 33, folder 2, LDS Church History Library.

48. JFS to Joseph R. Smith, 23 October 1899, JFS Papers, box 33, folder 2, LDS Church History Library.

49. JFS to Joseph R. Smith, 23 October 1899.

50. JFS to Joseph R. Smith, 23 October 1899.

51. JFS to Joseph F. Smith Jr., 23 October 1899.

52. JFS to Joseph F. Smith Jr., 5 February 1900, JFS Papers, box 33, folder 2, LDS Church History Library.

53. Telegrams, George Q. Cannon to Joseph F. Smith, 2 and 3 September 1898, JFS Papers, box 33, folder 1, LDS Church History Library.

54. Alexander, *Things in Heaven and Earth*, 330–31.

55. JFS to F. A. Wadleigh, 3 September 1898, JFS Papers, box 33, folder 2, LDS Church History Library.

56. JFS to David A. Smith, 23 May 1916, MS 23339, box 1, folder 1, LDS Church History Library.

57. JFS to David Eccles, 7 September 1898, JFS Papers, box 33, folder 1, LDS Church History Library.

58. "Consigned to the Tomb," *Deseret Evening News*, 8 September 1898, 1.

59. "Organization of the First Presidency," *Deseret Evening News*, 13 September 1898, 4.

60. Heber J. Grant Letterbook Journals, 4 January 1898, in D. Michael Quinn Papers, WA MSS S-2692, Beinecke Rare Book and Manuscript Library, Yale University.

61. Heber J. Grant Letterbook Journals, 4 January 1898, in D. Michael Quinn Papers, WA MSS S-2692, Beinecke Rare Book and Manuscript Library, Yale University.

62. Cannon Journal, 9 September 1898, Church Historian's Press, https://www.churchhistorianspress.org/george-q-cannon.

Notes to Pages 274–280   411

63. Cannon Journal, 9 September 1898, Church Historian's Press, https://www.churchhistorianspress.org/george-q-cannon.

64. Brigham Young Jr. Journal, 12 September 1898, in D. Michael Quinn Papers, WA MSS S-2692, Beinecke Rare Book and Manuscript Library, Yale University.

65. LeRoi C. Snow, "An Experience of My Father's," *Improvement Era* (September 1933): 677.

66. Apostolic Council, 5 April 1900, LDS Church History Library.

67. JFS to George Q. Cannon, n.d., recorded in George Q. Cannon Journal, 1 February 1899, Church Historian's Press, https://www.churchhistorianspress.org/george-q-cannon.

68. "Effect of Cannon's Death on Succession to Presidency," *Salt Lake Herald*, 13 April 1901, 2.

69. "Who Will be Chosen?," *Salt Lake Tribune*, 22 April 1901, 8.

70. The warning must not have shaken Young too much since he made the suggestion again in April 1901. Brigham Young Jr. Journal, 5 October 1898, 23 April 1901, in D. Michael Quinn Papers, WA MSS S-2692, Beinecke Rare Book and Manuscript Library, Yale University.

71. JFS to Anthony W. Ivins, 6 February 1900, JFS Papers, box 33, folder 3, LDS Church History Library.

72. JFS Sermon, general conference, 2 October 1898, in Hansen, *Thy Servants Speak*, 2:287.

73. JFS Sermon, general conference, 2 October 1898, in Hansen, *Thy Servants Speak*, 2:294.

74. "Leaders Urge Crusade Against Vice," *Salt Lake Herald*, 5 October 1901, 6.

75. JFS to H. H. Cluff and Benjamin Cluff Jr., 16 August 1902, typescript in "First Presidency Correspondence, 1899–1903," Scott G. Kenney Collection, MS 587, box 2, folder 11, Special Collections, Marriott Library, University of Utah.

76. First Presidency to F. S. Bramwell, 8 June 1900, typescript in "First Presidency Correspondence, 1899–1903," Scott G. Kenney Collection, MS 587, box 2, folder 11, Special Collections, Marriott Library, University of Utah.

77. Lucy Kimball Smith to Joseph F. Smith, 27 September 1898, JFS Papers, box 33, folder 2, LDS Church History Library.

78. JFS Journal, 31 March 1900, quoted in Smith, *Life of Joseph F. Smith*, 310.

79. "Meeting of the First Presidency and the Twelve," 5 April 1900, Historian's Office Journal History of the Church, vol. 374, CR 100 137, LDS Church History Library.

80. JFS Journal, 5 April 1900, quoted in Smith, *Life of Joseph F. Smith*, 310–11.

81. Brigham Young Jr. Journal, 5 April 1900, in D. Michael Quinn Papers, WA MSS S-2692, Beinecke Rare Book and Manuscript Library, Yale University.

82. 24 May 1899, Historian's Office Journal History of the Church, vol. 360, CR 100 137, LDS Church History Library.

83. Brigham Young Jr. Journal, 2 July 1899, in D. Michael Quinn Papers, WA MSS S-2692, Beinecke Rare Book and Manuscript Library, Yale University.

84. Entry for 2 July 1899 in *A Ministry of Meetings: The Apostolic Diaries of Rudger Clawson*, ed. Stan Larson (Salt Lake City: Signature Books, 1993), 70–71.

85. JFS Sermon, general conference, 6 April 1900, in Hansen, *Thy Servants Speak*, 21:328.

86. JFS Sermon, general conference, 6 April 1900, in Hansen, *Thy Servants Speak*, 21:328–29.

87. JFS, "Features of the True Gospel," sermon delivered 31 July 1898, in Hansen, *Thy Servants Speak*, 21:259.

412 *Notes to Pages 280–287*

88. JFS to Benjamin Cluff Jr., 6 February 1900, JFS Papers, box 33, folder 3, LDS Church History Library.

89. JFS to Joseph F. Smith Jr., 5 February 1900, JFS Papers, box 33, folder 2, LDS Church History Library.

90. First Presidency Minutes, 18 July 1900, Heber J. Grant Journal, 19 July 1900, in D. Michael Quinn Papers, WA MSS S-2692, Beinecke Rare Book and Manuscript Library, Yale University.

91. First Presidency Minutes, 9 August 1900, LDS Church History Library.

92. First Presidency Minutes, 9 August 1900, LDS Church History Library.

93. In *A Ministry of Meetings: The Apostolic Diaries of Rudger Clawson*, ed. Stan Larson (Salt Lake City: Signature Books, 1993), 247–48.

94. "Funeral of Wm. H. Folsom," *Salt Lake Herald*, 25 March 1901, 6.

95. JFS to Joseph F. Smith Jr., 2 April 1901, JFS Papers, box 33, folder 3, LDS Church History Library.

96. Brigham Young Jr. Journal, 6–7 February 1901, in D. Michael Quinn Papers, WA MSS S-2692, Beinecke Rare Book and Manuscript Library, Yale University.

97. JFS to George Q. Cannon, 7 April 1901, JFS Papers, box 33, folder 3, LDS Church History Library.

98. JFS to Joseph R. Smith, 11 April 1901, JFS Papers, box 33, folder 3, LDS Church History Library.

99. "President George Q. Cannon Dead," 18 April 1901, *Eastern Utah Advocate*, 1.

100. "The Obsequies," *Deseret Evening News*, 17 April 1901, 1.

101. Quoted in Bitton, *George Q. Cannon*, 449.

102. "Local and Other News," *Manti Messenger*, 20 April 1901, 4.

103. JFS to Joseph R. Smith, 14 May 1901, JFS Papers, box 33, folder 3, LDS Church History Library.

104. "Bishop Raleigh's Funeral," *Salt Lake Tribune*, 16 May 1901, 3.

105. Edward W. Tullidge, *History of Salt Lake City* (Salt Lake City: Star Publishing, 1886), 883.

106. JFS to Thomas Memmott, 3 February 1902, JFS Papers, box 33, folder 3, LDS Church History Library.

107. "Adjourned Conference," *Coalville Times*, 24 May 1901, 1.

108. JFS to Heber C. Smith, 16 February 1902, JFS Papers, box 34, folder 1, LDS Church History Library.

109. "President Smith Home from North," *Deseret Evening News*, 27 September 1901, 2.

110. JFS to Theodore Roosevelt, 24 September 1901, JFS Papers, box 33, folder 3, LDS Church History Library.

111. "Teton Stake," *Salt Lake Herald*, 6 September 1901, 4.

112. Dennis B. Horne, *Latter Leaves in the Life of Lorenzo Snow* (Springville, UT: CFI, 2012), 421.

113. Quoted in Horne, *Latter Leaves in the Life of Lorenzo Snow*, 421.

114. "Snow Begins His 88th Year," *Salt Lake Tribune*, 4 April 1901, 5.

CHAPTER 16

1. Edmund Morris, *Theodore Rex* (New York: Random House, 2001), 16–17.

2. JFS to Alvin Smith, 23 December 1902, JFS Papers, box 34, folder 1, LDS Church History Library.

Notes to Pages 287–295   413

3. JFS to Francis M. Lyman, 10 May 1888, MS 27013, box 1, LDS Church History Library.

4. Francis M. Lyman to JFS, 12 October 1901, JFS Papers, box 22, folder 1, LDS Church History Library.

5. JFS to Douglas Swan, 15 November 1901, JFS Papers, box 33, folder 2, LDS Church History Library.

6. JFS to Theodore Roosevelt, 24 September 1901, JFS Papers, box 33, folder 3, LDS Church History Library.

7. Lund Journal, 17 October 1901, Anthon H. Lund Papers, LDS Church History Library.

8. JFS to Martha Ann Smith Harris, 27 September 1895, MS 27013, box 1, LDS Church History Library.

9. Rudger Clawson Journal, 24 October 1901, in *A Ministry of Meetings: The Apostolic Diaries of Rudger Clawson*, ed. Stan Larson (Salt Lake City: Signature Books, 1993).

10. John Henry Smith Journal, 24 October 1901, in *Church, State and Politics: The Diaries of John Henry Smith*, ed. Jean Bickmore White (Salt Lake City: Signature Books, 1990).

11. Lund Journal, 7 April 1902, Anthon H. Lund Papers, LDS Church History Library.

12. Brigham Young Jr. to JFS, 22 December 1901, JFS Papers, box 23, folder 1, LDS Church History Library.

13. Joseph F. Smith, "Becoming Worthy to Enter the Temple," Salt Lake Stake Conference, 4 March 1893, in Hansen, *Thy Servants Speak*, 15:90.

14. The Second Great Awakening was a period of religious revival in the United States lasting from the late 1700s until the mid-1800s. It featured a shift from the dominant Calvinist soteriology to an Arminian model, with an emphasis on emotional expression and camp meeting revivals.

15. Christopher H. Evans, *The Social Gospel in American Religion: A History* (New York: NYU Press, 2017), 7.

16. JFS Sermon, 10 November 1901, in Hansen, *Thy Servants Speak*, 21:351.

17. JFS Sermon, 10 November 1901, in Hansen, *Thy Servants Speak*, 21:352.

18. First Presidency Minutes, 10 November 1901, LDS Church History Library.

19. JFS Sermon, 10 November 1901, in Hansen, *Thy Servants Speak*, 21:353.

20. J. Golden Kimball Journal, 10 November 1901, MS 1354, box 2, folder 2, LDS Church History Library.

21. JFS Sermon, 10 November 1901, in Hansen, *Thy Servants Speak*, 21:357–59.

22. Heber J. Grant to Charles W. Penrose, 28 February 1908, box 38, folder 19, LDS Church History Library.

23. JFS to Samuel Woolley, 2 February 1902, JFS Papers, box 34, folder 1, LDS Church History Library.

24. JFS to Richard R. Lyman, 27 December 1903, JFS Papers, box 34, folder 1, LDS Church History Library.

25. Most of the letters written to JFS are not easily available, but his responses usually also contain quotes from the original letters. His responses are easily accessed in the JFS Papers, MS 1325, Letterpress Copy Books.

26. JFS to L. B. Farr, 6 January 1902, JFS Papers, box 33, folder 3, LDS Church History Library.

414   *Notes to Pages 295–301*

27. JFS to Joseph J. Porter, 11 February 1902, JFS Papers, box 34, folder 1, LDS Church History Library.

28. Lund Journal, 19 May 1905, Anthon H. Lund Papers, LDS Church History Library.

29. JFS to William A. Smith, 23 January 1903, JFS Papers, box 34, folder 1, LDS Church History Library.

30. JFS to E. J. Wood, 5 October 1905, typescript in "First Presidency Correspondence," Scott G. Kenney Collection, MS 587, box 2, folder 11, Special Collections, Marriott Library, University of Utah.

31. JFS to Parowan Stake Presidency, 27 January 1912, typescript in "First Presidency Correspondence," Scott G. Kenney Collection, MS 587, box 2, folder 13, Special Collections, Marriott Library, University of Utah.

32. JFS to Frank Bellings, 17 February 1905, JFS Papers, box 34, folder 1, LDS Church History Library.

33. JFS to Charles Penrose, 29 November 1907. This letter mistakenly instructed Penrose to "disfellowship" guilty missionaries, but a letter from 27 April 1909 clarified that this had been a mistake, and the term "excommunication" should be used instead. Typescript in "First Presidency Correspondence," Scott G. Kenney Collection, MS 587, box 2, folder 13, Special Collections, Marriott Library, University of Utah.

34. Solomon C. Stephens, *The Philosophy of the Earth and of Man* (Ogden, UT: W. W. Browning, 1898).

35. JFS to Solomon C. Stephens, 28 July 1902, JFS Papers, box 34, folder 1, LDS Church History Library.

36. JFS to Lillie Golsan, 16 July 1902, JFS Papers, box 34, folder 1, LDS Church History Library.

37. JFS to J. Q. Adams, 11 February 1902, JFS Papers, box 34, folder 1, LDS Church History Library.

38. JFS to George Browning, 12 July 1902, JFS Papers, box 34, folder 1, LDS Church History Library.

39. JFS to Edward Bunker, 27 February 1902, JFS Papers, box 34, folder 1, LDS Church History Library.

40. JFS was allowing JFS Jr., under close supervision, to answer some doctrinal questions over JFS's signature as early as 1902.

41. JFS to Myers and Co., 24 December 1901, JFS Papers, box 23, folder 1, LDS Church History Library.

42. JFS to James T. Wilson, 13 January 1902, JFS Papers, box 33, folder 3, LDS Church History Library.

43. Joseph Irwin to JFS, 27 August 1902, JFS Papers, box 20, folder 1, LDS Church History Library.

44. First Presidency Minutes, "Apostolic Council," 4 November 1901, LDS Church History Library.

45. For a sense of the scope of such organizations in Utah, see "Women's Clubs," *Salt Lake Tribune*, 25 January 1903.

46. "Address of President Joseph F. Smith to Conference of the Women's Relief Society," in *Woman's Exponent*, 1 May 1903, 92–93.

47. "Address of President Joseph F. Smith to Conference of the Women's Relief Society," in *Woman's Exponent*, 1 May 1903, 92–93.

Notes to Pages 301–306   415

48. JFS to Melissa Smith, 24 July 1903, JFS Papers, box 34, folder 1, LDS Church History Library.

49. JFS to Melissa Smith, 24 July 1903, JFS Papers, box 34, folder 1, LDS Church History Library.

50. JFS to Edward Smith, 23 March 1903, JFS Papers, box 34, folder 1, LDS Church History Library.

51. JFS to Annie Barter, 26 April 1902, JFS Papers, box 34, folder 1, LDS Church History Library.

52. JFS to Heber C. Smith, 16 February 1902, JFS Papers, box 34, folder 1, LDS Church History Library.

53. JFS to Samuel Woolley, 4 July 1902, JFS Papers, box 34, folder 1, LDS Church History Library.

54. JFS to Coulson Smith, 10 July 1902, JFS Papers, box 34, folder 1, LDS Church History Library.

55. JFS to Coulson Smith, 6 January 1903, JFS Papers, box 34, folder 1, LDS Church History Library.

56. JFS to Walter Hoge, 14 March 1902, JFS Papers, box 34, folder 1, LDS Church History Library.

57. First Presidency Minutes, 27 May 1902, LDS Church History Library.

58. Brigham Young Jr. Journal, 30 December 1899, D. Michael Quinn Collection, WA MSS S-2692, Beinecke Rare Book and Manuscript Library, Yale University.

59. D. Michael Quinn, "LDS Church Authority and New Plural Marriages, 1890–1904," *Dialogue: A Journal of Mormon Thought* 18, no. 1: 86.

60. JFS, Anthon H. Lund, and John R. Winder, 7 March 1902, JFS Papers, box 34, folder 1, LDS Church History Library.

61. First Presidency Minutes, 1 December 1902, LDS Church History Library.

62. Abraham H. Cannon Journal, 7 October 1890, LDS Church History Library.

63. D. Michael Quinn, "LDS Church Authority and New Plural Marriages, 1890–1904," *Dialogue: A Journal of Mormon Thought* 18, no. 1: 87–88.

64. First Presidency Minutes, 1 December 1902, LDS Church History Library.

65. First Presidency Minutes, 13 February 1903, LDS Church History Library.

66. First Presidency Minutes, 2 February 1903, LDS Church History Library.

67. Rudger Clawson Journal, 10 January 1903, in *A Ministry of Meetings: The Apostolic Diaries of Rudger Clawson*, ed. Stan Larson (Salt Lake City: Signature Books, 1993), 533.

68. Telegram from Reed Smoot to JFS, 27 February 1903, JFS Papers, LDS Church History Library.

69. Quoted in Joseph Fielding Smith, *Life of Joseph F. Smith*, 382–94.

70. Telegram from JFS to Reed Smoot, 1 March 1903, JFS Papers, LDS Church History Library.

71. Reed Smoot to JFS, 5 March 1903, JFS Papers, box 34, folder 1, LDS Church History Library.

72. JFS to Charles W. Nibley, 20 May 1903, JFS Papers, box 34, folder 1, LDS Church History Library.

73. JFS to Samuel Woolley, 27 August 1903, JFS Papers, box 34, folder 1, LDS Church History Library.

74. JFS to Samuel Woolley, 27 August 1903, JFS Papers, box 34, folder 1, LDS Church History Library.

416   *Notes to Pages 307–312*

75. JFS to Samuel Woolley, 10 July 1903, JFS Papers, box 34, folder 1, LDS Church History Library.

76. JFS to Joseph H. Dean, 13 November 1903, translation mine, JFS Papers, box 34, folder 1, LDS Church History Library.

77. JFS to Reed Smoot, 28 January 1904, JFS Papers, box 34, folder 1, LDS Church History Library.

78. First Presidency Minutes, 9 February 1904, LDS Church History Library.

79. JFS wrote that "those dear souls who crossed the plains with handcarts deserve the greatest possible reward that Father can give." JFS to CCA Christensen, 16 November 1906, JFS Papers, box 34, folder 2, LDS Church History Library.

80. JFS to Gabriel Huntsman, 5 January 1904, JFS Papers, box 34, folder 1, LDS Church History Library.

81. JFS to Heber J. Grant, 23 August 1885, Grant Papers, box 34, folder 3, LDS Church History Library.

82. JFS to Elias Wesley Smith, 17 June 1909, JFS Papers, box 34, folder 3, LDS Church History Library.

83. *Proceedings Before the Committee on Privileges and Elections of the United States Senate in the Matter of the Protests Against the Right Honorable Reed Smoot, a Senator from the State of Utah, to Hold His Seat* (Washington, DC: Government Printing Office, 1906), 1:80.

84. *Proceedings Before the Committee on Privileges and Elections in the Matter of the Protests Against the Right Honorable Reed Smoot,* 1:84.

85. *Proceedings Before the Committee on Privileges and Elections in the Matter of the Protests Against the Right Honorable Reed Smoot,* 1:87.

86. Kathleen Flake, *The Politics of Religious Identity: The Seating of Senator Reed Smoot, Mormon Apostle* (Chapel Hill: University of North Carolina Press, 2004).

87. *Proceedings Before the Committee on Privileges and Elections in the Matter of the Protests Against the Right Honorable Reed Smoot,* 1:99.

88. JFS to O. C. Wixom, 25 March 1904, JFS Papers, box 34, folder 1, LDS Church History Library.

89. JFS to O. C. Wixom, 25 March 1904, JFS Papers, box 34, folder 1, LDS Church History Library.

90. JFS to O. C. Wixom, 25 March 1904, JFS Papers, box 34, folder 1, LDS Church History Library.

91. JFS to Reed Smoot, 9 April 1904, JFS Papers, box 34, folder 1, LDS Church History Library.

92. JFS to Reed Smoot, 7 April 1904, JFS Papers, box 34, folder 1, LDS Church History Library.

93. JFS to William Glasmann, 5 January 1905, JFS Papers, box 34, folder 1, LDS Church History Library.

94. Philip Loring Allen, "The Mormon Church on Trial," *Harper's Weekly,* 26 March 1904.

95. JFS to Isaac Smith, 11 October 1906, JFS Papers, box 34, folder 2, LDS Church History Library.

96. Lund Journal, 6 April 1904, Anthon H. Lund Papers, LDS Church History Library.

97. Lund Journal, 6 April 1904, Anthon H. Lund Papers, LDS Church History Library.

98. "Joseph Smith History," published as part of the Pearl of Great Price.

99. JFS, "Opening Address," April 1904 general conference, in Hansen, *Thy Servants Speak*, 21:415.

100. JFS, "Opening Address," April 1904 general conference, in Hansen, *Thy Servants Speak*, 21:415.

101. Lund Journal, 26 May 1904, Anthon H. Lund Papers, LDS Church History Library.

102. JFS to Reed Smoot, 20 March 1904, JFS Papers, box 34, folder 2, LDS Church History Library.

103. Heber J. Grant to JFS, 5 January 1906, Heber J. Grant Letterpress Copybooks, 42:145, LDS Church History Library.

104. JFS to Heber J. Grant, 12 April 1906, Heber J. Grant Letterpress Copybooks, 42:160, LDS Church History Library.

105. First Presidency to Stake Presidents and Counselors, 5 October 1910; reissued 31 January 1914, JFS Papers, box 24, folder 2, LDS Church History Library.

106. For more on the 1911 Taylor and Cowley cases, see Charles W. Penrose Journal, 10–11 May 1911, typescript in D. Michael Quinn Collection, WA MSS S-2692, Beinecke Rare Book and Manuscript Library, Yale University.

107. Circular published to Stake Presidents, 8 October 1910, copy in First Presidency Minutes, LDS Church History Library.

108. JFS to Charles Wolfenden [Woolfenden], 27 April 1910, JFS Papers, box 35, folder 1, LDS Church History Library.

109. David A. Smith, untitled reminiscences, 20 March 1939, David A. Smith Collection, MS 23339, box 1, folder 16, LDS Church History Library.

CHAPTER 17

1. "Mormons in Schools," *Washington Post*, 20 December 1904, 1–2.

2. "The Birdsall Land Case," *Salt Lake Tribune*, 22 December 1904, 2–3.

3. JFS to William Budge, 5 January 1905, typescript in "First Presidency Correspondence," Scott G. Kenney Collection, MS 587, box 2, folder 12, Special Collections, Marriott Library, University of Utah.

4. Lund Journal, 2 February 1907, Anthon H. Lund Papers, LDS Church Archives.

5. JFS to Reed Smoot, 11 January 1905, typescript in "First Presidency Correspondence," Scott G. Kenney Collection, MS 587, box 2, folder 11, Special Collections, Marriott Library, University of Utah.

6. Alexander, *Mormonism in Transition*, 109–19.

7. First Presidency to Samuel D. Fuller, 16 February 1907, typescript in "First Presidency Correspondence," Scott G. Kenney Collection, MS 587, box 2, folder 11, Special Collections, Marriott Library, University of Utah.

8. Alexander, *Mormonism in Transition*, 97.

9. JFS to Reed Smoot, 9 April 1904, JFS Papers, box 34, folder 1, LDS Church Archives.

10. JFS to Jesse N. Smith, 13 December 1904, JFS Papers, box 34, folder 1, LDS Church Archives.

11. JFS to Junius F. Wells, 4 January 1905, JFS Papers, box 34, folder 1, LDS Church Archives.

12. JFS to Ben E. Rich, 26 February 1905, JFS Papers, box 34, folder 1, LDS Church Archives.

418   *Notes to Pages 318–325*

13. For a thorough discussion of JFS's attitudes on this subject, see Craig James Ostler, "Joseph F. Smith on Priesthood and Church Government," in Manscill et al., *Joseph F. Smith*, 199–220; and Jonathan L. Stapley, "'The Last of the Old School': Joseph F. Smith and Latter-day Saint Liturgy," in Manscill et al., *Joseph F. Smith*, 233–47.

14. JFS to Horace Ensign, 19 March 1905, JFS Papers, box 34, folder 1, LDS Church Archives.

15. JFS to Archibald McFarland, 2 April 1905, JFS Papers, box 34, folder 2, LDS Church Archives.

16. JFS to Archibald McFarland, 2 April 1905, JFS Papers, box 34, folder 2, LDS Church Archives.

17. JFS to Junius F. Wells, 30 January 1905, JFS Papers, box 34, folder 1, LDS Church Archives.

18. JFS to Alvin F. Smith, 12 November 1906, JFS Papers, box 34, folder 2, LDS Church Archives.

19. Lund Journal, 20 February 1907, Anthon H. Lund Papers, LDS Church Archives.

20. JFS to Reed Smoot, 27 February 1907, JFS Papers, box 34, folder 2, LDS Church Archives.

CHAPTER 18

1. JFS to Edward A. Smith, 12 February 1904, JFS Papers, box 34, folder 1, LDS Church History Library.

2. JFS to D. J. Williams, 5 November 1905, JFS Papers, box 34, folder 2, LDS Church History Library.

3. Flake, *The Politics of Religious Identity*, 6.

4. JFS, "Address, October 1906 General Conference," in Hansen, *Thy Servants Speak*, 21:471.

5. JFS to Samuel Woolley, 16 May 1908, JFS Papers, box 34, folder 3, LDS Church History Library.

6. JFS to Wesley Smith, 22 July 1908, JFS Papers, box 34, folder 3, LDS Church History Library.

7. JFS to Joseph E. Robinson, 14 December 1907, box 34, folder 3, LDS Church History Library.

8. JFS made a similar remark to his wife Julina when she did not stop in to see Ina when passing through San Francisco en route to Hawaii in 1910. "You did not lose very much by not [visiting her]," he sniped. JFS to Julina Lambson Smith, 4 February 1910, JFS Papers, box 35, folder 1, LDS Church History Library.

9. Ina Coolbrith to John Smith, 28 July 1908, LDS Church History Library.

10. JFS to Ina Coolbrith, 29 December 1908, box 34, folder 3, LDS Church History Library.

11. JFS to Heber J. Grant, 11 April 1907, LDS Church History Library.

12. First Presidency to Lewis Anderson, 14 March 1907, typescript in "First Presidency Correspondence," Scott G. Kenney Collection, MS 587, box 2, folder 11, Special Collections, Marriott Library, University of Utah.

13. JFS, "Address, October 1906 General Conference," in Hansen, *Thy Servants Speak*, 21:471.

14. JFS, "Address, October 1906 General Conference," in Hansen, *Thy Servants Speak*, 21:471.

15. JFS, "Opening Address, October 1906 General Conference," in Hansen, *Thy Servants Speak*, 21:472–73.

Notes to Pages 325–333   419

16. Quoted in Brian Q. Cannon, "'Long Shall His Blood … Stain Illinois': Carthage Jail in Mormon Memory," *Mormon Historical Studies* 10, no. 1 (Spring 2009): 7.

17. JFS, "Opening Address, October 1906 General Conference," in Hansen, *Thy Servants Speak*, 21:468–73.

18. Charles W. Nibley, *Reminiscences of Charles W. Nibley* (Salt Lake City: privately published, 1934), 114–17, 124.

19. Nibley, *Reminiscences*, 114–17, 124

20. Nibley, *Reminiscences*, 114–17, 124.

21. Nibley, *Reminiscences*, 130.

22. JFS Journal, 18 February 1909, LDS Church History Library.

23. JFS Journal, 19 February 1909, LDS Church History Library.

24. JFS Journal, 20–21 February 1909, LDS Church History Library.

25. Nibley, *Reminiscences*, 136.

26. JFS Journal, 26 February 1909, LDS Church History Library.

27. JFS to Susa Young Gates, 5 March 1909, Susa Young Gates Papers, MS 7692, box 46, folder 30, LDS Church History Library.

28. JFS Journal, 5 March 1909, LDS Church History Library.

29. JFS Journal, 10 March 1909, LDS Church History Library.

30. JFS Journal, 13 March 1909, LDS Church History Library.

31. JFS Journal, 24 March 1909, LDS Church History Library.

32. "His Disgusting Grossness," *Salt Lake Tribune*, 4 August 1907, 7.

33. "Stop It," *Salt Lake Tribune*, 8 January 1807, 4.

34. "Sniveling Hypocrisy," *Salt Lake Tribune*, 3 May 1907, 6.

35. "Smith's Opening Address," *Salt Lake Tribune*, 6 October 1907, 7.

36. JFS, "Opening Address, October 1906 General Conference," in Hansen, *Thy Servants Speak*, 21:473.

37. "Joseph F. Smith and the Cartoons," *Salt Lake Tribune*, 9 January 1907, 5.

38. JFS to William Farrell, 10 January 1908, JFS Papers, box 34, folder 3, LDS Church History Library.

39. JFS to Edna Melissa Smith Bowman, 13 December 1907, JFS Papers, box 34, folder 3, LDS Church History Library.

40. JFS to E. Wesley Smith, 27 December 1907, JFS Papers, box 34, folder 3, LDS Church History Library.

41. JFS to E. Wesley Smith, 27 December 1907, JFS Papers, box 34, folder 3, LDS Church History Library.

42. JFS to Edna Melissa Smith Bowman, 26 December 1907, JFS Papers, box 34, folder 3, LDS Church History Library.

43. JFS to Richard R. Lyman, 28 December 1907, JFS Papers, box 34, folder 3, LDS Church History Library.

44. JFS to Edna Melissa Smith Bowman, 9 February 1908, JFS Papers, box 34, folder 3, LDS Church History Library.

45. JFS to Edna Melissa Smith Bowman, 6 March 1908, JFS Papers, box 34, folder 3, LDS Church History Library.

46. JFS to Emma Smith, 6 March 1908, JFS Papers, box 34, folder 3, LDS Church History Library.

47. JFS to Samuel Adams, 14 December 1907, JFS Papers, box 34, folder 3, LDS Church History Library.

48. JFS to Samuel Adams, 14 December 1907, JFS Papers, box 34, folder 3, LDS Church History Library.

420   *Notes to Pages 333–339*

49. JFS to Emma Smith, 11 January 1908, JFS Papers, box 34, folder 3, LDS Church History Library.

50. JFS to Samuel Adams, 11 May 1888, MS 27013, box 1, LDS Church History Library.

51. JFS to "My Dear Brother Marion," 18 May 1909, JFS Papers, box 34, folder 3, LDS Church History Library.

52. JFS to E. Wesley Smith, 30 March 1908, JFS Papers, box 34, folder 3, LDS Church History Library.

53. JFS to Edna Melissa Bowman Smith and Emma Smith, 30 March 1908, JFS Papers, box 34, folder 3, LDS Church History Library.

54. JFS to E. Wesley Smith, 10 August 1908, JFS Papers, box 34, folder 3, LDS Church History Library.

55. JFS to Mary Taylor Schwartz Smith, 17 June 1910, JFS Papers, box 35, folder 1, LDS Church History Library.

56. *Southwest Contractor and Manufacturer* 11, no. 19, 13 September 1913, 36.

57. JFS Notebooks, 1916–1918, JFS Papers, LDS Church History Library.

58. JFS to David A. Smith, 23 May 1916, MS 23339, box 1, folder 1, LDS Church History Library.

59. Nibley, *Reminiscences*, 117.

60. JFS to Calvin Smith, 6 September 1910, JFS Papers, box 35, folder 1, LDS Church History Library.

61. JFS to Franklin Smith, 10 December 1909, JFS Papers, box 35, folder 1, LDS Church History Library.

62. Joseph E. Robinson Journal, 6 April 1907, Joseph E. Robinson Papers, MS 7686, box 2, folder 2, LDS Church History Library.

63. Doctrine and Covenants, 124:91–95.

64. M. Russell Ballard, "Joseph F. Smith and the Importance of Family," in *Joseph F. Smith: Reflections on the Man and His Times*, ed. Craig K. Manscill et al. (Provo, UT: BYU Religious Studies Center, 2013), 4.

65. JFS to Ina Coolbrith, 19 May 1909, JFS Papers, box 34, folder 3, LDS Church History Library.

66. JFS to David A. Smith, 13 March 1917, MS 23339, box 1, folder 2, LDS Church History Library.

67. This particular statement was a favorite of JFS's when rebuking his missionary children for their lack of frugality. It may have been true for his first mission, but it certainly was not the case for his subsequent missions, for which he collected generous donations. JFS to Franklin R. Smith, 12 May 1909, JFS Papers, box 34, folder 3, LDS Church History Library.

68. JFS to Franklin R. Smith, 20 June 1909, JFS Papers, box 34, folder 3, LDS Church History Library.

69. JFS to Joseph Richards Smith, 3 May 1909, JFS Papers, box 34, folder 3, LDS Church History Library.

70. JFS to Joseph Richards Smith, 3 May 1909, JFS Papers, box 34, folder 3, LDS Church History Library.

71. JFS to Elias Wesley Smith, 17 June 1909, JFS Papers, box 34, folder 3, LDS Church History Library.

72. JFS to Franklin R. Smith, 20 June 1909, JFS Papers, box 34, folder 3, LDS Church History Library.

73. JFS to Ina Coolbrith, 24 March 1915, box 36, folder 1, LDS Church History Library.

74. JFS to Ina Coolbrith, 24 March 1915, box 36, folder 1, LDS Church History Library.

75. JFS to Wesley Smith, 24 March 1915, box 36, folder 1, LDS Church History Library.

76. JFS to Hyrum M. Smith, 4 August 1916, box 36, folder 1, LDS Church History Library.

77. JFS to A. S. Vincent, 20 October 1916, JFS Papers, box 36, folder 1, LDS Church History Library.

78. JFS to Hyrum M. Smith, 2 May 1916, JFS Papers, box 36, folder 1, LDS Church History Library.

79. JFS to Alice Kimball Smith, 11 July, 1916 , JFS Papers, box 36, folder 1, LDS Church History Library.

80. JFS to Alice Kimball Smith, 22 July 1916, JFS Papers, LDS Church History Library.

81. JFS to Alice Kimball Smith, 22 July 1916, JFS Papers, LDS Church History Library.

82. JFS to Wesley Smith, 9 November 1916, Scott G. Kenney Collection, MS 587, box 2, folder 11, Special Collections, Marriott Library, University of Utah.

83. JFS Sermon, "Why We Are Building a Temple in Canada," October 1916 general conference, in Hansen, *Thy Servants Speak*, 21:700.

84. Reed Smoot Journals, 1 June 2015, typescript in D. Michael Quinn Collection, WA MSS S-2692, Beinecke Rare Book and Manuscript Library, Yale University.

85. JFS to Samuel Woolley, 17 August 1915, JFS Papers, LDS Church History Library.

86. JFS to David A. Smith, 4 February 1910, JFS Papers, box 35, folder 1, LDS Church History Library.

87. JFS, "Remarks Given at his 75th Birthday Celebration," 14 November 1913, Susa Young Gates Papers, MS 7692, box 46, folder 29, LDS Church History Library.

88. Statement of the First Presidency, 21 April 1913, typescript in "First Presidency Correspondence," Scott G. Kenney Collection, MS 587, box 2, folder 14, Special Collections, Marriott Library, University of Utah.

89. Bates and Smith, *Lost Legacy*, 151–58.

90. JFS Address, April 1912 general conference, in Hansen, *Thy Servants Speak*, 1:606.

91. Quoted in Kent Walgren, "Inside the Salt Lake Temple: Gisbert Bossard's 1911 Photographs," *Dialogue: A Journal of Mormon Thought* 29, no. 3: 5.

92. James E. Talmage, *The House of the Lord: A Study of Holy Sanctuaries Ancient and Modern* (Salt Lake City: Deseret News, 1912).

93. JFS, "Remarks, 75th Birthday Celebration," 13 November 2013, JFS Papers, LDS Church History Library.

94. JFS to Martha Ann Smith Harris, 24 April 1909, JFS Papers, box 34, folder 3, LDS Church History Library.

95. JFS, "Peace on Earth Obtained Only Through Jesus Christ," *Liahona: The Elders' Journal* 12, no. 26 (22 December 1914): 403.

96. Susa Young Gates Journal, 6 September 1914, Susa Young Gates Papers, MS 7692, box 15, folder 4, LDS Church History Library.

97. JFS to Hyrum M. Smith, 19 February 1916, JFS Papers, box 36, folder 1, LDS Church History Library.

98. JFS to Isaac Russell, 11 January 1916, JFS Papers, box 36, folder 1, LDS Church History Library.

99. JFS to Hyrum M. Smith, 13 August 1915, JFS Papers, box 36, folder 1, LDS Church History Library.

422   *Notes to Pages 347–353*

100. Michael McGerr, *A Fierce Discontent: The Rise and Fall of the Progressive Movement in America* (New York: Oxford University Press, 2003), 83–84.

101. Reed Smoot Journals, 15 February 1909, typescript in D. Michael Quinn Collection, WA MSS S-2692, Beinecke Rare Book and Manuscript Library, Yale University.

102. Reed Smoot Journals, 15 February 1909, typescript in D. Michael Quinn Collection, WA MSS S-2692, Beinecke Rare Book and Manuscript Library, Yale University.

103. JFS to Martha Ann Smith Harris, 24 May 1909, JFS Papers, box 34, folder 3, LDS Church History Library.

104. JFS to Col. Ed. Loose, 15 February 1909, JFS Papers, box 34, folder 3, LDS Church History Library.

105. JFS to E. H. Callister, James H. Anderson, and Thomas Hull, 16 February 1909, JFS Papers, box 34, folder 3, LDS Church History Library.

106. Jonathan Stapley, "'Last of the Old School,'" in *Joseph F. Smith: Reflections on the Man and His Times*, ed. Craig K. Manscill et al., 234.

107. JFS, "Fashion and the Violation of Covenants and Duty," *Improvement Era* (August 1906): 813.

108. First Presidency, "The Origin of Man," *Improvement Era* 13, no. 1 (November 1909): 81.

109. Remarks of JFS at Temple Fast Meeting, recorded in Charles W. Penrose Journal, 5 March 1911, D. Michael Quinn Collection, WA MSS S-2692, Beinecke Rare Book and Manuscript Library, Yale University.

110. Joseph F. Smith, "Theory and Divine Revelation," *Improvement Era* 14, no. 6 (April 1911): 548.

111. JFS to Hyrum M. Smith, 1 July 1916, JFS Papers, box 36, folder 1, LDS Church History Library.

112. JFS to Dosil Smith, 13 October 1916, JFS Papers, box 36, folder 1, LDS Church History Library.

CHAPTER 19

1. Lund Journal, 31 August 1917, Anthon H. Lund Papers, LDS Church History Library.

2. Joseph E. Robinson Journal, 1 December 1917, Joseph E. Robinson Papers, MS 7686, box 3, folder 4, LDS Church History Library.

3. Lund Journal, 27 January 1917, Anthon H. Lund Papers, LDS Church History Library.

4. G. G. Richards to David A. Smith, 16 March 1918, David A. Smith Collection, MS 23/339, box 1, folder 4, LDS Church History Library.

5. David A. Smith to JFS, 11 March 1918, David A. Smith Collection, MS 23/339, box 1, folder 4, LDS Church History Library.

6. JFS to David A. Smith, 15 March 1918, David A. Smith Collection, MS 23/339, box 1, folder 4, LDS Church History Library.

7. Joseph E. Robinson Journal, 5 July 1918, Joseph E. Robinson Papers, MS 7686, box 3, folder 5, LDS Church History Library.

8. Lund Journal, 8 and 13 July 1918, Anthon H. Lund Papers, LDS Church History Library.

9. David A. Smith to Calvin F. Smith, 27 November 1918, David A. Smith Collection, MS 23/339, box 1, folder 4, LDS Church History Library.

10. Heber J. Grant to Reed Smoot, 28 August 1918, box 45, folder 9, LDS Church History Library.
11. Lund Journal, 20–22 July 1918, Anthon H. Lund Papers, LDS Church History Library.
12. Heber J. Grant to Reed Smoot, 25 September 1918, General Correspondence, box 44, folder 9, LDS Church History Library.
13. Heber J. Grant to Reed Smoot, 16 September 1918, box 45, folder 4, LDS Church History Library.
14. Grant Journal, 3 July 1918, D. Michael Quinn Collection, WA MSS S-2692, Beinecke Rare Book and Manuscript Library, Yale University. Grant's use of the letter from Woodruff is not without irony. Woodruff wrote the letter when Grant was lobbying for JFS to succeed John Taylor. He wrote it to protect his own primacy as president of the Quorum of the Twelve in the face of Grant's challenge. As president of the quorum in 1918, Grant had reason to agree with Woodruff and side against his own previous argument.
15. In *Cowboy Apostle: The Diaries of Anthony W. Ivins, 1875–1932*, ed. Elizabeth Anderson (Salt Lake: Signature Books, 2013), 575.
16. JFS Sermon, October 1918 general conference, in Hansen, *Thy Servants Speak*, 21:750–53.
17. Charles Penrose, address at October 1918 general conference, accessible online at https://archive.org/details/conferencereport1918sa/page/18/mode/2up.
18. Robinson here refers to Romania Pratt, who divorced Parley Pratt Jr. in 1881 and married Penrose as a plural wife in 1886. Robinson assumed the latter marriage to have been post-Manifesto, probably because it did not become public knowledge until 1905.
19. JFS Sermon, October 1918 general conference, in Hansen, *Thy Servants Speak*, 21:752.
20. JFS to Heber J. Grant, 19 October 1906, General Correspondence, box 44, folder 9, LDS Church History Library.
21. Joseph E. Robinson Journal, 4–10 October 1918, Joseph E. Robinson Papers, MS 7686, box 3, folder 5, LDS Church History Library.
22. Joseph E. Robinson Journal, 4–10 October 1918, Joseph E. Robinson Papers, MS 7686, box 3, folder 5, LDS Church History Library.
23. JFS Sermon, October 1918 general conference, in Hansen, *Thy Servants Speak*, 21:754.
24. Lund Journal, 31 October 1918, Anthon H. Lund Papers, LDS Church History Library.
25. Susa Young Gates Journal, 5 November 1918, Susa Young Gates Papers, MS 7692, box 15, folder 4, LDS Church History Library.
26. Anton H. Lund Journals, 713.
27. Emmeline B. Wells Journal, 21 November 1918, Vault MSS 510, L. Tom Perry Special Collections, Harold B. Lee Library, Brigham Young University.
28. Susa Young Gates Journal, 22 November 1918, Susa Young Gates Papers, MS 7692, box 15, folder 4, LDS Church History Library.

Bibliography

PRIMARY SOURCE COLLECTIONS (ARCHIVAL)

It should be noted that dozens, and sometimes hundreds, of individual documents have been drawn from the following collections. Readers should consult the relevant notes for references to specific documents.

Carole Call King Collection. MS 16763. LDS Church History Library.

Charles Ora Card Collection. MSS 1543. L. Tom Perry Special Collections, Harold B. Lee Library, Brigham Young University.

D. Michael Quinn Collection. WA MSS S-2692. Beinecke Rare Book and Manuscript Library, Yale University.

David A. Smith Collection. MS 23339. LDS Church History Library.

Gates, Susa Young. Papers. 1870–1933. MS 2692. LDS Church History Library.

George A. Smith Collection. MS 1322. LDS Church History Library.

Grant, Heber J. Papers. MSS 433. L. Tom Perry Special Collections, Harold B. Lee Library, Brigham Young University.

Hawaiian Mission Manuscript History and Historical Reports. 1850–1867. LR 3695. LDS Church History Library.

Joseph F. Smith Papers. MS 1325. LDS Church History Library.

L. Tom Perry Special Collections. Harold B. Lee Library, Brigham Young University.

LDS Church History Library. Church Historian's Office.

Lund, Anthon H. Papers. MS 1256. LDS Church History Library.

Mary Fielding Smith Collection. MS 2779. LDS Church History Library.

McKnight, James. Papers. MS 18504. LDS Church History Library.

Richards Family Collection. 1837–1961. MS 1215. LDS Church History Library.

Robinson, Joseph E. Papers. MS 7686. LDS Church History Library.

Sarah Ellen Richards Smith Collection. MS 2574. LDS Church History Library.

Scott G. Kenney Collection. MS 587. Special Collections, Marriott Library, University of Utah.

Smith, Hyrum. Papers. MS 14305. LDS Church History Library.

Smith, John Henry. Papers. Box 7 in George A. Smith Family Papers. MS 0036. Special Collections, J. Willard Marriott Library, University of Utah.

Smith, Joseph F. Papers. LDS Church History Library.

Smith, Joseph F. Correspondence. 1854–1918. LDS Church History Library.

Smith, Julina Lambson. Papers. MS 4364. LDS Church History Library.

426   *Bibliography*

Smith Family, George A. Papers. MS 0036. Special Collections, J. Willard Marriott
  Library, University of Utah.
Thatcher, Moses. Papers. 1866–1923 (COLL MSS 22). Special Collections Department,
  Utah State University.

PRIMARY SOURCE COLLECTIONS (PUBLISHED)

Anderson, Elizabeth, ed. *Cowboy Apostle: The Diaries of Anthony W. Ivins, 1875–1932.*
  Salt Lake City: Signature Books, 2013.
Cannon, George Q. Journal. Church Historian's Press, https://www
  .churchhistorianspress.org/george-q-cannon.
Clark, James R., ed. *Messages of the First Presidency.* 6 vols. Salt Lake City: Deseret Book,
  1965.
Joseph Smith Papers Project (JSPP). Salt Lake City: Church Historian's Press, 2008–
  present. https://www.josephsmithpapers.org.
Kelly, Charles, ed. *The Journals of John D. Lee, 1846–47.* Salt Lake City: Western Print-
  ing, 1938.
Larson, Stan, ed. *A Ministry of Meetings: The Apostolic Diaries of Rudger Clawson.* Salt
  Lake City: Signature Books, 1993.
Lyman, Edward Leo, ed. *Candid Insights of a Mormon Apostle: The Diaries of Abraham H.
  Cannon, 1889–1895.* Salt Lake City: Signature Books, 2010.
Nibley, Charles W. *Reminiscences of Charles W. Nibley.* Salt Lake City: privately pub-
  lished, 1934.
Orton, Chad M., ed. *The Journals of George Q. Cannon: Hawaiian Mission, 1850–1854.*
  Salt Lake City: Deseret Book, 2014.
Sillito, John, ed. *History's Apprentice: The Diaries of B. H. Roberts, 1880–1898.* Salt Lake
  City: Signature Books, 2004.
Smith, Joseph F., Jr., comp. *Gospel Doctrine: Selections from the Sermons and Writings of
  Joseph F. Smith.* Salt Lake City: Deseret News, 1919.
Van Wagoner, Richard S., ed. *The Complete Discourses of Brigham Young.* 5 vols. Salt Lake
  City: Smith-Pettit Foundation, 2010.
Vogel, Dan, ed. *The Journals of Wilford Woodruff.* 6 vols. Salt Lake City: Greg Kofford
  Books, 2021.
White, Jean Bickmore, ed. *Church, State and Politics: The Diaries of John Henry Smith,*
  ed. Salt Lake City: Signature Books, 1990.

SECONDARY SOURCES

Addams, R. Jean. "The Bullion, Beck, and Champion Mining Company and the
  Redemption of Zion." *Journal of Mormon History* 40, no. 2 (2014): 159–234.
Adler, Jacob, and Robert Kamins. *The Fantastic Life of Walter Murray Gibson, Hawaii's
  Minister of Everything.* Honolulu: University of Hawaii Press, 1986.
Allen, James B., and Glen M. Leonard. *The Story of the Latter-day Saints.* Salt Lake City:
  Deseret Book, 1992.
Allen, Philip Loring. "The Mormon Church on Trial." *Harper's Weekly,* 26 March 1904.
Alexander, Thomas G. *Mormonism in Transition.* Urbana: University of Illinois Press,
  1986.
Alexander, Thomas G. *Things in Heaven and Earth: The Life and Times of Wilford Wood-
  ruff, a Mormon Prophet.* Salt Lake City: Signature Books, 1991.
Alexander, Thomas G. *Utah, the Right Place.* Salt Lake City: Gibbs Smith, 2003.

Anderson, Devery S., and Gary J. Bergera, eds. *Joseph Smith's Quorum of the Anointed, 1842–1845: A Documentary History*. Salt Lake City: Signature Books, 2005.

Anderson, Devery S., and Gary J. Bergera, eds. *The Nauvoo Endowment Companies, 1845–1846: A Documentary History*. Salt Lake City: Signature Books, 2005.

Anderson, Lavina Fielding. "Lucy Mack Smith." In *United by Faith: The Joseph Sr. and Lucy Mack Smith Family*, edited by Kyle R. Walker, 62–66. American Fork, UT: Covenant Communications, 2006.

Bagley, Will. *Blood of the Prophets: Brigham Young and the Massacre at Mountain Meadows*. Norman: University of Oklahoma Press, 2002.

Bagley, Will, ed. *The Pioneer Camp of the Saints: The 1846 and 1847 Mormon Trail Journals of Thomas Bullock*. Logan: Utah State University Press, 2001.

Ballard, M. Russell. "Joseph F. Smith and the Importance of Family." In *Joseph F. Smith: Reflections on the Man and His Times*, edited by Craig K. Manscill et al. Provo, UT: BYU Religious Studies Center, 2013.

Bates, Irene M., and E. Gary Smith. *Lost Legacy: The Mormon Office of Presiding Patriarch*. Urbana: University of Illinois Press, 1996.

Baugh, Alexander L. "The Haun's Mill Massacre and the Extermination Order of Missouri Governor Lilburn W. Boggs." *Mormon Historical Studies* 10, no. 1 (Spring 2009): 22–31.

Baugh, Alexander L. "Was Joseph F. Smith Blessed by His Father Hyrum Smith in Liberty Jail?" *Mormon Historical Studies* 4, no. 3 (Spring 2003): 101–5.

Beckert, Sven. *Empire of Cotton: A Global History*. New York: Knopf, 2014.

Bennett, Richard E. *Mormons at the Missouri: Winter Quarters, 1846–1852*. Norman: University of Oklahoma Press, 1987.

Bitton, Davis. *George Q. Cannon: A Biography*. Salt Lake City: Deseret Book, 1999.

Bradley, James. *The Imperial Cruise: A Secret History of Empire*. Boston: Back Bay Books, 2010.

Brands, H. W. *Andrew Jackson: His Life and Times*. New York: Anchor Books, 2005.

Bringhurst, Newell G., and John Hamer, eds. *Scattering the Saints: Schism Within Mormonism*. Independence, MO: John Whitmer Books, 2007.

Britsch, R. Lanier. *Moramona: The Mormons in Hawaii*. Laie, HI: Institute for Polynesian Studies, 1989.

Buerger, David John. *Mysteries of Godliness: A History of Mormon Temple Worship*. Salt Lake City: Smith Research Associates, 1994.

Bushman, Richard Lyman. *Joseph Smith: Rough Stone Rolling*. New York: Knopf, 2005.

Butler, Jon. *Awash in a Sea of Faith: Christianizing the American People*. New Haven: Yale University Press, 1990.

Cannon, Brian Q. "'Long Shall His Blood ... Stain Illinois': Carthage Jail in Mormon Memory." *Mormon Historical Studies* 10, no. 1 (Spring 2009): 1-19.

Church of Jesus Christ of Latter-day Saints. *The Thatcher Episode: A Concise Statement of the Facts of the Case*. Salt Lake City: Deseret News, 1896.

Church of Jesus Christ of Latter-day Saints, First Presidency. "The Origin of Man." *Improvement Era* 13, no. 1 (November 1909).

Church of Jesus Christ of Latter-day Saints, First Presidency and the Quorum of the Twelve. "The Father and the Son: A Doctrinal Exposition." *Improvement Era* (August 1916): 934–42.

Clark, Christopher. "The Consequences of the Market Revolution in the American North." In *The Market Revolution in America: Social, Political, and Religious*

Expressions, 1800–1880, edited by Melvyn Stokes and Stephen Conway, 26–30. Charlottesville: University of Virginia Press, 1996.

Compton, Todd. *In Sacred Loneliness: The Plural Wives of Joseph Smith*. Salt Lake City: Signature Books, 1997.

Cummings, B. F., Jr. "Shining Lights." *Contributor* 16, no. 3 (January 1895): 174.

Darby, Robert. *A Surgical Temptation: The Demonization of the Foreskin and the Rise of Circumcision in Britain*. Chicago: University of Chicago Press, 2005.

Davis, Daniel. "Overland Travels." LDS History. http://history.lds.org/overlandtravels.

Eagleton, Terry. *Culture*. New Haven: Yale University Press, 2016.

Edwards, Rebecca. *New Spirits: America in the Gilded Age*. New York: Oxford University Press, 2006.

Ehat, Andrew F., ed. "'They Might Have Known That He Was Not a Fallen Prophet': The Nauvoo Journal of Joseph Fielding." *BYU Studies* 19, no. 2 (April 1979): 133–66.

Ellis, Joseph J. *American Sphinx: The Character of Thomas Jefferson*. New York: Vintage Books, 1998.

Ellis, Richard E. "The Market Revolution and the Transformation of American Politics, 1801–1837." In *The Market Revolution in America: Social, Political, and Religious Expressions, 1800–1880*, edited by Melvyn Stokes and Stephen Conway, 300–310. Charlottesville: University of Virginia Press, 1996.

England, Breck. *The Life and Thought of Orson Pratt*. Salt Lake City: University of Utah Press, 1985.

Esplin, Ronald K. "Hyrum Smith." In *United by Faith: The Joseph Sr. and Lucy Mack Smith Family*, edited by Kyle R. Walker, 125–29. American Fork, UT: Covenant Communications, 2006.

Esplin, Ronald K. "Joseph Smith and the Kirtland Crisis." In *Joseph Smith: The Prophet and Seer*, edited by Richard Holzapfel and Kent P. Jackson, 261–90. Salt Lake City: Deseret Book, 2010.

Evans, Christopher H. *The Social Gospel in American Religion: A History*. New York: NYU Press, 2017.

Faber, George. *Origin of Pagan Idolatry Ascertained from Historical Testimony and Circumstantial Evidence*. New York: F and C Rivingtons, 1816.

Firmage, Edwin Brown, and Richard Collin Mangrum. *Zion in the Courts: A Legal History of the Church of Jesus Christ of Latter-day Saints, 1830–1900*. Urbana: University of Illinois Press, 1988.

Flake, Kathleen. *The Politics of Religious Identity: The Seating of Senator Reed Smoot, Mormon Apostle*. Chapel Hill: University of North Carolina Press, 2004.

Fluhman, Spencer. *A Peculiar People: Anti-Mormonism and the Making of Religion in Nineteenth-Century America*. Chapel Hill: University of North Carolina Press, 2012.

Folkman, Kevin. "Letters from Joseph F. Smith to His Adopted Son Edward Arthur Smith." In *Joseph F. Smith: Reflections on the Man and His Times*, edited by Craig K. Manscill et al., 114–32. Salt Lake City: Deseret Book, 2013.

Gentry, Leland H., and Todd M. Compton. *Fire and Sword: A History of the Latter-day Saints in Northern Missouri, 1836–1839*. Salt Lake City: Greg Kofford Books, 2011.

Gibbons, Francis M. *Joseph F. Smith: Patriarch and Preacher, Prophet of God*. Salt Lake City: Deseret Book, 1984.

Gibbons, Francis M. *Joseph Fielding Smith: Gospel Scholar, Prophet of God.* Salt Lake City: Deseret Book, 1992.

Givens, Terryl L., and Matthew J. Grow. *Parley P. Pratt: The Apostle Paul of Mormonism.* New York: Oxford University Press, 2011.

Godfrey, Kenneth W. "Moses Thatcher in the Dock: His Trials, the Aftermath, and His Last Days." *Journal of Mormon History* 24, no. 1 (1998): 54–88.

Goodman, Ruth. *How to Be a Victorian: A Dawn to Dusk Guide to Victorian Life.* New York: W. W. Norton, 2013.

Gordon, Sarah Barringer. *The Mormon Question: Polygamy and Constitutional Conflict in Nineteenth-Century America.* Chapel Hill: University of North Carolina Press, 2002.

Grimsted, David. *American Mobbing, 1828–1861: Toward Civil War.* New York: Oxford University Press, 2003.

Gunn, Simon. "Urbanization." In *A Companion to Nineteenth-Century Britain*, edited by Chris Williams, 238–53. London: Blackwell, 2004.

Hahn, Steven. *A Nation Without Borders: The United States and Its World in an Age of Civil Wars, 1830–1910.* New York: Viking, 2016.

Haley, James L. *Captive Paradise: A History of Hawaii.* New York: St. Martin's, 2014.

Hansen, Jason, comp. *Thy Servants Speak.* 35 vols. Salt Lake City: 3rd Day, 2012.

Hill, Marvin S. "Mormon Religion in Nauvoo: Some Reflections." *Utah Historical Quarterly* 44 (Spring 1976): 170–80.

Hine, Robert V., and John Mack Faragher. *The American West: A New Interpretative History.* New Haven: Yale University Press, 2000.

Hollister, O. J. "The Supreme Court Decision in the Reynolds Case: An Interview Between President John Taylor and O.J. Hollister, Esq. Salt Lake City, Utah, January 18th 1879." *New York Tribune*, 18 January 1879.

Horne, Dennis B. *Latter Leaves in the Life of Lorenzo Snow.* Springville, UT: CFI, 2012.

Jenkins, Simon. *A Short History of England.* New York: Public Affairs, 2011.

Kenney, Scott G. "Before the Beard: Trials of the Young Joseph F. Smith." *Sunstone* 20 (November 2001): 20–42.

Khlevniuk, Oleg V. *Stalin: A New Biography of a Dictator.* New Haven: Yale University Press, 2015.

Kimball, Spencer W. *The Miracle of Forgiveness.* Salt Lake City: Deseret Book, 1969.

Kimball, Stanley B., and Violet T. Kimball. *Villages on Wheels: A Social History of the Gathering to Zion.* Draper, UT: Greg Kofford Books, 2011.

Launius, Roger D. *Joseph Smith III: Pragmatic Prophet.* Urbana: University of Illinois Press, 1988.

Lears, Jackson. *Rebirth of a Nation: The Making of Modern America, 1877–1920.* New York: Harper Perennial, 2009.

Leonard, Glen M. *Nauvoo: A Place of Peace, A People of Promise.* Salt Lake City: Deseret Book, 2002.

Lind, Michael. *Land of Promise: An Economic History of the United States.* New York: Harper, 2012.

Lyman, Edward Leo. *Political Deliverance: The Mormon Quest for Utah Statehood.* Urbana: University of Illinois Press, 1986.

Madsen, Carol Cornwall. *Journey to Zion: Voices from the Mormon Trail.* Salt Lake City: Deseret Book, 1997.

Maffly-Kipp, Laurie. "Assembling Bodies and Souls: Missionary Practices on the Pacific Frontier." In *Practicing Protestants: Histories of Christian Life in America, 1630–1965,* edited by Laurie F. Maffly-Kipp, Leigh E. Schmidt, and Mark Valeri, 51–77. Baltimore: Johns Hopkins University Press, 2006.

Manscill, Craig K. et al., eds. *Joseph F. Smith: Reflections on the Man and His Times*. Salt Lake City: Deseret Book, 2013.

Matthew, Colin. *The Short Oxford History of the British Isles: The Nineteenth Century*. New York: Oxford University Press, 2000.

May, Dean L. *Utah: A People's History*. Salt Lake City: University of Utah Press, 1987.

McConkie, Bruce R. *Mormon Doctrine*. Salt Lake City: Deseret Book, 1958.

McConkie, Mark L. "Joseph Smith, Sr." In *United by Faith: The Joseph Sr. and Lucy Mack Smith Family*, edited by Kyle R. Walker, 5–7. American Fork, UT: Covenant Communications, 2006.

McGerr, Michael. *A Fierce Discontent: The Rise and Fall of the Progressive Movement in America*. New York: Oxford University Press, 2003.

Meacham, Jon. *American Lion: Andrew Jackson in the White House*. New York: Random House, 2008.

Merry, Sally Engle. "Law, Culture, and Cultural Appropriation." *Yale Journal of Law and the Humanities* 10, no. 2 (1998): 575–603.

Mintz, Steven. *Huck's Raft: A History of American Childhood*. Cambridge, MA: Belknap, 2006.

Morris, Edmund. *Theodore Rex*. New York: Random House, 2001.

Newell, Linda King, and Valeen Tippetts Avery. *Mormon Enigma: Emma Hale Smith*. Urbana: University of Illinois Press, 1994.

Oaks, Dallin H. "The Suppression of the *Nauvoo Expositor*." *Utah Law Review* 9 (Winter 1965): 862–903.

Oaks, Dallin H., and Marvin S. Hill. *Carthage Conspiracy: The Trial of the Accused Assassins of Joseph Smith*. Urbana: University of Illinois Press, 1975.

Olsen, Nolan P. *Logan Temple: The First 100 Years*. Providence, UT: Watkins and Sons, 1978.

Osorio, Jonathan Kay Kamakawiwo'ole. *Dismembering Lahui: A History of the Hawaiian Nation to 1887*. Honolulu: University of Hawaii Press, 2002.

Osterhammel, Jurgen. *The Transformation of the World: A Global History of the Nineteenth Century*. Princeton, NJ: Princeton University Press, 2015.

Ostler, Craig James. "Joseph F. Smith on Priesthood and Church Government." In *Joseph F. Smith: Reflections on the Man and His Times*, edited by Craig K. Manscill et al., 200–220. Salt Lake City: Deseret Book, 2013.

Oxx, Katie. *The Nativist Movement in America: Religious Conflict in the Nineteenth Century*. New York: Routledge, 2013.

Park, Benjamin E. *Kingdom of Nauvoo: The Rise and Fall of a Religious Empire on the American Frontier*. New York: Liveright, 2020.

Parry, Jay A. "Called to Drink the Bitter Cup." In *Women of Faith in the Latter Days*, vol. 2, *1821–1845*, edited by Richard Turley and Brittany Chapman. Salt Lake City: Deseret Book, 2012.

Proceedings Before the Committee on Privileges and Elections of the United States Senate in the Matter of the Protests Against the Right Honorable Reed Smoot, a Senator from the State of Utah, to Hold His Seat. Washington, DC: Government Printing Office, 1906.

Pulham, Patricia. "The Arts." In *A Companion to Nineteenth-Century Britain*, edited by Chris Williams, 443–56. London: Blackwell, 2004.

Quinn, D. Michael. "LDS Church Authority and New Plural Marriages, 1890–1904." *Dialogue: A Journal of Mormon Thought* 18, no. 1: 9–105.

Raynor, Wallace Alan. *The Everlasting Spires: A Story of the Salt Lake Temple*. Salt Lake City: Deseret Book, 1965.

Ricks, Nathaniel R. "The Triumphs of the Young Joseph Smith." In *Joseph F. Smith: Reflections on the Man and His Times*, edited by Craig K. Manscill et al., 37–51. Salt Lake City: Deseret Book, 2013.

Roberts, David. *Devil's Gate: Brigham Young and the Great Mormon Handcart Tragedy*. New York: Simon and Schuster, 2008.

Rodell, Jonathan. *A Rise of Methodism: A Study of Bedfordshire, 1736–1851*. Rochester, NY: Boydell, 2014.

Seavoy, Ronald. *An Economic History of the United States From 1607 to the Present*. New York: Routledge, 2006.

Sessions, Gene A. *Mormon Thunder: A Documentary History of Jedediah Morgan Grant*. Draper, UT: Greg Kofford Books, 2008.

Siegel, Reva B. "'The Rule of Love': Wife Beating as Prerogative and Privacy." Faculty Scholarship Series. New Haven: Yale Law School, Yale University.

Slotkin, Richard. *The Fatal Environment: The Myth of the Frontier in the Age of Industrialization*. Norman: University of Oklahoma Press, 1985.

Smith, Jonathan Z. *Map Is Not Territory: Studies in the History of Religion*. Chicago: University of Chicago Press, 1978.

Smith, Joseph. *History of the Church*. 7 vols. Salt Lake City: Deseret Book, 1991.

Smith, Joseph. "The King Follett Discourse: The Being and Kind of Being God Is; The Immortality of the Intelligence of Man," sermon on 7 April 1844, in Smith, *History of the Church*, 6:302–17.

Smith, Joseph F. "Address of President Joseph F. Smith to Conference of the Women's Relief Society." *Woman's Exponent* (1 May 1903): 92–93.

Smith, Joseph F. Autobiographical entry in "The Twelve Apostles." *Historical Record* (May 1887).

Smith, Joseph F. "Boyhood Recollections of President Joseph F. Smith." *Utah Genealogical and Historical Magazine* 7, no. 2 (April 1916): 57–63.

Smith, Joseph F. "Fashion and the Violation of Covenants and Duty." *Improvement Era* (August 1906): 813.

Smith, Joseph F. "The Mormon Question." *Deseret News*, 10 March 1886, 121.

Smith, Joseph F. "Peace on Earth Obtained Only Through Jesus Christ." *Liahona: The Elders' Journal* 12, no. 26 (22 December 1914): 403.

Smith, Joseph F. "Sermon, 7 July 1878." *Journal of Discourses* 20, no. 28.

Smith, Joseph F. "Testimony." *Improvement Era* (August 1906): 308–10.

Smith, Joseph F. "Theory and Divine Revelation." *Improvement Era* 14, no. 6 (April 1911).

Smith, Joseph Fielding. *The Life of Joseph F. Smith*. Salt Lake City: Deseret News, 1938.

Snow, LeRoi C. "An Experience of My Father's." *Improvement Era* (September 1933): 667–69.

Staker, Mark Lyman. *Hearken, O Ye People: The Historical Setting of Joseph Smith's Ohio Revelations*. Salt Lake City: Greg Kofford Books, 2009.

Stapley, Jonathan A. "'The Last of the Old School': Joseph F. Smith and Latter-day Saint Liturgy." In *Joseph F. Smith: Reflections on the Man and His Times*, edited by Craig K. Manscill et al., 233–47. Salt Lake City: Deseret Book, 2013.

Stapley, Jonathan A. "Women and Mormon Authority." In *Women and Mormonism: Historical and Contemporary Perspectives*, edited by Matthew Bowman and Kate Holbrook. Salt Lake City: University of Utah Press, 2016.

Bibliography

Stephens, Solomon C. *The Philosophy of the Earth and of Man*. Ogden, UT: W. W. Browning, 1898.

Stevenson, Elder Edward. *Reminiscences of Joseph, the Prophet and the Coming Forth of the Book of Mormon*. 1893. Createspace Independent Publishing Platform, 2017.

Stuy, Brian H., ed. *Collected Discourses*. Burbank, CA: BHS, 1992.

Talmage, James E. *The House of the Lord: A Study of Holy Sanctuaries Ancient and Modern*. Salt Lake City: Church of Jesus Christ of Latter-day Saints/Deseret News, 1912.

Taylor, Samuel W. *The Last Pioneer: John Taylor, a Mormon Prophet*. Salt Lake City: Signature Books, 1999.

Thigpen, Jennifer. *Island Queens and Mission Wives: How Gender and Empire Remade Hawaii's Pacific World*. Chapel Hill: University of North Carolina Press, 2014.

Thorp, Malcolm R. "Early Mormon Confrontations with Sectarianism, 1837–40." In *Mormons in Early Victorian Britain*, edited by Richard L. Jensen and Malcolm R. Thorp, 49–69. Salt Lake City: University of Utah Press, 1989.

Tombs, Robert. *The English and Their History*. New York: Knopf, 2015.

Trevor-Roper, Hugh. *Archbishop Laud*. New York: Phoenix Press, 2001.

Tullidge, Edward W. *History of Salt Lake City*. Salt Lake City: Star, 1886.

Turner, John. *Brigham Young: Pioneer Prophet*. Cambridge, MA: Harvard University Press, 2014.

Tweed, Thomas A. *Crossing and Dwelling: A Theory of Religion*. Cambridge: Harvard University Press, 2006.

Unruh, John D., Jr. *The Plains Across: The Overland Emigrants and the Trans-Mississippi West, 1840–60*. Urbana: University of Illinois Press, 1979.

Van Orden, Bruce A. *Prisoner for Conscience Sake: The Life of George Reynolds*. Salt Lake City: Deseret Book, 1992.

Van Wagoner, Richard S. *Mormon Polygamy: A History*. Salt Lake City: Signature Books, 1989.

Utah Commission. *Report of the Utah Commission to the Secretary of the Interior*. Washington, DC: Government Printing Office, 1891.

Walgren, Kent. "Inside the Salt Lake Temple: Gisbert Bossard's 1911 Photographs." *Dialogue: A Journal of Mormon Thought* 29, no. 3: 1–5.

Walker, Ronald W. "Six Days in August: Brigham Young and the Succession Crisis of 1844." In *A Firm Foundation: Church Organization and Administration*, edited by David J. Whittaker and Arnold K. Garr, 162–96. Salt Lake City: Deseret Book, 2011.

Walker, Ronald W., Richard E. Turley, and Glen M. Leonard. *Massacre at Mountain Meadows*. New York: Oxford University Press, 2011.

West, Elliott. *Growing Up With the Country: Childhood on the Far Western Frontier*. Albuquerque: University of New Mexico Press, 1989.

Willes, Laura F. *Christmas with the Prophets*. Salt Lake City: Deseret Book, 2010.

Wilson, A. N. *The Victorians*. New York: W. W. Norton, 2003.

Woodger, Mary Jane. "The Ten Pioneering Missionaries of the Sandwich Islands, 1850–1854." In *Go Ye Into All the World: The Growth and Development of Mormon Missionary Work*, edited by Fred Woods and Reid Neilson, 16–182. Provo, UT: Brigham Young University Religious Studies Center, 2012.

Woods, Fred E. "The Palawai Pioneers on the Island of Lanai: The First Hawaiian Latter-day Saint Gathering Place, 1854–1864." *Mormon Historical Studies* (Fall 2004): 3–35.

Index

abortion, 295, 328, 333

abuse: animal, 160–61; JFS and, 359–60; of Joseph Smith Jr., 56, 69; sexual, 112; verbal, 50, 54; of women, 142

Adams, Samuel, 64–65, 73, 98, 114, 332–33

alcohol, 245, 266–67, 340, 353, 346–47: Alcoholic, 194, 196. *See also* Prohibition

American Party, 329, 347

American West, 41, 56–60, 74, 145, 198, 206, 262, 286

anger (of JFS): and anxiety, 168; and Buddy Smith correspondence, 271; and Coulson Smith, 341; displayed in British mission 109, 119, 126, 165, 178; and golf, 335; and grief, 150; and Hyrum's death, 37, 42; at Ina Coolbrith, 89–90; JFS childhood, 25; JFS and John Smith, 124; JFS fear of his own, 161; JFS and Mary Fielding Smith, 18; JFS in Utah territorial government, 154–55; and JFS mission call, 66; JFS preaches against, 284; and Levira Smith, 118, 137–38 (*see also* Smith, Levira: abuse victim); and Lott episode, 51, 54; and masculinity, 149; and the political manifesto, 258; and polygamy concerns, 199, 207, 210–11, 315; portrayed in press, 310–11, 331; righteous, 331, 333; and tithing office memories, 279. *See also* McKnight, James

apostasy (apostate), 71, 83, 85, 115, 143, 153–56, 189, 257, 265, 277, 291–92, 327

apostles (ancient), 22, 109, 130, 188–89, 228, 266

archives, 1–2

authority, 79, 112–13, 194, 237, 314; blessing, 305, 328, 357; cosmological, 23–24; and global male leadership, 185–86, 219, 253, 293; JFS ordination to Seventy, 98; local male leadership, 181, 193, 351, 359; Mormon conceptions of restoration, 188, 204–6; and politics, 252; and polygamy, 202; quorums, 29, 252; in ritual performance, 47–48, 211, 352; Walter Gibson sells offices in, 130; and women, 266, 301

baby blessings, 15–16, 348, 354

Ballard, M. Russell, 336–37, 360

baptism, 298: in Britain, 103, 112, 164; for the dead, 21, 126, 136, 159, 160, 228, 230; essential doctrine, 214, 298; Fielding family's, 8; in Hawaii, 76–78, 133; for health, 348; rebaptism, 94, 218–19, 295–96; and sealing concerns, 151

Baptists, 5–8, 105, 291

Baskin, Robert, 226

Beesley, Frederick, 209

Bellings, Frank, 296

Benson, Ezra T., 69, 131–34

Benton, Thomas Hart, 12

Bible, 7–8, 56, 80, 111, 159, 309, 349–50: Hebrew Bible, 7, 133, 205, 349: New Testament, 8, 21–22, 86, 205, 228, 298, 130, 356

Bigler, Henry, 83

Birdsall, Cora, 316

Black people: Africans, 44; African Americans, 92, 128, 222

Blaine, James, 203

Boggs, Lilburn W., 14, 44

433

434   Index

Book of Mormon: and America, 265, 346; Armenian translation, 324; Hawaiian translation, 73; Joseph Smith and, 6; JFS and, 75, 80, 159, 204, 209, 228; and polygamy, 89; Pratt editing with JFS, 187–88; and race, 83; rejected, 69; at the Smoot hearings, 309; and wealth, 175. *See also* Cluff, Benjamin, Jr.; Whitmer, David

Brigham Young Academy, 213, 280–81, 343
Brigham Young University, 280, 337, 350
British mission: Leeds, 104, 111; Liverpool, 55, 102–7, 111, 131, 164–65, 175, 180–184, 186, 345; London, 165, 183–84; Preston, 103–5, 164; Sheffield, 104, 107, 109, 112, 115, 122
Buchanan, James, 95, 251
Buddhists, 209
Bullock, Thomas, 135
Burdick, Alden, 51
Burrows, J. C., 306

Cain, John, 176
Calvinism, 5, 84–85, 90–91, 105
Canada, 7–10, 304, 310, 313, 324, 341–43
Cannon, Abraham H., 226, 242, 253, 303
Cannon, Angus, 218, 272
Cannon, Frank J., 248, 287–88, 318–19
Cannon, George Q.: arrest and imprisonment, 200, 211; and British mission, 110–11, 114–16, 127, 131, 178; and Church business, 220; and Cluff episode, 281; death, 281–85; as epitome of masculinity, 116–17; and Hawaiian mission, 72–76, 92; on Hawaiians, 84; Logan Temple dedication, 203; manages First Presidency business, 214–16, 289–90; and the Manifesto, 233–35; photo of, 148; and politics, 207, 246–48, 252, 258, 260; and the SLC Temple, 252–58; and succession, 186, 193–94, 217–18, 258, 273–78; in Washington, DC, 163
Cannon, John Q., 216, 218
capitalism, 70, 104, 191, 198–99, 207, 238, 263, 291
Carey, William, 200
Carrington, Albert, 176–80, 210, 218–19, 296, 331

childhood, 2, 58–60
China (Chinese), 5, 44, 70, 209
Christianity, 5–6, 22, 46, 56, 71, 75, 83, 85
Church Historian's Office, 135, 139–40, 144, 146, 154, 181–82, 187–88, 207
Church of England, 7, 104–5, 114
Citizens Party, 246
civilization (civilized): Americans views on, 46, 198, 347; in the Book of Mormon, 175; and Britain, 103; and Cluff expedition, 280; and Hawaiians, 79, 81, 83, 232; JFS and, 263; and missions, 73; Mormonism as, 221; Yankees and, 264; and World War I, 345
Civil War (U.S.), 128, 199, 207, 238, 249, 346
Clawson, Rudger, 223, 276, 284, 305, 312
Cleveland, Grover, 203, 256
Cluff, Benjamin, Jr., 280–81
Cluff, Harvey H. (H. H.), 231–32
Cluff, William (W. W.), 107, 109, 125, 157, 170, 214, 231–32
Coan, Titus, 85
colonialism, 2, 72, 206–7, 232, 280
Congregationalists, 5
Coolbrith, Ina Smith: JFS correspondence with, 88–92; JFS visits before traveling to Hawaii, 69, 131; Levira Smith stays with, 134–37; relationship becomes rocky, 322–24; visit with Julina, 327
Cooley, William, 200
Cowdery, Oliver, 188–89
Cowley, Matthias, 258, 313–14
Cullom, Shelby, 199

Davis, Daniel, 51
death, 151, 353–54, 357; European mission president, 336, 345–46; JFS's nightmare about, 168;
Democrats, 224, 244–52, 256, 259, 302, 341, 343
Denmark (Danish), 59, 107, 290
devil (*or* demon *or* Satan): astrology as evil, 99; in British mission, 112–13; evil spirits, 113, 352; exorcism, 112–13; federal government as, 225; JFS's enemies as, 12, 331; Smiths view as active in world, 8–9, 86, 120, 180, 192, 207, 255,

258, 317. *See also* Smith, Joseph F.: dualism

diaspora, 42–46, 50, 333

Doctrine and Covenants: and degrees of glory, 111; JFS work on, 185–88; and polygamy, 151, 202; publication in German, 176; sons of perdition commentary, 219, 298; on Presiding Patriarch, 293; in Smoot hearings, 309, 315; and succession, 192; and temples, 228. *See also* Smith, Joseph F.: Vision of the Redemption of the Dead

doctrine, systemization by JFS, 2, 79, 158, 188, 24, 206, 209, 228–29, 243, 258, 267, 271, 292, 297–99, 318, 348, 350, 357

Duncan, John, 147

Dyer, Frank, 207–8

Edlefsen, N. C., 247

Edmunds Act, 206–7

Edmunds–Tucker Act, 206, 233, 317

emigration: and the American West migration, 58–59; British to America, 55, 105–11, 122, 127, 164–66, 184; and citizenship, 236; end of LDS inducement to, 324; Fieldings to Toronto, 7; to Hawaii, 74; migration of Hawaiians to America, 84, 230; Perpetual Emigration Fund, 206; Walter Gibson and, 129. *See also* immigration

Endowment House: JFS service in, 24, 39, 136, 139, 146–49, 158–60, 181–82, 194; Julina and Edna work in, 174; and the Raid, 210

England. *See* British mission

Estee, Morris, 205, 234–35, 272, 300, 336

European mission, 79, 86, 116, 177, 180, 182, 186, 290, 336, 343, 345, 355

Everett, Addison, 188

evolution, 349–51

excommunication: of Albert Carrington, 218; in Britain, 109; Cora Birdsall, 216; in Hawaii, 78, 82, 95; of James McKnight, 161; and plural marriage, 295–97, 313–14; and sexual transgression, 295097; of Sidney Rigdon 40; of Walter Gibson, 131, 134; of William McLellin, 189

Farr, Enoch, 208–9

fasting, 85, 226, 267–68

femininity, 30, 166, 196

Fielding family, 4, 7–8, 17–18, 105, 126–27

Fielding, James, 17–18, 104, 126–27, 262

fire, 79–80, 128, 163–64, 167, 352

Fisher, Jane, 97–98

Folsom, William H., 281–82

food, 15, 48, 75, 80–81, 165, 261, 279, 327, 353

Ford, Thomas, 35, 40–41, 44

France (French), 70, 104, 201, 324

freemasonry, 36, 228

frontier, 13, 42, 47, 49, 56–60, 63, 69, 134

Gardo House, 194, 208, 213, 220

Gates, Susa Y., 157, 229–30, 233, 240, 264–67, 356–58

Gatewood, Mary, 254

gender roles, 2, 149. *See also* femininity; masculinity

Germany (German), 176, 189, 324, 344–45, 349, 353

Gibbs, George, 177

Gibson, Walter Murray, 129–34, 331

Glasmann, William, 311

Graham, John C., 249

Grant, Heber J.: businessman, 260, 331, 334; and Cluff expedition, 280–81; Democrat, 248, 347–48; on JFS work ethic, 294, 353–54; and JW Taylor, 313–14; ordained to Twelve, 201; relationship to GQ Cannon, 215–18; successor to JFS, 357

Grant, Jedediah, 95, 171

Grant, Ulysses S., 155, 163, 199

Great Britain. *See* British mission

grief, 9, 36–37, 100, 118, 149, 171, 179, 185, 196, 268, 331–34, 353

Griffin, Sarah Smith, 43, 182

Grinnells, Hannah, 64, 122

Grover, Asenath Richards, 62

Hammond, Mary, 75

handcart pioneers, 93–94, 308

Harris, Hyrum, 194

Harris, Martha Ann Smith: baptism, 61; birth, 28; correspondence with JFS,

436　　Index

Harris, Martha Ann Smith (*continued*) 74–75, 85–86, 89, 98, 160, 167, 268, 299, 344; early life, 25, 39; after Hyrum's murder, 43; on naming, 3; after Mercy's death, 62–65; wedding, 90
Harrison, Benjamin Henry, 241–42, 249
Hawaii: and colonization, 70–73; compared to British mission, 103–4, 108–9, 112–13, 122; Coulson Smith and, 301–302; GQ Cannon and, 72–76, 84, 92, 163, 208, 218, 282; "great dying", 70; Hawaiian language, 72–77, 109, 131, 208–10, 302, 328; Hyrum Harris and, 194; JFS district presidency in, 77, 99; JFS's first mission in, 73–80, 90–92; JFS friends from, 109, 125, 157, 176, 214, 231–32, 281; JFS's Hawaiian "Ma", 327–28; JFS's mission call to, 65–69; JFS on the lam in, 208–16, 266; JFS views of Hawaiian culture, 81–88; JFS visits as LDS Church President to visit, 324, 347–48, 352; Kuleana Act, 70; poi, 86, 132; pono, 70–71; Samuel Woolley and, 307, 322; and Walter Gibson episode (JFS second mission), 129–34; Wesley Smith in, 339; William Cluff in, 109, 125, 157, 214, 231–32, 281. *See also* Gibson, Walter Murray; Hawaii mission; Iosepa, Utah; Native Hawaiians; temples: Hawaii
Hawaii mission: formative for JFS, 67–68; JFS call to, 68–70; Hilo, 79, 85; JFS correspondence while in, 88–92, 213–14; JFS during first mission, 73–80; JFS on underground, 208–11; JFS views of Hawaiian culture, 81–88; Laie, 134, 208–9, 215, 328, 341–42, 352; Maui, 72, 75, 77, 81, 87; Molokai, 77, 79
Higbee, Chauncey, 35
Hill Cumorah, 83, 190, 322, 325
Holiness movement, 8
Hollister, O. J., 201
Holy Spirit *or* Holy Ghost: denying of, 219, 266, 298; Holy Spirit of Promise, 293; questions asked of JFS regarding, 229, 254, 270; key to revelation for JFS, 168, 185, 267, 310, 326, 355; and preaching, 77

Hovey, Joseph, 34
Huntington, Dimick, 36
Huntsman, Gabriel, 308
Hurst, Clem, 79
Hyde, Orson, 103–4, 147–48, 266

immigration, 11, 21, 27, 29, 40, 43, 50, 60, 94, 106, 263. *See also* emigration
Iosepa, Utah, 230–32, 281: Iosepa Agricultural and Stock Company, 231
Islam (Muslims), 209
Italy (Italian), 125, 189
Ivins, Anthony, 276, 281, 314–15, 356

Jackson, Andrew, 10, 12
Japan (Japanese), 130, 209
Jews *or* Jewish *or* Judaism, 7, 11, 44, 112, 205, 228, 240
JFS. *See* Smith, Joseph F.
Johnson, Benjamin F. (B. F.), 76

Ka'ahumanu, 70
Kamehameha I, 70
Kamehameha II, 70–71
Kamehameha III, 70, 83
Karren, Brother, 76
Kearns, Thomas, 303–5, 311, 318, 347
Keōpūolani, 71
Kimball, Derinda, 134–38
Kimball, Hazen, 136–37
Kimball, Heber C.: British mission 103–4, 164; family connection to JFS, 196; and JFS's mission call to Hawaii, 66; marriage to Mary Fielding Smith, 38; at Mary Fielding Smith's funeral, 61–62; at Winter Quarters, 47–48; and western exodus, 51–52; Yankee heritage, 264
Kimball, Hyrum, 241
Kimball, J. Golden, 294
Kimball, Solomon, 241
Kimball, Spencer, 241
King, William, 231, 341
Kirtland, Ohio: in early Mormonism, 6–9, 12–14, 28, 39, 51, 147, 269, 317; JFS visits, 190; polygamy in, 21; temple, 12, 23, 112, 148, 252, 254, 322, 325; and tithing, 157
Knowlton, Benjamin F., Jr., 271

Late Corporation of the Church of Jesus Christ of Latter Day Saints v. U.S., 233
Laub, George, 28–29
Law of Adoption, 62, 151, 230, 255, 267
Lectures on Faith, 270–71
Leilich, John, 306
Lewis, Philip, 74
Liberal Party, 244, 246, 310–11
Lincoln, Abraham, 199, 263
Lott, Cornelius, 51–56, 61, 331
Lund, Anthon H., 251–54, 288–91, 311–12, 319, 335, 352–58
Lyman, Amasa, 100, 106
Lyman, Francis, Jr., 341
Lyman, Francis M., 266, 276, 288
Lyman, Richard, 332
Lyons, Oscar, 66

Manifesto; political, 256–59; second, 313–14; Woodruff, 204, 206, 223, 235–43, 244, 280, 287, 290, 302–7, 312–14, 343, 355
Maori, 342
Martineau, James Henry, 203
Martineau, Netta, 203
martyrdom: George A. Smith as, 118; Hyrum Smith as, 62, 145, 196, 270, 332; John Taylor, 215; Joseph Smith as, 154–55, 170–71, 205; Mary Fielding Smith's sense of, 16–17; and Mormon identity, 12, 325; Parley Pratt as, 90; shapes JFS worldview, 32, 131, 224, 281, 288; Smith brothers, 56–57; Willard Richards as, 270; Wilford Woodruff as, 273
masculinity: JFS childhood, 30; JFS self–reflection on, 116–17, 149, 166, 179, 242; JFS hypermasculinity, 50; equated with religiosity, 116, 182; missions and, 301; and opposition to the state, 242–43, 263; and violence, 2, 56–57, 286, 331
materialism, 191, 238–42
McConkie, Bruce R., 241, 299
McKean, James B., 199–200
McKenzie, David, 179
McKinley, William, 284, 286
McKnight, James, 160–61, 194, 331
McLellin, William, 189–90
Merrick, D. M., 65

Merrill, Marriner W., 230
Methodists, 5–8, 18, 57, 105, 114, 192, 291, 306
Mexico, 184–85, 220, 280–81, 303–4, 314, 341, 355,
Millennial Star, 106–9, 122, 164–65, 184
Miller, O. P., 326
mining, 57, 217–18, 303, 329
Missouri: Caldwell, 20; Clay, 15; Daviess County, 14; Independence, 13, 20, 44, 189, 317; Jackson County, 13–14, 20, 44, 225, 234
Mitchell, F. A., 231
mobs, 1, 6, 11, 16, 18, 20, 30–36, 56, 128, 188, 250, 276, 317
Molen, Simpson, 91–92
Mormon Reformation, 78, 93–95
Mormon Trail, 47
Mormon War: Missouri, 14–15, 21; Utah, 94–97, 100
Morrill Act (1862), 187, 199–201, 206
Mountain Meadows Massacre, 91, 93–94

Napela, Jonatana, 76
Native Americans (Indians), 50–51, 57, 60, 88, 94, 165, 206–7, 232, 256
Native Hawaiians, 70–76, 80–85, 88, 91, 209, 232, 302, 327
nativism, 11
Nauvoo, Illinois: abandonment, 42–46; aftermath of martyrdom, 36–41; exodus, 47–48; founding, 20–24; Nauvoo, founded, 6, 20–24; JFS in, 19, 25–26; JFS visits to Nauvoo, 100, 325; life in, 26–32; and politics, 249; polygamy in, 152, 277; pre–martyrdom setting, 33–36; religion in, 28. *See also* temples: Nauvoo
Nelson, Joseph, 237
New Zealand, 342
Nibley, Charles: account of JFS's Hawaiian mission call, 65–66; in British mission, 186; friendship with JFS, 229, 335; and plural marriage, 233; travels with JFS, 324–28
Norway (Norwegian), 59
Nuttall, L. John, 171, 236

Owens, Alma, 20

438   Index

Paden, William, 302, 304
Palmyra, New York, 5, 190, 322
Partridge, Edward, Jr., 99, 208
patriarch (LDS Church officer), 24, 290,
     294, 354. *See also* Smith, Hyrum:
     as Church Patriarch; Smith, Hyrum
     G.; Smith, John, as Church Patriarch
patriarchal blessings, 20, 27, 63, 162
Pearl of Great Price, 80, 309
Penrose, Charles, 235, 248, 251–52, 343,
     352–56
People's Party, 244, 247–48, 310
persecution: of early Christians, 17;
     of Huguenots, 201; and JFS, 20, 46,
     56–57, 97, 205–6, 281, 292, 344–45;
     of Mary Smith, 55; and Methodism, 8;
     and Mormonism, 12, 91, 105–6, 203,
     251, 255, 317; of Mormons, 6–9, 34, 36,
     45; and polygamy, 211, 213, 215, 220, 227,
     311
Phelps, W. W., 21, 36
photography (photograph), 107, 126, 141,
     148, 229, 299, 311, 333, 344
Pickett, Agnes, 62, 92
Pickett, William, 69
Pierce, William, 62
plural marriage. *See* polygamy
polyandry, 33
polygamy: and the Book of Mormon,
     89–90; Brigham Young and, 42;
     in British press, 105; and Christian
     "hypocrisy", 91; cohabitation, 206, 208,
     303–6, 319, 355; complexities of, 174,
     212; convictions, 206, 272; and eternal
     families, 205–6; and exaltation, 156,
     202, 225; and emotion, 340; federal
     quest to end, 198–202, 206–7, 212, 214,
     221, 224–27; and First Presidency poli-
     tics, 290–91; JFS media campaign
     around, 223; JFS preaches on, 111, 287;
     John Smith and, 181; Joseph Smith's
     introduction of, 22–24, 33–35, 39, 145–
     46, 265; and Joseph Smith historical
     monument dedication trip, 321–22;
     LDS justification for, 228; and legal
     documents, 156; and Levira Smith, 140;
     and maintenance of family relation-
     ships, 232–33; men in hierarchy

practice, 144, 201–2; in Mexico, 303–4,
     355; and Mormon culture, 263–65; new
     and everlasting covenant, 203, 219;
     post–Manifesto, 280, 287, 303–7; 312–
     15, 355; and practicalities of religious
     survival, 344, 356; Progressives and,
     346–47; the Raids, 134, 206–7, 212, 226,
     273, 317, 333, 346; records of, 210; and
     religious freedom, 200; and the Repub-
     lican Party 1856 platform, 95–96, 249;
     RLDS and, 23, 145–46, 152–54, 190,
     204; and sex, 296–97; sexual caricature
     of, 240; and slavery, 92, 95, 106, 198,
     249–50, 291; statistics on, 302; suspen-
     sion theory, 221, 225, 234–35, 243, 265,
     292; topic at JFS final conference, 355;
     unauthorized as adultery, 184; and
     Utah statehood, 214–18, 244, 249–51,
     256, 292. *See also* Manifesto; Quorum
     of the Anointed; *Reynolds v. United
     States*; Smoot hearings
Pratt, Orson, 46, 147–48, 152, 158–59, 163,
     185, 187–93, 196, 266, 336
Pratt, Orson, Jr., 99
Pratt, Parley P., 8, 45–46, 69, 90, 94, 126,
     171, 229, 351
Presbyterians, 5, 291, 302, 306
Preston, William, 326
Progressives, 291, 330, 346–47
Prohibition, 347–48
Protestant: and Americanization, 207, 286,
     291, 309; antiwar, 346–47; evangelicals,
     5, 7, 198, 291; in Hawaii, 71–74, 81, 83,
     85, 90; low–church, 23–24; and Nativ-
     ism, 11; Reformation, 298; and religious
     freedom, 201; Second Great Awaken-
     ing, 5, 291; and sex, 241; Yankee, 175
Puritans, 4, 201, 264–65

Quorum of the Anointed, 23–24, 28,
     38–41, 47
Quorum of the Twelve Apostles: battle for
     authority with the First Presidency, 217,
     252, 273–75, 278, 293, 298–99; Car-
     rington scandal, 218–19; JFS ordained,
     144–45; and LDS Church business,
     220–22; and LDS Church President
     succession, 186, 192, 215–17, 256,

277–78, 289; and the 1844 LDS succession crisis, 39–40, 46; original, 29, 189; and the presiding patriarch, 305, 343, 354; as seers and revelators, 309; stipend, 220

race: and Americanism, 264; Hawaiian, 70, 83–84, 230; Lamanites as degraded, 83, 232; and missionary work, 130; racism, 76, 230–32. *See also* Black people; whites (whiteness)
Raleigh, Alonzo, 283
Rawlins, Joseph, 256
Redfield, Harlow, 18
Reed, J. C., 154–55
reform movements, 106, 198, 291–9, 300
Relief Society, 146, 155, 300–1, 317, 358, 359
religious freedom, 256, 265, 286
Reorganized Church of Jesus Christ of Latter Day Saints (RLDS Church), 114–15, 145–46, 153–54, 159, 190, 289, 321–22, 325
repentance, 34, 58, 78, 94–95, 214, 229, 270, 295–97, 317, 345: in the spirit world, 356
Republicans: 1856 platform, 95, 198; antipolygamy legislation, 198–99; JFS and, 224, 245–52, 263; and post–Manifesto politics, 244–45, 256–57; Utah legislative politics, 305, 319, 341, 347–48
revelation: and authority, 284, 297–98, 355; of Brigham Young, 57–58; concerning Missouri, 13, 20; and degrees of glory, 111; and dreams, 168; and the First Presidency, 192, 256, 354; GQ Cannon and, 218; and Hyrum Smith, 9, 27, 336; of John Seamount, 194; of Joseph Smith, 20, 111–12, 158–59, 228, 284, 346; in Mormon message, 8; and polygamy, 22, 24, 33–34, 42, 151–54, 201–5, 216, 224–27, 265; and the presiding patriarch, 293–94; and science, 350–51; at Smoot hearings, 309–10, 318; and temples, 228. *See also* Smith, Joseph F.: Vision of the Redemption of the Dead
Reynolds, Florence, 280
Reynolds, George, 164, 200–1

Reynolds v. United States, 199–201
Rich, Ben, 318
Rich, Charles C., 100, 196
Rich, David, 196
Rich, Joseph, 119
Richards, Franklin D., 186, 207, 216, 235, 248, 295
Richards, Franklin S., 248, 312
Richards, George F., 314
Richards, Heber J., 148
Richards, Henry, 170–71
Richards, Joseph, 163, 182–83, 240
Richards, Phineas, 34
Richards, Samuel W., 99
Richards, Willard, 31, 35–36, 99, 135, 146, 171, 270
Rigdon, Sidney, 31, 39–40
ritual: baby blessings, 15–16, 348, 354; and change, 19; for the dead, 112; dedication of prison cells, 211; endowment, 23–24, 29, 38, 41, 130, 136, 217, 228, 230, 297, 348; exorcism, 113; healing, 52–54, 150, 252, 348; initiatory (washing and anointing), 23–24, 38; JFS and, 79, 348–49, 357; Kirtland innovations, 12; liturgy, 23, 48, 292, 318; prayer, 47–48; ritual exchange, 231–32; sealing, 22, 24, 29, 38–41, 136, 139–40, 151, 153, 160, 171, 196, 202, 205, 207, 228–230, 255, 267, 269, 293, 295, 341; second anointing, 143, 205, 230, 324 temple dedication, 342; temple liturgy, 23–24, 29, 203, 228; and vengeance, 226; Walter Gibson and, 130–31. *See also* baptism; Law of Adoption
Roberts, B. H., 236–39, 248, 252, 271, 302–3
Robinson, Joseph, 323, 334, 355–56
Rockwell, Porter, 35, 97
Roman Catholicism (Catholic), 11, 73, 84, 105, 199, 205, 241, 298, 305
Roosevelt, Theodore, 267, 284, 286, 288, 305, 307, 330

sacrament, 28, 78, 94, 110
sacroscapes, 19–20
Salt Lake Tribune, 155, 161, 186, 235, 246, 258, 275, 287, 304, 316, 318, 322, 329–31

440 Index

Sandwich Islands. *See* Hawaii
Savage, Charles, 148, 291
Scandinavia, 80, 125–26, 290, 342
School of the Prophets, 147, 156, 181
Scotland (Scottish), 59
Seamount, John, 194
Second Coming of Christ, 20, 44, 112, 117, 162, 292
secularism, 28, 33, 56, 107–8, 209
Sessions, Perrigrine, 50
Seventy (LDS Office), 98, 201, 236, 238, 294, 317; Area Seventy, 110
sex: absent in some polygamous relationships, 38; birth control, 241; and criminalization, 106; JFS and, 2, 90, 117, 209–10, 219, 240–41, 296–97, 311, 346, 359; masturbation, 240–41; outlet in polygamy, 212; in political cartoons, 329; sexual abuse, 112; sexual sin, 219–20, 296–97
Shaffer, J. Wilson, 155
Shurtliffe, Louie, 150, 269
Sinclair, Peter, 177
Smith, Agnes, 63, 69, 136
Smith, Albert, 195–96
Smith, Alexander, 56, 144–46, 152, 261
Smith, Alfred Jason, 182, 196
Smith, Alice (daughter of JFS), 195, 268, 283
Smith, Alice Kimball, 196, 212–13, 261, 264, 271, 341
Smith, Alvin, 168, 262, 287
Smith, Bathsheba W., 41, 179, 250, 300–1
Smith, Calvin, 337–38
Smith, Clarissa, 208, 301
Smith, Coulson, 301–2, 337, 340–41
Smith, David (son of Joseph Smith), 144, 152, 154,
Smith, David A., 195, 326, 335–37, 340–43, 353
Smith, Don Carlos, 62, 69, 88, 322
Smith, Donnette (Nonie), 158, 210–13, 262, 268, 331–34
Smith, Edna (daughter of Edna), 195
Smith, Edna Lambson: children born, 182, 195; correspondence with JFS, 161, 167–70, 178, 183, 185, 210, 224; and David Smith, 353; death of children, 195, 268;

334; in Europe, 324; financial concerns, 261; marriage to JFS, 157–58; in Mexico, 281; and order, 268; plural wife strife, 173–74, 212–13
Smith, Edward, 127, 172, 301, 321
Smith, Elias Wesley, 210, 308
Smith, Emily, 268
Smith, Emma, 22–23, 35, 42, 152–54, 290, 301
Smith, Emma (JFS daughter), 332, 334
Smith, Franklin, 337, 339
Smith, Frederick, 321–22
Smith, George A.: and the British mission, 178; in Church Historian's Office, 135; correspondence with JFS, 75–76, 126, 154; death of, 118, 169–70, 179–80, 185, 287; JFS family connection to, 144; and JFS's mission call to Hawaii, 65–66; and John Smith, 125–26; note on naming, 2–3; tours Utah settlements, 155–56; in Washington, DC, 88
Smith, George A., Jr., 118
Smith, George Albert, 2–3, 323, 353
Smith, Heber John, 182
Smith, Hyrum: and adoption, 295; aftermath of murder, 36–40, 43, 46; arrest and incarceration, 14–16; assassination, 35–36, 215; birthdays noted, 321, 332; as Church Patriarch, 24, 27, 293, 343; JFS response to murder, 1; JFS sealed to, 255; and Joseph Smith Jr., 6–7, 31; marriage to Mary Fielding, 9–10; in Nauvoo, 26–31 and plural marriage, 22–24, 33
Smith, Hyrum, Jr., 16
Smith, Hyrum F., 343
Smith, Hyrum G., 343, 354
Smith, Hyrum M.: birth, 158; correspondence with JFS, 204, 240, 258, 262–68, 340, 350–51; note on naming, 2–3; ordained to apostleship, 289–90, 294
Smith, Ina (Josephine). *See* Coolbrith, Ina Smith
Smith, Jedediah, 60
Smith, Jerusha Barden, 7–10, 24, 38, 43, 61–62, 75, 100, 123, 182, 233
Smith, John (half–brother of JFS): autobiography, 37–38, 53; and Brigham

Index 441

Young, 62, 181–82, 289; correspondence
with JFS, 75, 80, 93–96, 208; death,
343; life before Utah, 16, 43, 48, 53, 55;
marriage to Helen, 97; meets JFS in
Midwest, 100; note on naming, 2;
patriarch, 162, 181; sets JFS apart as
LDS Church President, 289; suggested
for mission, 125–26; tension with JFS
over land, 123–26; weaknesses, 78
Smith, John (uncle of JFS), 63
Smith, John Henry: criticizes JFS, 258,
274; death of, 343; death of father, 169;
and the First Presidency, 288–89, 335–
36; note on naming, 2; and the political
manifesto, 247–49; and the presiding
patriarch, 254; travels with JFS, 284;
and the Woodruff Manifesto, 235
Smith, John Schwartz, 210, 226
Smith, Joseph, III, 17–18, 23, 115, 145–46,
153–54, 159, 204, 261, 321–22
Smith, Joseph, Jr.: and adoption, 230, 295;
and America, 45–46, 212; anger, 56;
arrest, 14; assassination, 35–36; attack
on, 12; beloved by Mormons, 179; birthplace monument, 318, 325; Brigham
Young remembrances of, 61; Council of
Fifty, 33; and eternal families, 151; and
the Fieldings, 8–9; First Vision, 6, 112,
321; and Ina Coolbrith, 89; JFS last LDS
Church President to know, 59, 287–88,
294; in JFS dream, 67; JFS memories of,
31–32; King Follett discourse, 33–34;
lack of succession plan, 39; in Liberty
Jail, 15–16, 25; and Missouri, 189–90;
Mormon message and, 75, 92, 156, 204–
6, 328; Mormon oath to avenge, 226;
note on naming, 2–3; political kingdom
of God, 33; and polygamy, 21–24, 38, 121,
152, 154, 202, 265; prelude to assassination, 33–37; and the Relief Society, 300–
1; 20, 111–12, 158–59, 228, 284, 346;; and
RLDS Church, 115, 144–46, 152–54,
159, 261, 321–22; and temple rituals, 217,
324, 348–49, 357; and truth, 28
Smith, Joseph, Sr., 2–5, 15, 27, 144
Smith, Joseph F. (JFS): anxiety and family
separation, 121, 136, 166–74, 210, 224,
232, 262, 301, 338; and astrology, 99;

back problems, 334, 340; beard, 237, 291,
302; birth, 10; birthdays, 116, 122, 229,
239, 268, 344, 352; and Brigham Young's
boosterism, 128–29; clothing, 102–3,
222–23; and the Commercial Club, 330;
competitive streak, 326–27; in Davis
County, 181–82; depression, 177–78, 185,
332, 223; disguised as Joseph Speight,
208; dislike of office work, 174–75;
divorce, 132, 136–37, 140–43, 146, 150;
dreams, 67, 86–89, 163–64, 168, 359;
dualism, 2, 9, 49, 85–86, 150, 180, 191–
92, 331; and education, 29, 64–65,
73–77, 116, 132, 165, 205, 209, 333; extrovert, 327; and fear, 25–26, 95, 115–21,
124, 132, 164–68, 171, 2224–25, 231–32,
262; frugality, 337; and golf, 335, 340,
352; and grit, 50, 77, 85, 183, 286; hand-
someness, 16, 140; hatred of media
leaks, 275; as herd boy, 50, 64; on high
council, 98–99, 144; homesickness, 95,
100, 122, 163, 166, 174–80, 183, 328;
humor, 81, 87, 113–16, 121; as Hyrum's
son, 69, 76, 106–7; intelligence, 16, 68,
76, 87–88, 191, 286, 308, 360; intimacy,
89–90, 163, 229, 262, 340; joins First
Presidency, 193; land ownership concerns while in England, 123–25, 218;
laying on of hands, 112–13, 252; love of
theatre, 108, 120, 136, 220; in the Nauvoo Legion, 96; in New York City, 100,
117, 128–31, 162–63, 190; note on names,
2–3; ordained to apostleship, 144–45;
as outsider, 4, 148, 256, 289; partisan
turn, 244; patriarchal blessings, 63,
162–63; physical prowess, 68, 87, 117, 169,
286; and political cartoons, 330; on politicians, 244; and posterity's righteousness, 151, 196, 336; premonitions, 185;
proposed successor to Brigham Young,
186; and record–keeping, 209; robbed,
161, 164; romanticism, 48, 68, 150;
on Salt Lake City Council, 155; self-
doubt, 115, 132, 165, 229, 288; sentimentality, 64, 68, 95, 99, 141, 166, 180, 328,
360; and Smith "blood", 32, 107, 145,
270, 288–89, 294, 336–37; in southern
California, 323, 334–35, 340, 352–53;

442   Index

Smith, Joseph F. (JFS) (*continued*)
    Sugar House Ward memories, 170;
    systemization of doctrine, 2, 79, 158, 188,
    24, 206, 209, 228–29, 243, 258, 267, 271,
    292, 297–99, 318, 348, 350, 357; in tears,
    149–50, 179, 208, 210, 255, 268, 288, 315,
    318, 325–28; tenderness, 89–90, 112, 127,
    166, 359–60; in territorial government,
    154–60; thrived under violence, 95; and
    trauma, 4, 18, 20, 30, 46, 62, 67, 86, 171–
    72, 264, 332, 338, 353, 360; and ven-
    geance, 16, 54, 63, 143, 167, 226; Vision of
    the Redemption of the Dead, 112, 171,
    356–57, 360; in Washington, DC, 163,
    220–25, 230, 244, 292, 307–13, 317, 333;
    and weakness, 66, 109, 116–17, 133, 166,
    168, 178, 206, 229; and wealth, 175–76,
    335; at the World's Fair, 307; Yankee
    heritage, 175–76. *See also* anger (of JFS)
Smith, Joseph Fielding, Jr., 1–3, 37, 65, 67,
    140, 182, 262, 336
Smith, Joseph Richards, 158, 240
Smith, Joseph Richards (Buddy), 182–83,
    240, 262, 269–71, 282, 337–39
Smith, JS, *Nauvoo Expositor* episode,
    34–35;
Smith, Julina Lambson: childbirth, 140,
    158, 182, 195; correspondence with JFS,
    161, 163, 167–68, 173, 175, 177, 183; death
    of children, 150; financial concerns, 193,
    261; in Hawaii, 208–14, 326; JFS
    funeral, 358; marriage to JFS, 140, 143;
    and plural marriage, 146, 157; plural
    wife strife, 173–74, 212–13; and the
    Relief Society, 300–1; Yankee, 264
Smith, Leonora (Nonie), 150, 158, 411, 237,
    331–34
Smith, Levira Kimball: abuse victim, 136,
    142–43, 186; in California, 134–39; cor-
    respondence with JFS in Britain, 100–
    2, 105, 107, 110–13, 116–20, 127; death,
    261–62; divorce, 141–43, 146, 150, 161;
    early relationship with JFS, 97–99; JFS
    alleges infidelity, 136, 141–42; JFS pro-
    vides for, 123–24; mental health, 98,
    120, 129–32, 136–37, 141; miscarriage,
    135; physical health, 120–22, 134–39;
    and polygamy, 139–41

Smith, Lot, 96
Smith, Lucy (sister of Joseph Smith), 190
Smith, Lucy Kimball, 277
Smith, Lucy Mack, 3–5, 25, 43
Smith, Mary, 150
Smith, Mary Fielding: auctions Nauvoo
    property, 43; and criticism, 26–27;
    death, 61; exodus to Utah, 51–55; held
    grudges, 18; and Hyrum's assassination,
    36–38; during Hyrum's incarceration,
    15–16; and Jerusha Barden, 123; JFS like
    his mother, 9; JFS standard for women,
    157, 169; life before marriage to Hyrum,
    7–10; marriage to Heber Kimball,
    38–39; mothering style, 16–18; naming
    conventions, 3; oxen healing narrative,
    52–54, 288; and plural marriage, 24;
    in Salt Lake Valley, 60–64; and snuff,
    53; at Winter Quarters, 48–50;
Smith, Mary Taylor Schwartz, 196, 210–
    14, 258, 261, 268, 271, 279, 319
Smith, Mercy Josephine (Jode), 140, 146,
    148, 196
Smith, Minerva, 195
Smith, Rachel, 268
Smith, Rhoda, 195–96
Smith, Robert (ancestor of JFS), 4
Smith, Robert (son of JFS), 195
Smith, Royal, 271–72
Smith, Ruth, 268
Smith, Samuel, 9, 97, 106
Smith, Samuel H. B., 109, 134, 139, 177
Smith, Sarah Ella, 148
Smith, Sarah Richards: childbirth, 158,
    182; correspondence with JFS, 165–68,
    172, 178–79, 210, 222, 236; death, 339;
    death of children, 148, 195–96, 283;
    finances, 261; first plural marriage,
    146–47; illness, 268, 270; plural wife
    strife, 173–74, 212–13; travels to
    England, 182–85; Yankee, 264
Smith, Silas, 74, 76, 83, 92
Smith, Willard, 262
Smith family, 4–10, 18, 27, 42, 62–63, 115,
    123, 190, 249, 289, 337
Smoot, Abraham O., 147, 194, 303
Smoot, Reed, 222, 264, 287, 292, 303, 326,
    342–48. *See also* Smoot hearings

Smoot hearings: and changes in Mormonism, 316–17; controversy, 222; criticism of JFS, 318–19, 329; early actions in, 305–9; end of, 319–20; prelude to, 303–5; JFS testifies, 309–11; JFS's presidency and, 287, 292; proposed dropping of Reed from apostleship, 313; and revelation, 309–10, 357; RLDS and, 321–22. *See also* Manifesto: second

Snow, Eliza R., 149, 176, 188

Snow, Erastus, 187

Snow, Lorenzo: becomes LDS Church President, 273–76; Buddy Smith correspondent, 271; and Cluff expedition, 280–81; and confession, 317; death, 286–90, 293–94; and George Q. Cannon's death, 283–85, 341; in Hawaii, 131–34; imprisoned, 211; and Moses Thatcher, 258; Ohio origins, 60; in photos, 148; and polygamy, 223, 302–3; and SLC temple, 252–53, 256; and succession, 277–78, 300; and tithing, 278–79

Spain (Spanish), 60, 70, 189, 213

Spanish flu, 358

Spencer, Claudius, 99

Spencer, Daniel, 50, 99

Staines, William, 175

Standing, Joseph, 276

Stephens, Solomon, 297

Steward, A. J., 69

succession (in LDS leadership), 39–40, 185, 215–216, 293, 354

Sunday School Union, 317

Sutherland, George, 341

Sweden (Swedish), 59, 189

Talmage, James, 271, 309, 344, 351

Tanner, Nathan, 84

Tayler, Robert W., 309–10

Taylor, David, 123–25

Taylor, John: Briton, 60; conversion to Mormonism, 7–8; and Davis County, 181; death, 215–16, 259, 274; and GQ Cannon, 256, 258, 289; and JFS's apostolic ordination, 144; and Joseph Smith's martyrdom, 34–36; Logan temple dedication, 203; marriage connections to JFS, 196; on underground,

207–10, 213–15; in photo, 148; and polygamy, 201–2; and Provo, 147; and succession, 185–87, 192–94, 217–20, 293

Taylor, John W., 258, 313–14

Taylor, Leonora, 8

Taylor, R. W., 307–9

Teasdale, George, 201

temples: blackmail attempt, 344; Cardston, Alberta, 324, 341–43; and cosmological priesthood, 23–24; feared confiscation, 235; garments, 23, 80, 210, 295, 348–49; Hawaii, 134, 324, 341–43, 352; and home, 172; JFS role in ritual development, 2, 24, 205; Kirtland, Ohio, 12, 23, 112, 148, 322, 325; Logan, Utah, 185, 203, 230, 247, 352; Manti, Utah, 220, 281, 290; Missouri, 13, 21, 190, 225, 234; Nauvoo, 23–30, 38–42, 100, 148, 281; SLC, 24, 96, 185, 220, 234, 252–56, 260, 269, 273, 278, 289–90, 344–45; St. George, Utah, 182; temple robes, 47, 177, 226, 275, 358. *See also* ritual: sealing

Thatcher, Moses, 215, 247–48, 251–52, 256–59, 280

theocracy, 198–99, 316

Thompson, Mary Jane, 169

Thompson, Mercy Fielding: criticism of, 24; death, 256; early life in Mormonism, 7–10, 15–17; exodus from Nauvoo, 43; JFS and, 167–70, 239; and polygamy, 24; temple rituals, 38; in Winter Quarters, 48, 50; in Utah, 60

Thompson, Robert, 8, 15, 24

Thompson, William, 279

tithing: as binding commandment, 279; in Britain, 109–11, 164, 186; collection, 48, 220; JFS family and, 187, 261, 337; JFS on, 157, 266–67, 299; labor, 27; LDS Church financial health and, 243, 260; payment in, 299; St. George drought and, 278–80

Tithing Office, 157, 174, 187, 207, 260, 279

tobacco, 53, 177, 181, 212, 261, 343

Trumbo, Isaac, 234–36, 241, 272

United Order, 225, 317

U.S. Army, 92, 95–97, 182, 251, 260, 317

U.S. Congress, 199, 201, 203, 206, 221–223, 235, 256, 302, 320, 347

444 Index

U.S. Constitution, 5, 46, 71, 176, 200–1, 263: amendment, 200–1, 206, 303; constitutional restorationism, 211–12, 264–65

U.S. Senate (Senator), 12, 264, 292, 302–7, 313, 318–20, 326, 347. *See also* Smoot, Reed; Smoot hearings

Utah: Cache Valley (Logan), 156–57, 202–3, 256, 347–50, 257, 331; Davis County, 181–82; Manti, 290, 316; St. George, 182, 278; Sugar House, 170

Utah Commission, 234–35, 246

Utah–Idaho Sugar Company, 287, 319, 333

Utah statehood, 88, 206, 214, 220–26, 230, 235–36, 244, 246, 250, 256, 260, 287, 292, 333, 343

Utah territory: dismantling of LDS control in, 198–99, 244, 257, 317; Democratic Convention, 247; economics, 93; federal takeover, 95–96; JFS in, 154–55, 163; penitentiary, 196, 211, 273, 276; and polygamy, 223, 232; Supreme Court, 200; and Whigs, 251

vaccination, 282

vigilantism, 35, 146, 166, 275

violence: against early Mormons, 12–16, 25; blood atonement, 95; domestic, 2, 98, 142–43, 284; JFS and, 18, 52–57, 63, 66, 95, 167, 282, 286; in LDS study manual, 359–60; after martyrdom, 41, 43; and masculinity, 2, 56–57, 286, 331; as Mormon characteristic, 50; and Nativism, 11–12; in Provo, 146; vigilantism, 35, 146, 166. *See also:* Smith, Levira Kimball: abuse victim; McKnight, James; mobs

Waite, Morrison, 200

Wales (Welsh), 59, 105, 189

Walker, Joseph, 60

Walker, Lovina, 43, 100

Walker, Lucy, 38

Webb, Ann Eliza, 176

Wells, Annie, 216

Wells, Daniel H., 155, 157, 176, 193, 217

Wells, Emmeline B., 47–48, 301, 358

Wells, Junius, 318–19

White, C., 137

whites (whiteness), 11, 72, 74, 81, 128, 182, 210, 230–32, 262–65, 328

Whitmer, David, 189–90

Whitmer, Jacob, 190

Whitney, Orson F., 349, 351

Widtsoe, John A., 351

Wilson, Woodrow, 341

Winder, John R., 248, 288, 290, 335, 343

Winter Quarters, 43, 48–51, 57, 60, 64

Wixom, O. C., 310

Woodruff, Abraham O., 312–13

Woodruff, Wilford: apocalypticism, 345; and the Brigham Young estate, 187; British mission, 106, 178; Carrington scandal, 219–220; and the Church Historian's Office, 135–36; death, 272–75; and doctrine, 266–67; and family separation, 166; and GQ Cannon, 283, 289–90; and Iosepa, Utah, 230–32; and John Taylor, 215–16; and the Law of Adoption, 151; and LDS Church businesses, 220–22; in Nauvoo, 21; and the political manifesto, 258–59; and politics, 245–48, 260; post–Smith assassination, 36, 42; pre–Manifesto decision making, 233–34; in Provo, 146–47; revelation, 226–27; and the SLC temple, 252–56; and succession, 193, 217, 293, 354; and Walter Gibson, 129–30; Yankee, 60. *See also* Manifesto: Woodruff

Woolley, Franklin, 99

Woolley, Samuel, 99, 307, 322, 342

Word of Wisdom, 53, 181, 261, 267, 343, 346. *See also* alcohol; tobacco

work: Hyrum and, 27; JFS as Church President, 287, 334, 340, 352–54; JFS as sergeant at arms, 99; JFS as teamster, 92, 99–100; JFS at Winter Quarters, 48, 50, 64; JFS children, 262; JFS in British mission office, 171–75; JFS in Hawaii, 208; JFS in Provo, 147; of JFS wives, 174, 210; of John Winder, 290; Mary Fielding Smith and, 61; morality of, 175, 263, 276; Mormons seek, 299; Smith family, 4–5; work ethic (JFS), 158, 224

World War I, 345–46

Young, Brigham: Adam—God teachings, 297, 351; Brigham Young Express and Carrying Company, 93; death, 185–87; and doctrine, 158–59; and economics, 93, 146–47; and emotion, 166; and British mission, 106–7, 122, 177–80, 183–85; evacuation of Nauvoo, 42–44; and Hawaiian colony, 73; JFS defense of, 69; and JFS Hawaiian mission, 65–66; JFS memory of, 31; at Mary Fielding Smith's funeral, 61–62, 283; and Mormon War, 96; only canonized revelation, 57–58; and the Order of Enoch, 176, 225; personality, 49–52; and polygamy, 24; and Reformation, 93–95; and the RLDS, 23, 144–45, 152–54; and the SLC temple, 253; and Succession, 36–42, 190; visit to small towns, 156–57; at Winter Quarters, 47–48; Yankee, 60

Young, Brigham, Jr., 147, 258, 274–78, 282, 290, 294, 313

Young, John W., 185, 221–23

Young, Joseph W., 77, 99

Young, Seymour B., 201, 223

Young, Zina D., 121, 300

Young Men's and Young Women's Mutual Improvement Association (YMMIA), 300, 317

Zane, Charles, 236, 241

Zion's Camp, 147

Zion's Cooperative Mercantile Institution (ZCMI), 146, 220, 261–62

Zion's Mercantile Bank, 196, 220, 237